International Trade in Financial Services: The NAFTA Provisions

International Banking, Finance and Economic Law

VOLUME 13

Series Editor

J.J. Norton
Centre for Commercial Law Studies
University of London
London Institute of International Banking,
Finance and Development Law
SMU Institute of International Banking and
Finance, Dallas, Texas
Asian Institute of International Financial Law
University of Hong Kong

Executive Editor

Christos Hadjiemmanuil
London School of Economics and
Political Science

The titles published in this series are listed at the end of this volume.

SMU Institute of International
Banking and Finance,
Dallas, Texas

Centre for Commercial Law Studies
University of London

Institute of International
Banking, Finance and
Development Law, London

Asian Institute of
International Financial Law,
University of Hong Kong

International Trade in Financial Services:
The NAFTA Provisions

by

K.N. Schefer

KLUWER LAW
INTERNATIONAL

THE HAGUE – LONDON – BOSTON

Published by
Kluwer Law International Ltd
Sterling House
66 Wilton Road
London SW1V 1DE
United Kingdom

Kluwer Law International incorporates
the publishing programmes of
Graham & Trotman Ltd,
Kluwer Law & Taxation Publishers
and Martinus Nijhoff Publishers

Sold and distributed in
the USA and Canada by
Kluwer Law International
675 Massachusetts Avenue
Cambridge MA 02139
USA

In all other countries, sold and distributed by
Kluwer Law International
PO Box 322
3300 AH Dordrecht
The Netherlands

ISBN 90-411-9754-0
CIP 99-00000
© Kluwer Law International 1999
First published 1999

British Library Cataloguing in Publication Data is available
A catalogue record for this book is available from the British Library

Typeset in 10/11 pt Palatino by EXPO Holdings, Malaysia
Printed and bound in Great Britain by Antony Rowe Limited, Chippenham and Reading

TABLE OF CONTENTS

PART II   CHAPTER FOURTEEN AND THE NAFTA PARTIES

PART III CHAPTER FOURTEEN AND NON-PARTIES—
EFFECTS ON THE INTERNATIONAL TRADE SYSTEM

International Trade in Financial Services: The NAFTA Provisions

K. N. SCHEFER
KLUWER LAW INTERNATIONAL, LONDON 1999

Inauguraldissertation zur Erlangung der Würde eines Doctor iuris der Rechts- und Writschaftswissenschaftlichen Fakultät der Universitär Bern. Die Fakultät hat diese Arbeit am 11. Juni 1988 auf Antrag der beiden gutachter, Prof. Dr. Thomas Cottier und Prof. Dr. Regula Dettling-Ott, als Dissertation angenommen, ohne damit zu den darin ausgesprochenen Auffassungen Stellung nehmen zu wollen.

Preface

GOAL OF THIS WORK

Since its beginnings, the debates about the North American Free Trade Agreement (NAFTA) within the Parties' communities have greatly over-shadowed the discussion of it outside North America. While inside Canada, Mexico, and the United States the Agreement is often seen in terms suggesting either doomsday for all involved or economic prosperity such as the world has never seen. In the non-American nations, NAFTA is rarely discussed, and when it is, then it is generally in a comparison with European integration. The Agreement, however, not only affects billions of dollars worth of traded goods and services, but it goes further than any other free trade zone[1] in sectoral coverage and depth of changes. The incorporation of a developing country's market within its scope just adds significance to NAFTA's attributes. In short, NAFTA cannot be ignored as it has too much potential to affect the way international trade and international trade law develops.

Chapter Fourteen has been selected as the object of study because of the importance of the financial service provisions to the NAFTA. Without the liberalization of financial services, trade in goods and services would be severely hindered, and the goals of the Agreement could never be fully achieved. I limit my study to the effects of the Chapter Fourteen provisions on the banking system in order not to compromise the depth of the analysis for breadth. Much of the analysis, however, can be adapted to the insurance and securities sectors.

I attempt to explain, in language understandable to non-specialists, the provisions' legal impact on non-Party banks, particularly in light of the new World Trade Organization's (WTO) regulation of trade in financial services. This is important as the findings reveal that there can be more effects on non-Party enterprises than arise directly from the text of the treaty. This opens the question of how an enterprise can minimize the competitive

---

[1] The term 'free trade zone' is used to indicate a particular type of economic integration area, namely one in which internal trade barriers are removed, but each member retains control over its own external trade frontiers. This is as opposed to a customs union, in which the members establish a common external trade regime as well as eliminating internal trade barriers.

disadvantages it faces on a regional market (a question perhaps for international business managers as much as for lawyers).

Finally, I aim to illustrate how two legal systems—the financial service law system and the international trade law system—are responding to the increasing invasion of each other's spheres of existence by means of the example set in NAFTA's trade in banking services regime. The NAFTA's use of trade law principles to regulate the intra-regional financial services trade was the first to do so within the context of purely economic integration. Whether the needs of the banking system have been taken into consideration to a sufficient degree remains to be seen. I begin to discuss how trade law principles will need to meld with the principles of banking law in order to spur further dialogue on how to ensure that trade in banking services (or trade in financial services) will be sustainable in the long term.

SUMMARY

The study of preferential integration areas has long been a topic of concern for international economic lawyers, and the effects of such areas on the multilateral trade system have been examined with economic analyses and philosophical legal arguments since the formal multilateralization of trading relations following the Second World War. Counterpoised to the long history of integration areas is the study of trade in services. Here, international economic law only began to address the legal framework in the late 1970s. Even newer is international economic law's attention on trade in financial services. The present study combines the old and the new in examining how a particular preferential trade arrangement addresses trade in financial services.

NAFTA establishes a free trade zone among the territories of Canada, Mexico, and the United States. Trade in goods, services, and investment, as well as the regulation of trade-related areas such as intellectual property protection and competition policy are to be progressively liberalized under the supervision of an intergovernmental committee. Among NAFTA's wide sectoral coverage is trade in financial services, regulated in Chapter Fourteen of the Agreement. Although the NAFTA itself has been the topic of much scholarly investigation, the effects of the Agreement on those not party to it has been given much less attention. Moreover, the financial services provisions—although integral to NAFTA—have not garnered the attention of legal analysts interested in the third country effects of the regionalization of North America. I chose these provisions to study in part out of a curiosity to discover if the near absence of other studies in the area was based on a finding that there was simply nothing to say or whether the effects or the areas of law relevant to such analysis were too complex to parcel or whether there was a reason based on a mixture of these two possibilities.

The work contained here presents the results of a close examination of NAFTA Chapter Fourteen. The substantive legal provisions are presented and analyzed mainly from the perspective of international trade law, with the incorporation of general international law principles and financial service law principles where I think appropriate. Chapter Fourteen's legal effects on NAFTA Parties' trade systems are then projected. More importantly, this book sets out to determine the legal effects of Chapter Fourteen on non-Party banks. In doing so, the current state of international law on trade in financial service must be considered, and I therefore set forth the present rules contained in the WTO's regulatory framework for trade in financial services to the extent necessary for my purposes. The provisions of the two agreements are then synthesized to determine where the NAFTA is compatible with the WTO laws and where the non-NAFTA WTO Members may encounter violations of their legally-protected rights under the law of the WTO.

The first two chapters, which make up Part I, give an overview of the context in which the Chapter Fourteen provisions are considered. Chapter 1 presents an account of the development of the Agreement, including the main forces for and against it within the Parties. It begins with an account of the Parties' historical bilateral relations, with an emphasis on early attempts to establish preferential trade agreements. This is followed by a short description of the Parties' multilateral trade relations. For readers not familiar with international economic law, there is an overview of the World Trade Organization legal system. This is intended to give the reader an introduction to the structure of the various agreements of the WTO and the ideology of the system. More detailed discussions of relevant WTO obligations are contained in subsequent chapters. Within the discussions of the multilateral relations, I set out each of the Parties' participation in the international trade law system of the General Agreement on Tariffs and Trade (GATT) and the current WTO. This is important for the later analysis of how the NAFTA obligations of the Parties interact with the WTO rules on financial services trade, and thus how the NAFTA affects third countries. Following these sections is an examination of the NAFTA negotiating process, with an emphasis on examining the domestic forces within each Party that helped or hindered passage of the NAFTA agreements within each national legislature. In Chapter 2 I cursorily explain each Party's banking system, in order that the reader realize how the treaty does (or does not) change the legal banking environment in the NAFTA territory.

Part II contains the core of the book. Chapter 3 focuses on the Chapter Fourteen provisions specifically. In this chapter, the individual provisions are explained and interpreted according to the general principles of international law on interpretation of treaties. Thus, the interpretation focuses on the plain language of the text and secondarily, as according to the context of the Parties and their goals in formulating the obligations contained in the chapter. In Chapter 4, I explain how Chapter Fourteen has changed the legal environment for Party banks, looking to the results of the Agreement's existence for banks in each Party's territory.

The chapters comprising Part III are detailed examinations of the NAFTA's role in the international economic law system and are thus of greatest interest to those studying the interaction of regional trade arrangements with the multilateral trade system. In Chapter 5, I present a discussion of how to determine whether a third party bank will be eligible for the NAFTA advantages, as the NAFTA's bank-nationality rules permit even non-Party-based institutions to benefit in many cases. Then the WTO rules on preferential trading arrangements are set forth to answer the question of whether NAFTA is a 'WTO-legal' agreement, and the effects of such a decision are explained to the extent possible given the lack of legal precedent. Chapter 6 compares the individual provisions of Chapter Fourteen with the provisions of the WTO. This includes a detailed account of the development and content of the financial services provisions of the WTO under the General Agreement on Trade in Services (GATS). I then review the NAFTA Parties' individual WTO commitments taken in the December 1997 round of negotiations on financial services. The provisions of the NAFTA and GATS/WTO are then categorized according to their compatibility with each other, in order to indicate where a non-Party WTO Member bank might have protectable rights under international law. Chapter 7 sets out the legal effects of NAFTA on non-Party banks. Here I place particular emphasis on the indirect effects of Chapter Fourteen—those effects that arise not from the Parties' obligations under the Agreement, but rather from the fact that the NAFTA exists and is developing its own system of laws, influenced by the non-governmental groups and individuals that involve themselves in promoting regional law as opposed to national or multinational law.

Part IV concludes the main investigation into Chapter Fourteen and its legal effects on banks. Chapter 8 contains a projection of how an expansion of NAFTA could affect banks. This short discussion considers the problem from two angles: that of a purely accession-driven expansion of NAFTA; and that of an incorporation of NAFTA into a hemispheric free trade area. Chapter 9 concludes the book. It first contains a summary of the results of my work, but then goes on to set out some final thoughts on the idea of regulating global financial services under an agreement based on trade law principles. I assert that the NAFTA Chapter Fourteen, as an example of such an agreement, must take into account the legitimate interests of both the international trade system and the financial services legal system if it is to accomplish its aim of promoting a liberal and secure framework for trade in financial services.

K.N. Schefer
August 1999

Part I
Background

1. Introduction

In just over three years, the proposal to form a United States-Mexico free trade area progressed from being an idea to becoming the North American Free Trade Agreement (NAFTA). Although various persons had suggested the formal economic unification of one or more North American countries at different times throughout the history of the nations, no serious consideration had been given this idea until the latter years of the 1980s. The official proposal to negotiate a comprehensive trade liberalization agreement was made by Mexican President Salinas de Gortari to United States President George Bush on 8 August 1990. Canadian Prime Minister Patrick Brian Mulroney signaled Canada's interest in joining the negotiations in the following month. By 1992, the main treaty text had been signed by the three leaders and the following year negotiations for the environmental and labor 'side' agreements were undertaken. On 1 January 1994, the NAFTA package went into effect for Canada,[1] Mexico,[2] and the United States[3]—ushering in a new era of continental relations.[4]

1.1   BILATERAL RELATIONS OF THE NORTH AMERICAN STATES

Although there was a rapid maturation of the NAFTA from conception of the idea until its coming into effect, the three years of development were hard ones for the NAFTA supporters. The intra-continental relations of the North American nations were themselves as much the product of misunderstanding and resentments as they were the result of mutual dependencies.

---

[1]   North American Implementation Act, Consolidated Statutes of Canada, 1993, c. 44 (assented to 23 June 1993). Section 242:1 of the Implementation Act sets 1 January 1994 as the date of NAFTA's coming into effect. The following subparagraph makes such coming into effect conditional on the treaty's acceptance by the United States and Mexico. *Ibid.* at § 242:2.

[2]   El Tratado de Libre Commercio en América del Norte, Executive Decree of 12-14-93 in *Diario Official* (hereinafter 'DO') of 20 December 1993.

[3]   North American Free Trade Implementation Act, P.L. 103-182 (signed 8 December 1993).

[4]   The English text of the North American Free Trade Agreement can be found in International Legal Materials, (1993) 32:2 ILM 289 (NAFTA Parts I–III and Annex 401); (1993) 32:3 ILM 605 (NAFTA Parts IV–VIII and Annexes). For a general consideration see Norton, J.J *et al* (eds), *NAFTA and Beyond. A New Framework for Doing Business in the Americas* (Maritinus Nijhoft, Dordrecht, 1995).

1.1.1   Mexican-United States Relations

The history of Mexican-United States relations is simultaneously one of mutual distrust and great dependence. Although the United States has been Mexico's largest trading partner and its most important source of foreign direct investment funds, the political relations between the two countries have always been rocky at best.

Mexico's history with the European colonial powers is both older and more violent than its history with the United States. Starting with Hernando Cortéz' overthrow of the Aztecs in 1521, when the Spanish conquistadores entered what is now Mexico, the inhabitants of the land, whether Indian or Spanish soldiers, were aware of their subordination to the Spanish Crown on both an individual and group level. As one author describes:

> The relationship began even before the two nations existed as such. It was born of a clash of cultures and imperial systems and included an admixture of greed, bigotry, and racism. By the eighteenth century Spain directed a great deal of its activity toward strengthening the northern frontier of New Spain (the region that was to become Mexico) politically and militarily against the intrusion of Anglo-Saxons and other foreign rivals. The concept of creating a buffer zone to protect the richer domains to the south continued into the nineteenth century.[5]

The uneasy coexistence of the colonies gave way to warring between the newly independent nations in the nineteenth century. Perhaps because the original Mexicans were subjected to this conquering power rather than the more benign settling sovereign that controlled the colonies of the North, the Mexican nation that emerged from its war for independence from Spain was less aggressive in its expansionary efforts than was the United States. The United States' (largely successful) attempts to take control of northern territories of Mexico in the middle 1800s resulted in more than the loss of nearly half of Mexico's territory, a great destruction of human life, and a wounded Mexican national pride:[6] it ruined for a century the possibility of deep trust between the neighbors.

---

5   Stanley Ross, 'Mexican-US Relations: An Historical Perspective', in Richard D. Erb and Stanley R. Ross (eds), *US Policies toward Mexico: Perceptions and Perspectives* (American Enterprise Institute for Public Policy Research, Washington, DC, 1979), pp. 5–14, at 6.
6   During the 'War of the North American Invasion', as the battle of 1846–48 between the United States and Mexico is known to many Mexicans, US troops were sent to what is now southern Texas in reaction to Mexico's insistence that that State's border lay at the Nueces River rather than, as Texans claimed, at the Rio Grande. When Mexico retaliated, the US proclaimed war.

> It would change political geography. [US General Zachary] Taylor swept into the city of Monterrey, … and in 1847 American troops under General Winfield Scott advanced from Veracruz to Mexico City, seizing the capital … The following year, in the Treaty of Guadalupe Hidalgo, Mexico was obliged to surrender a huge span of land—from New Mexico and Colorado to California, more than a million square miles—in exchange for a modest $15 million. Several years later the United States extended its holdings by obtaining an additional section of New Mexico and Arizona through the Gasden Purchase—a transaction remembered in Mexico for the application of US pressure, and therefore known as 'the imposition of La Mesilla' (el Tratado Impuesto de la Mesilla).

> Report of the Bilateral Commission on the Future of United States-Mexican Relations, *The Challenge of Interdependence: Mexico and the United States* (University Press of America, Lanham, MD, 1989), pp. 21–2.

Improved relations between the United States and Mexico during the late nineteenth century were short-lived. The Mexican Revolution of 1910 brought Mexican anger at the United States to the forefront once again.[7] This time the target of wrath was the foreign direct investment flowing southward across the border.[8] During Mexico's revolutionary era,[9] the United States understood the democratic aspirations of its southern neighbor, but feared the methods of the revolutionaries. Of particular concern to the United States government was Mexico's treatment of foreign property.[10] It was the issue of expropriation of American investments and banks that would resurface to again break relations between the countries in the 1970s and 1980s.

For its part, the Mexican government was less than enthralled at what it viewed as mistreatment by the US of Mexico and her population. A Mexican poet wrote of the relationship as, 'the relationship of strong and weak, oscillating between indifference and abuse, deceit and cynacism [*sic*]. Most of us Mexicans hold the justifiable conviction that the treatment received by our country is unfair'.[11]

Such convictions stem at least in part from the realization of Mexico's economic 'vulnerability' to the economic pressures exerted by the United States. The United States has been by far Mexico's largest export market, absorbing between 70 and 75 per cent of the Mexican products sent out of its borders. Investments by US corporations and individuals neared $21 billion in 1991, before the NAFTA (or the expectation of NAFTA) could have been decisive.

In looking at Mexican-US economic relations, one should not under-estimate the aspect of the Mexican and United States workforces. Migration of Mexicans to the United States has been a tradition throughout the history of the two countries. In 1990, legal migration of workers (not including non-working dependents) from Mexico to the United States was 120,000 persons

---

[7] Ross (note 5 *supra*), at 7.

[8] *Ibid*. at 6.

[9] Formally, the Mexican Revolution is considered to have lasted until 1917.

[10] Ross (note 5 *supra*), at 8. See also Victor L. Urquidi, 'A Mexican Perspective', in Erb and Ross (note 5 *supra*), pp. 23–30, at 23 ('The territorial expansion of the United States ... led eventually to the loss of half of Mexico's land after an unjust war, and Mexican diplomacy had to struggle against many predatory US ventures ... It is no wonder that the Mexican approach to relations with the United States is essentially one of mistrust').

[11] Ross (note 5 *supra*), at 10, citing Octavio Paz, 'Mexico and the United States: Positions and Counterpositions', address given in Washington, DC, 29 September 1978, p. 23. The most well-known expression of Mexico's exasperation with its forced relationship with the United States is as characteristic now as it was at the beginning of the twentieth century: 'Pobre México! Tan legos de Dios, tan cerca de los Estados Unidos!'. The saying, whose originator is unclear (it has been attributed to Porfirio Díaz, to Benito Juarez, and to John Canu, among others) became popular during the 1890s, when foreign investment into Mexico increased dramatically. By the early 1900s, the United States became Mexico's main trading partner, and began to increasingly try to link US economic interests with political pressure in Mexico. See The Report of the Bilateral Commission (note 6 *supra*), at 14. See also 'Liberalismo Contra Democracia: Recent Judicial Reform in Mexico' (1995) 108 Harv L Rev 1919, 1924–25; 'Latin American History: The Triumph of Neo-Colonialism' (text found on the internet at >www.emayzine.com<).

per year.[12] Estimates of illegal immigration suggest that between 1985 and 1990, nearly 2.3 million persons crossed the border to work as 'undocumented aliens'.[13] The effect of this migration has been to create a third labor market. According to economic research, some US and Mexican labor market segments are now so linked that employment levels, working conditions, and wages exist in a delicate balance that spans both sides of the border, and the social compacts in both countries have become intimately interdependent.[14]

1.1.2 Canadian-Mexican Relations

In 1990, Canadian experience with Mexico was very limited, economically and politically.[15] Throughout the colonial times, the Canadian and Mexican territories were kept uninvolved with the aggressions between England, France, and Spain. After independence, both countries were too involved with coming to terms with their large common neighbor to develop

---

[12] Raúl Hinojosa-Ojeda and Sherman Robinson, 'Labor Issues in a North American Free Trade Area', in Nora Lustig, Barry P. Bosworth and Robert Z. Lawrence (eds), *North American Free Trade: Assessing the Impact* (Brookings Institution, Washington, DC, 1992), pp. 69–98, at 75, in which Table 3 has figures taken from US Census data on economically active population, including unemployed. According to Census Report data, by 1996, 6.7 million of the 24.6 million foreign-born persons living in the United States were born in Mexico. US Census Bureau, *Current Population Reports, Special Studies P23-194: 1997 Population Profile of the United States* (US Department of Commerce, Washington, DC, 1998), p. 52.

[13] Hinojosa-Ojeda and Robinson (note 12 *supra*), at 75. The total of 'Mexican origin' members of the US workforce, including documented and undocumented immigrants and their descendants, from 1940 to 1990 is estimated to be 6.91 per cent of the entire US workforce. See also Richard D. Erb, 'Formulating US Policies toward Mexico: Problems and Complexities', in Erb and Ross (note 5 *supra*), pp. 15–20, at 15–17 (one should not underestimate the effect of the mass migrations from Mexico to the United States).

[14] Hinojosa-Ojeda and Robinson (note 12 *supra*), at 71.

[15] Canada's exports to Mexico were only valued at slightly more than US$1.1 billion in 1993. Yet, although total trade between the two countries increased by more than 13 per cent by the end of 1994, even in January 1998, Canadian Minister for International Trade Sergio Marchi remarked that '[t]he trading relationship between Mexico and Canada is in its early stages'. Department of Foreign Affairs and International Trade, 'Notes for an Address by the Honourable Sergio Marchi, Minister for International Trade, to the Opening Session of the Canada-Mexico Business Forum', 12 January 1998 (text found on the Department's internet site >www.dfait-maeci.gc.ca<); statistics from SECOFI, as reported in *Mexico, Economic and Business Overview: Mexico Your Partner for Growth* (1995), p. 22. Indeed, Canada's relations with all of Latin America have traditionally been limited. This is apparent by the Canadian Ministry of Foreign Affairs' report on Canada's relations with Mexico, which begins, 'Canada's relationship with Mexico is broader and more substantial than that with any other Latin American Country'. Department of Foreign Affairs and International Trade, 'Canada-Mexico Relations' (December 1996).

relations between themselves. In part this also has to do with the fact that politically and culturally Canadians have traditionally shown more of an affinity with Europe than they have with the Americas.[16]

While there was some trade between the two countries and while some direct investments were made by Canadian industry in Mexico, the relative importance of the two countries to each other was minuscule when compared to the relations of each with the United States.[17] In 1991, Canada's exports to Mexico accounted for only 1.6 per cent of Mexico's total imports[18] in comparison with the United States' 64.1 per cent in the same year.[19]

Before the NAFTA-spurred interest in trade between the two countries, the main product transfers between Canada and Mexico were manufactured goods. Shipments of Mexican-produced automobile parts made up by far the largest category of Canadian imports from Mexico (C$1.6 billion in 1991[20]), and Canadian-made machine parts were the largest category of Canadian exports to Mexico. Even this amount of trade, however, would not in itself justify negotiating a trade agreement, as about 80 per cent of the Mexican imports to Canada entered tariff-free and the rest paid tariffs that

---

[16] This is so even though Canada's biggest trading partner is the United States. Minister Marchi (note 15 *supra*), called attention to Canadians' changing perspectives on their position in the world as follows:

> … Canada's transition to this world view has not always been easy. It has required some fundamental restructuring of our economy, and it has involved a dramatic shift in our own sense of ourselves and our place in the world …

> Part of our transformation has seen Canada—a country with deep roots in Europe and with strong commercial ties to the United States—begin to recognize its natural affinity with the Pacific Rim and to see itself as a country of the Americas.

[17] In 1991, for instance, Canadian exports to Mexico were valued at C$2.58 billion and Mexican exports to Canada were worth just C$588.5 million. Statistics Canada (>www.docuweb.ca<). See also Gilbert R. Winham, 'NAFTA and the Trade Policy Revolution of the 1980s: A Canadian Perspective' (1994) XLIX:3 Int'l J 472, 492 ('… when Canada sought to join the Mexico-United States negotiation, its concern was not Mexico, or even less, Canadian-Mexican trade, which was insignificant …'.).

[18] European Parliament, Report of the Committee on External Economic Relations on the Free Trade Agreement between the United States of America, Canada and Mexico (NAFTA), DOC_EN\RR\217\217513 (18 November 1992), p. 7.

[19] Ted Chambers, 'Western Canada—Mexico Trade: Realizing Strategic Opportunities' (text found at >www.freenet.calgary.ab.ca<). Professor Chambers reinforces the paucity of trade between Canada's western provinces (British Columbia, Alberta, Saskatchewan, and Manitoba) and Mexico:

> These Mexican exports represent, on average, less than one-third of one per cent of western Canadian exports around the world in the period 1989–91. It is clear that in terms of commodity trade, the Mexican market is absolutely marginal for western Canadian business. In comparative terms, Western Canada and each of the four provinces sell less than one cent to Mexico for every $1 sold to the United States.

Canada did, however, offer Mexico GNP preferences under the GATT framework.

[20] Ronald J. Wonnacott, 'Canada's Role in NAFTA: To What Degree Has it Been Defensive?', in Victor Bulmer-Thomas, Nikki Craske and Mónica Serrano (eds), *Mexico and the North American Free Trade Agreement: Who Will Benefit?* (St Martin's Press, New York, 1994), pp. 163–75, at 174, n.6. Agricultural products as a whole and then computers formed the second and third largest categories of imports from Mexico.

averaged just slightly over 2 per cent.[21] The link to the United States was necessary. In 1993, after the signing of the NAFTA, the first Canadian trade office in Mexico was opened. This office, in Monterrey, was followed in 1995 with the opening of a second in Guadalajara.[22]

While there has been a lack of strongly positive relations between Canada and Mexico, there have also never been any seriously negative ones. Migration of workers from Mexico to Canada is small, due to the extreme distance between borders; the political interests of the countries have not conflicted directly; and the military threat that has intermittently shadowed relations of each with the United States is absent. The lack of problematic relations with each other, as well as the common interest in countering the United States, made co-operation during the NAFTA negotiations easier.[23]

1.1.3   Canadian-United States Relations

Canada's relations with the United States were, and are, often difficult. Culturally more similar to the United States than it is to Mexico, the uniqueness of Canada's history and political and social cultures is often overlooked by the US American.[24] The typical US citizen's assumption of Canadians as 'basically the same as us' remains a source of frustration for Canadians when interacting with their southern neighbors.[25]

Historically, the first European settlers of both Canada and the United States arrived as trappers and traders. However, the geography of the two lands quickly differentiated their populations. While Canada remained scarcely populated, with the population highly concentrated in the southern areas of its territory, the United States' expanses of arable lands encouraged many more immigrants to settle there and scattered the population throughout the territories.[26]

The population dynamics inevitably influenced the differences in political systems that arose. Not only do each of Canada's ten provinces have a much more distinct cultural identity than does an individual State of

---

[21] European Parliament (note 18 *supra*), at 8.

[22] Department of Foreign Affairs and International Trade, Canada-Mexico Relations.

[23] A Canadian (Chambers, note 19 *supra*), remarked on the benefits of this problem-free relationship as a potential for Canadian businesses to be at an advantage when doing business in Mexico under NAFTA: 'The Mexican attitude towards the United States remains ambivalent and, although the animosity of earlier decades has become muted, it is not extinct … Western Canadians with common sense and reasoned judgement, should be able with some frequency to take advantage of the fact that they are not Americans'.

[24] See also John Whalley and Colleen Hamilton, 'The Intellectual Underpinnings of North American Economic Integration' (1995) 4:1 Minn J Global Trade 43, 57 n.27, listing books and articles analyzing US-Canadian relations.

[25] See John Sloan Dickey and Whitney H. Shepardson, *Canada and the American Presence: The United States Interest in an Independent Canada* (New York UP, New York, 1975), p. xi: 'It is legendary that Canadians are born knowing that 'the United States will get you if you don't watch out' and that Americans die knowing nothing about Canada except that "it's cold up there"'.

[26] See *ibid.* at 4–6.

the United States, but the provinces' political autonomy is of a different echelon than the political authority reserved by the US States.[27] This difference between the two 'federal' systems of government could also have led to the unexpected difficulties in the negotiation or implementation of an international agreement that required the active or passive approval by the provincial governments in Canada.

The US population's widespread ignorance of Canada's history, culture, and geography as distinct from those of the United States has been at least partially responsible for the sometimes aggressive Canadian nationalism in both socio-political and economic arenas. Canadians' desire to maintain a distinct identity in the shadow of the United States has led to a conscious rejection of (or at least an attempt to minimize the influence of) many things 'American'. This rejection, whether of US magazines, movies, or investments, is then often complained about by the United States as being unfairly protectionist.[28] Such responses reinforce the Canadians' determination that the United States' vision of the relationship of culture, business, and trade should be kept out of Canada. In the words of Professor Robert Howse, an international trade law expert at the University of Toronto: 'there is still political capital to be made in Canada by standing up to American "bullying", and the American position is often expressed in the crude proposition that culture is a business like any other, and that the reasons for protecting it are simply bogus'.[29]

Unfortunately, the Canadian fear of an American cultural take-over may be more legitimate than the United States is able to recognize with its general ignorance of its closest neighbor. 'Americans', state two US researchers writing on United States-Canadian relations:

> may be helped in their understanding if they approach Canadian nationalism from two somewhat paradoxical premises: first, that despite the fact that Canada has over two hundred years of continuity as an evolving national society, much of her nationalism today has the self-conscious intensity of a newly created, somewhat uncertain, nation; second, that Canadian nationalism

---

[27] See *ibid.* at 6.

[28] See the recent dispute settlement proceedings between the United States and Canada in the World Trade Organization on the question (*inter alia*) of whether Canada's prohibition on the importation of 'split-run' editions of United States magazines violates Canada's national treatment obligation under the GATT. Canada—Certain Measures Concerning Periodicals, WT/DS31/R (14 March 1997) (panel report, appealed by Canada); AB-1997-2, WT/DS31/AB/R (adopted 30 July 1997). In the first instance, the panel found that the split-run magazines and other magazines could be 'like products', despite Canada's argument that a magazine's character must be determined by its content. WT/DS31/R at para. 5.26. The Appellate Body reversed the panel's finding, deciding instead that the two types of magazines are 'directly competitive or substitutable products'. WT/DS31/AB/R at 32. Thus, the end result was the same—the Canadian excise tax on these products was held to be a violation of the GATT Art. III:2 provision on national treatment. *Ibid.* at 39.

[29] Robert Howse, 'State Trading Enterprises and Multilateral Trade Rules: The Canadian Experience', in Thomas Cottier and Petros Mavroidis (eds), *State Trading in the Twenty-First Century* (University of Michigan Press, Ann Arbor, MI, 1998), p. 197. Professor Howse continues, 'If there are pressures for liberalization [in Canada] they come from within more than without …'. *Ibid.*

in its fundamental motivation is as old as the United States, in other words, that it is inescapably (and that is precisely the right word) a reaction to the American presence, past and current.[30]

1.2   MULTILATERAL RELATIONS OF THE NORTH AMERICAN STATES: THE GATT/WTO RELATIONS

The multilateral trade relations of the North American States are centered around each country's participation in the World Trade Organization (WTO) and, prior to this organization's establishment, the General Agreement on Tariffs and Trade (GATT). The history of the GATT/WTO system started with the end of the Second World War and continues to the present day. While Mexico joined the GATT system after Canada and the United States did, all are members of the WTO and are subject to the obligations found in that Organization's treaties.

1.2.1   Overview of GATT/WTO History

At the end of the Second World War, the victorious nations turned their attention to building a peaceful and prosperous international community. The tool chosen for this work was international trade. The belief that the high tariffs of the early 1930s had ignited the war by causing extreme economic depression committed the postwar states to the idea of free trade.

Free trade (or, more precisely, tariff-based freer trade) was to be ensured on a multilateral basis by the International Trade Organization (ITO), established to oversee its members' adherence to international commitments to liberalize the flow of goods into and out of its territory. In turn for giving up the right to levy tariffs on imports and exports, each member would gain the right to export its products to the other members.[31] The ITO would also have the authority to enforce the commitments of each member, thereby providing stability and predictability to the world economy, and would provide a forum for the non-violent settlement of disputes, thereby furthering the cause of peace.

1.2.1.1   The GATT 1947

The actual contract for the multilateral liberalization of trade was only one part of the foreseen ITO.[32] But, due to US Congressional resistance to the

---

[30] Dickey and Shepardson (note 25 *supra*), at xi.

[31] The trade organization was to be complemented by a monetary fund and a development bank in order to complete the toolbox for building worldwide economic prosperity and political stability. The result of such planning was the proposal of a triad of international economic institutions known as the Bretton Woods institutions: the International Bank for Reconstruction and Development (known as the World Bank); the International Monetary Fund; and the International Trade Organization.

[32] This contract was based on the document negotiated in Havana, Cuba in 1946, and is therefore known as the Havana Charter.

idea of subjecting the United States to any type of supranational organization, and to domestic political disputes between the Congress and the President, ITO was never formally established. Instead, it was only the contract that was to become the operating document, referred to as the General Agreement on Tariffs and Trade (GATT).

The GATT 1947, as the document is now known, set out the basic framework for trade in goods between and among its contracting parties. The idea was to liberalize trade in goods by voluntarily lowering tariffs and agreeing not to raise them above that level in the future. These 'bound' tariffs would, moreover, be valid for all GATT parties, as would any subsequent lowering of them. In addition, any trade benefits offered non-party states would be automatically extended to all other parties—expanding multilateralism was thus built into the system.

1.2.1.2   *Expansion of the GATT System*

Over nearly 40 years from 1947 to the mid-1980s, the ever more inclusive membership of the GATT met periodically to expand the scope of the General Agreement. They started in pursuit of lowering tariffs.[33] As the system grew, the Parties' attention turned increasingly to eliminating the non-tariff barriers to trade which were being used to circumvent the lowering of tariffs.[34] Successes included limiting the use of quantitative restrictions on imports and exports, regulating the use of technical standards to prevent protectionist closure of domestic markets to foreign goods, and declarations recognizing the distortions caused by subsidies.

While progress was made on tariff- and non-tariff barrier reductions in each of the GATT's first seven trade 'rounds', it was in 1986 with the Punta del Este Declaration opening the Uruguay Round of negotiations that the trading regime took a fundamental step forward in liberalizing world trade. At Punta del Este, and for the next eight years, the negotiators' focus was not just on how to further reduce restrictions on the trade of goods, but also on how to foster freer trade in services and on erecting a minimum level of intellectual property protection for all GATT member states.

---

[33] After the original meetings in Geneva in 1947, the GATT Contracting Parties met for negotiations in Annecy (France) in 1948 and in Torquay (England) in 1950 before another set of negotiations in Geneva in 1956. With double the number of governments taking part, the Dillon Round talks took place during 1960–61. The Kennedy Round was even longer, from 1964 to 1967. John H. Jackson, William J. Davey and Alan O. Sykes Jr, *Legal Problems in International Economic Relations* (3rd edn, West Publishing, St Paul, MN, 1995), p. 314.

[34] The Tokyo Round lasted from 1973 to 1979, and to a great extent changed the GATT structure. There were numerous substantive additions to the original Agreement, including 'tariff reduction protocols, nine special agreements, and four 'understandings' ... The overall impact of these results was to substantially broaden the scope of coverage of the GATT system'. Jackson *et al.* (note 33 *supra*), at 315, reprinted from John H. Jackson, *Restructuring the GATT System* (Royal Institue of International Affairs, London, 1990). See also *ibid.* ('The legal status of these various agreements and understandings, however, is not always clear').

1.2.1.3   The World Trade Organization

The resulting World Trade Organization (WTO) came into effect for most of its Members, including Canada, Mexico, and the United States, on 1 January 1995.[35] The WTO is the legal successor to the GATT, incorporating the GATT text[36] (while remaining separate from it), the so-called 'Understandings' or official interpretations of certain provisions,[37] as well as the dispute settlement panel decisions (the GATT 'case law') from the past 50 years[38] and exchanging the GATT Secretariat for the Secretariat of the WTO[39]. Members of the GATT that had ratified the Uruguay Round results by 1 January 1996 and the European Communities became original members of the WTO.[40] As of April 1999, there were 134 Members of the WTO. In addition, there were 31 observer states, 29 of which were in the process of applying for full membership.

1.2.2   United States Participation in GATT/WTO

The United States' participation in the GATT was active from the beginning of this international trade system. As a large exporting power after the Second World War, the US pushed for market access for its goods and was a strong proponent of the principle of 'unconditional MFN'. This is the form of most-favored-nation treatment that does not depend on reciprocal concessions. A trade partner that applies unconditional MFN will grant all the advantages of its trade regime to all partners equally, regardless if any—or only one—partner responds with market openings of its own.

Another indication of the central role of the United States in the GATT is indicated by its involvement in formal dispute settlements. The United States government was involved in 25 of the 52 dispute settlement cases heard by GATT panels, sometimes as the complainant and often as the complained-of party. Through this involvement, the United States was able to influence the

---

[35] There were 81 Members of the WTO on the Organization's coming into effect on 1 January 1995. *News GATT/WTO*, GW/13 (4 January 1995), p. 1. The European Communities
and the Member States had also completed the ratification process by that date. See also GATT, 'The WTO Enters into Force', *Focus GATT Newsletter*, No. 113 (December 1994), p. 1 ('The Implementation Conference, on 8 December, unanimously confirmed 1 January 1995 as the date of entry into force of the World Trade Organization with members pledging to make every effort to quickly conclude ratification of the WTO Agreement').

[36] Marrakesh Agreement Establishing the World Trade Organization, Art. II:4.

[37] *Ibid.* Art. II:2. These extra documents are termed 'associated legal instruments' in the Marrakesh Agreement.

[38] *Ibid.* Art. XVI:1.

[39] *Ibid.* Art. XVI:2.

[40] *Ibid.* Art. XI. For a more thorough description of the process of changing from the GATT to the WTO, see John Croome, *Reshaping the World Trading System: A History of the Uruguay Round* (WTO, Geneva, 1995); Terence P. Stewart (ed.), *The GATT Uruguay Round: A Negotiating History* (Kluwer Law and Taxation Publishers, Deventer, 1993) 3 vols; Garielle Marceau, 'Transition from GATT to WTO—A Most Pragmatic Operation' (1995) 29:4 J World Trade 147; Ernst-Ulrich Petersmann, 'The Transformation of the World Trading System through the 1994 Agreement Establishing the World Trade Organization' (1995) 6:2 Euro J Int'l L 161.

panel-made 'law' of the GATT (which has now been incorporated into the World Trade Organization). The US Trade Representative's arguments, while not always accepted, often became the 'other possible view' to solving a particular problem—inherently focusing the discussion of issues, and hence the development of the law, to suit US interests.

Being a frequent plaintiff in GATT dispute settlement, the United States also became a strong proponent for a move to a more 'legal' approach to dispute settlement. This was so at least until the mid-1980s, when the United States became a frequent object of complaint by its trading partners. The movement supporting the Dispute Settlement Understanding and the dispute settlement procedures (including the creation of the Appellate Body) during the Uruguay Round, was to a large degree the work of the United States.[41]

Perhaps even more significant in shaping the multilateral trade regime was the United States' commitment to broadening the GATT. Urging further liberalization in the goods sectors, the United States also looked to other sectors of the economy. The bringing of trade in services and the trade aspects of intellectual property under the multilateral rules of the GATT/WTO was made an issue for debate within the GATT by US insistence on these additions to the negotiating program of the Uruguay Round. Exploiting its position as the largest importer and exporter, the US Trade Representative threatened a walk-out from the trade negotiations unless it could be guaranteed attention would be paid to ensuring its growing services economy access to new markets. Similarly, it was United States' dissatisfaction with the lack of intellectual property protection afforded its exports that gave initial impetus to the TRIPs negotiations.

1.2.3 Canada's Participation in GATT

Canada, the United States' largest trading partner and northern neighbor played a less active role in the development of the GATT/WTO. Canada's GATT participation was, however, always supportive of the multilateral system. At the same time, Canada has been very active in the area of promoting a cultural exception to the GATT rules.

Particularly striking from the point of view of the NAFTA formation is the frequency with which the Canadian government has faced formal GATT dispute settlement proceedings against the United States. Starting in 1962, when the United States attacked the Canadian import regime for potatoes,[42] there were 15 cases between the neighbors up to 1994. This, in comparison to the total number of Canada's GATT history of 29 formal disputes, is particularly interesting. The coming into effect of the WTO has not lessened the frictions between the neighbors. Continued Canadian resistance to opening its cultural goods market and the United States' repeated use of unilateral threats of trade sanctions have led to renewed accusations of protectionism on either side.

---

[41] See Yong K. Kim, 'The Beginnings of the Rule of Law in the International Trade System Despite the US Constitutional Constraints' (1996) 17:4 Mich J Int'l L 967, 971–973.

[42] Export of Potatoes to Canada, 11S BISD 88 (adopted 16 November 1962).

1.2.4   Mexico's Participation in GATT

Mexico's participation differed from that of its northern neighbors. Given the opportunity in 1980, Mexico refused to become a Contracting Party of the GATT.[43] As economic reform gained momentum, the Mexican attitude toward the international trade system became more conciliatory and Mexico entered the GATT in 1986 under the leadership of then-President de la Madrid.[44] Under its Protocol of Accession, Mexico is characterized as a developing nation, and is thus eligible for benefits under the Generalized System of Preferences (GSP).[45]

Mexico's activity level in the GATT was relatively high until 1993. Although its Protocol of Accession required it to reduce its tariffs to 50 per cent, the Mexican government, eager to display its newly adopted policy of export-driven development, capped their tariff bindings at 20 per cent, with many falling to 10 per cent or even to zero. While Mexico never had a formal GATT dispute with Canada, it did apply to the dispute settlement organ twice for complaints it had with United States trade policy. The first was early in Mexico's GATT membership, in 1986–87, regarding US taxes on petroleum.[46] The second dispute started with consultations in 1990,[47] and ended unsatisfactorily when the United States refused to accept the panel decision finding the United States' prohibition on imports of Mexican tuna, as applied under national environmental law,[48] illegal.[49]

Under the GSP programs allowed under the GATT, developed nations were permitted (although not required) to grant imports from developing

---

[43] Alex E. Fernàndez Jilberto and Barbara Hogenboom, 'Mexico's Integration in NAFTA: Neoliberal Restructuring and Changing Political Alliances', in Alex E. Fernàndez Jilberto and André Mommen (eds), *Liberalization in the Developing World: Institutional and Economic Changes in Latin America, Africa and Asia* (Routledge, London, 1996), pp. 138–60, at 148.

[44] See Protocol for the Accession of Mexico to the General Agreement on Tariffs and Trade, L/6036 (1986).

[45] Report of the Working Party on the Accession of Mexico (L/6010) BISD 33S/57, 61, para.10:

> In acknowledging Mexico's status as a developing country, a number of members stated that the Working Party should seek to arrive at a mutually acceptable outcome that would take into account Mexico's development needs and enable Mexico to benefit from the full range of GATT rights, while upholding the principles and rules of the General Agreement. In this context it is the understanding of all members of the Working Party that the adoption of the Report of the Working Party (L/6010) and the approval of the Protocol of Accession of Mexico, confers on Mexico only such additional rights or privileges as are enjoyed by other developing contracting parties, and does not derogate in any way from obligations incumbent on developing contracting parties to the GATT.

> See also Protocol for the Accession of Mexico (*'Taking note* of Mexico's present status as a developing country, because of which Mexico shall enjoy the special and more favourable treatment which the General Agreement and other provisions deriving therefrom established for developing countries, …'.).

[46] See United States—Taxes on Petroleum and Certain Imported Substances, consultations with Mexico as recorded in L/6093 (10 November 1986).

[47] C/M/246 (5 November 1990).

[48] The law at issue was the United States Marine Mammal Protection Act of 1972. P.L. 92-522, 86 Stat. 1027 (1972), as amended.

[49] United States—Restrictions on Imports of Tuna, BISD 39S/155 (1991) (unadopted). The panel's decision can also be found in (1991) XXX:6 ILM 1594.

countries lower-than-MFN tariff rates. This deviated from the strict non-discrimination rules of the GATT in order to foster economic development of the developing countries.[50] The United States' GSP program, established in 1979, allowed many Mexican goods exported to the United States to benefit from tariff-free treatment, and others from preferential, or sub-MFN, tariffs. Receiving 48 per cent of the total US GSP benefits, the value of this treatment to Mexico was substantial in 1993, nearly five times more than the value of US GSP benefits going to the second-largest recipients, Brazil and Malaysia.[51]

In Canada, Mexican imports were minimal. Still, the Canadian GSP tariffs allowed for the Mexican imports to benefit from lower tariffs.[52]

1.3 BEGINNINGS OF THE NORTH AMERICAN FREE TRADE AGREEMENT

1.3.1 Early Proposals for a Free Trade Area of North America

While the first serious proposal for a free trade agreement of the entire North American continent was made by President Salinas de Gortari of Mexico to US President Bush in 1990,[53] the idea of a free trade area of, as well as bilateral areas within, North America was not original to President Salinas. There had been numerous attempts to foster trade from the beginnings of the independent nationhood in the New World.

1.3.1.1 From the Nineteenth Century to the Second World War

In the mid-nineteenth century, Canada (then the 'colonies of British North America') and the United States agreed to allow raw materials to pass the border freely under the Reciprocity Treaty.[54] Despite a short life span,

---

[50] The idea behind the GSP program was that developing countries needed preferential access to large developed markets in order to achieve economies of scale in their industries. Each developed country Contracting Party, therefore, was given the option to develop its own system of preferences to further this goal.

[51] See GATT, *Trade Policy Review: United States*, Vol. 1 (1994), p. 49 (Brazil and Malaysia each received 10 per cent of the US GSP benefits). The fact that GSP benefits were offered as a privilege and not as a right encouraged Mexico to undertake the NAFTA negotiations. See 1.3.2 *infra*.

[52] See Frank Stone, 'The Generalized System of Preferences', in Frank Stone, *Canada, the GATT and the International Trade System* (Institute for Research on Public Policy, Montreal, 1984), pp. 132–8, at 135–7, describing Canada's GSP program.

[53] See Letter from President of Mexico Carlos Salinas de Gortari to President of the United States George Bush, 21 August 1990. One of the Mexican NAFTA delegation leaders, Hermann von Bertrab recounts that the idea of a Mexican-US free trade agreement was first born at the World Economic Forum in Davos, Switzerland, in January 1990. Hermann von Bertrab, *Negotiating NAFTA: A Mexican Envoy's Account* (Center for Strategic and International Studies, Westport, CT, 1997), pp. 1–2.

[54] Reciprocity Treaty of 1854. The United States ended the treaty in 1866 as a signal of its dissatisfaction with Britain's role in the Civil War. Jeffrey Simser, 10 Banking & Fin L Rev at 191, n.14, citing R. White, *Fur Trade to Free Trade: Putting the Canada-US Trade Agreement in Historical Perspective* (Dundurn Press, Toronto, 1989), pp. 44, 55.

1854–66, the Reciprocity Treaty did help to foster trade between the nations. Only five years later, in 1871, Prime Minister John A. MacDonald proposed a new treaty, but it was short-lived. The year 1874 led to another unsuccessful attempt at Canadian-US free trade, as did 1911.

The years between the two World Wars began with a strong push toward internationalism, but the economic environment quickly became protectionist. The United States and Canada were both instigators and victims of the renewed mercantilism,[55] with raising of tariffs a major part of the foreign policy of each country, despite international calls to refrain from such actions.[56]

Even within the generally protectionist economic context of the 1920s, there were several developments in United States trade policy that would become important in the free trade movement later on. First, it was in 1923 that the United States adopted a policy of unconditional most-favored-nation treatment.[57] Thus, reciprocity was no longer necessary for the United States to reduce its own trade barriers. Secondly, the President was given authority to adjust tariffs in response to trading partners' actions.[58] The US trade policy was highly protectionist, and the intent of the 'flexibility' of tariffs was to *increase* them should terms of trade worsen for US products. This did not happen, however. The reason proposed by one commentator is that, 'an important principle had been conceded, namely, that the President could change tariffs without seeking further Congressional approval. The intended upward flexibility could become a downward flexibility in the future'.[59]

---

[55] See generally, Frank Stone, 'The Pre-War Background', in Stone (note 52 *supra*), pp. 5–17, at 7–8, explaining Canada-United States economic relations, focusing on the 1920s and 1930s:

> During most of the inter-war period, the United States followed import policies that were especially damaging to Canadian trade interests. Legislation passed by Congress in the early 1920s and in 1930 raised US tariffs to unprecedented heights: ... almost 50 per cent ...

> (T)he Hawley-Smoot tariff increases, imposed by the USA in 1930, provoked many other countries, including Canada, to raise new barriers to their imports ... In 1931 and 1932, Canadian tariffs were substantially increased; the average rate on dutiable imports rose ... to about 28 per cent.

[56] The League of Nations (of which the United States was never a member) had attempted to encourage its members to lower tariffs, change their quantitative restrictions on trade into tariffs, and extend to one another unconditional most-favored-nation treatment. Despite global economic conferences, the League's efforts were not enough to overcome the protectionist trends of the early 1930s. The World Economic Conference of 1927 addressed traditional trade issues such as the lowering of tariffs, the changing of quotas into tariffs, and the extension of unconditional most-favored-nation treatment to member states. The Monetary and Economic Conference of 1933 continued efforts to lower tariffs and added the issue of monetary policy to the agenda. Stone (note 55 *supra*), at 13.

[57] John H. Jackson, *The World Trading System: Law and Policy of International Relations* (MIT Press, Cambridge, MA, 1989), pp. 13–14. For a discussion of the principle of most-favored-nation obligation, see 3.10 *infra*.

[58] Nigel Grimwade, *International Trade Policy: A Contemporary Analysis* (Routledge, London, 1996), p. 7.

[59] *Ibid.* at 7.

Finally, the United States adopted a tariff-oriented approach to regulating trade. As a result, quantitative restrictions were no longer accepted as legitimate, due to their lack of transparency.[60]

In 1934, the United States changed its overall restrictive approach to trade. This in turn led to better economic relations with Canada, among others. Under the leadership of Franklin Roosevelt, the United States' economy began once again to focus on the encouragement of foreign trade. To achieve this, the Administration chose to lower tariffs under the authority of the Reciprocal Trade Agreements Act.[61] By the end of the 1930s, nearly 30 bilateral trade agreements were in effect in the United States, including two between the United States and Canada.[62] The 1935 Agreement included commitments not only to lower tariffs, but also to treat each other's goods according to the most-favored-nation obligation.[63] A 1938 Agreement built on the prior agreement, and included negotiations with the United Kingdom.

> The 1938 negotiations were 'triangular', in that the Canada-USA negotiations took place simultaneously with US-UK trade negotiations. These 1938 negotiations not only further liberalized trade among the three countries, but also set a pattern for future negotiations under GATT, since they involved a rudimentary 'multilateralization' of bilateral negotiations.[64]

The beginning of the Second World War limited the actual economic effectiveness of these trade agreements.[65] However, the ideology of free trade had been established.

1.3.1.2 The End of the Second World War to 1990

At the end of the Second World War, the Canadian and United States governments secretly drafted a protocol for free trade, despite a germinating preference for multilateral agreements.[66] The draft never developed into a formal agreement, as the Canadians withdrew in favor of the new General Agreement on Tariffs and Trade. In 1965, however, Canada and the United States entered into the Automotive Products Trade Agreement (known commonly as 'the US-Canada Auto Pact' or merely the

---

[60] *Ibid.* at 8.

[61] *Ibid.* at 5. The Reciprocal Trade Agreements Act of 1934 gave the President the power to negotiate trade agreements with foreign countries without the approval of Congress. The President could lower tariffs by up to 50 per cent under the terms of unconditional most-favored-nation treatment. 'The overall intent was to use the US tariff as a weapon to gain easier access for US manufacturers to the markets of other countries'; see also Stone (note 55 *supra*), at 11.

[62] Grimwade (note 58 *supra*), at 9; Stone (note 55 *supra*), at 11.

[63] Stone (note 55 *supra*), at 12. For an explanation of most-favored-nation treatment, see 3.10 *infra*.

[64] *Ibid.* at 12.

[65] Grimwade (note 58 *supra*), at 9.

[66] Murray G. Smith, 'Trade Policies in Canada', in Jorge Witker (ed.), *Legal Aspects of the Trilateral Free Trade Agreement* (Universidad Nacional Autonoma de Mexico, Mexico City, 1992), pp. 11–14, at 13.

'Auto Pact').[67] This agreement prescribed tariff-free trade in new autos and auto parts between the two countries.[68] Regarded as a success, the Auto Pact resulted in a complete restructuring of the North American auto manufacturing environment.[69]

The United States and Mexico had also had bilateral trade agreements since the end of the Second World War. One early agreement focussed on labor. Known as the Bracero Program, this agreement allowed migrant workers from Mexico to travel into the United States for seasonal work in agriculture. In 1965, the Mexican Border Industrialization Program (MBI) replaced the earlier Bracero Program.[70] As the name suggests, the MBI was a plan to industrialize the US-Mexican border region in hopes of keeping the one-time braceros on the Mexican side of the border, and at the same time offering US manufacturers a means to lower their production costs through cheaper labor. The 'maquiladora' industries that were established in the 20-kilometer strip of land south of the border were granted the right to import raw materials without paying tariffs, as long as the finished product would be exported back into the United States immediately.[71] The 'success' of the program is debatable,[72] but the number of United States factories to take

---

[67] For a detailed examination at the Auto Pact and the impact of capital mobility on trade, see Kenneth P. Thomas, 'Capital Mobility and Trade Policy: the Case of the Canada-US Auto Pact' (1997) 4:1 Rev Int'l Pol Econ 127.

[68] The Auto Pact was allowable under the GATT only as a waiver to the MFN obligations of Canada and the United States. See 'United States—Imports of Automotive Products', BISD 14S/37 (1966), decision of 20 December 1965. The waiver was conditional on the United States' agreement to enter into consultations with other GATT Contracting Parties who requested such consultations in order to prevent 'significant diversion of imports' from that country to imports from Canada. *Ibid*. at 38, para. 2.

[69] Thomas (note 67 *supra*), at 143–4 ('Consequences of the Agreement'). The sector-specific agreement also formed a model for one of the favored methods of negotiating commitments within the GATT/WTO context. Sectoral negotiations for liberalization are generally undertaken by the leading producer states and consumer states of that sector, and when agreement is reached, the results are extended to all other Member States on an equal basis. This method of negotiations has been used for negotiating trade conditions for chemical products and pharmaceuticals, furniture, paper, certain alcoholic beverages, non-ferrous metals, agricultural and construction equipment. Recently, the sectoral approach was also used in the WTO for liberalizing trade in information technology products. See Luzius Wasescha and Markus Schlagenhof, 'Information Technology Agreement (ITA)—Towards a New Area of Sectorial Market Liberalisation in WTO' (1998) 53:1 *Aussenwirtschaft* 113, 120–121. But see *ibid*. at 121–2, criticizing the sectoral approach as putting 'into question traditional elements of tariff negotiations' and for endangering multilateralism in favor of plurilateralism.

[70] For a concise account of the specific identity of the US-Mexican border area, see Ruth Buchanan, 'Border Crossings: NAFTA, Regulatory Restructuring, and the Politics of Place' (1995) 2 Global Leg Stud 371 (text found on the internet at >www.law.ind...<). See also Winham (note 17 *supra*), at 472, 476, relating that the main beneficiary of the Maquiladora program remained the textile manufacturers until the 1980s.

[71] A short history of the maquiladora industry can be found in Nacional Financiera's periodical *El Mercado de Valores*. 'Origins and Development of the In-Bond Exort Industry in Mexico' 4 *El Mercado De Valores* 19 (July–August 1996).

[72] The horrors of the working and living conditions in the settlements that have grown up around the maquiladora factories have been widely documented. See, e.g., Buchanan (note 70 *supra*), at n.43–5 and accompanying text:

advantage of the cheaper Mexican workforce increased rapidly, from 72 in 1967 to nearly 2,000 in 1992, and the number of Mexican workers jumped nearly one hundred-fold.[73] These maquiladora factories, no longer required to be located in the border region, continued to increase their supplying of export goods, even during the inward-looking years following the Mexican debt crisis of 1982.[74]

Meanwhile, the attempts to establish wider trade agreements continued. In 1977, the Canadian Progressive Conservative Duncan Edmonds unsuccessfully suggested the formation of an economic union of Canada, Mexico, and the United States.[75] In 1983, Canadian Prime Minister Pierre Trudeau, in attempting to attract more foreign investments, offered an idea of a bilateral US-Canada sectoral free trade agreement.[76] Four years later, under then-President Ronald Reagan, the dream of a US-Latin America trade zone was again expressed, this time by the United States, and this time the idea began to develop.

Following President Miguel de la Madrid's elections, Mexico's federal government began to interest itself in trade with its northern neighbor as well as with the rest of the world.[77] One of the first steps toward what is now the NAFTA occurred in 1987, when the Framework Understanding on Trade and Investment Relations was negotiated between the Reagan and the de la

---

(Contd.)

>...(A) number of troubling trends became apparent early in the program. It was women young, unmarried, and childless rather than the former braceros who were getting the jobs in these new plants ... The jobs generally entailed repetitive tasks, resulting in a high rate of employee injury, sickness, and turnover. The factories had few backward linkages to Mexican suppliers, and engaged in a minimal amount of worker training and minimal research and development in Mexico ...
>
>... The large influx of people to the border region ... has put enormous strain on the infrastructure of the border sites. Thousands live in makeshift settlements ... where there are no support services, and where water supplies are likely to be contaminated by sewage or hazardous waste. In 1991, the Mexican government acknowledged that fifty per cent of the maquiladora plants near the US border were producing toxic waste, and that the government had not enforced its regulations requiring that such wastes be returned to the United States.

[73] Kathryn Kopinak, 'The Maquiladorization of the Mexican Economy', in Ricardo Grinspun and Maxwell A. Cameron (eds), *The Political Economy of North American Free Trade* (1993), p. 141, cited in Ruth Buchanan (note 70 *supra*), at n.41 and accompanying text.

[74] See Preston Brown and Carolyn Karr, 'The Transformation of the Maquiladora Under the North American Free Trade Agreement', in Seymour J. Rubin and Dean C. Alexander (eds), *NAFTA and Investment* (Kluwer Law International, The Hague, 1995), pp. 37–63; *ibid.* at 50 (Maquiladora industry has been able to set up production outside of the border area since 1972).

[75] Donald Barry, 'The Road to NAFTA', in Donald Barry (ed.), *Toward a North American Community: Canada, the United States and Mexico* (Westview, Boulder, CO, 1995), cited in Winham (note 17 *supra*), at 473–4, n.2.

[76] Smith (note 66 *supra*), at 17 (Trudeau's proposal failed because the sectoral coverage desired by the United States and Canada differed).

[77] Mexico had acceded to the GATT in 1986 under the leadership of José López Portillo.

Madrid administrations.[78] This Understanding set out substantive and procedural norms to govern bilateral dialogues and conflicts in trade matters. Though the phrasing of the Understanding is general, the text addresses not only trade in goods,[79] but also trade in services,[80] investment,[81] technology transfer,[82] intellectual property protection[83], and the need for development of the border areas[84]—all areas contained in the NAFTA.[85]

In that same year, Canada and the United States intensified their trade relations with negotiations aimed at the formation of a bilateral free trade zone. The Canada-United States Free Trade Agreement (CUFTA) was the product of extremely difficult negotiations pushed forward by the Canadians.[86] The CUFTA came into force on 1 January 1989, creating a free trade area for goods and services of the two countries. The CUFTA is notable for its breadth. Not only manufactured goods, but also agricultural products, services, financial services, and investments were included in its trade liberalizing provisions. Moreover, government procurement, technical norms, rules of origin and temporary business travel were addressed. The CUFTA was the first free trade agreement to have such a broad reach, and surpassed by a large margin the multilateral trade rules in effect at that time.[87] Although not a descendant of the CUFTA, the NAFTA contains many provisions based closely on the earlier agreement's framework and text.

In October of 1989, ten and one-half months after the coming into effect of the CUFTA, the United States House of Representatives Committee on Ways and Means asked the International Trade Commission (ITC)[88] to

---

[78] Understanding Between the Government of the United States of America and the Government of the United Mexican States Concerning a Framework of Principles and Procedures for Consultations Regarding Trade and Investment Relations, done at Mexico City, 6 November 1987, found in (1998) 27 ILM 438 (hereinafter 'Framework Understanding').

[79] Framework Understanding (note 78 *supra*), I:4-7, (1988) 27 ILM 438, 439.

[80] *Ibid*. I:10.

[81] *Ibid*. I:11.

[82] *Ibid*.

[83] *Ibid*. I:12.

[84] *Ibid*. I:13.

[85] See, e.g., NAFTA, 'Preamble'; NAFTA Part II (trade in goods); NAFTA Part V (cross-border investment and trade in services); NAFTA Chapter Seventeen (intellectual property).

[86] Canada-United States Free Trade Agreement (done at Ottawa, 22 December 1987 and 2 January 1988, and at Washington, DC, and Palm Springs, 23 December 1987 and 2 January 1988). For the text of the agreement see (1988) XXVII:2 ILM 281, 293. For more on the CUFTA, see John D. Richard and Richard G. Deardon, *The Canada-US Free Trade Agreement: Final Text and Analysis* (CCH Canadian Ltd, New York, 1988), which contains a short explanatory summary and text of Agreement. There is a comparison of the CUFTA financial service provisions with those of the NAFTA in Chapter 4 *infra*.

[87] For an excellent bibliography of books, articles, and government documents on the Canada-United States Free Trade Agreement, see *External Affairs and International Trade Canada, Canada-United States Free Trade: A Bibliography* (5th edn, Library Services Division, Ottawa, 1989).

[88] The International Trade Commission is an independent agency of the United States. Six Commissioners compose the Commission, each appointed by the President for a nine-year term. One of the most important functions of the ITC is their preliminary study into whether safeguard remedies are called for under Section 201 of the Trade Act of 1974. John H. Jackson, William J. Davey and Alan O. Sykes Jr, *Legal Problems of International Economic Relations* (3rd edn, West Publishing, St Paul, MN, 1995), pp. 610–11.

conduct a study on the possibilities for economic relations with Mexico.[89] In its summary of results, the ITC noted that:

> [a]lthough many experts advocated a cautious, 'go-slow' approach in negotiations, the overwhelming majority of experts' [sic] supported the concept of [a free trade agreement (FTA)] as the most appropriate option for the United States and Mexico to pursue for the purpose of enhancing their bilateral trade relationship. Only if an FTA is not possible, did the majority recommend that the two countries engage in sectoral negotiations—and then only as an interim measure to keep moving toward the establishment of an FTA.[90]

The research, officially described as undertaken to allow 'US business leaders and policymakers ... a better understanding of the scope of the changes being undertaken by the Mexican leadership and their implications for future US-Mexican economic relations',[91] accurately foreshadowed the problems of negotiating traditionally non-trade issues such as environmental protection and labor rights. The results stated that 'a majority of participants expressed the opinion that non-trade issues have no place in trade negotiations'.[92]

Rejecting non-trade issues, the study concluded that a broad-based free trade agreement with Mexico would be to the advantage of US businesses' competitiveness overall.[93] Mexico was a market of 85 million consumers, over 60 per cent of whom were 24 years old or younger, under conditions of slowly but steadily growing hunger for products produced in the North.[94] The United States' own economy at the time was in recession, unemployment was high, and factory production was faltering.[95] The possibility to secure entry to new markets, urged US businesses, should be embraced.

Thus, by the time President Salinas made his offer of a Mexican-United States free trade zone to President Bush, the US Administration and Congress had already seen the background analyses of such a proposition and could be assured of support by the business community. Accordingly, President Bush welcomed the Mexican overtures.

---

[89] Letter from Dan Rostenkowski, Chairman, House of Representatives Committee on Ways and Means, to Anne E. Brunsdale, Chairman, United States International Trade Commission (12 October 1989); see also ITC, 'Executive Summary', in *Review of Trade and Investment Liberalization Measures by Mexico and Prospects for Future United States-Mexico Relations, Phase III: Summary of View on Prospects for Future United-States-Mexico Relations* (October 1990), p. iii, describing the request by the House Committee as for a survey of Mexico's trade and investment developments and a 'summary of experts' views on prospects for future United States-Mexican trade relations'.

[90] *Ibid.*

[91] Letter from Dan Rostenkowski (note 89 *supra*).

[92] ITC (note 89 *supra*), at 1–9.

[93] ITC (note 89 *supra*), Ch. 1: 'Summary of Views' at p. 1-1.

[94] Timothy J. Kehoe, 'Comment', in Lustig *et al.* (note 12 *supra*), pp. 58-63, at 63, in which Table 11 reflects 1990 population statistics from the Instituto Nacional de Estadística, Geografía e Informática in Mexico City); ITC (note 89 *supra*), Ch. 1: 'Summary of Views', at 1-13–1-14.

[95] Von Bertrab (note 53 *supra*), at 40, recalls that doubt about the US's ability to compete with Japan and Germany was a strong motivating factor for the responsiveness to Mexican trade overtures.

1.3.2   Mexican Initiative for a US-Mexico Free Trade Agreement

Under the leadership of President Carlos Salinas de Gortari, Mexico continued the process of economic reform begun by his predecessor Miguel de la Madrid.[96] The reduction of tariffs within the framework of the General Agreement on Tariffs and Trade (GATT) was just one part of Salinas' program of liberalization. In addition, state-owned enterprises were sold to private Mexican investors, inflation was lowered, and an emphasis on manufacturing started to reduce Mexico's historic reliance on oil exports. Most importantly, perhaps, Mexico started looking for foreign investors again.

President Salinas began a campaign for political reform to support the economic changes.[97] Domestically this included revising election procedures to attempt to reduce the appearance of election fraud by the ruling party. Internationally, Mexico re-entered the global trading system as an active member, acceding to the GATT in 1988.[98]

Witnessing the deepening of the European Communities' ties and the formation of the US-Canada Free Trade Agreement, by the early 1990s Salinas had become convinced of a global trend toward regional trading blocs. Only from within one of the blocs, he feared, could a state remain assured of reaping the advantages of trade.[99] Moreover, as the architect of Mexico's new economic internationalization, President Salinas wanted Mexico to join a free trade area as a way of firmly embedding the progress they had made in the previous ten years of economic liberalization.[100] In addition, Mexicans hoped that a free trade agreement with an industrialized country would lend credibility to the economic reforms, and in turn would make Mexico a more attractive market for foreign direct investment.[101]

---

[96]   For an overview of the Mexican government's foreign investment policies of the early 1980s, including a brief description of the National Development Plan of 1983, see Julio C. Treviño, 'Mexico: The Present Status of Legislation and Governmental Policies on Direct Foreign Investments' (1984) 18:2 Int'l Lawyer 297.

[97]   Ramesh Thakur, 'The North American Free Trade Agreement' (1993) 47:1 Australian J Int'l Aff 77, 79.

[98]   See 1.2.4 *supra*.

[99]   See Thakur (note 97 *supra*), at 79:

> ... Mexico discovered that a third option which could reduce overwhelming dependence on the US did not exist. South American countries form a relatively small market for Mexican goods, Asian markets remain impenetrable and prospects of accessing the European Community ... after 1992 were uncertain ... Mexico concluded that if the world was going to coalesce around trading blocs, then it was better to be inside a Fortress America than outside all blocs.

[100]   Simser (note 54 *supra*), at 193 ('For Mexico, NAFTA was a device to ensure that the economic reforms led by Salinas would survive the vicissitudes of a fragile polity').

[101]   Macario Schettino, *El TLC El Tratado de Libre Comercio: Qué es y Cómo Nos Afecta* (Grupo Editorial Iberoamérica, Mexico City, 1994), p. 39 ('uno de los principales objetivos del TLC era dotar a la inversión extranjera de un panorama màs estable en México'). Eduardo Gitli and Gunilla Ryd, 'Latin American Integration and the Enterprise for the Americas Initiative' (1992) 26:4 J World Trade 25, 35 ('The need to demonstrate that the reforms were not to be reversed is strongly felt by the Mexican authorities. In this regard, it is worth bearing in mind that the senior adviser to President Salinas, Mr José Córdoba, indicated, during the 1992 World Economic Forum in Davos, that Mexico wanted to use the free-trade agreement to lock-in deregulation, foreign investment and other policies, so that they could not be easily changed by future governments').

Traveling to Europe in 1990, Salinas tried to interest the leaders of the European Community (EC) in extending their network of trade agreements with Mexico.[102] The Community, however, was preoccupied with the Eastern European states' new market orientation, and decided against further additions from the New World.

Salinas was forced to the conclusion that if he were to bring Mexico into a regional trade group, the United States would be Mexico's only potential partner from whom there would be noticeable benefits.[103] Thus, reversing Mexico's traditionally hostile relations with the United States, Salinas approached US President George Bush with the idea of forming a US-Mexican Free Trade Area.

The United States was willing and eager to gain access to the expanding and promising Mexican market under conditions of competitive equality. Under President Reagan, the vision for developing US trade with all of Latin America had been expressed, with but little effect. George Bush, Reagan's successor, with the opportunity presented to him, agreed to act.

1.3.3 Canada's Entry into the Negotiations

The role of Canada in the formation of NAFTA is peculiar. Economic relations with the United States had historically been voluminous if not harmonious, and the experience of the Canadian-United States Trade Agreement[104] was mixed at best.[105] In terms of relations with Mexico, Canada was never very

---

[102] European Parliament (note 18 *supra*) at 6. In 1975, Mexico and the European Economic Community had signed a bilateral trade agreement extending most-favored-nation (MFN) treatment to goods and services. Agreement Between the European Economic Community and the United Mexican States, O.J.L. 247/11 (1975) ('EEC-Mexico Agreement'); Whalley and Hamilton (note 24 *supra*), at 63, n.50, and accompanying text. However, the EEC-Mexico Agreement provided exceptions to the MFN provision for customs unions and free trade area arrangements in Art. 2:2(b). With the 1986 accession of Spain, Portugal, and Greece to the EC, much of Mexico's preferential trade was diverted, and the EEC-Mexico Agreement became economically unimportant. See Therese M. Woods, 'The EEC-Mexican Agreement: Time for Reevaluation?' (1989) 12:3 Fordham Int'l LJ 541.

[103] Thakur (note 97 *supra*), at 79. The EEC-Mexico Agreement had originally been undertaken at least in part to lessen Mexico's dependence on trade with the United States. Woods (note 102 *supra*), at 544, referring to S. Weintraub, 'Free Trade Between Mexico and the United States?' (1984), p. 17.

[104] See 1.1.3 and 1.3 *supra*.

[105] Writing in the early 1990s, one commentator describes the the results of the CUFTA for Canada as 'difficult to seize or to judge'. Robert Bothwell, 'Free Trade and Its Discontents', in Bothwell, *Canada and the United States: the Politics of Partnership* (University of Toronto Press, Toronto, 1992), pp. 139–59, at 151. Mr Bothwell continues:

> Even the enthusiasts of free trade thought that some Canadian industries would suffer. They suffered more rather than less in 1989 and 1990. The Canadian dollar appreciated against its American counterpart, losing exports with every cent it gained. The Canadian government kept it high with interest rates a few per centage points above the American. Taken together, these policies were enough to drive the Canadian economy into a spate of plant closures and recession, by the end of 1990. How much worse, or better, things were because of free trade was a matter of lively dispute, in which the protagonists adopted entirely predictable positions.

Ibid. at 151–2. For further description on US-Canada pre-war relations, see Stone (note 55 *supra*).

actively involved with the third North American. The Canada-Mexico trade flows were a minuscule $3 billion in 1991.[106] Still, Canada's interest in joining the United States and Mexico was perhaps even more economically driven than the others.[107]

With respect to its manufactured goods, Canada's modern trade policy has traditionally been relatively liberal after a brief, yet disastrous, experiment with high tariffs in the first years of the 1930s.[108] After the Second World War, Canada supported the multilateral trade system of the GATT, lowering tariffs on goods and reducing non-tariff barriers for all trading partners. In 1965, the signing of the Auto Pact[109] avoided some of the damaging effects the two countries' countervailing duty schemes were having on their automobile industries.[110] However, despite its low tariffs, Canada's restrictions on investment began to be tightened during the 1970s.[111]

The United States and Canada were already co-partners in a regional trade arrangement in 1992. While the Canada-United States Free Trade Agreement did not eliminate all trade barriers between the two members, it did provide more liberalized trade than had before existed. More significantly, it addressed services (including financial services) and investment in addition to goods. At the same time, the animosity engendered among the CUFTA negotiators themselves and the resentment harbored by the Canadian population against their own government's yielding to the United States' non-concessional approach during the bilateral agreement's drafting left a bitter aftertaste to the completion of the negotiations.[112]

---

[106]   Dean Alexander, 'The North American Free Trade Agreement: An Overview' (1993) 11 Int'l Tax & Bus Lawyer 48, 49, cited in Simser (note 54 *supra*), at 199.

[107]   Simser (note 54 *supra*), at 192.

[108]   For a short history of Canada's trade policies, see Smith (note 66 *supra*), at 11–41.

[109]   See 1.3.1.2 *supra*.

[110]   Smith (note 66 *supra*), at 14.

[111]   *Ibid.* at 15.

[112]   For descriptions of the CUFTA negotiations see William S. Merkin, Ann H. Hughes, Ralph R. Johnson and Julius L. Katz, 'US-Canada Free Trade Agreement, 1986–1987' (1996) 1 Int'l Neg 257; Bothwell (note 105 *supra*), at 142–53. Both articles stress the different political importance placed on the negotiations by the two countries as well as the personal differences of the chief negotiators. See, e.g., Merkin *et al.* (*supra*), at 267 (Ann Hughs of the Commerce Department noted 'I have been involved in many negotiations, but have never been involved in one in which the chief negotiators grew to dislike each other so intensely. Even the team members on both sides grew to dislike each other'); *ibid.* at 259:

> On the US side, the negotiation was never given the priority or resources it deserved, and the process proved to be much more difficult, consequently, than it needed to be.
> In contrast, Canada gave much higher priority to the negotiation and it was 'front-page' news every day throughout the entire process.

Bothwell (note 105 *supra*), at 146:

> The two countries appointed chief negotiators: the Americans Peter Murphy, a youngish trade official, and the Canadians Simon Reisman, an abrasive veteran of forty years of trade negotiations. 'The Americans appointed somebody who couldn't talk, and the Canadians somebody who wouldn't listen', a bystander quipped ...
> ... Canada was the demandeur, in diplomatic jargon—the beggar at the feast. To the American side, that suggested a fairly hard line, in expectation of Canadian concessions ...
> ... Talks dragged along through the winter and spring of 1987, then through a painful summer. The Canadians raised issues, and the Americans evaded them. Time was the Americans' ally and delay their instrument ...

Consequently, when the plan for a United States-Mexico Free Trade Area was announced, the government of Prime Minister Patrick B. Mulroney was thrown into a dilemma. A national election was coming up, and was promising to be difficult for Mulroney's Conservatives. The Canadian economy was stagnant[113] and the Canada-United States Free Trade Agreement was a sore point with the voters. One author described the context in which Mulroney found himself when Salinas and Bush announced their agreement to co-operate on trade:

> Free trade had become the bogeyman of the Canadian economy as the unemployment rate shot up from 7.5 per cent in 1989 to 11.6 per cent in 1992. Books critical of [CUFTA] have been outselling those supportive of the deal, and cross-border battles over steel, autos, softwood lumber and beer have helped to keep trade issues in the public limelight. The nationalist Council of Canadians calculates that about 400,000 manufacturing jobs—almost 20 per cent of this sector—have disappeared since the FTA came into effect in 1989 ... There seems to be general agreement that the results of free trade have been a political disaster for the federal government. In an opinion poll published in May 1992, 66 per cent of Canadians expressed opposition to [CUFTA] and 64 per cent to NAFTA.[114]

Already characterized as 'slavishly pro-American',[115] the last thing Mulroney and the Conservatives needed was to have to restart negotiations for the extension of free trade with the United States.

At the same time, the Canadian government feared the secondary effects of a bilateral free trade agreement between Mexico and the United States. The so-called 'hub-and-spoke' model of trade agreements was of great concern to the Canadians.[116] They recognized that an hemispheric trade system of 'spoked' trade agreements between a US hub and lesser-developed, low-wage nations, would threaten the Canadians' own preferential trade relations with the United States. The Canadians assumed that any company wishing to do business in Canada and the United States would establish in the United States rather than Canada, as this would allow for the possibility of future entry into Latin American markets too.

A constellation such as this would have injured Canada's important automobile manufacturing sector,[117] divert textiles, and even more significantly

---

[113] It was not until 1994 that the Canadian economy started to emerge from the deep recession of the late 1980s. Wonnacott (note 20 *supra*), at 163–4. By 1994, unemployment was between 11 and 12 per cent and the gross domestic product had only reached its previous levels in 1993. *Ibid.*; 34th Meeting of Canada-US Interparliamentary Group, Congr. Report 13–17 May (1993). But see Wonnacott (note 20 *supra*), at 164, suggesting that the Canadian economy would have been worse without the existence of the Free Trade Agreement.

[114] Thakur (note 97 *supra*), at 86.

[115] Bothwell (note 105 *supra*), at 141, describing public opinion in the mid-1980s.

[116] Simser (note 54 *supra*), at 199. The term 'hub and spoke model' refers to a context in which one states creates multiple bilateral agreements on the same topic rather than a single multilateral agreement.

[117] Recent data relate that the automobile sector accounts for 10 per cent of all manufacturing jobs in Canada. See Syed Tariq Anwar, 'The Impact of NAFTA on Canada's Automobile Industry: Issues and Analysis' (1996) 19 *World Competition* 115, 117. But see Smith (note 66 *supra*), at 40 (Canadian trade barriers on Mexican auto parts were already very low, suggesting little potential diversion).

deflect foreign investment.[118] As a Canadian professor of government and political science stated, 'the analysis of the hub-and-spoke model was important regarding trade, but it became critical when applied to investment'[119] because capital would tend to flow to the United States, where it could access all three North American markets simultaneously (and among them the growing Mexican population).[120] Thus, the Canadians could not afford to let the United States turn its attention southward without assuring Ottawa of reciprocal trade privileges. At first, the Canadians noted the Mexican overture with concern,[121] and optimistically doubted the strength of Salinas' commitment to freer trade with the United States. They continued to hope 'that perhaps the whole thing might go away'.[122]

Yet the NAFTA did not go away. The Canadians were forced to begin examining their trading options and to begin planning a public relations campaign. To minimize public resistance to a possible NAFTA, the government realized they would have to move beyond emphasizing the immediate fears of trade diversion to Mexico. Instead, a campaign focussing on three positive aspects of new negotiations was put underway.[123] First, the government informed the people, NAFTA would give Canada an opportunity to deepen its relationship with the United States and improve on the existing commitments under the Canada-United States Free Trade Agreement.[124] Secondly, the government brought to light the previously unexplored profit opportunities of a liberalized Mexican market.[125] Finally, the Canadian

---

[118] Winham (note 17 *supra*), at 495 ('Investment was the greater concern of the Canadian government, and it was feared that ... a trade disadvantage would become an investment disadvantage'); Wonnacott (note 20 *supra*), at 165.

[119] Winham (note 17 *supra*), at 495; Wonnacott (note 20 *supra*), at 170.

[120] Thakur (note 97 *supra*), at 84–5.

[121] See Winham (note 17 *supra*), at 492 ('The idea of a free trade agreement between Mexico and the United States was not warmly received by the Canadian government').

[122] *Ibid.* at 493. See also Smith (note 66 *supra*), at 34 ('The future evolution of the US-Mexico or Canada-US-Mexico trade talks will also have implications for the multilateral trading system. Wonnacott has argued that a hub-and-spoke approach of bilateral FTAs is more trade diverting than a trilateral arrangement. Certainly, the trilateral approach of a core FTA lends itself more easily to plurilateral regionalism and would result in a much tidier set of arrangements than a series of parallel bilateral FTAs').

[123] Thakur (note 97 *supra*), at 87, writing that one Canadian official described the campaign as 'aimed to take 'the fear factor' out of the debate'. Professor Gilbert Winham, a member of several CUFTA dispute panels, explains (Winham, note 17 *supra*, at 478–9) that beyond the Canadian government's declared main goal of creating 'a trade and investment climate which could contribute ... to the creation of more and better employment opportunities', the aims of the NAFTA included the following:

> (1) the attainment of security of access through reducing the risks of United States contingency protectionism; (2) the improvement of access to ensure a sufficiently large market to realize economies of scale as well as access to world-class technology; and (3) the ordered adjustment towards a more competitive Canadian economy, particularly providing increased incentives for investment ... Another reason occasionally mentioned was the defensive strategy of gaining access to a regional trade agreement to counter similar movements in Europe and elsewhere.

[124] Thakur (note 97 *supra*), at 87; Simser (note 54 *supra*), at 199 ('NAFTA also presented Canada with an opportunity not only to strengthen and preserve the gains made under the [CUFTA] but also to open up new areas').

[125] Thakur (note 97 *supra*), at 87.

government played on the idea of improving the Mexican environmental standards and quality of life from within a trilateral trade arrangement (unlike the original ideas of the Mexican and US officials to keep these topics out of discussion).[126]

Mexico, formerly not very concerned with Canada as a trade partner, nevertheless saw the other as a useful third party in negotiations with the United States.[127] Canada's presence, Mexico hoped, would reduce the power differential between the countries and thus prevent the treaty from becoming one dictated by—or one perceived by the Mexican electorate as being dictated by—the United States.[128]

For its part, Canada was less interested in Mexico as a trade partner than alarmed by Mexico's potential to divert US trade interests away from it. While Canada did recognize some benefits stemming directly from a trade agreement with Mexico,[129] like Mexico, it viewed the NAFTA more as a way to protect its own economic alliance with the United States than as anything more.[130]

---

[126] *Ibid.*

[127] Simser (note 54 *supra*), at 198–9 ('It has been observed that NAFTA 'is a United States-Mexican solution to particular issues, with Canada an unnecessary but welcome third party"), citing M.W. Gordon, 'Economic Integration in North America—An Agreement of Limited Dimensions but Unlimited Expectations' (1993) 56 Modern L Rev 157, 164.

[128] Whalley and Hamilton (note 24 *supra*), at 61.

[129] See Thakur (note 97 *supra*), at 87, setting out five ways Canada would benefit from Mexico's involvement in a free trade agreement with the US and Canada. Professor Thakur notes the self-interest in a better Mexican economy because Canada could then reduce its developmental assistance payments; maintaining its 'global credibility' by supporting a developing country move to a market-driven economy; a reduction in refugees and drug trafficking that would result from Mexican economic improvements; and the 'moral obligation to work towards a more just society on a world scale'; Winham (note 17 *supra*), at 478–86, explaining in detail the motivations behind Canada's and Mexico's negotiating objectives and consequential negotiating behavior.

[130] Whalley and Hamilton (note 24 *supra*), at 56, describe this pressure by the 'small' NAFTA countries on the United States to join a trade agreement as stemming from the need for a 'safe haven'. Professor Winham (Winham, note 17 *supra*, at 485) asserts that the defensive interest lessened the Canadian and Mexican negotiators' interest in the negotiations as an overall balancing of concessions: 'Ultimately, what Canada and Mexico mainly wanted from the negotiations (namely, competitivenes and reform) they could have achieved unilaterally, and this allowed both governments to be somewhat indifferent to the relative "balance of concessions" in the negotiations'. See also Thakur (note 97 *supra*), at 84 ('Trade and Industry Minister Michael Wilson's officials acknowledged from the beginning that in the NAFTA talks they were less interested in increasing Canada's modest trade with Mexico than in defending their favoured status in the US under [the Canada-United States Free Trade Agreement]'); Wonnacott (note 20 *supra*), at 165, listing Canadian negotiating objectives, and commenting, 'Broadly speaking, … two objectives reflected the desire to achieve traditional gains from trade, while the other objectives were defensive, reflecting Canada's desire to avoid the costs of being excluded'; Robert A. Pastor, 'NAFTA as a Center of Integration Process: The Nontrade Issues', in Lustig *et al.* (note 12 *supra*), at 178 ('But it is clear that Canada has been less of an *actor* in the negotiations than a *defender* of the interests it acquired in the US-Canadian Free Trade Agreement') (emphasis in original). The Honourable Michael Wilson, Canada's Minister for International Trade, set out Canada's goals for the NAFTA negotiations as: gaining access to Mexico's markets on the same terms as the United States; ensuring Canada's continued viability as a target for foreign investment; and securing or improving upon the Canada-United States Free Trade Agreement provisions. Wonnacott (note 20 *supra*), at 165.

Within three months of President Bush's announcement of the US intention to enter trade negotiations with Mexico, Canadian Prime Minister Mulroney officially made the negotiations trilateral.[131]

1.4   FORCES ENCOURAGING THE FORMATION OF NAFTA

While the NAFTA was chiefly motivated by economic theory, there were certainly other factors motivating the parties that were only indirectly tied to economics.

1.4.1   Political Interest in Mexico's Economic Reform

The most significant of the non-trade factors facing the NAFTA Parties was the desire to 'lock in' the economically liberalizing changes made in Mexico in the preceding eight years.[132] This was a motivating force for the Salinas government in Mexico. In both the United States and Canada, too, the interest in Mexico's economic reforms was important, as the hope existed that economic and political reforms in Mexico would be mutually reinforcing.[133]

The international trade literature by proponents of the direct effect school[134] often asserts that international trade agreements offer governments a way of bringing economic programs into effect despite domestic opposition to such programs. This functions as a two-step process. First, the international negotiators can avoid the unpleasant necessity of voter approval as non-elected agents of the state, working to a large extent from non-public mandates in non-public meetings. Secondly, once agreed to by the negotiators, the agreement itself cannot be altered without damaging the state's future reliability in other arenas. Thus, the agreement can achieve goals a government may have that it would not be able to do through national legislation. As one NAFTA commentator writes, 'a free trade

---

[131] A nice overview of the negotiation process in general is given by the timeline found in Schettino (note 101 *supra*), at 6.

[132] Winham (note 17 *supra*, at 485) indicates that the Canadian government also had domestic reforms it wanted solidified through the NAFTA. Canada's openness to foreign investment was beginning to take hold in the 1990s, and the Mulroney government wanted to ensure that the liberalizations would not be reversed.

[133] Professor Winham (Winham, note 17 *supra*, at 483) draws an interesting contrast between the view of the NAFTA's ideology of free trade linked to government reform in Mexico and the Canadian government's view of free trade on its own political process. 'In Canada ... the government never enunciated a relationship between free trade and government reform. Instead, it emphasized politically safe economic aspects like employment creation ('jobs, jobs, jobs') and generally avoided comment on the politically sensitive issue of the impact of free trade on government practices'. The same could certainly also be said for the United States, where any suggestion that there be international influence on US governmental practice would be seen as heresy.

[134] These include such authors as Frederick M. Abbott, Werner Meng, Peter Moser, Pierre Pescatore, Ernst-Ulrich Petersmann, and the late Jan Tumlir.

negotiation offered a rationale for initiating and continuing domestic economic reform that would have been much more difficult to effect politically without the crutch of a bargained relationship'.[135]

While Canada and the United States have been relatively stable capitalist, market-driven democracies for over 100 and 200 years, respectively, Mexico's War of Independence was followed by the political instability of the Mexican Revolution, itself giving way to authoritarian 'democracy' accompanied by state control over the nation's economy. When threatened, either by political insurgence or external economic pressure, the Mexican government tended, until 1982, to tighten its hold on the economy and to solve fiscally what it could not allow to be solved democratically.

Presidents de la Madrid and Salinas ended the practice of turning inward in the face of economic troubles.[136] Instead, extreme domestic measures were used to rejuvenate the economy. Inflation was relentlessly fought by allowing more flexibility in the exchange rate,[137] with tight monetary policies, and with agreements between government, business, and labor to freeze wages and keep unemployment down. Foreign investment laws were relaxed and government-owned industries privatized.[138] In short, Mexican economic policy was completely altered. Yet, while strengthening the economy for the long-term, the immediate effects of the government's financial austerity program of reform were painful for many Mexicans. Political dissatisfaction was the result.

The governing party, Partido de Revolucionario Institucional (PRI) had had a stranglehold on Mexican elections for over 60 years.[139] Still, Salinas' domestic reforms posed a real threat to the PRI's future due to the extent of popular dissatisfaction with his economic reforms.[140] The

---

[135] Winham (note 17 *supra*), at 485, writing of the Canadian and Mexican ability to rely on the fact of an agreement with a 'large trading partner' to further governmental goals.

[136] The period 1988–94 is sometimes referred to as 'La Reforma de la Revolución' in Mexico, referring no doubt to Salinas' move away from the socialist ideals of the Mexican Revolution and toward a competitive economic system. Schettino (note 101 *supra*), at 91.

[137] This was accomplished by changing the fixed peso system to one of a 'crawling peg' to the dollar. The 'crawling peg' system for determining the exchange rate of the peso allowed for a 'gradual depreciation of the peso relative to the dollar'. GAO, *Mexico's Financial Crisis: Origins, Awareness, Assistance, and Initial Efforts to Recover*, GAO/GGD-96-56 (February 1996), p. 32.

[138] *Ibid.* at 33.

[139] The PRI had come into power in 1928, and never allowed itself to lose an election. One author, Mario Vargas Llosa, called the Mexican political situation the 'perfect dictatorship'. Simser (note 54 *supra*), at 195, also recalls that this 'comment ... led to his prompt exclusion from the country'.

[140] Although Salinas was a champion of economic reform, political reforms were less important to him. In 1991, the President commented upon his idea of 'Salinistroika':

When you are introducing such a strong economic reform, you must make sure that you build the political consensus around it. If you are at the same time introducing additional drastic political reform, you may end up with no reform at all. And we want to have reform, not a disintegrated country... The priority is economics.

Alina Rocha Menocal, 'The Myth of the Infallible Technocrat: Policy-Making in Mexico Under the Salinas Administration' (1998) 9 J Pub & Int'l Aff 167, citing an interview of Salinas that appeared in *New Perspectives Quarterly* 8 (1991) (text found on the internet at >wws.princeton.edu<).

only way to ensure that future governments would not revert to the old ways of economic nationalism was to bind Mexico in an international treaty.

> ... Once the trade patterns and dependencies created by increased exports under NAFTA became fixed, the cost of undoing both NAFTA and the attendant economic reforms might be too high for politicians of all stripes, particularly those with an interest in returning to the state doctrine of *Rectoria del Estado*.[141]

The United States was eager to ensure continued Mexican liberalization for its own benefit. The trade agreement would guarantee long-term access of US exports to the 85.8 million Mexican residents.[142] Moreover, with continued economic reforms and enhanced trade, wages and living standards should increase, lessening the relative attractiveness of the United States as a destination of illegal immigration.[143] Finally, the United States believed strongly in the power of economic liberalization to foster a capitalist political stability. The fear of political upheaval in a neighboring state was acute enough for the US government to overlook the non-democratic aspects of the Salinas regime, and hope that support for NAFTA would lead to his maintaining control.[144]

1.4.2   Reaction to Faltering Multilateral Trade Negotiations

Another reason for the NAFTA discussions was the ability to achieve progress in opening markets and securing fair trade bilaterally in the face of faltering multilateral trade negotiations. This was particularly important to the United States' Bush Administration, which wanted to flex its political muscle to force further market openings around the world, and so aid flailing US export industries.

Intended to mark the half-way point of the Uruguay Round that had started in 1986, the Mid-Term Review of 1989 made apparent the slow progress of the negotiations to reform the General Agreement on Tariffs

---

[141] Simser (note 54 *supra*), at 193. The principle of Rectoria del Estado is the constitutional right of the state to 'exercise stewardship over' the national economy.

[142] That was the 1990 population. Kehoe (note 94 *supra*), in Lustig *et al.* (note 12 *supra*), at 75 (Table 3). By 1997, the population was between 94.8 and 97.6 million and growing at a rate of 1.8 per cent annually. See the population figures given by the US-Mexican Chamber of Commerce at >www.usmcoc.org<.

[143] Simser (note 54 *supra*), at 196.

[144] Paul Krugman, 'The Uncomfortable Truth About NAFTA: It's Foreign Policy, Stupid' (1995) 72:5 Forg Aff 13. See also, Robert A. Pastor, 'NAFTA as the Center of an Integration Process: the Nontrade Issues' in Lustig, *et al.*(note 12 *supra*), pp. 176–99, at 196, discussing the differences between the Salinas 'first-world modernizers' and the opposition Cardenistas 'third-world progressives'; Pastor does not foresee the Cardenista victory in 1997 elections, but he does call attention to the likelihood of a change in Mexican foreign policy, and this discussion underscores the United States' interest in getting to an agreement with Salinas while the PRI still held power.

and Trade.[145] The Mid-Term Review took place in Montreal during 5–9 December 1988 and in Geneva during 5–8 April 1989. During these meetings, the GATT Contracting Parties agreed to continue working on liberalizations, but could only issue a list of decisions recognizing that the main principles the negotiations should aim to include in the future results. By the early 1990s, the Uruguay Round was so stalled that observers began to question whether there would ever be a successful end to the talks. The United States was particularly disappointed with the lack of progress on liberalizing trade in the cross-border service sectors, and was prepared to abandon the negotiations (and thus its historic emphasis on multilateral trade negotiations) and pursue trade concessions bilaterally with willing partners.

> Canada was also concerned with the potential collapse of the Uruguay Round negotiations, and it was partly in response to this concern that it entered the NAFTA negotiations. The importance of the multilateral trade system for 'small economies' (including small developed economies) has been brought out by numerous authors.[146] However, for Canada, with the United States as far and away its largest trading partner, the multilateral negotiations have a drawback when the main trading partner is reluctant to offer concessions.

Canada and Mexico share a unique element in their trade policy: they both have an overwhelming export dependency on the United States. That means that if either is going to liberalize trade through an international agreement, it can substantially accomplish that goal in an agreement with only one other country—the United States. Conversely, if either country seeks to liberalize trade through a multilateral agreement (for example, under the GATT), that agreement will be meaningful only in so far as it reduces protectionism *vis-à-vis* the United States.[147]

Canada therefore had to be concerned about the lack of progress in the Uruguay Round because the United States was concerned. If the US negotiators were not satisfied, the Canadians would be left with no improvements in their position unless they had a regional agreement as well.

Mexico had its own worries about the multilateral negotiations under the auspices of GATT. Although its participation in the GATT system had brought growth to the trading sectors of the economy, Mexican trade was still heavily skewed toward the United States. As a developing country member of the GATT, Mexico was eligible for beneficial treatment under national Generalized System of Preferences (GSP) schemes. It received such treatment from both the United States and Canada. However, under the

---

[145] See GATT, 'Decisions Adopted at the Mid-Term Review of the Uruguay Round', *GATT Focus* No. (May 1989), p. 61. The text may also be found in (1989) XXVIII:4 ILM 1023. The Uruguay Round negotiations were completed only at the end of 1993.

[146] For smaller economies, the world trading regime's legal system and principle of unconditional most-favored-nation treatment offers a degree of protection from an abuse of the large economic powers' advantageous bargaining positions.

[147] Winham (note 17 *supra*), at 486.

United States legislation authorizing the extension of GSP benefits, numerous factors determine which countries will receive duty-free trade with the United States. These factors include: 'competitiveness, general economic development, market access, protection of intellectual property rights, the presence ... of trade distorting investment practices and barriers to trade in services, and abidance by internationally recognized worker rights'.[148] In other words, the offer of GSP duty-free treatment by the United States was a political tool.

The Mexican government was eager to remove the threat of political retaliation for its actions by the US Congress' revocation of trade benefits. It saw its chance in entering into a free trade agreement that would give it non-conditional rights to trade benefits. Thus, the NAFTA negotiations were also motivated from the desire to secure existing tariff-free treatment in Mexico's US-bound trade in goods.

1.4.3   Individual Leaders' Personal Motivations

Finally, one would be naive to disregard the personal motivations of the leaders trying to bring the NAFTA idea into fruition. Presidents Salinas, Bush, and Clinton, as well as Prime Minister Mulroney, each had large political stakes in the acceptance of the treaty by their citizens. With the 1982 beginnings of economic liberalization and an emphasis on competition within the domestic economy, Mexico's government began a new approach to trade. By the end of the decade, President Salinas had completed the financial liberalization[149] and was being hailed internationally as the man who brought modern finance to Mexico. Salinas, anticipating stepping down from his powerful presidential position in 1994, wanted his achievements in opening the Mexican economy to remain in place. Salinas saw a treaty for a free trade area as a tool for ensuring that his market reforms would be maintained, even if his party was to fall from power.[150] In the wake of the European Union's rejection of Mexico's overtures, Salinas' personal pride, mixed with commitment to the free market ideology, moved Mexico to propose a trade pact with the United States.

In the United States, newly-elected President William J. Clinton had pledged during his election campaign to support passage of the NAFTA in Congress (as long as the environmental and labor side accords would be added). Failure to get this agreement implemented would have been disastrous for his credibility for the next four years.

Finally, in Canada, Prime Minister Mulroney, already facing popular resentment for the widely condemned CUFTA, also had an impending election to bolster with a trade success story. It was partly Mulroney's

---

[148] GATT, Trade Policy Review: United States (1994), p. 48.

[149] Fanny Warman and A.P. Thirlwall, 'Interest Rates, Saving, Investment and Growth in Mexico 1960–1990: Tests of the Financial Liberalization Hypothesis' (1994) 30:3 J Dev Stud 629, 634.

[150] One commentator writes that with the NAFTA, Salinas hoped to make Mexico a First World rather than a Third World country. Hans Werner Tobler, 'Das Verhältnis Mexiko-USA: Zwischen Konflikt und Kooperation' (text found on the internet at >www.fsk.ethz.ch<).

government's need for the pro-trade supporters in the business community that made Canada decide in favor of the economics of the NAFTA.

Indeed, given these personal motivations, as well as the sheer breadth of the Agreement, it is not surprising that what occurred during the process of formulating the NAFTA text and getting it ratified by the legislatures may be seen as a slight movement away from the pure economic orientation. Thus, the environmental movements in the United States, traditionally supportive of the Democratic Party, successfully pressured the Clinton Administration for inclusion of environmental protection assurances. This led to a 'side agreement' under which the Parties commit to require putting environmental considerations before monetary profit. Similarly, the labor side agreement was the product of workers' rights interests in all three countries wanting assurance of required minimal working conditions. Salinas', Clinton's, and Mulroney's need to get an agreement—*any* agreement—signed made each perhaps more willing to grant concessions (both positive and negative) than were dictated by economics.[151]

1.5   DOMESTIC CRITICISM OF THE NAFTA

Outside the three administrations, skeptics from all negotiating countries voiced concern over the idea of a free trade agreement. Much of the critique was based on the fact that two developed countries would be fusing their markets with that of a developing nation, but the opponents attacked the idea from many angles.[152]

1.5.1   Labor Groups' Opposition

In the United States and Canada, unions and workers' rights activists warned of the worsening of labor conditions in all three countries, due to

---

[151] Of course, concessions made under such conditions are endangered by a lack of commitment to implement them.

[152] Nikolaj Petersen's explanation of the 'integration dilemma' offers a theoretical perspective on the criticism to the NAFTA. See Nikolaj Petersen, 'National Strategies in the integration Dilemma: An Adaptive Approach' (1998) 36:1 J Common Mkt Stud 33. The dilemma comes from having to balance the benefits of integration with the losses such integration entails:

As rational actors, participants in regional integration must be presumed to want the benefits and avoid thedrawbacks of integration. However, difficult trade-offs have to be made, as benefits and drawbacks are closely intertwined and often two sides of one coin. Depending on the obtainable balance between perceived benefits and drawbacks the integration dilemma will appear more or less poignant. For [some] countries and decision-makers ..., trade-offs may seem uncontroversial and the integration dilemma may not even appear to be one. For others, ... the dilemma appears harsher and may be further complicated by splits in domestic opinion. In these cases decision-makers are placed in a 'strategic triangle' with sometimes impossible choices, where no equilibrium point may be possible.

cost-driven competition in attracting (or maintaining) investment. This 'race to the bottom' would begin due to the ease with which US and Canadian companies would be given permission to establish production centers in Mexico and re-import the products in the northern markets. As labor costs in Mexico are lower than in the United States or Canada, the fear among labor groups was that US and Canadian workers would also have to accept lower wages and/or longer working hours. Ross Perot, candidate for the US Presidency in 1992, led labor's charge against the NAFTA. In words that have become nearly immortal, he warned that the mass exodus of jobs moving South would cause a 'giant sucking sound' to be heard in the United States as soon as NAFTA was signed.[153]

The Canadian labor organizations lobbied against NAFTA too. The average cost of workers in Canada was already higher than the average in the United States, and the possibility of factories moving to Mexico would erode labor's position in Canada even further. Experiencing substantial job losses from the CUFTA, these groups looked at the NAFTA proposal as slightly ironic: '... NAFTA would stop their manufacturers from fleeing to the United States by ensuring that they relocated to Mexico instead'.[154]

Even the Mexican labor unions were not completely satisfied with the NAFTA. The Confederation of Mexican Workers, a union of five million men and women, are entitled to many social benefits that are stronger than Canadian benefits and which have no corollary in the United States. Their fears have been at least partially realized as the Mexican labor protections are being dismantled in the spirit of 'reform' promoted by the market openings.[155]

The opposition groups were strong enough to force an inclusion of labor issues on the negotiating agenda. The Agreement on Labor Cooperation became a part of the NAFTA package subsequent to the signing of the main treaty text.[156]

1.5.2   Environmental Protection Groups' Opposition

People from all three of the NAFTA Parties were active in opposing the formation of the NAFTA treaty as an agreement aimed solely at economic issues. In the United States and Canada, environmental protection organizations pointed to the attitude of the Mexican government toward the environment, and foresaw an exodus of industries from the North to Mexico

---

[153] Ross Perot, *Save Your Job, Save Our Country: Why NAFTA Must Be Stopped* (1993).
[154] Thakur (note 97 *supra*), at 85.
[155] Pastor (note 144 *supra*), at 187 (Mexican legislation requires the government to grant paid vacations and maternity leave, and employers may not hire non-union replacement workers during strikes).
[156] The English text of the Labor Agreement can be found in (1993) 32:6 ILM 1499.

to profit from lower pollution control costs.[157] Like the labor activists, environmental protection groups feared a movement of manufacturing southwards in response to the Mexican authorities' notoriously lax enforcement of environmental laws,[158] and to an even greater extent than labor, the environmental groups were wary of Mexican promises to protect the environment. Pointing to the relatively progressive environmental laws in existence in Mexico, those concerned doubted a true change for the better unless United States and Canadian oversight also existed to ensure their implementation. Within Mexico too, the 'Group of 100' organized a campaign to prevent the NAFTA from ignoring environmental concerns.

In addition, the environmentalists were united in their distrust of the trade orientation of the NAFTA. Even if there were to be opportunities for environmental protection measures to be implemented by the Parties, there was still the problem of viewing such protections as trade barriers. The possibility of an international trade-oriented panel hearing claims of environmental violations was suspect in itself: 'What, for example, if a Mexican company challenges a US law banning a pesticide that is permitted in Mexico, arguing that this is an unfair barrier to trade? The dispute might be referred to an international panel which will be more concerned with promoting free trade than guarding against hazardous chemicals in the food supply'.[159]

Resulting pressure on the leaders (and particularly on the Democratic majority in the US Congress), from a wide variety of non-governmental organizations, led to an agreement to form a co-operative council to draft a side agreement. The Council's resultant text was adopted as the Agreement on Environmental Cooperation and entered into force with the NAFTA.[160]

---

[157] Thakur (note 97 *supra*, at 92) writes of the environmentalists' fear of a 'fourfold damaging effect' of the NAFTA:

> First, companies could pressure Canadian and US governments to dilute environmental controls as unfair additions to cost inputs. Failing this, firms could relocate to Mexico in order to escape the more stringent and costly environmental controls north of the border. Third, increased industrial development in Mexico occurring alongside lenient environmental controls would worsen environmental degradation in Mexcio. As industrial development along the US-Mexican border has occurred faster than ... ability to construct environmental infrastructure, so toxic emissions and improper hazardous waste management have caused ... pollution in populated border communities. Fourth, since any further NAFTA-driven industrial development will be concentrated along the border, it will aggrevate trans-boundary air and water pollution in the United States itself.

[158] *Ibid.* at 93; Laura J. Van Pelt, 'Countervailing Environmental Subsidies: A Solution to the Environmental Inequities of the North American Free Trade Agreement' (1994) 29:1 Tex Int'l LJ 123, arguing that the Mexican government's non-enforcement of environmental rules amounts to a countervailable subsidy to producers located there.

[159] Thakur (note 97 *supra*), at 93.

[160] The English text of the Environmental Side Agreement can be found in (1993) 32:6 ILM 1480.

1.5.3 Human Rights Groups' Opposition

Human rights groups also joined the campaign to stop NAFTA. The most widespread complaints were focussed on the human rights violations of the Mexican government.[161] Mexico's one-party 'democracy', while not as despotic as many Latin American regimes, has a record of effectively suppressing opposition in a manner suggestive of widespread fraud,[162] corruption,[163] discrimination,[164] and the occasional 'political and other extrajudicial killing',[165] among other human rights violations.[166]

One of the most dramatic demonstrations of dissatisfaction with the treaty with the Mexican government came from the Mexicans themselves on the day the NAFTA came into effect. The uprising of indigenous peoples in the southern state of Chiapas on 1 January 1994, attracted worldwide attention on to the abuses the PRI government had inflicted on the Indian populations in the countryside.[167] The present signs of continuing human rights violations, as well as increasing militarization within Mexico validate the fears expressed by international social organizations prior to the NAFTA.[168]

---

[161] But see James F. Smith, 'NAFTA and Human Rights: A Necessary Linkage' (1994) 27 UC Davis L Rev 793, while referring in some portions of the article to Mexico, Smith argues mainly for a general incorporation of human rights in the NAFTA framework.

[162] See US Department of State, 'Mexico Human Rights Practices, 1995' ('The Institutional Revolutionary Party (PRI) has won every presidential election in the last 66 years, many of which involved credible allegations of fraudulent practices').

[163] *Ibid.*

[164] *Ibid.* Section 5, reporting widespread *de jure* and *de facto* discrimination against indigenous peoples, women, homosexuals, members of religious minorities, and the disabled.

[165] *Ibid.* Section 1:a (Peasants, church officials, governmental officials, political activists were often murdered by police or government-funded gunmen). PRI politician Luis Donaldo Colosio and José Francisco Ruiz Massieu were perhaps the most internationally noticed victims of their party's systemic quieting of political dissenters, his murder occurring late in Colosio's popular candidacy for the Presidency. Subsequent investigations have led to the arrest of Raúl Salinas de Gortari, brother of the Carlos Salinas, for masterminding the Massieu killing.

[166] A former legal adviser to the Mexican Secretary of Foreign Affairs states bluntly: 'Mexico has a reputation for respecting human rights that is less than enviable. Mexico's reputation as a violator of human rights is not of recent origin. To the contrary, this negative fame may be traced back a few decades'. Jorge A. Vargas, 'NAFTA, the Chiapas Rebellion, and the Emergence of Mexican Ethnic Law' (1994) 25:1 Cal W Int'l LJ 1, 27 (footnote omitted). Professor Vargas continues to cite a National Commission on Human Rights Annual Report that credits 89 of the 274 human rights violations (that affected nearly 900 individuals) to the Mexican Army. *Ibid.* at 30, citing Comisión Nacional de Derechos Humanos, *Informe Anual: Mayo 1993–Mayo 1994* (Mexico City, 1994).

[167] Professor Vargas (note 166 *supra*, at 12–13) claims that the Chiapas rebels feared that the NAFTA would destroy 'their economic sustenance, their culture and, in one word, their existence' while the Mexican elite would benefit.

[168] 'Zunehmende Militarisierung in Mexiko: Kontrast zur politischen Liberalisierung', *Neue Zürcher Zeitung*, 21–22 June 1997, p. 9, reporting that although the Mexican government is claiming improvements in their record on human rights, international organizations, including Amnesty International, find a worsening; the article also draws a connection between the peso-crisis and the increasing rate of crime in cities). The dispute between the Chiapas indians and the Mexican government also continues. 'Alleingang Zedillos bei den Indianerrechten: Ende der Verhandlungen mit den Zapatisten?', *Neue Zürcher Zeitung*, 20 March 1998, p. 9.

In addition to the concerns expressed over Mexico, during the NAFTA negotiations Mexico's government voiced criticism of the human rights violations in the United States. A primary target of such complaints was the US Border Patrol officers' abuse of Mexican nationals. According to the non-governmental watch group Americas Watch, US border patrollers were routinely involved in 'beatings, rough physical treatment, and racially motivated verbal abuse' of Mexicans.[169] Such acts, catalogued as well by the Mexican Commission for the Defense and Protection of Human Rights, exhibit the United States' crass disregard for internationally accepted norms of treatment of prisoners (not to mention of non-convicted persons).[170]

Another point of contention involved the methods used by the United States Justice system. Specifically complained about were the (Supreme Court-approved) kidnapping of a Mexican national from Mexican territory by US agents[171] and the regular carrying out of the death penalty by most US States.[172]

Less susceptible to foreign countries' criticism of how it handles its 'domestic affairs' than many states, the United States' policies have not changed since these complaints were made.

1.5.4 Sovereignty Concerns and Cultural Opposition

Perhaps more significant than economic worries was the outcry in both Canada and Mexico against the NAFTA's potential to further allow the spread of 'things American'. The size of the United States' commercial market and its economic strength has led to the acknowledgement that, for better or for worse, 'the United States has highly effective means to impact and influence other cultures'.[173] By neighboring the United States, Canada and Mexico are most directly exposed to the lifestyle of the US population. Free trade, many worried, would simply increase the amount of US influence, perhaps to the point at which the Canadian and Mexican cultures would no longer exist. Combating the cultural and political

---

[169] Pastor (note 144 *supra*), at 193, quoting *Americas Watch*, Brutality Unchecked: Human Rights Abuses Along the US Border with Mexico (1992).

[170] *Ibid*. at 193; James F. Smith, 'Confronting Legal Differences in the United States and Mexican Legal Systems in the Era of NAFTA' (1993) 1:1 US-Mex LJ 85, 106 n.133.

[171] See *United States v. Alvarez-Machain* 504 US 655 (1992), decision by US Supreme Court in which the incident of US Drug Enforcement Agents' entrance into Mexico and their forcible taking of Dr Alvarez-Machain to the United States to stand trial for murder was found to be not a violation of the US-Mexico extradition treaty in force at that time, because the treaty did not prohibit kidnapping (text of opinion can also be found in (1992) XXXI ILM 900).

[172] Pastor (note 144 *supra*), at 193–4; Smith (note 170 *supra*), at 104–5, 107 n.134.

[173] Henry W. McGee, Jr., 'Mexican Perspectives on Economic, Political and Cultural Implications of Free Trade' (1992) 12 Chicano-Latino L Rev 1, 3, summarizing the views of Victor Flores Olea, President of Mexico's National Council for Culture and Art.

influence of the US became key objectives for both Canada and Mexico during the NAFTA negotiations.[174]

In order to protect their cultural identity, the Canadians took an exception to the NAFTA obligations on non-discrimination to protect their right to offer Canadian magazines and television programming preferential treatment. In addition, Canada's government is presently actively pursuing further regional relations under its own initiative. The absence of the United States as a participant in these efforts is clearly and defiantly noted as of being unimportant in Canada's commitment to deeper hemispheric ties.

In Mexico, the idea of culture is often inextricably linked to the concept of sovereignty.[175] Amidst the fears that Mexico's interests would be subordinated to those of the United States should a free trade agreement come into force,[176] the Mexican government constantly reassured its citizens that Mexico's 'sovereignty' would not be sacrificed.[177] President

---

[174] Ruth Buchanan (note 70 *supra*, footnote omitted) states this idea well:

> One of the major ongoing themes surrounding the NAFTA is the extent to which a government's sovereign right to legislate over policy matters of domestic concern out to yield to the larger forces of globalization. Both the centrality and the slipperiness of conceptions of sovereignty were illustrated in the course of the NAFTA debates …
>
> The positions taken by the two sides to the debate were neither internally consistent nor coherent. … In this way, the distinction between a sovereign, domestic sphere and an increasingly integrated international sphere, while central, became very elusive during the NAFTA debates.

[175] See the discussion of 'sovereignty' in Kazuaki Sono, 'Sovereignty, This Strange Thing: Its Impact on Global Economic Order' (1979) 9:3 Ga J Int'l & Comp L 549; *ibid.* at 555:

> Under present international law, it is entirely up to the sovereign decision of each State which political system it chooses and which policies it implements … The United Nations Charter advocates appropriate international measures for matters of international concern …, but it also announces quite clearly in article 2(7) that essentially domestic matters are not to be interfered with by other nations. Today, however, most of the actions taken by a nation affect international society one way or another, and purely domestic problems are becoming rare.

> See also McGee (note 173 *supra*), at 10, setting forth Mexican historian Hector Aguilar Camín's ideas on the difference between sovereignty and autonomy; 'he argues that the concept of sovereignty is defensive, lacking in flexibility, and is incompatible with the process of economic integration …. [N]ational autonomy concerns that ability of citizens of a nation to determine their political life and to structure their internal political rules'.

[176] See Lorenzo Meyer, 'The United State and Mexico: The Historical Structure of Their Conflict' (1990) 43:2 J Int'l Aff 269–270 ('The political and cultural elite of Mexico fear that the resulting intense exposure to North American lifestyles could bring about a loss of national values, of national identity and of the nationalist sentiment that surged so greatly during the revolutionary period').

[177] One expression of a mild resentment of the Mexican government's acceptance of NAFTA reflects a fundamental dissatisfaction with the de la Madrid and Salinas political 'cozying up' to the United States: 'Mexico's recent entry in NAFTA represents the institutionalization of its "silent" integration in an area of US influence'. Alex E. Fernández Jilberto and Barbara Hogenboom, 'Mexico's Integration in NAFTA: Neoliberal Restructuring and Changing Political Alliances', in Alex E. Fernández Jilberto and André Mommen (eds), *Liberalization in the Developing World: Institutional and Economic Changes in Latin America, Africa and Asia* (Routledge, London, 1996), pp. 138–60, at 148.

Salinas strengthened his public opposition to any infringements on Mexico's sovereignty, stating that it 'is not subject to external evaluation'[178] and warning the United States from trying to affect Mexico's internal political structures through the negotiations[179]. Such promises did not satisfy the Mexican critics of the NAFTA, but there was a realization that the economic benefits of the agreement would outweigh the negative cultural consequences of free trade in the minds of most citizens.[180]

In the United States, the dominance of domestic law over NAFTA law was the key cultural issue at stake in the NAFTA. It is widely accepted that the US Congress would have refused to ratify the Agreement had direct effect of the provisions been included or left to judicial decision.

1.5.5 Economic Opposition

Although generally accepted by mainstream economists, opposition to the Agreement also came from certain economically oriented interests. The CUFTA had already increased trade between the countries, and many Canadians felt their deepening economic dependency was unhealthy. Canadian economists worried that membership in an hemispheric trade zone would bring Canada further from its goal of diversification of trade to lessen its dependence on the United States.[181]

The Mexican population was divided by their government's offering the United States the possibility of liberal trade. While most Mexican economists acknowledged the benefits NAFTA would have on stabilizing the peso and making Mexico more attractive to badly-needed foreign investment, Mexican owners of small- and medium-sized businesses (in particular financial service institutions) feared being overwhelmed and driven into either bankruptcy

---

[178] Pastor (note 144 *supra*), at 190.

[179] See Tod Robberson and Jackson Diehl, 'De Gotari Urges "Informed Debate" on Free Trade Pact', *Washington Post*, 23 February 1993 (text found on internet at >http://the-tech.mit.edu<, quoting Salinas as saying he would only negotiate on issues that 'make economic sense and do not infringe on our national sovereignty'.

[180] McGee (note 173 *supra*), at 12:

> This complex and often ambiguous debate among Mexican intellectuals about the cultural, social and even political impact of free trade markedly differs from the certitude which characterizes the assumption that the economic benefits to Mexico border on the undebatable. Indeed, it can be argued that the concerns about the collateral effects of free trade have been tempered by the enthusiasm for, if not duty to support, the new relationship with the United States.
>
> … Mexico appears eager to embrace the US as a 'free' trading partner, and the Mexican people are likely to link—no matter the cultural and social outcomes—their economic fortunes to those of the behemoth to the north.

[181] Winham (note 17 *supra*), at 493.

or merger by the invasion of large US competitors into their formerly protected markets.[182]

1.5.6   Subnational Government Opposition

Finally, subnational governments were also skeptical of the negotiations of the Free Trade Agreement, because, even more so than the Uruguay Rounds, NAFTA was affecting areas of traditional State/Province competence.

The States of the United States were uneasy, and the National Governors Association, along with regional governors' associations, anxiously monitored the negotiations for infringements of their areas of interest. Although some States, in particular Texas,[183] were strong supporters of the efforts to complete the NAFTA, discontent was voiced by many. One of the States' major complaints was their lack of involvement in the negotiations and the paucity of information given them both at the time of drafting and in the months following negotiations, when domestic policies were being adjusted.[184]

Canadian Provinces, traditionally enjoying much control over even foreign activities occurring in their territory, were even more troubled by their potential loss of control, as judicial doctrine on Canadian federalism has developed so as to give even more autonomy to the Provinces as US-style federalism does the States.[185] Partly as a result of the Provinces' far-reaching autonomy in forming economic policy, internal barriers to trade remain high within Canada. An international agreement obligating Canada to effectively liberalize trade, therefore, was viewed with suspicion by the subnational governments in general, and 'with outright opposition from New Democratic provincial governments'.[186]

---

[182] Mexico's view of sovereignty is not always identifiable with the common international law notion surrounding that (admittedly complex) term. Dr Regula Dettling-Ott in conversation with author. Rather, the term 'sovereignty' is more often used as a Levi-Straussian 'myth' as explained by Richard T. De George, 'The Many Faces of Sovereignty' (1997) 17 *Rechtstheorie* 93, 93:

> (I)n Levi-Strauss's sense of 'myth' … a myth encompasses a variety of different stories under the same name, in which a given myth is part of a large set of myths with which it is related and which help people make sense of and justify their practices, and in which some reality is revealed and illuminated at the same time that some aspects of reality are hidden and kept obscure.

[183] Texas' economic strength is tied closely to its position on the US-Mexican border. See Earl H. Fry, *The Expanding Role of State and Local Governments in US Foreign Affairs* (Council on Foreign Relations Press, New York, 1998), p. 44, noting that nearly 50 per cent of US exports to Mexico pass over the Texan-Mexican border.

[184] *Ibid.* at 113–14.

[185] Peter W. Hogg, *Constitutional Law of Canada* (2nd edn, 1985).

[186] Winham (note 17 *supra*), at 493; Matt Schaefer, 'Private Remedies in Domestic Courts' (1996–97) 17 NW J Int'l L & Bus 609, 617. A partial solution to the Provinces' desire to maintain their perogatives in trade and the federal government's need to liberalize commerce was worked out in the Agreement on Internal Trade of July 1995. The Agreement, however, has been called 'weak'. Schaefer (*supra*), at 617, n.33.

1.6   AIMS OF NAFTA

The NAFTA was conceived to be a free trade area agreement: a treaty to eliminate barriers to trade among the Party-states, but allowing each Party to keep its own external barriers to trade from non-Party sources. The original vision of NAFTA went beyond being just any other free trade area, though. Unlike the many trade agreements already in existence, NAFTA is not only aimed at eliminating tariffs on goods, nor is it merely to improve market access for Party-made products by minimizing non-tariff barriers (such as technical or sanitary standards). The idea goes further: NAFTA is to be the most comprehensive free trade agreement ever. In the words of one US Representative, 'NAFTA is more than just a US trade agreement with Mexico and Canada. It is [an agreement that is] vitally important for the continued economic growth of our country and for our future relationships with other trading partners'.[187]

More concretely, NAFTA is to ensure market access for services and service providers from other Parties under conditions no less favorable than those faced by nationals. It is to secure the effective enforcement of intellectual property protection in national courts for persons from its Parties. The NAFTA was planned to allow movement of business persons without visas within the area so that they might proceed unhindered with their work of stimulating the economies. It is to allow for freer movement of capital, not just through protection of foreign direct investment, but also through a liberalization of financial service regulations. And it is to do this in an agreement that treats its developing country party as a full and equal member with its developed country parties.

1.6.1   NAFTA Aims Compared With Those of the WTO and the European Union

Anyone not familiar with the state of trade agreements in 1992 may be somewhat underwhelmed by NAFTA goals. Indeed, the Uruguay Round was addressing the same topics, and the GATT principles have existed since 1947. The European Union is a second major example of a trade area that covers free movement of services and persons as well as free movement of goods, and it does so more thoroughly than does NAFTA, with formal supranational institutions and a court that can issue binding decisions. However, when NAFTA was created (and even now, though to a significantly lesser extent), it was much more comprehensive than the then-existing GATT agreement and is much less intrusive on its Parties' domestic policy-making ability than the European Communities.

---

[187]   Robert T. Matsui, 'Introduction' (1993) 27 UC Davis L Rev 791, introducing volume devoted to discussion of NAFTA legal issues.

1.6.1.1   NAFTA Compared With the GATT/WTO System

Unlike the GATT, which in 1994 was still an informal institution aimed at lowering tariffs on goods, the NAFTA contains a full trade liberalization program with strong institutional structures to promote further economic integration of its Parties' markets. Indeed, even today, over 50 years after the GATT first appeared, its successor, the World Trade Organization, does not address competition or investment rules in any meaningful way. In addition, it leaves the liberalization of many service sectors unfulfilled, contains only optional rules on government procurement, and has no effective mechanism for addressing the concerns of the environment and social rights. The NAFTA, in contrast, has full chapters on competition rules, investment rules (including separate dispute settlement provisions for investment conflicts) and government procurement, it liberalizes service sectors much more completely, and it has separate agreements on environmental and labor rights. Besides having broader coverage, the NAFTA's provisions are more specific than are those of the WTO—'There are thirty-eight articles in GATT; only one is industry specific ... In NAFTA, ... there are seventeen chapters, four of which are industry specific, and Chapter 3 has an Annex which adds two other industries, automotive and textiles trade'.[188]

In addition, the GATT/WTO system continues to offer developing country Members preferential terms of trade. The NAFTA, however, treats the lesser economically developed Mexico almost as an equal with Canada and the United States, and new Members will be expected to abide by the same rules. Although the principles of free trade are elemental to both the GATT/WTO and NAFTA, 'GATT allows foot draggers ... NAFTA does not'.[189]

1.6.2   NAFTA Compared With the European Union

The European Union, with its financial transfer payments to poorer Member states, also differs significantly from the NAFTA's treatment of the economic differences between the Parties. This is not the most important difference between the EU and NAFTA, however. The most significant difference between NAFTA and the European Union—a significance that permeates the entire treaty and one that must be taken account of when interpreting the treaty—lies in the fact that NAFTA is only a free trade area.[190]

---

[188] Michael W. Gordon, 'Some Comments and Comparisons: GATT and NAFTA' (1993) 1 US-Mex LJ 25, 27.

[189] *Ibid.*

[190] Linda Powers of the United States Department of Commerce emphasized this during her speech at a Symposium held on NAFTA prior to the Agreement's implementation:

> NAFTA is a free trade area only; it is not a common market. We are not aiming to develop the full spectrum of common internal policies that the European Community has developed, such as a common company law, a common social policy, a labor policy, and an agricultural policy. We are not aiming for common policies, just a free trade area.

Linda Powers, 'NAFTA and the Regulation of Financial and Other Services' (1993) 1:1 US-Mex LJ 65, 66.

The ideas behind the integration of European states that arose from the Second World War indicate important differences in the fundamental difference in approach to integration between the EU and NAFTA states.[191] Within the EU, the opening of markets and the economies of scale achievable through such openings certainly were seen as a benefit of integration, but the real driving force was the desire to avoid further armed conflicts.[192] The first trade agreement formed along the way to European Union, the Treaty Establishing the European Coal and Steel Community,[193] is a good example of an economic solution to a political problem. The treaty merged the coal and steel industries of participating countries, including France and Germany. Not only did this treaty end the use of trade barriers, thus rationalizing the market for producers and consumers, but by combining the resources under a multinational 'Authority', it also effectually eliminated the possibility that one member would build up a war machine to be used against another.[194] A further political unifier of postwar Europe was the threat of Josef Stalin's expansionary visions. Facing the Soviet Union, the West Europeans were ready to forgive their neighbors to allow for strength in the form of economic growth.

The importance of this military-political strain of the EU is also apparent in the rapid development of the political institutions of the Union. By 1957, the three original treaties of European Unification[195] each had an Assembly, a Council, a Commission, and a Court of Justice. In 1967, the Merger Treaty[196]

---

[191] For another overview of the differences between the NAFTA and the EU integrations, see *ibid.* at 64–7, particularly at 66–7:

> In Europe, the objectives underlying the Treaty of Rome were as much political and strategic as they were economic. Having experienced two wars earlier in the century, building economic interdependence as a way of underpinning new security arrangements was a key objective. This was to be done through a phased approach to institutionally based integration …
>
> In contrast, the North American FTAs followed after market-driven processes of integration [that] had already substantially increased US-Canada and US-Mexico trade … The objectives of Canada and Mexico seem to have been solely economic … These economic objectives, if anything, superceded possible political concerns for impairment of national sovereignty …
>
> In further contrast to Europe, future North American economic integration will probably continue to be driven by the market-oriented trade and investment forces, rather than by the intergovernmental institutional arrangements [as] in Europe.

[192] Derrick Wyatt and Alan Dashwood, *European Community Law* (3rd edn, Sweet & Maxwell, London, 1993), p. 3. See generally, P.J.G. Kapteyn and P. VerLoren van Themaat, *Introduction to the Law of the European Communities* (3rd edn, Kluwer Law International, London, 1998), pp. 1–7.

[193] 261 UNTS 140 (from 18 April 1951). For a further description of the treaty see Kapteyn and van Themaat (note 192 *supra*), at 7–9.

[194] Wyatt and Dashwood (note 192 *supra*), at 3.

[195] The three treaties composing the European Communities are those establishing the European Coal and Steel Community, the European Economic Community, and the European Atomic Energy Community. The finalization of the latter two treaties are described in Kapteyn and van Themaat (note 192 *supra*), at 14–17.

[196] Treaty Establishing a Single Council and a Single Commission of the European Communities (signed in April 1965, it came into effect in July 1967).

unified political institutions, and the basis of the modern European Council, Parliament, and Commission was established.[197]

Unlike those of the EU, the origins of NAFTA lie in the economics of comparative advantage and economies of scale set out in the writings of David Ricardo and in the Heckler-Olin theory of factor endowment: the elimination of trade barriers would, in fostering free trade, allow for the comparative advantage of each party, determined by the relative natural endowments of each partner, to be fully developed, thus resulting in more wealth for all.[198] One author, comparing the probable longer-term effects of the two regional arrangements, emphasizes the importance of the differing industrial structures among the states of the EU and the NAFTA as follows:

> The degree of regional integration ... can be measured by the share of intra-group trade in total trade. In 1992, intra-EC trade was 64 per cent of total EC trade as compared with 38 per cent for NAFTA. Thus, the EC seems to be much more economically integrated than NAFTA. One could argue that this is due to the fact that the EC has been in existence for over 25 years while NAFTA is only now beginning. But intra-EC trade was already 40 per cent of total EC trade in 1958, at a time when economic interdependence among nations was much less than today. With trade restrictions between the United States and Canada already very low, there is no room for a further major expansion of trade among them. Only trade between the United States and Mexico is likely to grow rapidly. Even so, it is not likely that intra-NAFTA trade as a percentage of total trade will become as high as in the EC anytime soon—if ever.[199]

He continues:

> The relative importance of inter-industry as compared with intra-industry trade in NAFTA means that there will be major problems of industrial restructuring and income redistribution in NAFTA countries, especially in Mexico. Since large income transfers from the United States to Mexico (as between the North and the South in the EC) are not contemplated, Mexico is likely to face major difficulties. In fact, the establishment of NAFTA, including as it does the largest and one of the most advanced economies in the world and a large nation in the early stages of development, represents one of the most daring and interesting economic experiments in modern economic history. According to the Stolper-Samuelson theorem, free trade is likely to

---

[197] Wyatt and Dashwood (note 192 *supra*), at 8-9.

[198] One author posits that '[n]o economic theory of trade has been more dominant in the last two centuries than David Ricardo's theory of comparative advantage' explained in his article 'On the Principles of Political Economy and Taxation'. Richard H. Steinberg, 'Antidotes to Regionalism: Responses to Trade Diversion Effects of the North American Free Trade Agreement' (1993) 29:2 Stan J Int'l L 315, 318–319. See also, Dominick Salvatore, 'NAFTA and the EC: Similarities and Differences', in Khosrow Fatemi and Dominick Salvatore (eds), *The North American Free Trade Agreement* (Pergamon, New York, 1994), pp. 15–30, especially at 26–8, comparing the EC and NAFTA in terms of trade effects, membership, and monetary policy.

[199] Salvatore (note 198 *supra*), at 26–7.

reduce the earnings of each nation's scarce factor. Thus, NAFTA is expected to reduce the average wages of low-skilled labor in the United States and the average return to capital in Mexico. Overall, however, average wages are not expected to fall in the United States. Furthermore, with wages rising faster in Mexico than in the United States, US-Mexican wages differences are expected to be reduced and this eventually is likely to slow the flow of Mexican migration to the United States.[200]

Even the political considerations of the NAFTA Party governments stemmed from economic considerations.[201] This is perhaps more clear from what was *not* discussed as from what was: regardless of the opponents' prophesying, at no time was the idea of giving up significant portions of sovereignty a real possibility. Even the most vocal opponents of the treaty did not start rumors of political union among the parties. Free movement of non-business persons (that is to say workers without higher education) was not discussed as a viable option. In fact, even harmonization of laws is not mandatory, appearing instead as a suggestion as the most efficient form of eliminating non-tariff barriers. One author states, '... outside of tariff elimination, NAFTA contains rearranged protection as well as substantive liberalization ... NAFTA, however, does not deal with any specific process for achieving further integration, and both its complexity and partly empty chapters equally pervade the agreement'.[202]

This is not to say political considerations and even personal aggrandizement did not come into play during the NAFTA negotiations, but the importance of political considerations was tied in with the economic

---

[200] *Ibid.* at 27.

[201] It is significant to study the history of the United States' relations with Mexico and the rest of Latin America, and to find that economic interests almost always prevailed over political interests. A scholar writing about the Latin American view of the American Revolution points this out:

> Historically, the image and influence of the United States [in Latin America] probably has been related more closely to its economic policies and system than to its political institutions. In this context, the ideals of economic liberalism of the men who made the American Revolution have had a direct relationship not only to Latin American conceptions of political and economic progress but also to inter-American relations. The preamble to the Franco-American Commercial Treaty of 1778 (based on the Model Treaty drafted by the Continental Congress in 1776) elaborated the liberal principles of 'the most perfect equality and reciprocity' and the 'founding of the advantages of commerce solely upon reciprocal utility and the just rules of free intercourse' [citation omitted] ...
>
> These ideals and principles of the American Revolution helped to shape the official US attitudes and policies toward the newly independent Latin American republics ... The Latin American policy of the Monroe and Adams administrations was aimed at establishing reciprocity as a key element in inter-American relations, and preventing the reestablishment of the old colonial order of economic mercantilism and political authoritarianism.

Robert Freeman Smith, 'The American Revolution and Latin America: An Essay in Imagery, Perceptions, and Ideological Influence' (1978) 20:4 J Interam Stud & World Aff 421, 434–435.

[202] Whalley and Hamilton (note 24 *supra*), at 55.

considerations. Military interests, it is fair to say, were non-existent.[203] One author comments on this constellation: 'Fortunately, among the US, Canada and Mexico, we have not gone out and killed 60 million of each other in this century. Consequently you do not have the same political drive that you had in Europe ... to have a more integrated unit'.[204]

Moreover, the degree of national autonomy yielded to the agreements by the participating states differs dramatically from the supranational EU to the regional trade agreement of the NAFTA. The European Union's Members agree to accept the decisions of the Commission, the Parliament, and the Court within their domestic legal and economic contexts. The NAFTA Parties refused to create any supranational institutions for legislating or executing NAFTA rules. Moreover, while they are accused by opponents of having given up some 'sovereignty', in reality each Party maintains control of deciding which, if any, of the treaty interpretations emanating from the dispute settlement panels it will accept.

Finally, the issue of movement of labor fundamentally distinguishes the EU from NAFTA. In the Treaty of Rome, movement of labor is anchored as one of the four 'fundamental freedoms' of the citizens of 'Europe'.[205] The ability of persons from all Member states to live

---

[203] Canada had been the target of the United States' military aggression. The American Revolution and the War of 1812 each included intrusions by colonial/US troops on Canadian soil. Moreover, while little attention is paid these wars in the United States, the memory of these events have contributed to the Canadians' historic distrust of their large southern neighbor. For a very good, concise account of these actions, see Dickey and Shepardson (note 25 *supra*), at 7–16, describing the tremendous effect the American Revolution and the War of 1812 had on Canadians' perceptions of the Canada-United States relationship. However, there is nothing to suggest that Canada has feared military aggression by the United States since Canadian nationhood in 1931. Although the United States had fought a fierce war with Mexico in 1846–48, and resentment of United States intrusion in Latin America formed the basis for some of the resistence toward the NAFTA in Mexico, there were no direct threats of armed conflict between the North American nations. For a short account of the Mexican-US conflicts over territory during the middle nineteenth century, see Bilateral Commission (note 6 *supra*), Ch. 1: 'The Nature of the Relationship', at 21–6. Nevertheless, the US defense industry strongly supported the NAFTA. In a report to the United States Trade Representative, selected industry leaders set out their opinion that while NAFTA 'will not directly impact the trade of defense goods and services among the United States, Canada and Mexico', it would permit better 'government trade relationships ... and should, therefore, be of long-term benefit to the US defense industry'. See Report on the North American Free Trade Agreement Submitted to the United States Trade Representative (31 August 1992) in Report of the Defense Policy Advisory Committee for Trade in the North American Free Trade Agreement (September 1992).

[204] Jonathon T. Fried, 'Two Paradigms for the Role of international Trade Law' (1994) 20 Can-US LJ 39, 58.

[205] ECT Art. 48. See, e.g., ECT Art. 48:

> 1. Freedom of movement for workers shall be secured within the Community by the end of the transition period at the latest.
> 2. Such freedom of movement shall entail the abolition of any discrimination based on nationality between workers of the Member States as regards employment, remuneration and other conditions of work and employment.

and work in any of the other Member states has been vigorously protected by the European Court of Justice, and indirect barriers to this flow of labor are struck down as violations of the Treaty of Rome.[206] In the NAFTA, the situation is completely different. Trade in goods, services, and investment is to take place without the movement of populations. While businesspersons are protected in their trade-creating travels, permanent residence is not encouraged, and mere 'labor' movements are not even considered by the Agreement. An expert summarizes:

> ... [The EC] agreement was based on the desire to move all workers across borders freely. There is an underlying sense that NAFTA is intended to *prohibit* the movement of any workers across borders. Although immigration is a prohibited word in the discussion of the Agreement, the concern of the United States over immigration from Mexico underlies the Agreement, and there is hope that NAFTA will improve jobs in Mexico and allow Mexicans an opportunity to prosper at home.[207]

1.6.3 NAFTA and the Regulation of International Trade in Financial Services

Trade in financial services is just one aspect of trade in services in general, and the newness of international agreements in the former is a direct result of the lack of regard for the latter as an area of economic interest up to the recent past. In order to grasp the significance of the NAFTA Parties' success in completing a substantive agreement to liberalize trade in financial services, a cursory review of the development of the services' regime in international trade is necessary.

1.6.3.1 Historical Development of the Concept of 'Trade in Services'

It was not until 1972 that the Organization of Economic Co-operation and Development (OECD) even conceived of the term 'trade in services'. Once labeled as such, it was nearly 20 years before the North American states would formally liberalize their cross-border service trade and several more years until the category of services would be included in the multilateral trading regime.[208] The reason for this neglect

---

[206] See, e.g., Case 118/75, *Watson & Belmann* (1976) ECR I-1185 (7 July 1976); Case 53/81 *Levin v. Staatssecretaris van Justitie* (1982) ECR I-1035 (23 March 1982); Case 267/83, *Aissatou Diatta v. Berlin* (1985) ECR I-567 (13 February 1985); Case 167/73, *Commission v. France* (1974) ECR I-359 (4 April 1974).

[207] Gordon (note 188 *supra*), at 25, 26 (emphasis added).

[208] See Report by the High Level Group on Trade and Related Problems (OECD, Paris, 1973). For an excellent and entertaining description of the process of making services a part of the WTO see generally Geza Feketekuty, 'Appendix: The History of a Campaign: How Services Became a Trade Issue', in Feketekuty, *International Trade in Services: An Overview*

of services was that prior to the 1970s, services were generally seen as non-productive for the economy as a whole.[209] Thus, services were neither very interesting to trade economists nor considered to be 'tradeable' in any sense familiar to trade lawyers and diplomats. These invisible trade-related transactions were often defined only in the negative: 'whatever is not included under agriculture, mining and manufacturing in systems of national accounting' or an 'intangible, invisible, non-transportable, non-storable, perishable, non-exhaustible, something you cannot drop on your feet'.[210]

It was at the urging of the United States that research was first undertaken on the importance of services to the economies of the world, and the United States Trade Act of 1974 was the first trade legislation to specify that 'the term "international trade" includes trade in both goods and services'.[211] Soon the other industrialized economies' service sectors were under investigation by their own governments in co-operation with the OECD. In 1975, Brian Griffith's book, *Invisible Barriers to Trade*[212] further changed the way international trade policy-makers and even most businesses thought about services.

As information emerged that services were becoming more economically important, interest grew in developing international rules for their

---

(Contd.)

and Blueprint for Negotiations (Ballinger, Cambridge, MA, 1988), pp. 295–322. Feketekuty relates that the OECD Report's trade in services chapter was written under the leadership of an American businessman Bill Eberle, Swedish economist Bertil Ohlin, and the British Sir Richard Powell, each of whom had extensive experience in trade leading to a shared conviction that barriers to trade in services needed to be addressed formally. *Ibid.* at 297–8. Without directly committing itself to promoting multilateral negotiations on trade in services, the Report states:

> Given that services are a sector which seems likely to expand rapidly in countries' economies, the main need is to avoid any tendencies to protectionism and to aim at achieving a more thorough liberalization
> … The Group considers that action should be taken by the developed countries to ensure liberalization and non-discrimination in the services sector … As in the case of goods, consideration might be given to allowing developing countries a limited time to adapt themselves before undertaking full commitments.

209 *Ibid.* at 32.
210 Phedon Nicolaides, 'The Problem of Regulation in Traded Services: the Implications for Reciprocal Liberalization' (1989) 44:1 *Aussenwirtschaft* 29, 31.
211 Trade Act of 1972, § 102 g(3), cited in Feketekuty (note 208 *supra*), at 300–1. Feketekuty reports that much of the domestic impetus for including services in the trade legislation came from Pan American Airlines and the American International Group, an internationally active US insurance company. Both of these businesses were facing entry barriers in foreign markets.
212 Brian Griffith, *Invisible Barriers to Trade* (Trade Policy Research Center, London, 1975). Feketekuty reports that Griffith, a scholar at the London School of Economcs, was given the assignment to do the research for the book by Australian Hugh Corbet, founder of the Trade Policy Research Center.

trade.[213] During the Tokyo Round of negotiations under the General Agreement on Tariffs and Trade, references to services made their way into the Agreement on Government Procurement, the Subsidies Agreement, and the Standards Code.[214]

The United States government, with the strong support of private enterprises and non-governmental institutions, continued the campaign to include services in the liberalization agenda of the next round of GATT negotiations.[215] After several years of funding intense public awareness programs and being subjected to just as intense political lobbying, the Office of the United States Trade Representative decided to bring the proposal for multilateral services negotiations to the GATT.

1.6.3.2 *Movement Toward International Regulation of Trade in Services*

In 1981, a group of leaders comprising the Consultative Group of Eighteen issued a Report to the other GATT Contracting Parties.[216] The Report addressed, among other topics, the issue of whether services should be included in future negotiations in the GATT. The text reveals the Group's own ambiguity on the question. While 'the Chairman suggested that trade-related services might ... be regarded as a proper concern of the GATT', 'some of those members stressed the complexity of this field, and suggested that the collection of information on work being done elsewhere should be the secretariat's first concern', and still others 'doubted the feasibility of extending GATT's activities in this area'.[217]

The next year, the GATT issued a Ministerial Declaration with a commitment that each Contracting Party investigate its service sector in order to decide whether multilateral negotiations for service trade liberalization should take place.[218]

In 1985, the Canada-United States Free Trade Agreement negotiations began, including a chapter on trade in services. That same year, the 25 parties to the GATT that were also members of the OECD

---

[213] One example of the importance given to services in the United States was that § 301 trade sanctions were granted to the President to use against countries that were found to be imposing restrictions on the importation of US services. Stewart (note 40 *supra*), at 2343. Despite the United States' leading role in making 'services' a topic of intense discussion among trade negotiators, sudies revealed that several European countries were more important traders of the group of services known as 'other' in international statistical records. Helena Stalson, *US Service Exports and Foreign Barriers: An Agenda for Negotiations* (National Planning Association, Washington, DC, 1985), pp. 14–15 (Great Britain, France, and Germany all had more exports of 'other' services than did the United States in the mid-1980s, and Belgium, the Netherlands, and Italy had nearly as many as the United States did, despite their enormous difference in size).

[214] Feketekuty (note 208 *supra*), at 304.

[215] *Ibid*. at 307–13.

[216] Report of the Consultative Group of Eighteen to the Council of Representatives, L/5210 (found in BISD 28S/71 (1980—81)).

[217] *Ibid*. at 74, para. 14.

[218] Ministerial Declaration, 'Services' L/5424 (adopted 29 November 1982) (found in BISD 29S/9, 21-22 (1981–82)).

decided that services were important enough to be discussed at the then-upcoming ministerial meeting of the GATT.[219] Discussion attempts faltered, however, due to opposition by the developing countries' representatives.[220] The idea of liberalizing the highly regulated areas of services within the GATT framework polarized North–South concerns even more than did the South's calls for open agricultural markets in the GATT.

Industrialized countries' insistent pressure combined with the developing country group's internal disputes finally succeeded in bringing the developing countries to the service negotiating table. Yet, even at the 1988–89 Mid-Term Review of the Uruguay Round, the developing countries' acceptance of negotiating a liberalization of trade in services seemed to be more of a token than a true commitment to the idea. They remained adamant that they not be made to fully liberalize their services.[221]

The extent of service liberalization and the rate at which the various service sectors would be liberalized soon became among the most hotly debated topics in pre-Marrakesh global trade relations.[222] While industrialized countries saw trade in services as a path for their future economic well-being,[223] developing countries saw the attempts to liberalize their less developed service sectors as another in a series of steps by the industrialized governments to invade their sovereignty while

---

[219] The United States, Canada, and Switzerland were among this group of 25 states, but Mexico was not yet a member of the OECD at that time, nor was any other developing country. See also Stalson (note 213 *supra*), and particularly at 2:

> Since the early 1980s, the US government has conducted a vigorous educational campaign, at home and abroad, emphasizing the changes that are taking place in industrial structures and employment in both advanced and developing countries, the technological innovations that are making traditional regulations irrelevant, and the dangers that can flow from inappropriate government intervention in the development of major service industries. The United States has urged the members of GATT to agree to global negotiations on trade generally and to include—for the first time—services as legitimate areas in which to negotiate international rules of behavior. The compelling motivation behind the US approach is the fear that, without a sense of movement toward a global trading system that offers more benefits to the United States, Congress will enact new protectionist legislation that will harm this country and others as well stifling the natural trend toward high valued trade in services.

[220] See Mexico's proposals for the services negotiations just after the Mid-Term Review. Murray Gibbs and Mina Mashayekhi, 'Elements of a Multilateral Framework of Principles and Rules for Trade in Services', in United Nations Conference on Trade and Development (ed.), *Uruguay Round: Papers on Selected Issues*, UNCTAD/ITP/10 (United Nations, New York, 1989), pp. 99–101.

[221] Nicolaides (note 210 *supra*).

[222] For an overview of the services negotiations, see Gibbs and Mashayekhi (note 220 *supra*), at 81–127.

[223] See also *ibid.* at 90–98, setting out the negotiating positions of the industrialized countries, all emphasizing MFN, NTO, and transparency.

assuring their own continued economic dominance.[224] Aversion to neo-colonialism on the part of the developing countries' representatives allowed them to only gradually recognize service trade as a major source of national income in their own economies, and finally agree to the inclusion of a General Agreement on Trade in Services (GATS) within the new World Trade Organization package of treaties.

The GATS negotiations, however, were not as successful in incorporating rules to regulate trade in financial services as they were in other service sectors. International trade in financial services is by no means a new phenomenon, but strictly limited market access for foreign banks, minimal capital requirements higher than for domestic banks, and limits on expansion within the territory are among the discriminatory banking regulations of virtually every nation of the twentieth century. General opposition to giving up sovereignty in an area so closely related to monetary policy, financial system-specific concerns about how liberaliza-tion would effect the systemic stability of a nation's banking sector, as well as fears by many states that more efficient foreign competitors would spur the collapse of domestic banking institutions all worked to prevent a final agreement on the extent to which financial services could be traded among the WTO Member states. By 1994, it was clear that there would not be a multilateral system for regulating trade in financial services by the time the WTO itself was scheduled to be formally established.[225]

1.6.3.3 NAFTA's Aims and Trade in Financial Services

Among the NAFTA Parties, the approach to trade in financial services was overwhelmingly one of a commitment to the principle of rapid liberalization. The strong interest of the United States financial sector in gaining access to the Mexican market and hopes of improving on the

---

[224] *Ibid.* at 81–3, setting out the factors affecting the developing countries' attitude toward the service negotiations). Gibbs and Mashayekhi (note 220 *supra*, at 98–9) refer to the develop-ing countries' statements on liberalization of services in the negotiations:

> Certain developing countries have made general statements on the economic and legal issues at stake.... Brazil, for example, has rejected the 'naive, theoretical assumption ... that liberalization should be adopted unilaterally as something intrinsically beneficial' and has stressed the 'asymmetry' in the situations of developed and developing countries, both in the economic sense and in their ability to adequately regulate services to meet national objectives. India has stressed that the mandate cannot be interpreted 'to warrant ... an open-ended scrutiny of all national regulation in services and subjecting it to multilateral detemination of its appropriateness or legitimacy'...
>
> The developing countries consider that the discussions should first focus on statistical issues, the definition of 'services' and 'international trade in services' and identification of sectors covered by the multilateral framework ... The only criterion against which all proposals for a multilateral framework on services could be tested should be the Ministerial Declaration and its mandate that the basic objective of a multilateral framework should be 'promoting economic growth of all trading partners and development of the developing countries'.

[225] See Chapter 6 *infra* for a more detailed account of the financial services negotiations in the WTO system.

existing commitments in the CUFTA propelled trade in financial services into its position as a critical area of negotiation. While the Mexican delegation was more hesitant, the negotiators were also familiar with the importance of financial services to future prosperity. Thus, even though they may have not volunteered to liberalizing their banking, insurance, and securities sectors, Mexico was willing to do so in order to partake of the many other economic benefits offered by the NAFTA 'Package'. Thus, NAFTA's solid economic base helped in ensuring the incorporation of the financial service sectors into the regional agreement, even where multilateral attempts to do the same had failed.

1.7   ACTUAL RESULTS OF NAFTA AFTER FIVE YEARS

After the hopes and fears gave way to the ratification of the NAFTA, the Agreement came into effect on 1 January 1994. Since then, the press (and therefore the public) seems to have lost much interest in the treaty.[226] To some extent this is justified: as often occurs following a polarized debate, the results do appear to be much less dramatic than anticipated. In the case of NAFTA, the Parties have neither fallen into the dire conditions of the industrial revolution nor have they succeeded in forming an unstoppable global competitor oozing wealth for each of its citizens. Macroeconomic indicators for each Party are mixed.

Statistics released by all three Party governments since the NAFTA went into effect suggest that the Agreement has fostered growth in intra-continental trade, with exports among the three Parties nearly doubling during 1993–98.[227] Governmental reports indicate that whereas US-Mexican trade reached over $100 billion in 1994[228] and $120.1 billion in 1995,[229] by 1998 the export and import figures totaled $197 billion (making Mexico the United States' second largest trading partner in 1998).[230] Canadian-Mexican trade has increased as well, from $4.1 billion in 1994 to nearly $10 billion by the end of 1998, moving Mexico into the number five position for Canada's trading partners in 1998.[231] The governments are claiming the increased

---

[226]   In early 1996, a newspaper in Austin, Texas asked a random sample of the city's inhabitants what three countries were the members of the North American Free Trade Agreement. Over 50 per cent were not able to answer correctly. Michele Kay, 'NAFTA Eludes Majority of Texans', *Austin-American Statesman*, 9 March 1996, p. B1.

[227]   Exports within North America in 1993 were estimated to be valued at $300 billion, and by 1998 had grown to around $510 billion.

[228]   'NAFTA Promotes US-Mexico Trade Gains', *NAFTA Works*, Issue 3 (March 1996), pp. 1–2, at 2.

[229]   'NAFTA Leads to Record Levels of Mexico-US Trade', *NAFTA Works*, Issue 11 (November 1996), p. 1.

[230]   Figures collected by the Embassy of Mexico in Canada, using SECOFI/Ottawa and Statistics Canada data; current trade figures are available over the internet at >www.embamexcan.com<.

[231]   Figures presented by SECOFI and Statistics Canada. Monthly updated trade figures are available over the internet at >www.nafta-mexico.org<.

trade as a NAFTA success, and point especially to positive growth rates in spite of the peso crisis.

In sectors such as textiles, where tariffs have been lowered due to the Agreement and rules of origin are particularly restrictive to non-Parties, trade among the Parties has grown significantly. The Mexico-US textile trade has increased 163 per cent since the end of 1993.[232] Agriculture trade among the three parties reached $1.8 billion by 1996,[233] and value of their trade in the automotive sector rose from $80.12 billion in 1993 to $94.21 billion in 1995.[234]

Statistics and their accompanying claims of the benefits of the regional agreement must be judged with skepticism, however, as the probability that other factors contributed to the increases in goods, services, and investments trade are high. Additional factors in assessing results of the agreement, that have, by wide acknowledgement, nothing to do with the NAFTA, are the Mexican peso crisis of January 1995 and the Asian financial crisis of 1998–99.

The results of NAFTA on employment have been less dramatic than the import-export results. Although extremely difficult to determine the extent to which the NAFTA itself has affected the number of positions created or ended, most available studies reveal almost undetectable changes in employment among the NAFTA Parties. The US Labor Department reported that as of December 1996, less than 90,000 persons had applied for federal retraining programs for workers dislocated by the NAFTA,[235] and while the non-government organization Public Citizen estimated that 300,000 jobs had been lost in the same period,[236] another economic study indicated an increase in employment due to NAFTA.[237] Even if any of these figures accurately predicts the effect of NAFTA on workers, however, it is small in comparison to the US economy-wide net gain of 3.5 million jobs in

---

[232] 'US-Mexico Textile and Apparel Trade Growing With NAFTA', NAFTA Works, Issue 4 (April 1996), pp. 1ff, at; see *ibid.* at 4, reporting that the gains in intra-NAFTA textile trade have come at the cost of trade with Asian textile exporters.

[233] 'Agriculture Leading NAFTA Trade Growth in 1996', *NAFTA Works*, Issue 6 (June 1996), p. 2. See also Tracy L. Cherpeski, 'Another Look at NAFTA: Political and Economic Implications and its Preliminary Effects on the Automotive Industry' World Business Conference (November 1997) (text found on the internet at >www.worldbusiness.net<, reporting that imports of autos and auto parts from Mexico to the United States has more than doubled since the NAFTA went into effect and that 'North America promises to become the world's largest exporter of inexpensive automobiles and trucks …'.

[234] 'NAFTA Auto Industry Expanding Markets', *NAFTA Works*, Issue 7 (July 1996), pp. 1–2, at 2.

[235] Nora Claudia Lustig, 'NAFTA: Setting the Record Straight', Brookings Policy Brief No. 20 (1997) (text found on the internet at >http://www.brook.E…olicy<).

[236] Robert Collier, 'NAFTA Stumbles Short of Expectations', *San Francisco Chronical*, 1995 (text found on the internet at >www.latinolink.com<). Mr Hufbauer's views are shared by NAFTA expert Nora C. Lustig at the Brookings Institute, 'the impact of NAFTA on gross job displacement in the United States has been negligible'. Lustig (note 235 *supra*).

[237] Lustig (note 235 *supra*), at n.2 and accompanying text, referring to Raúl Hinojosa *et al.*, *North American Integration Three Years After NAFTA: A Framework for Tracking, Modeling and Internet Accessing the National and Regional Labor Market Impacts* (UCLA, School of Public Policy and Social Research, December 1996).

1994. Economist and senior fellow at the Institute for International Economics in Washington, DC, Gary Hufbauer summed up the conclusions when he remarked, 'The best figure for the jobs effect of NAFTA is approximately zero', and added, 'the lesson for economists is that jobs forecasting is perilous and pretty misleading'.[238]

So do the increased trade effects and stable employment effects make NAFTA an overall success? Perhaps economically. But the effects of NAFTA cannot be discovered through quantitative analysis of the macro-economic indicators. Rather, the non-statistical results of the NAFTA are more important than the changes in trade and investment. Renowned economist Paul Krugman, shares this idea: 'So, where's the payoff from NAFTA ...? In foreign policy, not economics ...'.[239]

In terms of legal effects, it is the less tangible change in attitudes that make up the 'payoff'. Two other authors summarize one part of the change with their comment that '[t]he import of the North American Free Trade Agreement lies in its psychology ... [I]t is far more important as a symbol of change than as a structural method of tariff reduction'.[240] The second part of the attitude change takes the form of new efforts at co-operation, increased understanding, and perhaps above all in the short-term, the new awareness of one another that the Agreement forced upon the three Parties is being felt increasingly in the American business place. These intangible effects will be reviewed in the following chapters, and must be kept in mind in any—even a 'purely legal'—analysis of the NAFTA.

[238] Collier (note 236 *supra*).
[239] Paul Krugman, 'How Is NAFTA Doing? It's Been Hugely Successful—As a Foreign Policy', *New Democrat* (May–June 1996) (text found on the internet at >www.dlcppi.org<).
[240] Rober R. Amsterdam and Peter W. Klestadt, 'NAFTA: A Symbol of Change' (text found on the internet at >http://amperlaw.com<).

2. Banking Systems of the NAFTA Parties

Banks compose only one sector of the financial services industry. Yet, they play a very important—indeed perhaps the most important—part in the functioning of the financial systems. The banking systems of the NAFTA Parties contain elements of most of the prevalent banking environments, but each has special features that justify the following cursory review of them.[1]

A complete description of the banking systems of the NAFTA parties would be out of place in a book focussing on international and regional trade regimes. The purpose in the following chapter is to give a brief description of the structure of the banking systems of the United States, Canada, and Mexico in order to help the reader understand the national contexts onto which the NAFTA Chapter Fourteen provisions are built.[2] Thus, the following discussion is mainly focussed on the historical development of banking in that country, how banks are established, and the boundaries of a bank's permissible activities. The author also illustrates the unique aspects of each system that might affect the domestic banks' relation with foreign banks in that Party's territory.

2.1 UNITED STATES' BANKING SYSTEM PRE-NAFTA

There are two characteristics that have traditionally set the United States' banking system apart from the banking systems of most other countries: its openness and its complexity. The United States has had a long tradition of

---

[1] For a comprehensive guide to international banking, see Roy C. Smith and Ingo Walter, *Global Banking* (OUP, New York, 1997); Richard J. Herring and Robert E. Litan, *Financial Regulation in the Global Economy* (Brookings Institution, Washington, DC, 1995). Two books by the OECD have become classic treatises on the recent changes in the field of international banking; G. Bröker, *Competition in Banking* (OECD, Paris, 1989); OECD, *Banks Under Stress* (OECD, Paris, 1992). A more recent OECD study is equally valuable. OECD, *The New Financial Landscape: Forces Shaping the Revolution in Banking, Risk Management and Capital Markets* (OECD, Paris, 1995).

[2] For a non-technical explanation of why financial systems are structured as they are, see F. S. Mishkin, 'An Economic Analysis of Financial Structure', in *The Economics of Money, Banking, and Financial Markets* (4th edn, Harper Collins, New York, 1995), pp. 205–230.

allowing financial service providers unencumbered access to its market regardless of country of origin. Indeed, until the late 1970s, foreign banks were offered conditions of competition more advantageous than those allowed domestic banks for the reason that they were not regulated. Legislation has since been passed to 'level the playing field' for domestic banks, but the US regulators[3] maintain the policy of granting foreign banks the same opportunities to do business as are offered domestic banks. Today, approximately one-fifth of all banking assets in the United States belongs to foreign banks' branches and agencies.[4]

The United States' legal framework for banking regulation is also highly complex, with a peculiarly strong State-level banking system compared to other nations.[5] Basically a dual-system, with national- and State-licensed banks, there are also numerous additional characteristics that determine the particular rules governing a bank's daily activities—the type of bank/bank-like institution; whether a bank is a member of the Federal Reserve System of banks; and whether a bank receives Federal Deposit Insurance for its customers' deposits, to name just the major subcategories of regulation. This set of regulations has arisen as a product of the cultural and political history of the United States and continues to shape the legislative activity of today.[6]

There is, however, fervent discussion currently as to the future direction of regulation of financial services in the United States. Those supporting maintenance of the regulatory limits placed on banks point to the extraordinary changes brought about by technology and by liberalizations in other countries' banking markets. Such changes, they argue, are making supervision of the safety of depository institutions more difficult but no less necessary. Further liberalization complicates supervision, and thus increases the risks of financial system failures.

On the other side are those (including the Federal Reserve Board) who are convinced that the present structure of preventing banks from engaging in securities and insurance activities and the remaining limitations on

---

[3] States' regulators are in some instances significantly less generous with equal treatment of foreign banks. For more, see Chapter 3, 3.16 *infra*.

[4] In December 1994, 21 per cent of the domestic US banking assets were owned by foreign bank branches and agencies. GAO, *Foreign Banks: Assessing Their Role in the US Banking System*, GAO/GGD-96-26 (February 1996), p. 35; see also at p. 33, Fig. 2.3, showing the volume of various activities for domestic and foreign banks.

[5] For a general introduction into the US banking system in relation to foreign banking, see Henri Moudi, 'The State of US Banking in the Global Arena' (1992) 10:2 Bost Univ Int'l LJ 255.

[6] As stated in one text, 'If one were writing a clean slate, it is doubtful that such a regulatory structure would be designed. Nevertheless, each element of the regulatory structure has come about at least partly because of historical needs of [US] society responded to by Congress and the evolution of the American banking system since the eighteenth century'. Edward L. Symons, Jr. and James J. White, *Banking Law: Teaching Materials* (3rd edn, West Publishing, St Paul, 1991), p. 46. See also Edward L. Symons Jr, 'The United States Banking System' (1993) 19:1 Brook J Int'l L 1, 4–12, discussing the early history of the US banking system and the changes brought about by the Great Depression of the 1930s; Symons emphasizes the political influences that shaped banking law.

interstate banking is unnecessarily burdensome and harmful to the US banks' global competitiveness in an era of increasing competition. Liberalization would not mean abandoning regulation, they say, but would force the banks to be more responsive to the (impliedly more efficient) 'regulatory' forces of the market.

Although several attempts to change the laws governing these aspects of banking have failed to pass Congress, legislation continues to be introduced and agency regulations continue to be issued in a direction of liberalization. Despite the traditionalists and the wary, it is by no means certain that the US banking system of the 1990s will survive into the twenty-first century.

2.1.1 Supervisory Structure

2.1.1.1 *Federal Reserve System*

All nationally chartered banks are required to be members of the Federal Reserve System of banks. The Federal Reserve System, established in 1913 by the Federal Reserve Act, divided the country into 12 separate territories, or 'districts', each with nine directors to oversee that district's banks.[7] The entire system is co-ordinated by the Board of Governors of the Federal Reserve Bank ('the Board' or 'BOG').[8] This seven-member team is authorized to examine banks and scrutinize both the banks and the officers of the various districts. The Board uses its authority sparingly, however, allowing the District Banks and member banks to govern daily banking operations whenever possible, leaving itself more time to address the problems of the overall monetary policy of the United States.[9]

2.1.1.2 *Federal Deposit Insurance Corporation*

The Federal Deposit Insurance Corporation (FDIC) is a federally-owned company with the mandate of insuring private banks' deposits up to $100,000 per account. President Franklin Roosevelt authorized the establishment of the FDIC in 1931 to prevent a recurrence of the disastrous effects bank closures had on private individuals and families during the 1929–30 financial market crash. The FDIC has remained in place amidst

---

[7] The Districts are referred to numerically and are headed by a bank in a city located within the territory. The Districts, from one to 12 have their Federal Reserve Banks in: Boston; New York; Philadelphia; Cleveland; Richmond; Atlanta; Chicago; St Louis; Minneapolis; Kansas City; Dallas; and San Francisco. See *Board of Governors of the Federal Reserve System, Organization of the Federal Reserve System* (Board of Governors of the Federal Reserve System, Washington, DC, n.d.).

[8] The Board of Governors sits in Washington, DC. The Members of the Board are appointed by the President and approved by the Senate for a term of 14 years. BOG, *Organization of the Federal Reserve System* (organigram).

[9] Symons and White (note 6 *supra*), pp. 27–9.

growing concern of the 'moral hazard' it poses to bank owners at the cost of the US taxpayer.[10]

Until 1991, FDIC insurance was available to any bank in the United States, whether federally- or State-chartered, and whether domestic or foreign. Now, foreign banks that had not already joined the FDIC by 1991 are ineligible for FDIC-funded insurance of their accounts.

2.1.2   National Banks

2.1.2.1   *Controlling Legislation*

2.1.2.1.1   THE CONSTITUTION OF THE UNITED STATES

The United States Constitution is the 'Supreme Law of the Land', and as such is the first source for determining which branch of government as well as which level of government has legal authority for a particular area of law in the United States and its territories. The regulation of banking, however, is not addressed in the text of the Constitution. The effects of this omission in the form of a short history of the early development of the national government's competence to regulate banks can aid in understanding the rules of banking as they now exist in the United States.

The Drafters of the Constitution were well aware of the importance of banks to a nation's economy. By the late eighteenth century, banks in England were firmly established as an integral part of the industrialization process and the interconnections of trade and financial institutions were well recognized both in Europe and in the North American colonies. It is, then, remarkable that the matter of control over banks was left unexplained in the United States Constitution, and it was not long after the passage of the Constitution that the debate over the ability of the federal government to establish a bank led to heated public debate over the respective roles of the federal government and the State governments.[11]

Under the Constitution, the States retained a large fraction of their 'inherent' powers through the principle set out in the Tenth Amendment, ratified along with the Constitution, 'The powers not delegated to the United States by the Constitution, nor prohibited by it to the States, are reserved to the States respectively, or to the people'.[12]

---

[10] The term 'moral hazard' is used to describe the dilemma caused by a state-run insurance program for the private owners of a business. In banking, the moral hazard is that the FDIC program could encourage bank owners or bank managers to engage in excessively risky activities because if the activities are successful, the profit potential is higher than for low-risk ventures, and if the activities fail, the taxpayer-funded FDIC covers the losses.

[11] State governments under the Articles of Confederation were sovereign entities, and as such, possessed all powers of governance within their territories. The Constitution replaced the Articles of Confederation in 1789 and established a federal government with exclusive enumerated powers in the area of interstate commerce. Nevertheless, the issue of States' rights remains a political debating ground.

[12] US Constitution Art. 10.

So, when legislation was introduced in Congress in 1790 to create a national bank (in order to help finance the new nation and assist with revenue collection), the reaction was explosive.

Given that the proposal for a federally-chartered bank had no explicit constitutional basis, the two major strains of American political philosophies clashed over the issue of whether the Congress should be allowed such a competence.[13] Led by then-Secretary of the Treasury Alexander Hamilton, formerly one of the three vigorous authors of 'The Federalist Papers', the supporters of the formation of a national bank pointed to the powers explicitly granted Congress by the Constitution: the power to tax; the power to borrow money; the power to regulate trade; and the many other powers necessitating the spending of money. These enumerated powers, insisted Hamiltonians, implied a power to establish an institution which would make the charter possible.

Opponents to Hamilton's bank proposal were numerous. Among the most vocal protesters were the agricultural interests. They were wary of bankers' 'comity with commerce' and 'insistence on punctuality in paying debts, admission of foreigners to investment in America, and other miscellaneous mischief'.[14] Besides the farmers, many other citizens disliked the idea of a national bank, as there was a hardly-explainable, but general, distrust of finance among the early Americans.[15]

The political and legal implications of a national bank were another point of contention. The one-time Anti-Federalists, under the leadership of Thomas Jefferson, were loath to give the central government further powers than absolutely necessary to maintain a unified nation of States. Thus, they rejected Hamilton's broad reading of the Constitution. To support his own view on the inadvisability of granting Congress such secondary competences, Jefferson looked at the terms on which Congress had been granted its enumerated powers in the Constitution. Article I, section 8[18] states that Congress, in addition to its listed powers, may 'make all Laws which shall be necessary and proper for carrying into Execution the foregoing Powers, and all other Powers vested by this Constitution in the Government of the United States, or in any Department or Officer thereof'.[16]

The establishment of a national bank, the Anti-Federalists argued, is not 'necessary' and therefore the Congress should be prohibited from chartering it. Jefferson also pointed out the words of the Tenth Amendment. The express reservation to the States of non-enumerated powers was clearly set out, he argued. As banking powers were not explicitly granted the federal government, only States could charter and regulate banks.

Despite the arguments of Jefferson and his followers, the legislation was passed in 1791, creating the First Bank of the United States. In charge of

---

[13] Geoffrey Stone, Louis M. Seidman, Cass R. Sunstein, and Mark V. Tushnet, *Constitutional Law* (2d edn, Little, Brown & Co, Boston, 1991), p. 64
[14] Symons and White (note 6 *supra*), p. 7.
[15] *Ibid*. p. 11.
[16] US Constitution Art. I, § 8, cl. 18.

writing the charter for the Bank, Secretary Hamilton looked to the charter of the Bank of England and accommodated the specific conditions and concerns of the new nation in the text. As a result, the First Bank of the United States was carefully limited in its authority. It could not, for example, deal with goods or real estate, it could not buy United States stock, it could not demand interest of more than 6 per cent on its loans, and its life was limited to 20 years, upon which it could be renewed.[17]

Throughout its relatively successful 20 years, the First Bank of the United States was the only nationally-chartered bank among a growing number of State-chartered banks. Mainly commercial banks, the State banks concentrated first in the industrial centers and spread (to their misfortune) to the sparsely populated towns to the west. When the First Bank of the United States' bid for renewal was rejected by the Jeffersonian-majority in Congress in 1811, there was a period of five years in which there was no national bank.[18] During this time, the State banks, without either government (federal or State) oversight or the financial assistance of a large national bank, failed in great number.

In 1816, the Second Bank of the United States was chartered during Jefferson's Presidency. The public's recognition of the benefits of a national bank had not laid to rest the uncertainties of the division of competencies between the national government and the States in bank regulation, however. The landmark case of *McCulloch v. Maryland*, decided in 1819, finally ended the legal (if not the popular) dispute over the banking regulation question.[19] In *McCulloch*, Chief Justice John Marshall decided that Congress had acted within its constitutional powers when it issued the charter for a national bank. Marshall wrote that it is not the purpose of a constitution to set out the details of law, but rather to set out the framework of a legal system in language comprehensible by the public at large. Thus, the absence of an explicit grant of a particular power does not exclude the possibility that Congress may act. Marshall explained:

> The sword and the purse, all the external relations, and no inconsiderable portion of the industry of the nation, are entrusted to its government. It can never be pretended that these vast powers draw after them others of inferior importance, merely because they are inferior ... But it may with great reason be contended, that a government, entrusted with such ample powers, on the due execution of which the happiness and prosperity of the nation so vitally depends, must also be entrusted with ample means for their execution ... Let the end be legitimate, let it be within the scope of the constitution, and all

---

[17] Symons and White (note 6 *supra*), pp. 11–12.
[18] *Ibid*. p. 7:

> The combination of the substantial number of state-chartered banks and the cultural fear of concentration of power caused the bank not to be re-chartered, but rather to expire in 1811. A variety of economic problems occurred during and subsequent to the War of 1812, and as a result the Second Bank of the United States was chartered in 1816.

[19] *McCulloch v. Maryland* 17 US (4 Wheat.) 316 (1819).

means which are appropriate, which are plainly adapted to that end, which are not prohibited, but consist with the letter and spirit of the constitution, are constitutional.[20]

The Chief Justice went on to find that a State may not impose any special taxes or restrictions on a branch of a Congressionally-chartered bank. Marshall reasoned that a nationally-chartered bank is necessarily a creation of the entire US population, and thus, the people and government of a single State may not decide to apply their own laws to it. Although Chief Justice Marshall's legal analysis has been debated ever since *McCulloch*, the power of Congress to charter banks has not since been seriously challenged.

In 1863, the National Bank Act declared the near-independence of the State and federal banking regulatory systems. The constitutionality of the United States' dual system of banking remains accepted, although pre-emption of federal banking regulations over State regulations has been established and reaffirmed by judicial interpretation.[21]

Since the Federal Reserve Act of 1913, most State-chartered banks have been subjected to greater federal oversight, but the State regulatory systems remain firm. Nevertheless, the efficacy of the dual system is facing increasingly strong opposition from the banking industry, which would like to see a harmonization among State laws, if not a subsummation of them under a single federal statute. Modern arguments from the States resisting such pressure are reminiscent of the Jeffersonian claims. If the Federalist arguments again succeed, the magnitude of the changes in the US banking system will be tremendous.

2.1.2.1.2   UNITED STATES CODE TITLE 12

Second in the US hierarchy of legal authority are federal statutes, found in the United States Code (USC). The main pieces of legislation governing banks chartered by the US government are found in Title 12 USC. This Title addresses the banking industry's supervisory oversight organizations, the establishment and business rules of the national banks, the relationship to State banks, duties and liability of national banks, and the rules surrounding bank-like financial institutions, among other topics.[22]

For the present purposes, the most relevant aspects of Title 12 are those setting out the licensing procedure for national banks, the rules granting certain powers to national banks, the provisions covering the Federal Reserve system, and the articles specific to foreign banking in the United States.

---

[20] *Ibid.* at 421.
[21] See *Marquette National Bank of Minneapolis v. First of Omaha Service Corp.* 439 US 299 (1978), finding that federal regulation of national bank granting authority to charge the maximum rate of interest allowed in the bank's State of residence implied pre-emption of the borrower's State law on maximum rate of interest on a loan.
[22] See the outline of Title 12 at on the internet at >www.law.cornell.edu.uscode/12/<.

Licensing procedures   National banks are subject to the oversight of three federal agencies: the Office of the Comptroller of the Currency (OCC); the Federal Reserve System (the Fed); and the Federal Deposit Insurance Corporation. While each of these agencies is responsible for ensuring that the bank abides by the regulations and standards set by the agency, it is the OCC that is the 'primary regulator' from the beginning of the chartering process.[23]

The process for receiving a national bank charter is started when at least five persons sign Articles of Association setting out the purpose of their business and complete an organization certificate with the name of the bank[24] and the names and residences of the incorporators. The incorporators must capitalize the bank according to a statutory minimum based on the size of the community in which the bank will be established.[25] The funds for capitalization may come from the issuance of common or preferred stock, as long as the capital stock has been paid for prior to the bank's opening for business.[26]

The incorporators then send a copy of the Articles and Certificate to the Office of the Comptroller of the Currency. The OCC reviews the certificate on two basic levels: the individual application level and the overall, or systemic, level. There are several policies that the OCC has set out as their general guiding principles in the chartering decision:

> (1) the Comptroller has responsibility for maintaining a sound banking system; (2) the marketplace normally is the best regulator of economic activity; and (3) competition allows the marketplace to function and promotes a sound and more efficient banking system that better serves customers.[27]

These principles pervade both the aspects of individual bank suitability and systemic banking security.

Individual bank considerations. On the individual application level, the OCC is trying to assess whether the proposed bank will be a place where the customers' investments and savings will be secure. The Comptroller will check the capitalization of the association to determine whether there are sufficient funds available to the bank. The Comptroller also investigates the proposed management's personal qualifications and experience. In addition, the institution's planned business arrangements are reviewed to detect signs of unnecessary risks to potential investors and to indicate

---

[23] Symons and White (note 6 *supra*), pp. 65–6.
[24] The bank's name must include the word 'national'.
[25] 12 U.S.C. § 51.
[26] 12 U.S.C. § 53.
[27] See Symons and White (note 6 *supra*), p. 74, commenting that this is a change from the OCC's pre-1980 attitude of stressing 'community, economic and competitive factors, which seem to be treated as benefits that will naturally accrue if the factors listed in 12 C.F.R. § 5.20(c) are favorable'.

whether the bank's managers are likely to be serving the changing needs of the community in which the bank is located.[28]

Banking system considerations. On the systemic level, the Comptroller's assessment of a charter application must try to protect the integrity of the financial system as a whole. In order to fulfill this consideration, the Comptroller must decide how many banks should be a part of the financial system. To determine the optimum number of banks, the OCC balances having a substantial number of banks (to encourage competition among banks and to accommodate the public's desire for convenience) against limiting the number of banks to provide for more financial security through institutions with large capital bases. The belief in free-market principles that has led to deregulatory pressures throughout the US economy did not leave the banks untouched. Since the 1980s, the OCC has tended to give additional weight to the arguments stressing the advantages of competition.

Once the public's need for banks is assessed, the number of banks currently in the system is balanced against the optimal number. During times of saturated banking markets, the OCC may refuse to issue a license on grounds that the market cannot absorb another banking institution.

Finally, the Comptroller will determine which of the applicants at any given period ought to be admitted into the regulatory network. If an application is to be granted, the national bank will be allowed to begin doing business in the location for which it applied. The bank is then subject to the regulation of the various federal banking agencies as well as the Securities and Exchange Commission, and is restricted by the laws of the State in which it is established.

Establishment of a branch   Past rules on branching. Until the mid-1920s, national banks were restricted to operating out of one location. As State banks were often permitted to expand geographically throughout their State borders, fears of competitive disadvantage caused the National Bank

---

[28] Because the applicants will also be requesting FDIC insurance, the OCC will have to persuade the FDIC that the applicant bank is sound. The FDIC (and thus the OCC) is required to investigate seven factors in its decision to grant insurance:

    (1) The financial history and condition of the depository institution.
    (2) The adequacy of the depository institution's capital structure.
    (3) The future earnings prospects of the depository institution.
    (4) The general character and fitness of the management of the depository institution.
    (5) The risk presented by such depository institution to the Bank Insurance Fund or the Savings Association Insurance Fund.
    (6) The convenience and needs of the community to be served by such depository institution.
    (7) Whether the depository institution's corporate powers are consistent with the purposes of this chapter.

12 U.S.C. § 1816.

Act to be amended in 1927.[29] The present rules on national bank branching are found in Title 12, chapter 2 of the United States Code. Even with the more liberal branching rules, the number of branches in the United States compared to the total number of banks is relatively small: there are around 1,500 branches among the country's 14,000 banks.[30]

In 1927 Congress passed the first amendment to allow national banks to establish branches.[31] The amendment allowed for branching within the municipality of the main office if State banks were allowed to do the same. Then in 1933, a second amendment (now known as the McFadden Act) granted national banks the same rights as State banks to branch throughout the State, but it maintained the prohibition on branching outside of the State of establishment.[32]

If a national bank applies for a grant to establish a branch, the procedures for chartering the branch for a bank are similar to those of requesting a license for a new depository institution, but the considerations that the Comptroller makes are somewhat different. The OCC must judge the request on the basis of the respective State's bank branching regulations. The OCC's judgment is based on the words of the State's regulations as interpreted by the federal agency. Thus, the OCC, guided by the statutory policy of 'competitive equality' between national and State banks, may define 'branch' as according to federal rather than State law,[33] and may substitute its own judgment for the State banking authorities in determining whether the proposed branch in is the public interest.

Developments in branching. Since the NAFTA has come into effect, branching among national banks in the United States has been increasing. Pressure from the banking authorities as well as from foreign banking organizations has left Congress exposed to strong attempts at reform of the banking system to allow unlimited branching. Shortly before NAFTA came into force, the Riegle-Neal Interstate Banking and Branching Efficiency Act of 1994[34] was passed to allow banks to branch even into States that had previously required reciprocity from the home State. The three modes of interstate branching are:

1. interstate banking by acquisition: i.e., adequately capitalized bank holding companies (including foreign banks) are allowed to acquire a bank in any US State as from 29 September 1995;

---

[29] Symons and White (note 6 *supra*), p. 84.
[30] *Ibid.* pp. 85–6, commenting also on the difference in structure of the US banking market and the markets of most other countries.
[31] See 12 U.S.C. § 36. But see 2.1.4.2 *infra*.
[32] 12 U.S.C. § 36(c) (known as the McFadden Act).
[33] *First National Bank in Plant City v. Dickinson* 396 US 122, 133 (1969) ('We reject the contention made by amicus curiae National Association of Supervisors of State Banks to the effect that state law definitions of what constitutes 'branch banking' must control the content of the federal definition of § 36(f) [of the McFadden Act]').
[34] 103 P.L. 328; 108 Stat. 2338 (1994).

2. interstate banking by merger: i.e., States may approve an out-of-state bank to merge with an in-state bank and then allow the resulting bank to continue to operate branches, beginning 1 June 1997; and

3. interstate branching by *de novo* establishment of direct branches: i.e., a bank will be able to establish and operate a branch in a State in which the bank does not already operate, provided the host-state law expressly permits such interstate branching.[35]

Although there is a possibility for a State to positively reject (or 'opt-out') the merger-form of branching allowance, as of April 1996, only Texas had done so.[36]

2.1.2.2 Powers of National Banks: the Separation of Commercial Banking and Securities Activities

The narrow conception of 'banking activities' that arose in the eighteenth century remains the overriding theoretical principle of US banking regulation. Beyond 'deposit taking', 'credit granting', and 'credit exchange', banks are limited in their commercial activities.

2.1.2.2.1   GLASS-STEAGELL ACT

The Banking Act of 1933, commonly known as the Glass-Steagall Act, prohibits the combination of non-banking commercial activities and banking within the same institution.[37] Thus, insurance companies cannot own banks, and banks cannot own insurance companies. One of the most prominent, and controversial, provisions of the Glass-Steagall Act prohibits banks from 'underwriting' securities. Under the Securities Act of 1933, the federal law governing securities regulation in the United States, an 'underwriter' is defined as one:

> who has purchased from an issuer with a view to, or offers or sells for an issuer in connection with, the distribution of any security, or participates or has a direct or indirect participation in any such undertaking, or has a

---

[35] WTO, *Trade Policy Review: United States 1996* (WTO, Geneva, 1997), p. 160, para. 130.

[36] *Ibid.*

[37] The Banking Act of 1933. See in particular 12 U.S.C. §§ 24(7), powers and prohibitions regarding banks' securities activities; 78, governing personnel of banks and securities firms; 377, prohibiting banks from being affiliated with entities 'engaged principally' in underwriting and related activities, and 378, prohibiting the combination of taking deposits and underwriting securities. 12 U.S.C. § 335 extends the provisions to State banks that are members of the Federal Reserve system. The Act not only attempted to separate the commercial activities of banks from their investment activities, but it 'constituted the first step towards increasing the interrelationship of state and federal banking systems'. Symons and White (note 6 *supra*), p. 39. Part of this interrelationship arose from the Act's creation of the Federal Deposit Insurance Corporation, whose insurance is available to both federal- and State-chartered institutions. *Ibid.*

participation in the direct or indirect underwriting of such undertaking; but such term shall not include a person whose interest is limited to a commission from an underwriter or dealer not in excess of the usual and customary distributors' or sellers' commission. As used in this paragraph the term 'issuer' shall include, in addition to an issuer, any person directly or indirectly controlling or controlled by the issuer, or any person under direct or indirect common control with the issuer.[38]

In short, underwriting is the distribution of shares of an enterprise (the 'issuer') to buyers by a technique in which another company ('the underwriter', usually a securities firm or a bank) contracts to sell the shares to the public[39] while guaranteeing the enterprise a certain amount of financial funding at a certain time, in exchange for the profits of the sales. There are five basic types of underwriting—'old fashioned'; firm-commitment; best efforts; competitive bidding; and shelf registration[40]—and all would be denied banks under a strict reading of the Glass-Steagall Act.

Glass-Steagall's provisions have been severely criticized since their initiation, but particularly in the recent past.[41] The federal banking agencies, as well as the administration, have encouraged Congress to repeal at least some of the restrictions set out in the Act in order to promote a more liberalized financial services sector.[42] Indeed, many of the provisions have been interpreted so as to allow banks a wide range of activities in the

---

[38] 15 U.S.C. § 77(b)(11).

[39] The sales to the public may only begin after registration of the issuance with the Securities and Exchange Commission. Louis Loss and Joel Seligman, 'Securities Regulation' (3rd edn, 1989), pp. 317–72, reprinted in David L. Ratner and Thomas Lee Hazan (eds), *Securities Regulation: Cases and Materials* (5th edn, West Publishing, St, Paul, 1996), pp. 7681, at 77.

[40] See Loss and Seligman, *ibid.* at p. 77, describing the different underwriting techniques). Loss and Seligman note that firm-commitment underwriting has been the most common form of distribution, despite its non-insurance characteristics.

[41] See generally, Edward D. Sullivan, 'Glass-Steagall Update: Proposals to Modernize the Structure of the Financial Services Industry' (1995) 112 Banking LJ 977, 982–3, setting out the arguments of those who feel the Glass-Steagall separation should be repealed.

[42] The Department of Treasury is reportedly positively disposed toward 'the idea of wholesale financial institutions'. R. Christian Bruce and Pamela Atkins, 'Hawke Sketches Forthcoming Proposal to Modernize Domestic Financial Services' 67:19 BNA's Banking Rep 829 (19 November 1996), reporting on Treasury Department Undersecretary for Domestic Finance John D. Hawke Jr's address given to a banking lawyer's conference in November 1996. Explaining the effect of a Federal Reserve Board interpretation allowing for more interaction between banking and securities activities, a financial institutions expert said, 'I think the Federal Reserve is sending Congress a message that you better act … The Fed is saying, "If we're not going to get it done by Congress, then we're going to get it done by regulation"…'. Niles S. Campbell, 'Fed OKs Proposal Deleting Regulation R, Launching Glass-Steagall "Reg Reform"' 67:1 BNA's Banking Rep 3-4 (1 July 1996), quoting Diane Casey of Grant Thorton LLP.

securities markets.[43] The law, however, remains valid at time of publication.[44]

2.1.2.2.2   BANK HOLDING COMPANIES: A WAY AROUND THE GLASS-STEAGELL ACT

The legal form of a bank holding company (BHC) was introduced in the mid-1950s to circumvent the strict Glass-Steagall separation of banking from other

---

[43] See generally Campbell (note 42 *supra*), p. 3, reporting on the Federal Reserve Board's rescision of a previous interpretation of § 32 of the Glass-Steagall Act in order to allow bank holding companies to have affiliations with securities firms). See Sullivan (note 41 *supra*), pp. 978–9:

> As the debate over repeal is carried out, ... the Glass-Steagall 'wall' continues to crumble.
> Meanwhile, the commercial banking industry is carving out yet a bigger and bigger slice of financial products, specifically mutual funds ... For all practical purposes, banks are only disallowed from underwriting mutual funds. Permissible activities include:
> 1. Organizing a fund
> 2. Serving as investment advisor
> 3. Location of fund
> 4. Purchases of fund's share
> 5. Brokerage
> 6. Sweep arrangements
> 7. Shareholder services
> 8. Advertising
> 9. Establishment of master account arragements; [sic]
> 10. Sale of customer lists to distributor
> 11. Pooling of trust assets in mutual funds where provided by state law
> 12. Serving as custodian and transfer agent.

See also Campbell (note 42 *supra*), pp. 3–5; Niles S. Campbell, 'OCC Rule Expands Bank Business Lines; Operating Subsidiary Section Draws Fire' 67:20 BNA's Banking Rep 873–5 (25 November 1996); Philip A. Lacovara, 'Modernize Banking ... But With Care' (1992) 15 The GAO J 15, 18, (explaining the Federal Reserve Board's liberal interpretation of the 'engaged principally in' language of § 20 of the Glass Steagall Act); Donna Lance, 'Can the Glass-Steagall Act be Justified Under the Global Free Market Policies of the NAFTA?' (1995) 34:2 Washburn LJ 297, 307–18. The Supreme Court has also contributed to the weakening of the Glass-Steagall restrictions on banking activities. See particularly *Securities Industry Assoc. v. Board of Governors of the Federal Reserve System* 468 US 207 (1984), upholding the Federal Reserve's determinination that a company's trading of shares 'only as an agent' is 'closely related to banking' for purposes of § 20 of the Glass Steagall Act.

[44] The remaining limitations on the interaction of financial service institutions are due in large part to the strength of the political lobbies that would face increased competition from banks. The lobby of insurance industry members is reportedly one of the most powerful on Capitol Hill and the securities industry lobby is also able to influence policy. The reaction to a final rule promulgated by the OCC to allow national banks the competence to enter securities and insurance underwriting, among other commercial activities, was fierce:

> The [American Council of Life Insurance] vowed to wage an all-out war both judicially and legislatively to stop the OCC from allowing national banks to stray onto insurance industry turf ... Steve Judge, senior vice president of government affairs at the Securities Industry Association, said the new [rule] was part of the "piecemeal approach" to financial industry deregulation currently conducted by bank regulators ... The SIA, he said, is also considering legal and legislative options to block the OCC's decision.

Campbell (note 43 *supra*). See also Bruce and Atkins (note 42 *supra*), p. 829, reporting on the American Council of Life Insurance's ten-point list of demands it wanted in exchange for support on relaxing the legislative barriers between banking and insurance activities.

financial activities. By that time, the discrepancy in competencies allowed banks and other non-bank finance companies was apparent, and the Bank Holding Company Act of 1956 was one way to make the conditions of competition for capital more equal. Presently, almost all of the banks in the United States are owned by a holding company.

A bank holding company is defined under Title 12 USC as 'any company which has control over any bank or over any company that is or becomes a bank holding company by virtue of this chapter'.[45] That is, it is a company that owns or controls a subsidiary bank as well as other 'non-bank' subsidiaries that have bank-related commercial activities. As such, a BHC is subject to the provisions of chapter 18 of Title 12.

2.1.2.2.3 DEVELOPMENTS IN THE SEPARATION OF FINANCIAL SERVICE ACTIVITIES

The Glass-Steagall Act is under serious reconsideration by the US Congress. The banking community in the United States, including the Federal Reserve Board, strongly favors moves to allow themselves powers more equal to those they enjoy abroad. The Chairman of the House of Representatives Committee on Banking and Financial Services, James Leach, has introduced a bill that would repeal those sections of the Act that prevent financial service affiliations.[46] While in early 1999 there seemed to be bipartisan support for financial reform, and although the resistance posed by the insurance industry is showing some signs of dissipating,[47] the success of the reform proposals is not certain due to election-year Congressional distraction.[48]

As significant as legislative reform, although less visible, is the liberalizing effect the banking regulatory agencies are having on their own through rule-making and administrative proceeding opinions. The OCC, for

---

[45] 12 U.S.C. § 1841(a)(1). For purposes of the definition, 'control' means either the power to vote at least 25 per cent of the stock or the ability to determine who will become the majority of directors or trustees of a bank, or the ability and opportunity to influence decision-making. 12 U.S.C. § 1841 (a)(2).

[46] See Financial Services Competitiveness Act of 1995, H.R. 1062 (introduced 27 February 1995).

[47] See Linda Birkin Tigges, 'Functional Regulation of Bank Insurance Activities: the Time Has Come' (1998) 2 NC Banking Inst 455, 469–71; *ibid*. at 456, n.6, noting that the American Council of Life Insurance, according to its Vice President Roy Albertalli, 'reversed its policy on affiliations and hopes that this action will facilitate the development of legislation that is fair across the board'. But see *ibid*. at 483, n.173, citing a 'Life Agents Fear Entry of Banks into Insurance', *Best's Insurance News*, 23 September 1997.

[48] According to one report:

> Once again, the overriding question for the banking industry on the legislative front is whether Congress will pass legislation to overhaul the financial services laws. According to congressional, regulatory, and industry sources contacted by BNA, the good news is that much is left to build on from 1998, when legislators came closer than ever before, propelled by a consensus (still largely intact) among government and industry interests on what needs to be done. The bad news ... is that reform efforts may suffocate in a congressional session caught up in the trial of President Clinton, vitriolic partisanship, and election year dynamics.

72:4 BNA's Banking Rep 172 (25 January 1999),'Legislation' section.

instance, extended the exception for banks in small towns to sell insurance to permit the banks to sell insurance anywhere—as long as the bank itself was located in a small town. The extension withstood a challenge before the courts by insurance industry representative and has become accepted law.[49] In addition, OCC regulations effective as of the end of 1996 permit 'certain well-managed, well-capitalized banks … to have a subsidiary engage in activities that are part of the business of banking or incidental to banking, but that are not necessarily permissible for the bank itself', including insurance underwriting.[50]

2.1.3 State Banks

2.1.3.1 Introduction

States of the United States have the competence to charter and regulate financial institutions[51] independently of the national authorities. Each of the 50 States therefore has its own banking legislation and a regulatory body to oversee the network of banks and non-banks within its borders.[52]

States may charter both domestic banks and foreign banks or branches. Banks take advantage of this opportunity as shown by December 1995 figures: over 75 per cent of the 545 foreign bank branches and agencies in the United States at that time were operating under a State charter.[53]

Bank legislation varies widely from State to State, making it necessary for a potential financial service provider to investigate the particular rules in the State of establishment and compare those with both the national bank rules and the rules of other States to ensure the most favorable conditions for the particular business the bank wishes to conduct. For the present purposes, this chapter is limited to an introduction to the interaction of federal and State laws. A closer review of the laws of those States with the most active foreign bank communities is found in the chapter on the NAFTA Chapter Fourteen provisions.[54]

---

[49] *Independent Insurance Agents of America v. Ludwig* 997 F.2d 958 (D.C. Cir. 1993). In November 1996, the OCC sent an interpretive letter to a bank that reiterated this position. OCC Interpretive Letter 753, Establishment of Operating Subsidies to Engage in Insurance Agency Activities (4 November 1996).

[50] Tigges (note 47 *supra*), p. 468, describing the 'Operating Subsidies' rule, 12 C.F.R. 5.34 (1997).

[51] While States share the right to charter and incorporate banks and non-bank financial institutions with the federal government's equal power to do so, the States have the exclusive authority to regulate the insurance industry.

[52] Territories of the United States may also charter territorial banks. See, e.g., Guam Codes Annotated, Title 11, Division 4, § 100102 (definition of Territorial Bank); Compact of Free Association (between the United States of America and the Governments of the Marshall Islands and the Federated States of Micronesia) Art. II, § 121(b)(2).

[53] United States General Accounting Office (GAO), *Foreign Banks: Implementation of the Foreign Bank Supervision Enhancement Act of 1991*, GAO/GGD-96-187 (September 1996), p. 4.

[54] See 3.16 *infra*.

2.1.3.2   Controlling Legislation

2.1.3.2.1   FEDERAL PRE-EMPTION

Under the Supremacy Clause of the Constitution, federal laws pre-empt conflicting State laws.[55] This principle of US law is applicable to banking regulations as well as to every other area of law. Thus, the Commerce Clause of the US Constitution[56] prevents States from enacting any regulation that would hinder interstate trade. Similarly, those provisions of Title 12 of the United States Code that would affect State banks are binding on State-chartered banks in the same manner and to the same degree as they are binding on national banks.

2.1.3.2.2   CONCURRENT STATE REGULATION

The existence of federal pre-emption does not mean that States themselves are subsumed by federal banking policy, however. Rather, there is an official national policy of protecting the dual system through a principle of 'competitive equality' between national and state banks. This principle is evidenced, for instance, in the treatment of national banks' branching within the State in which it sits. There, the federal legislation expressly defers to the State's regulation of branching by State-chartered banks.[57] A national bank can establish branches to the extent that State banks can and no further.

In general, State laws provide that a bank may be established when an individual, a group of individuals, or a company applies to the State banking authorities for a charter. If granted, the charter allows for the establishment of a bank or non-bank, which will be subject to the supervision of the State banking authorities.

Beyond that, State-chartered banks may choose to join one or both of two federal systems: the Federal Reserve System and the Federal Deposit Insurance Corporation system. If either is joined, the bank is subject to the supervisory authority of the requisite federal body. That is, a State bank that is a member of the Federal Reserve System has the State banking authorities, the Federal Reserve Board, and the Office of the Comptroller of the Currency overseeing its activities. A State bank that offers Federal Deposit Insurance protection to its customers must answer to the FDIC as well as to the State. If a State bank is both a member of the FRS and FDIC, it is subject to all the respective authorities.

The burden of four or more agencies overseeing a single bank, with the frequent overlap of competencies, is a cause for concern among many State banks. Nevertheless, the competitive advantage that accompanies the federal program membership have had the result that today a great majority of State banks are members of the Federal Reserve System, and nearly all of the State banks have Federal Deposit Insurance Corporation protection.

---

[55] US Constitution Art. IV (known as the 'Supremacy Clause').
[56] US Constitution Art. I, § 8, cl. 3 (known as the 'Commerce Clause').
[57] 12 U.S.C. § 36(c) (McFadden Act).

2.1.4 Federal Regulation of Foreign Banks

Foreign banks have long been present in the United States. In 1818, for instance, the Bank of Montreal established an agency in New York, and by 1859 it had established a full bank in that city.[58] Since the nineteenth century, foreign banking has grown tremendously in the United States. As individual States began to pass laws to allow the establishment of foreign bank subsidiaries in the early 1900s, foreign banks began to enter in large number. It was New York's allowance of foreign branches in 1961, however, that ushered in the most rapid era of foreign bank growth in the country.[59] Since then, foreign banks have continued to establish and expand their US activities under a legal regime that is, in the main, non-discriminatory.

Today, the single most significant law for foreign banks in the United States is the Foreign Bank Supervision Enhancement Act (FBSEA), a part of the Federal Deposit Insurance Corporation Improvement Act (FDICIA) of 1991.[60] Passed in reaction to the mass of bank failures in the early 1990s, FDICIA allowed the Federal Deposit Insurance funds to be replenished, and simultaneously aimed to 'enhance the safety and soundness of the financial system'.[61] While a large portion of FDICIA targets domestic banks, foreign banking activity did not escape congressional scrutiny. Thanks in part to the Bank of Commerce and Credit International ('BCCI') fiasco, which itself was blamed in large part on the lack of co-ordination among banking regulators, the motivating principle behind the FBSEA provisions of FDICIA is the controlled entry of foreign banks into the United States markets and the consolidation of foreign bank supervision at the federal level.[62] Under the FBSEA, the federal supervisory offices are integrated into the oversight of all foreign banking operations in the United States, whether the bank is US-chartered or State-chartered.[63]

---

[58] Moudi (note 5 *supra*), p. 262, citing Faramarz Damanpour, *The Evolution of Foreign Banking Institutions in the United States* (1990).

[59] *Ibid.* p. 265, referring to Act of 14 April 1960, ch. 553 § 1, 1960 N.Y. Laws 1719.

[60] 12 U.S.C. § 3105(d)–(h) (Pub. L. No. 102-242 § 202(a), signed 19 December 1991). One of the best (and most easily available) sources for gaining an understanding of the FBSEA is the United States General Accounting Office's report to the House of Representatives Subcommittee on Financial Institutions and Consumer Credit. GAO (note 53 *supra*).

[61] See Lawrence G. Baxter, 'The Rule of Too Much Law? The New Safety/Soundness Rulemaking Responsibilities of the Federal Banking Agencies' (1993) 47 Consumer Fin LQ Rep 210.

[62] See Deborah Burand, 'Regulation of Foreign Banks' Entry into the United States Under the FBSEA: Implementation and Implications' (1993) 24:4 L & Pol'y Int'l Bus 1089, 1097, citing the Banca Nazionale de Lavoro scandal along with the Bank of Credit and Commerce International collapse as triggers to the implementation of the FBSEA; Cynthia C. Lichtenstein, 'US Restructuring Legislation: Revising the International Banking Act of 1978, For the Worse?' (1992) 60 Fordham L Rev S37, S41.

[63] Burand (note 62 *supra*), at 1098–9, n.50, explaining the changes the FBSEA made to the operational aspects of foreign banks in the United States, as opposed to the changed procedures for entry.

2.1.4.1   Entry of Banks

Foreign banks may establish operations in the United States in a variety of legal forms: subsidiaries; branches; agencies; representative offices; commercial lending companies; and bank holding companies.[64] Under the FBSEA, the Federal Reserve must approve every foreign bank's application to establish its branch or subsidiary, regardless of whether the final charter to be granted was sought from the OCC (as a federally-chartered branch) or from the State. Under the Act, 'establishment' includes opening an office in the United States, moving an US office to another State, expanding the functions of an office within the United States, including changing from a federal office or agency into a state office or agency; and for mergers and acquisitions of offices that have the effect of expanding or changing the powers of the office.[65]

The Federal Reserve has three required standards for judging whether a foreign bank may be established and four discretionary areas of examination. These standards are set out in the FBSEA and apply to each foreign bank application, regardless of the origin of the parent bank.[66]

2.1.4.1.1   REQUIRED STANDARDS FOR APPROVAL

The three required standards the Federal Reserve applies are best read as found in the statute:

> The Board may not approve an application under paragraph (1) unless it determines that—(A) the foreign bank directly engages in the business of banking outside of the United States and is subject to comprehensive supervision or regulation on a consolidated basis by the appropriate authorities in its home country; and (B) the foreign bank has furnished to the Board the information it needs to adequately assess the application.[67]

2.1.4.1.2   ENGAGED IN THE BUSINESS OF BANKING

The determination whether the bank is active in banking seems to be an objective evaluation and its intent is clear: the United States authorities want a bank to have experience in deposit-taking and the loaning of funds before they accept it into the banking system. The wording of the statute,

---

[64] During the early 1990s discussions of legislative changes to the rules governing foreign banks, the Department of Treasury proposed limiting the entry of foreign banks to the form of subsidiaries. As an alternative, Treasury suggested that only those foreign banks that had subsidiaries be given the possibility of engaging in securities and insurance activities, should such areas be opened to domestic banks in the future. See Financial Institutions Safety and Consumer Choice Act of 1991, S. 713, 102d Cong., 2d Sess. (1991) and H.R. 1505, 102d Cong. 2d Sess. (1991) (20 March 1991). The proposal was rejected after a joint study determined that the costs of such a change would outweigh any potential benefits to the soundness of the US banking system. See Burand (note 62 *supra*), at 1114–19; Lichtenstein (note 62 *supra*) at S37–S39, critically explaining the Treasury's 'branch roll up' proposal and the legislative response.

[65] Joseph T. Lynyak III, 'Foreign Bank Supervision: The Regulation K Amendments' (1994) 111 Banking LJ 464, 467–8.

[66] See 12 U.S.C. § 3105(d).

[67] 12 U.S.C. § 3105(d)(2).

requiring the bank to 'engage directly in the business of banking outside the United States', seems equally clear on a first reading.[68] The term 'directly' indicates that the bank itself, not simply an affiliate, must be active in banking. The 'business of banking', in the context of the legislation, refers to the taking of deposits and lending of assets.

Yet, the terminology 'business of banking' is certain to engender dispute. Specifically, it is unclear whether the 'business of banking' will be determined based on US law or on the foreign country's law in which the bank is active. The more limited view of banking in the United States could pose difficulties in interpreting this phrase.[69]

2.1.4.1.3   HOME COUNTRY CONTROL

The second test the foreign bank applicant must pass is the question of 'home country control'. This is more obviously problematic than is the question of the 'business of banking', and accordingly, has caused concern.[70]

The Federal Reserve Board has interpreted its assignment to require that the applicant bank's home country supervision must be checked twice each time an application is presented: first on a systematic level and then again on the individual bank level. The systematic level includes gathering information on 'the organization, operation, and effectiveness of the home country bank regulator'.[71] Then, because there is a presumption that foreign country authorities supervise each individual bank somewhat differently, the applicant must present data to satisfy the Federal Reserve's idea that consolidated supervision is viewed in reference to the individual

---

[68] 12 U.S.C. § 3105(d)(2)(A).

[69] See Lichtenstein (note 62 *supra*), at S51. It is beyond the scope of this work to analyze the provisions of the FBSEA. However, the Federal Reserve's interpretation of 'business of banking' under US principles in other contexts suggests a similar approach could be taken here. For instance, the phrase 'business of banking' found in the Competitive Equality Banking Act of 1987 § 2(h) has been interpreted in an Amero-centric way:

> ... [I]n its regulation defining what is meant by the 'banking business' for the purposes of 2(h), the Board in the past has considered in only the non-US entity's banking business that would be regarded as 'banking' under US conceptions, and has not been willing, until the most recent revision of Regulation K, to include any insurance business.

The Fed is likely to maintain a consistent view of the phrase, suggesting that only the US view of 'business of banking' will be taken into account in application review.

[70] The President of the Federal Bank of Atlanta has characterized the provision as the one that will prevent some foreign banks from entering the United States market because 'it significantly raised certain standards for entry into or expansion within the American market'. Robert P. Forrestal, 'Latin America's Economic Boom: The US Perspective', remarks at the Florida International Bankers Association, Miami, Florida, 15 September 1995 (text on the internet at >www.frbatlanta.org:80<); see *ibid*. continuing, 'Since enactment [of FBSEA], only a handful of applications from Latin American banks have been approved, a number have been withdrawn, and I have no doubt that many interested parties have not bothered even to apply after the track record to date'.

[71] Lynyak (note 65 *supra*), at 465–6.

applicant's parent bank, and thus must be re-studied even for applicants from the same home country.[72]

Even for those banks that can be secure in their ultimate admittance to the United States, according to one federal banking official this con-solidated home country supervision requirement has greatly increased the foreign banks' application approval times in the United States.[73] Whereas pre-FBSEA, applications for federal charters were generally approved within six months, the home country control test has extended that time to between 18 and 24 months. The Federal Reserve Board is maintaining files on each applicant, however, in order that the foreign banks that have already been approved may rely on previously collected information in any subsequent establishments within the United States.[74]

Further, in mid-1998, the Board of Governors sent a letter to each super-visory officer of the Federal Reserve System altering its Foreign Bank Organization Supervision Program.[75] Among the changes are several that reduce the disadvantages faced by an applicant foreign bank posed by the consolidated home country test. One, for example, allows 'Strength of Support Assessments' for similar foreign banks from a single country to be combined into one document.[76] Another limits the home country review requirement to an 'as needed' element (although annual updates will be performed).[77] As stated in the letter:

> … together, these modifications should enhance interagency communication and collaboration, alleviate burden on foreign banks, streamline the Federal Reserve's internal operations, and improve the communication of supervisory findings to home country supervisors.[78]

2.1.4.1.4   DISCRETIONARY STANDARDS

At its discretion, the Federal Reserve may look to other standards in deciding whether to approve an application for establishment. These optional standards are listed in § 3105(d)(3) and include looking to whether the home country authority has given its consent to the bank's US applica-tion for establishment. One standard that is regularly used is that of 'the financial and managerial resources of the foreign bank, including the bank's experience and capacity to engage in international banking'.[79] A US regulator noted that it is the credentials and experience of the proposed

---

[72] Discussion with Tim Sullivan, Office of the Comptroller of the Currency (Washington, DC, 24 January 1997).

[73] *Ibid.*

[74] Lynyak (note 65 *supra*), at 474.

[75] Letter from the Board of Governors of the Federal Reserve System to the Officer in Charge of Supervision and Appropriate Supervisory and Examination Staff at Each Federal Reserve Bank and Foreign Banking Organizations Supervised by the Federal Reserve, SR 98-13 (SUP.IB) of 3 June 1998.

[76] *Ibid.*

[77] *Ibid.*

[78] *Ibid.*

[79] 12 U.S.C. § 3105(d)(3)(B).

branch managers that are the target of scrutiny by the US supervisory authorities.[80] Thus, the bankers working in the United States must be qualified as well as the bank's employees at the head office in the home country.[81] Further, the application process is not one of consulting foreign banks how to be admissible to the US market.[82] Rather, the application is merely approved or rejected, although one author notes that '[i]n those cases in which the home country regulatory scheme does not meet the FBSEA requirement, the Board suggests that a representative office might constitute an alternative initial entry vehicle for a foreign bank'.[83]

The FBSEA additionally makes the Federal Reserve responsible for ensuring that each foreign bank branch is examined every 12 months. The Fed may, and has begun to, delegate this duty to the OCC and the relevant State authorities, with which it meets annually to discuss the focus of the year's examination, should have and ways to make the examination both thorough and not unduly burdensome for the bank.[84] If, during the examination, there are findings of illegal or unsafe practices by the bank or its officers, the Federal Reserve may impose civil fines or issue a cease-and-desist order. These 'formal' enforcement actions are generally undertaken by the OCC as a delegated agency when the foreign bank is federally chartered, and by the Federal Reserve itself if the bank is State-chartered. Informal enforcement mechanisms such as 'voluntary' commitments by the bank and memoranda of understanding between the bank and the Federal Reserve are also possible solutions to minor problems in a bank's compliance with standards.

Finally, if it is determined that continued existence of the bank would be against the public interest, the Federal Reserve has the authority under the FBSEA to force any foreign bank in the United States to close if the bank is guilty of violations of the law or unsafe practices. This authority to terminate a bank's activities extends to State-chartered institutions under the FBSEA, as well as to federally chartered ones.

2.1.4.2 Foreign Bank Operations

The US regulation of foreign banks *per se* is relatively new, although foreign banks have had a long presence in the country.[85] This is because prior to the International Banking Act of 1978, foreign banks operating in the United States were not subject to federal law. State banking legislation applied exclusively, allowing foreign banks to maintain activities throughout the territory of the United States, but with no federal supervision. The International Banking Act (IBA) altered the landscape of foreign branch

---

[80] Interview discussion with Tim Sullivan (see note 72 *supra*).
[81] *Ibid.*
[82] *Ibid.*
[83] Lynyak (note 65 *supra*), at 466.
[84] In order to ensure uniformity in the examination processes of the different examiners, the Federal Reserve, together with the OCC, FDIC, and State agencies wrote a manual in 1993. See GAO (note 53 *supra*), at 12.
[85] Symons and White (note 6 *supra*), at 743.

banking by reducing the advantages foreign banks enjoyed in the context of limited supervision. The IBA provides that foreign branches may choose to be chartered by either the federal government or by a State government.[86] In part, this was done to offer foreign banks the benefits of federal supervision, in part it was a reaction to calls from the US banking community to remove the advantages foreign branches enjoyed by not being regulated on the federal level.[87]

Once a foreign bank is licensed for activity in the United States, it is treated the same as any national or State bank except in a few areas. If a foreign bank incorporates a subsidiary in the United States, that subsidiary will be considered a US bank for all purposes. Only those assets that the subsidiary itself controls will be recognized as the bank's capital, however. The parent bank's funds are not attributable for purposes of capital reserves and loan-limiting standards. Thus, limitations on activities may arise from the lack of funds (but this is not directly related to the bank's 'foreignness').

The FBSEA goes further in changing the operational landscape of foreign banks in the United States. As stated above, foreign banks in the United States, whether branches, agencies, representative offices, or subsidiaries, may establish as either federally chartered or State-chartered institutions. If a foreign bank establishes a subsidiary in the United States, the separately-incorporated entity is simply treated as any other entity would be if owned by a US parent.[88] Thus, the FBSEA does not directly affect subsidiaries of foreign banking to any relevant degree.

By far the majority of the foreign banking institutions, however, choose to establish in the United States as a branch of the foreign parent.[89] The majority of those branches have a State charter (most are in New York) rather than a charter from the federal government. Since the 1978 International Banking Act (IBA) has been in effect, however, giving these branches the opportunity to choose to be subject to the federal government as their primary regulator.[90] The FBSEA did not change the IBA policy of national treatment of banks. However, it did shift the focus onto limiting

---

[86] 12 U.S.C. Chapter 31; Symons and White (note 6 *supra*), at 743.

[87] One of the advantages foreign banks enjoyed was that they did not have to maintain a particular level of required reserves The IBA changed that, putting 'most' branches of foreign banks on par with United States banks. GAO, *Statutory Requirements* (note 94 *infra*), at 4.

[88] GAO (note 4 *supra*), at 12—'Foreign-owned subsidiary banks have all the powers of US-owned banks, are insured by the Federal Deposit Insurance Corporation (FDIC), and are subject to all the rules and regulations governing US-owned banks'.

[89] Federal Reserve statistics revealed that in December 1994, there were 559 branches and agencies of foreign banks in the United States and 97 subsidiaries of foreign banks. GAO (note 4 *supra*), at 11 (Table 1.1).

[90] See *Conference of Bank Supervisors v. Heimann* No. 80-3284 (D.D.C. 30 September 1981), 'A principal purpose of [the IBA] was to give foreign banks "an important new option" in doing business in the United States; Congress understood that the federal chartering option might give overseas banks "opportunities which they do not now possess", even though it would also place new burdens of federal regulation on them. See Remarks of Mr. St. Germain, 122 Cong.Rec. 24403 (July 29, 1976)', quoted in *Conference of State Bank Supervisors v. Conover* 715 F.2d 604 (D.C. Cir. 1983).

the advantages that foreign banks had enjoyed in the United States that were not available to domestic banks. First, it extended the supervisory powers of the Federal Reserve over the life span of the bank from establishment, through its active business life, and potentially, to its termination. Secondly, the activities of foreign banks are restricted to ensure that the banks cannot engage in the types of profitable operations that are closed to domestic banking institutions.

The Federal Reserve now plays an active role in the entire life of a foreign bank, whereas prior to the FBSEA, State-chartered banks were substantially free of federal oversight. The FBSEA provisions include a requirement that the federal authorities make on-site examinations of all branches, agencies, and representative offices of foreign banks at least once a year.[91] Next, the Act now allows the Federal Reserve to terminate a State-chartered foreign bank's license in case of unsound or illegal practices.[92] Further, if a foreign bank decides to acquire more than 5 per cent of the voting shares of a US bank or bank holding company, the Federal Reserve must first give its approval. Finally, if a foreign bank (or an affiliate of the bank) makes a loan that is secured by 25 per cent or more of the securities of a US bank or bank holding company, the foreign bank must report the loan to the Federal Reserve.[93] These changes make the supervision of foreign banks in the United States more similar to the supervision that domestic banks undergo.

In terms of activities, even now if a foreign bank establishes a branch operation in the United States, the federally-chartered branch will be allowed to engage in substantially all the commercial banking activities that a domestic federally-chartered financial institution may (as well as having the advantage of using the parent bank's capital base for asset measurements).[94] However, since 19 December 1991, a branch of a foreign bank is subject to certain limitations. First of all, a foreign bank may no longer join the FDIC system. The consequences of this restriction are that the Directors of the FDIC cannot be voted on and new foreign banks may not accept retail deposits of less than $100,000. The lack of choice of FDIC directors

---

[91] 12 U.S.C. § 3105(b)(1)(A)–(B).

[92] 12 U.S.C. § 3105(e)(1)(A)–(B).

[93] 12 U.S.C. § 1817(j)(9). Attorney Burand explains that this FBSEA amendment to the Change in Bank Control Act was enacted 'to ensure that control over a depository institution is not exercised through loans secured by bank stock'. Burand (note 62 *supra*), at 1099, n.50.

[94] See Symons and White (note 6 *supra*), at 736–7; GAO, 'By the Comptroller General Report to the Congress of the United States: Statutory Requirements for Examining International Banking Institutions Need Attention', GAO/GGD-84-39 (11 July 1984), p. 2. The GAO describes the IBA:

> Under the IBA, foreign banking networks in the United States became subject to the same deposit restrictions as US commercial banks and their Edge Act corporations. This act required foreign banks operating in the United States to choose one state as their "home". Foreign banks are now permitted to accept domestic deposits only in branches within their home state. In branches elsewhere in the country, foreign banks can accept only those types of deposits allowed Edge Act corporations—that is, those predominantly international in character.

Ibid. at 3.

may have a disadvantageous effect on foreign banks in that the overall policy of this part of the banking system will be set without regard to the interests of these banks. The more significant difference in treatment is that of restricting retail deposit taking. While foreign banks are generally not interested in providing retail services, the technological changes of the last decade make individual account management an area with profit potential. If foreign banks are restricted from this market *ex ante*, there are certain competitive disadvantages from the rules. Importantly, however, the limitation was not retroactive. Thus, if a bank had already been a member of the FDIC in 1991, it may remain a member.[95] New applicants are the only ones who will be disadvantaged.

Another aspect of banking in the United States that the international banking industry complains about as discriminatory are the requirements under the Community Reinvestment Act (CRA).[96] The CRA requires banks to serve the entire local community, attempting to ensure that low- and middle-income neighborhoods receive bank loans. The administrative costs of complying with this regulation are considerable, as each bank must keep a geographic record of its loan activity as well as maintain a file on comments made by the public. When the CRA went into effect in 1977, foreign banks without insured deposits were exempt from the requirements of the program. This made sense insofar as their target clientele is generally the international business and trade community, and international banks are not usually in the business of granting small loans. Since 1994, however, the CRA does apply to foreign banks even if they have no insured deposit-taking activities. Under the Riegle-Neal Interstate Banking and Branching Efficiency Act, if a foreign bank merges with or acquires an out-of-State bank or branch that had been subject to the CRA, the foreign branch will continue to be bound by the obligations under the CRA.[97]

2.1.4.3   Foreign Bank Branching Within the United States

The International Bank Act of 1978 changed the former policy of unrestricted branching by foreign bank subsidiaries and branches. By subjecting foreign banks to federal regulation, the IBA also extended the limits of interstate branching to these institutions. At the same time, it was the IBA that allowed foreign banks to take advantage of the Edge Act provisions for establishing corporations to engage in international financial activities without being

---

[95] 52 foreign banks were grandfathered under the FBSEA, and therefore may take deposits as long as they remain insured. GAO (note 4 *supra*), at 42, n.8, and accompanying text.

[96] Community Reinvestment Act, 12 U.S.C. Chapter 29. For an overview of the legislation's requirements, see Symons and White (note 6 *supra*), at 168–76. Domestic banks also vigorously oppose the CRA. See generally, GAO, *Regulatory Burden: Recent Studies, Industry Issues, and Agency Initiatives*, GAO/GGD-94-28, (1994), pp. 48–51, setting out the content of the CRA, the industry's criticism of the legislation and consumer groups' responses, and regulators' and the administration's approach to solving the conflicts of interest.

[97] GAO (note 4 *supra*), at 19.

subject to the restrictive US banking laws, including, among others, that forbidding interstate branching.[98]

The Riegle-Neal Interstate Banking and Branching Efficiency Act of 1994 further liberalized foreign bank branching in the United States. The current regulations for international banks to branch or expand were summarized as follows:

> Foreign banks will be allowed to establish de novo full-service branches across state lines whenever US banks are allowed to establish de novo branches across state lines. Riegle-Neal will also allow foreign banks to expand across state lines by acquiring an existing bank or branch provided that the state also allows US banks to expand in such manner.[99]

The changes in banking regulation in the United States therefore benefit foreign banks as much as they do domestic banks. Thus, as of June 1997, the Riegle-Neal Act permitted both US and commercial banks to establish 'full-service branches' in the home State and throughout the rest of the United States.[100]

2.2 CANADIAN BANKING SYSTEM

Banks in Canada enjoy a highly developed, densely networked financial system that is subjected to minimal government intervention. Characterized by a high concentration of large banking institutions and a liberal policy toward non-banking activities, Canada's banking system is very different from that of the United States.[101]

2.2.1 Brief History of Canadian Banking

Canada's British colonial past has led to its inheritance of many elements of England's common law into the legal system. As in England, banks in Canada could only be established by an act of Parliament. An applicant would request a Charter for a limited liability company, and if granted, the Charter became the operational mandate of the bank. Generally, charters

---

[98] See GAO, *Statutory Requirements* (note 94 *supra*), at 4.
[99] GAO (note 4 *supra*), at 19.
[100] *Ibid.* at 44.
[101] The overview provided here is not intended to serve as an authoritative guide to banking in Canada. It is necessarily summary, and only highlights the most relevant aspects of the legal structure. See also Finance Canada, 'The Canadian Financial System' (1995); slightly outdated, but nevertheless helpful summary of the main aspects of the Canadian banking system put together by the Canadian Ministry of Finance; available on internet at >www.fin.gc.ca<; Hugh Thomas, 'Chapter 1: Banks and Other Deposit-Taking Institutions' in Finance Canada, *Financial Institutions Management* (draft of May 1996), text on internet at >www.business. mcmaster.ca<. For a detailed commentary on the Bank Act, see Brian Z. Gelfand, *Regulations of Financial Institutions* (Carswell: Scarborough, Ontario; looseleaf updated publication).

restricted lending by type of instrument and amount relative to paid-in capital, but there were no limitations on the maintenance of reserves.[102] Moreover, branching was unrestricted.[103]

With the British North America Act's grant of independence to the former colony came the federal Canadian government's exclusive power in banking regulation. The new government reacted to this grant of power with the implementation of the Bank Act of 1871. It was in this Act that the federal government assumed exclusive competence over the incorporation of banks.

Regulatory differences based on the categorization of a deposit-taking institution as a bank, a trust, or a loan company and the earlier separation of financial institutions' activities into securities, insurance, and banking are other characteristics the country inherited from the British. The regulatory interplay between federal and sub-national (in the case of Canada, Provincial) governments is common to Canada and the United States. However, the administrative division of competencies in Canada leaves the regulation of banking and insurance to the central government, while the securities industry is under the power of the Provincial governments. Thus, the banking system is not vertically bifurcated as it is in the United States. At the same time, the horizontal division of regulatory authority over the various financial service industry branches may make comprehensive financial liberalization more difficult for Canada than for countries without such a division of competencies.

The early characteristics of the banking system led to the current market structure of Canada's financial sector. There are relatively few large banks but each has an extensive branch network.[104] The high barriers to entry kept further competitors out of the market, while the unrestricted branching ensured that the existing banks could reach customers far removed from the head office.

---

[102] Angela Redish, 'The Government's Role in Payment Systems: Lessons from the Canadian Experience', in Catherine England (ed.), *Governing Banking's Future: Markets vs. Regulation* (Kluwer Academic Publishers, Deventer, 1991), pp. 161–80, at 163.

[103] *Ibid.*

[104] With the Department of Finance's rejection of a planned mergers between Royal Bank of Canada and Bank of Montreal (the largest and third-largest of the Canadian banks, respectively), and between the Toronto-Dominion Bank and the Canadian Imperial Bank of Commerce, the number of Canada's banks was kept at six. Together, these six already have a combined total of around 60 per cent of the consumer loans and personal deposits within Canada, and the former proposed merger would have given the new bank 27 per cent of the personal deposits and the same percentage of personal and credit card loans. 'Royal Wedding', *The Economist*, 31 January 1998, p. 85. Due to the relative size of the banks, the announcement of the mergers and the ensuing investigations spurred great attention. The merger issue became intermingled with the discussion of financial sector reform in general. Prime Minister Jean Chretien joined the Competition Bureau, the Office of the Superintendent of Financial Institutions, the Task Force on the Future of the Financial Services Sector, and the majority of parliamentarians in opposing the merger, calling it a proposal to be 'big to be big'. According to the Finance Minister Paul Martin, the rejection of the proposal was one 'that reflects the government's commitment to ensuring strong competition in the financial services sector'. Kenneth Pole, 'Canadian Bank Mergers Blocked; Officials Fear Too Much Concentration' 71:23 BNA's Banking Rep. 962 (21 December 1998).

Additionally, the strong reliance on self-regulation can be seen as an outgrowth of the market structure. The few Canadian banks have a deep foundation of capital assets. Therefore, they are less likely to fail due to their size and they carry tremendous political weight. Both characteristics help ensure that state supervision is kept to a minimum. In addition, their wide branching networks makes oversight of the individual branches administratively extremely burdensome—the Office of the Superintendent's staff of less than 30 persons is virtually forced to rely on the banks' own assessments of their soundness.[105]

Recent legislative changes in Canada's financial services system have reduced its resemblance to the current United States banking regime from another perspective—that of the allowed activities. Banks in Canada are now allowed to take part fully in securities market activities and to engage in some aspects of the insurance business.

In the light of its elements affecting trade in financial services, Canada's banking system is actually more similar to Mexico's system than it is to the United States'. The market maintains some entry barriers in the form of limits on foreign ownership of banks; the banking market is highly concentrated;[106] and the banks have a full range of banking activities, as well as a wide range of non-banking activities, allowed them. Additionally, although the traditional contestability of the Canadian banking market is low, there is a move toward increasing the competition among financial service providers. Thus, again like Mexico, foreign banks are being given numerous opportunities to establish and operate in Canadian territory under conditions equivalent to those enjoyed by domestic banks. For Canada's banking industry, NAFTA was just one step in an entire process of financial service liberalization that was (and is still) taking place nationally.

2.2.2 Controlling Legislation

2.2.2.1 Constitution

The Canadian Constitution is the supreme law of Canada. Federal and Provincial laws must adhere to the requirements of this document, as interpreted by the federal courts of the land and, as the final authority, the Supreme Court of Canada.

---

[105] Redish (note 102 *supra*), at 165 (reporting that in 1986 the staff of the Superintendent numbered just 21 persons).

[106] The steady trend toward consolidation of banks resulted in only 11 domestic banks remaining in the country in 1994, with the largest six possessing over 90 per cent of the total banking assets. The entire banking system, not just commercial banks, is facing the same consolidation trends. The June 1997 buyout of National Trust Co. by the Bank of Nova Scotia signalled the end of the privately-owned trust companies in Canada. *Neue Zürcher Zeitung*, 26 June 1997, p. 25.

Under the Canadian Constitution, the federal government is given authority to oversee the banking system. The Canadian Constitution sets out clearly:

> It shall be lawful for the Queen, by and with the Advice and Consent of the Senate and House of Commons, to make laws for the Peace, Order, Good Government of Canada, in relation to all Matters not coming within the Classes of Subjects by this act assigned exclusively to the Legislatures of the Provinces;
>
> ... and for greater Certainty, ... it is hereby declared that (notwithstanding anything in this act) the exclusive Legislative Authority of Parliament of Canada extends to all Matters coming within the Classes of Subjects next hereinafter enumerated; that is to say,
>
> ...
>
> 2) The Regulation of Trade and Commerce.
>
> ...
>
> 15) Banking, Incorporation of Banks, and the Issue of Paper Money.
>
> 16) Savings Banks.[107]

Although the constitutional division of powers between federal and Provincial governments is not so neat in reality,[108] it is accepted that it is only the federal government that has the competence to make most legislation and policy directly for banking (as opposed to trust and loan or non-bank financial institutions).[109]

2.2.2.2   The Bank Act

The Bank Act regulates the establishment and operation of banks in Canada, and as such is the piece of legislation most relevant to the topic of NAFTA's effects on banks.[110] The first Bank Act came into effect in 1871, and since then has been renewed in modified form approximately every ten years. The extent of the changes reflects the change in banking environment in both Canada and the world. The fundamental alterations of the banking system's structure that came out of the Bank Acts of 1980, 1991, and 1997 are symbols of the liberalizations taking place in banking regulation globally.

2.2.2.2.1   MAIN PROVISIONS OF THE MOST RECENT BANK ACTS

Bank Act of 1980   The Bank Act of 1980 introduced major changes to the financial service environment of Canada. It was only with this

---

[107] Constitution Act of 1867, Section 91.

[108] Discussions with Canadian lawyers reveals that the courts' interpretation of various clauses of the Constitution leaves the textual reading of the document to be a poor indicator of the true structure of the Canadian legal system. Conversation with Brian A. Smith, Counsellor (Finance), Canadian Embassy, Washington, DC (January 1997); conversation with John Craig, Berne, Switzerland (April 1997).

[109] Some banking activities are subject to provincial regulations. Trustee services and securities activities are the most common of these. 'The Canadian Financial System' (note 101 *supra*), at 2 ('Structure').

[110] The Bank Act can be found on the Government of Canada's website. Both English and French language texts can be located on the internet at >http://canada.justice.gc.ca<.

Act that banks were allowed to incorporate through an application to the Minister of Finance rather than by parliamentary decree.[111] Hence, the 'letters patent' procedure for obtaining a banking license supplanted the Charter procedure.

Even more importantly for purposes of NAFTA, the Bank Act of 1980 allowed foreign participation in Canadian banking for the first time. That Act divided bank ownership regulations into two groups, depending on the nationality of the bank: Canadian banks and foreign banks. No person (natural or legal person) is permitted to own or control more than 10 per cent of the shares of a Canadian bank for more than ten years.[112] Foreign bank subsidiaries, on the other hand, were allowed to have a 'significant shareholder'.[113]

Bank Act of 1992   During the late 1980s and early 1990s, the Government of Canada came under increasing domestic pressure to liberalize its financial services sector. All of the financial service sectors that had previously been separated by strict federal legislation—the banks, the trusts, the insurance companies, and the investment dealers—were urging the government to allow for more competition by permitting combined activities among the various industries.

After years of intensive study on the need for (and possibilities of) reform, the new Bank Act came into effect on 1 June 1992. Once again the legislation changed the Canadian banking environment dramatically. The focus of the Bank Act of 1992 was increased competition within the financial industries. Two paths to this goal were foreseen. First, banks would now be allowed to engage in various non-bank financial activities directly. As one commentator wrote, the Bank Act of 1992 'reflects the government acceptance of "one-stop financial shopping" as the economic key to the future'.[114] The newly allowed activities include portfolio management, fiduciary responsibilities, and investment advice.[115] Banks in Canada are allowed to add these areas to their operations from their offices and branches. In addition, the banks were given the right to issue insurance policies through separately incorporated subsidiaries.[116]

The second part of the Bank Act's competition promotion came through the liberalizations for foreign banks in Canada. The Bank Act of 1991 altered the former Act by dividing banks into Schedule I and Schedule II institutions, based on ownership structure rather than on nationality. Schedule I banks are required to be widely-held banks. That is, there can be no person (natural or legal) having a 'significant interest' (defined

---

[111] Redish (note 102 *supra*), at 164.
[112] Gelfand (note 101 *supra*), at 1–22, § 1.6(a), referring to Bank Act of 1980, s. 110(11), (13).
[113] *Ibid.*, referring to Bank Act of 1980, s. 110(12).
[114] M.H. Ogilvie, 'Financial Institutions Reform in Canada' (1992) J Bus L 615, 616.
[115] *Ibid.*
[116] The limitation on the right to sell insurance only through subsidiaries was a disappointment for the banks. The bankers had lobbied hard to include insurance sales among their allowable direct activities, but the government refused. See Ogilvie (note 114 *supra*), at 617.

as owning or controlling more than 10 per cent of the voting stock) in the bank for more than ten years. Schedule II banks are allowed to be closely-held, as long as the holder is either a non-bank, widely-held Canadian financial institution, a foreign bank, or a widely-held foreign non-bank financial institution.[117] However, the significant interest holder must 'control' the bank: that is the holder must be able to vote more than 50 per cent of the shares of the bank and elect a majority of the bank's directors.[118]

Foreign persons are also subject to a prescription on their total control of Canadian banking assets. First, 'non-residents'[119] may not own an aggregate of more than 25 per cent of any bank's voting rights (in addition to the 10 per cent limit on an individual's control of outstanding shares). The combination of these two limits is known as the '10/25 Rule'.

Secondly, foreign banks were still subject to the limitations on authorized capital. These limits restricted non-US foreign banks from accumulating more than 12 per cent of all domestic banking assets. This rule resulted in a great disadvantage to foreign banks because it prevented them from growing significantly. Without the possibility to control a bank or increase their authorized capital assets, many foreign financial institutions chose to avoid the Canadian market altogether or to establish investment companies rather than banks.

Currently, the cap on aggregated foreign financial assets in Canada no longer limits the scope of foreign banks to grow.[120] Although the United States had profited from this relaxation under the Canada-United States Free Trade Agreement, the Bank Act of 1992 extended the treatment to all banks.

Finally, the Bank Act of 1992 allowed US banks to benefit from the privilege of being permitted to maintain substantial control of a Schedule I bank for the first ten years following incorporation.[121] Subject to Minister of

---

[117] Gelfand (note 101 *supra*), at 1–23, § 1.6(a). Due to the term 'foreign institution' replacing the former 'foreign bank' in describing what types of institutions may have banking activities in Canada, the group of potential owners of foreign banks in Canada expanded. By definition, any of a wide variety of financial service companies might apply for a letters patent. Ogilvie (note 114 *supra*), at 619–20. Schedule I banks are required to have C$1 million paid-in capital while Schedule II banks are required to have C$2.5 million. These sums increase to requirements of C$10 million for each under the Bank Act of 1991 if the letters patent are requested from a federal trust, loan, or insurance company. See Gelfand (note 101 *supra*), at 1-6–1-5, § 1.2(a). Gelfand also notes that '[w]here the Minister issues letters patent on the application of a federal trust, loan, or insurance company, ... the letters patent may provide that shares of the bank will be exchanged on a share for share basis for shares in the company. The inclusion of this provision requires the approval of the Minister'). *Ibid.*, citing Bank Act of 1991, s. 29(1).

[118] *Ibid.* at 1–23, § 1.6(a), n.7, and accompanying text, citing Bank Act, S.C. 1991, c. 46, s. 374, s. 375, s. 3(1)(a)). Foreign Schedule II banks with C$750 million or more in equity are required to have at least 35 per cent of their stock widely-held. *Ibid.* at 1-27, § 1.6(c), discussing Bank Act, S.C. 1991, c. 46, s. 381–388.

[119] Defined in Bank Act, S.C. 1991, c. 46, s. 397. Paras 2 and 4 of this section exempt US residents from this rule, in compliance with CUFTA. Under the Bank Act revisions after NAFTA, Mexican residents were also exempted.

[120] Ogilvie (note 114 *supra*), at 622. The individual limits on holdings of bank shares remains in place for domestic and foreign banks. See 2.2.3 *supra*.

[121] *Ibid.* at 620.

Finance approval, this was a valuable concession to the US banks, which would otherwise have been limited to the 10/25 Rule prohibiting the control of a foreign bank by a single group of shareholders.

Bank Act of 1997 Due to the extent of the changes implemented by the Bank Act of 1992, it had a pre-determined life span of only five years The Bank Act of 1997 came into effect after the results of the earlier changes had been studied and analyzed in the context of increasing international pressure to liberalize financial service markets. Thus, while not as radical as the previous Act, the Bank Act of 1997 does introduce several noteworthy provisions.

The following presents a closer look at certain areas of Canadian banking law that are most important for the ultimate goal of analyzing the effects of NAFTA Chapter Fourteen on banks.

2.2.2.2.2 LICENSING PROCEDURES

The process All financial service providers in Canada must receive a license from the Minister of Finance before beginning to offer banking services.[122] Licenses for banks (called 'letters patent to incorporate a bank') are issued to either an individual or individuals or to a legal entity.[123] Since the Bank Act of 1992, the Minister of Finance ('the Minister') has the exclusive power to approve an application for the incorporation of a federal bank.[124] A person wishing to establish a bank begins the application process by announcing his or her decision to the public. The Bank Act requires that this announcement be in the form of a notice of intent to request a letters of patent published in both the official Canadian government circular (*Canada Gazette*) and in a newspaper circulating in the place where the head office of the proposed bank would sit.[125] Interested persons are thus able to know about the request and may try to influence the decision-making process.

Following the giving of notice, the applicant (or applicants[126]) submits a request to the Superintendent of Financial Institutions ('the Superintendent')

---

[122] Bank Act, S.C. 1991, c. 46 s. 32 ('A bank comes into existence on the date provided therefor in its letters patent').

[123] *Ibid.* at 2, 'entity', 'person'. The language 'one or more persons' indicates that the applicant may be either a natural person or a juridical person. See also *ibid.* s. 33. A government, an agent of a government, and a legal entity controlled by a government is prohibited from receiving letters of patent for the establishment of a Bank. *Ibid.* s. 23.

[124] *Ibid.* ss. 22, 35, in force 1 June 1992. Formerly, the power to approve incorporations resided with the Governor in Council. See Gelfand (note 101 *supra*), at § 1.2. Parallel powers are afforded the Provincial governments in the areas of local credit unions, provincial credit centrals, and securities markets. Department of Finance Canada, 1997 Review of Financial Sector Legislation: Proposals for Changes 19–20 (June 1996).

[125] To fulfil the notice requirement, the notice must be published at least once a week for four consecutive weeks 'in a form satisfactory to the Superintendent'. Bank Act s. 25.(2). But see Finance Canada (note 124 *supra*), at 32, proposing to amend the Bank Act ss. 14(5), 30, 37(2), 56(2), 229(3), 507(6), 514(6), 518(6), and 532 requirements that a notification be published in the *Canada Gazette* so that 'periodicals or electronic media readily available to the public' could be used instead.

[126] Bank Act s. 2.

to receive a letters of patent. The letter of application is to include a list of names of the proposed directors together with the necessary additional information for the Minister of Finance's decision on the application. This requires at least a showing of the applicant's experience in running a business, proof of the proposed managers' good characters and their ability to lead a bank,[127] proof of the applicant's financial resources available for the bank's business purposes, and a tentative plan of the bank's future business development.[128] The Superintendent is then to forward the application materials to the Minister.

If, within 30 days of notification, someone sends to the Superintendent a written objection to the applicant's request, the Superintendent must organize and carry out a public inquiry into the objection. The results of the inquiry will then be presented to the Minister before a decision can be taken on the application.[129]

The Minister's decision whether to grant the application for incorporation is to be based on 'all matters that the Minister considers relevant'.[130] Here, as in the United States, the Minister and Supervisor look to factors that can be grossly grouped into two categories: those looking to the stability of the individual bank, and those that aim to protect the stability of the overall banking system.

Individual bank considerations in general. One of the goals of the application investigation procedure is that of providing a level of certainty that the individual bank proposed will be a secure place of deposit for the individual customer. Thus, the investigators must determine whether the proposed bank structure and planned leadership are satisfactory in this regard. The Minister is required to look at:

(a) the nature and sufficiency of the financial resources of the applicant or applicants as a source of continuing financial support for the bank;
(b) the soundness and feasibility of plans ... for the future conduct and development of the business of the bank;
(c) The business record and experience of the applicant or applicants; [and]
(d) whether the bank will be operated responsibly by persons who are fit as to character, competence and experience suitable for involvement in the operation of a financial institution.[131]

The characteristics listed are all ones aimed at ensuring that there is expertise among those responsible for making business decisions, and that the decisions will not endanger the assets placed in the bank.

---

[127] See *infra*.
[128] Gelfand (note 101 *supra*) at § 1.2(a) at 1-5–1-6; see also Bank Act s. 27. Additional information may be required by the Superintendent. *Ibid.* s. 25.(1).
[129] *Ibid.* s. 26(1)–(3).
[130] *Ibid.* s. 27.
[131] *Ibid.*

Requirements for directors. Each bank must have a minimum of seven directors, one-third of whom are unaffiliated with the bank.[132] For Schedule I banks, 75 per cent of the directors must be residents[133] of Canada.[134] Foreign bank subsidiaries need only have one-half of the directors be Canadian residents.[135] Persons may be chosen who are already directors of a different financial institution. As one commentator notes, this is '[i]n furtherance of the dismantling of the four pillars, and in recognition of the fact that ownership ties are now permitted between different financial institutions'.[136]

The duties of the directors are to manage and supervise the bank.[137] Together with the restrictions on affiliation with the bank,[138] the inclusion of a duty to supervise the bank underscores the heightened need for self-regulation in a liberalized financial service environment. The supervision of banks must be taken over by the bank itself if the government's involvement in such oversight is to remain minimal.

Banking system considerations   The second major aim of the banking regulators' licensing requirements is ensuring the stability of the financial sector as a whole. Again, this systemic interest can be found in nearly every jurisdiction, and is based on the realization of the fundamental importance of financial institutions in the economy. The Bank Act requires the Minister to make a decision about an application for letters patent based on 'the best interests of the financial system in Canada'.[139] Determining what the 'best interests' are is a subjective decision, and as such might ideally be made by the legislature as a whole. Yet, it is the Ministry that is left to interpret this phrase. Although increased competition is certainly one of the system's interests, the stability consideration focuses as well on the regulatory aspects of the financial system. Among the considerations for whether an individual bank will be approved are whether the bank will contribute to a more efficient industry and whether the proposed location can support an additional bank.

One provision in the Bank Act that appears aimed at protecting the whole Canadian banking system is that setting out the quorum for meetings of the Board of Directors. Under this provision, the minimal quorum is half of the minimum required number of directors (that is, four).[140] Of those present, half

---

[132] For a definition of 'affiliated' as applies to bank directors, see Regulations Specifying the Circumstances Under Which a Natural Person is Affiliated With a Bank ('Affiliated Persons (Banks) Regulations'), SOR/92-325 (21 May 1992) s. 3.

[133] Bank Act s. 159(1). Before 1992, a majority of the directors had to be Canadian citizens. Gelfand (note 101 *supra*), at §1.5(b)(v), 1-15. Simser warns that the three-quarters residence rule is a violation of the NAFTA. Jeffrey Simser, 'Financial Services Under NAFTA: A Starting Point' (1994–95) 10 Banking & Fin L Rev 185, 208. For more see 4.4. *infra*.

[134] Bank Act s. 159(2).

[135] *Ibid.*

[136] Gelfand (note 101 *supra*), at § 1.5(b)(ii), 1-12.

[137] *Ibid.* § 1.5(b)(i) at 1-11, citing Bank Act of 1991 s. 157(1).

[138] See Bank Act s. 163–164.

[139] *Ibid.* s. 27(e).

[140] *Ibid.* s. 182(2). This is the majority of the minimum number of directors required. If the bank's bylaws so dictate, a higher quorum may be required.

of the directors of a foreign bank subsidiary must be residents of Canada and a majority of the directors of a Canadian bank must be resident.[141] The interest in having residents taking part in the making of management decisions and in overseeing the bank indicates the belief that the system will be better protected by persons who have a stake in its condition.

2.2.2.2.3   TYPE OF LICENSE

As stated earlier, the Bank Act of 1980 allowed the entry of foreign banks on to the Canadian financial service market for the first time.[142] Changes in the later Bank Acts have resulted in two distinct types of banking licenses that can be granted. One is the Schedule I bank license. The other is the Schedule II bank license.

The Schedule I license is for large, widely-held, domestic banks.[143] To establish a Schedule I bank, the incorporators must have at least C$750 million capital invested. In addition, no individual may own more than 10 per cent of any class of one of these bank's stock without permission from the Minister of Finance. Limits on aggregate foreign ownership of a Schedule I banks' assets to less than 25 per cent of the assets exist now only for banks from non-members of the World Trade Organization.

A Schedule II bank license was originally intended for small and foreign banks. Under the Bank Act of 1980, these banks were allowed to be wholly owned by a single person, without regard to the owner's nationality, and the capital of a Schedule II bank could not exceed C$750 million.

The revision of the Bank Act in 1991 changed the rules governing Schedule II banks. Now, even Schedule II banks are to be widely-held. The Minister of Finance must give approval for shareholdings in excess of the 10 per cent individual ownership limit unless the owner holds more than 50 per cent of the voting rights[144] The limits on capital are also lifted, but if the Schedule II bank does exceed the C$750 million level of assets, it must ensure that at least 35 per cent of its shares are widely-held.[145]

2.2.2.2.4   ESTABLISHMENT OF A BRANCH

Traditionally banks in Canada have enjoyed the power to engage in the business through branches throughout the territory of Canada.[146]

---

[141] *Ibid.* s. 183(1).
[142] See 2.2.2.2.1 *supra.*
[143] At present, the large Canadian Banks are all Schedule I banks.
[144] Ogilvie (note 114 *supra*), at 620.
[145] *Ibid.* at 621. The precise rules regarding Schedule II banks are much more detailed than are set out here.
[146] Bank Act, S.C. 1991 c.46, s. 15. -(3), in force 1 June 1992; GAO, *Bank Regulatory Structure: Canada*, GAO/GGD-95-223 (1995), p. 14; Ian F.G. Baxter, *Law of Banking* (4th edn, Thomson Canada/Carswell, Scarborough, Ontario, 1992), pp. 99–100. Wonnacott says potential comparative advantage of Canadian banks over US banks in Mexico, because of their greater experience with extensive branching. Ronald J. Wonnacott, 'Canada's Role in NAFTA: To What Degree Has It Been Defensive?', in Victor Bulmer-Thomas, Nikki Craske, and Mónica Serrano (eds), *Mexico and the North American Free Trade Agreement: Who Will Benefit?* (St Martin's Press, New York, 1994), pp. 163–75, at 166.

Indeed, the major Canadian banks have around 14,000 branches, spread over the entire geographic area of the country.[147]

To establish a branch, a Schedule I bank need not receive any additional license from the Ministry of Finance. A Schedule II bank, on the other hand, must apply for permission to establish more than one branch unless it is controlled by a United States or Mexican bank,[148] or, as of June 1999, the bank is controlled by a WTO Member state bank.[149]

2.2.2.2.5 POWERS OF A BANK

Canadian banks within Canada   Unless specifically limited in their business activities through the Bank Act, Canadian banks operating in Canada have the same rights and privileges, as do natural persons.[150] That said, one finds that the Bank Act contains several significant limitations.[151] Indeed, Article 409 reads clearly: '(1) Subject to this Act, a bank shall not engage in or carry on any business other than the business of banking and such business generally as appertains thereto'.[152]

The Bank Act sets out both the 'business of banking' activities and the other acceptable activities in a non-exclusive list, and grants the Governor in Council the power to make recommendations and changes to the regulations. The 'business of banking'[153] as set out in the statute includes 'providing any financial service',[154] acting as an agent[155] in financial matters,[156] giving investment advice to businesses or individuals,[157] and 'issuing payment, credit or charge cards and, in co-operation with others … operating a

---

[147] Ogilvie (note 114 *supra*) at 615; see also William R. White, *The Implications of the FTA and NAFTA for Canada and Mexico*, Technical Report No. 70 (Bank of Canada, Ottawa 1993), p. 16, stating that with 'approximately one bank branch per 2000 people', Canada has a per capita number of branches that is the same as that in the United States.

[148] It appears that the Ministry of Finance gives such special permission readily. In 1993 there were 564 branches of the 59 Schedule II banks. Department of Treasury, *National Treatment Study* (1994), pp. 122, 123. The Hongkong Bank of Canada is the only foreign bank in Canada involved in extensive retail banking, and it has a correspondingly large network of branches. *Ibid.* at 124; Finance Canada, *The Canadian Financial System*, Annex (1995) (in 1995, Hongkong Bank of Canada had 108 branches in Canada).

[149] Under Canada's obligations in the Fifth Protocol to the GATS, the government pledged to eliminate the permission requirement for WTO Member state banks. At the time the obligation was taken, it was made subject to the passage of the necessary legislation by Parliament. In February 1999, Bill C-67 was tabled, containing the relevant amendments to the Bank Act, as well as establishing a new regime for foreign bank entry directly through a branch.

[150] Bank Act, S.C. 1991 c.46, s. 15-(1), in force 1 June 1992; see also Ian F.G. Baxter (note 146 *supra*), 'Some Powers and Prohibitions'.

[151] Bank Act, Part VIII (Business and Powers).

[152] *Ibid.* s. 409-(1).

[153] *Ibid.* s. 409 -(2).

[154] *Ibid.* s. 409 -(2)(a).

[155] *Ibid.* s. 409 -2(b). See also *ibid.* s. 370 -(1)(a) (definition of 'agent' in relation to Canadian federal or provincial government for purposes of Ownership Provisions of the Bank Act); s. 370-(1)(b) (definition of 'agent' in relation to a foreign government for purposes of ownership provisions of the Bank Act).

[156] *Ibid.* s. 409 -(2)(b).

[157] *Ibid.* s. 409-(2)(c).

payment, credit or charge card plan'.[158] The other permissible banking activities include 'dealing' with land,[159] selling government lottery tickets,[160] and acting as a property's custodian[161] or as a 'receiver, liquidator, or sequestrator.[162]

The Bank Acts prescriptions on banks' activities go to both non-financial activities and non-bank financial activities. As to the non-financial activities, the Bank Act contains a general limitation: 'Except as authorized by or under this Act, a bank shall not deal in goods, wares or merchandise or engage in any trade or other business'.[163]

The Act has separate provisions for the non-bank financial activities such as securities, insurance, and leasing.

In 1992, the Canadian Parliament made extensive changes to the then-existing Bank Act. Among those changes were liberalizations to the previous separation of financial institution affiliations. With the 1992 Bank Act revisions, banks gained permission to form subsidiaries for insurance and trust business activity.[164] Thus, although banks are not allowed to establish bank holding companies, they may still engage in non-banking financial services.[165]

Securities activities. Canada has generally allowed banks to deal in securities through subsidiaries since the banking reform of 1987. This revision to the prior policy of strict separation of banking and securities activities found in the Securities Dealing Restrictions (Banks) Regulations of 1992 sets out the specific activities allowed and not allowed to banks as of June 1992.[166] The Regulations allow a bank to deal in securities for its own account[167] and to deal in the primary distribution of government[168] (and public utility)[169] debt obligations and the debt obligations of the bank itself.[170] These Regulations also allow the bank to offer 'investment counselling and portfolio management services'.[171] Moreover, a bank may underwrite securities as long as it is one of several members of a selling group.[172]

---

158 *Ibid.* s. 409-(2)(d).
159 *Ibid.* s. 410-(1)(a).
160 *Ibid.* s. 410-(1)(3)(iii).
161 *Ibid.* s. 410-(1)(f).
162 *Ibid.* s. 410 -(1)(g).
163 *Ibid.* s. 410-(2).
164 GAO (note 146 *supra*), at 12.
165 *Ibid.*, n.6, and accompanying text.
166 Regulations Restricting Dealing in Canada in Securities By a Bank ('Securities Dealing Restrictions (Banks) Regulations'), SOR/92-279 (14 May 1992) (amended SOR/92-364 (2 June 1992)).
167 *Ibid.* 3.(1).
168 *Ibid.* 3.(2)(a)(i), (iii).
169 *Ibid.* 3.(2)(a)(ii).
170 *Ibid.* 3.(2)(c).
171 *Ibid.* 3.(1).
172 *Ibid.* 3.(2)(h).

Insurance activities. The Bank Act's Regulations governing banks' insurance activities give a general authorization to banks to engage in 'any aspect of the business of insurance' except the underwriting of policies.[173] However, one commentator notes that, due to the limits on the banks' engagements in insurance, it 'remains a substantially discrete activity despite the integration of financial services otherwise enacted'.[174] Indeed, the affiliation must take the form of a subsidiary of the bank and branches of the bank are not allowed to house the offices of an insurance company owned by the bank.[175] Furthermore, the permission is qualified by certain limits for particular types of insurance[176] and by broad restrictions on the targeted 'promotion' of insurance companies,[177] insurance agents or brokers,[178] or insurance policies.[179] Finally, banks and their affiliates are prohibited from giving insurance companies information about customers or customers' representatives.[180] Thus, barriers continue to prevent the full integration of banking and insurance.

Canadian banks outside Canada If a Canadian bank does business outside the country, it is free to engage in business to the extent the foreign law allows.[181] An exception to this principle of host-country rules is that under no circumstances may a Canadian bank underwrite insurance.[182]

---

[173] Regulations Respecting the Extent to which a Bank May Undertake the Business of Insurance and Relations Between Banks and Entities that Undertake the Business of Insurance, Insurance Agents and Insurance Brokers, SOR/92-330 (21 May 1992) (amended by SOR/95-171 (4 April 1995)).

[174] Ogilvie (note 114 *supra*), at 617.

[175] *Ibid.*

[176] The Regulations distinguish between 'authorized type of insurance', personal accident insurance, and group insurance policies. Insurance Business (Banks) Regulations 2.(a)–(h). A list of 'authorized type[s] of insurance', consists of:

  (a) credit or charge card-related insurance;
  (b) creditors' disability insurance;
  (c) creditors' life insurance;
  (d) creditors' loss of employment insurance;
  (e) creditors' vehicle inventory insurance;
  (f) export credit insurance;
  (g) mortgage insurance; or
  (h) travel insurance.

Under the Regulations, banks may provide detailed advice and recommendations about policies and risks, insurance companies, and particular brokers only in regards to authorized types of insurance. *Ibid.* 5–7.

[177] Promotion of non-authorized types of insurance must take place outside the premises of the branch of the bank and must not be targeted to particular customers. *Ibid.* 6.

[178] *Ibid.*

[179] *Ibid.* 7.

[180] *Ibid.* 8.

[181] Bank Act, S.C. 1991 c.46, s. 15.-(4), in force 1 June 1992.

[182] Insurance Business (Banks) Regulations 3.

2.2.2.3   Canadian Deposit Insurance Corporation

Every bank is required by The Bank Act to be a member of the Canada Deposit Insurance Corporation (CDIC) if it wants to accept deposits.[183] The CDIC came into being in 1967 as a government-owned ('Crown') corporation. It guarantees bank deposits for up to C$60,000 per account, and so is intended to provide security to small depositors in case of bank failure.[184] The CDIC also is responsible for the procedures of liquidating unsound banks.[185]

The CDIC has an active role in the supervision of Canadian banks in addition to its role as protector of deposits. Issuing legally-binding bylaws on matters related to sound financial practices, the corporation helps the banks judge their activities in such a way as to encourage effective risk management in the self-regulatory environment.[186]

The bank's management and directors are responsible for assessing their compliance with the CDIC standards through an annual self-assessment report.[187] If the standards are not being upheld, the CDIC may cancel the bank's insurance.[188]

2.2.3   Specific Provisions for Foreign Banks

Canadian banks have traditionally dominated the Canadian banking market. In the past, this was due to the high barriers to entry. When the barriers were lowered, foreign banks began to enter, but currently the foreign bank activity in Canada is still much lower than in many industrialized countries: only about 10 per cent of the banking assets in Canada stem from the foreign banks; only one foreign bank has retail activities in the country; and an increasing number of banks are indicating an interest in serving the Canadian market by means of cross-border banking.[189]

The Bank Act defines a 'foreign bank' to be:

> an entity incorporated or formed by or under the laws of a country other than Canada that
> (a) is a bank according to the laws of any foreign country where it carries on business,
> (b) carries on a business in any foreign country that, if carried on in Canada, would be, wholly or to a significant extent, the business of banking,

---

[183] Bank Act, s. 413.
[184] Redish (note 102 *supra*), at 170.
[185] See GAO (note 146 *supra*), at 31, describing briefly the possible actions the CDIC may take to 'resolve' a bank.
[186] See *ibid*. at 29.
[187] *Ibid*. at 27. There are two forms of report, a simplified and a detailed report. If the CDIC is not satisfied with the simplified report, a detailed report may be required. *Ibid*. n.21, and accompanying text.
[188] *Ibid*. at 26.
[189] See note 210 *infra*.

(c) engages, directly or indirectly, in the business of providing financial services and employs, to identify or describe its business, a name that includes the word 'bank', 'banque', 'banking' or 'bancaire' ...,

(d) engages in the business of lending money and accepting deposit liabilities transferable by cheque or other instrument,

(e) engages, directly or indirectly, in the business of providing financial services and is affiliated with another foreign bank,

(f) controls another foreign bank, or

(g) is a foreign institution, other than a foreign bank within the meaning of any of paragraphs (a) to (f), that controls a bank named in Schedule II, but does not include a subsidiary of a bank named in Schedule I ... .[190]

As mentioned above, until 1980, the Canadian banking system was highly restrictive *vis-à-vis* foreign banks, refusing to allow for foreign control of banks.[191] The definition of control at that time excluded foreign ownership of more than 50 per cent of the voting stock of any bank.

After the Bank Act of 1980 allowed for majority ownership of subsidiaries in Canada by foreign banks, the Canadian market became attractive to investors. There were however still high barriers to entry and disadvantageous operating conditions preventing an extensive development of foreign banks in Canada. A foreign investor could not own more than 25 per cent of any Schedule I bank's total assets, Schedule II banks could not exceed a capital limit of C$750 million, and branching of Schedule II banks was limited to a single branch.

2.2.3.1 Foreign Banking Under CUFTA

A slow opening of Canadian financial service markets began in the late 1980s with the initiation of talks with the United States to form a bilateral free trade area. The Canada-United States Free Trade Agreement (CUFTA) negotiations included talks on liberalizing the trade between the Canadian and US banks and non-bank financial institutions other than insurance companies.[192] Under Chapter 17 of the resulting agreement, the two Parties promised narrow improvements in market access rules and operating limitations, and they exchanged commitments to further co-operation on liberalization measures in the future. Importantly, however, the Article 17 rights were limited to institutions of which at least 50 per cent of the issued voting shares were controlled by persons of one of the two Parties.[193]

Procedurally, the CUFTA financial service provisions set out requirements for transparency in legislation and regulations.[194] Substantively, the CUFTA provides that under certain conditions banks in the United States

---

[190] Bank Act s. 2 ('foreign bank'). The Minister of Finance may exempt any foreign bank from the status of foreign bank. *Ibid.* s. 12(1).

[191] GAO (note 146 *supra*), n.9 and accompanying text.

[192] For more on CUFTA, see Chapter 1 *supra*.

[193] CUFTA Art. 1705:2; see also Art. 1706 (definition of 'controlled').

[194] CUFTA Art. 1704 (Notification and Consulation).

will have right to deal in Canadian-government debt obligations[195] and that Canadian banks will be assured of both no worse treatment than currently offered them in the United States[196] and would benefit from liberalizations that might take place on the US domestic banking regulation front.[197]

Canada in turn removed several significant market access barriers for US banks interested in entering the Canadian market.[198] Also, under the condition that the government in Washington would continue to negotiate liberalizations on the permissible activities of its own banks, Canada agreed to grant US institutions all further liberalizations that Canadian banks would enjoy if regulatory changes were to occur there.[199]

2.2.3.1.1   RESTRICTIONS ON MARKET ACCESS

The market access concessions that Canada offered included a lifting of restrictions on foreign ownership of financial institutions whose shares are more than 50 per cent controlled by Canadian residents.[200] Equally significant was Canada's agreement to allow US-controlled subsidiaries of Canadian banks be excluded from Canada's foreign bank asset limits[201] and to allow their branching inside Canada without prior approval from the Ministry of Finance.[202]

At the time the NAFTA was under negotiation, the banking market in Canada still discriminated against foreign (including US) banks. Beyond the prohibition on direct branching into the Canadian market, the application process for establishing a subsidiary was notoriously complicated and slow. Once a subsidiary was established, it operated at a disadvantage relative to Canadian banks, because the parent bank's assets were not included in assessments of financial capital against which loans are made. Neither could foreign bank subsidiaries enter the retail banking market without specific permission from the Minister.

---

[195] Federal and provincial government-backed debt obligations may be offered by banks in the United States to the extent that US government-backed debt obligations may be offered, as long as the liability for the payment of the obligations remains 'ultimately and unconditionally' on the respective government. CUFTA Art. 1702:1.

[196] This was particularly significant as regards the US branching regulations. These, CUFTA Art. 1702:2 states, would remain at least as liberal as those in place on 4 October 1987.

[197] A general provision covered both the non-regression and the future possibility of better treatment. CUFTA Art. 1702:4. Specifically, the CUFTA provided that potential changes in US banking legislation that prevent banks from undertaking securities activities would be extended to Canadian banks. Art. 1702:3, referring to 'the *Glass-Steagall Act* and associated legislation and resulting amendments to regulations and administrative practices'.

[198] CUFTA Art. 1703:1, Art. 1703:2.

[199] CUFTA Arts 1703:3, 1703:4, including the phrase, 'subject to normal regulatory and prudential considerations'.

[200] CUFTA Art. 1703:1 see also CUFTA Art. 1706 (definition of Canadian-controlled).

[201] CUFTA Art. 1703:2.

[202] CUFTA Art. 1703:2(c).

2.2.3.1.2 OTHER BARRIERS

Restrictions on the composition of the bank's management were additional barriers to foreign subsidiaries in Canada. Up to 50 per cent of the Board of Directors of foreign banks may be composed of non-residents of Canada, but the other half must be residents.[203] Moreover, at each meeting, at least half of the Board members present must be residents.[204] Therefore, there could be a subtle Canada-orientation to business decisions made by the Board.

Finally, the Bank Act restricts the transfer of information for data processing out of the country. This inflicts an additional cost on foreign bank subsidiaries that have a central data processing center in the territory where the parent bank is located.

2.2.3.2   Post-1997 Reforms and Remaining Barriers

The financial reforms contained in the Bank Act of 1997[205] move Canada's banking system closer to their stated goal of a 'level playing field',[206] but discriminations remain. Significantly, however, in 1999 the issue of direct branching seems to have been resolved by the proposed legislative changes coming in the wake of financial system reform.

The 1997 Act divides foreign banks into 'regulated foreign banks' and 'near banks', depending on whether a foreign institution is regulated as a bank in its home country. Regulated foreign banks, that is those that 'are regulated as banks in their home jurisdiction and for which financial services constitute a large part of their operations',[207] may operate either as a regulated financial entity[208] or as an unregulated entity.[209] Unregulated entities may not accept deposits and must keep their Canadian assets under C\$200 million in return for being exempted from federal or provincial supervisory requirements.

In December 1996, the government established a Task Force on the Future of the Canadian Financial Services Sector to investigate this (and other) banking system problems. Among their results, the Task Force recommended that foreign banks be allowed to establish a banking presence in Canada through direct branches as well as through

---

[203] Bank Act s. 159(2).
[204] *Ibid.* s. 183 (if the Board is of a Canadian bank, a majority of those present must be resident Canadians, but if the bank is a subsidiary of a foreign bank, only 50 per cent of those present must be residents).
[205] Act to Amend Certain Laws Relating to Financial Institutions, S.C. 1997, c. 15 (previously Bill C-82).
[206] Finance Canada, Foreign Bank Entry Policy I, available on the internet at >www.fin.gc.ca<.
[207] *Ibid.* at III.
[208] The permissible regulated forms of entities are bank subsidiary, trust, loan, or insurance company, and securities dealer. *Ibid.*
[209] *Ibid.* 'An "unregulated" entity (for purposes of this paper) is a financial entity other than the above-listed regulated financial institutions, which is not subject to solvency-based federal or provincial regulation'.

subsidiaries.[210] The Foreign Bank Entry Bill, put before Parliament in early-1999, contained the Task Force's recommended changes within a comprehensive framework for regulating such branches.[211] The new framework will allow foreign banks to petition the OFSI for permission to open either a full-service branch or a lending branch in Canada. Full-service branches will be allowed to take deposits of C$150,000 or more and make loans. Lending branches will only be authorized to make loans.[212] Neither type of branch is eligible for CDIC membership (and this fact must be signalled to customers),[213] but full-service branches would have access to the Canadian Payments Association. The government expects the new framework to increase competition in the non-retail banking market, but has made provisions for protecting the safety and soundness of the banking system as a whole by retaining discretion in the application process and by subjecting the branches to regular supervision.[214]

---

[210] The Final Report was released 14 September 1998, and contained 124 recommendations. The reforms are meant to improve competitiveness and increase competition, to 'empower' financial service consumers, to ensure fair corporate practices, and to improve the structure and process of institutional regulation. 'Financial Services Deregulation Urged by Canadian Task Force' 71:10 BNA's Banking Rep 427 (21 September 1998). The recommendations were made in the face of a declining presence of foreign banks in Canada and the global movement toward greater liberalization of financial services trade. See Finance Canada, 'Backgrounder on Foreign Bank Entry Bill', News Release 99-016:

> Since reaching a peak of 59 in 1987, the number of foreign bank subsidiaries in Canada has declined to just 45 in 1998. Their share of total banking assets, which stood at about 12 per cent in 1990, fell to just under 10 per cent by the end of 1998. Foreign banks have indicated that existing regulatory requirements make it difficult for them to compete. In order to help sustain a viable foreign bank presence in Canada, the options available to foreign banks wanting to do business in Canada need to be broadened.

At the same time, a response to the Task Force's Report by the Standing Senate Committee on Banking, Trade and Commerce maintains that body's continued commitment to a financial institutions framework that will 'foster Canadian control of the key institutions in the financial services sector'. 'A Blueprint for Change: Response to the Report of the Task Force on the Future of the Canadian Financial Services Sector' (December 1998), on the internet site of the Canadian Parliament at >www.parl.gc.ca<.

[211] Bill C-67, tabled 11 February 1999. For a description of the contents of the bill, see OFSI, Guide to Foreign Bank Branching (draft of 2 February 1999). See also 'Government Introduces Legislation Opening Doors to Foreign Bank Branches' 72:8 BNA's Banking Rep 351 (22 February 1999), describing a disappointed reaction from the CBA's Schedule II Foreign Banks Executive Committee chairman Gennaro Stammati, who commented that the legislation makes an '… openness that is half-open, not completely open'.

[212] Bill C-67 will require that the OFSI and the Superintendent of Financial Institutions each approve an application for the establishment of a branch. The OFSI may only give its approval if it has evidence that, *inter alia* 'the authorized foreign bank will be capable of making a contribution to the Canadian financial system'. Guide to Foreign Bank Branching (draft), p. 5, referring to the language of the Bank Act s. 524(3).

[213] See Notices (Authorized Foreign Banks) Regulations (draft 19 February 1999), including example notices that must be posted in each branch and requiring notices also be placed in certain advertisements.

[214] See New Regulations Applicable to Authorized Foreign Banks: Regulatory Impact Analysis Statement (draft 19 February 1999), the text of which is on the OSFI internet site at >www.osfi-bsif.gc.ca<.

As will be discussed, the NAFTA provisions on transparency and the Board of Directors alleviate some of the remaining discriminations faced by US and Mexican banks in Canada, but for other countries' banks, these restrictions remain. In addition, the bank management and board quorum requirements have not been altered by the 1997 legislation or the 1999 proposals.

2.3 MEXICO'S BANKING SYSTEM

Any study of NAFTA Chapter Fourteen's effects on banks must highlight the characteristics of the Mexican banking system before and after the Agreement. As foreign banks had faced a closed banking system before the NAFTA, the results of liberalizations under Chapter Fourteen should be the greatest for the NAFTA Party banks going to Mexico. The following highlights the Mexican banking market's qualities that are likely to influence the actual impact of the NAFTA provisions on both Party and non-Party banks.[215]

2.3.1 History

During Spain's colonial rule over Mexico, there were no true banks in Mexico.[216] Rather, moneylenders were merchants or individuals who held deposits for others and lent funds to their own profit.[217] This early system of moneylending continued to be the main form of 'banking' even following the newly independent nation's implementation of a commercial code.[218] However, government chartering of banks did begin to take form in the second half of the nineteenth century. A uniform system was enacted by the Mexican legislature in 1873, and was strengthened in 1884.[219] Although the Commercial Code of 1884 recognized only one type of bank, pressure for liberalizing the financial system led to a new General Statute of Credit Institutions of 1897 and three types of bank charters.[220] Unfortunately for the

---

[215] Again, this is not intended to be a comprehensive review of Mexico's banking laws and should not be relied upon to the exclusion of other information sources.

[216] Roberto Molina Pasquel, 'The Mexican Banking System' (1956–57) 11 Miami LQ 470.

[217] Valerie J. McNevin, 'Policy Implications of the NAFTA for the Financial Services Industry' (1994) 5 Colo J Int'l Env'l L & Pol'y 369, 396.

[218] The Ordinances of Bilboa were a codification of the Spanish mercantile laws. See Pasquel (note 216 *supra*), at 470, n.2, and accompanying text.

[219] *Ibid*. at 470.

[220] *Ibid*. at 470–71. The first type of bank to be allowed was the 'bank of issue', one serving as a public depositary institution exchanging money for certificates payable upon demand to the bearer. The three types of banks certified under the General Statute of Credit Institutions were: a national bank of issue; mortgage banks; and banks of agriculture and industry.

development of the financial system, a financial collapse ended the early banking experiment.[221]

Mexico's banking system began taking on its modern form after the Mexican revolutionary period of 1910–17. The Constitution of 1917 placed regulation of the banking system in the competence of the federal government once again. The National Bank Law was passed in 1924 and the National Banking Commission was organized as the primary regulator of banking that same year. In 1925, the Central Bank of Mexico was established to fulfil the macroeconomic policy-setting role typical of such institutions. In addition, the Central Bank was to act as the lender of last resort.[222]

2.3.1.1   First Stages of Banking Law Reform (1976–82)

Until 1976, Mexican banks were severely restricted in their activities. Much like the US and Canadian financial institution systems, the Mexican regulations had carefully separated financial service providers into insurance providers, securities dealers, and banking institutions. In 1976, however, the government revised the law, allowing for 'multiple' banking. This law effectively unified commercial banks and permitted banks to create separately incorporated subsidiaries for insurance and securities activities in hopes of promoting the growth potential of the entire financial sector.[223]

Unexpectedly, macroeconomic conditions prevented the fulfillment of these expectations: the Mexican economy's continued struggle with inflation and its effects prevented the banks' newly acquired areas of activity from achieving their potential. The inflation rate had begun to rise in 1972 after remaining stable for over 20 years following the Second World War.[224] In addition, both the fiscal deficit and the current account deficit were increasing throughout the 1970s. The inflation of the peso

---

[221] Pasquel (note 216 *supra*), at 471, describes the collapse as a consequences of the early system's three-part structure:

> The [mortgage banks and the banks of agriculture and industry] engaged mainly in large loans to the big land owners, and as a result, the entire banking system collapsed in 1908. The directors, who were at the same time owners of both the banks and the mortgaged farms, had permitted indefinite renewal of loans with the result that their portfolios became completely frozen. Since the loans had been made for the purposes of financing consumption rather than production, interim measures remained without success. This serious crisis was teminated by the more violent one culminating in the Mexican Revolution of 1910.

[222] See *ibid.* for more details on Mexican banking laws up to the Second World War, and *ibid.* at 472–7 for details on Mexican banking in the decade after the Second World War.

[223] The 1976 legislation maintained the distinction between commercial and investment banks. James E. Ritch Jr, 'Legal Aspects of Lending to Mexican Borrowers' (1981) 7:3 NC J Int'l L & Com Reg 315. It was not until 1990 when new legal reforms of the banking system created the 'financial institution' that this separation was removed. Marilyn E. Skiles, 'Stabilization and Financial Sector Reform in Mexico' (1991) Fed Res Bank of New York Research Paper No. 9125 at 13–14.

[224] GAO, 'Mexico's Financial Crisis: Origins, Awareness, Assistance, and Initial Efforts to Recover', GAO/GGD-96-56, p. 29 (February 1996)

coincided with the fear of an unstable balance of payments and led investors to take their funds out of the country.[225] Despite outgoing President Luis Escheverría's lowering of the peso's official exchange rate in September 1976, the country sank into a deep recession by the end of the year.[226]

The following six years under the administration of President Jose Lopez Portillo were marked by further peso depreciation. This was accompanied by large foreign borrowings backed by Mexico's oil prospects.[227] Inflation continued to rise, as did the federal deficit, but Mexico's large offshore oil reserves allowed the economy to maintain high rates of growth despite the dangerous fiscal conditions.[228] When oil prices fell in 1982, Mexico's ability to finance itself with foreign funds ended. What followed was economic chaos:

> Faced with dwindling foreign reserves and massive capital flight, once again an outgoing Mexican administration resorted to devaluation. This time, the peso was devalued by almost 500 per cent against the dollar over the course of the year. The country was plunged into a disastrous economic and financial crisis. Inflation reached an annual rate of over 60 per cent. A series of protest strikes and work stoppages paralyzed economic activity. The Mexican stock market plummeted. The Bank of Mexico (Mexico's central bank) ran out of foreign currency reserves, and in August, Mexico temporarily suspended repayment of principal on its foreign debt.[229]

Despite the need for domestic funds for investment, the Mexican banks maintained a tight credit policy, refusing to extend loans to Mexican citizens. Simultaneously, speculation on the peso's devaluation through the purchase of foreign currency was offering much larger profits to prosperous Mexicans than was the losing prospect of investing in traditional accounts. The banks were quick to create exchange services for those transferring their account funds into foreign money.[230] The speculation itself spurred further devaluation.[231] This cycle of devaluation, combined with the massive transfers of money out of the country, gave private banks huge profits: from 1977 to 1982, the banks' profits grew by 1,156 per cent.[232]

---

[225] *Ibid.* at 29.
[226] *Ibid.*
[227] *Ibid.* at 30. Mexico is placed eighth in the world for size of their oil reserves, with 65 billion proven barrels in 1995. See *Mexican Investment Board, Economic and Business Overview 1995: Mexico* (1995), p. 5.
[228] GAO (note 224 *supra*), at 30.
[229] *Ibid.*
[230] See Bronwen Davis, 'Mexico's Commercial Banking Industry: Can Mexico's Recently Privatized Banks Compete with the United States Banking Industry After Enactment of the North American Free Trade Agreement?' (1993) 10:1 Ariz J Int'l & Comp L 77, 81, n.31. 'By August 1982, the banks were earning 49 per cent of their gross profits from exchange operations'.
[231] *Ibid.* at 80.
[232] *Ibid.* at 80–81, n.29, and accompanying text.

In August 1982, the Mexican government attempted to bring the economy under control by decrees aimed at an international stabilization of the peso. However, neither the creation of a special fund of foreign currency for the state and key importers[233] nor the imposition of an official peso exchange rate for foreign currency debts[234] were able to halt the capital flight.[235] More drastic steps needed to be taken.

2.3.1.2   *Nationalization of Banks*

On 1 September 1982, President Portillo voiced his dramatic resolution to Mexico's economic turbulence. He spoke to the people of Mexico: 'Mexico's private banking system has postponed the nation's interest, and it has promoted, propitiated, and even instrumented speculation and capital flight …'.[236] The solution, he said, was to nationalize the banks.

The legislature passed the 'Decreto que establece la nacionalizacion de la banca privada'[237] to bring Mexico's entire commercial banking assets (an amount estimated to be three trillion pesos)[238] under government ownership.

During the four full years of nationalization,[239] the government controlled Mexican banks. As a result, they faced no competition from the outside or from each other. The government set mandatory interest rates and controlled exchange rates. Yet, due to the huge foreign debts Mexico owed, capital continued to flow out of the country, inflation rose, and the exchange rate dropped to new lows. In 1987, the peso-to-dollar ratio was approximately 3,000:1.[240] Annual inflation was over 150 per cent.[241]

---

[233] Decreto que establece reglas para atender requiremientos de divisas, a tipos de cambios especiales, 373 *Diario Official de la Federación* (18 August 1982), p. 2.

[234] Decreto para proveer la adecuado observancia del articulo 80 de la ley monetaria de los Estados Unidos Mexicanos, en los casos a que hace referencia, 373 *Diario Official de la Federación* (18 August 1982), p. 6.

[235] Davis (note 230 *supra*), at 81–2, n.35.

[236] *Ibid.* at 83, footnotes omitted, citing John P. Cogan Jr, 'Privatization of the Mexican Banking System: Quetzalcoatl and the Bankers' (1992) 23 St Mary's LJ 753, 756.

[237] 374 *Diario Official de la Federación* (1 September 1982), p. 3. In November 1982, the Mexican Constitution was amended to require that the government (and only the government) provide banking services to the Mexican people. Decreto que modifica el articulo 73 en sus fracciones X y XVIII, y adiciona los articulos 28 y 123, apartado B de la Constitucion Politica de los Estados Unidos Mexicanos, 375 *Diario Official de la Federación* (17 November 1982), p. 7.

[238] Davis (note 230 *supra*), at 83, n.42, citing Ewell E. Murphy Jr, 'Expropriation and Aftermath: The Prospects for Foreign Enterprise in the Mexico of Miguel de la Madrid' (1983) 18 Tex Int'l LJ 431, 444.

[239] There were a few exceptions from the nationalization, significantly Citibank NA and the representative offices of foreign banks. See generally Davis (note 230 *supra*), at 82–4; *ibid.* at 83, n.47, referring to the fact that the choice of which banks were not nationalized was never adequately explained by the government.

[240] GAO (note 224 *supra*), at 31.

[241] *Ibid.*

2.3.1.3   Reprivatization

It was in the face of near economic catastrophe that President Miguel de la Madrid's administration decided to allow 34 per cent of the bank's non-voting shares to be sold to the public in order to raise much needed capital and build investor confidence in Mexico.[242] The 1987 reprivatization offerings, however, were limited to Mexican buyers.

When Carlos Salinas de Gortari assumed the Presidency in December 1988, the Mexican government committed itself to continuing and deepening de la Madrid's program of economic reform based on privatization. In May 1989, Mexico enacted a new foreign investment law, liberalizing the requirements on government approval of foreigners' plans for investing and extending the available investment opportunities for full foreign ownership. In December 1989, the Mexican stock market was opened to foreign investors. This liberalization furthered the influx of foreign funds to Mexico and reinforced the country's commitment to complete financial market reforms.[243] Seven months later, in June 1990, Mexico began to completely privatize its banks.[244] In 1992, the last of the 18 government-owned banks was sold.[245]

2.3.2   Mexico's Banks in the Early 1990s

2.3.2.1   Banking Market Structure

Mexico's banking system during the NAFTA negotiations was entirely owned by private Mexican investors, but was still suffering from the non-competitive, government-controlled banking environment of the nationalized period. Consequently, Mexican banks were widely viewed as much less developed than their counterparts in Canada and the United States were. The asset bases of the banks were weak due to portfolios burdened with a high (and increasing) percentage of overdue loans;[246]

---

[242] Davis (note 230 *supra*), at 86, n.68, and accompanying text, citing Cogan (note 236 *supra*), at 761.

[243] See generally GAO (note 224 *supra*), at 33–4, discussing Mexico's investment liberalizations of the late 1980s and early 1990s; Skiles (note 223 *supra*).

[244] Privatization was made legally possible through an amendment of the Constitution in June 1990. Decreto que deroga al parrafo quinto del articulo 28, 441 *Diario Official de la Federación* (27 June 1990), p. 2. Besides allowing for private ownership of banks, the Amendment also replaced the pre-nationalization procedure of granting a concession for bank establishment with a procedure requiring government authorization. Under the concession rules, the end of a concession resulted in the bank's loss of its assets to the government. Now with the authorization rules, banks are able to retain their assets even if authorization to continue operating is withdrawn. Davis (note 230 *supra*), at 87–8, n.79.

[245] The last bank to be privatized, Banco del Centro SA, was sold for 4.65 times more than its book value. The other banks also brought much higher than expected prices, and in the end, Mexico earned $12.9 billion on the sales—more than twice the original estimate by Salomon Brothers. See Cogan (note 236 *supra*), at 762–3.

[246] GAO (note 224 *supra*), at 48, reporting that the overall percentage of past due loans increased from 3.5 per cent in December 1991 to 8.5 per cent in March 1994. The number of overdue loans required Mexican banks to charge interest rates of 15–20 percentage points above the short term Mexican government treasury certificates. This in turn led to the danger of more defaults.

the number of products offered was limited, partially because of legal restrictions[247] and partially because of lack of expertise and technological infrastructure; and the use of new technologies and mechanization were far below that of developed countries' banking systems. Nevertheless, in terms of profitability, with between 0.9 per cent and 4.5 per cent rates of return on their assets, the Mexican banks of the late 1980s far surpassed the three largest US banks' returns of –0.6 to 1.1 per cent and the three largest Canadian banks' returns of 0.3 to 0.5 per cent during the same time frame.[248]

2.3.2.2   *Reasons Behind the Underdevelopment of Mexican Banking*

2.3.2.2.1   MACROECONOMIC FACTORS

Mexico's banking market itself, while growing, is small in comparison to even small developed countries. One of the reasons the banks were not able to develop lies in the economics of inflation and government borrowing that combined to drive the private sector to other financial institutions in search of funds. After the nationalizations of 1982, the Mexican banking authorities were able to raise the required capital reserve levels, and in this way garnered for the government a source of funds. The high interest rates of the mid-1980s, however, worsened the federal deficit problems and caused further inflation. Those private persons and businesses that were able to took their capital out of Mexico. Others began to invest in assets that were not as susceptible to inflation, such as government bonds. For financing, the private sector increasingly relied on non-bank sources of financing, with the result that the securities brokers experienced a tremendous growth at the expense of the banks.[249]

In addition, the economic recession's high inflation rates of the late 1980s combined with the economic reforms of the 1990s to lead to increases in private domestic consumption.[250] In 1991, out of a population of 81 million,

---

[247] Banks in Mexico cannot, e.g., offer clients repurchase agreements with some securities or hold open foreign exchange positions for customer portfolios. See Ignacio Trigueros, 'The Mexican Financial System and NAFTA', in Bulmer-Thomas *et al.* (eds), *Mexico and the North American Free Trade Agreement* (note 146 *supra*), at 51.

[248] Sidney Weintraub, Chandler Stolp and Leigh Boske, 'Banking', in *US-Mexican Free Trade: The Effect on Textiles and Apparel, Petrochemicals, and Banking in Texas*, Policy Report No. 5 (US-Mexican Policy Studies Program, Austin, TX, 1993), at 81–2, citing figures from Gary C. Hufbauer and Jeffrey J. Schott, *North American Free Trade: Issues and Recommendations* (Institute for International Economics, Washington, DC, 1992), at 313.

[249] One author reports that in the six years approaching 1990, the brokerage industry experienced a real growth of nearly 1,000 per cent. Skiles (note 223 *supra*) at 8, n.3 (net worth of brokerage firms between 1984 and 1990 increased from 14 billion pesos to 3.7 trillion pesos).

[250] For more on the specifics of the banking reforms of the 1980s and 1990s financial sector reforms, see *ibid*.

only 3.6 million Mexicans had bank accounts,[251] and brokerage firms' offers of money market investment plans were luring away many of the banks' customers that did exist.[252] In 1992, the private domestic savings rate as a percentage of GDP was 8.9, only half of what it was in 1988 (when it was 18.1).[253]

2.3.2.2.2   HIGH CONCENTRATION OF BANKING ASSETS

A second factor limiting the development of the Mexican banking market is a direct result of the nationalistic investment policies that have kept the foreign bankers out. Until the NAFTA increased competition for banking services from foreign bankers, the Mexican banking environment was highly concentrated and almost purely Mexican, with the large Mexican banks owned by a small number of extremely powerful families. Foreign investors were not interested in the allowed 34 per cent ownership of banks, as this was not enough to meet the threshold for minority share-holder rights under Mexico's law governing corporations. Of the nationally-owned banks, the largest three (Banamex, Bancomer, and Banca Serfin) owned one-half of the total banking assets in Mexico and more than one-half of all loans.[254] The one foreign commercial bank allowed to operate in Mexico immediately prior to the coming into effect of NAFTA, Citibank, was likely also deeply enmeshed with the inner circle of Mexican powerholders.[255]

---

[251] Davis (note 230 *supra*), at 104, n.181, citing Janet Duncan, 'Mexican Banks Begin 2nd Private Year With Optimism', Reuters, 1 July 1992, (available in LEXIS NSAmer Library, Mexico File).

[252] Weintraub *et al.* (note 248 *supra*), at 86.

[253] GAO (note 224 *supra*), at 44, (Bank of Mexico, chart 'Mexico's Private Domestic Savings Rate as a Percentage of GDP 1987–94'); Davis (note 230 *supra*), at 105, n.187 and accompanying text.

[254] Hufbauer and Schott (note 248 *supra*), at 308–9 (table 15.1). See Fernando Solís Soberon and Ignacio Trigueros, 'Bancos' in United Nations, *Mexico: Una Economia de Servicios*, UNCTAD/ITP/58, (United Nations, New York, 1991), pp. 93–113, at 94, reporting on the concentration of the Mexican banking market at the beginning of the 1990s, and indicating that the six national banks at that time owned 95.9 per cent of all banking assets in Mexico). See also *ibid*. at 95:

> Una excepción a lo anterior podría ser lo relacionado a las operaciones activas tradicionales de la banca. Dado que las instituciones más grandes se especializan en el financiamiento corporativo, en el que también las casas de bolsa tienen una participación intensa, el índice de concentración de la banca tendería a subestimar el grado de concentración verdadero.

noting that the degree of concentration underestimates the true extent market power, because of the competition banks face from securities brokerages in giving corporate loans.

[255] Citibank, as the only foreign bank not affected by the 1982 nationalization of banks, had six branches in Mexico, with assets of 1.4 per cent of the whole Mexican banking market. Department of the Treasury (note 148 *supra*), at 139.

In addition, the trend to further consolidate was strong. Banks merged with each other and started merging with stock brokerages to form 'financial groups', further concentrating the market for financial services.[256] Profitability soared, with a gross margin of profit at 10.2 per cent of assets in 1989–90.[257]

2.3.2.3   Strengths of the Mexican Banking System

Despite all of its weaknesses, in comparison to other developing countries, Mexico's banking system has been called 'among the most structurally advanced'.[258] Since 1976, Mexican banks have enjoyed the freedom of a universal banking system, allowing them to engage in securities underwriting as well as deposit-taking. In addition, branching is unlimited for Mexican-owned banks. Mexico's challenge, then, was to build on the structural framework of its banking legislation in such a way that both market concerns (efficiency, competitiveness) and safety concerns (stability of the system, soundness of individual banks) would be addressed.[259]

2.3.3   Controlling Legislation

The Mexican banking regulations have been in a state of great development since the commercial bank reprivatization of 1990. Commercial law principles as well as civil (and even criminal)[260] law principles govern various aspects of contract and securities law associated with banking,[261] and it is of great importance to determine into which of these frameworks any particular legal issue fits before attempting to solve it locally.[262]

---

[256] Trigueros (note 247 *supra*), at 43.
[257] Skiles (note 223 *supra*), at table 7 (OECD data).
[258] Weintraub *et al.* (note 248 *supra*), at 84.
[259] For a review of recent initiatives to improve the stability of the Mexican banking system through both strengthening the banks and by improving supervision by the government, see Christopher R. Rowley, 'Searching for Stability: Mexico's 1995 Banking System Reforms' (1998) 4:3 NAFTA: L & Bus Rev Am 30, 42–9.
[260] One article warns, 'In addition to the previously discussed legal requirements, the foreign creditor in Mexico should exercise caution with respect to the following: the somewhat gray distinction between the civil and criminal law and the use of charges of fraud and prejudgment incarceration as a negotiating tool ...'. David W. Banowsky and Carlos A. Gabuardi, 'Secured Credit Transactions in Mexico' (1994) 28:2 Int'l Law 263, 286, citing Dianne Solis, 'Commercial Risks, In Mexico, a Dispute Over a Business Deal May Land You in Jail', *Wall Street Journal*, 27 September 1993, p. 1.
[261] Banowsky and Gabuardi (note 260 *supra*), at 264. However, the authors warn, the particular subject matter of the contract 'will determine the particular statutes that govern such contract, the manner of enforcing the contract, and with respect to the pledge of personal property, will determine the manner of perfection'.
[262] Banowsky and Gabuardi (note 260 *supra*), at 286, encourage lawyers to be aware of both sets of laws, but to attempt to design projects to be subject to the Code of Commerce rather than the Civil Code if possible.

2.3.4 Constitution

The Mexican Constitution is the supreme law of the land.[263] It puts the power to charter and control banks with the federal government. As Mexican federal authorities are also in charge of overseeing the securities and insurance markets, Mexico has a single layer of banking authorities at the national level, unlike the US system of dual banking systems and the Canadian system where Provincial authorities have competencies over the non-bank financial activities. Theoretically, at least, complete financial service liberalization should encounter fewer legal barriers.

2.3.5 Ley de Instituciones de Crédito

The primary legislation governing bank establishment is the Ley de Instituciones de Crédito (the Credit Institutions Act of 1990; 'LIC').[264]

---

[263] The Mexican Constitution of 1917 was based to a large extent on the US Constitution, incorporating a three branch presidential-led government and principles of federalism. However, the actual balance of power within the government is quite different from the United States' version of republicanism. For an excellent overview of the Mexican legal system see James F. Smith, 'Confronting Differences in the United States and Mexican Legal Systems in the Era of NAFTA' (1993) 1:1 US-MexJ 85; note, '*Liberalismo Contra Democracia*: Recent Judicial Reform in Mexico' (1995) 108 Harv LJ 1919, describing the PRI's judicial reform program of 1994. See also Robert Freeman Smith, 'The American Revolution and Latin America: An Essay in Imagery, Perceptions, and Ideological Influence' (1978) 20:4 J Interam Stud & World Aff 421, discussing how the American Revolutionaries influenced the early Creole intellectuals; but see Carlos del Río Rodríguez, 'Judicial Review Seen from a Mexican Perspective' (1989–90) 20 Cal W Int'l LJ 7—'First I would like to make perfectly clear that the frequently repeated assertion found in text books on constitutional law, ... that the Mexican constituents of 1825 copied the badly translated copy of the United States Constitution ... is erroneous. In 1824 Mexico already had a rich constitutional tradition that could serve as a basis for drawing up the new constitution ...'.

James Smith emphasizes the strength of the executive in the Mexican governmental system as being one that not only heavily influences the promulgation of laws and regulations, the way public funds are spent, and the commercial policy of the nation domestically and internationally, but also one that plays a significant role in the decision-making of the Mexican Supreme Court. See Smith (*supra*), at 98–104. For more on the historical development of the Mexican court system see generally del Río Rodríguez (*supra*). See also '*Liberalismo Contra Democracia*' (*supra*) at 1928–31; *ibid*. at 192–9:

> Prior to the Judicial Reform, the Supreme Court of Mexico consisted of twenty-one Justices (*Ministros de Justicia*) and up to five additional *supernumerario* Justices. [footnote 64: The appointment of the five *supernumerario* Justices depended on circumstances, such as the case load of the Court or absences of regular members. In effect, however, the ability of the President to add the *supernumerario* Justices gave him a power to 'pack' the Court at will ..., adding to the President's immense power to replace Justices.] ... It was thought that the large number of Justices, sitting either en banc or on panels, would alleviate backlog. In practice, this assumption proved false and may have served to dilute the power and prestige of the Court, making individual Justices less accountable for their jurisprudence and more vulnerable to pressures from the executive and legislative branches.

[264] Text of the LIC can be found on the Mexican government's internet site at >www.cnvv.gov.mx<. See also Weintraub *et al.* (note 248 *supra*) at 95.

In legislating for the reprivatization of Mexico's banks, the LIC provides for two types of banks: 'multiple' (or commercial) banks and development banks[265] and sets out the ownership restrictions and permissible activities of each.[266] The LIC is based on attempts by the Mexican legislature 'to guarantee competent, Mexican-majority ownership of Mexican banks at a fair price'.[267] A summary review of the Act's provisions proves that at least the majority-ownership aim was achieved. If projections are correct, the NAFTA should assist in achieving the other two goals.

2.3.5.1   Establishment of Mexican Banks

Under the LIC, the Mexican banking authority responsible for the licensing of banks is the Secretaría de Hacienda y Crédito Público (SHCP). The SHCP may allow a bank to establish itself under a license as a national, regional, or multi-regional institution.[268] The decision as to which license to give is generally based on the desired area of activity, and consequently is left to the business planners of the applicant bank. While the national banks are typically engaged in all areas of commercial banking, including retail and investment banking, corporate financing, trade financing, and portfolio management, the multi-regional banks tend to specialize in particular industrial sectors and in creating financial packages for local industry.[269] Regional banks are similar to the multiregional institutions, in that they exist mainly to assist local businesses, but development banks have an additional role of furthering the government's attempts to decentralize financial activities.[270]

In order to approve a license application, the SHCP must ascertain that the applicant complies with the standards set out in the LIC. The applicant must, for instance, deposit at least 10 per cent of the minimum operating capital and the net capital must remain at least 6 per cent of the institution's total active and passive loan business and risked assets.[271]

Second, the applicant may not, with the proposed grant of a license, own more than 5 per cent of the total commercial banking capital in Mexico unless the SHCP specifically grants an exception to this rule. In no case may the individual own more than 10 per cent of the total.[272]

Finally, the proposed board of directors must be composed exclusively of Mexican nationals. The applicants must also show that each director is known for having high moral standards (*reconocida calidad moral*).[273]

---

[265] Solís Soberon and Trigueros (note 254 *supra*), at 98.
[266] Weintraub *et al.* (note 248 *supra*), at 95.
[267] *Ibid.*
[268] Department of the Treasury (note 148 *supra*), at 142.
[269] Soberon and Trigueros (note 254 *supra*), at 94–5; Olin L. Wethington, *Financial Market Liberalization: The NAFTA Framework* (Shepard's/McGraw-Hill, New York, 1994), p. 25, n.12.
[270] *Ibid.*
[271] Soberon and Trigueros (note 254 *supra*), at 99.
[272] *Ibid.*
[273] *Ibid.*

2.3.5.2 Branching

Mexico has no prohibition on the establishment of branches by Mexican-owned banks. While the banking license restricts the geographic market which the particular bank may serve, there are no further limits on the establishment of branch offices to serve customers. Indeed, the 19 commercial banks that existed in Mexico in 1990 had a network of 4,487 branches throughout the country in that year.[274] Significantly, the concentration trend that occurred following the reprivatization did not affect the number of banking locations. The large banks' numbers decreased, but the branches remain open. This not only allows the large banks to attract customers in all regions, but also permits them to absorb many of the market's new customers, further contributing to the high concentration of asset ownership in Mexico's banking system.[275]

2.3.6 Ownership of Banks

The rules governing the ownership of banks are divided into two categories: those for development banks and those for commercial banks.

2.3.6.1 Development Banks

Development banks were required to be wholly owned by Mexican nationals. In view of their limited purpose, one can view this restriction as a protection of the Government's control over macroeconomic policy. The main development bank, Nacional Financiera (Nafinsa), owns 49 per cent of all the assets of the seven development banks.[276] Another 24 per cent of the entire assets are owned by the national export finance bank Bancomext.[277]

2.3.6.2 Commercial Banks

At the time of the NAFTA negotiations, ownership of commercial banks was no longer subject to the same restrictions as it was for development banks. This reflects the realization by the de la Madrid and Salinas administrations that the financial service landscape of Mexico needed greater foreign participation if the Mexican economy was to be able to attract much needed foreign investment. The possibility to reign-in such foreign participation, however, remains in the law.

Under the 1990 law, foreign investment could comprise a minority ownership of the shares of commercial banks. In one of the two investment structures available for a Mexican bank, there was an allowance to authorize up to four different forms of stock issuance for voting shares: 'A', 'B', 'C', and 'L'

---

[274] Weintraub *et al.* (note 248 *supra*), at 86.
[275] Soberon and Trigueros (note 254 *supra*), at 94, 'Sin embargo, si se considera el número de bancos, se tiene que la operación de la banca comercial en México es relativamente muy intensiva en sucursales'.
[276] Department of the Treasury (note 148 *supra*) at 143.
[277] *Ibid.*

shares. A fifth form of stock was newly created to apply to foreign controlled banks.

'A' stock was required to make up 51 per cent or more of the total issuance. As the most powerful shares by virtue of their majority ownership, A stocks could only be owned by Mexican individuals, the Mexican government, development banks (which are in turn owned by Mexicans), and financial holding companies.[278]

The second group of shares, 'B' stocks, could represent the ownership of up to 49 per cent of the bank. Any legal person qualifying for 'A' stock was permitted to also own 'B' stock, as could wholly-Mexican corporations and institutional investors.[279]

The final type of voting stock authorized under the Credit Institutions Act of 1990 was 'C' stock. These shares could be offered to foreigners, but the total issue was not to exceed 30 per cent of the ownership of the bank.[280]

The issuance of 'L' shares was permitted in an amount equal to 30 per cent of the voting capital. 'L' shares could also be offered to foreigners, but were required to be non-voting, and thus were interesting only from the passive investment perspective.

The second possible investment regime did permit majority ownership of banks by foreigners. With the 'F' class of shares, at least 51 per cent of a foreign bank's subsidiary established in Mexico could be owned by non-Mexican nationals.[281] There were other limits on such investments, however. First, all such majority foreign ownerships must have been authorized by the Ministry of Finance. In addition, the ownership was restricted to 6 per cent or less of the aggregate capital in the Mexican banking market, and to 25 per cent or less 'as a proportion of total market size'.[282]

2.3.7   Scope of Permissible Activities

2.3.7.1   Development Banks

Development banks are limited to providing funds to and for the government. Besides funding public works, the development banks are mainly involved with financing agriculture, foreign trade, and small businesses through loans and advisory services.[283] If needed, however, the development banks may purchase direct equity ('temporary direct equity participation').[284]

2.3.7.2   Commercial Banks

Commercial banks, the more common type of bank in Mexico, may engage in various banking activities. Before Mexico's law reform of 1975 changed

---

[278] Weintraub *et al.* (note 248 *supra*), at 96.
[279] *Ibid.*
[280] *Ibid.*
[281] Mexican Investment Board (note 227 *supra*), at 36.
[282] *Ibid.*
[283] *Ibid.* at 35.
[284] See Nacional Financiera for more.

the banking system, there was a legal requirement of the separation of banking activities among specialized banks similar to that existing in the United States today. Although even at that time 'affiliations' between banks could be made in the form of limited banking groups, the 1975 reform allowed for the complete consolidation of banking activities in 'multiple',[285] or universal, banks.[286] Whereas prior to 1975, Mexican banks were 'deposit banks' or 'savings banks', 'mortgage banks', 'savings and loans', or 'trusts', or 'financial societies' or 'capital societies',[287] since the reform commercial banks have been allowed to take retail deposits and issue loans as well as to participate in investment banking activities and the selling of securities, to deal in government securities, and to offer cash management services.[288] Insurance activities by banks are still restricted to separately incorporated subsidiaries of the banks.

Before the nationalization of Mexico's commercial banks by the government, these multiple banks were able to form arrangements with other financial institutions to provide for a variety of services. In 1990, the new Law for the Regulation of Financial Groups once again granted commercial banks the right to form financial groups. In connection with at least two other financial service providing institutions, the banks may form an umbrella organization called a *grupo financiero*. These financial groups combine a commercial banking institution with at least two different types of related institutions: a securities brokerage; an insurance company; a leasing company; a foreign exchange firm; or non-banks. These are then legally arranged in a holding company structure to separate liability.[289] In reality, the result has been 'a blurring of functions between banks and brokerage firms, as activities previously conducted by brokerage firms, such as money market operations and foreign exchange trading, have been transferred to the bank in the financial group'.[290]

---

[285] In Spanish, 'bancas múltiples'. See Soberon and Trigueros (note 2:54 *supra*), at 98.
[286] Department of the Treasury (note 148 *supra*), at 140, reporting that the first multiple bank began operating in 1978.
[287] *Ibid.*
[288] Weintraub *et al.* (note 248 *supra*), at 98.
[289] Mexican Investment Board (note 227 *supra*), at 38.
[290] Department of the Treasury (note 148 *supra*), at 141. See also statements of Robert Lyon, Head of International Department, Mexican Bankers Association, at the First Meeting of Representatives of the USCIB, the Mexican Bankers Association, and the Canadian Bankers Association for the Drafting of Guidelines for the Clearing and Return of Checks between Canada, the United States and Mexico, 27–28 July 1992 (Tuscon, AZ):

> The financial system is becoming much more compact and the operational needs of Mexican banks will expand greatly from a strictly commercial banking operation to a more universal banking operation. There are basically two structures: one is a holding company structure which allows for a financial holding company to own the bank, a brokerage house, a leasing company, a factoring company, or a warehouse in terms of different financial entities. Formerly, we had a structure similar to the Glass-Steagall law in the US ... The services offered now by the holding company structure or by the association structure, which is very similar, will completely broaden the activities.

> in Mordy Karsch and Boris Kozolchyk (transcript eds), *Towards Seamless Borders*, Vol. 1. p. 357 (Appendix).

Furthermore, a 1993 amendment to the LIC permits financial leasing activities by banks in an attempt to increase the Mexican banks' global competitiveness.[291]

2.3.8   Specific Provisions for Foreign Banks

As set out above, prior to the NAFTA, foreign banks (with the exception of Citibank NA) had no active role in the Mexican banking system following the nationalizations of 1982. Though allowed in the form of representative offices, foreign commercial banks were limited in their ownership of total assets in Mexico and could only own a minority share in any banking institution. With no possibility of controlling a bank and its management, the result was that—despite extraordinarily high profit margins—Mexico was not an attractive market for foreign banks.

Since the NAFTA, the regulations governing non-NAFTA foreign banks have been liberalized significantly. First, the general banking law was expanded upon with a chapter devoted to the topic of foreign bank subsidiaries. Secondly, the allowance for foreign participation in Mexican bank ownership has been progressively extended.

2.3.8.1   Foreign Bank Subsidiaries

In 1993, the Mexican government announced that the LIC was to be adjusted in accordance with NAFTA.[292] Among the adjustments was the addition of provisions governing foreign banking subsidiaries. These provisions, found in the Second Title, Chapter III ('De las Filiales de Instituciones Financieras del Exterior') provides that the SHCP is authorized to grant licenses to foreign banks to establish subsidiaries in Mexico, subject to the existence of an international agreement between Mexico and the government of the foreign bank.[293] This chapter gives the guidelines for foreign banking participation in the Mexican market.[294]

The changes mandated by NAFTA are discussed in detail in Part II, and so will not be discussed here. What is important at this point, however, is the fact that the Mexican government has exceeded its obligations under the NAFTA by permitting greater ownership of Mexican banking assets than required and by affording investors from more than merely Canada and the United States the opportunity to take part in the Mexican banking system.

---

[291] Department of the Treasury (note 148 *supra*), at 143.

[292] 'Motivos de las Reformas y Adiciones a La Ley de Instituciones de Crédito', decreed 14 December 1993 (published in *Diario Official*, 23 December 1993), and text is on the Mexican
banking regulators' internet site at >www.cnbv.gov.mx<.

[293] See LIC Art. 45A-D.

[294] There are parallel provisions for other forms of financial institutions. See, e.g., Ley General de Organizaciones y Actividades Auxiliares del Crédito, the Second Title, Chapter III*bisI* (Art. 45*bis* allowing for foreign subsidiaries of credit auxiliaries, capitalized with 'F' shares and, optionally, 'B' shares).

2.3.8.2   Foreign Ownership of Mexican Banks

The amendments to the LIC in 1995 and 1998 were among the most significant changes to the law.[295] Among the relevant changes for commercial banks was the elimination of 'C' shares, the broadening of access to 'B' shares to foreigners, and the granting of 'L' shares limited voting rights.[296] In particular, these changes had the effect of opening up a foreigner's ownership in a Mexican bank to 49 per cent.[297] In addition, the normal individual ownership limit is now 5 per cent of the bank's capital, with a possibility that the SHCP can authorize an individual to own up to 20 per cent of the capital.[298] The individual limit on owning aggregate banking assets in Mexico was also raised: now a single foreign entity may acquire up to 6 per cent of the net banking assets.[299]

2.3.8.3   Remaining Restrictions

Several elements of the banking law have not changed, however. First, development banks are still off-limits to foreign investors.[300] Secondly, the general director of a commercial bank must still be a Mexican citizen.[301] And, perhaps most importantly, there is still an official policy of 'keeping the Mexican banking landscape in Mexican hands'.[302]

---

[295] For a review of the 1995 Amendments, see Rowley (note 259 *supra*), at 39–42.
The Mexican Executive Branch issued a bulletin announcing proposed changes to the LIC in March 1998. *Boletín de Prensa* 004/98 (24 March 1998). Among the changes signalled would be the integration of the differing ownership categories into a single series of shares. *Ibid*.

[296] See LIC, Second Title, Chapter III, Arts 14–15.

[297] See *ibid*. at Art. 11 (requiring 'A' shares to compose a minimum of 51 per cent of a bank's ownership, but allowing the remaining 49 per cent to be composed of 'B' shares or a combination of 'A' and 'B' shares).

[298] *Ibid*. at Art. 17.

[299] *Ibid*.

[300] *Ibid*. at Art. 33.

[301] *Ibid*. at Art. 24.

[302] See *ibid*. at Art. 17 ('Al efecto, la citada Secretaría tomará en cuenta la composición del capital de la institución de que se trate y la participación extranjera en la misma, *a fin de que el sistema de pagos del país esté en todo tiempo controlado por mexicano*s') (emphasis added).

Part II
Chapter Fourteen and the NAFTA Parties

3. NAFTA Financial Service Provisions

'The heart of the NAFTA is contained in Chapter 14'[1]

3.1 OVERVIEW

Chapter Fourteen of the NAFTA deals exclusively with financial services.[2] Its provisions set out a framework for a controlled liberalization of trade in banking, insurance, and securities services over 15 years. While a 15-year 'transition period' may seem a long time for achieving even those trade preferences that are promised (which is not complete integration of markets), the agreement to Chapter Fourteen is, in itself, a major achievement: for the first time an extensive liberalization of financial services was placed in the context of an economically-oriented trade agreement.

Incorporating by reference parts of NAFTA Chapter Eleven (Investment), the Labor and Environmental Side Agreements, several of the Canada-United States Free Trade Agreement provisions on financial services, and subject to an extensive annex, Chapter Fourteen is more substantive than it appears from its relatively brief main text.

In this Part, the terms and provisions of Chapter Fourteen are set forth individually. Most of the Agreement's drafting is clear, and in the absence of any official interpretative opinions to suggest otherwise, almost all of the terms can be reasonably interpreted through a plain meaning reading. There are important exceptions to this generalization, however. Although the approach taken here to address these problematic provisions is one heavily influenced by the norms of international trade

---

[1] Valerie J. McNevin, 'Policy Implications of the NAFTA for the Financial Services Industry' (1994) 5 Colo J Int'l Env'l L & Pol 369, 371. Ms McNevin then adds, 'This is where the real action under the NAFTA and job creation will be'. *Ibid.* n.12.

[2] This is unlike the financial service regulatory structure in the World Trade Organization (WTO). In the WTO, financial services are included within the scope of the General Agreement on Trade in Services. Although there is a special annex with specific rules for trade in financial services, the banking, insurance, securities, and other financial industries are subject to the same basic framework as are all other services.

law, it is recognized that financial service law might understand them to have a slightly different meaning. Therefore, where possible, an interpretation of terms that combines the goals of the different legal systems of trade law and financial services law is suggested.

Structurally, the Chapter Fourteen provisions are presented to a large extent in the order found in the Agreement, but there are departures from this order in certain instances for the sake of clarity of explanation. After an introductory note on the process of negotiating the Chapter, for example, there is a discussion of the institutional structure of the financial services provisions of the NAFTA, followed by a portion setting out the scope of the application (the text of the Chapter itself begins with the scope of the agreement).

3.2   THE NEGOTIATING OF CHAPTER FOURTEEN

The NAFTA negotiations were driven from the beginning predominantly by the economic interests of the Parties.[3] The Mexican government wanted secured access to the US market for Mexican goods, the United States wanted the opportunity to invest in a stable Mexican economy, and the Canadian government wanted to be included in the liberalizations of the other North American markets so as not to jeopardize its trade preferences with the United States. The negotiations on Chapter Fourteen reflected these interests. According to one of the negotiators, '[a]ll three participating countries believed that a liberal financial services regime would facilitate the efficient flow of capital between the countries and thereby promote economic growth',[4] so from the outset some degree of liberalization of the Mexican financial sector was foreseeable. The issues of contention became how much liberalization and how soon.[5]

---

[3]   See *supra* Part I. But see Jeffrey Simser, 'Financial Services Under NAFTA: A Starting Point' (1994–95) 10 Banking & Fin L Rev 185, 188, claiming that '(d)espite the spirited debates on the economic impact of NAFTA ..., NAFTA is neither a piece of domestic legislation designed to create jobs, nor a mere agreement designed to foster trade among three nations. NAFTA is a carefully conceived foreign policy product'.

[4]   Olin L. Wethington, *Financial Market Liberalization: The NAFTA Framework* (Shepard's/McGraw-Hill, New York, 1994), p. 4.

[5]   *Ibid.* at 18–19, observations 1 and 2 that negotiating teams were in general agreement as to the significance of their goal of liberalizing financial services throughout the NAFTA area and that the failure of the negotiations would be the worst possible scenario); *ibid.* at 55:

> Much of the NAFTA negotiations in the financial services sector concerned the elements of the transition period—its length, the speed of the liberalization during the transition, the extent of market share for United States and Canadian firms ... and certain special rules that would apply only to the transition period.

Two of the most prominent US trade economists, writing before the NAFTA was completed, recommended a 'rapid liberalization' of the Mexican financial services economy for the benefit of all Parties, but acknowledged that this would be accompanied by problems. They write:

While it is generally acknowledged that the NAFTA Party who will benefit the most from the NAFTA package is Mexico,[6] in financial services it was Mexico that conceded the most, to the overwhelming benefit of the Canadian and US financial service industries (and to the short-term detriment of the Mexican financial service industry). Chapter Fourteen thus represents the price paid by Mexico for the rest of the NAFTA.[7] As one commentator said,

---

(Contd.)

Rapid liberalization would quickly bring the benefits of a highly competitive financial system, but it runs into three practical difficulties. First, it would hasten the default of thinly capitalized and weakly managed local insurance companies and multiregional banks. Second, it could overwhelm the vital, but still small, Mexican securities firms. Third, and this refers mainly to the banking system, it would strike at the heart of Mexican 'financial sovereignty'.

Gary Clyde Hufbauer and Jeffrey J. Schott, *North American Free Trade: Issues and Recommendations* (Institute for International Economics, Washington, DC, 1992), p. 324. But later, after the financial crises in Asia, two other authors emphasized the dangers of liberalizing the financial system without ensuring that there are sufficient supervisory structures in place first:

The culprit in these crises was not internationalization per se. The culprit was not that Indonesia or Thailand had opened their capital accounts … The culprit was weaknesses in domestic financial systems that should have been corrected before or during internationalization. These weaknesses included inadequate oversight and supervision of financial institutions, inadequate risk assessment by banks, and directed lending. In addition, exchange rates were allowed to become overvalued … More financial reform preceding internationalization, not less, might have reduced or even eliminated the full-blown financial and economic crises that followed the currency depreciations.

Wendy Dobson and Pierre Jacquet, *Financial Services Liberalization in the WTO* (Institute for International Economics, Washington, DC, 1998), pp. 10–11.

[6] See, e.g., US International Trade Commission, Pub. No. 2596, 'Potential Impact on the US Economy and Selected Industries of the North American Free-Trade Agreement' (January 1993), p. viii (long-term gains to the United States and Canada estimated to be 0.5 per cent GDP or less while the gains to Mexico's GDP are estimated to be anywhere from 0.1 per cent to 11.4 per cent in the long-term). See also Sidney Weintraub, 'Modeling the Industrial Effects of NAFTA', in Nora Lustig, Barry P. Bosworth and Robert Z. Lawrence (eds), *Assessing the Impact: North American Free Trade* (Brookings Institution, Washington, DC, 1992), pp. 109–33, explaining and analyzing the various economic models used to predict the effects of the NAFTA on the Parties' industrial sectors.

[7] Professor of international law and trade in financial services specialist Joel Trachtman is also of this view. See Joel P. Trachtman, 'Trade in Financial Services Under GATS, NAFTA and the EC: A Regulatory Jurisdiction Analysis' (1995) 34 Colum J Trnsnt'l L 37, 58. Beside its commitment to liberalizing its financial services sector, Mexico had many other adjustments to make in implementing the NAFTA. See Sergio López-Ayllón, 'Comments', in Paul Demaret, Jean-François Bellis, and Gonzalo García Jiménez (eds), *Regionalism and Multilateralism After the Uruguay Round: Convergence, Divergence and Interaction* (Institut d'études Juridiques Européennes, University of Liège, Liège, 1997), pp. 251–64, at 255 ('It should be noted that the 'cost' Mexico had to pay to prepare for and adapt to the new circumstances, including the negotiation and implementation of NAFTA, was very significant … Mexico had to modify nearly 75 per cent of its domestic legal system as a result of the new orientation of the economic growth model and opening of trade').

'From a political standpoint, the [US] perspective is that if there were no financial services agreement, there would have been no NAFTA'.[8]

The Chapter Fourteen negotiating teams were established early in the overall negotiation process by the ministries of finance in each Party. The Canadian team consisted of Bill Bryson, Nicholas LePan, and Pierre Sauvé, and was led by Frank Swedloff for the Canadian Department of Finance. The United States team, composed of members of the Department of Commerce and the Department of the Treasury, was under the leadership of attorney Olin Wethington and the legal guidance of Keith Palzer. The Mexican Ministry of Finance and Public Affairs created a negotiation team with Guillermo Ortiz Martinez and Jose Angel Gurría as chief negotiators.[9]

Unlike many of the areas of NAFTA that were hotly and openly debated, the negotiations on Chapter Fourteen were accomplished quietly among the government officials and interested industry members with little attention from the press or consumer groups. In the United States for example, the negotiation's decision-making body included a formal advisory committee composed of the Department of Commerce and the Office of the US Trade Representative combined with an Industry Advisory Committee. This trilateral group was formally responsible for the details of drafting. Informally, industry organizations such as the Coalition of Service Industries, the American Financial Services Association, the Finance Companies Organization, and the major commercial and investment banks were very active in promoting policy goals that would be to their benefit.[10] Assisted by periodic updates from the Executive Branch on the status of the negotiations, as well as by individual meetings with the negotiators, the industry members were able to follow the negotiations 'like hawks' and ensure that the end result would address their competitive needs.[11]

From the perspective of trade law, it is significant that the NAFTA negotiations on financial services took place contemporaneously with the financial services negotiations under the World Trade Organization's

---

[8] Comment of Ms. Powers, 'Discussion of the Regulation of Financial Services Under NAFTA' (1993) 1:1 US-Mex LJ 81, 83.

[9] The Mexican negotiators' personal conviction of the need to liberalize Mexico's financial sector was significant for the relatively smooth process of drafting Chapter Fourteen. The mainly-US educated Mexican negotiators had a faith in the benefits of free capital markets that was left unswayed by popular sentiments not to accede to US and Canadian desires for Mexico's opening its doors to northern financial firms. The governmental system of Mexico, under the leadership of economic-reform minded President Carlos Salinas de Gortari, allowed the negotiators to avoid political retaliation from the banking community for promises made under Chapter Fourteen.

[10] See Letter from Mr Llewellyn Pascoe to The Honorable Henry B. Gonzales (25 October 1993) and attached list of private sector organizations consulted during the negotiations of Chapter Fourteen, found appended to 'Abuses Within the Mexican Political Regulatory and Judicial Systems and Implications for the North American Free Trade Agreement (NAFTA)' 103d Cong., 1st Sess. 53, 57–76 (8 November 1993).

[11] Telephone interview with Keith Palzer, legal consultant for US negotiating team on Chapter Fourteen and GATS financial service provisions (10 October 1996).

General Agreement on Trade in Services (GATS).[12] Some of the negotiators were involved in both sets of discussions, and all were at least aware of the proposed GATS texts. Moreover, the NAFTA negotiators worked consciously to make the NAFTA text GATS-compatible.[13] The ideas of ensuring a right of establishment and providing national treatment to Party financial institutions, for example, as well as the exceptions for prudential concerns are crafted to dovetail with those of the GATS.[14]

The NAFTA and WTO approaches to financial services are not identical, however. The underlying perspective of Chapter Fourteen differs from that in GATS. In GATS, the obligations set out a rule-oriented framework for liberalization of trade in services.[15] In NAFTA the approach is more specific with institutionally-based obligations.[16] That is, rather than setting out principles of liberalization, the NAFTA focuses on how institutions are to be treated.[17] The coverage is thus more comprehensive, while less flexible.[18] Moreover, as the NAFTA only had to take into account the interests of three countries, two of whom already had close financial relations, the NAFTA negotiators were able to achieve a much greater degree of detail and completeness than were the 83 states represented at the multilateral trade negotiations in Geneva.

---

[12] Simser (note 3 *supra*), at 201–2. The GATS negotiations were accomplished under the Uruguay Rounds of negotiation. The Uruguay Rounds were started with the Punta del Este Declaration of Ministers in September 1986. Most of the negotiations were ended with the signing of the Marrakesh Agreement on 15 April 1994.

[13] Telephone interview with Keith Palzer. See Simser (note 3 *supra*), at 202 ('observers should not be too suprised to discover a number of parallels between the approaches taken in NAFTA and in GATT').

[14] The United States' ultimate rejection of the GATS' unconditional MFN provision in the Uruguay Round came only after the completion of the NAFTA.

[15] See generally Simser (note 3 *supra*), at 202–11, explaining NAFTA Financial Service provisions, with references to differences to the GATS approach to similar concepts.

[16] Wethington (note 4 *supra*), at 67, commenting that the institutional perspective was a disappointment to the United States; the US negotiators urged a 'financial activities' approach to 'provide a more secure route in drafting terms to comprehensive coverage of the financial services field'.

[17] A Mexican author notes that the Chapter Fourteen focus on institutions (as opposed to products) is similar to the regulatory focus in Mexico. Ignacio Trigueros, 'The Mexican Financial System and NAFTA', in Victor Bulmer-Thomas, Nikki Craske and Mónica Serrano (eds), *Mexico and the North American Free Trade Agreement: Who Will Benefit?* (St Martin's Press, New York, 1994), pp. 43–57, at 48.

[18] It is questionable how appropriate an institutions-based financial service agreement is in light of the changes in the industries that come under this framework. In the United States, for example, although much of the financial services legislation is aimed at banking, insurance, or securities companies, these sectors show an increasing interest in supplying similar products. Some commentators now propose a product-oriented regulatory framework. Craig A. Simmons and Stephen C. Swain, 'Girding for Competition' (1992) GAO J No. 15, 3, 9:

> But it is important to remember that, in the long run, what is least important about modernization is the particular institutional arrangement that provides financial services … The truth may be that, in time, it will no longer be important whether banks, securities firms, or any other kinds of institutions are the ones that will eventually serve the public—only that the public be served.

From the perspective of financial services law, the NAFTA Chapter Fourteen provisions are more foreign. As most of the negotiators came from a trade or free-market economic background, the main Chapter Fourteen provisions demonstrate a firm commitment to the principles of free trade (market access, non-discriminatory treatment, arbitration-based dispute settlement procedures) and a lesser consideration of the interests of financial service regulators and practitioners. The exceptions and reservations to the trade principles are the purest examples of truly 'financial service' rules in the Chapter.

However, despite this heavy trade-orientation to Chapter Fourteen, disputes arising from financial service industry concerns are to be decided by financial experts.[19] Therefore, the financial services approach to the trade terms must be considered as extremely important in the interpretation of Chapter Fourteen provisions from a practical perspective.

3.3   LEGAL STATUS OF CHAPTER FOURTEEN PROVISIONS

3.3.1   International Legal Status of Chapter Fourteen

As an international agreement, the NAFTA binds the Parties to their obligations as sovereign states. Thus, Chapter Fourteen, like the other NAFTA Chapters, is subject to the trilateral dispute settlement procedures.[20] These provisions ensure that implementation of the Agreement by one Party can be challenged by another Party if former Party believes the Agreement to be violated. If the judges, or panelists, agree with the charges, the Party can be held liable for action or fines. However, none of the Parties can be forced to abide by the treaty, as none has acknowledged giving up any national sovereignty to the NAFTA institutions.

International law itself does not have a hierarchy among international agreements. Rather, all international treaties, unless otherwise qualified, have the same level of validity.[21] Thus, when two international treaties require efforts in one area of law that have an impact on another area of law so as to

---

[19] See discussion of dispute settlement, 3.18 *infra*.

[20] For more details on the dispute settlement provisions applying to Chapter Fourteen, see 3.18 *infra*.

[21] The question of the validity of contradictory treaty norms among treaties enacted at different times poses some problems in international law. The Vienna Convention sets out a 'later in time' rule (*lex posterior*) for 'treaties relating to the same subject matter', but the general principle that the subsequent treaty prevails must logically fail when the main subjects regulated by the treaties are different. Rules of speciality (*lex specialis*) and the nature of the provision in dispute (protection of fundamental rights or the securing of business interests), for example, affect the heirarchy of treaty provisions.

jeopardize one or the other agreements, problems arise.[22] The interaction of other international law obligations with the NAFTA provisions is provided for in large part by the Agreement itself, such as the trumping of several international environmental agreements[23] and the continued effectiveness of bilateral tax treaties despite potential conflicts with the NAFTA terms.[24]

A significant example of the potential conflict between international law instruments that is not addressed by the NAFTA text is the existence of the Canada-United States Free Trade Agreement. That bilateral treaty is officially suspended by implementing legislation.[25] If, however, either the Canadian or United States government decides to withdraw from the NAFTA, the CUFTA will resume effectiveness upon the date of withdrawal.[26]

3.3.2 Status of Chapter Fourteen Within the Parties' National Courts

The question of how to ensure the effectiveness of international trade agreements within a participating state is the subject of a great deal of literature and debate. One of the main lines of thought draws on the idea of direct effect, or self-execution of treaty provisions within the national law framework of a Party to the treaty. It is unnecessary to put forth the arguments of those supporting the direct effect of treaties and those opposing direct effect here.[27] What is important for present purposes is to know that the NAFTA does not enjoy direct effect in the United States and Canada, but does in Mexico.

---

[22] While the WTO was being negotiated (1986–93), and indeed after it was was negotiated, there were governmental studies undertaken to remedy or prevent conflicts between the trade rules and the obligations facing states under multilateral envionmental agreements. The Committee on Trade and Environment met periodically until 1997, when it became temporarily inactive, but did not come to any final consensus on the problems investigated. The March 1999 High Level Symposium on Trade and Environment was also a disappointment, with a mere repetition of the same arguments that had been made since the topic emerged.

[23] NAFTA Art. 104 (Relation to Environmental and Conservation Agreements); see discussion of this provision, 3.15.5 *supra*.

[24] NAFTA Art. 2103:2 (general exception for provisions of international tax conventions).

[25] See Office of the President of the United States, The North American Free Trade Agreement Implementation Act Statement of Administrative Action B(1)(c) at 8. As most of CUFTA's provisions were incorporated in an expanded form, the effect of the suspension is not noticeable.

[26] See *ibid*. ('The suspension will remain in effect for such time as the two governments are parties to the NAFTA').

[27] For the major debating positions about self-execution in international trade law see, e.g., John H. Jackson, 'Status of Treaties in Domestic Legal Systems: A Policy Analysis' (1992) 86 Am J Int'l L 310; Ernst-Ulrich Petersmann, 'The Dispute Settlement System of the World Trade Organization and the Evolution of the GATT Dispute Settlement System Since 1948' (1994) 31 Common Mkt L Rev 1157; Piet Eeckhout, 'The Domestic Legal Status of the WTO Agreement: Interconnecting Legal Systems' (1997) 34 Common Mkt. L. Rev. 11; Thomas Cottier and Krista Nadakavukaren Schefer, 'The Relationship of WTO Law, National and Regional Law' (1998) 1:1 J Int'l Econ L 83; Giorgio Sacerdoti, 'The Application of GATT by Domestic Courts, European and Italian Case Law' (1976) 2 Italian YB Int'l L 225. For a more general discussion of direct effect, see Noemi Gal-Or, 'Private Party Direct Access: Comparison of the NAFTA and EU Disciplines' (1998) 21 BC Int'l & Comp L Rev 1, discussing 'direct' and 'non-direct' access to the agreements' provisions by non-state actors.

3.3.2.1   *Canada and the United States: No Direct Effect*

In Canada and the United States implementing legislation was needed before any of the provisions of NAFTA became effective.[28] Such legislation was passed promptly in both countries.[29] Canadian implementing legislation sets out that the law creates no private rights.[30] Thus, individuals

---

[28] Canada is, like the UK, a dualistic nation as regards the legal effect of international treaties. The CUFTA and the Uruguay Round Agreements are also non self-executing. See Canada-United States Free Trade Agreement Implementation Act, 1988, c. 65, s. 5; WTO Agreement Implementation Act, 1994, c.47, ss. 5 and 6. Canada's Constitution gives the federal government an exclusive authority to form treaties, but the federal political structure requires that certain areas of legislating be performed exclusively by Provincial governments. Thus, an international agreement such as the NAFTA, where the treaty extends to subject matters lying in both central and Provincial governmental spheres, is only viable for implementation if both levels of government are in agreement. This has been called the 'politics of accoMmodation'. Debra P. Steger, 'Canadian Implementation of the Agreement Establishing the World Trade Organization', in John H. Jackson and Alan Sykes (eds), *Implementing the Uruguay Round* (Clarendon, Oxford, 1997), pp. 243–83, at 243. Ms Steger also explains the 'double aspect doctrine' of Canadian Constitutional law, another result of the complex federalism in Canada:

> Sections 91 and 92 (of the Constitution, setting out the exclusive powers of the federal government and of the Provincial governments, respectively) are worded so generally that, even though the courts may try to be as definitive as possible, some powers inevitably overlap and conflict ... It is not always possible to define federal and provincial powers in a mutually exclusive manner ...
>   International trade obligations tend to be all-pervasive in the economy ... The double aspect doctrine enables the federal government to obtain jurisdiction over an international aspect of an otherwise wholly provincial or local subject-matter. However, it also means that the provinces retain their rights to legislate with respect to the same subject matter, as long as the legislation affects a local aspect.

Ibid. at 265. The United States is not firmly either monistic or dualistic. Instead, it is traditionally monistic, but in the recent past Congress has explicitly conditioned its approval of major international trade agreements on the denial of the agreements' direct effect. The NAFTA was one of the treaties that is non-self-executing by legislative decree.

[29] See The North American Free Trade Agreement Implementation Act, Stats. Can. 1993, c. 44; The North American Free Trade Agreement Implementation Act of 1993, P.L. 103–182; 107 Stat. 2057. Prompt passage is not meant to imply that it was an easy passage. In the United States, the NAFTA was introduced as a Congressional-Executive Agreement, and therefore only required a majority approval in both chambers of Congress. The House voted for the Agreement with a vote of 234 to 200, and the Senate followed with a vote of 61 to 38. 139 Cong. Rec. H10,048 (daily edn 17 November 1993); 139 Cong. Rec. S16,712-13 (daily edn 20 November 1993). Had the NAFTA been introduced as a treaty, US Constitutional law would have required approval by two-thirds of the Senate (i.e., a possible 66 Senators' votes). US Const. art. II, § 2[2] ('[The President] shall have Power, by and with the Advice and Consent of the Senate, to make Treaties, provided two-thirds of the Senators present concur'). Although perhaps the President would have garnered enough votes (by virtue of more directed canvassing or by the absence of some Senators on the day of the vote), it is at least questionable whether a North American Free Trade *Treaty* would have been passed. For more on the treaty-Congressional-Executive agreement distinction, see Bruce Ackerman and David Golove, 'Is NAFTA Constitutional?' (1995) 108:4 Harv. L.Rev. 799.

[30] Canada, NAFTA Implementing Act s. 6.

cannot appear before a Canadian court with a claim that the NAFTA has been violated.[31]

According to the United States' implementing legislation, only the federal government can invoke the NAFTA before courts of law in that country.[32] While States will be encouraged to co-operate with the federal government's regulations, State laws and prudential regulations are not superseded by the NAFTA Chapter Fourteen obligations.[33] Finally, private persons may not invoke NAFTA provisions except in the case of a Chapter Eleven investor-state dispute.[34]

For banks and other financial institutions, the non-direct effect of the Agreement in the United States and Canada means that the main substantive provisions cannot be enforced in those countries without the backing of the institution's government in a full and formal dispute settlement process. Thus, if Canada denies a US bank market access, it is only the government of the United States (not the bank) that can call on Canada's obligations under the treaty to contest the Canadians' denial.

Of great importance in the United States' banking context is the assurance given to the States by the federal administration that 'NAFTA does not automatically "preempt" or invalidate State laws that do not conform to NAFTA's rules—even if a NAFTA dispute settlement panel were to find a state measure inconsistent with the NAFTA'.[35] Thus, despite the requirements set out in the Agreement itself, in the United States, the States remain free (to a large extent) to act contrary to the provisions of the treaty, and private persons in a State must obey the State laws despite the laws' possible violation of the NAFTA.[36] Moreover, although the

---

[31] Steger (note 28 *supra*), at 281.

[32] See generally, The North American Trade Implementation Act of 1993, P.L. 103–182; 107 Stat. 2057 at § 102 (relationship of NAFTA provisions to domestic law). For a better understanding of how the United States approaches international trade policy dometically see John H. Jackson, 'US Constitutional Law Principles and Foreign Trade Law and Policy', in Meinhard Hilf and Ernst-Ulrich Petersmann (eds), *National Constitutions and International Economic Law* (Kluwer Law and Taxation Publ., Deventer 1993), pp. 65–89; David W. Leebron, 'Implementation of the Uruguay Round Results in the United States', in John H. Jackson and Alan Sykes (note 28 *supra*), pp. 175–242, at 177–201.

[33] The North American Trade Implementation Act of 1993 at § 102(b)(1). See Statement of Administrative Action at 9 ('The Administration is committed to carrying out US obligations under the NAFTA, as they apply to states, through the greatest possible degree of state-federal consultation and cooperation ...'.).

[34] The North American Trade Implementation Act of 1993 at § 102(c). The US courts are to adhere to the practice of interpreting national legislation so as to conform to the country's international treaty obligations, but it is unclear how beneficial this is in practice. For a concise and somewhat dated, but thorough, analysis of Supreme Court jurisprudence in the area of international treaty law, see James C. Wolf, 'The Jurisprudence of Treaty Interpretation' (1998) 21:3 UC Davis L Rev 1023.

[35] NAFTA Statement of Administrative Action at 9.

[36] Manuel O. Méndez and John H. Knox, 'NAFTA's Effect on State Agencies and Administrative Law', paper pressented at 7th Annual Advanced Administrative Law Course, September 1995, p. 7. The legislation implementing the WTO Agreements also contains the jurisdiction limitation allowing only the United States itself to use the Agreement as a cause of action. Uruguay Round Agreement Act, Pub. L. No. 103-465, 108 Stat. 4809, § 102(b)(2) (1994). David Leebron comments that this is not suprising, as 'many of the general implementation provisions of the URAA were drawn from the NAFTA'. Leebron (note 32 *supra*), at 189.

federal government does reserve the right to force a State into compliance,[37] in its NAFTA Statement, the Executive committed itself to undertaking consultations with the violating State before bringing legal action, thus reducing the potential for full-fledged legal proceedings under the implementing legislation's provision.[38] The United States as a Party will, however, remain bound by its obligations *vis-à-vis* the other Parties. Thus, the nation as a whole may incur retaliation if a State refuses to comply with the Chapter Fourteen provisions. Consequently, it may be that other States or even groups of constituents will bring political pressure from within to change the non-complying behavior in order to protect their own region's industry.

3.3.2.2   Mexico: Direct Effect

Mexican constitutional law provides that international treaties have direct effect.[39] Thus, the Chapter Fourteen provisions bind the Mexican government without necessitating further actions by the national lawmakers.[40] A Supreme Court of Mexico decision from 1994 reaffirmed this principle.[41] As a result, if there is a violation of the NAFTA provision, persons in Mexico may invoke the provisions in legal actions against the government as long as the complaining investor has not yet begun an arbitration proceeding under the auspices of Chapter Eleven.[42]

However, one commentator warns that the fact that the NAFTA is self-executing does not clarify what position the treaty has *vis-à-vis* subsequently implemented federal laws that 'emanate' from the Constitution which would contradict the NAFTA:

> ... me parece que lo único que puede concluirse con certeza es que los tratados y las leyes emanadas de la Constitución tiene igual jerarquía, y que en caso de conflicto entre ellos no puede aplicarse el principio de que la ley

---

[37] The North American Trade Implementation Act of 1993, § 102(b)(2). The US Supreme Court has long upheld the right of the Federal government to sue a State government to bring the State into compliance with an international treaty. *Sanitary District of Chicago v. United States* 266 US 405 (1925).

[38] See Leebron (note 32 *supra*), at 224–31, explaining how the Uruguay Round Agreement Implementation Act's strengthened federalism functions. Leebron also points out that this more prominent role of State sovereignty was new with the NAFTA. *Ibid.* at 228, n.203 ('This is another instance in which the evolution primarily occurred between the implementation of the [CUFTA] in 1988 and NAFTA in 1993').

[39] Mexican Constitution, Art. 133.

[40] Mexico is a monistic land. The Mexican Constitution considers all 'tratados', or treaties, the supreme law of the land. 'Acuerdos', or agreements, are not, as the executive can form them without consulting the legislature. Treaties, on the other hand, must be approved by two-thirds of the Mexican Senate. For a discussion of the relationship of the NAFTA to the Mexican Consitution and federal legislation, see Jorge Adame Goddard, 'Relaciones entre el Tratado De Libre Comercio y la Legislación Mexicana' (1992) 16 Rev Investigaciones Jur 9.

[41] *Contradicción del Tesis 3/92*, Pleno de la Supreme Corte de Justicia (2 March 1994), cited by NAFTA Dispute Panel In the Matter of: The Mexican Antidumping Investigation into Imports of Cut-to-Length Plate Products from the United States, MEX-941904-02, at n.46 and accompanying text.

[42] NAFTA Annex 1120.1(a).

posterior deroga a la anterior, ya que si una ley posterior deroga un tratado se contradice el principio fundamental de que los tratados deben cumplirse (*pacta sunt servanda*), y si un tratado posterior derogara una ley se contradiría el artículo 72-f de la Constitución que exige que las leyes sean derogada con aprobación de ambas cámaras.[43]

This hugely important issue of the hierarchy of laws and treaties within a domestic legal system has only begun to be examined in the trade law context and its resolution is far from settled.[44]

Perhaps even more troubling than the hierarchy of NAFTA as subordinate to the Constitution in Mexican law is the character of the Mexican Constitution. Whereas the US Constitution is regarded as setting forth principles that are to be followed, the Mexican Constitution is thought of as setting out ideals for which to strive, but which are not necessarily currently achieved. As one author wrote, 'The Mexican Constitution has been consistently characterized by Mexican constitutional scholars as a project to be accomplished, a statement of revolutionary ideals that is nominal in that there is no intended immediate congruency between its stated aspirations and reality'.[45]

If this general statement applies to the provisions of direct effect of treaties, individuals calling upon the NAFTA in Mexican courts may encounter unexpected difficulties. Although this is unlikely, given Mexico's traditional adherence to international law, there is a possibility that nominal direct effect will not benefit the individual claimant in an actual dispute with the government.[46]

---

[43] Goddard (note 40 *supra*), at 26–7.

[44] See John H. Jackson, 'Status of Treaties in Domestic Legal Systems: A Policy Analysis' (1992) 86 Am J Int'l L 310, 313:

> One of the basic conclusions of this article is that there are sound policy reasons for a national legal system with typical democratic institutions to avoid the combination of direct domestic law application of treaties and higher status for those treaty norms than later-enacted statutory law. This conclusion depends greatly on the relative degree to which constitution drafters trust international institutions and treaty-making processes compared with national institutions and legislative processes. But, in any event, the premise here is that these relationships and policies are too little understood and that gaining an understanding of them can have vital consequences both within national systems and beyond.

[45] James F. Smith, 'Confronting Differences in the United States and Mexican Legal Systems in the Era of NAFTA' (1993) 1:1 US-Mex. L.J. 85, 94, citing Jorge Capizo, *La Constitución Mexicana de 1917* (1986), p. 125; Raphael de Pina, Vara, *Diccionario de Derecha* (1984) pp. 272–3; and Jorge Capizo, 'La Democracia y la Clasificación de las Constituciones una Propuesta' (1982) IX Anuario Jur 360.

[46] See Smith (note 45 *supra*), at 98, n.69, translating Cesar Sepulveda, *Derecho Internacional* (1986) p. 79:

> The examination of the Mexican practice reveals that no norm has existed that attempts to limit compliance with an international treaty, nor have the courts established binding precedent, in any case, to place the Constitution over treaties. Also, it is certain that the Mexican nation has complied in good faith with all of its obligations derived from the international legal order, despite its effect on its internal interests. The logical consequence is that in [sic] general International Law is superior to the norms of the Mexican state.

3.3.2.3   *For All Parties, Investor-State Disputes Allow for Limited Direct Effect*

The domestic legal status of the NAFTA makes no difference in those situations in which a bank or its investors are harmed by a State enterprise or a monopoly in contravention to the Party's obligations in Chapter 15.[47] For such cases, the bank and/or its investors may request that the Party in question submit to arbitration based on its alleged violation of NAFTA obligations. Due to the fact that Mexico allows direct effect anyway, there is a special provision limiting investors to bringing their complaints either before Mexican national courts or to arbitration under Chapter Eleven.[48]

3.4   INTERPRETATION OF THE NAFTA CHAPTER FOURTEEN PROVISIONS

The formal rules of interpretation for the financial service provisions of the NAFTA are in no way extraordinary. The Parties and the dispute settlement panelists are to interpret the Agreement as they would other international legal rules. According to the general rules governing the NAFTA, the Parties are to interpret the provisions of the Agreement 'in the light of its objectives set out in paragraph 1 [of Article 102] and in accordance with applicable rules of international law'.[49] As all of the Parties either are signatories to, or accept as customary international law, the Vienna Convention on the Law of Treaties, this Convention forms the basis for interpretation of the NAFTA.[50]

Applying Articles 31 and 32 of the Vienna Convention, the NAFTA panels are to interpret the NAFTA provisions 'in good faith in accordance with the ordinary meaning to be given the terms of the treaty in their context and in the light of its objects and purpose'.[51] One panel has already interpreted this to mean that as a first step, the ordinary meaning of the terms are to govern interpretation.[52] As the NAFTA text has three official versions (English, French, and Spanish) the ordinary meaning of the word in one language must correspond to the ordinary meaning of the words in the other two languages.

---

[47] Chapter Fifteen regulates State enterprises and monopolies, requiring, among other things, national treatment and most-favored-nation treatment in such enterprises' granting of licenses, handling of expropriations, and in fulfilling its regulatory duties. Art. 1503:2. See also discussion of Chapter Eleven arbitration process, *infra*.

[48] See Annex 1120.1(a). Financial insitutions themselves may not invoke the Party-Investor arbitration process at all, but must go to national courts. Annex 1120.1(b).

[49] NAFTA Art. 102:2.

[50] See, *In the Matter of: Tariffs Applied by Canada to Certain US-Origin Agricultural Products*, NAFTA Arbitral Panel Established Pursuant to Art. 2008, CDA-95-2008-01, at 30–33, paras 118–24 (2 December 1996) ('Approach to Interpretation'; setting out the Vienna Convention Arts 31 and 32 as applicable to the NAFTA dispute settlement panel interpretations).

[51] Vienna Convention on the Law of Treaties, U.N. Doc. A/CONF. 39/27, Art. 31:1 (concluded at Vienna on 23 May 1969; entered into force 27 January 1980).

[52] *Tariffs Applied by Canada* (note 50 *supra*), at 31, para. 119 ('The Panel must therefore commence with the identification of the plain and ordinary meaning of the words used').

This does not generally cause problems, but can be an issue when nuances in one language indicate a different interpretation than do the connotations of the term in another language.[53]

Moreover, the ordinary meaning, under NAFTA Article 201:2, is to be read in 'light of [the NAFTA's] objectives'.[54] The objectives of the NAFTA are set out in Article 201:1. Those most relevant to trade in financial services include promoting 'conditions of fair competition' and increasing 'substantially investment opportunities'. Thus, these characteristics should govern the interpretation of the Chapter Fourteen provisions. A NAFTA panel, faced with interpreting several agricultural trade provisions of the NAFTA categorized such objectives as 'trade liberalization' goals.[55] A Chapter Fourteen panel need not adopt a similar categorization, but it would be likely to do so.

Defining the ordinary meaning of the term in question also requires that the context of the treaty be taken into consideration.[56] The 'context' of the

---

[53] Facing a 'technical failure to specifically mention international treaties of direct application as a source of Mexican antidumping law' in English, the NAFTA dispute panel in *Mexican Antidumping Investigation into Imports of Cut-to-Length Plate Products* had to interpret the treaty in view of more than just the ordinary usage of a term in one language. To solve this problem, the opinion states:

> [The] Panel notes that under the official Spanish language version of NAFTA Article 1904(2), this does not appear to poes a significant problem. In that version, 'leyes' is referred to as a source of antidumping law in Mexico, and the term 'leyes' is well-known pursuant to the Constitution to include treaties to which Mexico is a party. However, under the official English language version of Article 1904(2), which utilizes the words 'relevant statutes', the omission of a reference to treaties may be of some moment. Nevertheless, the Panel concludes that there is ample support for the proposition that these treaty documents are an important source of Mexican antidumping law … and that it is appropriate in this context to rely upon the Spanish language version of Article 1904(2).

In the Matter of: the Mexican Antidumping Investigation into Imports of Cut-to-Length Plate Products from the United States, MEX-941904-02, pp. 10–11 (opinion decided under Chapter Fourteen Procedures of NAFTA) (footnotes omitted). The text of this decision is found in James R. Holbein and Donald J. Musch (eds), *North American Free Trade Agreements: Dispute Settlement: Binational Panel Decisions under the North American Free Trade Agreement* (Oceana, Dobbs Ferry, NY, 1995).

[54] *Tariffs Applied by Canada* (note 50 *supra*), at 31, para. 119 ('In [determining the ordinary meaning of the terms used], the Panel will take into consideration the meaning actually to be attributed to words and phrases looking at the text as a whole …'.).

[55] The majority elaborated:

> … as a free trade agreement the NAFTA has the specific objective of eliminating barriers to trade among the three contracting Parties. The principles and rules through which the objectives of the NAFTA are elaborated are identified in NAFTA Article 102(1) as including national treatment, most-favoured-nation treatment and transparency. Any interpretation adopted by the Panel must, therefore, promote rather than inhibit the NAFTA's objectives.

Ibid. at 32, para. 122.

[56] Vienna Convention on the Law of Treaties Art. 31:1.

treaty, as defined by the Vienna Convention, is broader than merely the chapter of the treaty in which the disputed term is found. It is even broader than the overall agreement. Rather, the 'context' includes all agreements and instruments formed among the Parties in relation to the Agreement.[57] Moreover, separate agreements and actions taken after the completion of the original agreement are to be considered in interpreting a provision of the treaty as well.[58] In a dispute between NAFTA Parties, then, the definition of a phrase found in Chapter Fourteen ought to be interpreted in light of the Environmental and Labor Side Accords, as well as in view of the Border Bank. If Mexico and the United States are the disputants, interpretations should even be made in light of the Monetary Assistance package offered Mexico in the wake of the peso-crisis of 1996, as it constitutes an 'action taken' by one Party to directly affect (in this case to aid) another Party.

If after taking into account the context of the Agreement, the meaning of the words of a particular provision remains unclear, ambiguous, or would lead to 'manifestly absurd or unreasonable' results, the negotiating history of the Parties and the 'circumstances of [the Agreement's] conclusion' are to be considered.[59] In the case of NAFTA Chapter Fourteen provisions, use of negotiating history is difficult, as it was so poorly recorded. The negotiations, as stated above, took place to a great extent away from the public's view, and although one book has been written by a US negotiator,[60] the other members of the drafting teams have remained unobtrusive.

Finally, NAFTA panels will look to national courts' decisions on related questions and for interpretations. The dispute settlement panels established under the United States-Canada Free Trade Agreement often looked to the domestic case law of the Parties to assist in interpretation of provisions, and there is no indication that the practice will not continue in the NAFTA dispute settlement arena. Within the Parties' own court systems, national law will govern the interpretation of the provisions. Thus, the role of the administrative bodies and the normal courts will vary with the Party.[61]

---

[57] *Ibid*. Art. 31:2.
[58] *Ibid*. Art. 31:3(a).
[59] *Ibid*. Art. 32.
[60] See Wethington (note 4 *supra*). Mr Wethington was the lead negotiator for the United States in the NAFTA Chapter Fourteen negotiations.
[61] In Canada, the Department of Finance will be the primary body to interpret the Chapter Fourteen provisions. In reviewing agency decisions, Canadian courts are likely to defer to the agency's interpretation, but may overrule the interpretation if the judge feels a different interpretation would be better. In Mexico, the Ministry of Finance and Public Credit (SHCP) has been given the competence to interpret the Chapter Fourteen provisions. In the United States, the Department of the Treasury, along with the Office of the Comptroller of the Currency, the Federal Reserve Board, and the Federal Deposit Insurance Corporation will all have input as to how the different terms should be applied. The standard of review of the agency interpretations will therefore be that of the so-called 'Chevron Doctrine'. This doctrine, set out by the Supreme Court in *Chevron USA v. Natural Resources Defense Council* 467 US 837 (1984), gives deference to reasonable agency findings of law unless Congress has addressed the specific issue directly. Thus, even if a court would have interpreted the passage of a treaty differently, the agency's decision will be upheld unless it there is a showing that it was arbitrarily made.

3.4.1   Stare Decisis?

In the NAFTA there is no formal doctrine of *stare decisis*.[62] Thus, a panel is not bound to interpret phrases of the Agreement in the same way a previous panel has done. However, it is to be expected that panels will take note of prior decisions and strive to maintain a consistency in the NAFTA jurisprudence.[63] A primary argument for the use of *stare decisis* is the need for predictability in the law. While certainly not unique in this respect, actors in the trade arena are highly sensitive to stability and instability in the legal framework of import/export and investment rules. Financial services markets are even more sensitive. If a bank faces uncertainty in whether its activities will be permitted on a particular day or in the near future, many opportunities of trade will be ignored. In this way, random decision-making can act as a non-protectionist trade barrier.

---

[62] *Stare decisis* is the doctrine by which courts adhere to the judgments made by earlier courts in factually similar cases. *Black's Law Dictionary* includes references to United States case law defining the phrase. *Black's Law Dictionary* (6th edn, 1990), p. 1406, citing, e.g., *Neff v. George* 4 N.E.2d 388, 390–391 (Ill. 1936) ('Policy of courts to stand by precedent and not to disturb settled point'); *Otter Tail Power Co. v. Von Bank* 8 N.W.2d 599, 607 (N.D. 1943) ('Doctrine is one of policy, grounded on the theory that security and certainty require that accepted and established legal principle, under which rights may accrue, be recognized and followed, though later found to be not legally sound, but whehther previous holding of court shall be adhered to, modified, or overruled is within court's decision under circumstances of case before it'). But see Christopher J. Peters, 'Foolish Consistency: On Equality, Integrity, and Justice in Stare Decisis' (1996) 105:8 Yale LJ 2031, 2033–34:

> ... if strictly observed, the scope of stare decisis can extend far beyond a single unjust decision. Its effects can be cumulative: A [sic] single erroneous court decision, if followed, becomes two erroneous decisions, then three, and soon a 'line' of cases. In this way, stare decisis has the potential to import injustice irremediably into the law.

[63] The WTO dispute settlement practice refuses to commit to the principle of *stare decisis* as well. The Appellate Body of the WTO explained its approach to the issue of *stare decisis* in an historical context:

> Although GATT 1947 panel reports were adopted by decisions of the CONTRACTING PARTIES, a decision to adopt a panel report did not under GATT 1947 constitute agreement by the CONTRACTING PARTIES on the legal reasoning in that panel report. The generally-accepted [sic] view under GATT 1947 was that the conclusions and recommendations in an adopted panel report bound the parties to the dispute in that particular case, but subsequent panels did not feel legally bound by the details and reasoning of a previous panel report.
>
> We do not believe that the CONTRACTING PARTIES, in deciding to adopt a panel report, intended that their decision would constitute a definitive interpretation of the relevant provisions of GATT 1947. Nor do we believe that this is contemplated under GATT 1994.

Japan—Taxes on Alcoholic Beverages, WT/DS8/AB/R, WT/DS10/AB/R, WT/DS11/AB/R 13 (4 October 1996).

The NAFTA's goal of promoting liberalized trade among the Parties would thus be hindered.

The likelihood of that a *de facto* following of *stare decisis* will occur is increased by the legal cultures of two of the Parties.[64] The national courts of Canada and the United States, as common law jurisdictions, adhere to *stare decisis.* Yet even within these common law Parties' court systems, adherence to the principle is not absolute. There are different emphases placed on the competing interests. In Canada, the goal of consistency and predictability of the law is valued, but at least within regulatory contexts, the need for competent decision-making is more highly regarded. When an administrative court hears a case, '(i)t is a matter of applying rules, or principles, to facts. The essence of the matter is not to determine in some scientific fashion whether a decision is consistent with a claimed precedent but to determine who should decide'.[65] It is thus possible that past decisions will be regarded with interest, but not with reverence by

---

[64] The US Supreme Court supported its refusal to overturn a past decision by capsulizing the reasons that have been given for adhering to *stare decisis*:

> The Court has said often and with great emphasis that 'the doctrine of stare decisis is of fundamental importance to the rule of law'. *Welch v. Texas Dept. of Highways and Public Transportation,* 483 US 468, 494 (1987). Although we have cautioned that 'stare decisis is a principle of policy and not a mechanical formula of adherence to the latest decision', *Boyds Markets, Inc. v. Retail Clerks,* 398 US 235, 241 (1970), it is indisputable that stare decisis is a basic self-governing principle within the Judicial Branch, which is entrusted with the sensitive and difficult task of fashioning and preserving a jurisprudential system that is not based upon 'an arbitrary discretion'. The Federalist, No. 78, p. 490 (H. Lodge ed. 1888) (A. Hamilton). See also *Vasquez v. Hillery,* 474 US 254, 265 (1986) (stare decisis ensures that 'the law will not merely change erratically' and 'permits society to presume that bedrock principles are founded in the law rather than in the proclivities of individuals').

Patterson v. McLean Credit Union 491 US 164, 172 (1989). In Canada, *stare decisis* is also a governing principle of judicial decision-making. *Domtar Inc. v. Quebec* (Commission d'allel en matière de lésions professionnelles) (1993) 2 S.C.R. 756, at V:B.1.2 ('... the requirement of consistency is also an important objective. As our legal system abhors whatever is arbitrary, it must be based on a degree of consistency, equality and predictability in the application of the law'). While not every panel member from these Parties will be a trained judge, they will most likely be so familiar with the system of *stare decisis* that past decisions will continue to be regarded with great deference. An example of one NAFTA panel's regard for the common law principles can be found in its support of the principle of *res judicata* over the application of the results of an unadopted GATT panel report. See *In the Matter of Gray Portland Cement and Clinker from Mexico* USA-95-1904-02, 19 (13 September 1996) ('... to give effect to the unadopted GATT panel report would violate statutorily-imposed US procedural laws ... and would undermine established principles of *res judicata.* Both legal doctrines are of enormous importance in common law jurisprudence, and should not be cast aside in favor of a recommendation of questionable legal status').

[65] H. Wade MacLauchlan, 'Some Problems with Judicial Review of Administrative Inconsistency' (1984) 8 Dalhousie LJ 435, 441.

Canadians.[66] United States case law on *stare decisis,* on the other hand, tends to adhere more strongly to the principle of consistency than it does to arguments of expertise in decision-making. The Supreme Court writes:

> Our precedents are not sacrosanct, for we have overruled prior decisions where the necessity and propriety of doing so has been established ... Nonetheless, we have held that 'any departure from the doctrine of stare decisis demands special justification'. [Citation omitted] We have said also that the burden borne by the party advocating the abandonment of an established precedent is greater where the Court is asked to overrule a statutory interpretation, for here, unlike in the context of constitutional interpretation, the legislative power is implicated, and Congress remains free to alter what we have done.[67]

No NAFTA Chapter Fourteen provisions have yet been addressed by a panel or court, leaving the precedential power of final decisions open to speculation. In view of the various legal backgrounds of the Parties, it is likely that the future decisions will carry some weight beyond the immediate dispute context in which they arise. Yet, it is to be expected that the effectiveness of the liberalization measures, and not the prior decisions, will be the critical point of any particular decision.

3.4.2 Interpretation of a Trade in Financial Services Agreement

The final point on interpretation has to do with the characteristics of the Chapter as an agreement to liberalize trade in financial services. The NAFTA text seems to presume its own adequacy to formulate rules for trade in financial services. It is not, however, so clear that the rules adopted (mainly trade principles) can be faultlessly imposed upon their subject (the regulation of financial services). Because trade law and financial service law

---

[66] A CUFTA panel puts the Canadian state of law on this issue perhaps a little too bluntly:

> There is no administrative *stare decisis* in Canadian law. Thus, even if (the prior case) did describe a specific analytic methodology, the Tribunal could not be bound to that methodology in the (subsequent dispute).

In the Matter of: Certain Hot-Rolled Carbon Steel Plate and High-Strength Low-Alloy Plate, Heat-Treated or Not, Originating in or Exported from the USA CDA-93-1904-06, 23 (20 December 1994). See also *Domtar* (note 64 *supra*), at 799–800 ('the search for consistency is not an absolute one ... (T)he consistency objective must be pursued in keeping with the decision-making autonomy and independence of members of the administrative body ... (C)ertainty of the law and decision-making consistency are chiefly notable for their relativity'); *Consolidated-Bathurst Packaging Ltd. v. IWA* (1990) 1 S.C.R. 282, 328 ('the decision of one panel cannot bind another panel and the measures taken by the Board to foster coherence in its decision-making must not compromise any panel member's capacity to decide in accordance with his conscience and opinions').

[67] *Patterson* (note 64 *supra*) at 172–173 (1989); *Hilton v. South Carolina Public Railways Commission* 502 US 197 (1991), re-affirming *Patterson* findings on *stare decisis.*

are two separate legal systems, the combination of the two systems in the NAFTA Chapter Fourteen necessitates that the interpretation of the Chapter's provisions take into account both the trade perspective and the financial services perspective.[68]

3.5   INSTITUTIONAL STRUCTURE OF THE NAFTA FINANCIAL SERVICES PROVISIONS

The Parties established a Financial Services Committee (FSC) to oversee the functioning of NAFTA Chapter Fourteen.[69] To the discredit of the Parties' efforts, the FSC is only minimally defined as to its composition and role in the implementation process. The 'cryptic descriptions' contained in the Article 1412 provisions leave much room for interpretation.[70]

The FSC has no fixed number of members, but each Party is to include 'an official' of the responsible national body for financial services as its chief representative.[71] For the existing NAFTA parties, the responsible bodies for Canada, Mexico, and the United States are the Department of Finance of Canada, the Secretaría de Hacienda y Crédito Público, and the Department of the Treasury and the Department of Commerce, respectively.[72] The term 'official' is left undefined by the treaty, and will presumably be decided by each Party according to national law.[73] At a minimum, however, each 'official' ought to have the authority to make binding commitments for their governments and to be able to ensure the enforcement of whatever decisions are taken.

---

[68]   The question of how these two systems interact is futher developed in the final portion of this book. See Chapter 9 *infra.*

[69]   NAFTA Art. 1412:1, 2.

[70]   McNevin (note 1 *supra*), at 387. Ms McNevin, from the legal division of the Federal Deposit Insurance Corporation, writes:

> The tools given to this august body with which to work its secret magic are practically nonexistent. The carve-out provisions of 1410, along with the lack of tools, structure, and authority, paint a picture of a ghost with no substance, accountability, defined internal or external expectations, credibility, or legitimacy. This is particularly disturbing since it is this group which has been entrusted by the NAFTA with supra-national responsibilities. Yet it is unclear who governs this body, how it is governed, on what basis it is governed, who appoints the members ..., on on what basis and to whom the individual members ... or its bodies are accountable.

[71]   NAFTA Art. 1412:1. It is not clear with whom the authority lies to choose the particular members of the Commission. See McNevin (note 1 *supra*), at 388.

[72]   NAFTA, Annex 1412.1. In the United States, the Department of the Treasury is responsible for the banks and securities industries, while the Department of Commerce is the authority responsible for the insurance companies under the NAFTA.

[73]   In the United States Constitution, an 'official' is one appointed to a position by the President with the advice and consent of the Senate. US Constitution Art. II, § 2. The Supreme Court has declared that an official is therefore only removeable by the President or by a Congressional impeachment process. *Bowsher v. Synar* 478 US 714 (1986).

Under the supervision of the Free Trade Commission,[74] the FSC is to supervise the implementation and elaboration of the Chapter provisions, 'consider issues' that the Parties bring to its attention as regards financial services, and issue reports or decisions on the validity of a claim of exception in dispute settlement.[75] While supervising the implementation of the norms and consulting on issues of contention is a somewhat intangible role, the FSC's role in dispute settlement is potentially powerful: its decision on the validity of an exception's invocation is binding on the Tribunal hearing the case.[76] In effect, it is the FSC that determines whether a violation of the treaty is legitimate.

Finally, the FSC is to meet each year to 'assess the functioning' of the NAFTA as it affects financial services.[77] It is not clear how this role differs from that of supervising the implementation of the Chapter. Certainly, however, this final provision reinforces the idea of on-going review and encourages the active making of suggestions for improvements in the liberalization process.

3.6   SCOPE OF APPLICATION (ARTICLES 1401 AND 1402)

The scope of NAFTA Chapter Fourteen has three dimensions: who must abide by the obligations; who/what is protected by the provisions; and who has standing to bring a claim. The short answers to these questions are: the Parties, their subnational units, and self-regulatory organizations must abide by the obligations; investors in financial services that are nationals or permanent residents of the Parties are protected; and both the Parties and the institutions and their investors may have standing to bring a claim.[78]

To determine how these dimensions of scope are to work, one must address the particular terms of the relevant provision: Article 1401. Because there have been no panel judgements interpreting these provisions, it is important to keep in mind the underlying goal of the Chapter: the negotiating parties wanted the Chapter Fourteen provisions to form a comprehensive framework for liberalizing all financial service activity throughout the NAFTA territory.

Chapter Fourteen of the NAFTA sets out that its provisions apply to:

Measures adopted or maintained by a Party relating to:
(a) financial institutions of another Party;
(b) investors of another Party, and investments of such investors, in financial institutions in the Party's territory; and
(c) cross-border trade in financial services.[79]

---

[74] NAFTA Art. 2001:2(d).
[75] NAFTA Art. 1412:2.
[76] NAFTA Arts 1412:2(c), 1415:2.
[77] NAFTA Art. 1412:3.
[78] This standing is not absolute. Only the Parties may take part in a formal dispute settlement proceeding. See 3.18 *infra*.
[79] NAFTA Art. 1401:1.

However, the provisions do not to form a barrier to a Party's reservation of certain public services to itself and its public entities. Those providers of financial services that are a 'public retirement plan or statutory system of social security' and 'activities or services for the account or with the guarantee or using the financial resources of the Party, including its public entities' are specifically excluded from the scope of Chapter Fourteen.[80]

It is with the basic provision of Article 1401 that one must begin the investigation into the scope of the Chapter. This starts with an individual examination of each term.

3.6.1 'Measures adopted or maintained'

3.6.1.1   Wide Definition of 'Measures'

As defined in Chapter Two of the NAFTA, for purposes of the entire Agreement 'measure' refers to more than just laws and regulations.[81] It includes a 'procedure, requirement or practice' as well.[82] Thus, any existing or new mode of influencing financial institutions must be compatible with NAFTA Chapter Fourteen provisions, whether legislatively approved, authorized by the executive, or adopted by a regulatory agency as rule or policy. Moreover, even if never officially endorsed, a pattern of behavior should be considered a 'practice' and thus subject to the Chapter Fourteen obligations. A pattern might appear, for instance, if a bank supervisory agency repeatedly subjected the banks of only one Party to certain tests. Even if administering such tests were within the agency's discretion, and even if there were no explicit policy to discriminate, such a pattern of behavior, from the perspective of the examined institutions, would inflict competitive disadvantages.

3.6.1.2   Rule for Existing Measures

NAFTA allows non-compatible existing measures to be continued as long as the inconsistencies are set out in one of the treaty's annexes as a reservation.[83] However, while these measures may be renewed, they cannot be altered so as to further deviate from the Party's NAFTA obligations.[84]

---

[80] NAFTA Art. 1401:3. If a Party grants such activities to a private entity, it may do so in a way that favors domestic entities, but the Party remains bound by the other obligations of the Chapter. See NAFTA Art. 1410:3. Under NAFTA Chapter Ten (Government Procurement), Canada and Mexico have excluded financial services from their obligations to liberalize government procurment activities. See NAFTA Annex 1001.1b-2, Section B (Schedule of Canada; Schedule of Mexico). The United States did not take an exception for financial services in Chapter Ten, but allows itself the privilege under Chapter Fourteen to discriminate for pension plan and social security activities. See NAFTA Annex 1001.1b-2, Section B (Schedule of the United States). Subnational units are not automatically included in the Chapter Ten obligations. NAFTA Art. 1024:3.

[81] NAFTA Art. 201:1 ('measure')

[82] NAFTA Art. 201:1 ('measure').

[83] NAFTA Art. 1409:2. See NAFTA Annex VII, Sections A and B for each of the Parties.

[84] NAFTA Art. 1409:1(a), (b).

Provisions allowing for the continued effect of incompatible national laws are common in international trade law.[85] However, the NAFTA does improve upon the unenumerated 'standstill' provisions of the Canada-United States Free Trade Agreement and the GATS through its attempt to form a list of excepted measures.[86]

3.6.2　'By a Party'

There is no definition of 'Party' in the NAFTA. Yet throughout the NAFTA the term is used in a way that makes obvious that it refers to all signatories that have ratified the NAFTA. The obligations accepted by each Party also extend to the sub-national political units and the self-regulatory organizations of each.[87]

3.6.2.1　National Governments

Upon the going into effect of the Agreement, Canada, Mexico, and the United States were the Parties to the NAFTA. The provision on accession indicates that a Party must be a 'country or group of countries'.[88] Thus, formal statehood is a minimal requirement.[89] Similarly, a Party may be a regional trade arrangement such as Mercosur or the European Communities. The scope of obligations under the Agreement does not, however, extend between Parties if one Party objects to the accession of another as Party.[90]

3.6.2.2　Subnational Units

In the past, there has not been much attention paid to the issue of sub-national governments' role in international trade. However, it is an area of growing significance, as the 'new' trade issues (services, government procurement, technical standards, etc.) are often within the competence of

---

[85] The process of 'grandfathering' legislation serves the purpose of ensuring that treaty provisions may be included in the overall agreement, while also allowing politically sensitive programs to be continued domestically. Professors Jackson, Davey, and Sykes describe grandfather rights and note that grandfather rights in the WTO are much less important than they were in the General Agreement on Tariffs and Trade 1947. John H. Jackson, William J. Davey, and Alan O. Sykes Jr, *Legal Problems of International Economic Relations: Cases, Materials and Text* (3rd edn, West Publishing, St Paul, MN, 1995), pp. 300–301.
[86] See discussion of reservations, see 3.16 *infra*.
[87] NAFTA Art. 105.
[88] NAFTA Art. 2204:1.
[89] The Membership provisions of the WTO are more liberal. There, statehood is not a requirement. Rather, a functional test of 'possessing full autonomy in the conduct of its external commercial relations and of the other matters provided for in [the WTO Agreements]' is deciding. Marrakesh Agreement Establishing the World Trade Organization, Art. XII:1.
[90] NAFTA Art. 2204:2.

subnational governments.[91] Unlike the prior Canada-United States Free Trade Agreement's provisions on financial services, NAFTA Chapter Fourteen applies to subnational governments.[92]

The original text of NAFTA Chapter Fourteen realizes the importance of these subunits in North America, and shapes the scope of the obligations accordingly. NAFTA Article 105 provides that the Parties are to 'ensure that all necessary measures are taken in order to give effect to the provisions of this Agreement, including their observance, except as otherwise provided in this Agreement, by state and provincial governments.

That is, as drafted, the text requires that Provincial and State governments, as well as county, city, and municipal governments, adhere to the NAFTA provisions.[93]

The extension of trade liberalization provisions to subnational units is particularly important in the case of financial regulation in North America. In both the United States and Canada, States and Provinces, respectively, have an important role in the regulation of the various types of financial institutions.[94] Without binding governmental authorities below the national level, any commitments taken are much less effective. Stressing the importance of subnational actors in the federal systems of the large trading nations, particularly in respect to investment and services agreements, one author asserts, '… these non-tariff and new area topics of negotiation are matters in which sub-federal governments are active regulators. Constraining sub-federal actors in the United States, Canada, and other economically powerful federations may be more important to world welfare than constraining central government action in smaller nations'.[95]

In practice, however, the coverage is not uniform throughout the subnational units. The Annex VII Schedules provide the present Parties with

---

[91] See, e.g., Earl H. Fry, *The Expanding Role of State and Local Governments in US Foreign Affairs* (Council on Foreign Relations Press, New York, 1998); Matt Schaefer, 'Are Private Remedies in Domestic Courts Essential for International Trade Agreements to Perform Constitutional Functions with Respect to Sub-Federal Governments?' (1996–97) 17:2/3 NW J Int'l L & Bus 609; Fred L. Morrison and Rüdiger Wolfrum, 'The Impact of Federalism on the Implementation of International Trade Obligations', in Meinhard Hilf and Ernst-Ulrich Petersmann (eds), *National Constitutions and International Economic Law* (Kluwer Law and Taxation Publishers, Deventer, 1993), pp. 519–35; H. Patrick Glenn, 'Reconciling Regimes: Legal Relations of States and Provinces in North America' (1998) 15 Ariz J Int'l & Comp L 255.

[92] Compare NAFTA Arts 1402, and 105 with CUFTA Art. 1701:2.

[93] For a discussion of the domestic legal status of NAFTA in sub-national units, see Schaefer (note 91 *supra*), at 611 ('Private remedies in domestic courts are perhaps the most persuasive means of ensuring compliance by sub-federal governments with international trade norms. Indeed, private remedies are in certain respects better suited to perform constitutional functions *vis à vis* sub-federal governments as compared to central governments').

[94] Manuel O. Méndez and John H. Knox, 'NAFTA's Effect on State Agencies and Administrative Law', paper presented at the State Bar of Texas 7th Annual Advanced Administrative Law Course; September 1995.

[95] Schaefer (note 91 *supra*), at 614, citing Matt Schaefer, 'Federalism and Regional Free Trade in the Americas: Searching for Pareto Gains' *(forthcoming)*. See also Earl H. Fry, 'Sovereignty and Federalism: US and Canadian Perspectives' (1994) 20 Can-US LJ 303, 308.

certain reservations in respect to the adherence of their sub-national units to the obligations.[96] Canada, for instance, reserved the right to allow its Provinces to maintain non-conforming measures in their handling of financial services.[97] Similarly, the United States has reserved the right to list and maintain its States' non-conforming measures.[98]

3.6.2.3   Self-Regulatory Organizations

In addition to the Parties and the Parties' subnational units, the Chapter Fourteen provisions apply to measures used by self-regulatory financial organizations if a Party requires that:

> ... a financial institution or a cross-border financial service provider of another Party to be a member of, participate in, or have access to, a self-regulatory organization to provide a financial service in or into the territory of that Party, the Party shall ensure observance of the obligations of this Chapter by such self-regulatory organization.[99]

This is another example of the Parties' concern with equalizing the actual competitive conditions facing banks.

At present there are numerous separate offices that must adhere to the NAFTA provisions: in the United States, there are at least four national financial service authorities in charge of the banking sector (Department of Treasury, Department of Commerce, Office of the Comptroller, the Federal Reserve Banks under the leadership of the Board of Governors of the Federal Reserve, and the Federal Deposit Insurance Corporations), with a possible fifth (the Securities and Exchange Commission), as well as the individual State authorities. The general provisions of the NAFTA cover measures taken

---

[96] Annex VII, Section A.

[97] NAFTA Annex 1409.1:1 ('Canada may set out in Section A of its Schedule to Annex VII by the date of entry into force of this Agreement any existing non-conforming measure maintained at the provincial level').

[98] This reservation expired for six States on 1 January 1994, and for the other 34 States on 1 January 1995. The six States with the earlier deadline are those that have the greatest foreign banking activity: California, Florida, Illinois, New York, Ohio, and Texas. NAFTA Annex 1409.1:2. Since the signing of the Agreement, dissatisfaction from the subnational units has led to even more deviation from their original inclusion. On 1 April 1996, the Parties agreed by letter to allow the States and Provinces to make a blanket grandfathering of their service and investment measures, excluding financial service measures, that do not conform to the NAFTA and that were in existence on 1 January 1994. 'NAFTA Parties to Protect Existing Sub-Federal Measures Indefinitely' 3:7 *Inside NAFTA* 1 (3 April 1996). By adding text to the Annex I reservations of each Party, the method of specific listing of grandfathered measures has been ended for non-financial services and investment measures at the sub-national level. This significant regression in the overall liberalization process does not directly relate to banking, but as one US State official reportedly said, 'a 'catalyst' for liberalization may have been lost because of the decision'. To what extent this will affect banking indirectly remains to be seen. 3:7 *Inside NAFTA* at 15. See also Frederick M. Abbott, 'The NAFTA as Architecture for Political Decision' (draft of 21 May 1997), p. 10 (manuscript on file with author).

[99] NAFTA Art. 1402.

by these offices. Article 1402 focuses on those non-governmental organizations closely involved with the provision of the financial service in the Party's territory. Each of these must also develop policies and practices that are consistent with the Party's obligations under Chapter Fourteen. An organization such as the United States' Securities and Exchange Commission is a clear example of an organization that would have to abide by the provisions of Chapter Fourteen.[100] All companies which want to be listed on the national stock exchanges in the United States must be registered with, and abide by the rules of, this Commission. The other Parties' stock exchange authorities are also subject to the rules of NAFTA. The Mexican Securities Exchange, for which applicants must pay large sums of money to join, is proving a contentious organization for just this reason. The US and Canadian stock traders allege that the high seat fees are discriminatory and in that way are a violation of Mexico's NAFTA obligations.

More of a question arises with the 'quasi-public' Canadian Payments Association, responsible for the Canadian clearing system.[101] This Association took over its duties from the private Canadian Bankers Association in 1980,[102] and remains organizationally separate from the government. Nevertheless, the public role it plays in the Canadian financial environment would suggest that it too must abide by the rules of the NAFTA, and answer to the government if it violates them.

Professional associations such as the American Bankers Association (ABA) and the Canadian Bankers Association (CBA) should be included in the scope of Chapter Fourteen from an international trade viewpoint, but are not. Both the ABA and the CBA are voluntary groups composed of industry members who pay a membership fee. Membership provides the benefits of gaining access to the processes that form the official policies of the organization. These policies, in turn, are presented to the national legislators with the backing of the organization. These and similar organizations also provide individual members with a marketable qualification. All else equal, consumers will tend to visit a business with a recognized affiliation rather than one without such affiliation, because there is an assumed level of competence stemming from the membership. Yet, if viewed as solely a professional lobbying organization, neither association would need to adhere to the principles of non-discrimination in the marketplace set out by NAFTA because the state is not involved in the organization's governance, funding, or admission policies.

There is, of course, the ever-present issue of *de facto* necessity of membership. It would be plausible to argue that there is a *de facto* need for a bank to be a member of the ABA or CBA in order to remain competitive. If this is the case, these associations ought to be bound by the NAFTA financial service provisions. Yet, the wording of Article 1402 prevents a reasonable interpretation from extending the scope of the Chapter so far. The words

---

[100] Simser (note 3 *supra*), at 203.
[101] US General Accounting Office, *Bank Regulatory Structure: Canada* (September 1995), p. 14 (GAO/GGD-95-223).
[102] *Ibid.*

clearly refer to only those organizations to which a bank must belong because a Party requires it. As the Parties do not require membership in the professional banking associations, joining is 'merely' a competitive measure. Thus, although it would be a welcome step for the professional associations to adopt internal guidelines that further the Chapter's goal of actual (as opposed to theoretical) liberalization of the financial services market, such a step cannot be demanded on the basis of NAFTA.

3.6.3 'Relating To'

There is no information on the directness with which the measures adopted by a Party must affect financial institutions. The treaty does not define the term 'relating to', nor is it discussed in the main interpretive works written on Chapter Fourteen.[103] While many measures that one could imagine a government applying would either directly affect a financial institution or be covered in another part of the treaty, there is nevertheless legitimate cause for concern that disputes could arise, the resolution of which will depend on the interpretation of 'relating to'.

As NAFTA has three official versions, in interpreting the phrase 'relating to' in English, one first must notice the wording of the Spanish and French texts to see whether the ambiguity is absent in one or both of those versions.[104] In this case, the interpretive process is not helped: 'relativa a' and 'concernant', are legitimately defined as 'relating to', and the nuances are not indicative of a different meaning.

The interpretation is further hampered when the phrase is sought in other parts of the NAFTA. Searching for the words 'relating to' in the English text reveals several instances of its use. These same passages in the Spanish and French versions, however, are not uniform in their use of words. While the language of Chapter Eleven (Investment) defines its scope as applying to measures *'relativas a* (a) los inversionistas de otra Parte'*, these are not the words used in the Spanish version of Chapter Ten on Government Procurement ('El presente capítulo se aplica a las medidas que una Parte adopte o mantenga *con relación a* las compras ...'.) or in Chapter Thirteen on Telecommunications ('Este capítulo se refiere a: (a) las medidas que adopte o mantenga una Parte, *relacionadas con* el acceso a y el uso de redes o servicios públicos de telecomunicaciones ...'.).

Analogies drawn from the use of the same phrases in the NAFTA Parties' domestic courts[105] leads to a conclusion that a broad reading may be called for. In 1993, the Canadian Supreme Court had to interpret the phrase 'relating to'. Faced with determining if a particular judicial proceeding fell within an exemption of a law, the Justice for the majority found the scope of the exception to be very broad. He based his determination mainly on the fact that 'relating to' is a term to be widely laid out. First addressing the

---

[103] See, e.g., Wethington (note 4 *supra*); Simser (note 3 *supra*).
[104] See 3.4 *supra* (interpretation).
[105] On the use of national court decisions by NAFTA panels, see 3.3.2 *supra*.

phrase 'in respect of', the Justice comments, '(t)he phrase "in respect of" is probably the widest of any expression intended to convey some connection between two related matters'.[106] He then continues, 'In my view, these comments are equally applicable to the phrase "relating to" … This breadth of meaning is confirmed when one examines the French version of the section which contained the expression "ayant trait a"'.[107]

Thus, in Canada, 'relating to' indicates a very wide reach of the law.

Recently, the United States' Supreme Court reaffirmed an earlier finding that the phrase 'relates to' should be interpreted broadly.[108] In the 1996 case, a nationally chartered bank wanting to sell insurance in a small town was forbidden by the State Insurance Commission from doing so. The federal statute governing such sales of insurance in small towns contained an 'anti-pre-emption' clause unless the conflicting federal statute 'relates to' the insurance business. In determining whether the anti-pre-emption clause were called for in this case, the unanimous Court states, '(t)he word "relates" is highly general, and this Court has interpreted it broadly in other pre-emption contexts'.[109] In a subsequent portion of the opinion, the Court also recalls that a statute may 'specifically relate to more than one thing'.[110] Taken together with the plain meaning of 'specifically' (indicating a more limited group of elements than otherwise), it can be presumed that a law can 'relate to' many things at once. Hence, a broad definition is given this phrase in United States jurisprudence also.

3.6.3.1 Panel Interpretations of 'Relating To' and 'Affecting' as Found in the WTO Agreements

3.6.3.1.1 INTERPRETATION OF GATT ARTICLE XX(G)

In the international trade agreements of the World Trade Organization (WTO) and General Agreement on Tariffs and Trade (GATT 1947), the definition of 'relating to' becomes more problematic. 'Relating to' is seldom used in the various WTO Agreements, the scope of which are mostly set out by the word 'affecting'. The phrase 'relating to' does exist in GATT-lex, however, and has itself been the object of a dispute settlement panel's attention. In the argument between Mexico and the United States over the

---

[106] *Slattery (Trustee of) v. Slattery*, Canadian Supreme Court [1993] 3 S.C.R. 430 at V.3.
[107] *Ibid.*
[108] *Barnett Bank of Marion County v. Nelson* 517 US 25, 116 S.Ct. 1103 (1996), reaffirming the finding of *Pilot Life Insurance Co. v. Dedeaux* 481 US 41, 47 (1987), in which 'relate to' means to have 'a connection with or reference to'; *Metropolitan Life Ins. Co. v. Massachusetts* 471 US 724, 739 (1985); *Shaw v. Delta Air Lines* 463 US 85, 97 (1983); *Morales v. Trans World Airlines* 504 US 374, 383–384 (1992)).
[109] *Barnett Bank* (note 108 *supra*), at 38. The court continues by citing 'See, e.g., *Pilot Life Ins. Co. v. Dedeaux*, 481 US 41, 47 (1987) (words "relate to" "have broad common-sense meaning, such that a state law 'relate(s) to' a benefit plan" … if it has a connection with or reference to such a plan"), quoting *Metropolitan Life* (note 108 *supra*), at 739 and *Shaw* (note 108 *supra*), at 97; *Morales* (note 108 *supra*), at 383–384, interpreting similarly the words 'relating to' in the Airline Deregulation Act.
[110] *Barnett Bank* (note 108 *supra*), at 41.

US law prohibiting imports of tuna, the panel had to interpret the extent of the GATT 1947 general exception for environmental protection measures.[111] Article XX of the GATT states that '… nothing in this Agreement shall be construed to prevent the adoption or enforcement by any contracting party of measures … (g) relating to the conservation of exhaustible resources …'.[112] In interpreting 'relating to', the panel noted that it agreed with an earlier panel, '… that the term 'relating to' should be taken to mean "primarily aimed" at the conservation … on the understanding that the words' primarily aimed at' referred not only to the purpose of the measure, but also to its effect on the conservation …'.[113]

Thus, 'relating to' under the GATT, at least in so far as the words are used in the general exceptions, is to be interpreted to *narrow* the scope of the provision.

3.6.3.1.2   INTERPRETATION OF GATS ANNEX ON FINANCIAL SERVICES USE OF 'AFFECTING'

In the framework of the WTO's regulation of services, the General Agreement on Trade in Services (GATS) Annex on Financial Services sets out the scope by the phrase 'measures *affecting* the supply of financial services' rather than by saying 'measures relating to the supply of financial services'. Yet the meanings are logically the same. One panel decision defining the term 'affecting' as used in GATT's Article III obligation of National Treatment is perhaps indicative of how the GATS term 'affecting' can be interpreted:

> The selection of the word 'affecting' would imply, in the opinion of the Panel, that the drafters of the Article intended to cover … not only the laws and regulations which directly governed the conditions of sale or purchase but also any laws or regulations which might adversely modify the conditions of competition between the domestic and imported products on the internal market.[114]

Here, the panel's interpretation of the phrase *broadens* the scope of the provision—the opposite of what the *Tuna* panel did for GATT Article XX(g)'s use of 'relating to'.

3.6.3.2   *Interpretation Based on Goals of Agreement*

The difference in the terms 'relating to' and 'affecting' as laid out by the GATT dispute settlement panels is subtle. It is not clear whether the panels' different interpretations of linguistically similar terms are based on the words themselves or on the underlying goal of the GATT to foster non-discrimination. The narrowness of scope attributed to the term 'relating to'

---

[111] United States—Restrictions on Imports of Tuna (text of the opinion can be found in 33:4 ILM 839 (1994)).
[112] GATT Art. XX(g).
[113] United States—Restrictions on Imports of Tuna, 33:4 ILM at 893.
[114] Italian Discrimination Against Imported Agricultural Machinery, BISD 7S/69, 64 (1959).

and the accompanying broadness of the term 'affecting', while not explicitly stated, must be seen in context: the general goal of the GATT is non-discrimination. Thus, the scope of Article III's national treatment obligation, containing the term 'affecting' is interpreted to encompass anything having to do with the conditions of competition. The use of exceptions allowing deviation from the national treatment obligation, including Article XX(g), using the same analysis, needs to be restricted: hence, a narrow reading of 'relating to' in the GATT panel opinion defining that term.[115] The NAFTA's Chapter Fourteen use of the term 'relating to' is, therefore, better compared to the description of the GATS' 'affecting'—that is, widely defined as a general principle.

Moreover, in the NAFTA context, the Parties' national courts' broad reading of 'relating to' is very influential evidence that the NAFTA's term should be interpreted in this way. Adding strength to a wide interpretation of the term 'relating to' in Chapter Fourteen is the recognition of the mixed character of the provisions. The provisions, as mentioned earlier, are not purely trade obligations. Rather, they are trade principles applied to financial services. Thus, a financial service perspective must be taken into account in the interpretation of the Chapter's terms. The case law of the Parties that give 'relates to' (or 'relating to') a broad reach are cases specifically addressing financial services. They therefore gain a heightened significance.

Accepting that the provisions of a treaty must be interpreted in the overall context of the agreement leads to the conclusion that the interpretation of 'relating to' as the indicator of the scope of NAFTA Chapter Fourteen will not necessarily be the same as it was for the GATT. Thus, instead of requiring that the measures be primarily aimed at financial institutions in order to be subject to the rest of the Chapter's provisions, NAFTA dispute settlement panels are likely to find that the NAFTA's goal of comprehensive coverage would require a broad interpretation of the term to be consistent with the overall context. A measure will 'relate to' financial institutions of another Party if the measure has some reasonable connection with financial institutions.

3.6.4   'Financial Institutions'

The NAFTA focuses on measures relating to 'financial institutions' rather than on those relating to financial products.[116] The institutional

---

[115] See also, *Tariffs Applied by Canada* (note 50 *supra*), at 32, para. 122 ('Any interpretation by the Panel must … promote rather than inhibit the NAFTA's objectives. Exceptions to obligations of trade liberalization must perforce be viewed with caution').

[116] NAFTA Art. 1401:1 states 'This Chapter applies to measures … relating to: (a) financial institutions of another Party'.

approach is significantly different than the service approach taken by the GATS.[117]

Under the definitions provided at the end of Chapter Fourteen, a financial institution is 'any financial intermediary or other enterprise that is authorized to do business and regulated or supervised as a financial institution under the law of the Party in whose territory it is located'.[118]

The language of this definition suffers from certain circularity, referring as it does to 'financial' intermediary and even to 'financial institution'. From most perspectives, the definition indicates an assumed spontaneous recognition. However, from the financial services regulatory perspective, the definition has an important function. This circularity allows the Parties to maintain ultimate control of what will be affected by the obligations of Chapter Fourteen.[119]

Presently, the definitions of financial institutions in Canada, the United States, and Mexico clearly include banks, thrifts, savings institutions, insurance companies, and non-finance (or limited finance) companies. Thus, such regulated industries may take advantage of the liberalizations Chapter Fourteen offers. The Parties' need to ensure a continued stability of their financial markets requires that they are able to oversee the actors affecting these markets. Hence the provision that to be within the scope of Chapter Fourteen a 'financial institution' must be recognized as such by its national government. A government's refusal to domestically recognize an enterprise

---

[117] Compare NAFTA Art. 1401:1 with GATS, Annex on Financial Services 1(a) ('This Annex applies to measures affecting the supply of financial services'). The CUFTA takes the institutional approach as well. See, e.g., CUFTA Art. 1702:1 ('… the United States of America shall permit domestic and foreign banks, including bank holding companies, … to engage in the dealing in, underwriting, and purchasing of debt obligations to a comparable degree by Canada …'.); CUFTA Art. 1702:2 (the United States 'shall not adopt … any measure under federal law that would accord treatment less favourable to Canadian-controlled banks …'.); CUFTA Art. 1703:2 ('Canada shall exempt United States-controlled Canadian bank subsidiaries … from limitations on the total domestic assets …'.); CUFTA Art. 1703:3 ('Canada shall not use review powers governing the entry of United States-controlled financial institutions …'.).

[118] NAFTA Art. 1416 ('financial institution'). The GATS Annex on Financial Services contains the following definition: 'A financial service is any service of a financial nature offered by a financial service supplier of a Member. Financial services include all insurance and insurance-related services, and all banking and other financial services (excluding insurance)': Annex on Financial Services 5(a). There follows a non-exclusive list of specific types of services that are included in the definition. The definition of 'financial service supplier' is not given in the Annex. Instead, 'service supplier' is found in the body of the GATS itself: "service supplier' means any person that supplies a service'. GATS Art. XXVII(g). It is the footnote included with this definition that is more interesting than the completely unhelpful definition. The footnote states that not only are juridical persons covered as suppliers, but branches, representative offices, and 'other forms of commercial presence' that are the indirect suppliers of services come under the definition as well. Thus, the obligations of the GATS are likewise applicable. GATS Art. XXVII(g), n.12.

[119] One commentator recalls that the definition of 'financial institution' is difficult to make more specifically because of the differences in how the Parties regulate their own financial institutions. While Canada has 4 different types of financial institutions, Mexico has 17 and the United States has around 100. Macario Schettino, *El TLC El Tratado de Libre Comercio: Qué Es y Cómo Nos Afecta* (Grupo Editorial Iberoamérica: México 1994), p. 48.

as a financial institution would prevent the application of the non-cross-border trade[120] liberalizations under Chapter Fourteen.[121] While such a non-recognition is unlikely to occur for a traditional bank or bank holding company, a new form of institution that is not allowed under the national laws of a party would not have rights granted by virtue of the NAFTA. For companies which do not fit the label of 'financial institution' within the Party, the NAFTA definition of 'financial intermediary' and 'financial enterprise' is determinative.

3.6.4.1   *'Financial Intermediary'*

The term 'financial intermediary' is nowhere defined in NAFTA. One is left to rely on other methods of interpretation. To interpret this by means of plain language, one must combine the definitions of each word. As there is no indication that 'financial' acts as anything more than a descriptive qualifier of 'intermediary', an additive definition is appropriate. A definition given in Black's Law Dictionary for 'financial' is 'relating to finances'[122] and 'intermediary' refers to a 'broker; one who is employed to negotiate a matter between two parties'.[123] Thus, a financial intermediary, based on a plain meaning interpretation, would be a financial broker. Taking the interpretation one step further, one defines a 'broker'. The usual broker is an individual, acting independently or as an agent. Thus, the term 'financial intermediary' indicates a natural person who negotiates matters relating to finance between two persons.

3.6.4.2   *'Financial Enterprise'*

The next term, 'financial enterprise' can be similarly defined. The qualifier 'financial' has the same meaning as above. Yet the term 'enterprise' indicates a legal person (the commercial firm). Chapter Two of NAFTA gives a general definition of 'enterprise': '... any entity constituted or organized under applicable law, whether or not for profit, and whether privately-owned or governmentally-owned, including any corporation, trust, partnership, sole proprietorship, joint venture or other association'.[124]

Therefore, a financial enterprise is a non-natural person that exists as a legal person and which has something to do with money and other forms of finance. The question of whether a branch is included is left unaddressed.[125]

---

[120] Cross-border trade liberalizations are available to 'financial service providers', which in turn need not be recognized by governments as 'financial service institutions'. See discussion of cross-border trade at 3.8 *infra*.

[121] The protections would then have to arise out of Chapter Eleven (Investment). See Wethington (note 4 *supra*), at 69.

[122] *Black's Law Dictionary* (note 62 *supra*), at 630.

[123] *Ibid.* at 815.

[124] NAFTA Art. 201 ('enterprise').

[125] While one could postulate that even branches are 'constituted or organized' under law, the non-mentioning of branches in the definition gives cause for questioning whether the branch form of business qualifies for the definition of an enterprise. See also discussion of 'financial institution of another Party', at 3.6.5 *infra*.

3.6.4.3 Finance Corporations

The unregulated financial institutions known as finance companies, so strong in the United States financial markets, were unknown under Mexican law during the NAFTA negotiations. Although the Mexican government promised to pass legislation to recognize financing companies under the category of 'limited finance corporation', some US auto-financing firms did not fall under this rubric, and therefore were excluded from the Chapter Fourteen benefits within Mexico.[126] These firms must rely on Chapter Eleven provisions to protect their market access and ability to undertake the competitive activities of their choice.[127]

3.6.5 'Financial Institutions of Another Party'

Generally, the benefits of Chapter Fourteen are offered exclusively to financial institutions 'of another Party'. The definition of 'of another Party' is very important but somewhat complicated. A 'financial institution of another Party' is a financial intermediary or enterprise '... including a branch, located in the territory of a Party that is controlled by persons of another Party'.[128]

3.6.5.1 Branch

The specific inclusion of branches of financial institutions is significant in several aspects. First, it indicates that the general definition of 'financial institution' *does not* include branches, but is limited to separate legal entities. In addition, the inclusion of branches means that the banks' provisions of services in Canada's and Mexico's highly networked banking systems will not be burdened by measures designed to ensure that the services offered in other Party territories or to other Party persons originate from the parent office. Finally, the United States' allowance of foreign banks to directly branch into the US market has the result that these branches may be eligible for NAFTA benefits if they are 'controlled by persons of another Party'.[129]

3.6.5.2 Territory of a Party

Under Chapter Two (General Definitions), the territory of each Party is set out, and for the existing NAFTA Parties includes the customs territories of

---

[126] Cross-border trade is the exception. See 3.8 *infra*.

[127] Wethington (note 4 *supra*), at 69, n.2.

[128] NAFTA Art. 1416.

[129] As US law on control of banks recognizes 25 per cent ownership of stock as legal control, a minority shareholding by NAFTA Party persons may be sufficient for a branch of a foreign bank to reap the benefits of Chapter Fourteen. Canada's 1999 financial reform legislation allowing for direct branching by all WTO Member banks will extend the NAFTA benefits to those branches that can pass the control test as well.

Canada, the United States, and the States of Mexico.[130] In addition, the territory includes the territorial seas of each Party and Mexico's islands and the seas adjacent to them.

3.6.5.3   *Persons of Another Party*

For purposes of the NAFTA in general, a 'person of another Party' may be either a natural or juridical person.[131] A branch of a company, however, is not a 'person of another Party'.[132]

3.6.5.3.1   NATURAL PERSON

A natural person is considered a 'person' under the NAFTA. To receive the benefits of the Agreements, the individual must be either a citizen or a permanent resident of a Party.[133] A 'person of a Party' also includes 'a national or citizen' of Mexico as defined by the Mexican Constitution's Articles 30 and 34,[134] and 'a national of the United States' as defined by the US Immigration and Nationality Act for persons who were United States nationals as of 1 January 1994.[135]

3.6.5.3.2   JURIDICAL PERSON

If the 'person' is a juridical person, it includes 'any entity constituted or organized under applicable law' of a Party,[136] including government-owned and privately owned enterprises.[137]

3.6.5.3.3   DUAL TEST

To determine whether an enterprise is a 'person of a Party', the NAFTA has two tests: the residency test and the control test. Generally, NAFTA provisions recognize enterprises as persons of a Party as long as the enterprise is incorporated in the territory of a Party or under the territory's law. This is the residence rule, and is valid in Mexico and the United States.

Canada employs the control test in its domestic legal regime. Consequently, it took a reservation to the financial service liberalization to ensure that only enterprises that are ultimately controlled by Party persons can benefit from NAFTA liberalizations in Canada. Thus, only if a person or parent company that is in the territory of Canada for at least 183 days per year owns or directs at least 50 per cent of the stock of a financial institution, will the enterprise benefit from the NAFTA Chapter Fourteen liberalizations.[138] The result is that if a bank located in Canada is only

---

[130] NAFTA Annex 201.1 ('territory').
[131] NAFTA Art. 1416 ('person of a Party'); NAFTA Art. 201 ('person of a Party').
[132] NAFTA Art. 1416 ('person of a Party').
[133] NAFTA Art. 201 ('person of a Party').
[134] NAFTA Annex 201.1 ('national' (a)).
[135] NAFTA Annex 201.1 ('national' (b)).
[136] NAFTA Art. 201 ('enterprise of a Party').
[137] NAFTA Art. 201 ('enterprise').
[138] See NAFTA Annex VII, Schedule of Canada, Section B (2) (use of control test for purposes of foreign ownership limits and limits on foreign financial assets benefits under NAFTA).

nominally owned by either Mexican or United States citizens, but its activities are actually directed by a non-NAFTA Party person, the bank may be refused the NAFTA benefits.[139]

Shell corporations, or entities established in one Party by non-Party incorporators for the sole purpose of entering another Party, may also be denied benefits of the NAFTA.[140]

3.6.5.4 Treatment of Branches as 'Financial Institutions' and 'Financial Institutions of Another Party'

Whether or not branches of financial institutions are to be extended the benefits of Chapter Fourteen is not always clear from the text of the Agreement. The definition given for 'person of a Party' specifically excludes branches of non-Party enterprises from its reach.[141] The 'financial institution of another Party' definition specifically includes branches of financial institutions within its scope.[142] At the same time, there is nothing in the general definition of 'financial institution' to indicate either the inclusion or the non-inclusion of branches, thus bringing this ambiguity to the fore. The reference to branches in the more specific definition (financial institution of another Party) suggests that the Parties meant to leave branches out of the scope of the general definition (financial institution). With no positive textual basis for this suggestion, however, principles of general corporate law could be invoked. In US corporate law, for example, a branch is an integral part of the corporation as a whole. This would lead to an inclusion of branches of financial institutions in both the general and the NAFTA Party specific definitions.

However, based on the context of Chapter Fourteen (with the mentioning of branches in another provision) and the presumed intent of the Parties to limit the benefits of the Agreement to NAFTA Party institutions, there is a strong argument to be made that branches are only to be included when specifically mentioned. Thus, references to 'financial institutions' in the Agreement would not refer to branches, while references to 'financial institutions of another Party' would.

Whether branches are or are not 'financial institutions' generally will be unimportant to the outcome of a particular case. The differential treatment of branches according to the nationality of the parent entity reflects the influence of the European Union's Second Banking Directive on the drafting of the financial service provisions of NAFTA. The Second Directive requires the establishment of subsidiaries in the territory of a European Member State in order to benefit from the internal market liberalizations. The NAFTA terms attempt to reciprocate with a similar

---

[139] The provision on Denial of Benefits provides another instrument for ensuring that non-Party persons do not have actual control over financial institutions benefitting from the NAFTA. See 3.15.4 *infra* (discussion of NAFTA Art. 1113).

[140] See 5.4.2 *infra*.

[141] NAFTA Art. 1416 ('person of a Party').

[142] NAFTA Art. 1416 ('financial institution of another Party').

limitation on branching by external institutions.[143] However, in examining the Chapter Fourteen provisions, one realizes that generally the term used in reference to obligations is 'financial institution of another Party' and there is no instance in which the use of 'financial institution' makes a resolution of the branch/no branch question decisive. Thus, while it would, in this author's view, be incorrect to say either that branches are or are not included as 'financial institutions', the mistake would have no impact on the working of the Chapter. Therefore, the question will be left unanswered.

3.6.6 'Investor of Another Party'

The NAFTA provides no definition for 'investor of another Party'. It does, however, give definitions for the various terms of the phrase, and from these separate definitions, one can discern the intended meaning. An 'investor' is a Party, person, or enterprise that is attempting to set up, or that has set up, 'an enterprise' or that has committed 'capital or other resources' in a territory of a Party in order to undertake economic activities in that territory.[144] An 'investor of a Party' is an investor that is a Party or that is a national or permanent resident of that Party, or an investor that is organized under the laws of a Party.[145]

An 'investor of another Party' is thus, presumably, an investor from a Party that seeks to set up economic activities in one of the other Parties' territories.[146] Further, an 'investor of another Party' may be a Party, person, or enterprise that has 'an interest in an enterprise' that gives the owner a right to share either the income or profits of the enterprise or a right to a share of the

---

[143] For more detailed information on the Second Banking Directive, see Barbara C. Matthews, 'The Second Banking Directive: Conflicts, Choices, and Long-Term Goals' (1992) 2:1 Duke J Comp & Int'l L 89; Jane Louise Powell, '1992: Single European Market Implications for the Insurance Sector' (1990) 13:2 BC Int'l & Comp L Rev 371; Christine Rossini, 'Cross-Border Banking in the EC: Host Country Powers Under the Second Banking Directive' (1995) 4 Europ Rev Private L 571; Craig M. Scheer, 'The Second Banking Directive and Deposit Insurance in the European Union: Implications for US Banks' (1994) 28:1 Geo Wash J Int'l L & Econ 171 (note); Shari Siegel, 'Slouching Toward Integration: International Banking Before and After 1992' (1989) 11:1 Cardozo L Rev 147; Gerhard Wegen, 'Transnational Financial Services: Current Challenges for an Integrated Europe' (1992) 60:6 Fordham L Rev S91.

[144] NAFTA Art. 1416 ('investor of a Party', 'investment'); NAFTA Art. 1139 ('investment' (a)–(d)). For a comparison of the definitions of 'investment' in the NAFTA, the GATS, and the Energy Charter Treaty, see Pierre Sauvé, 'Qs and As on Trade, Investment and the WTO' (1997) 31:4 J World Trade 55, 63–65, explaining that the definitions in NAFTA and the Energy Charter Treaty are much broader than in GATS, indicating a more effective framework for liberalization.

[145] NAFTA Art. 1416 ('investor of a Party').

[146] 'Investor of another Party', like 'financial service provider of another Party' and 'cross-border financial service provider of another Party' are used in the Agreement's text, but are not specifically defined in the Art. 1416 Definitions. There, the terms are defined for 'investor of a Party', for example. A reasonable assumption is that 'another Party' refers to a NAFTA Party from which the investor does not originate.

[147] NAFTA Art. 1139 ('investment' (e)–(h)).

[148] NAFTA Art. 1139 ('investment' (d)(i)).

assets when the enterprise is dissolved.[147] A Party, person, or enterprise that is attempting to have or that has a debt security of or loan to an affiliated non-state enterprise[148] or a debt security 'where the original maturity ... is at least three years' is also an 'investor' for purposes of Chapter Fourteen as long as the debt security or loan 'issued by a financial institution ... is treated as regulatory capital by the Party in whose territory the financial institution is located'.[149]

The unwieldy definition of 'investor of another Party' is based on the characteristic of a Party, person, or enterprise that has an 'investment', as defined by the Chapter of the Agreement that deals with investments (Chapter Eleven). As the terms of this definition address investments themselves, they are best understood from the perspective of the financial service law. Unlike trade law's traditional 'enterprise-based scope' to investment,[150] NAFTA uses the more financial 'asset-based approach':

> ... the NAFTA (Article 1139—Definitions) ... define[s] investment using an asset-based approach which covers a wide range of direct and portfolio investments, including ownership and other interests in an enterprise, as well as interests that entitle an owner to share in the income or profits of an enterprise, real estate and all forms of tangible and intangible property. This includes physical assets, intellectual property rights, goodwill, securities, long-term loans linked to an investment, joint-ventures, concession agreements, licensing agreements and similar rights arising undercontracts.[151]

Thus, the difference in the financial characteristics of the capital flow is important for determining whether the particular flow will benefit from the liberalizing terms of the NAFTA.[152]

One of the motivating interests in creating a free trade area for financial services, it should be remembered, was Mexico's need to attract more long-term capital investment.[153] During the NAFTA negotiations, therefore, the Mexican government strove to ensure that foreign capital flows to Mexico (at least those from the NAFTA partners) would be increasingly in the form of infrastructure development and economically productive activities. This consideration certainly played a role in the drafting of the asset-based

---

[149] NAFTA Art. 1139 ('investment' (d)(ii)).

[150] Sauvé (note 144 *supra*), at 64.

[151] *Ibid.* at 65.

[152] The placing of investments and the treatment of Party investments, on the other hand, are governed by the trade-oriented establishment and NTO provisions of Chapters Fourteen and Eleven.

[153] Mexico's economic collapse of 1995 is widely believed to have been caused in large part by the magnitude of foreign capital invested on the stock exchange. When inflation increased, the highly liquid funds were rapidly withdrawn, leaving a devestated economy as the only trace of prior foreign moneys. A Mexican economist noted that there are problems from increased foreign capital flows as well as benefits. Jaime Ros, 'Financial Markets and Capital Flows in Mexico', in José Antonio Ocampo and Rober to Steiner (eds), *Foreign Capital in Latin America* (Interamerican Development Bank, Washington, DC, 1994), pp. 193–239, at 193–4 stated as follows:

definition of 'investment'. Among the most important definitional criteria is the requirement that extensions of credit for commercial transactions be for longer than three years if they are to be considered an 'investment'.[154] Such characteristics not only encourage the input of funds to building a viable economic system for the future, but they also attempt to prevent the massive withdrawal of investment capital from the country should economic instability increase.[155]

Finally, the NAFTA definition of 'investment' excludes loans issued by states.[156] Thus, sovereign debt does not qualify as an investment.[157]

3.6.7   'Cross-Border Trade in Financial Services'

The term 'cross-border trade in services' refers to the bringing of a service, a service provider, or a service consumer across a national border. Cross-border trade is the only form of international trade in products, but is a relatively new addition to the law of trade in services.[158] The concept is important to trade law due to the intangible nature of most services. The following is a brief introduction to the term. The provisions on cross-border trade in financial services are discussed fully in the discussion on Article 1404.[159]

3.6.7.1   Cross-Border Trade

There are three basic constellations of financial service trading that constitute protectable 'cross-border trade' for Chapter Fourteen. Each involves a combination of the service provider of one nationality and a customer of another nationality, and each has certain limitations.

(Contd.)

> First, to the extent that they cause appreciation of the real exchange rate and greater fluctuations thereof, their impact on exports and the import-substitution sectors is negative, thus creating new macroeconomic adjustment problems in the medium term. This subject is of particular importance in the current climate of trade liberalization.
>
> If, in addition, the flows are concentrated in highly liquid financial assets, the process of real exchange rate appreciation must be dealt with in conditions of growing financial instability. Finally, they may be inadequately regulated and thus result in a poor allocation of resources (between consumption and investment, financial and physical assets, and among various economic sectors).

[154] Wethington (note 4 *supra*), at 72–3.

[155] For an economic analysis of how liberalizations in developing countries affect investment, see Kanhaya L. Gupta and Robert Lensink, *Financial Liberalization and Investment* (Routledge, London, 1996).

[156] NAFTA Art. 1139 ('investment' (c): 'does not include a debt security ... of a state enterprise'; (d): 'does not include a loan ... to a state enterprise').

[157] Wethington (note 4 *supra*), at 72.

[158] Cross-border trade in financial services was not provided for under the Canada-United States Free Trade Agreement. See CUFTA Chapter 17.

[159] See 3.8 *infra* (cross-border trade).

One of the constellations of cross-border trade is the 'providing' of a financial service from one Party's territory into the territory of another Party. An example of this would be the loaning of funds from a Canadian bank account to a corporation in Mexico.[160] Here, the service itself crosses the border.

The second type of activity covered by cross-border trade provisions is the service given by a Party national in that Party's territory to a national of another Party. Thus, a United States banker could give investment advice to a Mexican citizen in the banker's New York office. In this case, the consumer of the service crosses the border.

The third constellation for cross-border trade under the NAFTA is when a Party national provides a financial service in another Party's territory. In this case, a Mexican banker could travel with her customer to Montreal to advise him on investment possibilities in Canada. Here, the service provider crosses the border.

Specifically excluded from the definition of cross-border trade under Chapter Fourteen is the provision of a financial service in the territory of a Party by an investment in the same territory.[161] This is so even if the investor is of a different Party as the Party in which the investment is placed. As one author explains:

> ... the provision of investment advisory services by the Mexico city subsidiary of a New York investment firm to a Mexican citizen in Mexico City would not be cross-border trade in financial services. However, the provision of investment advisory services by a United States national visiting Mexico, but employed by a New York firm, to a Mexican national in Mexico City would be considered cross-border trade in financial services.[162]

Because there is no crossing of a border by either the service, the consumer of the service, or the service provider, such a transaction would be regulated by domestic authorities under a national law framework.

3.6.7.2 *Financial Service*

A financial service is any service that is 'of a financial nature'.[163] Thus, banking and similar loan activities are covered. Moreover, the NAFTA term includes insurance services. Although insurance services are generally considered financial services, in the CUFTA context, such services were excluded from the trade liberalizations.[164]

Under NAFTA, 'financial service' also includes the incidental and auxiliary services related to the financial-natured services.[165] Therefore, the

---

[160] Wethington (note 4 *supra*), at 73.
[161] *Ibid.* at 73, 74.
[162] *Ibid.* at 74.
[163] NAFTA Art. 1416 ('financial service').
[164] Canada-United States Free Trade Agreement excluded insurance underwriting services and the selling of insurance from the definition of financial service, and thus from the Chapter 17 provisions' coverage. CUFTA Art. 1706 ('financial service').
[165] NAFTA Art. 1416 ('financial service').

delivery of banking records from one financial institution to another may be considered a 'financial service', because it is auxiliary to the provision of banking services.

It is important to note that whether a service is a financial service or not depends, for purposes of cross-border trade, on the type of activity itself. It does not depend, as it does in other parts of the Agreement, upon the provider's status as a regulated service provider.[166] Thus, the delivery company responsible for the transfer of banking records would enjoy NAFTA cross-border trade benefits. More significantly, the US financial companies (such as those the American auto industries control) would be eligible for the benefits of cross-border trading possibilities contained in NAFTA, whereas they would not be eligible for the other types of benefits found in Chapter Fourteen (such as establishment).

3.7   ESTABLISHMENT OF FINANCIAL INSTITUTIONS (ARTICLE 1403)

The term 'establishment' of an institution refers to the setting up of a physical or legal presence in a territory. More person-oriented than trade in goods, service trade in some cases requires a physical presence of the provider to be economically viable. Even when a service provider could perform a service from abroad, the establishment of service facilities in foreign territories has been increasingly used as the service delivery mode of choice for international business because it offers the provider the advantages of close contact with the customers and a better 'feel' for the local business context.[167] Such considerations are particularly important for most types of financial services. Thus, establishment has become a basic tool used in international trade law to increase the flow of services around the world.[168] The NAFTA Parties' agreement to grant access to their markets by establishment was an important component of the negotiations and the principle of establishment set out in Article 1403 is one of the most significant elements of NAFTA regulation of trade in financial services.[169]

Article 1403:4 provides the basis for the right of NAFTA Party investors to establish financial service institutions in the other Parties' territories: 'Each Party shall permit an investor of another Party that does not own or

---

[166] See Wethington (note 4 *supra*), at 73, n.18.

[167] The desire to establish locally in the service market is particularly prevalent among US service providers. WTO, *Trade Policy Review: United States 1996*, WT/TPR/S/16 (1996), p. 13, para. 24.

[168] The concept of offering foreign firms a right to establishment together with the allowance of cross-border service trade corresponds to the two main methods used to increase the trade in goods, namely the reduction of tariffs and restricting the use of quotas.

[169] One set of authors call financial institution's right of establishment 'an issue of threshold importance for providers and their governments' even though they see the possibility that in the future long-distance banking may become widespread even in the retail business. Richard J. Herring and Robert E. Litan, *Financial Regulation in the Global Economy* (Brookings Institution, Washington, DC, 1995), p. 89.

control a financial institution in the Party's territory to establish a financial institution in that territory'.[170]

This right of establishment is subjected to each Party's national regulatory framework that may set out the legal form of the new establishment[171] and other 'terms and conditions on establishment'.[172] These conditions must adhere to the national treatment obligation, however.[173] As such, the NAFTA right to establishment is a vast improvement over the past.[174]

Specifically, under Article 1403, each Party agrees to open its market to investors from another Party that want to form a financial service institution from which to conduct business in that territory. Due to the historic limitations on foreign bank access to the Canadian market and the nearly complete prohibition of foreign financial service providers from the Mexican market since 1982, Article 1403 is of great symbolic importance: opening the world's financial markets between developed economies and an emerging economy on a nearly equal basis, it marks a leap forward in the globalization of financial services.

The hortatory language and narrowness of the obligations that do exist, however, dampen the radical idea behind the Article.[175] The paragraphs governing the legal form of the established financial institution and the post-establishment extensions begin, '[t]he Parties recognize the *principle …*'.[176]

Viewed from a negotiating process perspective, Article 1403 provisions can be explained by both 'the importance of maximizing the win-set of counterpart negotiators in the other countries' and the '[l]owest common denominator bargaining' that took place among the financial service negotiating teams from all three countries.[177] The United States' lead negotiator for financial services pointed to Article 1403 as the product of the Parties' desiring to come to a mutually-agreeable agreement more than their wishing to have an entirely satisfactory agreement:

---

[170] NAFTA Art. 1403:4.

[171] That is, whether a foreign bank may be established as a branch of the foreign parent or whether it must be separately incorporated as a subsidiary. NAFTA Art. 1403:4(a).

[172] NAFTA Art. 1403:4(b).

[173] *Ibid.* The national treatment obligation of NAFTA Art. 1405 is discussed at 3.9 *infra*.

[174] Whether the General Agreement on Trade in Services (GATS) provisions for market access are subject to the national treatment obligation of that Agreement is debatable. While most commentators assume that the former obligation does extend to the latter, an expert from the Trade in Services Division of the WTO is unsure if this is necessarily so from a plain reading of the GATS text. See Aaditya Mattoo, 'National Treatment in the GATS: Corner-Stone or Pandora's Box?' (1997) 31:1 J World Trade 107, 113–19 (Section B entitled 'GATS: Text versus Context').

[175] Wethington writes that the provisions are 'significant statements of principle which the NAFTA Parties recognize as important guidelines to future action, but they do not constitute binding obligations'. Wethington (note 4 *supra*), at 83.

[176] NAFTA Art. 1403:1 (emphasis supplied). In context, the paragragh reads: 'The Parties recognize the principle that an investor of another Party should be permitted to establish a financial institution … in the juridical form chosen by such investor'. NAFTA Article 1403:1. See also NAFTA Art. 1403:2 ('The Parties recognize the principle that an investor of another Party should be permitted to participate widely …'.).

[177] Wethington (note 4 *supra*), at 21. Mr Wethington adopts the terminology of negotiation analysis formulated by Robert D. Putnam in 'Diplomacy and Domestic Politics: The Logic of Two-Level Games' (1998) 42 Int'l Org 427.

> Absent a willingness to use coercive tactics to compel assent to particular provisions or a willingness to construct side-payment deals outside the negotiation, the Parties, in the financial services arena, preserved their sovereign rights to continue the existing regime … Only if an issue rose to the level of a deal-breaker could a solution be forced—again to avoid a noagreement scenario. Once core principles were established, the desire to produce an agreement drove disposition of specific secondary issues.[178]

Yet even with each Party unwilling or politically unable to concede particular aspects of its national law during the negotiations, the establishment provisions remain essential to the entire Chapter Fourteen framework. Moreover, the provisions are open to more liberalizing modification should domestic banking laws of the Parties change.[179]

3.7.1   'Investors of Another Party'

For purposes of Article 1403, the term 'investor of another Party' refers only to investors that are financial service providers in another Party.[180] Thus, by implication, only those investors with experience in and (perhaps more importantly from a banking regulator's perspective) with a record of operating financial institutions will benefit from the new openings of the financial service markets. The treaty language does not indicate how long the investor must have 'engaged' in business in the home Party's territory, but the requirement effectively excludes a non-Party investor from establishing a shell financial corporation in one Party and using it as a stepping stone into the next.[181]

3.7.2   Parties' Disagreement on the Extent of the Establishment Obligations: Direct Branching and Securities Activities

It is the first several provisions of Article 1403 that set out the Parties' areas of non-agreement. The provisions of Article 1403:1, 1403:2, and 1403:3, set out aims rather than obligations. Nevertheless, these provisions are

---

[178] Wethington (note 4 *supra*), at 21–2.
[179] See 3.7.3 *infra*.
[180] NAFTA Art. 1403:5.
[181] In an interview, Robert Herzstein, counsel for Mexico during the NAFTA negotiations, said that the requirement of prior engagement in financial service operations was the request of the Mexican government. Interview with Mr Herzstein, January 1997. The inference that this author draws from such a statement is that the Mexican government feared the United States' liberal establishment policy toward foreign banks. They wanted an exclusion for shell corporations to be expressed as a separate provision rather than merely implied by the prudential regulation provisions because otherwise the US policies could have been used by non-Party members to gain entry to the Mexican market. See also Wethington (note 4 *supra*), at 72.

important indicators of the Parties' desire to continue working toward increased liberalization.[182]

Tentatively worded, Article 1403:1 provides that the NAFTA Parties 'recognize the principle' that Parties' investors 'should' be able to establish a financial institution in any legal form.[183] At issue here is the question of whether a Party may require an investor of another Party to establish a financial service institution as a branch or a subsidiary of an existing institution in the home country. While the United States (and most States of the United States) allows foreign banks to establish as a branch, Mexico's post-NAFTA market and Canada's required the subsidiary form of establishment for foreign financial institutions.[184] The United States had long complained of Canada's subsidiary-rule, seeing the cost-efficiencies of branches as outweighing the disadvantages of not having all the assets within the host country. Article 1403:1 thus reflects a long-standing dispute among the Parties (although the dispute has been partially resolved by Canada's financial reform laws allowing direct branching as of 1999). Just why the drafters inserted such language is unclear in view of the continuing disagreement. However, the explicit expression that the issue was left undecided ensures that in the future no judicial interpretation will incorrectly find that silence on the matter meant one outcome or the other.

In the next paragraph, the Parties again 'recognize' that Party investors should be allowed to engage in diverse financial service activities and to spread their commercial operations throughout the country.[185] The language of this passage is clearly aimed at the United States' legislative prohibitions on the combination of investment banking and deposit-taking activities.[186] It also points to the US restrictions on inter-State branching for financial service institutions.[187] Canada and Mexico, both having national banking systems that allow financial institutions to offer universal service, would have liked the United States to commit itself to removing its internal barriers, but their efforts in this direction were to no avail. There are no provisions in Chapter Fourteen to require the United States to allow for nation-

---

[182] Wethington (note 4 *supra*), at 83:

> It was not possible ... in the context of the NAFTA negotiations to reach agreement on these various elements because of their regulatory and political complexity. Instead, the Parties sought to capture in a statement of principle the direction toward which future evolutions on government policy should aspire. The statement of principles ... is carefully worded to balance competing sensitivities and objectives of the three NAFTA Parties.

[183] NAFTA Art. 1403:1.

[184] Canada and Mexico were concerned about the financial stability of a branch, and wanted the assets of the institution located in their territory to be reliant on its own assets. Since the going into effect of NAFTA, Canada has changed its banking legislation to permit direct branching. See 2.2.2.2.4 *supra*.

[185] NAFTA Art. 1403:2.

[186] See discussion of the Glass-Steagall Act restrictions on bank-securities relationships, 12 U.S.C. §§ 24(7), 78, 377, 378; see 2.1.2.1 *supra* (US banking law).

[187] See discussion of the McFadden Act, 12 U.S.C. § 36, at 2.1.2.1.2 *supra* (US banking law).

wide branching, nor is there an obligation for the US to permit universal banking. The United States' two neighbors settled for the agreement to once again 'recognize the principle' of the preference for investors to 'be permitted to participate widely in a Party's market'.[188]

3.7.2.1   Effects of Article 1403

The immediate tangible effects of the NAFTA Article 1403 right to establishment are twofold. First is the ability of NAFTA banks to establish in Mexico, and the signaling of a fundamental change in Mexican government policy toward foreign financial service providers. Secondly are the effects relating to the procedural guarantees of non-discriminatory treatment during the process of establishment. Although the Parties may limit the legal form of establishments, the commitment to continue negotiations for further liberalizations is an achievement in itself. Such progress is not to be underestimated for the future landscape of financial services.

3.7.3   Exceptions to Establishment Obligations

Finally, it is important to note the Parties' Annex VII reservations to their establishment obligations.[189] An integral part of the NAFTA, Annex VII sets out the particulars of the Agreement's coverage for each Party in a three part 'schedule'. The provisions of Mexico's schedule regarding establishment are particularly important to financial service institutions wishing to set up commercial activities in that country.[190] A cursory description of the Canadian and United States schedules will be given as well.

3.7.3.1   Canada's Exceptions to Establishment

3.7.3.1.1   FEDERAL RESTRICTIONS ON ESTABLISHMENT

Under the Chapter Fourteen provisions, NAFTA Party financial institutions may establish in Canada only in the legal form of a separately incorporated subsidiary. (This has since been changed to permit direct branching.) Beyond this restriction, Canada has only one provision in its Annex VII schedule that limits its obligations to offer financial service providers of another Party the right to establish in Canadian territory. Section C, paragraph 1 of the Canadian schedule promises to afford the same treatment to Mexican residents and financial institutions as it does United States

---

[188]   NAFTA Art. 1403:2. The United States in turn had to accept that the Mexican and Canadian governments maintain certain ownership requirements in contravention of the most-favored-nation obligation.

[189]   See NAFTA Annex VII.

[190]   It should be noted that Mexico periodically revises its laws to accomodate the progressive liberalization schedules of the NAFTA. Therefore, anyone interested in entering Mexico should consult the latest official figures before doing so.

residents and institutions as regarding the Canadian limits on foreign ownership of financial assets.[191]

Referring to several domestic laws governing banking, insurance, and investment companies, the Canadians effectively exempt Mexicans from the 25 per cent maximum on aggregate foreign holdings of widely-held financial institutions required by the Canadian investment rules.[192] At the same time, Canada maintains its restrictions on the level of the individual, providing that no person may own more than 10 per cent of any single widely-held institution.[193]

3.7.3.1.2   PROVINCIAL RESERVATIONS

There are many restrictions on financial institution establishment imposed by the individual Canadian Provinces. These do not affect commercial bank establishment, but do extend from insurance and securities firms to credit unions, loan institutions, and trust corporations. The reservations often have residency in the Province as a prerequisite for establishment. Because Canadian banks may have insurance subsidiaries, however, there might be a discriminatory effect on foreign banks' ability to provide a full range of services. Still, the rules for insurance and securities firms are more likely to be a barrier to trade than are those for bank-like institutions.[194]

3.7.3.2   *Mexico's Exceptions to Establishment*

Mexico's commitments under the NAFTA Chapter Fourteen provisions were a great change from its foreign financial institution policies of the

---

[191] NAFTA Annex VII, Schedule of Canada, Section C, para. 1.

[192] This exemption had been granted to the financial service providers of the United States under the Canada-United States Free Trade Agreement, Art. 1703.

[193] See Kenneth L. Bachman, Scott N. Benedict and Ricardo A. Anzaldua, 'Financial Services Under the North American Free Trade Agreement: An Overview', in Judith H. Bello, Alan F. Holmer and Joseph J. Norton (eds), *The North American Free Trade Agreement: A New Frontier in International Trade and Investment in the Americas* (ABA, Washington, DC, 1994), p. 229.

[194] As an example, note the following reservations:

> *Alberta*—incorporation of a credit union in Alberta is limited to residents, and mortgage brokers must have lived in Canada for three months prior to registration and maintain residency in Alberta for registration. Credit Union Act, R.S.A. 1980, c. C-31.1; Mortgage Brokers Regulation Act, R.S.A. 1980, c. M-19. Individuals applying for registration as portfolio investment intermediaries or as securities brokers and dealers must have lived in Canada for one year and be a resident of the Province on the date of application. Securities Act, S.A. 1981, c. S-6.1, as amended.
>
> *British Columbia*—the provincial Minister of Finance may refuse to charter a trust company or an insurance company if he or she has reason to believe that the applicant either has control over 10 per cent or more of the voting interests in the trust or if, it is not in the public interest that the person have such control or influence. The Minister's decision on what the public interest is may, and does, 'take into account the degree of foreign ownership and discriminate[s] on that basis'. Financial Institutions Act, S.B.C. 1989, c. 47. Credit unions may only be established if the subscribers are residents of British Columbia. Credit Union Incorporation Act, S.B.C. 1989, c. 23.

1980s. Moreover, Mexico is a developing country, whose domestic financial institutions are weak from the years without competition and with the heavy control of the state. It is not surprising, therefore, that Mexico's obligations to offer establishment to its NAFTA partners' financial institutions are softened by extensive reservations.[195]

First, any financial institution of another Party must establish itself as a separately incorporated subsidiary. Branches do not enjoy the advantages of the right to establish in Mexico.

The most significant reservations set out in Mexico's schedule are those regarding the limits on the foreign financial assets of other Party nationals. According to Part B of the Schedule, the maximum capital an individual was to be allowed to own is 1.5 per cent of the aggregate capital of commercial banks, casualty insurance firms, or life and health insurance companies. The limit is set at 4 per cent for securities firms. These limits have since been raised.

In Section B, paragraph 14, the Mexican government limits establishment to persons of other Parties that are already 'directly or through any of its affiliates, engaged in the same general type of financial services in the territory of the other Party'.[196] A securities brokerage established in Vancouver, therefore, would not have a right to be given permission to incorporate a life insurance company in Acapulco. However, once a financial service provider of a Party establishes (or acquires) a commercial bank or securities company, that provider may form a 'financial holding company'. Through the holding company, the provider of one type of financial service may establish or acquire other financial service institutions in accordance to laws governing Mexican nationals.[197]

Further, Mexico may adopt measures that would prevent the other Parties' investors from establishing 'more than one institution of the same type in Mexico'.[198] This means that while branches of a commercial bank

---

(Contd.)

> *Manitoba*—only Canadian residents will be eligible for a license to act as an insurance agent or broker. Insurance Act, C.C.S.M. 140.
>
> *Ontario*—foreign persons are subject to an ownership limit of 10 per cent for individuals and 25 per cent in the aggregate for various bank-like companies, trust companies, consumer loan companies, business financing companies, mortgage companies, and mortgage brokers. Mortgage Brokers Act, R.S.O. 1990, M. 39; R.R.O. 1990, Reg. 798.

Provincial reservations may be found in 'Appendix N: Provincial Reservations of Canada', in Wethington (note 4 *supra*), at 322–421.

[195] See Stephen T. Zamora, 'Comments on the Regulation of Financial and Legal Services in Mexico Under NAFTA' (1993) 1:1 US-Mex LJ 77 ('The partial opening of Mexican financial markets to foreign financial institutions is a welcome development, but the Financial Services Chapter of NAFTA contains numerous qualifications, and a staged process of liberalization, [footnote omitted] that demonstrate the concern of the Mexican government in proceeding cautiously in this area. Because the financial system lies at the heart of all economic activity, this caution is well deserved').

[196] NAFTA Annex VII, Section B, para. 14.

[197] NAFTA Annex VII, Section C, para. 5. See also Bachman *et al.* (note 193 *supra*), at 222.

[198] NAFTA Annex VII, Section B, para. 14.

may be established anywhere, the owners of that bank do not have the right to open several commercial banks, each separately incorporated as subsidiaries of the foreign parent.

3.7.3.3   United States' Exceptions to Establishment

3.7.3.3.1   FEDERAL RESTRICTIONS ON ESTABLISHMENT

Establishment of a financial institution in the United States is subjected to virtually no discrimination on the basis of nationality. Additionally, either a subsidiary or a branch of a foreign bank is a permissible form for entering the US banking market. Under its Annex VII Schedule, the United States therefore takes no reservations regarding establishment of national banks.

---

[199] State reservations to Chapter Fourteen taken at the close of the negotiations can be found in 'Appendix O: State Reservations in the United States', in Wethington (note 4 *supra*), at 422–524. Possible reservations would allow the following laws to be maintained:

California—non-US banks and bank holding companies are subject to a reciprocity requirement in order to acquire more than a 5 per cent ownership interest in a California bank or bank holding company. California Financial Code, §§ 3750–3761. Substantial reciprocity is also required for non-US banks in California to establish State-chartered branches. Cal. Fin. Code § 1753(b)(7); 10 Cal. Code Reg. §§ 10.14100-10.14188. Foreign bank branches in California have limited trust powers. Cal. Fin. Code §§ 1503, 1755(b). Foreign banks and the banks under foreign control must receive the approval of the Superintendent before they may acquire a majority of the capital stock of an international and foreign banking and financing corporation, while US citizens may do so without approval. Cal. Fin. Code § 3514. A supermajority residency requirement for the board of directors may be imposed as a condition of approval of an application for a State charter for a commercial bank. Cal. Fin. Code §§ 350, 361, 362.

Florida—Only foreign banks that either have a minimum of $25 million in capital or that is one of the five largest banks in its home country may establish an office in Florida as a State-chartered agency. Fla. Stat. § 663.055. A hearing before the State Department of Banking and Finance is required for the establishment of a bank, trust company, or capital stock savings association in which a non-US citizen owns or controls more than 10 per cent of any class of voting stock. Fla. Stat. § 120.60.

Illinois—foreign banks may establish a State branch in Illinois only if US and Illinois banks may own and operate banks in the home country of the applicant bank and foreign bank branches may only have one office in the central district of Chicago unless the bank is designated as a World Trade Center. Ill. Forg. Banking Office Act §§ 3, 6. In addition, foreign bank branches and agencies are restricted from investing in correspondent banks and in banks that offer banking services to other financial institutions. 205 ILCS 110/8, 110/14(7), as amended).

New York—no reservations on banks' establishment possibilities.

Ohio—foreign banks and bank holding companies are subject to reciprocity requirements for establishment privileges in Ohio and the State banking authorities determine the principle place of business of a foreign bank holding company to be that State in which the company has a subsidiary bank outside its 'home State' under the International Banking Act (this could disadvantage the foreign bank because domestic holding companies must be treated according to the treatment of the home State. Ohio Rev. Code § 1101.05.

3.7.3.3.2 STATE RESERVATIONS

State governments' banking regulators sometimes impose added restrictions on the institutions they charter compared to the national authorities.[199] The reservations to the establishment provisions listed in Annex VII of NAFTA are therefore not complete for the United States banking landscape. In most States, the reservations are requirements of reciprocity rather than a complete bar to foreign ownership. Moreover, the reservations usually apply to out-of-State US enterprises as well as to non-US persons, but this is not always true.

3.8   CROSS-BORDER TRADE (ARTICLE 1404)

3.8.1   Introduction to the Concept of 'Cross-Border Trade'

The idea of cross-border trade of services is complex.[200] Moreover, it is a concept that was developed by international trade lawyers and only later applied to financial services. During the NAFTA Chapter Fourteen negotiations, with experts of both disciplines involved, the concept of cross-border trade became very important, even at a time when technology was removing the barriers to international financial transactions on its own. Whether or not all of the NAFTA negotiators understood why they were drafting Article 1404,[201] and indeed whether or not the provision is going to remain important in the future, the cross-border trade provision at present is certainly one of the foundations of the Financial Services chapter.

The term 'cross-border trade', or 'trade in services',[202] refers to the sale or purchase of a good or service by a person of one party to a person of another party in the territory of one of the parties to the agreement. Thus, there is a temporary relocation factor involved in the commercial exchange.

(Contd.)

> *Texas*—foreign corporations may not engage in banking activities in the State (but bank subsidiaries may be owned by foreign investors). Texas Constitution Art. XVI, § 16(a). See also Opinion of Texas Attorney General, No. JM-630 (1987). Permission for foreign banks to establish State agencies is conditioned on reciprocity; foreign banks may not have more than one office in the State and are limited to counties which have at least 1.5 million residents. Tex. Rev. Civ. Stat. Arts 342-1001–342-1011.

[200] An abbreviated discussion of the cross-border trade provisions is given in the discussion of the scope of Chapter Fourteen, 3.8 *supra*.

[201] When asked about the cross-border trade provisions in NAFTA, one lawyer involved in the negotiations commented with amusement, 'nobody really knew what cross-border services were, but the trade people wanted to provide for their free movement'. Interview with author, January 1997 (identity of speaker protected). Such comments, even though not to be taken entirely seriously, do indicate the ideological separation between the financial service camps and the trade camps in the NAFTA negotiations. See also Chapter 9 *post*.

[202] See GATS Art. I:2; see also GATS Art. XVI:1, n.8, referring to a Member's obligation to allow for the 'cross-border movement of capital' where that capital is necessary to take advantage of the Member's obligations on market access.

This movement of factors distinguishes cross-border trade from establishment, where the person of one Party moves into another Party's territory permanently. Although both are related to market access, the liberalization of cross-border trade extends the benefit of selling or buying a product to non-residents without engendering the additional costs that accompany the establishment of a formal presence in a foreign territory (including rent, redundant labor costs, infrastructure costs, etc.).

The NAFTA Article 1416 definition of cross-border trade in financial services is:

> The provision of a financial service:
>
> (a) from the territory of a Party into the territory of another Party,
> (b) in the territory of a Party by a person of that Party to a person of another Party, or
> (c) by a national of a Party in the territory of another Party,
>
> but does not include the provision of a service in the territory of a Party by an investment in that territory.[203]

Referring to purchases of financial services from 'financial service providers', Article 1404:2 extends the freedoms of cross-border trade to consumers of financial services as well.[204]

To understand how this cross-border trade scheme applies to a particular situation, one can consider the following: under Article 1404:1, a representative of a Canadian bank (the financial service provider from one Party) may not be stopped from travelling to Acapulco (the territory of another Party) to provide a Mexican business person (a financial service consumer of the second Party) with a loan to build a beach hotel there.

Alternatively, under Article 1404:2, this same Mexican business person would be allowed to travel to Montreal to discuss the loan with the bank's representative. In this case, it is the consumption that moved rather than the service supplier.

However, due to the fact that there is a restriction set out in Article 1404:1 that cross-border trade 'does not include the provision of a service in the territory of a Party by an investment in that territory', the Mexican business person would not be covered by Article 1404 if she traveled to the United States to receive advice about insurance coverage for her hotel (provision of a service in the territory of a Party) from a subsidiary of a Canadian insurance company incorporated in Chicago (investment in the territory). By incorporating in Chicago, the subsidiary is 'an investment' in the territory of the same Party in whose territory the service is provided, and thus is not protected under NAFTA.

---

[203] NAFTA Art. 1416 ('cross-border provision of a financial service or cross-border trade in financial services').

[204] 'Each Party shall permit persons located in its territory and its nationals wherever located, to purchase financial services from cross-border financial service providers of another Party located in the territory of that other Party or of another Party'. NAFTA Art. 1404:2.

Under NAFTA Article 1404:1, the Parties to the Agreement are not to restrict cross-border trade in the provision of financial services more than the restrictions existing on 1 January 1994 unless reservations are taken in Annex VII, Section B. The Parties' reservations in that Section are few. Canada refused to limit its right to 'adopt any measure relating to cross-border trade in securities', the United States reciprocates this reservation *vis-à-vis* Canada, and Mexico reserves the right to disregard the obligation to allow the provision of or purchase by a Mexican from a person of another Party in Mexico 'if such transactions are denominated in Mexican pesos'.[205]

Additionally, the provisions of Article 1404 stipulate that the Parties may require the registration of both cross-border financial service providers and 'financial instruments'. The term financial instrument is not defined in the Chapter, and, together with the use of 'financial service provider', Article 1404 stands apart from the rest of the Chapter. One negotiator writes that the choice of terms 'instruments' and 'providers' indicates a deviation from the overall 'financial institutions' approach to regulation.[206] Article 1404 uses a 'financial activities' approach.[207] Thus, non-regulated sellers of financial services may be subjected to the obligation of registration, as are regulated financial service providers.

3.8.2   Limitations on the Provision of Cross-Border Services

3.8.2.1   *Doing Business and Soliciting*

Under Article 1404:2, as noted above, the Parties agreed to allow the purchase of cross-border trade in financial services as well as the provision of these services. However, the article states, 'This obligation does not require a Party to permit such providers to do business or solicit in its territory'.

Thus, while purchasing is protected, the use of sales techniques to attract buyers is not. Moreover, the provision continues to allow that 'each Party may define "doing business" and "solicitation" for purposes of this obligation' as long as it does not further restrict the provision of cross-border trade by financial service providers of another Party. A Party, therefore, can define an activity as either 'doing business' or as 'solicitation' and then prohibit financial service providers from other Parties from engaging in this activity without violating its obligations under NAFTA.

Viewed in combination with the 'financial activities' approach of the Article, provisions 1404:2 and 1404:3 show the Parties' concern with maintaining oversight of the financial service industries operating within their territories. Robert Herzstein, legal representative for Mexico during the negotiations, explained that it is his belief that these provisions were inserted to 'draw line between establishment and doing business'.[208]

---

[205] NAFTA Annex VII, Schedule of Mexico, Section B.
[206] Wethington (note 4 *supra*) at 73, n.18.
[207] *Ibid.*
[208] Interview with author, January 1997.

Support for this theory comes from Mexican financial services trade expert Ignacio Trigueros. Mr Trigueros writes that cross-border trade was 'intended to be discouraged' by Mexican authorities, perhaps in order to maintain more control over the financial service products offered in their territory.[209] This is not necessarily limited to the Mexican government. All of the Parties wanted to ensure that if a financial service provider or an unregulated seller of financial instruments is active in their territories, they are aware of the existence of the seller, in order to be able to monitor what it is doing. The use of self-definition of 'doing business' and 'soliciting' are based on consumer protection concerns, and by potentially limiting an institution's freedom to most effectively market its services, it leaves Party governments with another tool for retaining regulatory oversight.

3.8.2.2 'Subject to Paragraph 1'

The standstill language of Article 1404:2 ('Subject to paragraph 1') was inserted to protect the many investment bankers that were already operating in Mexico from the United States prior to the NAFTA negotiations. Their activities would have been in danger of being curtailed had the standstill not been included.[210]

As discussed below, the provision of cross-border trade in financial services is protected by the obligations of national treatment and most-favored-nation treatment. With these principles, the danger of abusing the discretionary definitions of the terms of Article 1404:2 is minimized.

3.9.   NATIONAL TREATMENT (ARTICLE 1405)

The national treatment obligation (NTO) is one of two main international trade principles describing how a government is to regulate a foreign provider, consumer, good, or service in its territory. The principal aims to ensure that foreign goods or services suffer no commercial disadvantages compared to similar domestically-produced goods or services in a particular market. A 'pure' national treatment obligation would require exactly the same treatment of foreign and domestic goods or services (or their producers). In practice, the obligation is usually less rigid.[211]

---

[209] Trigueros (note 17 *supra*), at 51.
[210] Interview with author, January 1997.
[211] For a discussion of the national treatment obligation in general and as it applies to trade in services, see Christoph Stadler, *Die Liberalisierung des Dienstleistungshandels am Beispiel der Versicherungen: Kernelemente bilateraler und multilateraler Ordnungsrahmen einschliesslich des GATS* (Duncker & Humblot, Berlin, 1992), pp. 80–82. Dr Stadler writes:

> Es ist wichtig festzustellen, dass nicht alle Abkommen dieselbe Inländerbehandlungsklausel beinhalten … Das Verbot der Schlechterbehandlung kann mit unterschiedlicher Schärfe greifen, je nachdem welche Ansprüche die Klausel an die Vergleichbarkeit der Situationen stellt und je nachdem wie sie das Gebot der 'Gleich'behandlung definiert. Vor allem aber bedeutet

Chapter Fourteen's national treatment obligation mandates that its Parties offer one another's financial services, financial service suppliers, and the investors in financial services 'treatment no less favorable' than each does for its domestic industry.[212] This allows for differences in treatment as long as the foreign product is not competitively disadvantaged by the difference.[213]

The NAFTA Parties also agreed to not adopt the principle of 'mirror-image reciprocity', or strict comparable treatment, that was found in the European Union's first proposal of their Second Banking Directive.[214] This principle would have restricted foreign financial institutions' activities to those that the institution's home country allows its own foreign institutions. Potentially that would be less advantageous than national treatment.

There have been many articles written and disputes formed around the specifics of national treatment in the context of the GATT obligations since the early years of the modern international trade regime.[215] The national

---

(Contd.)

Inländerbehandlung in der Regel nicht, dass die Vergleichssubjekte in jeder Hinsicht gleich behandelt werden müssen.

Ibid. at 81 (footnotes omitted).

[212] The General Agreement on Trade in Services, like the General Agreement on Tariffs and Trade and the Agreement on Trade-Related Aspects of Intellectual Property Rights, also uses the modified (i.e., 'no less favorable') form of national treatment obligation. GATS Art. XVII:1; GATT Art. III:4; TRIPs Art. 3:1.

[213] For example, a foreign financial service supplier may have to apply to a federal authority for a permit to do business while a similar domestic supplier could be approved locally. As long as the two application processes are equally burdensome, the modified national treatment obligation would be fulfilled despite the different treatment.

[214] Proposal for a Second Banking Directive on the coordination of Laws, Regulations and Administrative Provisions Relating to the Taking-up and Pursuit of the Business of Credit Institutions and Amending Directive 77/780, Eur. Commission Doc. (COM No. 715 final) (1988). See Wethington (note 4 *supra*), at 106; Scheer (note 143 *supra*), at 177, n.49:

Initially, the Second Banking Directive required that comparable treatment be afforded to EU banks by third countries before their banks could be given Union-wide banking privileges. In response to protests from US banking groups, the comparable treatment provision was amended to its present form, so as to not exclude the banks of third countries, such as the United States, that cannot provide comparable treatment to EU banks but do afford them national treatment;

Siegel (note 143 *supra*), at 159–64.

[215] For a general overview of the use of the national treatment principle in the GATT/WTO system, see John H. Jackson, *World Trade and the Law of GATT* (Bobbs-Merrill, Indianapolis, 1969), Ch. 12; Kenneth W. Dam, *The GATT: Law and International Economic Organization* (University of Chicago Press, Chicago, 1970), Ch. 7. For a more up-to-date analysis of the principle as applied by GATT/WTO dispute settlement panels, see WTO, *Analytical Index: A Guide to GATT Law and Practice*, Vol. 1 (WTO, Geneva, 1995), pp. 121–207; William J. Davey, 'The WTO/GATT World Trading System: An Overview', in Pierre Pescatore, William J. Davey and Andreas F. Lowenfeld (eds), *Handbook of WTO/GATT Dispute Settlement* (Transnational Publishers, Irvington-on-Hudson, NY, looseleaf collection, updated June 1997), pp. 28–35.

treatment obligation of Chapter Fourteen is sufficiently similar to the GATT obligation to draw legitimate comparisons where there are likely to be differences of opinion.

3.9.1 Scope

The NAFTA Article 1405 begins:

> Each Party shall accord to investors of another Party treatment no less favorable than that it accords to its own investors, in like circumstances, with respect to the establishment, acquisition, expansion, management, conduct, operation, and sale or other disposition of financial institutions and investments in financial institutions in its territory.[216]

The next two clauses extend the obligation of 'treatment no less favorable' to financial institutions and investments of another Party, and to cross-border service providers:

> 2. Each Party shall accord to financial institutions of another Party and to investments of investors of another Party in financial institutions treatment no less favorable than it accords to its own ... .
> 3. ... where a Party permits the cross-border provision of a financial service it shall accord to the cross-border financial service providers of another Party treatment no less favorable than it accords to its own ... .[217]

The extent of the national treatment obligation is extremely wide: for the Parties, the 'treatment' that must be non-discriminatory includes more than just 'measures' (that is laws, regulations, procedures, requirements or practices). Instead, anything that affects the conditions of competition could legitimately be contained within the term 'treatment'. Omissions, for instance, can be 'treatment' as well.[218]

However, the scope of 'treatment' is not unlimited. First, consumer preference for domestic-financial service providers should not normally be considered 'treatment', as this would make any difference in profitability sufficient grounds for an allegation of a national treatment violation.[219] Even if

---

[216] NAFTA Art. 1405:1. There is a great similarity between the NAFTA language and the wording of the various WTO Agreements.

[217] NAFTA Art. 1405:2, 3.

[218] To illustrate this concept, one can look to GATT disputes. One GATT panel found that the United States' procedures for alleging patent law violations violated the GATT national treatment obligation, because, among others, the holder of a foreign patent had no choice of forum to which to bring a complaint and there was no counterclaim offered by the procedures available to the holder of a foreign patent. United States—Section 337 of the Tariff Act of 1930, BISD 36S/345, 391 (1989).

[219] GATT panels have noted that the non-discrimination principles of NTO and MFN cannot be used to ensure market share, but rather only secure market opportunities. The first declaration of this principle was made in the very first report adopted by the Contracting Parties to the GATT in 1949. Brazilian Interal Taxes, II BISD 181 (adopted 30 June 1949). A WTO Panel reaffirmed this principle in 1997. Canada—Certain Measures Concerning Periodicals, WT/DS31/R at para. 5.26 (14 March 1997).

a consumer preference stems from official actions or inaction such as 'buy national' campaigns, subsidies for consumers, or perhaps official endorsements, the complainant ought to be required to fulfill a high standard of proof, showing strong preferences by the nationals, as well as a causal link between the Party's (in)action and the preferences enjoyed.

Secondly, because the definition of financial institution and cross-border financial service provider encompass only regulated providers of financial services, non-regulated providers of financial instruments are not afforded national treatment protection under NAFTA.[220]

3.9.1.1   Obligation of Subnational Units

The NTO obligation of subnational units are specifically included in Article 1405, paragraph 4. Unlike the general NAFTA requirement that Parties ensure that their subunits abide by the provisions of the Agreement,[221] Article 1405:4 has a complex standard prescribing what level of treatment fulfills that of 'treatment no less favorable'. Basically, Article 1405:4 states that if the subnational units of the Parties somehow affect the conditions of competition of financial institutions or their investors, the obligation of 'national' treatment also extends to these subunits.[222] Again, it is both the investor of a Party as a legal person[223] and such an investor's investment[224] in a financial institution that is protected.

In itself, this concept is not difficult to understand—it is merely an extension of the NTO treatment to subnational units for Canada and Mexico. However, complexity arises due to the characteristics of the United States' banking system, which has a dual supervisory scheme. Particular passages were inserted to assuage concerns voiced by the State governments in the United States when they were faced with a potential loss of sovereignty to the federal government.[225]

According to Article 1405:4, a State has the following responsibilities:

– if a bank owned or controlled by a person of another Party is establishing or is established in only one State, the State must treat the institution, an

---

[220] See NAFTA Art. 1416.
[221] NAFTA Art. 105.
[222] NAFTA Art. 1405:4.
[223] NAFTA Art. 1405:4(a).
[224] NAFTA Art. 1405:4(b).
[225] See Wethington (note 4 *supra*), at 108:

> The need for a distinct formulation of the national treatment principle in the financial services chapter is, in large part, the result of the fact that bank regulation in the United States takes place at several different levels of government and the fact that states have differing rules with respect to entry of foreign institutions and interstate banking. The United States negotiators took the position that the interstate banking restrictions required a special framework.

> Recall that in the United States banking system the States retain a great deal of regulatory competence over financial services, including the right to charter foreign-owned banks. See *supra*. See also *supra* (subnational units' resistance to the NAFTA).

investment in the financial institution, and the investor in the financial institution no less favorably than it does its own institutions, investments, and investors in financial institutions;[226]

- if a bank owned or controlled by a person of another Party is already established in another State (the 'home State'), and wants to establish or is established in another State, this other State must treat the institution, an investment in the institution, and the investor in the financial institution no less favorably than the institution's home state does institutions, investments in financial institutions, or investors in financial institutions from that home State;[227]

- if a bank owned or controlled by a person of another Party is already established in several other States, and wants to establish or is established in a third or fourth (for instance) State, that third or fourth State must treat the institution no less favorably than it would any other institution from the State from which the Party institution is 'directly established'.[228]

In the context of an investor who has invested in a financial institution that is located in more than one other State, the rule for treatment of the *investor* of a financial institution is slightly different than the rule for treatment of the investment or the institution. In such a case, the investor must receive treatment no less favorable than he or she receives in any of the other States instead of treatment depending on the treatment received in the State from which the new establishment will be made.[229] The individual investor is thus assured the most beneficial treatment in every jurisdiction, regardless of in which jurisdiction the last investment was made.

The extent to which the United States will apply the provisions of Article 1405:4 as intended depends greatly on the familiarity of the interpreters with the negotiating background of the passage. As such, international law (mandating a plain reading interpretation whenever possible and relegating legislative history to a last resort) may not support the 'correct' use of the provision.

3.9.2 'Treatment No Less Favorable'

As mentioned above, NAFTA does not use a pure form of the national treatment obligation.[230] Instead of mandating that Parties treat all financial institutions, investments in the institutions, and investors the same, Article 1405 prescribes 'treatment no less favorable' than that offered Party nationals. If a Party has different rules for other Party nationals than it does for its own, then, the definition of what is less favorable must be discovered.

---

[226] NAFTA Art. 1405:4(b).
[227] NAFTA Art. 1405:4(a); see also Wethington (note 4 *supra*), at 108, explaining Art. 1405:4(a).
[228] See Wethington (note 4 *supra*), at 108, explaining Art. 1405:4(d).
[229] See *ibid.*, explaining Art. 1405:4(c).
[230] See 3.9.1 *supra*.

The broad idea of non-discrimination incorporated in the term 'treatment' is furthered by the phrase 'no less favorable'.[231] The NAFTA Parties had learned from the disputes between GATT parties over the term 'no less favorable'[232] (as well as from similar concepts in their own domestic systems)[233] and included a definition of it in Article 1405 so as to avoid similar disputes.[234] This paragraph stipulates that for purposes of the national treatment obligation, the term is to be interpreted to mean treatment that 'affords equal competitive opportunities'.[235]

The clarification of 'equal competitive opportunities', in turn, is found in the following paragraph. There one finds that, as used in Chapter Fourteen, 'equal competitive opportunities' means that there is to be no relative disadvantage in a foreign institution's or a cross-border financial provider's ability to provide financial services because of the Party's treatment of it.[236]

---

[231] See United States—Section 337 of the Tariff Act of 1930, BISD 36S/345, 386, para. 5.11 (adopted 7 November 1989):

> The Panel noted that, as far as the issues before it are concerned, the 'no less favorable' treatment requirement set out in Article III:4, is unqualified. These words are to be found throughout the General Agreement and later agreements … as an expression of the underlying principle of equality of treatment of imported products … The words 'treatment no less favorable' in paragraph 4 call for effective equality of opportunities for imported products in respect of the application of laws, regulations and requirements affecting the internal sale, offering for sale, purchase, transportation, distribution or use of products.

[232] See, e.g., *ibid.*; Italian Discrimination Against Imported Agricultural Machinery, BISD 7S/60 (1958) (panel found that Italian consumer subsidy for buying domestically produced machines a violation of the national treatment obligation); EEC—Measures on Animal Feed Protein, 25S/49, 66, para. 4.12 (1978) (panel found that administrative measures serving to enforcement mechanisms were not 'treatment less favorable' because there were different, but equivalent requirements placed on domestic sellers); United States—Imports of Certain Automotive Spring Assemblies, 30S (1983) (panel left unaddressed Canada's claim that patent law protection in the US violated national treatment because foreign producers had to engage in two legal proceedings instead of one proceeding); United States—Restrictions on Imports of Tuna, 39S/155 (1991) (unadopted) (panel accepted Mexico's complaint that United States environmental law to protect dolphins resulted in treatment less favorable to Mexican-caught tuna than domestic tuna). See also 1 Analytical Index at 162–71.

[233] Under the United States Constitution, States are not allowed to create barriers to inter-State trade. The 'Commerce Clause' jurisprudence, interpreting US Constitution Art. IV, and the 'Dormant Commerce Clause' jurisprudence, often adress the same problems as do the international trade dispute settlement bodies. See, e.g., *Minnesota v. Clover Leaf Creamery* 449 US 456 (1981), finding a State statute prohibiting the sale of milk in plastic non-returnable containers constitutional because of State's interest to encourage recycling and not to discriminate against out-of-State milk producers; *Tupman Thurlow Co. v. Moss* 252 F.Supp. 641 (D.C. Tenn. 1966), holding a State law requiring meat sellers to label foreign meat with country of origin unconstitutional.

[234] NAFTA Art. 1405:5.

[235] NAFTA Art. 1405:5.

[236] NAFTA Art. 1405:6.

Finally, the idea of competitive equality is elaborated upon in the next passage. Article 1405:7 indicates that market share, profitability, and size may be used as evidence of competitive disadvantage, but that standing alone, these aspects of a financial service provider are not sufficient to establish 'treatment no less favorable'.[237]

Despite the extent of detail included in the text to define the 'treatment no less favorable' requirement, one negotiator warns of the likelihood of disagreement as to its concrete use.[238] Olin Wethington writes:

> [t]he application of the obligation of equal competitive opportunity may prove difficult in the future. Over time, one might expect extensive consultation and even dispute settlement with respect to its application. The interpretation of this provision within the consultation and dispute settlement process may be required in order to give it more specific meaning.[239]

Indeed, it would be impossible to define 'equal competitive conditions' in the abstract. The difficulty in creating a legitimate interpretation of the phrase arises when the concrete case is viewed in an attempt to determine whether the treatment actually afforded was 'less favorable' or not. Hindsight often cannot rid itself of the realization that the complainant is presently suffering, and the parcing of factors may be neglected in an after-the-fact assumption of discrimination.

3.9.3 'In Like Circumstances'

The national treatment obligation of 'treatment no less favorable' only makes sense if the comparison of different treatment is made in the context of the situation in which the treatment is afforded.[240] In the words of international trade, the analysis depends on treatment of like products or services in 'like circumstances'.

The NAFTA contains the phrase 'like' to qualify the obligation of offering national treatment to financial institutions and their investors and

---

[237] NAFTA Art. 1405:7.

[238] Wethington (note 4 *supra*), at 110.

[239] *Ibid*. n.15.

[240] But see Australia-New Zealand Closer Economic Relations-Trade Agreement, Protocol on Trade in Services (1988). In this Protocol (Art. 4), the national treatment obligation does not make mention of either 'like services' or 'like circumstances' for market access. Instead it states simply: 'Each Member State shall grant to persons of the other Member State and services provided by them access rights in its market no less favorable than those allowed to its own persons and services provided by them'. One author surmises that this lack of a comparison was used to equalize all companies in both countries as regards market access. Stadler (note 211 *supra*), at 141.

investments to circumstances that are comparable.[241] This is similar to the WTO agreements,[242] but while the WTO Agreements use the term 'like' to define the *target* of the obligation (like products, like services, and like service suppliers), NAFTA Chapter Fourteen looks to the *situation* in which the pre-defined financial service provider acts ('Each Party shall accord to investors of another Party treatment no less favorable than that it accords to its own investors, in like circumstances ...').[243]

In defining 'like circumstances', the dispute panel history of the GATT/WTO is not suitable for lending much guidance to future Chapter Fourteen panel members. Although the GATT has a plethora of cases analyzing whether two products are 'like', the resulting panel decisions have generally decided the question on one of two bases: whether the products themselves are physically similar; or whether consumers' behavior suggests that the products are similar.[244] The current definition for likeness given by the WTO

---

[241] NAFTA Art. 1405:1. In the Spanish text, the provision reads:

> Cada una de las Partes otorgará a los inversionistas de otra Parte trato no menos favorable del que otorga a sus propios inversionistas, *en circunstancias similares,* respecto al establecimiento, adquisición, expansión, administración, conducción, operación y venta u otras formas de enajenación de instituciones financieras e inversiones en instituciones financieras en su territorio.

(emphasis added). The French text reads:

> Chacune des Parties accordera aux investisseurs d'une autre Partie un traitement non moins favorable que celui qu'elle accorde à ses propes investisseurs, *dan des circonstances analogues,* en ce qui concerne l'établissement, l'acquisition, l'expansion, la gestion, la direction, l'exploitation et la vente ou autre aliénation d'institutions financières, et d'investissements dans des institutions financières, sur son territoire.

(emphasis added).
[242] See GATT Art. III:4 ('The products of the territory of any contracting party imported into the territory of an other contracting party shall be accorded treatment no less favourable than that accorded to like products of national origin ...'.); GATS Art. XVII:1 ('... each Member shall accord to services and service suppliers of any other Member, in respect of all measures affecting the supply of services, treatment no less favourable than that it accords to its own like services and service suppliers'). The Agreement on Trade-Related Aspects of Intellectual Property Rights (TRIPs) does not use a 'likeness' criteria for its national treatment obligation, as the obligation in the TRIPs context extends to the individual holders of intellectual property. The protected 'nationals' are therefore assumed to be 'like' nationals of other Members. TRIPs Art. 3:1 ('Each Member shall accord to the nationals of other Members treatment no less favorable than that it accords to its own nationals with regard to the protection of intellectual property ...'.) (footnote omitted).
[243] NAFTA Art. 1405:1. Paras 2 and 3 contain identical terms of 'in like circumstances'.
[244] A third approach, used by only a few panels prior to the coming into effect of the WTO, is that examining whether the treatment prescribed by the national legislature intended that the products be considered similar. See Manfred Wagner, 'The Interpretation of the Term 'Like Product' in Paragraphs 2 and 4 of Article III GATT 1994' (manuscript on file with author). Wagner characterizes the panel reports as using either a 'physical characteristics or textual' approach or an 'aim-and-effects' approach, grouping the consumer preference approach with the textual approach. The aims-and-effects approach, however, has been repeatedly rejected by subsequent panels, and is not the approach taken by the Appellate Body. See also Aaditya Mattoo and Arvind Subramanian, 'Regulatory Autonomy and Multilateral Disciplines: the Dilemma and a Possible Resolution', *WTO Staff Working Paper* TISD9802.WPF (January 1998) including a critique of both the 'textual', or physical characteristics, test and the 'contextual', or aims-and-effects, test.

Appellate Body, relies heavily on a composite of the two tests in determining 'likeness'.[245]

In the Financial Services arena of NAFTA it is not the financial institutions themselves, nor their investors or the investments, nor even the services they provide, that are 'like', but rather the 'circumstances' in which the financial institutions or providers find themselves. Thus, there are no physical characteristics worthy of comparison. One could, perhaps look to geographic location as a physical characteristic, but such a basis for comparison would be less than satisfactory at best (as in a characterizing of institutions located in the same metropolitan area as 'in like circumstances'), and arbitrary at worst (as in all institutions located on a corner lot are 'in like circumstances').

Neither is consumer taste very appropriate for determining 'likeness' in the context of NTO for financial services. This is so because tastes normally have to do with the service itself rather than with the circumstance of the provider.

Thus, determining whether a financial institution of one Party finds itself 'in like circumstances' to the circumstances another Party's financial institution is likely to prove to be even more problematic than the already heavily disputed determination of whether a tangible product is 'like'. While one could imagine that a 'line of business' test could be a criterion for 'like circumstance', the Article's provision does not mention how narrowly the various fields of financial services can legitimately be drawn. Article 1405, for instance, does not specify how a dispute panel would compare a commercial bank with a life insurance company or with a thrift.[246]

Referring to the French and Spanish versions of the Agreement's text tends does not support such an interpretation, either. The 'dans des circonstances analogues' and 'en circunstancias similares' seem to go more to the external environment in which the institution (or investor) finds itself than to the institution itself.[247]

The OECD national treatment requirement may be of significance in this respect, as it requires treatment no less favorable for foreign enterprises

---

[245] See Japan—Taxes on Alcoholic Beverages, WT/DS8, 10, and 11/R at para. 6.22 (1 November 1996), panel report as modified by Appellate Body Report, using test physical characteristics/end-use test for determining 'likeness' of products under GATT Art. III:2; United States—Standards for Reformulated Gasoline, WT/DDS2/R at para. 6.8–6.9 (29 January 1996), as modified by the Appellate Body Report, applying physical characteristics test to determine 'likeness' of products under GATT Art. III:4; Korea—Taxes on Alcoholic Beverages, WT/DS75/AB/R and WT/DS84/AB/R para. 118 (18 January 1999), affirming the findings of Japan—Alcoholic Beverages that the term 'like product' must be narrowly defined. See also Mattoo (note 174 *supra*), at 124-9, explaining the concept of 'likeness' in GATT Art. III and comparing it with the same term as used in GATS Art. XVII.

[246] Not comparing the institutions themselves is interesting from the point of view of the discussions going on in the WTO about production process methods ('PPMs'). The PPM debate is centered on whether products can be considered 'like' or 'unlike' based not only on their final physical characteristics, but also on how they were produced. While the US representatives to the WTO tend to support the consideration of PPMs in determining likeness, and could conceivably (though not inevitably) extend this view to NAFTA, Mexico and Canada do not accept PPMs as legitimate differentiating factors.

[247] See note 241 *supra*.

than treatment afforded domestic enterprises 'in like situations'.[248] The OECD view is that at a minimum, this indicates enterprises in the same sector. Beyond that, 'general considerations' could give additional qualifications to the meaning of like situation.[249]

3.9.3.1   Proposed Test for 'Like Circumstances'

For the NAFTA, defining 'in like circumstances' so as to lend some degree of foreseeability to Parties when developing regulatory structures is going to require looking to the basic principle of the national treatment obligation as set out in Chapter Fourteen. That principle aims to achieve equal competitive conditions for foreign and domestic financial services. Under such a view, it would seem logical that a panel ought to look at the question of 'like circumstances' by considering the overall issue of national treatment and asking whether, if the financial institution, investment in the institution, or investor were owned, controlled by, or were a national rather than a person of another Party, would it face better competitive opportunities due to the Party's actions or inaction.

3.9.4   Annex VII Exceptions to National Treatment Obligation

In Annex VII of the NAFTA, the Parties set out exceptions to their obligation to give the financial institutions, the investments in financial institutions, and the investors with investments in financial service institutions of other Parties the benefit of national treatment.

3.9.4.1   Canadian Exceptions

3.9.4.1.1   FEDERAL RESTRICTIONS ON NATIONAL TREATMENT

While Canada does not set out any specific exceptions to national treatment in Annex VII, in Section C of that Annex, it offers Mexico the same treatment it gives US persons in respect to limits on foreign ownership of Canadian-controlled banks. This treatment removes from the Mexican banks the aggregate foreign investment limits on widely-held banks.[250]

3.9.4.1.2   PROVINCIAL RESERVATIONS

Because the Canadian Provinces do not have wide powers over commercial banks, there are no specific NTO reservations taken that apply to such foreign institutions. There are some NTO reservations for credit unions, trust companies, and securities dealers, but these are limited and mainly

---

[248]   OECD, National Treatment for Foreign-Controlled Enterprises (OECD: Paris 1993).
[249]   *Ibid.* at 22, cited in Mattoo (note 174 *supra*), at 133, n.52.
[250]   See 2.2.2 *supra* (discussion of Canadian Banking Regulations).

apply to residency requirements.[251] Moreover, the reservations tend to be as discriminatory against extra-Provincial institutions as they are against non-Canadian entities.

3.9.4.2   Mexican Exceptions

3.9.4.2.1   SECTION A OF ANNEX VII

Mexico's exceptions to the national treatment obligation are more extensive than Canada's and are more substantive than the United States'. For those relating to banks, one of the most significant is the limit placed on other-Party financial institution investments in Mexican-owned commercial banks located in Mexico. Mexico reserved the right to restrict the majority ownership of these banks and the majority ownership of holding companies to Mexicans. More specifically, Mexico may legislate that local Mexican commercial banks and holding companies not be permitted to have more than 30 per cent of their common stock (*'capital ordinario'*) owned by non-Mexican investors. Foreign financial affiliates, defined as 'financial institution(s) established in Mexico and owned and controlled by an investor of another Party',[252] are excepted from the ownership limitation. There is no phase-out provision on this reservation.[253]

It is widely recognized that Mexico took this particular reservation as a way to prevent the external foreign control of any of Mexico's largest commercial banks.[254] The exception to this reservation is particularly significant in this respect. The reservation does not apply to 'foreign financial affiliates'. Thus, the main reservation on foreign ownership over 30 per cent in reality is very narrow—financial institutions that are established in Mexico and owned or controlled by other-Party investors may be wholly owned by other Party investors. This reinforces the belief that the reservation aims narrowly at maintaining Mexican ownership of the large banks.

A second set of reservations Mexico took to Article 1405 is the complete exemption of foreign investments in foreign exchange firms, credit unions,

---

[251] Examples of the non-residency requirement reservations include:

> *Alberta*—non-Provincial credit unions may only engage in collecting or enforcing obligations within Alberta;
> *Manitoba*—non-Provincial credit unions may not carry on the 'ordinary business of deposits and loans' (The Credit Union and Caisse Populaires Act, sec. 129); shares in a trust company that are owned by a non-resident of Canada may not be used in voting unless registered (The Corporations Act, secs. 345–6);
> *Ontario*—voting rights of non-residents in a trust company are limited (Loan and Trust Corporations Act, R.S.O. 1990, L. 25);
> *Prince Edward Island*—registration fee for non-resident securities salespersons is higher than for residents (Securities Act, R.S.P.E.I. 1988).

[252] Annex VII, Schedule of Mexico, 'Definitions' (definition of a 'foreign financial affiliate').
[253] This limit has now been raised to 49 per cent ownership. See 2.3 *supra*.
[254] See, e.g., Wethington (note 4 *supra*), at 126.

and development banks.[255] Such institutions may be required to be wholly owned by Mexicans. If the foreign exchange firms or credit unions are foreign financial affiliates, however, this restriction will not apply.[256] Again, there is no phase out for these reservations.[257]

In another reservation applying to securities firms, financial leasing companies, investment companies, and bonding companies, among others, the Mexican government prohibits Party governments and state enterprises from investing (directly or indirectly) in the covered financial institutions. For investments in commercial banks, the reservation goes further, prohibiting any non-Mexican Party 'entities that exercise governmental functions' from making direct or indirect investments. For these restrictions, it is important to remember that the definition of 'investment' does not include either a Party or a Party's state enterprise's issue of a debt security[258] or trade financing or other extensions of credit 'in connection with a commercial transaction'.[259]

Finally, non-Mexican development banks and all commercial banks are prohibited from fulfilling certain public functions. Specifically, Mexican development banks are given the exclusive competence to hold securities and cash from the 'administrative and judicial authorities' and goods seized 'according to Mexican measures'.[260]

3.9.4.2.2   SECTION B OF ANNEX VII

In Section B of their Annex VII Schedule, the Mexican negotiators set out further reservations to the Chapter Fourteen provisions in order to shield the domestic banks from a sudden influx of highly competitive US and Canadian banks. Some of the reservations expire on 1 January 2000 (the end of the transition period) while others will continue indefinitely.

Until 1 January 2000, no other-Party investor owning or controlling a commercial bank established in Mexico will be granted a capital authorization for the bank in excess of 1.5 per cent of the total capital of all commercial banks in Mexico.[261] This rule cannot be avoided by an acquisition of a pre-existing financial institution by such an investor, as the reservation provides that the authorized capital of each institution will be added and contributed to the investor.[262] Mexican investors are free to own or control

---

[255] Annex VII, Schedule of Mexico, Section A.
[256] See *supra* (definition of foreign financial affiliate).
[257] Annex VII, Schedule of Mexico, Section A
[258] NAFTA Art. 1416.
[259] NAFTA Art. 1139.
[260] Annex VII, Schedule of Mexico, Section A.
[261] This Section also provides that although at the time of establishment, the Mexican government will not authorize capital in excess of the paid-in capital, the amount of paid-in capital after establishment may fall below that authorized. Foreign financial affiliates will be treated no less favorably than their Mexican counterparts in the post-establishment decision of maximum size of operations: the government will decide based on 'the lesser of its capital or its authorized capital'. Annex VII, Schedule of Mexico, Section B, para. 3(a).
[262] Annex VII, Schedule of Mexico, Section B, para. 2.

the remainder of the authorized capital of banks. A security firm controlled by an investor of another Party is allowed to control up to 4 per cent of the aggregate capital of all security firms in Mexico.[263]

Another limit on authorized capital is based on the sum of the authorized capital of all foreign financial affiliates.[264] Increasing each year until 2000, these percentages are based on the total capital of all financial institutions of the type in Mexico. For other Party commercial banks, the Mexican government need not authorize more capital than 15 per cent of the total capital in all commercial banks in Mexico until 1 January 2000.[265] For securities firms, the comparable figure is 20 per cent until the end of the transition period.[266]

Following the transition period, the limits on the capital authorization for individual financial institutions will be increased to 4 per cent[267] and those on the aggregated foreign financial institution presence in Mexico will be removed entirely.[268] However, if between the end of the transition period and 1 January 2004, other Party controlled commercial banks are highly active in Mexico and obtain 25 per cent of the aggregate capital of all commercial banks in Mexico, the Mexican government may freeze the authorized capital at 25 per cent for up to three years.[269] For security firms, the threshold is 30 per cent of the aggregate.[270]

Finally, non-Mexican owned and controlled branches or subsidiaries of other Party financial institutions are prohibited from issuing subordinated debentures to anyone other than its own controlling investor.[271]

Among its non-expiring Section B reservations, Mexico reserved the right to require that foreign financial affiliates be 'wholly-owned by an investor of another Party'.[272] Practically, this would potentially prevent a branch of a non-Party investor located in Canada or the United States from acquiring a financial affiliate in Mexico. Further, it is possible for the Mexican government to refuse to issue licenses for establishing a financial institution to Party investors if the investors are not already active in the 'the same general type' of activity in their home territory.[273]

Moreover, Mexico may prevent the investor and its affiliates from owning or controlling more than the one financial institution of the type

---

[263] Annex VII, Schedule of Mexico, Section B, para. 2.

[264] Annex VII, Schedule of Mexico, Section B, para. 5.

[265] *Ibid*. In calculating the aggregate foreign financial affiliate capital at any set time, the Mexicans agreed not to include the amount that Citibank had in Mexico on 1 January 1996.

[266] *Ibid*.

[267] Annex VII, Schedule of Mexico, Section B, para. 13.

[268] Annex VII, Schedule of Mexico, Section B, para. 9.

[269] *Ibid*.

[270] *Ibid*. There is little likelihood that this limit will be surpassed. As of December 1997, the NAFTA-Party bank presence in Mexico was a mere 6.15 per cent of the aggregate industry assets. 'Mexico Updates Capital Limits for US, Canadian Subsidiaries Under NAFTA', 71:5 BNA's Banking Rep. 229 (3 August 1998). Due in part to the peso crisis of 1995, in part to better investment opportunities elsewhere in the world, the level of financial investments has remained below Mexican expectations.

[271] Annex VII, Schedule of Mexico, Section B, para. 4.

[272] Annex VII, Schedule of Mexico, Section B, para. 12.

[273] Annex VII, Schedule of Mexico, Section B, para. 14.

authorized,[274] and 'may also restrict [them] from establishing agencies, branches, or other direct or indirect subsidiaries in the territory of any other country'.[275] Thus, Mexico apparently was concerned with the concentration of financial power in non-Mexican hands and was likewise displeased with the thought of becoming a stepping-stone for other North American investors looking to free-ride on Mexico's agreements with other countries.

3.9.4.3   *United States' Exceptions*

3.9.4.3.1   FEDERAL RESTRICTIONS ON NATIONAL TREATMENT

The United States' exceptions to its national treatment obligations of Article 1405 are mainly based on the US negotiators' refusal to commit the United States government to changing the laws regulating financial service institutions.

3.9.4.3.2   SECTION A OF ANNEX VII

The United States maintained the national bank regulators' deference to State regulation by making a reservation that it would not authorize the formation of a bank subsidiary in State 1 (the 'target State') by a full-service foreign branch located in State 2 (the 'home State') if the target State does not have an explicit legislative allowance for domestic bank holding companies based in the home State to acquire or establish banks there.[276] This reservation applies to national, State, and 'other' commercial banks, branches and agencies of foreign banks.[277] This reservation similarly extends to foreign bank holding companies. These companies may not acquire or establish a bank subsidiary in a target State unless the laws of that State 'expressly permit' this type of transaction with holding companies from the home State.[278]

The reservation continues to identify potential situations in which foreign banks located in one State would not be treated as favorably as a national bank holding company from that same State. Again, the lack of national treatment depends on the particular laws of the target and home States. Mentioned expressly (but not exclusively) are constellations in which regional holding company laws either explicitly or implicitly prohibit foreign banks from owning other banks[279] and the possibility that the definition of bank holding company under State banking law would prohibit foreign banks from acquiring a local bank if it does not already own a bank subsidiary.[280] This clearly and significantly limits the benefits of the United States' offer to extend national treatment more broadly than

---

[274] *Ibid.*
[275] Annex VII, Schedule of Mexico, Section B, para. 12
[276] Annex VII, Schedule of the United States, Section A.
[277] *Ibid.*
[278] *Ibid.*
[279] Annex VII, Schedule of the United States, Section A, (a), (b).
[280] Annex VII, Schedule of the United States, Section A, (c).

it already did. Finally, there is a possibility that a target State will apply the more restrictive treatment to a foreign bank that has a principle place of business different from (and more restrictive *vis-à-vis* bank holding companies than) its home state.[281]

The United States also reserved the right to discriminate against financial institutions owned or controlled by another Party in its limitation of Edge corporations to 'foreign banks and US subsidiaries of foreign banks'.[282] Because Edge corporations may have owners that are domestic bank holding companies and certain domestic non-bank companies,[283] this restriction would violate the 'no less favorable' criteria of Article 1405.

If a foreign bank was not an insured deposit-taking institution on 19 December 1991, the United States banking authorities may require it to establish a subsidiary insured by the Federal Deposit Insurance Corporation before it may accept domestic retail deposits of less than $100,000.[284] Moreover, unless the foreign bank is in the form of a subsidiary rather than a branch or agency, it is not eligible to be a member of the Federal Reserve System at all. Therefore, foreign branches and agencies cannot vote for Federal Reserve directors.[285]

The dealing in US government debt obligations and the acting as a sole trustee for securities are exempted from the national treatment requirement in so far as there is no reciprocity with the foreign bank's home government. Under the Primary Dealers Act, reserved in Section A, the United States must refuse foreign commercial banks the right to be primary dealers in US bonds unless the bank's home country grants US firms 'the same competitive opportunities as are accorded to domestic firms in the underwriting and distribution of government debt instruments'.[286] Similarly, but giving the United States discretion in its decision, a foreign financial institution outside the country may be denied the authority to act as 'the sole

---

[281] Annex VII, Schedule of the United States, Section A, (d).

[282] Annex VII, Schedule of the United States, Section A. See also definition of Edge Act corporations, 2.1.4.3 *supra*.

[283] Annex VII, Schedule of the United States, Section A. US non-bank companies that wish to own Edge corporations must limit themselves to activities 'closely related to banking' but foreign non-bank companies are not allowed to own Edge corporations at all. See 12 U.S.C. § 619:

> Except as otherwise provided ..., a majority of the shares of the capital stock of any [Edge corporation] shall at all times be owned by citizens of the United States ... Notwithstanding any other provisions of this subchapter, one or more foreign banks, institutions organized under the laws of foreign countries which own or control foreign banks, or banks organized under the laws of the United States, the States of the United States, or the District of Columbia, the controlling interests in which are owned by any such foreign banks or institutions, may, with the prior approval of the Board of Governors of the Federal Reserve System ... own and hold 50 per centum or more of the shares of the capital stock of any corporation organized under this subchapter ...

[284] Annex VII, Schedule of the United States, Section A; 12 U.S.C. § 3104(c).

[285] Annex VII, Schedule of the United States, Section A; 12 U.S.C. §§ 221 (definitions), 302, 321.

[286] Annex VII, Schedule of the United States, Section A; Primary Dealers Act of 1988, 12 U.S.C. §§ 5341–2. This is an example of a reciprocity requirement, and as such goes against the basic national treatment obligation principles contained in Chapter Fourteen.

trustee under an indenture for debt securities sold in the United States if US institutional trustees cannot act as sole trustees for securities sold in the foreign firm's home country'.[287]

Finally, if a bank offers security advisory services, it is only the foreign banks that must register with the government authorities. Domestic banks need not register, as provided for in the law governing the giving of such advice.[288]

3.9.4.3.3   STATE RESERVATIONS

There are numerous State reservations taken to the national treatment obligation provisions of Article 1405. Most reservations were taken to the NTO based on a State reciprocity requirement.[289] Another general group of reservations was taken in order to protect the right to determine the level of treatment of foreign banks by regarding the treatment given the State's own banks in the foreign bank's 'principal place of business' rather than in its home State.[290] Other purely discriminatory reservations were taken as well, however.[291]

---

[287] Annex VII, Schedule of the United States, Section A; Trust Indenture Act of 1939, 15 U.S.C. § 77jjj(a)(1).

[288] Annex VII, Schedule of the United States, Section A; see Investment Advisers Act of 1940, 15 U.S.C. §§ 80b-2, 80b-3.

[289] See Wethington (note 4 *supra*), Appendix O., e.g.,

> *California*—'substantially equivalent' treatment required from the foreign country for a foreign bank to receive a license to establish an agency, branch, or wholly-owned subsidiary in California (Cal. Fin. Code § 1753(b)(7)); 'substantial reciprocity' required before a foreign bank or an out-of-State bank holding company may acquire a California bank or BHC, acquire more than 5 per cent of the voting shares of a bank or BHC, acquire 'substantially all' of the assets of a California bank or BHC, take over deposits from, or merge with a California bank or BHC (Cal. Fin. Code §§ 3750–61);
>
> *Illinois*—for a foreign bank to establish an office in Illinois, the home country must allow Illinois banks to establish a bank office in the country and to wholly own banking organizations in that country (Foreign Banking Office Act, § 3);
>
> *Ohio*—foreign banks may establish or acquire a subsidiary in Ohio only if the 'principle place of business' of that bank allows Ohio banks to establish or acquire banks and BHCs 'on terms that are substantially no more restrictive' than Ohio's (Ohio Rev. Code, § 1101.05);
>
> *Texas*—foreign banks cannot establish agencies in Texas unless Texas banks can engage in activities to the same extent in the home country (Texas Rev. Civ. Stat., Art. 342-1001–342-1011).

[290] E.g., California (based on Cal. Fin. Code §§ 3750–61); Ohio (based on Ohio Rev. Code, § 1101.05). Wethington (note 4 *supra*), Appendix O.

[291] Among the more important reservations of the six foreign banking centers are, as in Wethington (note 4 *supra*), Appendix O:

> *California*—foreign bank branches and agency have few trust powers (Cal. Fin. Code §§ 1503, 1755(b)); foreign banks must have Superintendent's approval before more than 50 per cent of their shares may be controlled by a foreign bank (Cal. Fin. Code § 3514); sale of payment instruments by agencies and branches of foreign banks must have a license unless they are selling foreign currency payment instruments that are not money orders or travelers checks (Cal. Fin. Code §§ 33700, 33761); foreign banks are subject to usury laws if it has assets of less than $100 million and is lending cross-border (Cal. Fin. Code § 1716);

3.10 MOST-FAVORED-NATION TREATMENT (ARTICLE 1406)

Most-favored-nation (MFN) treatment is the third of the three main principles used to achieve non-discriminatory trading conditions (the others are establishment and the national treatment obligation). Like the national treatment obligation, the requirement of MFN treatment obliges the Party to give 'treatment no less favorable' to the target of the liberalization. The difference with NTO is that MFN treatment compares treatment afforded to services or products of another Party *vis-à-vis* other trading partners rather than *vis-à-vis* like domestic services or products.

3.10.1 Basic Rule: Unconditional MFN

In NAFTA, the basic MFN rule states:

> Each Party shall accord to investors of another Party, financial institutions of another Party, investments of investors in financial institutions and cross-border financial service providers of another Party treatment no less favorable than that it accords to the investors, financial institutions, investments of investors in financial institutions and cross-border financial service providers of any other Party or of a non-Party, in like circumstances.[292]

(Contd.)

  Florida—foreign bank agency offices must have either $25 million in capital or be one of the five largest banks in the home country, and they have limited deposit-taking powers (Fla. Stat. § 663.055); hearings are required for a foreign national to own or control 10 per cent or more of a bank for which a license is sought (Fla. Stat. § 120.60);
  Illinois—foreign branches may not engage in trust activities (Forg. Banking Office Act § 6); foreign bank branches and agencies must register to deal in securities (Ill. Sec. Law § 2.7); foreign bank branches and agencies may not invest in correspondent banks (Ill. Fin. Instit. Banking Act §§ 8, 14(7)).
  New York—foreign banks are not exempt from broker-dealer registration, as national and State banks are (Gen. Bus. Law §§ 359-e(1)(e), 359-e(14)(g)(iv));
  Ohio—foreign banks are not exempt from broker-dealer registration, as national and State banks are (Ohio Rev. Code § 1707.01(X));
  Texas—foreign bank branches and agencies are required to register investment advisers whereas national or state banks need not do so (Tex. Rev. Civ. Stat. art. 581-4(C)); foreign bank agencies are subject to prejudgment seizure although other financial institutions that lend money or extend credit may not be subject to such seizures (Tex. Rev. Civ. Art. 342–609); foreign bank agencies may not accept deposits or act as fiduciaries except to the extent necessary to fulfill an executor role of a non-US citizen who left property in Texas (Tex. Rev. Civ. Art. 342–1011, Tex. Prob. Code § 105A); foreign banks that are not agencies licensed by Texas require a license to exchange currency in Texas (Tex. Rev. Civ. Stat. Art. 350) or to sell checks (Tex. Rev. Civ. Stat. Art. 489d).
[292] NAFTA Art. 1406:1.

Comparing Article 1406:1 with Article 1405:1 (basic NTO rule), one sees the similarities of phrases used. Indeed, it is not merely the words that are the same, the intent of the paragraphs are the same: to provide all Parties' financial service providers with the same competitive opportunities within and throughout the free trade zone and to ensure that this is the best treatment available.

3.10.1.1 'Treatment No Less Favorable'

Based on the same fundamental motive, it is not surprising that the words of the basic MFN requirement also share the same meaning as the identical words when used in the national treatment provision. The phrases 'treatment no less favorable' and 'in like circumstances' can only reasonably be interpreted to mean that a Party has the responsibility to ensure that any financial institution, investment in that institution, or investor in a financial institution be given equal competitive opportunities as any other, regardless of which Party it is a national.[293]

Significantly, the principle of MFN adds another dimension to the extension of 'treatment no less favorable' by bringing in a comparison of a Party's treatment of non-Party financial service providers. Stated clearly at the end of the clause, the MFN requires treatment no less favorable than that given to any foreign financial service provider, including those of states not party to the Agreement: 'Each Party shall accord to investors of another Party, ... treatment no less favorable than that it accords to investors ... of any other Party *or of a non-Party* ...'.[294]

Such a comprehensive MFN obligation ensures fidelity to the preferential trade partners and encourages outsiders to join.

3.10.1.2 Unconditional Extension of Benefits

Also significant is the fact that the MFN obligation of Article 1401 is 'unconditional'. That means a Party's extension of MFN treatment to another Party's financial service institution may not be dependent on considerations of reciprocity. Based on the language of Article 1406:1, a Party's equal treatment of other Parties is independent from how the Party itself is treated by each of the others. The obligation to extend the benefits of more liberal treatment to each other Party requires that all co-Parties will share the benefits, even if the benefit extended was

---

[293] See *supra*.

[294] NAFTA Art. 1406:1 (emphasis added). The plainness of the inclusion of non-Parties as a measure of the MFN level of obligations is in contrast to the more subtle wording of the GATT provision. That Agreement says '... any advantage, favour, privilege or immunity granted by any contracting party to any product originating in or destined for any other country shall be accorded ...'. GATT Art. I:1.

in exchange for benefits from one Party and one or more of the other co-Parties does not reciprocate with any liberalizations or benefits.[295]

3.10.2 Recognition of Prudential Measures: Conditional MFN

Paragraphs 2, 3, and 4 of NAFTA Article 1406 set out a framework for one Party to accept another's prudential measures as adequate to fulfill the former's own prudential standards.[296] A Party can offer this acceptance or 'recognition' unilaterally[297] or reciprocally,[298] or two or more Parties can agree to harmonize their prudential standards.[299] Like the basic treatment of Article 1406:1, the recognition provision extends beyond the NAFTA Parties, allowing a NAFTA Party to recognize a non-Party's standards.[300] A Party need not automatically recognize every co-Party's prudential standards if it decides to accept another Party's or non-Party's standards as equivalent. (That is, this is not an 'unconditional' MFN obligation as is the Party's treatment of financial service providers themselves.) The Party may

---

[295] The inclusion of 'unconditional MFN' in the NAFTA is significant to the extent that the United States refused to accept the WTO's obligation of unconditional MFN in the GATS' Annex on Financial Services until December 1997. In the context of the Uruguay Round, the United States complained that offering unconditional MFN to all countries of the international trade regime would be unfair as many of the other members did not allow US financial service providers entry to, or equal competitive opportunities in, their markets. This has since changed, but only in response to other WTO Members' agreement to further liberalize their financial service markets. In the NAFTA Chapter Fourteen negotiations, all Parties obviously felt that none was free-riding on the others, and that an unconditional MFN clause was the optimal choice for ensuring further liberalizations in the financial services markets of North America. The fact that the NAFTA negotiations on financial services were mainly at the cost of Mexico's financial service industry, which itself later ratified the unconditional MFN provisions of the GATS, helps explain the different US position as well. It is difficult to postulate whether the same result would have occurred had the NAFTA negotiating group been larger, including for example, all of the South American countries, many of which have maintained relatively restrictive financial service markets throughout GATS negotiations.

[296] Bilateral or minilateral 'Mutual Recognition Agreements' (or MRAs) have become increasingly important in international economic relations, as they offer a way of eliminating non-tariff barriers to trade in goods or services while maintaining ultimate national control over imports. For a review of the existing MRAs as well as the theoretical basis for (and problems with) such agreements in World Trade Organization law, see Kalypso Nicolaïdis, 'Mutual Recognition of Regulatory Regimes: Some Lessons and Prospects', in OECD (ed.), *Regulatory Reform and International Openness* (OECD, Paris, 1996), pp. 171–203.

[297] NAFTA Art. 1406(2)(a).

[298] NAFTA Art. 1406(2)(c).

[299] NAFTA Art. 1406(2)(b).

[300] NAFTA Art. 1406:2 ('Such recognition may be ... (c) based upon an agreement or arrangement with the other Party or non-Party'); NAFTA Art. 1406:3, referring to para. 2, including the provisions on non-Party standards recognition; NAFTA Art. 1406:4 (see note 301 *infra*). Cf. NAFTA Art. 1406:1.

unilaterally extend the benefits of recognition or it may harmonize its prudential standards with another Party or non-Party on the condition that the other Party offers it a similar concession in return. In non-trade terminology, a demand for reciprocity is permissible.

3.10.2.1   Limits on Conditionality

The 'conditional' form of most-favored-nation treatment, as this reciprocal form of MFN is called in international trade literature, does result in certain obligations under the NAFTA, however.[301] First, a Party that recognizes another state's (Party or non-Party) standards by means of an 'agreement or arrangement' must offer every co-Party an 'adequate opportunity' to prove that the co-Party's prudential standards are as effective in protecting the financial system as those that are recognized in the agreement or arrangement are under existing circumstances.[302]

If the co-Party can provide evidence that the effectiveness of its prudential standards are equal to those accepted by the other Party in the recognition agreement, then the Party that accepted the prudential standards originally must offer the co-Party an 'adequate opportunity … to negotiate' for its own standard's recognition.[303] This opportunity to negotiate, standing alone, cannot guarantee that a recognition agreement will come into effect. Therefore it is of questionable importance from a viewpoint of coercive power. It does, however, help to further the principle of equal treatment for equivalent financial service suppliers for which the NAFTA Chapter Fourteen strives.

Because the recognition obligation of Chapter Fourteen is conditional, a Party has no right to recognition if it cannot provide sufficient evidence of its prudential standards' equivalence to those recognized by another Party.

---

[301] NAFTA Art. 1406 states in part:

> 3. A Party according recognition of prudential measures … shall provide adequate opportunity to another Party to demonstrate that circumstances exist in which there are or would be equivalent regulation, oversight, implementation of regulation, and if appropriate, procedures concerning the sharing of information between the Parties.
> 4. Where a Party accords recognition of prudential measures [based on an agreement or arrangement with the other Party or non-Party] and the circumstances set out in paragraph 3 exist, the Party shall provide adequate opportunity to another Party to negotiate accession to the agreement or arrangement, or to negotiate a comparable agreement or arrangement.

[302] NAFTA Art. 1406:4.
[303] *Ibid.*

3.10.2.2 *Interpretation of Recognition Provisions*

On a plain reading of its words, Article 1406:2–4 is open to wide interpretation. (The French and Spanish texts are equally open.)[304] The passages of the recognition provision that are most likely to cause dispute among the NAFTA Parties in applying it are: first, what is an 'equivalent' level of prudence or supervision;[305] secondly, what will be considered 'adequate' opportunity for demonstrating the existence of circumstances where the prudential standards of the Party are (or would be)[306] sufficiently effective to be recognized;[307] and finally, what will be considered 'adequate' opportunity for negotiating for similar recognition.[308] The interpretation of these terms must necessarily be highly fact-specific. Each case will have to carefully balance the considerations of national control over the stability of a domestic financial market with the need to avoid unfounded discrimination or hidden protectionism.

The Chapter Fourteen provisions, reflecting the concerns of all the NAFTA Parties, vigorously protect the safety of the financial services sectors of each economy. As the NAFTA inherently assumes that it is the Party's own financial system supervisors that are best positioned to judge the needs of its system, the independence of the governmental supervisory authorities' ability to maintain control of the quality of financial service providers in the Party territory is the main means by which NAFTA assures that continued emphasis can be placed on the value of safety and security of the financial system. Therefore, the individual Party's right to choose for itself what standards to apply and, in turn, what standards to accept as equivalent to its own in a process of recognition must be scrupulously protected in any dispute over the recognition clause of Chapter Fourteen.

---

[304] As an example, the Spanish text of Art. 1406:4 reads:

> Cuando una Parte otorgue reconocimiento a las medidas prudenciales de conformidad con el párrafo 2(c) y las circunstancias dispuestas en el párrafo 3 existan, la Parte brindará oportunidades adecuadas a otra Parte para negociar la adhesión al acuerdo o arreglo, o para negociar un acuerdo o arreglo similar.

The same provision in French reads:

> Lorsqu'une Partie reconnaît des mesures prudentielles aux termes de l'alinéa (2) c) et que les circonstances évoquées au paragraphe 3 existent, la Partie ménagera à une autre Partie une possibilité adéquate de négocier son adhésion à l'accord ou à l'arrangement, ou de négocier un accord ou un arrangement comparables.

[305] NAFTA Art. 1406:4.
[306] NAFTA Art. 1406:3 provides that the Party requesting recognition must have an opportunity to demonstrate 'that circumstances exist in which there are or would be equivalent regulation, oversight, implementation of regulation, and, if appropriate, procedures concerning the sharing of information between the Parties'. This suggests that a promise to raise current standards could be sufficient to fulfill the evidentiary burden.
[307] NAFTA Article 1406:3.
[308] *Ibid.*

At the same time, the interest of the Parties in the non-discriminatory liberalization of trade in financial services throughout the NAFTA territories requires that the individual Party's decision to recognize certain standards and not others are subject to oversight. In order to accomplish both of these aims, factors of examination should focus more on the procedural steps taken by the Parties in their comparison of standards and less on the substance of the standards themselves.[309]

3.10.3   Exceptions to MFN

3.10.3.1   Canadian Exceptions

3.10.3.1.1   FEDERAL RESTRICTIONS ON MOST-FAVORED-NATION TREATMENT

Canada only maintains one reservation to the MFN obligation. This reservation is Canada's right to offer the United States financial institutions more limited opportunity to engage in cross-border trade in securities, or even stop such trade entirely. While Canada's reservation permits such limitation or stop against Mexico as well, they need not treat the United States at least as favorably.[310]

---

[309] The US Securities Exchange Commission (SEC) and several Canadian Provinces' securities commissions have an agreement to implement a 'Multijurisdictional Disclosure System' (MDS). The MDS allows for a relaxation in registration requirements for securities firms, and so results in a favored position for the firms that are subject to one of the participating commissions. Because this is a mutual recognition agreement, under Chapter Fourteen a Mexican securities commission does not have an automatic right to have its own members granted equal privileges in like circumstances. However, the Mexican securities commission does have the right to be granted an adequate opportunity to prove that its standards for membership are equivalent to those of the provincial governments' or of the SEC's. Subsequently, if this evidence is provided, the Mexican commission would then have the right to negotiate for equivalent recognition. The results of such negotiations would most likely depend on the extent to which the Mexican commission agreed to reciprocal recognition of US and Canadian firms. Simser (note 3 *supra*), at 206, n.63, and accompanying text. See also Joel P. Trachtman, 'Unilateralism, Bilateralism, Regionalism, Multilateralism, and Functionalism: A Comparison with Reference to Securities Regulation' (1994) 4:1 Transnat'l L & Contemp Probs 69, 91–95, explaining the MDS in more detail. See also Simser (note 3 *supra*), at 207, saying, somewhat imprecisely, that recognition means that an 'arrangement does not have to be extended to Mexico unless Mexico agrees to extend unique treatment'. Another example of how the recognition provision of Art. 1406:3 should function would be the following. Suppose the Canadian Ministry of Finance and the US Office of the Comptroller of the Currency agreed to recognize one another's standard of judging the qualifications of a bank applicant's proposed management team. If Mexico wanted to have its qualifications standards recognized by Canada as well, arguing that its standards achieved 'equivalent aspects such as Mexico's thoroughness in informing Canada of its own standards and reasons for using its criteria should be factors in deciding whether Mexico had an adequate opportunity for demonstrating its standards' equivalence.
[310] Annex VII, Schedule of Canada, Section B, para. 1.

3.10.3.1.2 PROVINCIAL RESERVATIONS

There were nearly no reservations taken by the provincial governments to the MFN obligation in respect to banking institutions.[311]

3.10.3.2 Mexican Exceptions

Mexico also only sets out one reservation to Article 1406 in its Annex VII Schedule. This exception excludes the benefits of Chapter Fourteen from being enjoyed by 'a foreign bank branch existing in Mexico on the date of entry into force of this Agreement', until the branch would convert into a subsidiary.[312] Because the only foreign bank branch in Mexico at the time of the NAFTA negotiations was a US institution, this provision discriminates in fact by disadvantaging that US enterprise when no Canadian enterprise is affected. For purposes of a legal analysis, however, this provision is irrelevant to the principle of MFN in the context of Chapter Fourteen.

3.10.3.3 United States' Exceptions

3.10.3.3.1 FEDERAL RESTRICTIONS ON MOST-FAVORED-NATION TREATMENT

The United States, like Mexico, was much more limited in its exemptions to the most-favored nation treatment provision of Chapter Fourteen than it was with the exceptions to national treatment obligations. Under the US Schedule in Annex VII, the MFN reservations include the maintenance of the reciprocity provisions of the Primary Dealers Act of 1988 and the Trust Indenture Act of 1939.[313] In addition, the United States extends better treatment to broker-dealers whose principle place of business is Canada than for such dealers whose main country of business is anywhere else.[314] For the former, the broker's required reserves can be kept in a Canadian-supervised bank, while all others must hold reserves at a bank in the United States.[315] Finally, the United States mirrors the Canadians in reserving the right to impose restrictions on the cross-border trade of securities between the two countries.[316]

3.10.3.3.2 STATE RESERVATIONS

The reciprocity requirements that were reserved under the establishment and NTO provisions of NAFTA are listed as reservations to the MFN by

---

[311] The major reservation arises from Quebec's trilateral arrangement with Great Britain and Ireland to afford their financial institutions (as well as those from the other Canadian Provinces) the same rights as Quebec corporations (Loi sur les sociétés de prêts et de placements, L.R.Q., c. S-30).

[312] Annex VII, Schedule of Mexico, Section B.

[313] Annex VII, Schedule of the United States, Section A. See 3.9.4.3 *supra* for discussion of these two reservations as applicable to national treatment obligation.

[314] Annex VII, Schedule of the United States, Section A.

[315] *Ibid.*

[316] Annex VII, Schedule of the United States, Section B.

several States.[317] Beyond these, there are few MFN reservations by the six largest foreign banking States in respect to banking institutions.[318]

3.11   NEW SERVICES AND DATA PROCESSING (ARTICLE 1407)

While US and Canadian banks derive an high percentage of their profits from the introduction of new financial packages, Mexican banks have been slow to innovate, mainly because they had no need to in the protected pre-reform market. The more highly developed banks in the United States and Canada also increasingly rely on electronic data transfer in order to minimize the costs of information analysis by having a single information processing center. The fact that Mexico's banking system was not as developed as the systems of the United States and Canada (either in size, coverage, or methods) led to fears among the two northern Parties that many of their banking activities would be excluded from Mexico. Of particular concern to the US and Canadian banking communities was their ability to provide a full range of services on each Party's market and the right to transfer information over electronic systems from one Party territory to another.[319] Concern arose because of the nature of the national

---

[317]   See note 289 *supra* (reciprocity reservations by California, Illinois, Ohio, and Texas).
[318]   The other reservations include:

> *Florida*—if a foreign bank applicant for an agency office does not have $25 million in capital for the office, it must be one of the largest five banks in its home country to establish an agency office in Florida. This could mean that a bank with less capital than another Party's bank be able to enter due to the home market's lesser development (Fla. Stat. § 663.055);
>   *New York*—securities guaranteed by the government of any of the Canadian Provinces or municipalities need not register such securities, whereas other governments' securities may only be exempted at the national level (Gen. Bus. Law § 352-f(1)(c));
>   *Texas*—securities guaranteed by the government of any of the Canadian Provinces or municipalities need not register such securities, whereas other governments' securities may only be exempted at the national level (7 Tex. Admin. Code §§ 139.4, 139.5).

[319]   The President and Chief Officer of the Federal Reserve Bank of Atlanta captured the connection between innovations, technology and competitiveness in banking:

> … the pace and impact of technological change in the last 10 to 15 years have been nothing short of breathtaking. If there is a concise way to express what both of these mean to the banking industry, I think it is that bank services have become more like commodities. In a commodities business, it is difficult to provide uniqueness, and competition occurs mainly in the realm of prices. In many respects, banking is moving in this direction because of technology … [T]ools for processing and transmitting information have become enormously more powerful … As a result, products can be mass produced. Hence, to stand out, a bank needs new products or a marketing angle.

Robert P. Forrestal, 'Banking Outlook' 23 October 1995 (remarks to the Bank Administration Institute, New York).

treatment obligation that disadvantages foreign innovation. The Canadian and United States banking communities feared the Mexican government could have exploited this 'loophole'.

3.11.1 Article 1407 as a Loophole in Chapter Fourteen's NTO

The national treatment obligation only protects foreign service providers from discrimination between domestic and foreign financial service providers. Thus, there would be no violation of the 'treatment no less favorable than that it accords to its own' rule of NTO if a Party would forbid a particular activity for all banks (domestic and foreign) equally. The other NAFTA Parties feared that the Mexican government could therefore prohibit the supply of any new banking activities and restrict the transfer of data across its borders. Not competitive in these areas anyway, Mexican banks would not be harmed by such a measure. Domestic political pressure would therefore not alter the government's actions. On the other hand, US and Canadian banks would be competitively disadvantaged by the inability to act in those areas where they have the greatest profit potential. Nevertheless, they could not bring a claim of NAFTA violation, because the treatment itself would be *de jure* and *de facto* 'no less favorable'. At the same time, none of the Parties were willing to allow the final control of their financial service markets be determined by others. Mexico was the most vocal on the issue of maintaining 'sovereignty', but Canada and the United States were also unwilling to let new services and electronic information enter their markets without some measure of control.

Chapter Fourteen provides a partial solution to this dilemma by including an article on New Financial Services, under which the introduction of banking innovations is specifically protected.[320] Article 1407 also provides for rules on electronic transfers of information across national borders.[321] This provision serves to protect the ability of banks to continue to rely on their extensive and growing electronic information transfer systems for normal operations.[322]

---

[320] NAFTA Art. 1407:1.

[321] NAFTA Art. 1407:2.

[322] The conglomeration of rules governing New Products and those on Data Processing is not, as it may seem at first, random. A recent study into the effects of information technology on certain service sectors shows that there is a strong link between technology development and, particularly, delivery of products. Georg Licht and Dietmar Moch, 'Innovation and Information Technology in Services', Discussion Paper No. 97-20 (ZEW May 1997). Licht and Moch write:

> Our inability to measure productivity changes in services owing to new technologies' use in service sectors may be due to the fact that unlike in manufacturing, innovation in services often is neither represented by new services nor by process improvements which increase output or decrease inputs. Innovation in service is often closely connected to the way products are delivered. E.g. technical change is connected to the number of hours during which a service can be delivered or to improvements in the spatial dimension of the services (e.g. home banking).

The following will address first the new services obligation and secondly the data processing provisions of Article 1407.

3.11.2   New Services

The provision on new services states:

> Each Party shall permit a financial institution of another Party to provide any new financial service of a type similar to those services that the Party permits its own financial institutions, in like circumstances, to provide under its domestic law. A Party may determine the institutional and juridical form through which the service may be provided and may require authorization for the provision of the service. Where such authorization is required, a decision shall be made within a reasonable time and the authorization may only be refused for prudential reasons.[323]

3.11.2.1   Scope

3.11.2.1.1   TO WHOM/TO WHAT

Article 1407 applies to 'financial institutions'. Because the term stands alone here, in contrast to in other provisions such as the NTO and MFN clauses, this highlights the exclusion of protection for 'investments' and 'investors in financial institutions' under the new product rule.[324] Therefore, only supervised financial institutions (including branches of financial institutions) controlled by nationals or enterprises of a Party have the right to offer new financial services in another Party.[325]

Moreover, cross-border financial institutions are not included in the scope of Article 1407. This means that any financial institution that wants to offer new financial services in a Party must establish in that Party's territory. This is significant, as it has the result that the institution will be subject to the Party's regulatory scheme—an important concession for the Mexican government in its efforts to maintain oversight of the domestic banking market. A Party can

---

(Contd.)

> *Ibid.* at 6. See also 67:17 BNA's Banking Rep. 768 (4 November 1996) ('Technological innovation is also changing the financial marketplace, with interest booming in the Internet as a site for financial transactions'); Susan Phillips 'Supervisory and Regulatory Responses to Financial Innovation and Industry Dynamics', 25 November 1996, remarks by member of the Board of Governors of the Federal Reserve System to the Seminar on Regulatory Policy Changes ('Advances in telecommunications and computer technology have provided banks and their competitors with new and more efficient opportunities to expand regionally, nationally and globally. At the same time financial innovation has enabled institutions to fine tune and expand product lines and activities').

[323] NAFTA Art. 1407:1.

[324] See discussion of the terms 'financial institution', 'investor in a financial institution', and 'investment in a financial institution', *supra.*

[325] See NAFTA Art. 1416 (definition of 'financial institution').

therefore still monitor the use of the new service and control its marketing in such a way as to maintain the safety of the domestic system and protect the individual purchasers of such services.

3.11.2.1.2   OBJECT OF PROTECTION: NEW FINANCIAL SERVICES

Secondly, Article 1407 applies to financial services that are 'new'. Article 1416 ('Definitions') provides the relevant definition of what a 'new financial service' is: 'new financial service means a financial service not provided in the Party's territory that is provided within the territory of another Party, and includes any new form of delivery of a financial service or the sale of a financial product that is not sold in the Party's territory'.[326]

Under this definition, the phrase does not require the service to be 'new' in the ordinary meaning of the word.[327] Rather, 'new' indicates that the particular financial service is not being offered within the territory of the target Party at the present time.

Indeed, a complete innovation in financial services is not covered by either the definition in Article 1416 or by the national treatment obligation of Article 1407. By definition, the service must be being offered in one of the other Parties (suggesting that creativity may have to be restricted to a bank's home office). A financial service that had at one time been offered in the target Party but is no longer offered there is considered a 'new' financial service by NAFTA if offered in another Party.[328]

Third, the service to be offered must be 'of a type similar' to services already offered in the target Party.[329] There is no definition set out to indicate what is meant by a 'similar' type of financial service, leaving it open to judgment to what extent the service must resemble those already present on the target market. One suggestion is that the phrase:

> contains a common sense meaning referencing categories of financial products going well beyond single product offerings. For example, foreign exchange forwards of any currency might be viewed as a 'type' of service, whereas peso forwards arguably would be too narrow a product to fit the definition of a 'type'. At the other extreme, all derivative products would probably be too expansive a category to fit the meaning of 'type'.[330]

Another possible interpretation would be based on products that are economic substitutes for each other. Under this method, the consumer of

---

[326] NAFTA Art. 1416 ('new financial service').
[327] *Webster's Dictionary* defines 'new' to mean: 1. of recent origin, production, purchase, etc.; having but lately come or been brought into being .... 2. of a kind now existing or appearing for the first time; novel ...; *Webster's Encyclopedic Unabridged Dictionary of the English Language* (Random House, New York, 1994 edn), p. 961.
[328] Wethington (note 4 *supra*), at 118.
[329] NAFTA Art. 1407:1. The Spanish definition given is 'nuevo servicio financiero de tipo similar a aquellos que esa otra Parte permite prestar a sus instituciones financieras ...'.; the French definition is 'nouveau service financier d'un type semblable aux service qu'elle autorise ses propres institutions financières ...'.
[330] Wethington (note 4 *supra*), at 119.

financial services would determine what services are similar to others. If a consumer would purchase one service instead of another based on price, the services would be considered 'similar' for purposes of Article 1407:1, even if not 'similar' from the producer's viewpoint. The use of 'directly competitive or substitutable' qualities is already used in NAFTA in reference to determining what are 'like' goods.[331] This type of comparison therefore has the added advantage of offering consistency in the method of analysis throughout the treaty,[332] and allows trade lawyers to work with concepts that are more familiar to them than are descriptions of banking products.

An analysis of 'type similar' that might be the most preferable from the viewpoint of banking system regulators (as opposed to trade experts) could be based on an assessment of the risk levels of various financial instruments. The interpretive tools would have to change as supervisory methods change, but would therefore be highly suited to achieving the goals of safety and soundness of the national banking system of a Party.

Assuming that the qualification of the obligation to allow new services to services of a 'type similar to those services a Party permits' already was made to ensure that national authorities could adequately supervise the provision of new services, the normal analysis of banking regulators may also be the appropriate framework for comparing banking services in Article 1407. Since the early 1990s, financial supervision practices around the world have been changing from rules restricting behavior to principles to guide practice. In the words of one United States regulator:

> In earlier years, supervisors used guidance for relatively narrow purposes—typically to advise examiners or bankers on interpretations of existing regulations or procedures for compliance. Today, guidance is moving from narrow, compliance-oriented prescriptions toward the identification and dissemination of sound practices for managing the risks involved in the various activities banks conduct.
>
> ...
>
> For example, examiners are now placing more emphasis on evaluating the soundness of a bank's process for managing and controlling risks ... This change reflects the importance we place on sound management and adequate internal controls.[333]

---

[331] NAFTA Art. 301:2 (the idea of NTO for like products in reference to state or provinces' treatment 'shall mean, with respect to a state or province, treatment no less favorable than the most favorable treatment accorded ... to any like, directly competitive or substitutable goods, as the case may be ...').

[332] The concept of similarity or likeness is found throughout the NAFTA and throughout international trade law instruments as well. In NAFTA, the term 'like circumstances' is used for comparing investors and cross-border service providers; the adoption of the GATT rules for NTO in NAFTA trade in goods means that 'like products' must be defined there too.

[333] Phillips (note 322 *supra*), at 6–9.

Regulators also place an increased emphasis on the transparency of innovative tools.[334] Such risk and transparency criteria are in part responses to the deregulatory changes occurring in many banking markets, and are in part a necessity in a time of increasingly rapid development of complex and often custom-made financial instruments.

The NAFTA provisions aiming at protecting supervisors' ability to regulate might therefore be best interpreted with similar approaches. A new financial service could be a 'similar type' of banking service as one that involves the same level of risk, allows for the same level of risk management, and that is as transparent—regardless of the services' other characteristics. The innumerable other variations, while of utmost importance to the individual customer, are less interesting to the regulator. Comparing banking services by factors that are significant from a regulator's point of view thus requires a more abstract analysis than one of detailed assessment of the service's or instrument's concrete characteristics.

3.11.2.2 Basic Rule: National Treatment for New Financial Services

The basic principle applied to the NAFTA Parties' regulation of new financial services is the same national treatment obligation as is found in Article 1405 for financial services in general.[335] Article 1407 states in part: 'Each Party shall permit a financial institution of another Party to provide any new financial service of a type similar to those services that the Party permits its own financial institutions, in like circumstances, to provide under its domestic law'.[336]

This requirement strikes a balance between allowing for foreign innovation and allowing each Party government to decide the outer limits of financial service activity within its territory.

3.11.2.2.1 'IN LIKE CIRCUMSTANCES'

In providing for national treatment for new financial services, the term 'in like circumstances' (and *'en circunstancias similares'* or *'dans des circonstances analogues'*) appears once again.[337] Even more so than in the context of Articles 1405 (NTO) and 1406 (MFN), the Article 1407 concept of 'like circumstances' leaves room for different interpretations. It would seem that the only option for interpretation would be for a decision maker to examine 'in like circumstances' independently of the offering of new financial services. Instead, she would rely on the basic national treatment obligation intent of equal competitive opportunity for financial institutions of all

---

[334] Susan Phillips, 'New Approaches Aid Risk Measurement, Management', 8:4 *Financial Update* 1, 5 (October–December 1995). Bulletin published by the Federal Reserve Bank of Atlanta reporting on US and international efforts to increase the transparency of new financial products, including references to the Bank for International Settlements, 1994 Fisher Report and a joint report issued by the Basle Committee on Bank Supervision and the International Organization of Securities Commissions Technical Committee in 1995.

[335] See discussion of the national treatment obligation of Article 1405, *supra* 3.9.

[336] NAFTA Art. 1407:1.

[337] *Ibid.*

Parties. The other possible approach would be of little practical use: if a particular financial service is not offered in a Party, a discussion of that Party's financial institutions being in 'like circumstances' with a financial institution of another Party as regards the offering of such services is too theoretical to be a suitable tool.

3.11.2.3 Obligatory Legal Form and Authorization for New Financial Services

Article 1407 does not grant complete freedom to financial institutions wanting to offer new financial services. A Party may require that the new service be provided through a particular 'institutional and juridical form'.[338] So, even though a branch is protected by the overall provision for offering new financial services by virtue of the definition given for 'financial institution of another Party',[339] the drafters seem to intend that other legal forms (such as partnerships or limited liability companies) may be required to offer or be prohibited from offering new services.

Moreover, the target Party may require that the financial institution providing a new service apply for authorization before engaging in the activity.[340] Article 1407 does not specify a particular authorization procedure to protect the financial institution other than that it must be completed 'within a reasonable time'.[341] Although 'reasonable time' is not further defined, assuming that a new financial service is a subset of all financial services, a 'reasonable time' must be within 120 days of the applicant institution's submission of all required information to the regulatory agent.[342]

The target Party's ability to refuse a request for authorization is limited by the provision that authorization must be granted unless prudential reasons can be given as a basis for the denial.[343] Together with the time limitation on decisions, the restrictions on authorizations function to ensure that new financial services are admitted liberally and rapidly.[344] It is unnecessary to specifically refer to the allowance for denial based on prudential reasons, given the general exceptions later in the chapter. Still, it is symbolically important as a reinforcement of the Parties' prerogative to maintain national control over the banking systems of their territories.

---

[338] *Ibid.*
[339] NAFTA Art. 1416.
[340] NAFTA Art. 1407:1.
[341] *Ibid.*
[342] See NAFTA Art. 1411:4.
[343] NAFTA Art. 1407:1.
[344] See Wethington (note 4 *supra*), at 119 ('... [the time limitation and refusal for prudential reasons only] provision represents a political statement as to the importance of extending market access to the full array of rapidly evolving financial products').

3.11.3 Data Processing

Electronic transfer of information is very important to the economically efficient functioning of modern banks.[345] Financial institutions collect and have to analyze enormous amounts of monetary and economic information daily simply to be able to function normally. Increasingly, the processing of bank data is done electronically. If the processing can be centralized in a single location, the costs of the processing can be lowered due to savings in capital investment and wages. In addition, the transfer of information within a financial group eliminates the costs associated with collecting and analyzing information more than once by related users.

Absent a provision such as 1407:2, under the NAFTA a Party could negate (or seriously impair) the Chapter Fourteen intent of liberalizing financial service trade simply by restricting the amount or type of electronic exchanges that could take place across its borders. The necessity of protecting transfers of data stems from this danger. As with the protection of new services, the data processing paragraph of Chapter Fourteen reduces the potential for protectionism that arises from the unequal levels of development that exist between Canadian and United States banks on the one side and Mexican banks on the other. Article 1407:2 aims at protecting the convenience and potential cost savings from the transfer of electronic information needed for data processing.

Article 1407 provides, '... each Party shall permit a financial institution of another Party to transfer information in electronic or other form, into and out of the Party's territory, for data processing where such processing is required in the ordinary course of business of such institution'.[346]

3.11.3.1 Scope of Application

Like the preceding paragraph on new services, the scope of the data processing provision is limited to financial institutions (including branches)

---

[345] One US banking supervisor has indicated that it is the bank's ability to collect and process large amounts of information that is their main area of competitive advantage over non-bank financial companies. Robert P. Forrestal, 'Banking Outlook', 23 October 1995, remarks by the President and Chief Executive Officer of the Federal Reserve Bank of Atlanta to the Bank Administration Institute, New York ('banks still have the edge in gathering, processing, and monitoring information'). See also, 31 CFR 208 (16 September 1997); part of the US Government's Electronic Fund Transfer 99 program, this proposed rule would require all federal agencies to use exclusively electronic funds transfers for federal payments other than tax payments.

[346] NAFTA Art. 1407:2. In United States banking law, the Financial Institutions Regulatory and Interest Rate Control Act of 1978 is the source of provisions on, among other areas, electronic fund transfers. P.L. 95-630, 92 STAT. 3641. Data processing has also been the focus of several rules and regulations by the United States banking supervisors. See 12 C.F.R. § 7.3500 (bank regulations); 12 C.F.R. § 225.25(b)(7) (for bank holding companies). There are also court decisions reviewing the Federal Reserve's application of these rules. See, e.g., *Association of Data Processing Service Organizations, Inc. v. Board of Governors of the Federal Reserve System* 745 F.2d 677 (D.C. Cir. 1984), affirming the Board's decision to allow a bank to sell its excess data processing capacity and computer hardware on the basis of the data processing's being 'closely related to banking'.

established in the territory of the Party. Neither does Article 1407:2 grant any rights to cross-border financial service providers.[347] In addition, the transfer of any information that is either 'related to the financial affairs and accounts of individual customers' or 'confidential' may be restricted under an exception found in a subsequent provision.[348]

3.11.3.2   Data Processing Allowed If 'In Ordinary Course of Business of Such Institution'

The limitations on information transfers are based on the end-use of the information. The provisions require that the information be destined for 'data processing' that is 'required' in the 'ordinary course of business of such institution'. Each of these terms will be discussed below.

3.11.3.2.1   DATA PROCESSING

'Data processing' is not defined in the NAFTA text. In normal usage, the term refers to the systematic collection, organization, and/or analysis of information. As there is nothing to indicate a deviation from the usual definition, under international law the usual definition must be applied.

3.11.3.2.2   'REQUIRED'

The data processing itself must be 'required'[349] by the institution's regular functioning. The choice of the word 'required' is interesting because it limits an institution's right to transfer information.[350] Thus it hinders the full rationalization of the financial markets. As an inherent barrier to trade within a treaty aimed at liberalizing trade, the term must be carefully examined.

With the growing linkages between different types of financial service providers, there is an economic benefit to transferring client information among the financial group to minimize analysis costs. This type of information transfer is certainly not 'necessary' for business under a narrow view of the concept.[351] Nevertheless, it is economically efficient. The spectrum of possible interpretations of 'required' is wide: is data processing only 'required' if a bank could no longer function as a bank? Or is the data processing 'required' if the institution would become less profitable without the information collection? Or should 'required' be interpreted even more

---

[347] See 3.8 *supra*.
[348] See Art. 1411 (Transparency) and discussion of Art. 1411:5 at 3.13.5 *infra*.
[349] See also the Spanish text, using the term 'necesario' and the French text, using 'nécessaire'.
[350] It is also puzzling why the word 'necessary' was not used, in light of the Spanish and French versions of the text. See note 349 *supra*.
[351] Indeed, in some countries this type of transfer of information is a violation of privacy laws, and can result in criminal penalties. See, e.g., Bundesgesetz über die Banken und Sparkassen Art. 47(1) (Swiss banking law provision criminalizing the release of information by bank employees and officers).

broadly, to mean that if the bank could not achieve its maximum profitability without the data processing that it 'requires' the processing?

Based on the plain text meaning of 'required', a strict view of the obligation would be reasonable under international law principles of interpretation. The term 'required' in English generally indicates a necessary condition for existence. Thus, the strict view of Article 1407:2 would allow a Party to refuse to allow transfers of electronic information if that transfer was done 'only' for purposes of cost-saving.

However, such a narrow interpretation of 'required' would contradict the overall movement toward a liberal market in financial services and negate the purpose of the provision itself. Under the viewpoint of the treaty's goal, a more liberal interpretation is more suitable. Because it limits the overall goals of the treaty, the concept of 'required' should be treated as an exception, and applied narrowly enough to allow for achieving the goals of the treaty without making the term useless in practice. 'Required' should be identified with economic practicability: between the question of whether the bank could continue to exist without the information and the question of whether the bank could reach its maximum profitability with the information.

3.11.3.2.3 'ORDINARY COURSE OF BUSINESS'

Another term to be defined is that of 'ordinary course of business'.[352] The term 'ordinary course of business' has no specifically 'trade'-orientation in Article 1407, so the plain meaning of the words should govern its interpretation. In the context of Chapter Fourteen, one may assume that 'ordinary course of business' will be defined in terms of the sub-industries regulated by the Chapter: banks' ordinary course of business will include deposit taking, issuing loans, and investing deposits; insurance companies' ordinary course of business will include issuing and paying out premiums; and securities firms' ordinary course of business will include buying and selling shares on the world stock exchanges and futures markets. It will be the outer limits of their activities that will give rise to disputes over interpretation of 'ordinary'.

Because the statutory frameworks governing the Parties' financial institutions permit banks different areas of activities, the characterization of whether the data processing is in the 'ordinary course of business' will depend on the Party in which the institution is established. In Canada and Mexico, for instance, banking institutions' analysis of securities transactions should be considered 'ordinary'. Thus far in the United States, these same activities might not be 'ordinary' even for related banks.[353]

---

[352] The Spanish version of this phrase is 'llevar a cabo las actividades ordinarias de negocios'. The French version is 'la conduite des affaires courantes'.

[353] The US Federal Reserve Board has a list of activities it considers 'usual' for purposes of Regulation K. See 12 C.F.R. § 211.5(d) and § 211.23(c)(2) (1991). This list is used to determine whether the foreign commercial activities of a financial institution are 'banking' activities. For more on the effects of Regulation K see Joel P. Trachtman, 'Recent Initiatives in International Financial Regulation and Goals of Competitiveness, Effectiveness, Consistency and Cooperation' (1991) 12 NW J Int'l L & Bus 241.

It would be possible that the definition of what is a financial institution's 'ordinary course of business' evolves into a negative description. The panel would ask what is *not* the ordinary course of business rather than what is. While this approach may be usable for the first several disputes raising the issue of data processing information, such a framework does not promote the legal security needed for long-term stability in the international financial markets.

Another possibility for addressing the term 'ordinary course of business' would be the 'I know it when I see it' test.[354] Here, a panelist would hear the facts of a disputed action and decide on the ordinariness from a subjective 'feeling' about the case. While such an approach could be workable for the beginning stages of an international trade in services jurisprudence, it is less than ideal as a long-term judicial principle. First, as with the negative test, the need for legal security discredits the use of such an interpretive non-method. Financial service institutions would have to guess at a subjective standard. Secondly, the quality of the decision would be inextricably based on the panelists' individual expertise in the subject matter of the particular dispute. In a dispute settlement context where panelists are not full-time employees of the NAFTA, placing such reliance on specific knowledge should be avoided, despite their required expertise in financial services.[355]

A better approach for interpretation is certainly a positive test for what is 'in the ordinary course of business'. To develop such a test, the case law of each Party can give helpful insight on what is considered ordinary in a particular jurisdiction. As national judges have experience in interpreting such terms, their already-established parameters form a logical starting point for NAFTA interpretations of this concept. In addition, an interpretation of Chapter Fourteen provisions that is compatible with national law will allow the NAFTA Party financial service institutions to assess more readily whether their need for data transfer will be protected under the NAFTA.

In United States courts, for example, a determination of whether an action is in the 'ordinary course of business' depends on the reasonable expectations of others. A two-dimensional test has developed in the jurisprudence: a vertical test and a horizontal test. A recent opinion from the Court of Appeals of the Second Circuit[356] explains:

> Under this two-part analysis, 'the touchstone of "ordinariness" is thus the interested parties' reasonable expectations of what transactions the debtor in possession is likely to enter in the course of its business' ...

---

[354] The phrase 'I know it when I see it' originates in US Supreme Court Justice Stewart's comments on determining what is obscenity. *Jacobellis v. Ohio* 378 US 184, 197 (1964), concurring opinion; 'I shall not attempt to define the kinds of material I understand to be embraced within that shorthand description; and perhaps I could never succeed in intelligibly doing so. But I know it when I see it ...'.

[355] For more on the dispute settlement panels required by Chapter Fourteen, see 3.18.2.2 *infra*.

[356] The federal court system in the United States is composed of 94 District Courts, four specialized courts (Tax Court, Court of Federal Claims, Court of Veterans Appeals, and the Court of International Trade), 13 Circuit Courts, and the Supreme Court. Circuit courts hear appeals from the District Courts, and review only issues of law. The Second Circuit Court sits in New York.

Under the vertical test, the court views the disputed transaction from the vantage point of a hypothetical creditor and inquires whether the transaction subjects a creditor to economic risks of a nature different from those he accepted when he decided to' enter into a contract with the debtor.

...

The horizontal test involves 'an industry-wide perspective in which the debtor's business is compared to other like businesses. In this comparison, the test is whether the postpetition [*sic*] transaction is of a type that other similar businesses would engage in as ordinary business'.[357]

To use this bifurcated view of what is ordinary business, a NAFTA panel would look first at what types of data bank customers in the NAFTA territory would expect a bank to process. The Second Circuit's emphasis on the specific context of the action is even more important in a plurilateral setting such as the NAFTA than in a single nation's system.

The panel would follow the vertical test with an application of the horizontal test. Here, the views of other banks would be taken into account to determine if the industry as a whole would treat the action as 'in the ordinary course of business'.

Again, the specific context of a dispute must be taken into account after looking at the general claim. What might be an ordinary course of business in most cases may not be ordinary in the circumstances of a given dispute: 'Some transactions either by their size, nature or both are ... extraordinary'.[358] Here the inclusion of the phrase 'of such institution' must be more carefully considered. The subjectiveness lent by this phrase makes a detailed examination of the particular facts of the transaction *in the context of the bank in question* necessary.

Of course, Canadian courts' and Mexican courts' approaches must also be taken into account in developing a test for 'ordinary course of business'. However, this US jurisprudence could form a useful starting point for an 'ordinary business' analysis under the NAFTA for banks located in the United States. The goals of legal predictability and security are preserved, and the decision maker need not have more expertise in the particular business context than what he or she can glean from the evidence submitted by the Parties.

3.11.3.2.4 HARD CASE

Recently there have been several alliances formed between banks and information service companies.[359] An interesting question for the NAFTA

---

[357] *In Re: Jeffrey E. Lavigne* 114 F.3d 379, 384–385 (2d Cir. 1997), quoting from *In re Dant & Russell* 853 F.2d 700, 705 (9th Cir. 1988).

[358] *Ibid.*

[359] See 'Bank Technology News—Article 6' (found on internet at >www.banking.com<), reporting on Swiss Bank Corporation's purchase of a part of Perot Systems Corp, an information outsourcer; reporting also that Alltel Information Services contracted with Metropolitan Bank and Trust Co of the Philippines; on EDS Corp's arrangement with NationsBank to electronically deliver government benefits; and on Fiserv Inc's agreement to work together with Chase Manhattan Bank to sell data center services.

Chapter Fourteen is whether such alliances can claim that their data processing services require transfers of information 'in the ordinary course of business' of the bank. If the data processing activities are sold as services on their own, their ordinariness to their banking activities becomes less clear. At the same time, because the services would be provided by a 'financial institution', the Chapter Fourteen rules, rather than the rules of Chapter Eleven seem to be the most appropriate to apply.

The aims of the financial service perspective of Chapter Fourteen may not extend far enough to cover transfers of information for non-financial service use. Although one banker pointed out that 'as a financial services institution, we're in the information business, not necessarily the money business',[360] data processing services that are sold separately should not be protected by the provisions of Article 1407. Such an interpretation of the 'ordinary course of business' language could prevent a further liberalization of trade in banking services, but the supervision of such activity is not within either the intended realm of financial services or the reasonable competence of the financial authorities.

3.11.4   Annex VII Reservations

3.11.4.1   Canadian Reservations

Canada has no Annex VII reservations on the application of Article 1407.

3.11.4.2   Mexican Reservations

Mexico has no Annex VII reservations on the application of Article 1407.

3.11.4.3   United States' Reservations

The sole reservation maintained on Article 1407 in Annex VII is that by the United States on onions.[361] Under the Commodity Exchange Act, futures contracts, options, and options on futures contracts on onions may not be offered for sale or sold.[362] This law is not altered by the new financial services provisions of NAFTA.

3.12   MANAGEMENT AND DIRECTORS (NAFTA ARTICLE 1408)

To achieve a liberal market in financial services, the NAFTA Parties extended the market access and non-discrimination rights to those in charge of the financial institutions. Because residency and nationality

---

[360] Randle in Bob Curley, 'Charting Virtual Territory'.
[361] Annex VII, Schedule of the United States, Section B.
[362] Commodity Exchange Act, 7 U.S.C. §§ 2, 13-1.

requirements have long been complained about in the area of foreign investment in general, the NAFTA Article 1408 attempts to eliminate such protectionism as regards business management.

3.12.1 Senior Management and Essential Personnel

The Parties agreed to prohibit themselves from requiring that the positions of senior management and essential personnel of financial institutions are filled by persons of their own nationality. The first paragraph of Article 1408 reads: 'No Party may require financial institutions of another Party to engage individuals of any particular nationality as senior managerial or other essential personnel'.[363]

It is not clear how far down the hierarchy of a financial institution's employment structure this obligation reaches, but certainly it would ensure that those responsible for determining the overall business strategies might be of any nationality.

It is interesting to note, however, that the provision does not prohibit placing residency requirements on senior management or essential personnel. A Mexican vice president of a Mexican bank located in Chicago may therefore still be subjected to a requirement to live within the Chicago city limits. The Article 1408 implicit allowance on residency restrictions is another example of the Chapter Fourteen's general protection of national prudential interests. The reasoning is apparently that if a person is 'essential' to the operation of a bank, the person should be regularly near the bank. Safety and soundness of the banking system as well as of the individual institution are in this way better maintained. Further, in case of investor or depositor losses, the management will be within the jurisdiction of the authorities responsible for the legal disputes that could follow.[364]

3.12.2 Board of Directors

The Board of Directors of a NAFTA Party financial institution, compared to the management, may be subject to greater restrictions by the Parties. 'No Party may require that more than a simple majority of the board of directors of a financial institution of another Party be composed of nationals of the Party, persons residing in the territory of the Party, or a combination thereof'.[365]

---

[363] NAFTA Art. 1408:1.
[364] The issue of bankruptcy law is not addressed by the NAFTA. The increase in business activity among the NAFTA Parties, however, has led to an increased realization that the differences in the bankruptcy laws can cause great difficulties for the individual businessperson. See Charles A. Beckham, Jr. and Roberto Fernandez, 'Cross-Border Insolvency: the Bridge You Never Want to Cross' (1998) IV:1 NAFTA: L & Bus Rev Am 50. See also Alex D. McElroy, 'Report Calls for Global Framework to Resolve Multinational Financial Crises', 71:4 BNA's Banking Rep 182 (27 July 1998), discussing the Group of Thirty's July 1998 report on 'International Insolvencies in the Financial Sector'.
[365] NAFTA Art. 1408:2.

Like the previous provision for management, the liberalization of the board of director requirements attempts to ensure that NAFTA financial service providers may operate as they choose within the NAFTA Parties' territories. Because the Board of Directors determines the overall approach to be taken by a bank, an assurance that nationals of the banks' country of origin can be a substantial part of the board allows for the character of the bank to be maintained.

Although it is worded in the negative, Article 1408:2 still allows a Party to legislate that half of the members of a Board be either its nationals, residents of the Party, or a combination of nationals and residents.[366] The fact that Canada, Mexico, and the United States each had restrictions of these sort at the time of negotiation explains why there is not an obligation to allow non-residents or non-nationals access to full control of the Board.[367] The national restrictions on full board control stem in turn from perceptions of the significance of banks in society as a whole. Non-residents are presumed to have less of an interest in the bank's local community, and if all directors were non-residents, their decisions could be made at the cost of the community. This risk is supposed to be minimized if half of the directors are nationals or residents.[368]

3.12.3   Annex VII Reservations

The reservations to Article 1408 are copious, but limited to the United States.

3.12.3.1   *Canadian Reservations*

Canada maintains no Annex VII reservation to Article 1408.[369]

3.12.3.2   *Mexican Reservations*

Mexico maintains no Annex VII reservation to Article 1408.

3.12.3.3   *United States' Reservations*

The United States took an exception to the entire Article 1408,[370] and many of the States—by which most foreign banks are chartered—have reservations to the provisions as well.

---

[366] *Ibid.*
[367] Wethington (note 4 *supra*), at 120.
[368] One can question the validity of the premise that allows a national living in another part of the territory to be eligible for a position for which a foreigner is not eligible regardless of ties to the region.
[369] Simser (note 3 *supra*), at 208, notes that the Bank Act of 1991 requires a three-quarters majority of the directors of a bank be Canadian. Bank Act of 1991 § 159. If not amended, this presents a claim of action for a possible dispute settlement proceeding.
[370] NAFTA Annex VII, Schedule of the United States, Section A.

3.12.3.3.1　FEDERAL RESTRICTIONS ON MANAGEMENT AND DIRECTORS'
REQUIREMENTS

On the national level, Annex VII reserves the United States' right to maintain both citizenship and residency requirements on the directors of any foreign bank or branch.[371] If a national bank is affiliated with, or a subsidiary of, a foreign bank, US citizens must compose at least a majority of the board of directors.[372] Moreover, two-thirds of the directors must have lived for at least one year before election to the board and must continue to live either in the State where the bank is located or within 100 miles of the bank itself.[373]

Finally, the United States set out its Trust Indenture Act's reciprocity requirement as an exception to Article 1408.[374] That Act allows the United States to refuse to permit a foreign enterprise the right to act as a 'sole trustee under an indenture for debt securities sold in the United States' unless United States firms can participate in these activities in the foreign institution's home country.[375]

3.12.3.3.2　STATES' RESERVATIONS

Among others, the States of Florida, Illinois, New York, and Texas—all major jurisdictions for foreign bank chartering—took reservations to NAFTA rules on financial service institutions' directors. Although several of the States require supermajorities rather than a simple majority of the directors to be residents of the State, nationality is not required in any of these four jurisdictions for commercial banks.[376] For other bank-like financial institutions, nationality is sometimes required.[377] The laws of the particular jurisdiction must therefore be checked closely.

---

[371] *Ibid.*

[372] National Bank Act, 12 U.S.C. § 72; Annex VII, Schedule of the United States, Section A.

[373] *Ibid.*

[374] Annex VII, Schedule of the United States, Section A. Trust Indenture Act of 1939, 15 U.S.C. § 77jjjj(a)(1).

[375] James R. Holbein and Donald J. Musch, *NAFTA: Final Text, Summary, Legislative History & Implementation Directory* (Oceana Publications, New York, 1994), p. 937, summarizing the exceptions.

[376] *Florida*—Fla. Stat. § 658.33 requires that a minimum of 60 per cent of a bank's board of directors have been resident of Florida for at least one year before becoming director, and that in-State residency continue throughout the term of office.

> *Illinois*—Ill. Banking Act § 16(2)(a) requires that a minimum of two-thirds of a bank's board of directors maintain in-State residency or have a residence within 100 miles of the 'main banking premises'. See 25 ILCS 105/3–4(a);
> *Texas*—Texas requires that a majority of the board of directors of a commercial bank must be residents of Texas. Tex. Rev. Civ. Stat. Art. 342–404, § 2; Art. 342–912, § 4.

[377] Wethington (note 4 *supra*), Appendix O:

> *Illinois*—regulations require two-thirds of the directors of Savings and Loans, savings banks, Illinois association mutual holding companies, and that all of the directors of an Illinois development credit corporations to be residents of the State. Savings Bank Act § 408; 38 Ill. Admin. Code § 1075.1220(c); 805 ILCS 35/14.
> *New York*—New York requires that all directors and management committee members of credit unions be US citizens and that all the trustees of mutual savings banks and mutual savings and loans be citizens. Banking Law §§ 246(3), 397, 450.

3.13   TRANSPARENCY (ARTICLE 1411)

The term 'transparency' when used by international trade lawyers refers to the ready availability of laws and regulations affecting trade, as well as a willingness and ability of a government or an organization to efficiently assist those who request information or the opportunity to participate in the trade system (whether as a trader or as a contributor to trade-policy discussions). If one accepts that NAFTA's primary goal is to improve living standards in its Parties, and that the chosen means to accomplish this goal is to increase the flow of goods, services, and investments, then the Parties' emphasis on transparency can be seen as a 'meta-means' (a means to a means). The existence of a provision such as Article 1411, which promotes the flow of information relevant to financial service investment, is one aspect of the efforts to achieve this goal.

NAFTA Chapter Eighteen on the Publication, Notification and Administration of Laws sets out the general treaty rules to encourage Parties' transparency. Article 1411 is a special provision governing transparency in financial service regulation. As a set of rules for a specific area, Article 1411 in part trumps the provisions of Chapter Eighteen and in part is additive.[378] The Article's six subparagraphs contain four main concepts: transparency in rules (widely defined); transparency in the administration of applications; transparency in the functioning of Chapter Fourteen as a whole; and exceptions to the transparency obligation.

3.13.1   Scope: 'Interested Persons'

Before delving into the four concepts, the scope of the transparency obligation must be made clear, as it is unusual. The language of Article 1411, like that of Chapter Eighteen, generally refers to 'interested persons'[379] rather than to 'persons of a Party':

1. ... each Party shall, to the extent practicable, provide in advance to all interested persons any measure of general application that the Party proposes to adopt in order to allow an opportunity for such persons to comment on the measure. ...
2. Each Party's regulatory authorities shall make available to interested persons their requirements for completing applications relating to the provision of financial services.

---

[378] NAFTA Art. 1411:1 ('in lieu of Art. 1802(2) (Publication), each Party shall ...'.).
[379] The Spanish and French terms are not distinguishable from the English ('personas interesadas' and 'personnes intéressées', respectively).

3. On the request of an applicant, the regulatory authority shall inform the applicant of the status of its application. ...

...

6. Each Party shall maintain ... one or more enquiry points ... to respond ... to all reasonable inquiries from interested persons regarding measures of general application covered by this Chapter.[380]

The use of 'person' without the qualification that the person is of a Party indicates that the transparency provisions of NAFTA can be invoked by nationals or enterprises of either a Party or by those persons of a non-Party.[381] The transparency benefits of the Agreement thus extend farther than do most of the other NAFTA provisions. Such an extension is particularly curious in a free trade area agreement, where the inherent purpose of the agreement is to limit the benefits of liberalization to reciprocal members. One must surmise that the interest in transparency is so great as to have moved the Parties to subject themselves to a wider scrutiny than necessary.

In Article 1411, qualification of the scope of the obligations with the phrase 'interested persons' is also noteworthy. In deciding how broadly to interpret the phrase, the financial and administrative burden of notification must be taken into account and balanced against the value the information has to the individual and the financial industry as a whole. If interpreted widely, the term 'interested persons' could include all potential financial service providers of another Party. The interest in a well-informed public would call for such an approach.[382]

The phrase 'interested person' may, however, legitimately be interpreted more narrowly. This narrower approach would limit the requirement such that a Party is only required to respond to persons who actively request the information. Several of the provisions' text would support a narrow interpretation of the transparency obligations. The requirement that a Party tell the status of the application '[o]n request of an applicant'[383] and inform the applicant if it needs more information to make a decision on the application,[384] for instance, refers to persons who have actively availed themselves of the NAFTA protections and have a stake in the decisions of a national authority. In addition, a definition of 'interested person' limited to actively interested persons would be a more reasonable balancing of the burdens and benefits of transparency as applies to Chapter Fourteen. Applying the same idea as in the more relaxed

---

[380] NAFTA Art. 1411.
[381] See NAFTA Art. 201.
[382] In US administrative law, there is a rule requiring agencies to allow 'interested persons' to be able to participate in rule-makings. Administrative Protection Act § 553 (c). According to one author, 'it seems to be understood that anyone who claims to be interested is interested for this purpose; or at least, an attempt to exclude anyone under this language has never been litigated'. Walter Gellhorn, Clark Blyse, Peter L. Strauss, Todd Rakoff and Roy A. Schotland, *Administrative Law: Cases and Comments* (8th edn, Foundation Press, Mineola, NY, 1987), p. 331.
[383] NAFTA Art. 1411:3.
[384] NAFTA Art. 1411:3.

approach to 'publication', one can reasonably approach the Article 1411 obligations in such a way as to allow for minimizing their the financial and administrative burdens.[385]

3.13.2   Transparency in Rules (Widely Defined)

Article 1411:1 requires that Parties are to give interested persons information about, and a chance to comment upon proposed measures of general application. The term 'measures', as elaborated earlier, has a very wide definition, covering laws, rules, and practices. The Article 1411 provision, unlike Chapter Eighteen's general transparency obligation, does not require that all proposed measures be published. Rather, financial service measures may be published, written, or given 'in such other form as permits an interested person to make informed comments'.[386] Thus, it is imaginable that oral information, perhaps in a conference of industry leaders or over the telephone, would satisfy this provision. The logic of this more informal requirement may be grounded in the relative narrowness of the financial service sector. Most measures that will affect financial services are simply not of interest to the wider public to make the administrative cost of publication commensurate with directly supplying the information to all persons in a Party territory.

Including a wide transparency in rules requirement in the NAFTA Chapter Fourteen is as important for ensuring an awareness of the rules governing bank activities in the United States and Canada as it is for those doing business in Mexico. Although both Canada and the United States have well developed systems for publicizing formal legislation, the rules from supervisory agencies and commissions are at times only accessible to (or understandable by) a few of the largest domestic institutions. The complex regulatory process facing banks in day-to-day operations makes more transparency in these agency and commissions necessary for a truly liberalized and non-discriminatory market. In the United States, for example, the Federal Reserve Board practice of making rulings on the individual bank level has come under criticism for being non-transparent.[387] This is especially disturbing as 'the rulings of (the Board), which contradict the provisions of Glass-Steagall, 'suggest that the powers of US Banks in the securities area are being changed substantially by the discretion of the regulators without a change in laws''.[388] In Canada, there

---

[385] See 3.13.2 *infra* under 'Transparency in Rules'.
[386] NAFTA Art. 1411:1.
[387] Simser (note 3 *supra*), at 207.
[388] *Ibid.*, quoting J. Chant, 'The Financial Sector in NAFTA: Two Plus One Equals Restructuring', *The NAFTA Network* (1993), p. 179. This is a bulletin of the Fraser Institute of Vancouver; see also Gerald T. Dunne, 'The Glass-Steagall Wall: Subtle Hazards Revisited' (1994) 111 Banking LJ 115 ('Demolition of the Glass-Steagall 'wall' [has been] undertaken by the federal judiciary and bank supervisors without a word of change in the basic statute ...'.).

are similar concerns about a lack of transparency in the Office of the Superintendent of Financial Institutions.[389]

3.13.3 Transparency in the Application Process

The transparency requirements of Article 1411 also extend to making the application process more accessible and understandable to the ordinary person. This is in order to protect the feasibility of Chapter Fourteen's establishment provisions and other liberalizations. Thus, paragraph 2 requires that the authorities provide interested persons with information on the requirements for completing any application 'relating to the provision of financial services'.[390]

Moreover, the Party authorities are to ensure that every application is processed efficiently. The potential investor is to be informed of the stage at which the application is in examination, and ought to be furnished with a decision within four months of submitting all necessary application information. Once an applicant gives sufficient information to the requisite authorities to satisfy the application and 'all relevant hearings are held', the Party's authorities have 120 days to make a decision on the application unless they notify the applicant that meeting the deadline is not feasible.[391] If the decision is postponed, Article 1411 provides that the authorities 'endeavor' to come to a decision within a 'reasonable time thereafter'. This is a safeguard for the applicants, who might otherwise be effectually prevented from entering another Party's market simply due to administrative languor. The strength of this protection, of course, depends on how strictly the terms 'endeavor' and 'reasonable time' are interpreted.

3.13.4 Transparency in the Functioning of Chapter Fourteen

Article 1411:6 contains a requirement that each Party set up an inquiry point to which questions on implemented measures of general application can be directed.[392] In an attempt to ensure the effectiveness of these inquiry points, the provision requires that all 'reasonable' questions are to receive a written reply 'as soon as practicable'.[393]

---

[389] Simser (note 3 *supra*), at 207, quoting J. Robinson, 'NAFTA and Doing Business with Mexico: Financial Services Under NAFTA' (Canadian Institute Conference, Toronto, 13 January 1994), p. 13, stating that the OSFI regulatory practices 'do not comply with NAFTA's transparency obligations'.
[390] NAFTA Art. 1411:2.
[391] NAFTA Art. 1411:4.
[392] NAFTA Art. 1411:6.
[393] *Ibid.*

3.13.5   Exceptions to the Transparency Obligations: Privacy Provisions

In contrast to the other provisions of Article 1411, the provisions of paragraph 5 are not directly related to transparency. Paragraph 5 contains a Chapter-wide exception from obligations to offer or transfer information if restrictions on such flows are needed to protect the privacy of individuals and businesses:

> Nothing in this Chapter requires a Party to furnish or allow access to:
>
> (a) information related to the financial affairs and accounts of individual customers of financial institutions or cross-border financial service providers; or
> (b) any confidential information, the disclosure of which would impede law enforcement or otherwise be contrary to the public interest or prejudice legitimate commercial interests of particular enterprises.[394]

This provision reflects the current concern about how to best balance privacy considerations with the free flow of information that is necessary if financial liberalization is to succeed.[395] It exempts Parties from any duty to release information about 'individual customers' of financial institutions or cross-border financial institutions.[396] Such information is protected to some extent by national bank secrecy laws, and reference to it in the NAFTA is to ensure there is no confusion as to the status of such norms.[397]

---

[394] NAFTA Art. 1411:5.
[395] *Ibid*. The rule of Art. 1407:2 on transfer of information for data processing is also exempted when the information is about an individual's financial affairs. The OECD developed Privacy Guidelines in 1980 to influence the 'collection, uses and security of personal information on people who make money transactions electronically'. OECD, 'Electronic Commerce at the OECD', News Release (30 April 1997) (text found on internet at >www.oecd.org<).
[396] NAFTA Art. 1411:5(a).
[397] In the USA, see, e.g., Right to Financial Privacy Act of 1978, Pub. L. 95-630, 92 Stat. 3697 (12 U.S.C. §§ 3401–22), governing the yielding of customer financial records by a financial institution and its personnel to government agencies; see in particular at § 1102 (12 U.S.C. § 3402):

> Except as provided by [the following provisions], no Government authority may have access to or obtain copies of, or the information contained in the financial records of any customer from a financial institution unless the financial records are reasonably described and [list of requirements such as the receipt of explicit customer permission, an administrative or judicial subpoena, or a search warrant].

In Canada, Common Law protects the confidentiality of bankers' information on their clients:

> It is an implied term of the contract between a bank and its customer in Canadian law that the bank will maintain secrecy with regard to the customer's account and banking affairs and will not disclose to other persons information pertaining to the account status or the customer which the bank may acquire in the course of its relationship with that customer. This duty continues relating to such information even after the banker-customer relationship ends.

This provision on protecting privacy and is not controversial in and of itself.[398] Its use, however, may well cause dispute, particularly if it is used to limit the cross-border transfer of data processing information. The high degree of electronic commerce involved in the provision of financial services increases the need to develop rules on the protection of individual privacy in this area,[399] but it remains to be seen to what extent Article 1411:5 will achieve this goal.

Article 1411 also exempts Parties from the duty of releasing information if this would 'impede law enforcement', 'otherwise be contrary to the public interest', or injure a business' competitive advantages.[400] The Parties' interest in not hampering potential or on-going criminal investigations is a generally accepted reason for withholding of information.[401]

The extent of 'otherwise contrary to the public interest' is more difficult to determine, but assumedly goes to legitimate non-prudential concerns that a government has in protecting its citizens. The determination of what is in the public interest is notoriously difficult for an external observer. There is always a danger that when and international body must scrutinize a state's motivations, any negative decision will be rejected. Within the Chapter Fourteen framework, a panel would have to

---

(Contd.)

Dale Ursel, 'Bank Confidentiality in Canada' (1992) 14 Comp L YB Int'l Bus 239, at 241. The Canadian courts have adopted four significant exceptions to the confidentiality rules set out in the English case of *Tournier v. National Provincial & Union Bank* [1923] 1 KB 641 (Court of Appeal). See *Bank of Montreal v. A.G. of Quebec* 1 SCR 565, 570–572 (1979). The exceptions to the non-disclosure principle are: client consent (express or implied); duty to the public; self-interest of bank; and compulsion by law.

[398] Compare GATS Art. III*bis*:

Nothing in this Agreement shall require any Member to provide confidential information, the disclosure of which would impede law enforcement, or otherwise be contrary to the public interest, or which would prejudice legitimate commercial interests of particular enterprises, public or private.

[399] See also discussion of electronic transfers of information, *supra*.

[400] NAFTA Art. 1411:5(b).

[401] The Canadian Evidence Act grants courts the power to make an 'order of the Court made for special cause' to a bank so as to gain access to bank records. The order for special cause may only be granted by a court if a litigant 'can satisfy the court that it is reasonable, under the circumstances of the particular case, that the bank be put under an obligation to divulge certain documents or information otherwise inaccessible to the applicant'. Ursel (note 397 *supra*), at 243. See *ibid.* at 243–6, for a discussion of case law on banks and the Canadian Evidence Act; see *ibid.* at 252, for a discussion of Proceeds of Crime Act, in 1992 still a proposed bill, in which banks are required to keep records on the identities of customers for purposes of criminal investigations. A US official made a statement to the House of Representatives' Committee on Banking, Finance and Urban Affairs asserting that law enforcement agencies do not make sufficient use of the Currency Transaction Reports that banks are required to submit under the Bank Secrecy Act of 1970. See Statement of Henry R. Wray, 'Money Laundering: The Use of Bank Secrecy Act Reports by Law Enforcement Could Be Increased', GAO/T-GGD-93-31 (released 26 May 1993).

be very careful in rejecting a Party's assertion that certain information cannot be disclosed due to the public interest. Yet an automatic acceptance of such an assertion could effectively negate any obligation to liberalize the flow of information.

The protection of business advantages by the Parties' ability to withhold information that could 'prejudice legitimate commercial interests of particular enterprises' is a safeguard against requests for confidential information by competitors, and is in keeping with the overall treaty goals. Again, similar exceptions are found in both national rules to foster transparency[402] and in international agreements.[403]

3.14   INCORPORATION OF CHAPTER ELEVEN INVESTMENT AND CHAPTER TWELVE SERVICE PROVISIONS (ARTICLE 1401:2)

Chapter Fourteen incorporates certain Chapter Eleven (Investment) provisions and makes them applicable to financial services.[404] Specifically, these are the Investment Chapter's articles addressing transfers related to an investment;[405] expropriation and compensation;[406] formalities and information requirements;[407] the denial of benefits to investors of a non-Party enterprise;[408] and environmental measures.[409] The Chapter Twelve provision on denial of benefits is also brought into Chapter Fourteen,[410] as are the investor dispute settlement articles of Chapter Eleven for claims arising under its incorporated provisions.[411]

---

[402] Administrative Procedure Act § 552(b)(4) (exempting 'trade secrets and commerical or financial information obtained from a person and privileged or confidential' from the rules on making administrative information available to the public).

[403] See, e.g., GATS Art. III*bis*; TRIPs Art. 39.

[404] NAFTA Art. 1401:2. For a more detailed discussion of NAFTA Chapter Eleven, see Michael Gestrin and Alan M. Rugman, 'The North American Free Trade Agreement and Foreign Direct Investment' (1994) 3:1 Transnat'l Corp 77; Sauvé (note 144 *supra*), at 63–5, reviews, *inter alia*, of how the definition of 'commercial presence' in NAFTA Chapter Eleven interacts with the GATS definition of the same term); Friedrich Oschmann, 'Das Investitionsrecht des NAFTA-Abkommens—Mexikos Kehrtwende im Recht der Auslandsinvestitionen?' (1997) 96:3 *Zeitschrift für vergleichende Rechtswissenschaft* 242, a general overview of the provisions of Chapter Eleven. See also Rojas, Miguel Jauregui, 'A New Era: The Regulation of Investment in Mexico' (1993) 1:1 US-Mexico LJ 41, 48–51, explaining the NAFTA investment rules from a Mexican legal perspective, in the context of Mexican investment law.

[405] NAFTA Art. 1109.

[406] NAFTA Art. 1110.

[407] NAFTA Art. 1111.

[408] NAFTA Art. 1113.

[409] NAFTA Art. 1114.

[410] NAFTA Art. 1401:2.

[411] *Ibid.*

3.14.1 Transfers (Article 1109)

The basic rule on transfers set out in Chapter Eleven as applied by Chapter Fourteen is that NAFTA Parties, their subnational units, and financial service self-regulatory organizations are not to restrict flows of money between an investor and an investment. 'Each Party shall permit all transfers relating to an investment of an investor of another Party in the territory of the Party to be made freely and without delay ...'.[412]

A 'transfer' for purposes of the NAFTA may be either a transfer *per se* or an international payment.[413] The flows of monies that are covered by Article 1109 (and therefore Chapter Fourteen) are contained in an exclusive list:

(a) profits, dividends, interest, capital gains, royalty payments, management fees, technical assistance and other fees, returns in kind and other amounts derived from the investment;
(b) proceeds from the sale of all or any part of the investment or from the partial or complete liquidation of the investment;
(c) payments made under a contract entered into by the investor, or its investment, including payments made pursuant to a loan agreement;
(d) payments made pursuant to [compensation for expropriation]; and
(e) payments arising [from the settlement of an investment dispute].[414]

The Parties may not restrict transfers directly (by limiting the types of funds that may be transferred) or indirectly (by requiring the funds to be of a certain currency). Nor are the Parties to force the repatriation of funds stemming from investments in the territory of another Party. Further, the Parties are to allow payments to be made in any major currency converted at a market exchange rate.[415] This prevents a government from mandating a *de facto* bar on trading by disallowing payments in the seller's desired form and it also hinders a false exchange rate from being imposed on cross-border payment transactions.

3.14.1.1 Permissible Limits on Transfers

There are certain exceptional situations that allow a Party to impose limits on the transfers, as long as these limits are applied non-discriminatorily. For instance, a Party may completely prevent the transfer of funds through an 'equitable, non-discriminatory and good faith application' of domestic laws relating to bankruptcy procedures,[416] to activities having to do with securities,[417] and to 'reports of transfers of currency or monetary instruments'.[418] Additionally, criminal law provisions can be called upon to

---

[412] NAFTA Art. 1109:1.
[413] NAFTA Art. 1139 ('transfers').
[414] NAFTA Art. 1109:1.
[415] NAFTA Art. 1109:2.
[416] NAFTA Art. 1109:4(a).
[417] NAFTA Art. 1109:4(b).
[418] NAFTA Art. 1109:4(d).

prevent transfers,[419] as can judicial settlements.[420] Transfers in kind may be limited on the same grounds.[421]

3.14.2   Expropriation and Compensation (Article 1110)

The expropriation of foreign investments through nationalizations has long been a source of conflict in North American relations.[422] Concerns of the modern United States banking community have been particularly strong as regards investing in Mexico since 1982. In that year, the Mexican government nationalized all foreign bank properties for the second time this century.

Before NAFTA, the Mexican government adhered to the Calvo Doctrine.[423] This stance, named after the Argentinian international law expert Carlos Calvo, states that foreigners are limited to the same treatment as nationals.[424] Thus, the Mexican government refused to hear private claims for compensation under any law but its own.[425] The Calvo Doctrine led to much dissatisfaction among foreign investors, as these investors had to accept the risk of uncompensated nationalizations if they brought assets into Mexico.

The incorporation of the NAFTA investment protections found in Article 1110, including an agreement to submit to investor-Party arbitration proceedings under the rules set out in the NAFTA, is thus as politically and symbolically significant as it is legally important for encouraging financial service movement among NAFTA Parties. Their incorporation into Chapter Fourteen is also a signal of the particular character of the chapter as a mixture of the trade and financial service systems. Expropriation, as long as it does not discriminate among the properties based on nationality, is beyond the concern of pure international trade law. Although there is a potential that trade would be affected, there are no explicit provisions on

---

[419] NAFTA Art. 1109:4(c).

[420] NAFTA Art. 1109:4(e).

[421] NAFTA Art. 1109:6.

[422] See G.H. Hackworth, (1942) 3 Dig Int'l L 655–665, with letters between US and Mexican governments regarding Mexico's expropriation of foreign oil companies in 1937).

[423] See John P. Bullington, 'Problems of International Law in the Mexican Constitution of 1917' (1927) 21 Am J Int'l L 685. The Calvo Doctrine was promoted by all Latin American States, and even by the United States. 'It is an interesting aside to note that the United States in its formative years, as an importer of European capital, had experiences similar to the ones which developing countries presently have … But, after its emergence as a regional economic power, it insisted that its Latin American neighbors should provide treatment in accordance with international standards to foreign investors'. M. Sornarajah, *The International Law on Foreign Investment* (Grotius/CUP, New York, 1994), p. 11.

[424] Sornarajah (note 423 *supra*), at 11, n.32, refers to the passage in Calvo's multi-volume work *Le Droit International* (5th edn, 1885), Vol. 6, p. 231: 'Aliens who established themselves in a country are certainly entitled to the same rights of protection as nationals, but they cannot claim any greater measure of protection'. See also Rudolf Dolzer, *Eigentum, Enteignung und Entschädigung im geltenden Völkerrecht* (Springer, Berlin, 1985), pp. 19, 20. Mr Dolzer cites at 20, n.29, D. Shea, *The Calvo Clause* (1955) as the basic text on this doctrine.

[425] Wethington (note 4 *supra*), at 152.

nationalization or expropriation in the General Agreement on Tariffs and Trade or in the many other WTO agreements (that include the agreement on Trade-Related Investment Measures). For investment and the functioning of the financial service industries, however, the inclusion of an expropriation provision is of critical importance. Market access and the assurance of national treatment are little more than worthless if uncompensated nationalizations are allowed to take place regularly. The qualifications that Article 1110 sets out for the allowance of expropriations, on the other hand, do fulfill certain objectives of trade law.

The NAFTA rules limiting expropriation and nationalization are similar to the formulation of law historically promoted by the United States.[426] That is to say, expropriations and nationalizations are acknowledged to be among the legitimate competencies of sovereign states, but the injured investor must be compensated for the loss suffered.

The NAFTA states this rule in the negative ('No Party may ... nationalize or expropriate ... except ...'), indicating a disapproval of expropriation while not forbidding them completely. Article 1110 begins:

> No Party may directly or indirectly nationalize or expropriate an investment of an investor of another Party in its territory or take a measure tantamount to nationalization or expropriation of such investment ('expropriation'), except:
> (a) for a public purpose;
> (b) on a non-discriminatory basis;
> (c) in accordance with due process of law and Article 1105(1); and
> (d) on payment of compensation in accordance with paragraphs 2 through 6.[427]

In order to understand the NAFTA view of the law of expropriation and nationalization, one must answer three questions: what is an expropriation or nationalization? Under what conditions is the taking of property legal? And what is just compensation? These three questions have been examined extensively in the financial service and investment literatures, and it is from there that the terms must be interpreted.[428]

3.14.2.1   What is an Expropriation or a Nationalization?

First of all, under NAFTA Article 1110, expropriation or nationalization are both referred to by the term 'expropriation'. Although this is not necessarily

---

[426] William W. Bishop Jr, 'E. The Problem of Expropriation', in *International Law: Cases and Materials* (3rd edn, Little, Brown, Boston, 1971), pp. 851–99, containing substantial portions of the diplomatic correspondence between the United States and Mexico during 1938–40 over the Mexican expropriations American-owned interests.

[427] NAFTA Art. 1110:1.

[428] For a detailed study of expropriation in international law, see Sornarajah (note 423 *supra*), at 277–322, 357–414, Ch. 7, 'Taking of Foreign Property', and Ch. 9, 'Compensation for Nationalisation of Foreign Investment'; Dolzer (note 424 *supra*), at 35–50, with a concise treatment of the jurisprudence and state practice regarding expropriation and compensation; Ignaz Seidl-Hohenveldern, 'Internationales Enteignungsrecht', in Alexander Lüderitz and Jochen Schröder (eds), *Internationales Privatrecht und Rechtsvergleichung im Ausgang des 20. Jahrhunderts: Bewahrung oder Wende? Festschrift für Gerhard Kegel* (Alfred Metzner, Frankfurt, 1977), pp. 265–84.

in accordance with international law, the Parties seem not to distinguish between the two. Secondly, there is no clear definition given for either term. Thus, a basic understanding from the international law on investments may be assumed. An expropriation for purposes of NAFTA is (by default): an action by a Party to negate, in whole or in part, the ownership of, control over, or profitability of an investment owned by an 'investor of another Party'.[429]

The scope of the provision is broad, including actions that either 'directly or indirectly' expropriate an investment as well as 'a measure [taken that is] tantamount to' expropriation.[430] This means that not only are forced takings of an enterprise considered an expropriation, but so are so-called measures of 'creeping expropriations'[431]—regulatory takings that are '[i]nterferences with the exercise of property or ownership rights by the host state'.[432] The broad definition of 'investment' given at the end of Chapter Eleven[433] has the result that the forced sale of stock in an enterprise[434] and even the breach of state contracts 'involving the presence of an investor's property in the territory of the Party'[435] or those 'where remuneration depends substantially on the production, revenues or profits of an enterprise'[436] are compensatory takings.[437]

---

[429] For greater clarity, Art. 1110:8 emphasizes that 'a non-discriminatory measure of general application shall not be considered tantamount to an expropriation of a debt security or loan covered by this Chapter solely on the ground that the measure imposes costs on the debtor that causes it to default on the debt'.

[430] NAFTA Art. 1110:1.

[431] Sornarajah (note 423 *supra*), at 283.

[432] Sornarajah (note 423 *supra*), at 294, lists the types of measures that categorize 'creeping expropriation':

> (1) forced sales of property; (2) forced sales of shares; (3) indigenisation measures; (4) exercising management control over the investment; (5) inducing others to physically take over the property; (6) failure to provide protection when there is interference with the property of the foreign investor; (7) administrative decisions which cancel licenses and permits [sic] necessary for the foreign business to function within the state; (8) exorbitant taxation; (9) expulsion of the foreign investor contrary to international law; (10) acts of harassment such as the freezing of bank accounts, promoting of strikes, lockouts and labour shortages.

But see note 429 *supra*, referring to NAFTA Art. 1110:8, excluding non-discriminatory measures of general application that impose costs on a debtor of a debt security or loan).

[433] NAFTA Art. 1139 ('investment').

[434] NAFTA Art. 1139 ('investment' (b); 'equity or debt securities').

[435] NAFTA Art. 1139 ('investment' (h)(i)).

[436] NAFTA Art. 1139 ('investment' (h)(ii)). See also *supra*, discussion of definition of investment.

[437] This is by no means always, or even normally, the case in the law of expropriation. Mr. Sornarajah points out that the International Court of Justice's decision in the *Barcelona Traction Case* from 1970 is still the governing law on the matter of forced sale of shares. Case Concerning the Barcelona Traction Light and Power Company (*Belgium v. Spain*), ICJ 1970, p. 4. The case is reprinted in (1970) IX:2 ILM 227. The Court in that case rejected the claims of disinvested Belgian shareholders of a Canadian company operating in Spain for compensation after the Franco government took over the Spanish operations. The Court based its decision on the legal distinction between rights of a limited liability company

However, Article 1110 excludes certain aspects of intellectual property rights from the scope of the expropriation provisions. For example, if a Party complies with the NAFTA intellectual property rights provisions set out in Chapter Seventeen, the issuance, termination, or limitation of those rights is not to be affected by Article 1110.[438]

3.14.2.2 Under What Conditions Is the Taking of the Property Legal?

A basic view of modern international law is that an expropriation or a taking is 'prima facie lawful'.[439] Acknowledgement of this idea is based on the sovereignty of a state as well as on the balancing of the interests of an individual against that of the public good in national policy-making. The lawfulness of a particular taking under international law, however, is subject to certain conditions being fulfilled. These conditions include the existence of a public interest in the taking and some amount of compensation being offered the injured person.[440]

Under NAFTA rules on expropriation of investments, the emphasis is on the conditions of the taking as opposed to emphasizing the basic lawfullness of the act by the government. Thus, the rule is that an expropriation is only legal if it is done to further a public purpose;[441] if it is made non-discriminatorily;[442] if it is done in accordance with procedural guarantees of

---

(Contd.)

and its shareholders ('the mere fact that damage is sustained by both company and shareholder does not imply that both are entitled to claim compensation', para. 44 at 36; in ILM at 262) and on the general international law existing on diplomatic protection:

> ... where it is a question of an unlawful act committed against a company representing foreign capital, the general rule of international law authorizes the national State of the company alone to make a claim.
>
> ...
>
> Thus, in the present state of the law, the protection of shareholders requires that recourse be had to treaty stipulations or special agreements directly concluded between the private investor and the State in which the investment is placed.

paras 88, 90 at 47, 48; in ILM at 272. The widespread dissatisfaction with the decision, as well as the many bilateral investment treaties that include protection for shareholders may signal a change in the future, but '[d]espite these distinctions, it is best to be cautious and proceed on the basis that international law has not yet devised an adequate rule on the protection of shareholdings'. Sornarajah (note 423 *supra*), at 286–9, 289, including a footnote citing G. Sacerdoti, 'Barcelona Traction Revisited: Foreign-Owned and Controlled Companies in International Law', in Y. Dinstein (ed.), *International Law in a Time of Perplexity* (1989), p. 699.

438 NAFTA Art. 1110:7.
439 Sornarajah (note 423 *supra*), at 315.
440 Mr Sornarajah characterizes the international law on expropriation as divided between the 'views of the capital-exporting states' and the 'views of the capital-importing states'. See Sornarajah (note 423 *supra*), Ch. 9, 'Compensation for Nationalisation of Foreign Investment', at 357–414.
441 NAFTA Art. 1110:1(a).
442 NAFTA Art. 1110:1(b). Note that this is important for the trade system's interests and for overall equity, but is not as important to the financial service system.

fairness;[443] and if it is followed by compensation.[444] While the shift in emphasis could be seen as merely a difference in wording, the shift is a further indication that NAFTA aims to protect investors more than does general international law. This is yet another sign that it was the United States and Canadian interests that 'won' the negotiations on investments (including financial service investments).

3.14.2.2.1   PUBLIC PURPOSE

Under NAFTA Article 1110:1, all expropriations must be undertaken to further a 'public purpose'.[445] Nowhere defined in the Agreement, this requirement is consistent with most agreements on the protection of foreign investments. However, the actual use of the condition is limited, as the practice of international tribunals reveals a nearly complete acceptance of the expropriating state's declaration that an action is done for a public purpose[446], and it is not to be expected that a NAFTA dispute settlement body, whether in arbitration or in a formal panel proceeding, would be any less deferential.

One problem in defining 'public purpose', like that of defining 'public interest' or 'public good', lies with defining the relevant 'public'. Is the public the government, of a territory? The people of a subnational unit? The residents of a geographic region? Or all of the persons of the world?[447] A convincing answer to the question of defining 'public' can rarely be made in the abstract. Because 'the public' is so amorphous, it is equally difficult for a national court, let alone a plurilateral panel of decision makers, to

---

[443] NAFTA Art. 1110:1(c).

[444] NAFTA Art. 1110:1(d).

[445] NAFTA Art. 1110:1(a).

[446] The Restatement on Foreign Relations Law 'Commentary' indicates the non-use of the public purpose requirement:

> The requirement that a taking be for a public purpose is reiterated in most formulations of the rules of international law on expropriations ... That limitation, however, has not figured prominently in international claims practice, perhaps because the concept of public purpose is broad and not subject to effective re-examination by other states.

Rest. 2d Forg. Rel., Art. 712(1)(a). But see the discussion of 'indigenisation' in Sornarajah (note 423 *supra*), at 291–3, particularly at 291:

> Indigenisation measures involve a progressive transfer of ownership from foreign interests into the hands of the local shareholders. They were undertaken in many African and Asian countries after they achieved independence to ensure that the termination of political control also meant the termination of economic control and the passing of such control into the hands of local entrepreneurs. One factor that sets indigenisation measures apart from outright takings is that there is no vesting of any property in the hands of the state or the state organ. There is no direct or even indirect enrichment of the government as a result of the measures.

[447] A Member of the American Association of Law Schools posed similar questions in the context of determining the interests of the 'State of California':

deny the validity of a state's claim of acting in the public interest. Thus, it will be only in an extreme case, such as if a Party would expropriate a bank in order to benefit an individual or single enterprise, that the public purpose requirement would have any chance of causing the expropriation to be declared illegal. As a consequence, 'it is unlikely that [the public purpose requirement] will constitute more than a subsidiary, throwaway argument for illegality'.[448]

3.14.2.2.2   NON-DISCRIMINATORY

A second requirement for a legal expropriation is that it be undertaken non-discriminatorily. In the context of the Chapter Fourteen this means that a Party may not expropriate only the financial institutions of another Party, as this would be discriminatory. Instead, all financial institutions, those owned by the Party's own nationals, as well as those owned by the other Parties' nationals, must be affected equally.

In the international law on expropriation, 'discriminatory' takings also refer to racially-directed expropriations. Actions that take away ownership rights of a group of people based on ethnic or racial grounds are thus illegal.[449] Although unlikely to occur in such a way that NAFTA would be invoked, the absence of any text to the contrary allows one to assume that the idea of discrimination will not be limited to the trade law definitions.[450]

3.14.2.2.3   DUE PROCESS

The NAFTA requirements for expropriation are unusual in that they provide that such actions must adhere to 'due process of law and Article 1105(1)'.[451] There is no definition of 'due process' or indication of what

---

(Contd.)

> Is [the 'State'] the territory within its physical boundaries? Or is it a particular legal system enforced in its courts? Or is it the euphoria of its residents induced by its climate and its vineyards? And once the State is defined, how will the courts grapple with *its* interests, and not those of the parties?

Remarks of Yntema, quoted in Friedrich K. Juenger, 'Governmental Interests—Real and Spurious—in Multistate Disputes' (1988) 21:3 UC Davis L Rev 515, 518, n.27, and accompanying text, quoting Letter of 2 April 1986 from Dr Vera Bolgar to Juenger.

[448] Sornarajah (note 423 *supra*), at 316–17. Mr Sornarajah explains that the public purpose requirement developed when state interventions in investments were rare, and when there was a clear distinction between confiscation of foreign property and nationalization of foreign property. The former case (taking of property without a public interest) was illegal. Now, when states regulate the daily activities of enterprises far more, 'it will be difficult for tribunals sitting outside the state to question the motives behind the taking'.

[449] *Ibid.* at 320. Examples of such instances are the Nazi takings of Jewish properties in the 1930s and the expropriations of Indians' properties in Uganda under the regime of Idi Amin.

[450] This provision could not be used to protect native peoples' properties, however, as national measures against citizens of that Party do not come within NAFTA.

[451] NAFTA Art. 1110:1(c).

exactly is meant by 'fair and equitable treatment' within the text of the NAFTA. Because this is an Anglo-American legal concept, however, one can surmise that procedural fairness, such as the right to an independent decision-maker, the right to have access to information regarding the expropriation itself, and the right to participate in the decision-making process by presenting arguments against an expropriation are included.[452] In the dispute settlement context of the World Trade Organization, an Appellate Body decision has identified the goal of due process as giving 'the parties and third parties [to a dispute] sufficient information concerning the claims at issue in the dispute in order to allow them an opportunity to respond to the complainant's claim'.[453] Thus, the idea of information and an possibility to present views has been attached to the term due process in the multilateral trade context, giving credibility to the thesis that the NAFTA's use of the term should be similar.

The other provision mentioned, Article 1105:1, lays out the 'Minimum Standard of Treatment' Parties are to give investors, and says, 'Each Party shall accord to investments of investors of another Party treatment in accordance with international law, including fair and equitable treatment and full protection and security'.[454]

Once again, the NAFTA text leaves this provision open to interpretation without providing any guidance. International law on treatment of investors, as mentioned above, is not uniform, and is actually in some

---

[452] See *Marshall v. Jerrico*, 446 US 238, 242 (1980):

> The Due Process Clause entitles a person to an impartial and disinterested tribunal in both civil and criminal cases. This requirement of neutrality in adjudicative proceedings safeguards the two central concerns of procedural due process, the prevention of unjustified or mistaken deprivations and the promotion of participation and dialogue by affected individuals in the decision making process ... At the same time, it preserves both the appearance and reality of fairness ... .

> See also *Mathews v. Eldridge* 424 US 319 (1976). In Mathews, the Supreme Court summarized the content of the due process clauses: 'The fundamental requirement of due process is the opportunity to be heard "at a meaningful time and in a meaningful manner"'. *Ibid.* at 233, quoting *Armstrong v. Manzo* 380 US 545, 552 (1965). The Court indicated several interests, or factors to be considered in each case: 'the degree of potential deprivation that mapotential deprivation that may be created by a particular decision' (at 341); 'the possible length of wrongful deprivation of ... benefits' (*ibid.* at 341, quoting *Fusari v. Steinberg* 419 US 379, 389 (1975)); 'the fairness and reliability of the existing pre-termination procedures, and the probable value, if any, of additional procedural safeguards' (*ibid.* at 343); and 'the public interest [which includes] the administrative burden and social costs' (*ibid.* at 347). The Court refined its conclusions by saying:

> [f]inancial cost alone is not a controlling weight in determining whether due process requires a particular procedural safeguard prior to some administrative decision. But the Government's interest, and hence that of the public, in conserving scarce federal and administrative resources is a factor that must be weighed.

Ibid. at 348.
[453] Brazil—Desiccated Coconut, WT/DS22/AB/R, p. 22 (21 February 1997).
[454] NAFTA Art. 1105:1.

areas quite contentious. That said, the idea of equitable treatment in the context of expropriation would indicate a stronger consideration of the investor's interests. The phrase 'full protection and security' is also vague, but considering that expropriations are allowed under the Agreement, it must be inextricably tied to the concepts of due process of law and just compensation (discussed below).

3.14.2.3   What is Just Compensation?

3.14.2.3.1   COMPENSATION FOR LEGAL EXPROPRIATIONS

Each expropriation of an investor of another Party's investment must be followed by compensation.[455] The most contentious of the issues surrounding expropriations on an international level is that of how much compensation must be paid by a government. NAFTA answers this question in Article 1110:2. The fair market value of the investment is clearly set out to be the measure of the payments required for non-discriminatory measures taken for a public purpose, under conditions of due process and fair treatment:

> Compensation shall be equivalent to the fair market value of the expropriated investment immediately before the expropriation took place ('date of expropriation'), and shall not reflect any change in value occurring because the intended expropriation had become known earlier. Valuation criteria shall include going concern value, asset value including declared tax value of tangible property, and other criteria, as appropriate, to determine fair market value.[456]

In addition, if the expropriation is to be legitimate under Chapter Fourteen (and Chapter Eleven), compensation must be made 'without delay'.[457] These requirements are substantially the same as the dominant theory of compensation among developed countries: payment should be 'adequate, effective and prompt'.[458]

The discussions of what constitutes 'fair' market value, while not precisely defined, is also relieved of the uncertainty of whether to include the possible decline in market value that occurs due to the knowledge that nationalization would occur and avoids making the actual market price the

---

[455]   NAFTA Art. 1110:1(d).
[456]   NAFTA Art. 1110:2.
[457]   NAFTA Art. 1110:1(d); NAFTA Art. 1110:3. It is interesting to note that the Spanish phrase 'sin demora' ('without delay') is not a legal term in Mexican law. M. Schettino (note 119 *supra*), at 43. Mr Schettino thus interprets the phrase to demand 'immediate' payment. ('… no existe el término sin demora en la jurisprudencia mexicana. Gracias a la siguiente frase, 'completamente liquidable' es como se pueden defender los inversionistas de otra parte para exigir un pago inmediato'). Mr Schettino's view is not completely warranted, as 'immediate' and 'without delay' are not necessarily the same, immediate being more absolute. This is another instance of ambiguities arising from linguistic subtleties.
[458]   The 'Hull formula' originated in a note from Secretary of State Cordell Hull to the Mexican Ambassador in Washington, DC, from 3 April 1940.

relevant measure of the amount to compensate.[459] Moreover, the compensation amount is to include a 'commercially reasonable' rate of interest for the time between expropriation and actual payment, regardless of the currency in which compensation is paid.[460] Finally, the Party who expropriated an investment must give the investor an award that is 'freely transferable as provided in Article 1109' upon payment.[461]

3.14.2.3.2   PAYMENTS FOR ILLEGAL EXPROPRIATIONS

The NAFTA does not have a system of damage payments for illegal expropriations. Instead, the Agreement only addresses compensation for legal takings. This implies that illegal takings would be subject to dispute settlement provisions under Chapter Twenty. The NAFTA dispute settlement rules would therefore require compensation in the amount of the damage done to the investor. This supports a decision of the Permanent Court of International Justice (PCIJ) from early in the twentieth century, which wrote:

> ... it is a principle of international law, and even a general conception of law, that any breach of an engagement involves an obligation to make reparation ... (R)eparation is the indispensable complement of a failure to apply a convention, and there is no necessity for this to be stated in the convention itself.[462]

The Court continued, holding that international law would find that the measure of damages for an illegal taking, or confiscation, should be based on principles of restitution.[463] The amount of the reparations was limited to

---

[459] The literature on the issue of 'fair' or 'just' compensation is vast. A very good article for non-economists into the economic theory of this question is William A. Fischel, 'The Offer/Ask Disparity and Just Compensation for Takings: A Constitutional Choice Perspective' (1995) 15:2 Int'l Rev L & Econ 189.

[460] NAFTA Arts 1110:4, 1110:5.

[461] NAFTA Art. 1110:6. See also discussion of transfers, 3.14.1 *supra*.

[462] *The Case Concerning certain German interests in Polish Upper Silesia*, PCIJ Rep. Series A, No. 7, at 22 (1926). In this case, the PCIJ faced a claim for breach of the Geneva Convention of 1922 by Poland. Poland was charged with confiscating a factory owned by German nationals when Upper Silesia returned to Polish control under the Treaty of Versailles. Although the Convention allowed for nationalization under certain conditions, the Court found that the taking of the lands and factory at issue was a confiscation in violation of the Convention.

[463] *Case Concerning the Factory at Chorzòw*, (1928) PCIJ Rept. Series A, No. 13, 46. In this subsequent proceeding, the PCIJ faced the issue of monetary award. Characterized as a taking in contravention to the Parties' agreement, the Court found that the action complained of was a confiscation, rather than an expropriation or nationalization, and thus, required that Poland pay more than simply 'compensation'. Instead, the government was called on to pay 'damages', going beyond the present market value of the investment. The Court writes:

> The action of Poland ... is not an expropriation—to render which lawful only the payment of fair compensation would have been wanting; it is a seizure of property, rights and interests which could not be expropriated even against compensation, save under the exceptional conditions (set out in Convention) ... reparation is in this case the consequence.

The PCIJ continued to explain (at 47), 'The essential principle contained in the actual notion of an illegal act ... is that reparation must as far as possible wipe out all the consequences of the illegal act and re-establish the situation which would, in all probability, have existed if that act had not been committed'.

'only the value of property, rights and interests which have been affected and the owner of which is the person on whose behalf compensation is claimed, or the damage done to whom is to serve as a means for gauging the reparation claimed ...'.[464]

As is apparent by combining the PCIJ's opinions and those provisions NAFTA sets forth with the non-explained terms, NAFTA's general treatment of illegal takings is in line with international law and is suitable for applying the details of international law in those areas that need interpretation.

3.14.3   Formalities and Information Requirements (Article 1111)

Like Chapter Fourteen, the Chapter Eleven provisions on investment include the Parties' obligation to offer each other's investors and investments national treatment[465] and most-favored-nation treatment.[466] Yet, these obligations do not prohibit a Party from imposing certain 'formalities', or restrictive conditions, on the investments by investors of other Parties.[467] Such restrictions may include a residency requirement or a legislated legal form of the investment. The critical factor for determining whether the formalities impose are permissible under the Agreement is that they must not 'materially impair the protections afforded' the investments and investors of the other Parties. Whether a residency requirement on a financial institution would reach the requisite level of 'material' impairment depends on the specific sphere of activity in which the institution is involved. However, regardless of whether it would materially or only somewhat impair the Chapter Eleven protections, according to Chapter Fourteen, a residency requirement may not extend to more than one half of the institution's board of directors.[468]

Requirements as to the form of establishment of investments are permitted as well.[469] A point of heated disagreement, the form of establishment for financial institutions was not finalized. However, there are

---

[464] *Ibid*. at 31.
[465] NAFTA Art. 1102. See, e.g., NAFTA Art. 1102:1 ('Each Party shall accord to investors of another Party treatment no less favorable than that it accords, in like circumstances, to its own investors with respect to the establishment, acquisition, expansion, management, conduct, operation, and sale or other disposition of investments').
[466] NAFTA Art. 1103. See, e.g., NAFTA Art. 1103:1 ('Each Party shall accord to investors of another Party treatment no less favorable than that it accords, in like circumstances, to investors of any other Party or of a non-Party with respect to the establishment, acquisition, expansion, management, conduct, operation, and sale or other disposition of investments').
[467] NAFTA Art. 1111:1.
[468] NAFTA Art. 1408.
[469] NAFTA Art. 1111:1.

more specific rules on this topic in Chapter Fourteen,[470] and they would logically supercede the general investment rules of Chapter Eleven under international law's interpretive rule of *lex specialis*.

Under Article 1111, Parties to the NAFTA may also require extra information to be produced by investors of other Parties without becoming liable for a violation of NTO and MFN.[471] This is a protection of the national oversight function, and is thus of particular significance to the heavily regulated banking (and other financial) industries. The information requested by the Party in accordance to this Article must, however, be 'routine' and 'concerning' the investment.[472] Moreover, the data may only be collected and used for 'informational or statistical purposes'.[473] In using the information, the Party is to particularly protect business information which would upset the competitive position of either the investment or the investor.

3.14.4   Denial of Benefits to Investors (Article 1113 and Article 1211)

3.14.4.1   *Denial of Benefits in Chapter Eleven (Article 1113)*

If an enterprise of a Party is owned or controlled by investors of a non-Party, the other NAFTA Parties may refuse to grant such investment the benefits of NAFTA liberalizations. The Party can withhold such benefits if the non-Party is a country with which the Party 'does not maintain diplomatic relations' or if the Party 'adopts or maintains measures with respect to the non-Party that prohibit transactions with the enterprise or that would be violated or circumvented if the benefits ... were accorded to the enterprise or to its investments'. Each will be examined in turn.

3.14.4.1.1   DIPLOMATIC RELATIONS

Under Chapter Fourteen, the United States and Mexico will generally accept as a NAFTA Party bank any subsidiary or affiliate of a foreign bank established in one of the other NAFTA Party territories. The denial of benefits provision of Article 1113 modifies this generality to prevent benefits from being offered to subsidiaries whose parent company is a national of a state considered a political 'enemy'. The provision states:

---

[470]   See discussion on establishment, *infra*.
[471]   NAFTA Article 1111:2.
[472]   *Ibid*.
[473]   *Ibid*.

1. A Party may deny the benefits of this Chapter to an investor of another Party that is an enterprise of such Party and to investments of such investor if investors of a non-Party own or control the enterprise and the denying Party:
(a) does not maintain diplomatic relations with the non-Party ...[474]

The NAFTA contains no definition of diplomatic relations. Under the Vienna Convention on Diplomatic Relations (to which all NAFTA Parties are a party), the term 'diplomatic relations' refers to the presence of an embassy and an official government presence of a state in the territory of another state.[475] Whether a state has diplomatic relations with another state is a purely political decision: relations can be annulled and renewed at will, albeit often with severe consequences for commercial activity in one or both territories.[476] The denial of benefits provision for denial on the basis of no diplomatic relations thus reasserts the Parties' commitment to maintaining their own sovereignty.

Because Canada and Mexico have diplomatic relations with almost all states,[477] it is the United States that is most likely to invoke the claim of denial of benefits.[478] In the present state of political relations, for instance, this provision would certainly be used by the United States to prohibit Cuban-controlled investments in Canada or Mexico from being treated as NAFTA-Party investments. As of March 1999, however, there has been no use of this provision by any Party.

3.14.4.1.2 MEASURES THAT WOULD BE VIOLATED OR CIRCUMVENTED'

If a Party has laws, regulations, or policies with a non-Party that could not be implemented or that would be avoided by offering Chapter Fourteen benefits to the other state's financial institution subsidiaries (or affiliates),

---

[474] NAFTA Art. 1113:1(a). Compare this to the similar provision in GATS: GATS Art. XXVII(a), (c). The first clause of GATS Art. XXVII states: 'A Member may deny the benefits of this Agreement: (a) to the supply of a service, if it establishes that the service is supplied from or in the territory of a non-Member or of a Member to which the denying Member does not apply the WTO Agreement'.

[475] T.I.A.S. No. 7502, 500 U.N.T.S. 95 (adopted at Vienna, 14 April 1961, entry into force on 24 April 1964). The Convention does not explicitly define the term 'diplomatic relations', but such a definition can be implied from the whole of the treaty. See also *ibid*. Art. 1, defining 'diplomatic agent' as 'the head of the mission or a member of the diplomatic staff of the mission'.

[476] One international law expert observed that the cancellation of diplomatic relations is generally used as a 'punishment', and as such is only interesting for large powers. Professor Walter Kälin, discussion with author (November 1997).

[477] There is no country with which Canada does not maintain diplomatic relations. Mexico also has diplomatic relations with every state in its adherence to the 'Estrada Doctrine'. Jorge Castanares, El Director de Asuntos Economicos con Norteamerica (Director of Economic Affairs with North America), Secretaría de Relaciones Exteriores (Mexico), correspondence with author from 13 December 1997 ('Essence of this policy is the no interference in any form with the domestic affairs of sovereign countries').

[478] Alhough the United State's list of countries with which it has broken diplomatic relations changes, in recent years the United States has had no diplomatic relations with Cuba, Iran, Iraq, Libya, North Vietnam, and Sudan.

Article 1113 allows the Party to refuse to extend such benefits to the institution even if the institution is located in the NAFTA territory.[479] The scope of application of this provision is wide: there are no limits put on the acceptable reasons for the Party's measures with the non-Party. Such an approach is also consistent with the protection of state sovereignty that is apparent elsewhere in the NAFTA.

3.14.4.1.3   'SUBSTANTIAL BUSINESS ACTIVITIES'

Finally, the Party can deny the benefits of Chapter Fourteen (and Chapter Eleven), on the basis that the owning or controlling investors have no 'substantial business activities' in the territory of the Party in which it is organized:

> Subject to prior notification and consultation ..., a Party may deny the benefits of this Chapter to an investor of another Party that is an enterprise of such Party and to investments of such investors if investors of a non-Party own or control the enterprise and the enterprise has no substantial business activities in the territory of the Party under whose law it is constituted and organized.[480]

As long as a Party gives prior notification 'to the maximum extent possible',[481] it may restrict the entrance and operation of 'shell corporations' in its territory. The need for such a provision arises from the NAFTA's characteristic as a free trade zone, as opposed to a customs union.[482] As each NAFTA Party maintains its own external trade relations, the movement of non-Party goods, services, and investments must be distinguished from Party goods, services, and investments at each of the internal borders. Essentially a form of rule of origin, this denial of benefits provision is designed to limit the entry of non-Party entities into a Party's territory through the taking advantage of another Party's more lax rules on market access. Thus, it keeps the benefits of the Agreement in the control of the several Parties.

---

[479] NAFTA Art. 1113:1(b). Compare the corollary to this provision under the GATS Art. XIV(c):

> Subject to the requirement that such measures are not applied in a manner which would constitute a means of arbitrary or unjustifiable discrimination ... nothing in this Agreement shall be construed to prevent the adoption or enforcement of measures:
>
> ...
> (c) necessary to secure compliance with laws or regulations which are not inconsistent with the provisions of this Agreement ...

> One notices that the similar provision, found in the GATS' list of general exceptions, does not afford a Member as much latitude in refusing to act according to its obligations as the NAFTA does.

[480] NAFTA Art. 1113:2.
[481] NAFTA Arts 1803:1, 1113:2.
[482] See *supra*.

3.14.4.2 Denial of Benefits Provision of Chapter Twelve (Article 1211)

Under Chapter Twelve's regulation of trade in non-financial services, there is a denial of benefits provision substantially the same as that found in Chapter Eleven.[483] Article 1211 is a part of Chapter Fourteen by virtue of the incorporation clause in Article 1401:2. According to this provision, a Party may deny the benefits of the Chapter to a service provider of another Party if non-nationals of a Party own or control the enterprise providing the service and either the Party does not 'maintain diplomatic relations with the non-Party' or the denying Party's national laws or procedures would be violated if the NAFTA provisions were to apply to the non-Party's enterprise.[484] Also similar to the other denial of benefits provisions, if a service provider is of another Party, but the enterprise is owned or controlled by persons of a non-Party and has no substantial business activities in the territory of any Party, the benefits of NAFTA may be denied. Such a denial is subject only to the giving of prior notification and an opportunity for consultations.[485]

There are some small variations to ensure the non-circumvention of the Agreement in certain services,[486] but they do not have an appreciable affect on financial services.

3.14.5 Environmental Measures (Article 1114)

A Party may impose environmental protection measures on investments of investors of another Party[487] and is under a positive obligation to maintain its adherence to health, safety, and environmental standards without regard to attracting new or expanded investments.[488] If one Party 'considers' that another Party is weakening its environmental protection in order to be a more attractive place for investments, the Party may request consultations, and 'the two Parties shall consult with a view to avoiding any such encouragement'.[489]

The incorporation of an environmental protection clause such as Article 1114 into the financial services framework of NAFTA is more of an

---

[483] See discussion of Art. 1113, 3.15.4 *supra*.
[484] NAFTA Art. 1211:1.
[485] NAFTA Art. 1211:2.
[486] For example, the application of the provision to 'service providers' rather than to 'investors'. Also, the denial of benefits is allowed if a cross-border transportation service provider is found to be 'using equipment not registered by any Party'. NAFTA Art. 1211:1(b).
[487] NAFTA Art. 1114:1 ('Nothing in this Chapter shall be construed to prevent a Party from adopting, maintaining or enforcing any measure otherwise consistent with this Chapter that it considers appropriate to ensure that investment activity in its territory is undertaken in a manner sensitive to environmental concerns').
[488] NAFTA Art. 1114:2 ('… a Party should not waive or otherwise derogate from, or offer to waive or otherwise derogate from, such measures as an encouragement for the establishment, acquisition, expansion or retention in its territory of an investment of an investor').
[489] NAFTA Art. 1114:2.

indication of the Parties' recognition of public concerns voiced about the state of the environment in general than it is a provision that will actively promote the health of the environment.

First, financial service industries are not the most likely targets of environmental regulations, as they are inherently less damaging (or at least less directly damaging) to the environment than are other types of investments.[490]

Secondly, even if there are fears of the environmental damage caused by financial services, Article 1114 is not very progressive in allowing for controls. In the first paragraph, a Party's competence to enforce environmental sensitivity as it 'considers appropriate' would seem to give the Parties great discretion, but this is almost nullified by the qualifying phrase 'any measure otherwise consistent with this Chapter'.[491] If the measure is truly 'otherwise consistent', then there should be no complaints about it from the other Parties to begin with. In short, the first paragraph says very little.

Moreover, the provisions of Article 1114:2 are little more than wishes. The passage begins with a recognition 'that it is *inappropriate* to encourage investment by relaxing domestic health, safety or environmental measures', and continues with the hortatory 'a Party *should* not waive ... such measures as an encouragement ...'.[492] While there is a final requirement that a Party enter consultations upon request, there is nothing to mandate the withdrawal of such encouragement. While the incorporation of this provision does show some desire to protect the environment, the legal weakness of the Article calls into question the unanimity of that desire.

3.14.6   Settlement of Disputes Between a Party and an Investor of Another Party (Articles 1115–1138)

The NAFTA is unusual as an international trade agreement in its inclusion of a dispute settlement mechanism for individuals injured by a Party's violation of the Agreement.[493] While the investor-Party dispute mechanism does not give the NAFTA direct effect,[494] it does subject the Parties to an accountability to individuals for breaches of the Agreement.[495] Chapter Fourteen of the NAFTA incorporates the investor-Party dispute procedures for violations of the incorporated articles of Chapters Eleven and Twelve.

---

[490] As one author writes, '... Art. 1114 would appear to have greater practical application to sectors outside of financial services ...'. Wethington (note 4 *supra*), at 78.

[491] NAFTA Art. 1114:1 (emphasis added).

[492] NAFTA Art. 1114:2 (emphasis added).

[493] The Investor-Party dispute mechanism does not hinder a Party from bringing a claim before a NAFTA dispute settlement panel on the same facts. NAFTA Art. 1115. ('Without prejudice to the rights and obligations of the Parties under Chapter Twenty ...'.).

[494] See discussion of the direct effect of NAFTA, at 1.4.1 *supra*.

[495] The first use of this procedure was the case brought by the Mexican chemical manufacturer Signa against the Canadian government for Canada's prohibition of Signa's sales of its generic antibiotic in Canada. Canada NewsWire, 'First-Ever Use of NAFTA By Individuals. New Type of Lawsuit Leads to $50 Million Claim Against Canada', news release of 13 March 1996.

The stated purpose of the investor-Party dispute settlement procedure is to ensure 'both equal treatment among investors of the Parties in accordance with the principle of international responsibility and due process before an impartial tribunal'.[496] (Remembering the history of United States investors in Mexico, one is struck by the change in attitude the Mexican government must have undergone before accepting such a provision.) Although an investor is to undergo consultations or negotiations with the Party first,[497] the individual now may have her claim heard according to the rules of international arbitration rather than under the laws of, and in the courts of, the government accused of wrongdoing.

Any individual may bring an investor-Party dispute action on behalf of himself as an investor of a Party.[498] In addition, if he is an investor of a Party, the investor may bring an action on behalf of an enterprise of another Party owned or controlled by him.[499] However, the investment itself cannot make a claim for arbitration.[500]

For financial service institutions and investors, a claim under Chapter Eleven procedures is limited to another Party's alleged breaches of the NAFTA provisions on transfers, expropriation, denial of benefits for investments, and environmental measures affecting investment.[501] Other disputes must be pursued in the Party-to-Party consultations of the Chapter Twenty dispute settlement procedures.

The statute of limitations for calling an arbitration process is three years 'from the date on which the investor first acquired, or should have first acquired, knowledge of the alleged breach and knowledge that the investor

---

[496] NAFTA Art. 1115.

[497] NAFTA Art. 1118.

[498] NAFTA Art. 1116:1 ('An investor of a Party may submit to arbitration under this Section ...'.).

[499] NAFTA Art. 1117:1 ('An investor of a Party, on behalf of an enterprise of another Party that is a juridical person that the investor owns or controls directly or indirectly, may submit to arbitration under this Section ...'.).

[500] NAFTA Art. 1117:4.

[501] NAFTA Art. 1401:2 (incorporating the Investor-Party dispute settlement procedures 'solely for breaches by a Party of Arts 1109–1111, 1113 and 1114, as incorporated into this Chapter'). For non-financial service investors, the scope of the Investor-Party dispute settlement procedure is broader, extending to all of the Chapter Eleven obligations as well as certain provisions of Chaper Fifteen (Competition Policy, Monopolies and State Enterprises). The passage states in relevant part:

> An investor of a Party may submit to arbitration under this Section a claim that another Party has breached an obligation under:
> (a) Section A or Article 1503(2) (State Enterprises), or
> (b) Article 1502(3)(a) (Monopolies and State Enterprises) where the monopoly has acted in a manner inconsistent with the Party's obligations under Section A ...

NAFTA Art. 1116:1. The provision for claims by the owner/controller of an enterprise of another Party is the same. See NAFTA Art. 1117:2.

has incurred loss or damage'.[502] Thus actual knowledge of the breach and the loss or damage starts the running of the statute.[503] While this acts to lessen the bringing of claims from the far past, the combination of the two elements of 'knowing' the breach and 'knowing' of the damage stemming from the breach protects the investors.

Additionally, there is an objective standard for the statute ('*or should have* first acquired'), placing a duty of care on the investor in overseeing the investment.[504] Quite common in the Anglo-American legal systems, this reasonable person standard strengthens the bar to claims from the past, and works to the advantage of the Party. Unclear from the text is a determination of the standard to be used to judge whether the investor 'should have first acquired' the knowledge. Because the investors who could avail themselves of these provisions are most likely going to be experienced usinesspersons (particularly so in the case of financial service investors), any interpretation of the phrase by future arbiters should result in a level of care dependent upon a reasonably prudent investor rather than the lower standard of a mere reasonable person who does not necessarily have any specialized knowledge of finances.

3.14.6.1   *Arbitration Procedure*

The remaining provisions of the investor-Party dispute framework set out the procedural aspects of the arbitration itself. The process is to start with consultations and negotiations to settle the dispute. If that does not achieve an acceptable solution, the investor must, to begin with, send a notification that a claim will be submitted to arbitration, including the relevant details of the allegations and what the investor is requesting as relief.

3.14.6.1.1   REQUEST FOR ARBITRATION AND PANEL SELECTION

No sooner than six months after the Party's complained-of action, the investor can request a formal arbitration under the general international rules on arbitration. If the complained-of Party gives its written consent to submit to arbitration[505] and the investor (and enterprise upon whose behalf the investor may be acting) waives her rights to any

---

[502] NAFTA Art. 1116:2 (for investor acting on own behalf); Art. 1117:2 (for investor acting on behalf of an enterprise).

[503] It is interesting to note that a claim for arbitration cannot be submitted until six months after the alleged violation has occurred. See NAFTA Art. 1120:1. This effectively narrows the window for bringing claims to thirty months from the time of the violation if one assumes that the investor knew or should have known of the violation and the resulting damage on the same day as the action occurred.

[504] NAFTA Art. 1116:2 (emphasis added).

[505] Consent must be given so as to fulfill the requirements of the ICSID Convention and the Additional Facility Rules, the New York Convention for an agreement in writing, and the Inter-American Convention for an agreement. NAFTA Art. 1122:2.

other proceedings to collect damages,[506] the claim may be submitted to arbitration.[507]

The framework of the arbitration is determined by whether both parties to the dispute are members of the Convention on the Settlement of Investment Disputes between States and Nationals of other States ('ICSID Convention') or if only one is.[508] If both are members, the ICSID rules are to apply, and if only one is a member,[509] the Additional Facility Rules of the ICSID will apply.[510] Alternatively, the investor may request that the United Nations Commission on International Trade Law (UNCITRAL) Arbitration Rules be applied.[511]

Generally, the arbitration panel will consist of three members, one appointed by each disputant and the third agreed upon by both disputants.[512] In case of irreconcilable differences of opinion on who the third arbitrator should be, the Secretary-General may select the third person.[513] Alternatively, the disputants may agree to abide by the ICSID rules on appointment of arbitrators.[514]

3.14.6.1.2 ARBITRATION PROCESS

The actual arbitration process is set out to include the use of expert reports,[515] the exchange of evidence and written arguments,[516] and the opportunity for the arbitral tribunal (Tribunal) to request assistance from the NAFTA Commission (Commission) on matters of interpretation of the Agreement.[517] If such a request is made, the Commission's response is binding on the Tribunal. If there is an argument that seeks to defend a breach on the basis of a reservation or exception, the Tribunal must ask

---

[506] However, 'proceedings for injunctive, declaratory or other extraordinary relief, not involving the payment of money' may be subsequently brought. NAFTA Art. 1121:1(b); 1121:2(b). Further, no waiver is necessary if the investor claims that a Party has 'deprived [the investor] of control of an enterprise' and, if the alleged wrongdoer is Mexico, the investor may (despite Annex 1120.1(b)) also claim that Mexico violated the Chapter Fifteen provisions on State Enterprises and Monopolies. NAFTA Art. 1121:4.

[507] Both consent and waiver must be in writing. NAFTA Art. 1121:3.

[508] As of 1 January 1998, the United States was a member of the ICSID Convention, while Canada and Mexico were not members to that Convention.

[509] NAFTA Art. 1120:1(a).

[510] NAFTA Art. 1120:1(b).

[511] NAFTA Art. 1120:1(c). As of 1 January 1998, Canada and Mexico had accepted the UNCITRAL rules. The United States does not accept UNCITRAL rules. The rules can be found on the T.M.C. Asser Institute's website >www.asser.nl<.

[512] NAFTA Art. 1123.

[513] NAFTA Art. 1124:2. The procedure for the selection of the third arbitor by the Secretary-General is given in detail in NAFTA Art. 1124 as is the obligation to create and maintain a roster of potential presiding arbitrators. See Art. 1124:4.

[514] NAFTA Art. 1125.

[515] NAFTA Art. 1133.

[516] NAFTA Art. 1129:1. The cost of abiding by the request of the Party for this information rests with the investor.

[517] NAFTA Art. 1131:2. The parties may also submit proposals for interpretation of the Agreement's text to the Commission *sua sponte*. NAFTA Art. 1128.

the Commission for an opinion on the issue. Again, the Commission's interpretation will be binding on the Tribunal, as long as it is submitted within 60 days.[518]

3.14.6.2   Tribunal Decisions

The arbitrators are bound to decide issues presented according to the NAFTA and 'applicable rules of international law'. For financial services, this includes the rules set out in the General Agreement on Trade in Services and the Marrakesh Agreement Establishing the World Trade Organization, as well as those stemming from the Basle Committee, and general principles of international law (such as good faith and the principle of protection of legitimate expectations).

The Tribunal may precede a final decision by an 'interim measure of protection' to ensure that evidence is not destroyed and that the final decision will be effective. However, the Tribunal is explicitly forbidden from attaching property or from preventing 'the application of a measure alleged to constitute a breach' of the rules on state enterprises or monopolies, or any other provision of Chapter Eleven.[519]

3.14.6.2.1   AWARDS

The final decision of a Tribunal may consist of compensatory damages and/or restitution.[520] No punitive damages may be awarded or enforced.[521] Moreover, once the decision is issued, the Tribunal's role is at an end.

3.14.6.2.2   ENFORCEMENT OF THE DECISION

Enforcement of the decision rests with each Party[522] and a Party's failure to pay the investor can be remedied by the investor's complaint to its own government.[523] That government then may request the Commission to start an arbitration proceeding under NAFTA Chapter Twenty to investigate the other Party's non-payment.[524]

---

[518] NAFTA Art. 1132. The 60-day limit is measured from the 'date of delivery of the request' for interpretation. The choice of this date could be problematic in the case of a request that is delivered to the office of the Commission but is not seen by the Commission members until sometime later. However, it is to be expected that in such a case, receipt by the Commission is to be implied as of the date of delivery to the office. That this is indeed what the Parties intended is indicated by Annex 1137.2, which requires each Party to select and publish 'the place for delivery of notice and other documents'. Further support comes from the need to uphold the interest in speedy resolution of disputes. See also the UNCITRAL Arbitration Rules 2:1, recognizing the delivery to the home or business address of the target to be equivalent to receipt. In fact, even a reasonable attempt to make a delivery, regardless of whether the person actually receives the information, is sufficient to give notice.

[519] NAFTA Art. 1134.

[520] NAFTA Art. 1135:1-2.

[521] NAFTA Art. 1135:3.

[522] NAFTA Art. 1136:4.

[523] NAFTA Art. 1136:5.

[524] NAFTA Art. 1136:5.

The investor can alternatively or simultaneously attempt to enforce the decision under the ICSID Convention, the United Nations Convention on the Recognition and Enforcement of Foreign Arbitral Awards (known as the New York Convention), or under the Inter-American Convention on International Commercial Arbitration.[525]

3.14.6.2.3 PUBLICATION OF ARBITRATION AWARDS

An Annex to Chapter Eleven sets out the Parties' agreements on whether the Tribunal's award may be made public.[526] Either disputant allows the publication of awards where the complained-of Party is the United States or Canada.[527]

If Mexico is the Party involved in the dispute, the investor and Mexico are to follow the rules on publication set out in the arbitration rules under which the matter was decided.[528] Under the UNCITRAL arbitration rules, both disputants must give consent to allow the results to be published.[529] Under the Additional Facility Rules of ICSID, the law of the country in which the award was made determines whether the award will be registered.[530]

3.15 RESERVATIONS TO CHAPTER FOURTEEN PROVISIONS

Chapter Fourteen provisions are subject to numerous exceptions. Some are set out in the Chapter Fourteen text at Article 1410. Others are general exceptions, applying to the entire NAFTA. These are found in Chapter Twenty-One. Finally, there are the country-specific exceptions. These are found in Annex VII to the Agreement.

3.15.1 Annex VII

Annex VII ('the Annex') is a portion of the NAFTA that expands on the principles set out in Chapter Fourteen. The Annex contains a 'Schedule' composed of three sections for each Party listing the Party's reservations, non-compatible domestic laws, and commitments in reference to Chapter Fourteen obligations.

---

[525] NAFTA Art. 1136:6. The ICSID Convention was done at Washington, DC on 18 March 1965. The New York Convention was done at New York on 10 June 1958. The Inter-American Convention was done at Panama on 30 January 1975.

[526] NAFTA Annex 1137.4 ('Publication of an Award').

[527] *Ibid.*

[528] *Ibid.*

[529] UNCITRAL Arbitration Rules, Art. 32:5 (adopted by UNCITRAL 28 April 1976).

[530] ICSID Rules of Procedure for Arbitration Proceedings, Section C Arbitration (Additional Facility) Rules, Rule 53(3).

3.15.1.1   Section A

Section A of the Schedule contains the Party's reservations to the provisions for Establishment, Cross-Border Trade, National Treatment, Most-Favored-Nation Treatment, New Services and Data Processing, and Senior Management and Boards of Directors.[531] Each reservation sets out the sector, sub-sector, and industry classification that a particular existing law affects, and then identifies the Chapter Fourteen obligation the measure violates and the date at which the measure will be brought into compliance with the Agreement (if at all).

To make this Section more easily understandable, the level of government implementing the measure, submeasures 'adopted or maintained under the authority of and consistent with the measure',[532] and a description of the measures' non-conformity are all included for each reservation. The explanatory note accompanying the Schedules also notes, 'In the interpretation of a reservation, all elements of the reservation shall be considered. A reservation shall be interpreted in the light of the relevant provisions of the Chapter against which the reservation is taken'.[533]

The Annex, this indicates, is to be interpreted in accordance with the Vienna Convention principles on interpretation of treaties.[534]

3.15.1.2   Section B

Section B of the Schedule, in accordance with Article 1409:2, contains a list of reservations that the Party has taken to the above-mentioned obligations. These lists include measures that are in effect or will be adopted and that will not be modified to abide with the Agreement. To facilitate the use of the schedules, each reservation also sets out the provisions of Chapter Fourteen with which it is not compatible.

3.15.1.3   Section C

Section C contains the Party's commitments to future liberalization.

3.16   GENERAL EXCEPTIONS TO CHAPTER FOURTEEN (ARTICLE 1410)

One of the main problems faced by the drafters of any financial service liberalization agreement—whether in a national parliament, in bilateral treaty negotiations, or in a multilateral negotiation to establish an international

---

[531] See NAFTA Annex VII:1.
[532] NAFTA Annex VII:2 (explanatory note preceding the Parties' schedules).
[533] NAFTA Annex VII:3 (explanatory note preceding the Parties' schedules).
[534] See 3.4 *supra* (interpretation of Chapter Fourteen, setting out Vienna Convention on the Law of Treaties' principles of interpretation in light of the entire context of the Agreement and the relations of the Parties).

organization—is the issue of how to allow freer flows of financial services and investments while maintaining a reasonable level of financial and monetary system security.[535] Unlike some aspects of trade, in which precautionary measures can be compatible with, if not support, freer flows of goods and services, in the area of financial services there is an inherent trade-off between lower barriers to trade and greater security for the consumer of financial services.[536] The negotiators of the NAFTA were not the first to approach this balance by providing for prudential exceptions.

Though not particularly long, Article 1410 sets out in some detail the legitimate objectives a Party may pursue in its financial regulatory laws and practice. At the same time, there are repeated references to the idea of non-discriminatory application of the regulation within the Party's sphere of sovereign interest.

3.16.1 Basic Rule: Exception for Prudential Measures

Article 1410:1 provides that the obligations found in Chapter Fourteen will not be effective in preventing a Party from using 'reasonable' prudential measures to maintain a sound financial system. It states:

> Nothing in this Part shall be construed to prevent a Party from adopting or maintaining reasonable measures for prudential reasons, such as:
>
> (a) the protection of investors, depositors, financial market participants, policy-holders, policy-claimants, or persons to whom a fiduciary duty is owed by a financial institution or cross-border financial service provider;

---

[535] For an overview of the goals and problems of financial regulation on a domestic and international level, see generally Roy C. Smith and Ingo Walter, *Global Banking* (OUP, New York, 1997), pp. 153–84, Ch. 6, 'Regulatory Issues'.

[536] Smith and Walter (note 535 *supra*), at 156 write:

> There are no 'free lunches' in this respect. Greater safety and stability almost always entail less static and/or dynamic efficiency in terms of criteria such as those listed [previously in the text]. At the same time, some of the most easy-to-supervise regulations such as capital adequacy rules may cause significant efficiency losses, while difficult-to-supervise rules like 'fitness and properness' criteria—that is, who is fit and proper to run a bank or to work in a bank—may be able to create safety and soundness with minimal efficiency losses. And finally, more intensive supervision almost always entails higher compliance costs and an erosion of efficiency.
>
> It is not difficult to see why optimizing across the trade-offs ... is so difficult, especially when gains or losses in static and dynamic efficiency are often exceedingly difficult to measure, and when the costs of underregulation or undersupervision do not become apparent until it is too late. Nor is it difficult to see why, under such conditions, there is a persistent tendency for overregulation in the financial services sector.

[537] NAFTA Art. 1410:1.

(b) the maintenance of the safety, soundness, integrity or financial responsibility of financial institutions or cross-border financial service providers; and

(c) ensuring the integrity and stability of a Party's financial system.[537]

The intent of Article 1410:1 is to allow the financial regulators of each Party to continue to protect consumers of and investors in financial services by ensuring that the financial institutions operating in the Party's territory are economically healthy. Thus, market access through establishment, national treatment, and most-favored-nation treatment can be withheld legitimately from one or more Party institutions if there is a 'prudential reason' for regulating the affected institutions, investors, or investments less liberally than the provisions of Chapter Fourteen would otherwise dictate. Regulations requiring other-Party institutions to submit additional information files prior to establishment, for example, would likely be excused under Article 1410:1(a) and (b), as long as the information is relevant to the supervisory process and not more burdensome than necessary. The requirement that the discriminatory prudential measures be 'reasonable' should prevent Parties from abusing the use of the exception.

Added to the language is a reference to the maintenance of the stability of the financial system as a whole.[538] It is the policy around the world to base regulatory oversight not just (or even mainly) on protecting individual banks from failing (and thus to protect individual investors), but to supervise financial institutions in order to maintain the stability of the financial system overall.[539] By allowing Parties the freedom to protect the systemic aspect of financial service provision as well as allowing for the individual entities composing the system to be supervised, NAFTA Article 1410 codifies the universal goals of regulation.

The Parties are not prohibited from having measures that are for the purpose of addressing the prudential concerns of soundness of the financial system and individual financial institutions. Such measures, however, must be 'reasonable'.[540] The objective reasonableness standard is not further defined, nor is there an indication given as to the level of deference to be afforded the Party government by a dispute settlement panel. Given the tension between the need for regulation of financial systems and the desire for reducing trade barriers, it is likely that determining what is 'reasonable' to protect a financial system will lead to disputes.

There is no doubt that the Bank of International Settlement and the Basle Committee standards will be of relevance in determining what is reasonable to protect a financial system. However, there has been criticism raised that capital adequacy standards are not a valid measure of the security of a

---

[538] NAFTA Art. 1410:1(c).

[539] Smith and Walter (note 535 *supra*), at 155, characterizing the dual objectives of banking regulation as 'maintenance of a safe and sound banking system—one that is resistent to collapse—yet without precluding the failure of institutions that are not competitively viable or are poorly managed'.

[540] NAFTA Art. 1410:1.

bank. A US bank regulatory official points out the shortcomings of the Basle standards in the modern international banking environment:

> Certainly, the Basle capital standards did the job for which they were designed, namely stopping the secular decline in bank capital levels that, by the late 1980s, threatened general safety and soundness. But the scope and complexity of banking activities has proceeded apace during the last two decades or so, and *standard* capital measures, at least for our very largest and most complex organizations, are no longer adequate measures on which to base supervisory action for several reasons:
> - The regulatory capital standards apportion capital only for credit risk and, most recently, for market risk of trading activities. Interest rate risk is dealt with subjectively, and other forms of risk, including operating risk, are not treated within the standards.
> - Also, the capital standards are, despite the appellation 'risk-based', very much a 'one size fits all' rule. For example, all non-mortgage loans to corporations and households receive the same arbitrary 8 percent capital requirement. A secured loan to a triple-A rated company receives the same treatment as an unsecured loan to a junk-rated company. In other words, the capital standards don't measure credit risk although they represent a crude proxy for such risk within broad categories of banking assets.
> - Finally, the capital standards give insufficient consideration to hedging or mitigating risk through the use of credit derivatives or effective portfolio diversification.[541]

Another commentator criticized the competitive effect capital adequacy standards may have on banks:

> The bank supervisors' 'love affair' with capital adequacy will undoubtedly continue in the short-term. But what is unfolding is an incongruity and density of approaches as the regulators try to objectively measure non-credit risks within an all-embracing capital adequacy formula. Already, it has become clear that any such formula will probably *not* achieve the policy objective of competitive equality; [footnote: See H. Scott and S. Iwahara, 'In Search of a Level Playing Field: The Implementation of the Basle Capital Accord in Japan and the United States' (Group of Thirty, 1994)] that any forced convergence in such areas as market risk … will most probably lead to divergency; that the burdens and expenses imposed by such 'high-tech' capital adequacy formula may well exceed the benefits; and that the growing density of such a formula is becoming counterproductive to the residual policy objective of increased transparency. [*Footnote*: See, e.g., 'Greenspan Says As Banking Changes, Regulators Need to Change With The Times' (1994) 62 BNA Bank.Rep. 859.] As has been rightly noted by a leading international supervisor: 'Bank supervision is not a science, but an art'. [*Footnote*: See Remarks By E. Gerald Corrigan, President Federal Reserve Bank of New York at the 7th International Conference of Banking Supervisors, Cannes, France (8 Oct. 1992).]

---

[541] Alice M. Rivlin, 'Optimal Supervision and Regulation of Banks', comments of the Vice-Chair of the Board of Governors of the Federal Reserve System at The Brookings Institution National Issues Forum, Washington, DC, 19 December 1996, pp. 5–6.

The relevance and importance of capital adequacy should be kept within the bounds of this perspective. Obviously, it is an important factor of supervision, but an over-tinkering with capital regulation may simply lead to over-complexity and an increase of marketplace innovations designed to take advantage of inevitable distortions in the capital regulations. As suggested by the Chairman of the US Federal Reserve Board, Alan Greenspan, the bank regulators need to gain a better perspective on the range of risks inherent in such products and a better understanding of the relationship among different risk types. [*Footnote*: See Greenspan Says …, *supra*.][542]

Thus, as the financial environment changes and becomes increasingly international, the possibilities for disputes over necessary regulation of the financial marketplace will change.[543]

Inevitably, however, the prudential exceptions of Chapter Fourteen present an opportunity for discrimination, the taking advantage of which by the Parties will be difficult to stop. Because the idea of 'integrity and stability' of a system, particularly a financial system, is so comprehensive and intangible, it is quite likely that in a given dispute settlement proceeding, the decision makers will be required to accept the arguments of the regulatory body against whom a complaint is lodged. Otherwise the decision makers risk disregarding the evidence presented by the most

---

[542] Norton, 'Trends' (1994) 48 Consumer Fin LQ Rep 415, 418. See also Alan Greenspan, 'Banking in the Global Marketplace', Remarks by the Chairman of the Board of Governors of the Federal Reserve System to the Federation of Bankers Associations of Japan; Tokyo, 18 November 1996, pp. 13–14 ('The decision to craft a bank's capital requirements for trading activities around acceptable and verifiable internal risk measures was an important step in the supervision and regulation of large, internationally active banks … Time and again, though, events are demonstrating that despite the complexity of transactions and the alleged sophistication of management systems, it is the lack of simple basic policies and controls that so often lead to problems at banks … We must never forget that no matter how technologically complex our supervisory systems become, the basic unit of supervision on which all else rests remains the human judgement of the degree of risk on a specific loan, based on the creditworthiness and character of a borrower'). See also Office of the Comptroller of the Currency, 'Newsrelease: Revised OCC Derivatives Handbook Focuses on Strong Risk Management and Emphasizes Importance of Internal Controls', 23 January 1997 (revision of supervisor's handbook emphasizing the need for bank management to ensure the soundness of their bank's activities based on risk measurement); William J. McDonough, 'Achieving Bank Safety and Soundness: A Central Banker's Perspective', remarks by the President of the Federal Reserve Bank of New York to the Joint Conference of Argentine Bankers Association, the Institute of International Finance, the Inter-American Development Bank, and the World Bank, Buenos Aires, 23 March 1996 (emphasizing the need for private sector involvement in the supervision of bank soundness, with a focus on risk management by the bank's own board of directors and management).

[543] This is where the dispute settlement panel composition will play a role of great significance. The financial service experts that are to be selected will bring with them a background that favors or disfavors regulation. One could expect that panelists who have worked with government banking authorities will be more likely to be sympathetic to arguments legitimizing the invocation of the exception while experts from the banking community will be more likely to favor adherence to the general principles of the Agreement, namely liberalization of the markets. It is to be hoped that such generalizations may be avoided by the careful selection process that recognizes the dangers of unintended bias.

competent authorities who could determine the question.[544] Thus, the use of the prudential exception in a way compatible with the liberalizations of Chapter Fourteen is left in large part to the good faith of those supervisory authorities it is intended to control.

3.16.2 Specific Exceptions

3.16.2.1 Chapter Fourteen Exceptions

The other clauses of Article 1410 refer to specific exceptions to rules other than the non-discrimination principles. Here, the significance of maintaining adherence to the principle of national treatment is clear. Article 1401:2 allows the Parties to take 'non-discriminatory measures of general application' to further national monetary and credit policies or exchange rates without fear of violating Chapter Fourteen provisions.[545] The ability to control monetary policy is widely held to be an inviolable sovereign competence. Thus, this provision was particularly important to Mexico, which feared outsiders' domination of its economy. Still, the references to non-discrimination and measures of general application provide an underlying legitimacy for such an exception within the bounds of the NAFTA as a whole.

Under Article 1410:3, a Party may also give a financial institution a monopoly over the services required for the national pension plan or social security system.[546] Although this sort of exception would excuse a complete violation of the non-discrimination principles, it is one that is widely accepted in international trade law.[547]

---

[544] This same dilemma is present in Art. 1411:5(b) language that allows for an exception to the transparency and other Chapter Fourteen rules for reasons of 'public interest'. See 3.13.5 *supra*.

[545] NAFTA Art. 1410:2.

[546] NAFTA Art. 1410:3; NAFTA Art. 1401:3(a).

[547] The WTO's GATS does not include government supplied services within its scope. General Agreement on Trade in Services, Art. I:3(b) (''services' includes any service in any sector except services supplied in the exercise of governmental authority'); GATS Annex on Financial Services 1(b):

> For the purposes of subparagraph 3(b) of Article I of the [GATS], 'services supplied in the exercise of governmental authority' means the following:
> (i)   activities conducted by a central bank or monetary authority or by any other public entity in pursuit of monetary or exchange rate policies;
> (ii) activities forming part of a statutory system of social security or public retirement plans; and
> (iii) other activities conducted by a public entity for the account or with the guarantee or using the financial resources of the Government.

But see GATS Annex on Financial Services 1(c):

> For purposes of subparagraph 3(b) of Article I of the [GATS], if a Member allows any of the activities referred to in subparagraphs (b)(ii) or (b)(iii) of this paragraph to be conducted by its financial service suppliers in competition with a public entity or a financial service supplier, 'services' shall include such activities.

Finally, a Party can restrict or even refuse to allow transfers by financial institutions or cross-border financial service providers to related persons.[548] This provision has the intent of allowing Parties to maintain a viable system of comprehensive control over the assets of a bank. The avoidance of another BCCI-type supervisory failure can only be accomplished if a Party can track funds. This, in turn, can only be possible if transfers between related institutions can be restricted.

To prevent the circumvention of the goals of Chapter Fourteen as much as possible, Article 1410:4 requires that the restriction or refusal be effectuated by non-discriminatory measures. Thus, a Party cannot simply burden another Party's institutions with limited rights of transferring funds while allowing its own banks freedom to move funds from one bank to another.

Moreover, it is explicitly stated that the restrictive measures are only to be used to protect the 'safety, soundness, integrity or financial responsibility of financial institutions or cross-border financial service providers'.[549] This provision reinforces the language of Article 1410:1 ('for prudential reasons') and clarifies its relationship to the transfer provisions found in Chapter Eleven (Investment).[550]

3.16.2.2   *NAFTA-Wide Exceptions*

The NAFTA Chapter Fourteen's basic coverage is limited not only by the exceptions in Article 1410 and the specific reservations set out in the Annexes, but also by general exceptions for all NAFTA provisions found in Chapter Twenty-One. Similar to the exceptions set out in other international financial agreements, the NAFTA exceptions have been characterized as being 'in general, widely recognized as reserved for governments and are not particularly controversial'.[551] The following is only a summary explanation of the exceptions and their relation to Chapter Fourteen.

3.16.2.2.1   NATIONAL SECURITY (ARTICLE 2102)

The national security exception of NAFTA is similar to that found in virtually every international agreement.[552] Yet, unlike some national security

---

[548] NAFTA Art. 1410:4.
[549] *Ibid.*
[550] See NAFTA Art. 1109.
[551] Wethington (note 4 *supra*), at 68.
[552] Compare, e.g., GATT Art. XXI ('Nothing in this Agreement shall be construed (a) to require any contracting party to furnish any information the disclosure of which it considers contrary to its essential security interests; ...'.); GATS Art. XIV*bis*:1 ('Nothing in this Agreement shall be construed: (a) to require any Member to furnish any information, the disclosure of which it considers contrary to its essential security interests; or (b) to prevent any Member from taking any action which it considers necessary for the protection of its essential security interests ...'.); TRIPs Agreement Art. 73 (Security Exceptions; same wording as in GATS); United Nations Charter Art. 51 ('Nothing in the present charter shall impair the inherent right of individual or collective self-defense if an armed attack occurs against a Member of the United Nations, until the Security Council has taken the measures necessary to maintain international peace and security'); United States-Japan Friendship, Commerce and Navigation Treaty Art. XXI:1 ('The present Treaty shall not preclude the application of measures ... (d) ... necessary to protect its essential security interests').

clauses found elsewhere, the NAFTA provisions are more descriptive in what is considered 'national security' and also set out what sorts of actions are excused. In the first clause, Parties may refuse to give access to information it finds would compromise its 'essential security interest'.[553] Further, a Party is free to disregard the NAFTA provisions if it feels the need to act to protect its security interests in trade in war goods and services, and in technology to support its military.[554] Actions during war or 'other emergency in international relations' are excused from NAFTA restrictions,[555] as are acts taken to implement policies or multilateral treaties for the nonproliferation of nuclear weapons.[556] Finally, any actions a Party takes under the United Nations Charter to maintain 'international peace and security' are exempted from the NAFTA provisions.

Although any national security exception is open to misuse based on the impossibility of 'proving' a Party's need for invoking it, it would be hard to imagine an international treaty where the signatories did not allow themselves the option to avoid their obligations in times of military need.[557] However, interpretation of the national security exceptions remains an underdeveloped area of trade law, with many aspects left unaddressed.[558] In the context of Chapter Fourteen, the interesting issue is to what extent 'essential security interests' can relate to the economic stability of, and control over, financial services. The United States has, for instance, taken a blanket national security exception for its investment review procedures.[559] Although this procedure will mainly be used for investment in high technology industries, it is at least conceivable that investment in a bank could also come under scrutiny. Should the investment be denied, a question would arise on the reviewability of the scope of the exception. The United States and Canada differ in their views on this:

> The United States position is that all national-security-related decisions are not subject to dispute resolution under the terms of NAFTA. However, article 1138 of the investment chapter states that only the decision to allow or disallow an investment on the basis of national security considerations is

---

553 NAFTA Art. 2102:1(a).
554 NAFTA Art. 2102:1(b)(i).
555 NAFTA Art. 2102:1(b)(ii).
556 NAFTA Art. 2102:1(b)(iii).
557 One could postulate that this is a sign that the realist school of political theory is right, and that 'might makes right' did not die at the end of the Cold War. Here, however, is not the place for discussing this possibility.
558 See John H. Jackson, 'Helms-Burton, the US, and the WTO' *ASIL Insight* (March 1997) (text found on internet at >www.asil.org.insight7.htm<)discussing the security exceptions of the WTO Agreements in the context of the United States' Helms-Burton legislation penalizing persons, including foreign persons, for having commercial relations with Cuba.
559 Gestrin and Rugman (note 404 *supra*), at 86–7.

excluded from the review process. The Canadian position is therefore that, apart from the specific exclusion of article 1138, any other matter related to article 2102, such as the question as to what constitutes a legitimate national security concern in the first place, is subject to the Agreement's dispute settlement provisions.[560]

Should such a question arise, a dispute settlement panel will be responsible for determining the scope of the exception. It is, however, likely that a panel—whether it ought to or not—would refrain from examining a Party's internal decision-making on matters of national security.[561] It will therefore be left to the good faith of the Parties to ensure that the 'considerable' potential for discrimination contained in this exclusion remains latent.[562]

3.16.2.2.2   TAXATION (ARTICLE 2103)

Taxation measures are broadly excluded from the scope of the NAFTA,[563] and the obligations under any tax conventions of which a Party might be a member are to be superior to NAFTA obligations. However, certain provisions remain in place in so far as newly promulgated tax laws would disadvantage persons of another Party.[564]

Absent any contrary tax convention obligations, the Chapter Fourteen provision on national treatment remains effective for 'taxation measures on income, capital gains or the taxable capital of corporations',[565] and the parts of Mexico's 'Ley del Impuesto al Activo' (Asset Tax Law)[566] which 'relate to the purchase or consumption of particular services'.[567] Likewise, unless there is a tax convention which would dictate a Party to do otherwise, the national treatment and MFN obligations of Chapter Fourteen 'shall apply to all

---

[560] Gestrin and Rugman (note 404 *supra*), at 87. See also Jackson (note 558 *supra*). Professor Jackson noting that in the WTO framework, 'a key interpretation question for the national security exception is whether this exception permits a WTO member to decide for itself, to 'auto-determine', whether the criteria for invoking the exception exist. If the answer is yes, then arguably a government only need to invoke the exception to end a proceeding against it, no matter what the underlying facts of the case are'.

[561] Jackson (note 558 *supra*), recalls that there have been 'some GATT practice' that tended to support a goverment's right to determine the use of the national security exception without being subject to panel review.

[562] Gerstin and Rugman (note 404 *supra*), at 86–7, warn, 'Since most advanced technologies have military and civilian use, the discriminatory potential ... is considerable. While this potential has not yet been realized, the continued erosion of the United States position in high-technology manufacturing could give rise to calls for a more active role for the Committee on Foreign Direct Investment ...'.

[563] NAFTA Art. 2103:1.

[564] The national treatment and MFN obligations of Chapter Fourteen incorporated into this Article do not apply to existing tax measures or to the measures' renewal or amendments that do not make the measure less conforming with the NAFTA than they were at the time of ratification of the Agreement. NAFTA Art. 2103:4(d), (e), and (f).

[565] NAFTA Art. 2103:4(a).

[566] NAFTA Annex 2103.4(1).

[567] NAFTA Art. 2103:4(a).

taxation measures, other than those on income, capital gains or on the taxable capital of corporations, taxes on estates, inheritances, gifts and generation-skipping transfers and those taxes [in Mexico's 'Ley del Impuesto al Activo'].[568] In short, the NTO and MFN obligations apply to virtually all tax measures taken by a Party that would affect the purchase or use of a financial service (unless a separate international tax convention would require otherwise), but it still leaves much room for creative discrimination by the Parties' tax authorities.

Finally, Article 1110 on expropriation and compensation, incorporated into Chapter Fourteen, is to apply to taxes as well.[569]

3.16.2.2.3 BALANCE OF PAYMENTS (ARTICLE 2104)

Functioning as a safeguard against infringement of a Party's economic sovereignty, Article 2104 reserves to the NAFTA Parties the right to contravene Chapter Fourteen for purposes of maintaining the national balance of payments. This is an exception of particular importance to Mexico's acceptance of the Chapter.

> Nothing in this Agreement shall be construed to prevent a Party from adopting or maintaining measures that restrict transfers where the Party experiences serious balance of payments difficulties, or the threat thereof, and such restrictions are consistent with paragraphs 2 through 4 and are:
>
> ...
>
> (b) consistent with paragraphs 6 and 7 to the extent they are imposed on cross-border trade in financial services.[570]

As a whole, this provision allows a Party to take action that would be contrary to the NAFTA provisions if faced with a balance of payment crisis. The referred to paragraphs 2 through to 4 set forth the requirements the Party is obliged to complete if action is taken under this exception. Through procedural and substantive rules, these paragraphs safeguard to the greatest extent possible the other Parties' interests in continuing free trade.

Procedurally, the Party must submit itself to IMF supervision,[571] consulting with the organization[572] and implementing the results of the discussions[573] in order to take advantage of the balance of payments exception. If the measure taken by a Party to restore its balance of payments restricts cross-border trade in financial services, the Party is obliged to work with the other Parties as well as with the IMF. Specifically, the Party may not restrict more than one transfer without having been advised to do so by the IMF.[574] Also, the Party is to 'promptly notify and consult with'[575] the other Parties in order to assess

---

[568] NAFTA Art. 2103:4.
[569] NAFTA Art. 2103:6.
[570] NAFTA Art. 2104:1.
[571] NAFTA Art. 2104:2(a).
[572] NAFTA Art. 2104:2(b).
[573] NAFTA Art. 2104:2(c).
[574] NAFTA Art. 2104:6(a).
[575] NAFTA Art. 2104:6(b).

the problem and the measures used to relieve the situation. Included in this assessment will be the severity of the Party's balance of payment 'difficulties',[576] the 'external economic and trading environment',[577] and other possible solutions to the problem.[578] The Parties will then, under the condition that 'all findings of statistical and other facts ... relating to foreign exchange, monetary reserves and balance of payments' given by the IMF are to be assumed true,[579] consider whether the adopted measures are compatible with the exception.[580] The phasing-out of the measures is further highlighted as particularly important.[581]

Substantively, the measures taken by the Party to relieve its balance of payments problem must be narrowly tailored to the aim of relief, keeping the negative effects on other Parties' interests to a minimum.[582] This includes progressively canceling or lessening their severity as the need for them is reduced.[583]

Another important aspect for the other Parties is the obligation that all measures are to be applied with the better of national treatment or most-favored-nation treatment.[584] Not only does this provision fit with the framework of the NAFTA as a whole, but also it will limit the potential for abuse of the exception. A related limitation on the content of a measure is set out in the provision stating that even if particular services need more advantageous treatment, measures are not to be imposed 'for the purpose of protecting a specific industry or sector unless the measure is consistent with [the policies suggested by the IMF during consultations] and with Article VIII(3) of the Articles of Agreement of the IMF'.[585] If a measure is taken, it cannot be so selective as to be a barrier to trade for only one Party.

3.16.2.2.4   PRIVACY OF PERSONS AND LAW ENFORCEMENT NEEDS (ARTICLE 2105)

Individual privacy as well as national police efforts are protected by a general exception aimed mainly at NAFTA's transparency rules fostering information flows. Article 2105 permits a Party to refuse to give out information if such publication would either 'impede law enforcement or would be contrary to the Party's law protecting personal privacy'.[586] Significantly for Chapter Fourteen, this exemption explicitly includes a Party's laws on the privacy of financial affairs and the privacy of customer accounts in financial institutions.[587] The inclusion of this exception in Chapter Twenty-One is very similar to the clause in Article 1411:5(b), but here exempts 'information' requests

---

576   NAFTA Art. 2104:6(b)(i).
577   NAFTA Art. 2104:6(b)(ii).
578   NAFTA Art. 2104:6(b)(iii).
579   NAFTA Art. 2104:7(b).
580   NAFTA Art. 2104:7(a).
581   *Ibid.*
582   NAFTA Art. 2104:3(a), (b).
583   NAFTA Art. 2104:3(c).
584   NAFTA Art. 2104:3(e).
585   NAFTA Art. 2104:4.
586   NAFTA Art. 2105.
587   *Ibid.*

under any of the NAFTA provisions, while the Chapter Fourteen exception more narrowly applies to requests for 'confidential information' in the context of the transparency provision.

3.16.2.2.5 ENVIRONMENTAL MEASURES (ARTICLE 1114)

Incorporated into Chapter Fourteen, Article 1114 provides the Parties with the opportunity to call upon protection of the environment as a reason for taking actions that would otherwise violate the financial service provisions. The measures taken to ensure environmental sensitivity must, however, be 'otherwise consistent' with the remainder of the Chapter.[588]

The second paragraph reflects the popular concerns that a Party would use low environmental standards to attract other Party investors.[589] The provision states: 'The Parties recognize that it is inappropriate to encourage investment by relaxing domestic health, safety or environmental measures. Accordingly, a Party should not waive or derogate from, or offer to waive or derogate from, such measures as an encouragement ...'.[590]

Phrased as a moral responsibility rather than a legal obligation, there is not any textual indication that the avoidance of the standards would be grounds for formal dispute settlement. However, if another Party believes that a lowering of the standards did occur, consultations may take place.[591] In addition, if such encouragements are offered so as to discriminate among financial service institutions or providers based on nationality, a possibility still exists for basing a complaint on national treatment or most-favored-nation treatment clauses.[592]

3.16.2.2.6 LABOR STANDARDS?

Although not referred to within the NAFTA general exceptions or in Chapter Fourteen's specific exceptions, it is credible that the protection of labor standards could also be invoked as grounds for deviating from the provisions of the Chapter. The North American Agreement on Labor Cooperation's Preamble states in part: 'RESOLVED to promote, in accordance with their respective laws, high-skill, high-productivity economic development in North America by: ... fostering investment with due regard for the importance of labor laws and principles'.[593]

This language could be interpreted to allow preferences to be given to financial services that create better conditions for their employees than do others. Discrimination in granting licenses or in offering tax advantages may be justified thereby.

---

[588] NAFTA Art. 1114:1.
[589] NAFTA Article 1114:2.
[590] *Ibid.*
[591] *Ibid.*
[592] It would, however, most likely require proof of a pattern of encouragement to the financial service providers of one of the other Parties.
[593] North American Agreement on Labor Co-operation Between the Government of Canada, the Government of the United Mexican States and the Government of the United States of America, Preamble (final draft 13 September 1993).

3.17   DISPUTE SETTLEMENT

Disputes under Chapter Fourteen are to be settled within the general framework of NAFTA dispute settlement found in Chapter Twenty. Thus, co-operation and consultations are the preferred method of resolving differences between or among the Parties.[594] If there is a dispute about the interpretation or application of Chapter Fourteen that cannot be solved by alternative means, there are two possible fora for settling the differences. Subject to certain limitations, a Party may invoke either the World Trade Organization dispute settlement procedures or the NAFTA procedures.

3.17.1   WTO Procedures

If the complaining party feels that the issue at stake is one best addressed in a multilateral trade forum, under the NAFTA it may elect to use the General Agreement on Trade and Tariffs (GATT 1947) or its successor agreement's procedures for settling disputes. As the NAFTA was written prior to the establishment of the World Trade Organization, the reference to the successor agreement is somewhat vague for purposes of disputes on financial services. The GATT 1994 is the true successor agreement to the GATT 1947, but under the framework organization of the World Trade Organization (WTO), the General Agreement on Trade in Services (GATS) is the proper treaty for addressing financial service disputes. However, because of the inclusion of an 'Understanding on Rules and Procedures Governing the Settlement of Disputes' (DSU), the basic dispute settlement framework is the same for all of the treaties included in the WTO structure.[595] The difference comes in the recourse to suspension of concessions in case of non-obeying of a panel decision.

Before the Party requests a panel in the WTO, it must inform all other NAFTA Parties of its actions.[596] The third Party can then consider whether it has related claims, and if so, whether it would rather have them heard within the NAFTA. If the third Party would indeed prefer to bring its case before a NAFTA panel, 'normally' the dispute will be settled in the NAFTA context.[597]

Under WTO dispute settlement procedures, the complainant has the opportunity to present its case to a three- or five-person panel[598]

---

[594] NAFTA Art. 2003.
[595] For an overview of the legal process of WTO dispute settlement as well as several reviews of the specific aspects of the process, see Ernst-Ulrich Petersmann (ed.), *International Trade Law and the GATT/WTO Dispute Settlement System* (Kluwer Law International, London, 1997).
[596] NAFTA Art. 2005:2.
[597] *Ibid.*
[598] WTO, Understanding on Rules and Procedures Governing the Settlement of Disputes (DSU) Art. 8:5.

composed of trade experts.[599] The decision of a panel is binding on the disputing Members unless the decision is appealed by one of the disputants.[600]

The WTO's appellate process is a change from the GATT dispute settlement system.[601] It is a separate level of review from the panel decision, looking only to the legal reasoning of the appealed decision. The decision-making group, the Appellate Body, is a standing group of seven persons who serve in rotating groups of three to review panel reports when necessary.[602] Unless rejected by a unanimous decision of the WTO membership as a whole, the appellate decision is final and binding.[603] If the Member against whom a decision is issued does not undertake the required actions within 15 or 18 months,[604] the Dispute Settlement Body may allow the winning Member to retaliate by withholding trade benefits.[605]

3.17.2 NAFTA Dispute Settlement

If the disputing NAFTA Parties either choose to settle their differences in a NAFTA proceeding[606] or are forced to settle the problem in the NAFTA because of a third Party's interest in the matter[607] or because the dispute is to be solved under either of the Side Agreements or Standards Chapters of the NAFTA,[608] the process is governed by the NAFTA dispute procedures set out in Chapter Twenty, Section B (as adopted by Chapter Fourteen).[609]

---

[599] The panelists are supposed to be selected from a roster kept by the WTO Secretariat. See DSU Art. 8:4. In reality, however, the roster is only one source for panel candidates.

[600] See DSU Art. 16.

[601] See generally Ernst-Ulrich Petersmann, *The GATT/WTO Dispute Settlement System: International Law, International Organizations and Dispute Settlement* (Kluwer Law International, London, 1997). Within the volume, see particularly Ch. 2, 'The GATT Dispute Settlement System 1948–1995: An Overview'; Ch. 5, 'The New Dispute Settlement System of the 1994 WTO Agreement'. See also William J. Davey, 'The WTO/GATT World Trading System: An Overview', in Pierre Pescatore, William J. Davey and Andreas F. Lowenfeld (eds), *Handbook of WTO/GATT Dispute Settlement* (Transnational Publishers, Irvington-on-Hudson, NY, 1997), pp. 70–74; Pierre Pescatore, 'Drafting and Analyzing Decisions on Dispute Settlement' in Pescatore *et al.* (*supra*), pp. 3–54.

[602] See generally DSU Art. 17 (Appellate Review/Standing Appellate Body).

[603] DSU Art. 17:14.

[604] DSU Art. 21:4.

[605] DSU Art. 22:2,3.

[606] See NAFTA Art. 2005:1.

[607] NAFTA Art. 2005:2.

[608] NAFTA Art. 2005:3.

[609] NAFTA Art. 1414:1. There is also a separate dispute settlement procedure for NAFTA Parties' use of antidumping/countervailing duty measures. An explanation of this mechanism is found in Kristin Moody-O'Grady, 'Dispute Settlement Provisions in the NAFTA and the CAFTA: Progress or Protectionism?' (1994) 18:1 Fletcher Forum World Aff 121.

3.17.2.1   Consultation (Article 1413)

The first step to NAFTA dispute settlement in the case of financial service disagreements is consultation.[610] In this phase, the Parties' representatives (including at least one member from the responsible administrative agencies)[611] exchange information in hopes of coming to a mutually acceptable solution.[612] During this period, all 'confidential or proprietary' materials that are exchanged are to remain confidential,[613] and the interests of other Parties are not to be damaged.[614] The results of the consultations are to be reported to the Financial Services Committee.[615]

3.17.2.2   Dispute Settlement by Panel (Article 1414)

3.17.2.2.1   INITIATION OF PANEL PROCEEDINGS

If the consultations do not bring about a resolution of the dispute, either of the Parties may write a request that the Commission meets to initiate formal panel proceedings to fix a settlement.[616] In the request, the Party is to note which of the Articles of the NAFTA has allegedly been violated as well as other relevant provisions.[617]

Upon receiving a request, the Commission's work consists of aiding the Parties' attempts to find a satisfactory solution. To accomplish this task, the Commission is authorized to ask for expert opinions, form working groups, use various forms of alternative dispute resolution procedures, and recommend actions to be taken by the disputants.[618]

3.17.2.2.2   FORMATION OF PANEL

If, within 30 days,[619] the Parties do not resolve their dispute, either (or any) of them may request that an arbitral panel be formed.[620] The

---

[610] One author argues that the NAFTA's pragmatic, consultation orientation to dispute resolution is harmful to Mexico because of that Party's lack of bargaining power. Michael Barber, 'NAFTA Dispute Resolution Provisions: Leaving Room for Abusive Tactics by Airlines Looking Southward' (1996) 61 J Air L & Commerce 991.

[611] NAFTA Art. 1413:2. The responsible agencies are the Canadian Department of Finance, the Meixcan Secretaría de Hacienda y Crédito Público, and the US Department of the Treasury (or the US Department of Commerce, if the dispute involves insurance services). NAFTA Annex 1412.1.

[612] NAFTA Art. 2006:5.

[613] NAFTA Art. 2006:5(b).

[614] NAFTA Art. 2006:5(c).

[615] NAFTA Art. 1413:1.

[616] NAFTA Art. 2007:1(c), as incorporated by NAFTA Art. 1414:1.

[617] NAFTA Art. 2007:3, as incorporated by NAFTA Art. 1414:1. The form of complaint known in international trade law as the 'non-violation complaint' is not available to NAFTA Parties under Chapter Fourteen. NAFTA, Chapter Twenty, Annex 2004:1. For a discussion of the non-violation complaint in the WTO agreements, see Thomas Cottier and Krista Nadakavukaren Schefer (note 595 *supra*), 'Non-Violation Complaints in WTO/GATT Dispute Settlement: Past, Present and Future' in Petersmann (note 595 *supra*), at 145–83.

[618] NAFTA Art. 2007:5.

[619] Alternatively, a panel is to be formed within 'such other period as the consulting Parties may agree'. NAFTA Art. 2008:1(c).

[620] NAFTA Art. 2008:1.

Commission 'shall establish' such a panel.[621] The panel for a Chapter Fourteen dispute will consist of five individuals,[622] usually to be selected by the Parties from a roster of 15 persons with an expertise in financial services law.[623] The panelists may be persons with no special knowledge of financial services if one of the Parties to the dispute so requests.[624] If the dispute is between two Parties, each Party will choose two panelists, both citizens of the other Party.[625] If there are more than two Parties to the dispute, the complained-against Party is to choose a panelist from each of the other Parties, and the complaining Parties are to choose two panelists who are citizens of the complained-against Party. The chairperson of the panel is to be selected by mutual agreement, or, failing that, by random drawing.[626]

3.17.2.2.3 INITIAL REPORT

This panel will hear the arguments of the Parties using the Model Rules of Procedure,[627] hearing expert evidence if needed,[628] and will issue an 'initial report' within 90 days (unless the Parties agree otherwise).[629] The initial report is to contain a portion setting forth the facts of the dispute, a finding of whether the complaint is a violation of the NAFTA provisions or of the legitimately-expected benefits of the Agreement, and the panel's recommendations for settling the dispute.[630] The report may include separate opinions from the panelists if there is disagreement as to the findings or recommendations,[631] but the authors of both the majority report and the dissents and/or concurrences are to remain anonymous.[632]

Once the report is circulated to the disputing parties, the Parties have two weeks in which to make written comments for the panel to consider before completing its final report.[633] After receiving and taking into consideration the Parties' reactions to its initial report, the panel should next write and send its final report and any separate opinions to

---

[621] NAFTA Art. 2008:2.
[622] NAFTA Art. 2011.
[623] NAFTA Art. 1414:3. The panelists may be either from private practice or from regulatory agencies, and are not required to be lawyers, as long as they are objective, reliable, and independent.
[624] NAFTA Art. 1414:4.
[625] NAFTA Art. 1414:4(b)(i).
[626] NAFTA Art. 2011:2.
[627] NAFTA Art. 2012:2.
[628] NAFTA Art. 2014.
[629] NAFTA Art. 2016:2.
[630] *Ibid.*
[631] NAFTA Art. 2016:3.
[632] NAFTA Art. 2017:2.
[633] NAFTA Art. 2016:4.

the Commission. This is to occur within 30 days of presenting the initial report to the Parties.[634]

3.17.2.2.4   PUBLICATION OF THE REPORT

The final report is to be published within 15 days of the Commission's receipt of it.[635] As with the initial report, the published final report may contain separate opinions of panelists that are in concurrence with the majority or who dissent from the final opinion. However, also as with the initial report, the identity of the authors of all opinions is to remain unknown to non-panelists.[636]

3.17.2.2.5   IMPLEMENTATION OF THE REPORT

The final report's proposed resolution is then to be implemented by the disputing Parties. The Agreement is not as strongly worded as to the implementation of the report as it is to the prior procedural rules and to the fact that the disputants must resolve their differences, however: 'On receipt of the final report of the panel, the disputing Parties shall agree on the resolution of the dispute, which *normally* shall conform with the determinations and recommendations of the panel …'.[637]

In a case where the panel finds for the complaining Party, if possible the implementation is to consist of the removal or non-implementation of the measure that violates the text or spirit of the NAFTA.[638] If that is not possible, compensation may be given to the complaining Party.[639]

3.17.2.2.6   SANCTIONS

When a Party refuses to abide by a final report's recommendations, the injured Party may retaliate by suspending trade benefits that it would have granted the other Party under the NAFTA framework. Under the general dispute settlement provisions of Chapter Twenty, the suspended benefits should be from the same sector as the violation (cross-sectoral sanctions are permissible if that is not practicable, however) and they should be of the same amount as the damage suffered.[640] The provisions on dispute settlement for Chapter Fourteen are more strictly limited to the financial service sector. Article 1414:5 states:

> In any dispute where a panel finds a measure to be inconsistent with the obligations of this Agreement and the measure effects:
> (a) only the financial services sector, the complaining Party may suspend benefits only in the financial services sector;

---

[634] NAFTA Art. 2017:1.
[635] NAFTA Art. 2017:4.
[636] NAFTA Art. 2017:2.
[637] NAFTA Art. 2018:1 (emphasis added).
[638] NAFTA Art. 2018:2.
[639] *Ibid.*
[640] NAFTA Art. 2019:2.

(b) the financial services sector and any other sector, the complaining Party may suspend benefits in the financial services sector that have an effect equivalent to the effect of the measure in the Party's financial service sector; or

(c) only a sector other than the financial services sector, the complaining Party may not suspend benefits in the financial services sector.[641]

These provisions make it clear that the preference in Chapter Fourteen is to isolate the financial service industry from the use of retaliatory sanctions. Not only can a Party only use retaliation in the financial services sector when the violating measure affected the financial services sector, but even if the effects of the violation were broader, the sanctions within the financial service sector may not exceed the amount of the effects the measure had in that sector. Cross-sanctions in the traditional sense are not allowed under Chapter Fourteen.

---

[641] NAFTA Art. 1414:5.

4. Effect of Chapter Fourteen on NAFTA Members

It was widely proclaimed that the coming into effect of the NAFTA signaled a new era for North American relations. Among the members of the financial service industries in the three partner states there was a curious mix of feelings. In official accounts, the United States and Canadian bankers were jubilant, anticipating the financial rewards they could reap from Mexico's commitments to liberalize its financial service market. The Mexican bankers supposedly were apprehensive, fearing a rush of more highly developed financial service providers from the North under whose onslaught many Mexican banks would fall.[1]

The reality, not surprisingly, was more differentiated than the media accounts.[2] In the United States, one banking lawyer discounted the importance of the Chapter Fourteen provisions, commenting that all NAFTA really does is 'grease the wheels' for trilateral trade in financial services among the banks of the three Parties, not in itself make trade

---

[1] See, e.g., Advocate Group, 'NAFTA-Chapter 14' (text found on the internet at >www.accent.net<) ('The financial services chapter, one of the priorities of US negotiators, has created much excitement in the affected US industry—and as much anxiety in its Mexican counterpart—as any NAFTA provision'); Department of Foreign Affairs and International Trade Canada, 'NAFTA-Financial Services' (text found on the internet at >http://strategis.ic.gc.ca<) (in description of 'Benefits to Canada': 'Significant new expansion opportunities for Canadian financial institutions in the developing Mexican market').

[2] One observer criticizes the Clinton administration's use of the mass media to 'sell' NAFTA to the US voters. This 'media blitz campaign' discredited the Agreement itself as well as the Administration.

> Rather than resolve the credibility issue, the administration exacerbated the situation … Because of the media hype, the public was left with exaggerated and extravagant expectations regarding the possible negative and positive effects of the NAFTA … Because of the manner in which it was introduced to the public, the NAFTA was not, and still is not, supported wholeheartedly on a grassroots level by any of the signing countries.

> Valerie J. McNevin, 'Policy Implications of the NAFTA for the Financial Services Industry' 5 Colo J Int'l Env'l L & Pol 369, 382 (footnotes omitted).

possible.[3] Other observers recall that trade in financial commodities is so highly technologized that, while official trade barriers are a nuisance, they are not so great an obstacle to such transactions that liberalization will be decisive in the placement of financial service investments.[4] Likewise, in Mexico, certainly not all of the banks felt the same way. Some bankers were perhaps fearful of the NAFTA (or resentful of what the NAFTA threatened to do to their profit margins), but other experts looked forward to the opportunity to be forced into efficiency and to gain opportunities to learn about new technologies and teach others what they knew.[5]

---

[3] Discussion with author (Oxford, September 1996); Rudi Dornbusch, 'Why the US Needs to Nail Down NAFTA', *Business Week*, 26 April 1993, p. 18 ('all the hype notwithstanding, the NAFTA merely applies the finishing touches to trade relations between the US and Mexico that are already basically open'), in McNevin (note 2 *supra*), at 378, n.41. A Mexican expert echoed these sentiments but put his emphasis on the potential lack of future benefits developing from the NAFTA legal structures, writing that '[e]ven if one accepts that it is the presence of legal barriers that explains the absence of widespread trade in financial services, the elimination of those barriers does not guarantee the materialisation of gains from trade'. Ignacio Trigueros, 'The Mexican Financial System and NAFTA', in Victor Bulmer-Thomas, Nikki Craske and Mónica Serrano (eds), *Mexico and the North American Free Trade Agreement: Who Will Benefit?* (St Martin's Press, New York, 1994), pp. 43–57, at 47.

[4] 'Task Force on the Future of the Canadian Financial Services Sector', Discussion Paper (1997), at 1.9. In section on 'Limits on What Government Can Do', the Task Force notes, '… the scope within which Parliament can act effectively is being narrowed, primarily by the impact of technology …'.

[5] See generally Fernando Solís Soberon and Ignacio Trigueros, 'Bancos', in United Nations, (ed.), *México: Una Economia de Servicios*, UNCTAD/ITP/58 (1991), pp. 93–113, at 104–5, setting out (on 104) the views of 15 commercial banks and three development banks in Mexico about the opening of the Mexican banking market:

> Cinco bancos (30 por ciento) no consideraron ventajosa la importación de servicios, mencionando que su nivel de eficiencia no les permitía hacer frente a la competencia externa. Por otra parte, de los bancos que están a favor de la importación de servicios, la mayor parte considera que la competencia externa es beneficiosa pues trae consigo una mejor calidad de los servicios y transferia de tecnología.
>
> En cuanto a la conveniencia de la inversión extranjera directa, el 20 por ciento de los bancos la considera negativa porque su nivel de competitividad no es adecuado y uno de los bancos porque valorativamente considera que este sector debe permanecer en manos de los mexicanos. El 80 por ciento restante considera que ésta es beneficiosa porque implica más recursos y transferencia tecnológica.
>
> En relación a los servicios en los que se consideran competitivos, la mayor parte de los bancos se refirieron a las operaciones de inversión que realizan en las mesas de dinero. Respecto a los menos competitivos, 4 de los bancos mencionaron que ninguno o no especificaron, 4 consideran a la captación tradicional y 6 el financiamiento de divisas y las transacciones internacionales.
>
> En cuanto a la infraestructura y calidad del personal, la encuesta arroja los siguientes resultados: 4 de los bancos consideran que su infraestructura es adecuada, 7 la consideran medianamente adecuada y 4 la consideran insuficiente. En relación al personal las proporciones son similares. Además, la mayor parte de los bancos consideran que les tomaría entre uno o dos años el lograr que la infraestructura y los recursos humanos estén en niveles adecuados.

It is certain that the increase in trade flows between, and economic activity within, Canada, Mexico, and the United States as a result of NAFTA provide all banks in this region with profit-making opportunities that did not exist previously. The legal effects of Chapter Fourteen on NAFTA Party banks, however, differ significantly among the Parties due to the advantages existing in the earlier Canada-United States Free Trade Agreement and the specific reservations taken by each Party. And, perhaps even more importantly, the direct legal effects of NAFTA are potentially far outweighed by the indirect effects of the Agreement.

4.1   BANKS GOING TO CANADA

For the NAFTA Party banks establishing and operating in Canada, there have been certain substantial changes brought about by the Agreement. As banking services were covered by the Canada-United States Free Trade Agreement, the extent to which the Canadian commitments in the NAFTA benefit the Mexican banks is greater than it is for US banks.

4.1.1   United States Banks in Canada

The United States had approached the NAFTA negotiations with Canada in hopes of improving on the financial service provisions of the Canada-United States Free Trade Agreement without changing its own laws.[6] From Canada's perspective, then, it is not surprising that the benefits accruing to US banks under the NAFTA are not a great deal different from those under the CUFTA. United States persons had already been assured of national

---

(Contd.)

See also Trigueros (note 3 *supra*), at 55 ('The liberalisation package negotiated by Mexico under NAFTA constitutes an important step in terms of promoting (a much needed) greater efficiency in the Mexican financial system ...'.); comment of Ms Powers, 'Discussion of the Regulation of Financial Services Under NAFTA' (1993) 1:1 US-Mex LJ 81, 82 ('Remember, it is not a situation of excess capacity in finance in Mexico; rather, it is a situation of a shortage of capacity that could very well become a bottleneck to their development. So yes, the newly privatized [Mexican] banks are going to grapple with the new competition. Mexico needs the additional financial capacity which the banks will develop and, with technology, they will become more competitive'). Economic literature on integration supports the idea that one of the main benefits of trade areas is the gains stemming from increased competition between firms. See Brigitte Guggisberg, *Das Protektionspotential der EG und die Effekte auf Drittstaaten* (Verlag Rüegger, Zurich, 1997), p. 20. 'Pro-competitive' effects arise from unhindered entrance of new producers and from the reduced power of firms to wield market power as monopolies or oligopolies. *Ibid.* citing Alasdair Smith and Anthony J. Venables as the creators of this term. See also Alasdair Smith and Anthony J. Venables, 'The Cost of Non-Europe: An Assessment Based on an Formal Model of Imperfect Competition and Economies of Scale', *Survey on the Cost of Non-Europe*, Studie Nr. 21 (Commission of the European Communities, Luxembourg, 1988).

[6]   See discussion of negotiation of Chapter Fourteen in Chapter 3, 3.2 *supra*.

treatment in the Canadian government's review of applications for establishing financial service institutions in Canada.[7] Additionally, the United States had secured for its banks the right to no less advantageous treatment in the future.[8] The US banks also benefited by an exemption from the Canadian cap on foreign assets on financial services and by the ability to branch within Canada without receiving prior approval from the Minister of Finance under the CUFTA. Thus, the parallel provisions of NAFTA Chapter Fourteen confer no new advantages on the US banks in Canada in these respects.

At the same time, the Canadians' unfulfilled requests for a more liberalized US inter-State branching regime and for permission that banks are permitted to engage in commercial banking and securities or insurance resulted in their unwillingness to extend further liberalizations just to appease the United States. Consequently, securities trade remains excluded from the NAFTA, against the strong wishes of the United States. Perhaps more importantly, under the NAFTA United States banks were still only permitted to establish a presence in Canada through the form of a subsidiary.[9] In these ways, the NAFTA did not improve the CUFTA treatment to the extent the United States' Chapter Fourteen negotiators had hoped it would.

And yet, the NAFTA does make several significant improvements over the CUFTA's relatively summary chapter on financial services. First, the scope of NAFTA is much broader than that of the quasi-provisionary CUFTA. A major novelty in the NAFTA is the inclusion of insurance activities in its scope. Combined with the Canadian financial liberalization allowing banks to engage in limited insurance activities through subsidiaries, the NAFTA's broader scope is important for the competitive equality of United States banks on the Canadian market. The US banks can now be protected by Chapter Fourteen's principles of NTO and MFN if they choose to broaden their financial activities beyond pure banking.[10]

Next, subnational political units and self-regulatory organizations are subject to a Party's NAFTA obligations, whereas under the CUFTA only national governments were included.[11] And, even if some subnational political units are specifically exempted from certain NAFTA obligations, the national level is now more completely liberalized. Moreover, NAFTA's

---

[7] CUFTA Art. 1703:3 ('Canada shall not use review powers governing the entry of US-controlled financial institutions in a manner inconsistent with the aims of this Part').

[8] Based on that which the US banks enjoyed at the time of coming into effect of the CUFTA.

[9] In Fall 1997, Canada published proposals to change its banking legislation to allow for direct branching of foreign financial institutions. See Finance Canada, *1997 Review of Financial Sector Legislation: Proposals for Change* (text found on the Department's internet site at >www.fin.gc.ca<). In 1999, these proposals were accepted, and came into effect on 1 June 1999.

[10] This is almost a corollary to the protection of new banking services that the United States and Canada imposed on Mexico. See discussion of NAFTA Art. 1407:1 (see new services, 3.11 *supra*).

[11] Compare NAFTA Art. 105 and NAFTA Art. 1402 with CUFTA Art. 1701:2 ('The provisions of this Part, ... shall not apply to any measure of a political subdivision of either Party').

specific reference to self-regulatory organizations demonstrates an aware-ness of the practical barriers to trade in services that can be erected by non-national governments.

Finally, the cross-border trade form of financial service provision is included in NAFTA, as is commercial presence.[12] The CUFTA focused on the commercial presence mode of supply, but did not elaborate on the rules regarding cross-border trade.[13] The inclusion of cross-border liberalizations is important for banks that find it more efficient to provide services from their home country, and at least in some respects reduced the dis-advantages imposed by Canada's requirement that establishment were to be in the form of incorporated subsidiaries. The unhindered provision of cross-border banking services is also of increasing import due to the development of technologies that allow services to be supplied over inter-active electronic networks. In this, the data transfer protections of NAFTA are a further advantage to the Parties.

What is also very new and, from a trade law perspective very important, for United States banking institutions under the NAFTA, is the ability to invoke full-fledged dispute settlement proceedings in case of alleged violations of the Agreement.[14] Under the CUFTA, Parties could only request consultations with one another when complaints arose under the financial services provisions.[15] Under NAFTA, there are two possible dispute settlement fora for banking disputes: the normal NAFTA dispute settlement process between the Parties (contained in Chapter Twenty) and the special investor-Party dispute settlement procedures (incorporated from NAFTA Chapter Eleven). The change from informal consultation to binding consultations under formal procedural rules of the dispute settlement mechanism signals a movement away from the political solution and toward a legal solution. With a formal interpretation of Chapter Fourteen provisions to look upon as authority, NAFTA Party banks and their lawyers will have a more predictable legal space within which to operate. While the likelihood of formal dispute settlement being called upon by a Party bank has been estimated at approaching zero,[16] there remains a benefit for banks—parti-cularly small or new institutions—in being assured of receiving legal protection of their right to non-discriminatory treatment should they choose to invoke it.

---

[12] See discussion on NAFTA Art. 1403 (establishment) and NAFTA Art. 1404 (cross-border trade), 3.7 and 3.8 *supra*.

[13] See generally CUFTA Art. 1702 (Commitments of the United States of America); Art. 1703 (Commitments of Canada). See, e.g., CUFTA Art. 1702:2 (The US 'shall not adopt or apply any measure ... with respect to [Canadian banks'] ability to establish and operate ...'); CUFTA Art. 1703:2(a) (Canada shall 'not refuse to incorporate a United States-controlled Canadian bank subsidiary ...').

[14] See 3.18 *supra*.

[15] NAFTA Art. 1404.

[16] Interview with an official at the American Bankers' Association (Washington, DC, January 1997). The official, a non-lawyer, voiced the opinion that banks would be hesitant to initiate formal dispute settlement proceedings, preferring to work out problems away from the public's view. When a formal settlement would be requested, it would be only for a very large dispute.

Another important procedural improvement NAFTA brings to the Parties is the transparency requirement. While the CUFTA did provide for the publication of laws and regulations,[17] the NAFTA includes these requirements and more. The NAFTA's increased specificity in its rules on how notification of laws and proposals are to be made gives banks in the Parties a firmer basis for controlling the implementation of the Parties' obligations. Of particular importance to new banks are the transparency obligations regarding time limits of application reviews. The strict deadlines for NAFTA Parties were absent from CUFTA, yet are decisive in ensuring a more liberalized financial market for purposes of daily operations.

The privacy protections offered by NAFTA, as well as the required establishment of information points to which 'interested persons' can turn for help, are new also. The benefits of these protections potentially extend beyond the immediate banking community to the public at large.

NAFTA also brings material differences in its obligations. Perhaps the main difference to the CUFTA is that NAFTA includes both a wide and detailed national treatment obligation and a most-favored-nation obligation for all Party banks. Thus, US banks can be assured that the treatment they receive is at least as good as that received by any other bank in Canada 'in like circumstances'. In strategic planning, such *de jure* obligations are helpful even if usual practice had long been to grant *de facto* equal treatment. The great changes taking place in the financial sectors around the globe make such assurances even more valuable.

Next, the movement of businesspersons for banking-related activities is liberalized in the NAFTA, unlike in the CUFTA. Potentially of great importance for the transfer of expertise from parent company to subsidiary, the NAFTA provisions should prevent unnecessary refusals of requests for temporary entry into a Party territory from becoming a tool of disguised discrimination.[18]

4.1.2   Mexican Banks in Canada

For Mexican banks wanting to operate in Canada, the competitive conditions have improved greatly. Formerly not a Party to the Canada-United States Free Trade Agreement, Mexican banks now enjoy the benefits of that agreement as well as those of the NAFTA due to the former's incorporation into Chapter Fourteen. Thus, due to this incorporation, Mexican banks are no longer subjected to the maximal Canadian investment limits on foreign banking capital. Nor are they limited to the aggregate 25 per cent of banking investments cap placed on non-Canadian (and non-US) banks as they were before 1994.

---

[17] The comment period on proposed laws was also provided under CUFTA. See CUFTA Art. 1704:1 ('to the extent possible').
[18] See 3.12 *supra*.

Another significant improvement is that under NAFTA's adoption of CUFTA obligations, Mexican banks may branch throughout Canada, like US banks, without receiving prior approval from the Canadian authorities.[19] Having experience in extensive branching in their home market, the Mexican banks may benefit from this liberalization even more so than do the United States-based institutions.

Finally, all of the new Chapter Fourteen benefits accruing to the United States financial service institutions and investors will be enjoyed by their Mexican counterparts who wish to take advantage of the opportunities in Canada. Transparency and dispute settlement procedures, for instance, are as valuable to Mexican banks (or even more valuable, as they may be less familiar with Canadian governmental structures) as they are to US banks.[20]

4.2   BANKS GOING TO MEXICO

4.2.1   Canadian and US Banks' Enjoyment of Liberalizations

Certainly the most celebrated effects that NAFTA has had on its Party banks are those surrounding the opening of Mexico's banking markets.[21] Under NAFTA Chapter Fourteen, Mexico committed itself to granting the banks of the other Parties a protectable right to establish and operate under non-discriminatory conditions of competition within its territory. The benefits to the United States banks and the Canadian banks are legally identical. Moreover, the provisions found in NAFTA, as the first externally-oriented financial services liberalizations, are significant indicators of how Mexico's banking regulators will treat other foreign banks.[22]

Although under the NAFTA development banks remain off-limits for foreign investors, Mexico committed itself to allowing progressively increasing levels of foreign ownership of commercial banks. Since the coming into effect of the NAFTA, Mexico has updated its capital limits as required by the Agreement. The updates take place twice a year and 'reflect changes in the amount of capital and assets held by institutions in Mexico, as well as changes in the percentage of the Mexican market

---

[19] Canada's GATS obligations taken under the Fifth Protocol foresee an extension of this benefit to all GATS Members as of 1 June 1999. See 6.1.4.1 *infra*, discussion of Canada's GATS obligations.

[20] See 4.1, and 4.1.1 *supra* (NAFTA's effect on US banks going to Canada).

[21] See, e.g., David W. Banowsky and Carlos A. Gabuardi, 'Secured Credit Transactions in Mexico' (1994) 28:2 Int'l Law 263.

[22] Many of Mexico's financial liberalizations have indeed been extended to all foreign banks, whether through the GATS negotiations or through other bilateral or regional preferential arrangements. Yet, the experience of the NAFTA negotiations as a first opening results in a good chance that future interpretations of the new laws will have a NAFTA-orientation.

that foreign institutions can hold based on a sliding scale established under NAFTA'.[23]

In addition, the 1995 peso crisis spurred the Government to offer foreign banks the opportunity to purchase majority shares of Mexican banks up to a 49 per cent ownership of the aggregate Mexican banking market.

If a foreign bank does not purchase the majority share of a Mexican bank, the NAFTA limits are effective. In mid-1996, the aggregate of foreign banks still owned only 5.8 per cent of the net Mexican banking system capital, around $650 million below the then-available ownership limits of 10.8 per cent.[24] In terms of assets, commercial banks and limited-scope financial institutions owned only 0.21 per cent of the allowable 3 per cent limit, resulting in a $4.3 billion potential for expansion in Mexico.[25] By 1998 these figures had improved, although the allowable limits were still not reached. While the permissible aggregate foreign subsidiary ownership of banking assets available until 31 October 1998 was 13.6 per cent of the net capital, or around $1.7 billion, the actual ownership was only 6.15 per cent, or $969 million.[26] For system-wide assets of foreign-owned commercial banks and limited-scope financial institutions, the figures were more extreme: of the three percent ownership available (approximately $4.2 billion), the foreign financial service providers had only taken advantage of 0.1 per cent ($200 million).[27]

In addition, under Chapter Fourteen, US and Canadian banks are now able to ensure that their Mexican subsidiaries (and their investors) will have a right to operate under equal competitive conditions with their Mexican competitors. They may, therefore, engage in securities underwriting and exchange, in sales of insurance, and in the purchase of holding companies (as well as normal commercial banking activities). Moreover, the NAFTA Party nationals' banks may branch throughout the geographic territory of Mexico without limit.[28]

As significant as the market access and non-discrimination commitments are, the incorporation of international law protections on investments contained in NAFTA Chapter Eleven are equally important for Party banks.

---

[23] John Nagel, 'Mexico Updates NAFTA Limits On Capital From Foreign Institutions' 67:18 BNA's Banking Rep 814 (11 November 1996).

[24] *Ibid.* at 814.

[25] *Ibid.* at 816.

[26] 'Mexico Updates Capital Limits for US, Canadian Subsidiaries Under NAFTA' 71:5 BNA's Banking Rep 229 (3 August 1998).

[27] *Ibid.*

[28] The commercial possibilities for any new bank—foreign or domestic—in Mexico is great, particularly with respect to the small and medium sized business customers. 'In Mexico, virtually the entire private sector has been denied credit for over ten years … Access to credit is just as important to Mexican companies as to United States companies, particularly small and medium-sized companies'. John E. Rogers, 'The Prospects for Modernization of Financing of Mexican Business' (1994) 2 US-Mex LJ 139. To capture the profit opportunities this market holds will be to the great advantage of the Mexican economy in general as well as to the monetary advantage of the bank or banks that does/do it.

Chapter Eleven, through its incorporation in Chapter Fourteen, abolishes the Calvo Doctrine for NAFTA Party banks.[29] Potential nationalizations of NAFTA Party investors' property by the Mexican government are now protected by the due process and fair compensation provisions found in Chapter Eleven. Failing the fulfillment of such obligations, Mexico will be subject to the formal dispute settlement framework of Chapter Twenty. The investor-Party arbitration mechanism is also a step forward.

What NAFTA does not change about Mexican banking is also important for banks to consider. Even beyond the transition period, the Mexican government retains the right to require the incoming banks to establish as incorporated subsidiaries of the parent banks. Additionally, joint ventures in non-insurance financial services between nationals of the other NAFTA Parties and Mexicans may be refused by the Mexican government.[30] Thus, although licenses for wholly-owned enterprises must be approved if fulfilling the other criteria, Canadian and United States investors may be prevented from attempting to capitalize on local know-how by buying only a majority of a Mexican banking institution.

Finally, and very importantly from a trade law perspective, Mexico may limit the other Party-owned or -controlled financial service institutions from branching outside the Mexican market. Thus, the benefits of the North American Free Trade Agreement may not be allowed to be extended through Mexico's other bilateral or multilateral arrangements.

4.2.1.1   The Concerns About 'Country Risk'

A separate consideration when examining the effects of the NAFTA on banks going to Mexico is the country-risk factor. Prior to the NAFTA, many foreign investors would not have chosen to enter the Mexican banking market even if they were allowed to do so. The political (as well as economic) situation was simply too unstable to make investment in financial services industries attractive. The NAFTA effort was, in part, an attempt by Mexico to win credibility with investors as a stable financial market. Indeed, to some extent, the Agreement with two developed economies does lessen the risks of investing in Mexico, as government financial policies are more likely to be influenced by the demands of the country's northern neighbors. As a US or Canadian bank, therefore, the Mexican market becomes more interesting.

---

[29] For an explanation of the Calvo Doctrine, see 3.15.2 *supra*.

[30] Insurance companies are an exception to this reservation. Mexico agreed to allow joint venture projects between Canadian and United States investors and Mexican insurance companies. Such foreign participation was particularly necessary in the insurance sector, as it was particularly underdeveloped in comparison to the world insurance market. Hufbauer and Schott, writing in 1992, had already encouraged this sort of liberalization. See Gary C. Hufbauer and Jeffrey Schott, *North American Free Trade: Issues and Recommendations* (Institute for International Economics, Washington, DC, 1992), p. 325 ('In the insurance sector, easily the weakest of the three major Mexican financial sectors, the need for foreign capital and expertise is greater. The resources and technical skills of foreign companies far exceed the levels of the Mexican industry. The solution is association on a large scale between Mexican and foreign firms').

However, as the peso crisis of 1995 forcefully demonstrated, the NAFTA does not eliminate investment risks. Political instability remains a powerful, if somewhat suppressed, threat to Mexico's financial markets, and the sheer newness of the competitive system there should make more cautious bankers think twice before entering again with large investments. In the first three years of the NAFTA, United States banks were more reserved than might have been expected about entering the Mexican markets. Canadian banks were more active, but only one has established a full service institution in Mexico.[31]

4.3 BANKS GOING TO THE UNITED STATES

Besides the implementation of the formal dispute procedures under NAFTA Chapter Twenty and the investor-Party arbitration possibilities of Chapter Eleven, Canadian and Mexican banks wanting to establish and operate in the United States face few differences in the legal landscape due to the ratification of NAFTA by the US Congress. Establishment of a foreign-owned bank is still open to any applicant that fulfills the criteria of adequately experienced leadership and community need, and the operational activities of incorporated subsidiaries are subject to the same rules as are those of a US-citizen controlled bank.[32] Thus, NAFTA did not lessen the traditional legal openness of the United States banking market.

Neither, however, did NAFTA further *open* the United States' financial market for the NAFTA Party banks. Those regulations for national banks that were discriminatory previous to NAFTA remain in place: full inter-State branching remains the exception, and the law separating commercial banking from securities and insurance activities is still in force, despite Canadian and Mexican pressure to remove these barriers. Non-affiliated and non-foreign owned national banks' directors must still be US citizens, and if affiliated with or owned by a foreign bank, more than one-half of a bank's board of directors must be US citizens, two-thirds of whom must reside in the State in which the bank is established or within 100 miles of the bank. Many State regulations also provide for residency requirements, at a minimum during the time in office, and sometimes for a period of time prior to becoming a director. The 'Primary Dealers Act of 1988' requires reciprocity for a bank to be designated a 'primary dealer' whether that other bank is a Party bank or a non-NAFTA Party bank, and a broker dealer with its principle place of business in Canada may maintain required residency in a bank in Canada, under Canadian supervision. Other broker dealers, including those from

---

[31] The Bank of Nova Scotia is perhaps the most active Canadian bank in Latin America as a whole, possibly looking to gain a sphere of expertise in the southern countries of the Americas (as well as in Asia). 'Canadian Finance: Freedom Fighters', *The Economist*, 19 July 1997, pp. 72–3.

[32] As set out earlier, the US banking environment has traditionally been very open to foreign banks. See Chapter 3 *supra*.

Mexico, must maintain reserves in the United States. Finally, it remains the law that NAFTA Party banks, like all other foreign banks, must register as investment advisers if they want to provide securities advisory services in the United States. On the State level, discriminatory banking laws are maintained as exceptions in the annexes.[33]

In addition, the United States' acceptance of cross-border banking activities remains subject to the Article 1410:1 exception based on prudential, or 'safety and soundness', concerns.[34] Under its interpretation of this provision, the US Federal Reserve requires proof of 'effective consolidated supervision' before it will allow a bank to provide cross-border services. The result of this interpretation is, for Mexican banks in particular, a dramatic reduction in the actual NAFTA liberalizations in the cross-border supply of services.

Yet amidst this sea of constancy, there are two major positive changes that NAFTA brought Mexican and Canadian banks in the United States that should not be overlooked. The first is the important provision in NAFTA that the United States must ensure that its NAFTA partners' banks receive all the benefits of future changes in the regulatory landscape. This goes beyond the most-favored-nation obligation that Canadian and Mexican banks newly receive under the NAFTA. With the bank regulations in the United States undergoing such serious, fundamental re-thinking, the potential benefits of this promise grow daily. Ever more liberal decisions by the Federal Reserve Board toward bank expansion and bank engagement in the areas of the securities and insurance sectors are just the most obvious of the areas of US banking law that are likely to change in the not-too-distant future.[35]

The second significant legal change is NAFTA's application to sub-national governments and self-regulatory organizations. How much the inclusion of these additional decision-making layers with result in actual benefits to the other NAFTA Parties remains to be seen—particularly in light of the fact that the incompatible rules of several important international banking States of the United States are exempted from the Agreement. Yet, it is important to have the recognition of the States and banking organizations contained within the treaty. Such recognition, even though it carries with it limiting obligations, also gives the named entities a stake in the implementation of Chapter Fourteen and in the interpretation of its terms. Thus, the 'language' of Chapter Fourteen has a broader base from which to develop.

---

[33] The Executive's Statement of Administrative Action that accompanied the NAFTA implementing legislation gives perhaps the most apt description of the effect of the NAFTA on US laws. Under the heading 'Action Required or Appropriate to Implement NAFTA', the following stands alone: 'Chapter Fourteen does not require any legislative change'. The North American Free Trade Agreement Implementation Act, US Statement of Administrative Action, B:1.

[34] See discussion of Art. 1410, 3.17 *supra*.

[35] When the NAFTA was negotiated, the GATS provisions on financial services were not in effect, and indeed until 1997, the United States had a reservation to its MFN commitments on New Financial Services. See 6.1.4 *infra*.

4.4 THE EFFECTS OF CHAPTER FOURTEEN ON PARTY BANKS

In the financial services industries, the changes that have occurred due to NAFTA in first five years of implementation are more subtle than are the changes in the goods sectors.[36] Subtlety, however, does not necessarily indicate insignificance. The NAFTA Parties' banking markets have certainly become more contestable—whether there has been an accompanying increase in other-Party banking activity in those markets or not.

Statistics on banking entities in each country do not give a complete picture of the improved openness of the markets. Given the minor changes in number of institutions (which themselves cannot necessarily be attributed to the NAFTA alone), one is prone to dismiss the NAFTA Chapter Fourteen as unimportant. Certainly, the relatively minor effects of the Chapter one-third of the way into liberalization indicates that financial liberalization is not going to succeed to either catapult an otherwise dormant economy into success or to decimate an entire economic sector of a nation. Yet, an assessment that NAFTA Chapter Fourteen has not affected and will not affect the Parties' banking industries would be incorrect.

First, many of the changes contained in Chapter Fourteen are not yet effective. Two authors have noted that short-run changes contained in a formal agreement are likely to be minor in comparison to the long-run changes because the actions implemented first are likely to be the less controversial ones.[37] What is described in the setting of private international commercial transactions is just as true in public international law treaties. In the case of NAFTA, the major openings are scheduled to be implemented over the span of up to 15 years. Combined with the relatively liberal treatment given by the US and Canada to each other already under CUSFTA, the majority of the NAFTA-mandated alterations of the North American banking systems are indeed only slight variations of the former *status quo*, and the noticeable immediate results of such adjustments are therefore equally slight.[38]

---

[36] See discussion of general changes due to NAFTA, *supra*.

[37] Ralph Folsom and Michael Gordon, *International Business Transactions*, Vol. 1 (West Publishing, St Paul, MN, 1995), p. 577.

[38] Even in the much more thoroughly integrated economies of the European Union, and despite the liberalizations in the provision of banking services there, integration of the banking market are far from complete. Florus Wijsenbeek, a European Parliament deputy from the Netherlands, commented:

> Possibly in response to the advent of monetary union, there has been a wave of mergers of financial institutions. Nevertheless, the banking sector ... is still a highly fragmented market.
> Even the largest European banks ... do not account for more than one or two per cent of the total volume of banking services at Union level.

Arthur Rogers, 'EU Parliamentarians Weigh Changes to Allow Freer Cross-Border Banking Activity' 70:20 BNA's Banking Rep 826 (18 May 1998).

Secondly, many of the areas of NAFTA's regulation of financial services are 'invisible'—that is, the provisions will make banking more efficient (and perhaps more secure), but will not necessarily have much of an impact on the number of banks that are active in the marketplace. Here, the concept to keep in mind is that of market contestability. Contestability refers to a market's openness to new entrants, embodying a qualitative rather than a merely quantitative dimension to openness.[39] Contestability is thus a more satisfactory measure of the benefits of international integration than is the idea of 'free trade'.[40] What the NAFTA Chapter Fourteen can be seen to have done is to have enhanced the contestability of the Parties' banking systems: it has made them more open to potential entrants[41] by reducing some large, but many more small, barriers to trade. It is the removal of a plethora of smaller barriers that are mistakenly overlooked because they will not always be enough to cause detectable changes in the market structure.[42] Chapter Fourteen's rules on transparency or data processing, for example, are certainly improvements on the markets' contestability, but will not inevitably attract more entries or even necessarily more investment (although it probably will).

Yet, the changes that are not reflected in trade figures may be even more important indicators of the success of the NAFTA at fostering long-term trade flows between the Parties than are the changes in number of banks being established throughout the Party territories. At the same time, particularly in the area of financial services, external conditions exert tremendous influence on the way firms behave. That the peso crisis of 1995 had the result that interested Canadian and US banks decided against establishing operations in Mexico is not provable, but is reasonably surmisable.

Thirdly, it ought also to be remembered that many of the changes arising from the NAFTA (Chapter Fourteen and the whole of the Agreement) lie more in attitudes than in statistics. The NAFTA is the first free trade arrangement to treat a developing country on a nearly equal basis as the developed country partners. The idea for an Enterprise of the Americas is

---

[39] The following discussion of contestability is based on the work of Edward M. Graham and Robert Z. Lawrence, 'Measuring the International Contestability of Markets' (1996) 30:5 J World Trade 5. Further insight was gleaned from Edward M. Graham, 'The (Not Wholly Satisfactory) State of the Theory of Foreign Direct Investment and the Multinational Enterprise', in Jerome L. Stein (ed.), *The Globalization of Markets: Capital Flows, Exchange Rates and Trade Regimes* (Physica-Verlag, Heidelberg, 1997), pp. 99–122.

[40] Graham and Lawrence (note 39 *supra*), at 5.

[41] Graham and Lawrence (note 39 supra), at 7, remind the reader that 'operationalizing and measuring contestability is not easy, precisely because it reflects potential rather than actual entry'.

[42] For two studies on what factors small- to medium-sized firms take into account when investing in another country see Andrew Solocha and Mark D. Soskin, 'Canadian Direct Investment, Mode of Entry, and Border Location' (1994) 34:1 Mgmt Int'l Rev 79; Andrew Solocha, Mark D. Soskin and Mark J. Kasoff, 'Determinants of Foreign Direct Investment: A Case of Canadian Direct Investment in the United States' (1990) 30:4 Mgmt Int'l Rev 371. Both studies find that technology existing in the foreign market and domestic market concentration played large roles in the movement or non-movement of smaller- to mid-sized Canadian firms to the northern areas of the United States.

thus supported by positive experiences.[43] Mexico too is benefiting by its willingness to negotiate with developed countries without asking for highly preferential treatment. On 13 May 1996, the European Union made public its willingness to negotiate with Mexico on an Agreement of Economic Association and Political Coordination and German Chancellor Helmut Kohl's visit to Mexican President Zedillo indicates that the Mexican-European relationship is progressing. Canada, under the leadership of Prime Minister Chretien has also assumed attractiveness for foreign business investment that it did not enjoy before.[44]

Finally, the indirect results of the NAFTA will have a significant positive effect on NAFTA banks moving within the NAFTA territory.[45] One example of such changes is the greater awareness of how to trade with, or do business in, the other NAFTA parties. With the Agreement and its tariff reductions and rules of origin came NAFTA information desks, official NAFTA question-takers in the customs offices, and increased press coverage on the opportunities and pitfalls of trading across the border. These governmental 'Know Your NAFTA' programs are complemented by private initiatives in making the residents of one Party familiar with the ways of life of the other Party.

The NAFTA's high profile in all Parties has left in its wake not only domestic anger, but also—for the long run much more important—a desire for better regional understanding. The business communities of Canada and the United States in particular, are gaining an awareness of the legal environment and business culture of their Mexican neighbors to an extent never before realized. By reducing perceived risks and transaction costs, it is such awareness that may be the most significant outcome of the NAFTA as a whole.

The NAFTA banks going to other Parties are profiting by such informal results. On their own initiative or spurred by clients interested in moving to take advantage of new regional liberalizations, banks from each Party are forming relationships with banks in other Parties to ease NAFTA transactions, and are simultaneously undergoing a more or less perceptible metamorphosis from being 'Canadian-', 'Mexican-', and 'US-banker', into being 'North American bankers'.[46] Legal issues surrounding the daily aspects of banking are being discussed at the level of individual groups of bank professionals and banking attorneys as well as among academics. While the NAFTA framework limits itself to the larger legal problems of

---

[43] The Enterprise for the Americas Initiative is discussed more fully in Chapter 8 *infra*. See 8.2 *infra*.

[44] Wonnacott asserts that the greatest benefit of the NAFTA is the improved ability to compete with the United States producers in the United States market. Ronald J. Wonnacott, 'Canada's Role in NAFTA: To What Degree Has It Been Defensive?', in Bulmer-Thomas *et al.* (note 3 *supra*), at 167.

[45] This concept is discussed in terms of its negative effects on non-Party banks in Chapter 7 *infra*.

[46] See Steven Miller, 'Citibank has jump on competition', *NAFTA Watch*, reporting the comments of Murray Resini, international lawyer in Maryland, 'The most important aspect of banking that entrepreneurs need to know to start doing business in Mexico is the relationship between their US bank and a Mexican bank'.

market access and operational equality, many conferences, symposia, exchanges, and discussion groups have been formed to identify potential difficulties in cross-border banking activities and to consider how daily transactions can be facilitated—whether through harmonized business practices or merely through explanations as to how the rules of one Party operate in comparison with similar rules in the other Parties.

The dialogues and common search for information that are the offspring of NAFTA will certainly have major impacts on how banking is done in North America in the future. As the regional markets develop, the interactions will continue to respond in an increasingly 'North American' way.[47] Laws and practices are likely to become more similar and, more importantly, even where the rules themselves vary, they will be better understood by the other Parties who are involved in the genesis of the new legal sphere of the Chapter Fourteen market.[48] The comments of one Mexican lawyer encapsulates the breadth of the NAFTA changes among the Parties: 'I believe that NAFTA will generate a tremendous amount of energy between Canada, the United States, and Mexico in all respects, which will create a different environment in doing business, in conducting law practice, and in settling disputes'.[49]

---

[47] A more thorough discussion of this view is contained in Chapter 9 *infra*.

[48] See Carlos Angulo Parra, 'Comments on the Potential Influence of NAFTA on Procedures for the Settlement of Disputes' (1993) 1 US-Mex LJ 29, 29–30, explaining how the Mexican judicial system traditionally has focused more on the procedural norms in bringing a case to trial than on the legal substance of the dispute and projecting that the NAFTA dispute settlement process might change this, bringing Mexican judicial procedures in line with those of Canada and the United States, and pointing to the NAFTA's emphasis on arbitration as a possible catalyst for the wider use of arbitration in Mexico's domestic commercial environment).

[49] *Ibid*. at 29.

Part III
Chapter Fourteen and Non-Parties—Effects on the International Trade System

5. Effect of Chapter Fourteen on Third Country Banks

Sir:

I wish you well on your studies, however, I cannot imagine anything less relevant to financial services (or anything else) than the NAFTA agreement. NAFTA esta muerto, as we say in Mexican; it is without effect. To the extent that NAFTA has made some people invest in Mexico when they might otherwise have avoided such risks, then one may conclude that some effect did occur.

NAFTA is not law; it is an act of political wishful thinking between two nations; one pretends to abide by the rule of law, the other does not even try to pretend.

Saludos[1]

5.1 INTRODUCTION

As a regional agreement, at its most basic level the NAFTA does not have direct effects on third parties. The Parties themselves, in forming a free trade area rather than a customs union, did not aim to harm third countries' terms of trade.[2] However, as numerous articles by trade economists and lawyers point out, preferential agreements have an inherent potential

---

[1] R.C. Whalen, Legal Research International Inc (e-mail to author from 23 July 1996).

[2] While both a free trade area and a customs union eliminate trade restrictions among party states, free trade areas differ from customs unions in the formers' maintenance of separate external trade policies. A customs union has unified customs and trade regulations for non-party states, while the free trade area members each keep control over their own trade policies with respect to non-area states. See the definitions given in GATT Art. XXIV:8(a) (custom's union) and Art. XXIV:8(b) (free-trade area). In the context of the Canada-United States Free Trade Agreement, one Canadian commentator set out the Parties' adherence to the value of maintaining good multilateral relations through the development of a free trade area as opposed to a custom's union. The value is equally valid for the NAFTA:

> The crucial difference between a free trade area and a customs union is that in a free trade area each member maintains control over commercial policy for, and trade negotiations with, third countries. Canada (and also the United States) recognizes that the members of a free trade area have a continuing interest in the international trade rules which provide the framework for managing trade relations and trade disputes. Each member continues to have separate trade relations with third countries, and important elements of the multilateral rules continue to govern bilateral trade.

either to create or to divert trade.[3] While a rigorous analysis of trade creation or diversion[4] requires large amounts of quantitative data and long-term projections (for which a non-economist is not qualified to make), generally it is safe to assume that any agreement covering an entire sector would do a bit of both.[5] Quantitative results, moreover, cannot reveal all

---

(Contd.)

Murray G. Smith, 'Trade Policies in Canada', in Jorge Witker (ed.), *Legal Aspects of the Trilateral Free Trade Agreement* (Universidad Nacional Autónoma de México, Mexico City, 1992), pp. 29–30.

[3] See, e.g., 'Multilateral and Regional Efforts to Integrate Markets: The Uruguay Round, NAFTA, Asia Pacific Economic Cooperation Initiatives and the European Communities', in Proceedings of the 87th Annual Meeting, (1993) Am Soc'y Int'l L 340–356. (Mark David Davis, Reporter); Frederick M. Abbott, 'Regional Integration Mechanisms in the Law of the United States: Starting Over' (1993) 1 Global Legal Stud J 155; Chris Alan Johnson, 'Protectionism Toward Transplants and Obligations Under GATT, FCN Treaty and OECD Instruments: Trojan Horse or Engine for Growth?' (1994) 4:1 Transnat'l L & Contemp Probs 279 (Symposium: Regional Economic Integration in the Global Marketplace); Phedon Nicolaides, 'Trade Policy in the 1990s II: Avoiding the Trap of Regionalism' 46:5 *The World Today* 85 (May 1990); Richard H. Steinberg, 'Antidotes to Regionalism: Responses to Trade Diversion Effects of the North American Free Trade Agreement' (1993) 29:2 Stanford J Int'l L 315; Kevin A. Wechter, 'NAFTA: A Complement to GATT or a Setback to Global Free Trade?' (1993) 66:6 So Cal L Rev 2611.

[4] The terms 'trade creation' and 'trade diversion' were popularized in the trade community through Jacob Viner's work, *The Customs Union Issue* (1950). The two terms are meant to describe the quantitative effects a free trade area has on the member countries' production and consumption patterns in relation to the non-members' production and sales in the area. Trade creation occurs if the lowered barriers to trade spur greater demand for a lower-priced foreign product that had previously been artificially too expensive due to tariffs. Trade diversion is the result of demand for an integration partner's products becoming relatively cheaper than a non-partner's like product as a result of preferential (rather than general) tariff reductions.

There is, however a third possible scenario that has been set forth by trade economist Robert C. Hine. Hine suggests that if a free trade area creates new demand for a product, by improving the economic well-being of the inhabitants the overall demand after the integration may be so great as to offset the potential negative effects of trade diversion even for non-partners. See Robert C. Hine, 'International Economic Integration', in David Greenaway and Alan L. Winters (eds), *Surveys in International Trade* (Blackwell, Oxford, 1994), p. 237, discussed in Brigitte Guggisberg, *Das Protektionspotential der EG und die Effekte auf Drittstaaten* (Verlag Rüegger, Chur, 1997), p. 16.

[5] Indeed, the NAFTA has both created and diverted trade in numerous sectors of the North American economy, even acknowledging the many political and economic factors independent of a trade agreement that affect a nation's trade statistics. Automotive parts trade between the NAFTA Parties has been enhanced while trade in textiles from the Caribbean Basin states has declined, for example. See US Department of Commerce, *Second Annual Report to Congress: Impact of the North American Free Trade Agreement on US Automotive Exports to Mexico* July 1996: 'NAFTA benefitted all segments of the US automotive industry in 1994, with US exports of automotive products to Mexico increasing by $850 million over pre-NAFTA levels … the US automotive market was healthy in 1995, with demand dropping only slightly from strong 1994 sales …'. See also *ibid.*, reporting that United States imports of passenger vehicles from Mexico rose by 70 per cent during 1995–96; Alejandro Ferraté, 'Foreign Direct Investment in Costa Rica After the "Death" of CBI' (1996) 2:2 J Int'l Leg Stud 119, attributing the decline in interest in the Caribbean and Central American countries' textile industries by foreign investors to the NAFTA and the Multi-Fiber Agreement; United States International Trade Commission, 'Potential Effects of a North American Free Trade Agreement on Apparel Investments in CBERA Countries', USITC Pub. 2541, Inv. No. 332-321 (1992).

the changes brought about by integration. Some of the results of a trade agreement stem from the informal exchanges that arise during and after the negotiating process and from the fact of having an agreement.[6]

The economic models created prior to the implementation of the NAFTA revealed expectations of very little trade diversion and similarly modest trade creation in all but a few manufacturing and agricultural sectors.[7] These quantitative results are in congruence with the results that would be expected on a basic theoretical level. Trade economists generally believe that the more trade barriers that existed between any given free trade area's members prior to the formation of such an area, the more trade diversion will occur from the rest of the world ('ROW'). The opposite is presumed true as well, making the results of the NAFTA's ROW economic analyses in large part consistent with each other.

Based on the very low (mainly zero) tariffs imposed between Canada and the United States under the Canada-United States Free Trade Area regime and the nearly as low tariffs imposed by Canada and the United States on Mexican products under the Generalized System of Preferences (GSP) programs, analysts tend to discount the possibility of either significant trade creation or trade diversion stemming from NAFTA. Well-known economist Jeffrey Schott sums up the current thinking with an understandable example:

> Concern that NAFTA will lead to a substantial diversion of trade has been relatively muted, for two reasons. First, existing barriers to the US market (which accounts for about 85 per cent of the North American region) are quite low. Indeed, under the Canadian-US agreement, some firms have ignored the CUSFTA preferences, because the paperwork to qualify for the reduced tariffs was more expensive than paying the minimum duty![8]

---

[6] These aspects are addressed at the end of this chapter.

[7] See generally, Mattias Busse, 'NAFTA's Impact on the European Union' (1996) 51:3 *Aussenwirtschaft* 363, examining effects of NAFTA on manufactured goods only; Richard H. Steinberg (note 3 *supra*), at 315, explaining how seven manufacturing sectors in Asia may be affected by the NAFTA; Drusilla K. Brown, 'The Impact of a North American Free Trade Area: Applied General Equilibrium Models', in Nora Lustig, Barry P. Bosworth and Robert Z. Lawrence (eds), *North American Free Trade: Assessing the Impact* (Brookings Institution, Washington, DC, 1992), pp. 26–57; Sidney Weintraub, 'Modeling the Industrial Effects of NAFTA', in Lustig *et al.* (*supra*), pp. 109–32.

[8] Jeffrey J. Schott, 'Comment', in Lustig *et al.* (note 7 *supra*), pp. 238–41, at 238. See also Gary Clyde Hufbauer and Jeffrey J. Schott, 'Is NAFTA Trade Diverting?', in Lustig *et al.* (eds), North American Free Trade: Issues and Recommendations (Institute for International Economics, Washington, DC, 1992). pp. 113–14, at 114 ('… the scope for trade diversion is limited because of the relatively unfettered access that Mexico already enjoys in the US market'). Note that most of the economic studies done on the effects of NAFTA on world trade use models developed for studying trade in the goods sectors. See, e.g., Brown (note 7 *supra*), at 56–7 ('… the differentiated product-CRS models show small welfare gains of less than 1 per cent GNP, though the welfare effects are positive for the participating countries'); Tim Josling, 'NAFTA and Agriculture: A Review of the Economic Impacts', in Lustig *et al.* (note 7 *supra*), pp. 144–68, at 168, concluding his review of the main models for NAFTA's effect on agriculture by stating that '[t]he overall picture then is one of rather modest developments … stemming directly from a NAFTA and some quite dramatic changes in Mexico (to the benefit of US exporters) if Mexico continues to liberalize its internal markets for agricultural products'; Dean Alexander, 'The Likely Impact of NAFTA on Investment in Selected Goods and Services Sectors in Mexico, Canada, and the US', in

Carlos Primo Braga, a trade expert from the World Bank, noted that the beliefs that NAFTA will be either world trade neutral or perhaps even world trade positive, may be the reason the rest of the world has paid so little attention to NAFTA's formation.[9] Braga warns, however, that this inattention may be too optimistic. Elaborate rules of origin such as those for textiles[10] and safeguard mechanisms that leave room for administrative discretion are just two areas of trade in goods that hold the potential for less-than-benign NAFTA effects.[11] He writes:

> ... the focus on static trade diversion generated by preferential tariff cuts that characterizes most of the analyses of NAFTA's implications for non-member countries seems to be missing important dimensions of the problem ... Accordingly, the apparent lack of concern with NAFTA's potential for discrimination could alternatively be interpreted as a sign that the rest of the world has not yet fully grasped (or that it has preferred to overlook) the real contours of NAFTA.[12]

The area on which NAFTA's externalities are most likely to be felt economically by the rest of the world is not in the goods arena, but in the diversion of investment. Global trade in capital has been expanding at nearly twice the rate that trade in goods has, and an estimate by McKinsey & Co sets the

---

(Contd.)

Seymour J. Rubin and Dean Alexander (eds), *NAFTA and Investment* (Kluwer, Boston, 1995), pp. 207–17, containing very summary statements of predicted effects of NAFTA, including 'NAFTA's short-term impact on Mexico's automobile and auto parts sector is expected to be both minor and positive' (at 152). One expert's statement suggests why industrial goods have been the focus of most NAFTA effect analyses:

> Customs union theory was developed primarily by examining merchandise trade. Trade creation-trade diversion, the Viner concept to assess the welfare effect of a customs union, the potential for economies of scale, and, more recently, the literature on learning by doing deal essentially with manufacturing.

Sidney Weintraub (note 7 *supra*), pp. 109–32, at 109.

[9] Carlos Alberto Primo Braga, 'NAFTA and the Rest of the World', in Lustig *et al.* (note 7 *supra*), pp. 210–34, at 211–12.

[10] See NAFTA Annex 300-B and Appendix 1.1 (Textiles and Apparel Goods rules under NAFTA).

[11] But see Jeffrey J. Schott (note 8 *supra*), at 239, commenting that discriminatory rules of origin could pose more problems to third countries' exports of particular products and '(t)his problem should be the focus of much more attention than the concern raised by Primo Braga'. A potential for discrimination against outsiders exists even in the interpretation of facially non-discriminatory, but ambiguous provisions of a trade agreement. Under the Vienna Convention on the Law of Treaties, interpretation is to be made in light of the objectives of the treaty. However, third party interests are virtually never included in a treaty's objectives. Discrimination in interpretation of a regional agreement may therefore occur in a way completely compatible with international law. This becomes a particular problem when the treaty provisions combine two different areas of law into a new area. The new area's language, as determined by the treaty, then begins to develop within this closed system, preventing non-members from giving input. See *infra* (discussion of Chapter Fourteen as a new system with its own language).

[12] Braga (note 9 *supra*), at 212–13, suggesting that if NAFTA becomes an exercise in managed trade, the discriminatory effects against non-Parties might be significant.

amount of the projected global financial market of the year 2000 at $83 trillion.[13] Thus, the more careful NAFTA researchers have not ignored the potential for diversion of capital. Indeed, the possibility that investors would tend to move away from Canada and to the United States was one of the motivating forces in Ottawa's desire to join the trade area negotiations between Mexico and the United States.[14] Similarly, the potential movement of investment capital to Mexico and away from the Pacific Basin caused the newly industrializing Asian countries to voice concern over North America's 'sneaky protectionism' subsequent to NAFTA's official notification.[15]

Closely connected to movement in investment is trade in financial services. The transfer of funds, necessary for setting up a business and engaging in international transactions, as well as repatriation of profits or income across national borders requires the interaction of banks, non-bank financial institutions, insurance corporations, and security brokerages on either side of the border, if not around the world. By following their globalizing corporate customers with the establishment of subsidiaries or branches, financial institutions facilitate multinational commercial activities by minimizing transaction costs in making foreign direct investments.

Until the 1990s, however, financial service institutions were often strictly limited in the services they could provide in a foreign country. Combined with export controls on currencies, the limits on foreign financial service offerings posed high cost barriers to further investment. This was particularly so in many of the less developed countries around the world. In many of these states (including Mexico), US corporations were forced to create elaborate payment systems and invest in expensive local legal advice to secure their ability to repatriate the profits from their commercial activities in those territories.

At the same time, the US financial services industry was facing difficulties at home and saw potential profits abroad if the foreign markets could be opened.[16] The US negotiators of the NAFTA were therefore adamant to include banking service liberalization as an accompaniment to the investment liberalization chapter of the treaty.

---

[13] Jessica T. Mathews, 'Power Shift' (1997) 76:1 Foreign Aff 50, 57.

[14] See 1.3.3 *supra*.

[15] Braga (note 9 *supra*), at 212 (the Asian countries 'are the only major economic partners of NAFTA countries, outside the Western Hemisphere, that seem to be more directly concerned with the possibilities of trade and investment diversion'). With Mexico's credibility as a safe growth area enhanced through NAFTA membership combined with the free movement of goods from Mexico to the United States market, investors would, all other factors being equal, be more likely to invest in Mexico than they were prior to NAFTA.

[16] In 1990, financial services contributed a 16.2 per cent share of the national income, 6.0 per cent of the nationwide employment and exported a total of $6.7 billion. In 1993 and 1995, these figures were 17.2 and 17.1 per cent of the national income, 5.9 and 5.8 per cent employment, and $6.0 and $7.5 in exports, respectively. WTO, *Trade Policy Review: United States 1996*, WT/TPR/S/16 (1996), p. 8, citing US Department of Commerce, Survey of Current Business, various issues). Securities and commodities brokers had a real value growth of 50 per cent during 1992–94. WTO (*supra*), p. 7.

Despite the North American banks' sharp attention to the structuring of the NAFTA financial services provisions,[17] outside of North America economic and legal experts have not shown much interest in these provisions. There are a few preliminary studies on the topic,[18] but in the specific area of banking services, if the number of analyses made is any indication, the effects of NAFTA on third country financial providers are likely to be even less dramatic than those in the case of goods. This leads one to wonder whether this nonchalance is warranted.

There are clear positive effects that are likely to be felt. First, the increased economic activity that has been the result of the NAFTA's liberalization in the trade in goods and non-financial services will almost certainly have a positive impact on all banks that are occupied with corporate loans and trade financing in these countries.[19] Such increases should occur whether the bank is controlled by foreign or by NAFTA-party investors. Second, the high degree of contestability that existed in the United States banking market prior to the NAFTA, combined with the non-exclusivity of the NAFTA financial service benefits for banks in the markets, will allow the openings of the Mexican banking market to be available to most internationally active commercial banks, whether controlled by US or Canadian residents or others, as long as the bank itself is established as a subsidiary.

At the same time, there are potential negative effects from the NAFTA. These could arise either as absolute disadvantages or as relative disadvantages for non-Party banks.[20] The traditional static models of integration effects for NAFTA did not always take into consideration either the pro-competitive effects of the 'negative integration' on the Parties (stemming from national treatment obligations) or the absolute disadvantages that non-Parties could face from 'positive integration' (due to harmonization of regulations). These two effects on outsiders have been considered in the

---

[17] Private participants in the Chapter Fourteen negotiations in the United States included the American Financial Services Association, the Coalition of Service Industries, and the Bankers' Association for Foreign Trade (with members Bankers Trust Co, Bank of Boston, Chase Manhattan Bank, Chemical Banking Corp, Citicorp/Citibank, Commerce Bank, Morgan Guaranty Trust Co, and NationsBank), and the Texas Bankers Association. See Hearing Before the Committee on Banking, Finance and Urban Affairs House of Representatives, 'Abuses within the Mexican Political Regulatory and Judicial Systems and Implications for the North American Free Trade Agreement (NAFTA)', Serial No. 103-93 (103d Congress, 8 November 1993) at pp. 57, 50–71.

[18] Hufbauer and Schott (note 8 *supra*), at 128–9. This, of course, does not reflect the number of studies done on financial service liberalization effects in general, or those on the NAFTA's effects within the NAFTA territories.

[19] Christine Castleberg, interview with author (March 1997). But see also Thomas Hagdahl, 'Doing Business in a Wider Europe', in Mary Robinson and Jantien Findlater (eds), *Creating a Common European Economic Space: Legal Aspects of EC-EFTA Relations* (1990), pp. 229–37, at 233 ('… less and less financial service transactions are related to trade in goods. This is a service sector which is now expanding without having any direct relationship to underlying transactions in manufacturing or other service sectors').

[20] Relative disadvantages from integration arises from 'negative integration'. Absolute disadvantages occur when integration partners take 'positive integration' measures. See Guggisberg (note 4 *supra*), at 51, 57–63.

context of European integration, but are not commented upon as often in the NAFTA framework.[21]

Negative integration causes a relative worsening in the competitive position of non-Parties through the offer of national treatment to other Parties' nationals. The relative disadvantage occurs to the extent that Parties are benefited by the treatment given to all other Party-persons. Such disadvantages are most likely to be felt by newly-expanding banks. The Canadian banking market, for instance, has more restrictive rules of entry than the United States' and thus it offers profit potential to NAFTA-Party banks that exceed the opportunities available to other foreign banks. The opening of Mexico's banking system, too, could prove to be an advantage enjoyed only by NAFTA Parties.

Positive integration refers to the harmonization of laws and regulations. Its effects are potentially more damaging to non-Parties than is negative integration because the danger is one of harming non-Parties absolutely (not just relatively). The cause of the danger lies at the political level of policy-making, where non-Parties are not represented (or not represented adequately). Thus, it is also harder to remove the cause of the disadvantages through adjudication. Finally, harmonization or standardization can occur either through formal government co-operation, through national legislative procedures in each of the Parties, through administrative rulemakings, or, significantly, through informal agreements. The latter method of standardization is not subject to a Party's international law obligations, and yet may be as important for the daily competition facing industry participants as formal laws are. Thus, it is in such informal decision-making circles that many of the effects of the NAFTA on non-Party banks may arise.

The economic effects of Chapter Fourteen are not, however, the only way that the Agreement will impact non-Party banks. The provisions of the Chapter also have legal ramifications. Depending on the particular financial service provider, the NAFTA framework may affect it either by giving rise to new legally protectable rights or by violating existing legal rights. Alternatively, the NAFTA may not alter the rights of the third country bank at all. In analyzing the legal effects of NAFTA on third country banks, and

---

[21] Fully reviewing the economic literature on trade integration areas is beyond the capacity of this author and the bounds of this book. An understandable commentary on the economic effects of European Communities' trade integration, including further references, is Guggisberg (note 4 *supra*). For the study of negative integration effects, Dr Guggisberg cites Ulrich Tigges, *Zur Aktualität nichttarifärer Handelshemmnisse im europäischen Binnenmarkt, Dargestellt am Beispiel mittelständischer Betriebe im deutsch/französischen Aussenhandel* (Nomos, Baden-Baden, 1991); Dennis Swann, 'Standards, Procurements, Mergers and State Aids', in D. Swann (ed.), *The Single European Market and Beyond: A Study of the Wider Implications of the Single European Act* (Routledge, London, 1992), pp. 53–80, at 54ff; for positive integrations Jan Tumlir, 'Strong and Weak Elements in the Concept of European Integration', in Fritz Machlup, Gerhard Fels and Hubertus Mueller-Groeling (eds), *Reflections on a Troubled World Economy: Essays in Honour of Herbert Giersch* (Macmillan, London, 1983), pp. 29–56. For a somewhat dated, but conceptually useful comparison of the positive and negative integration effects of the European Community and the CUFTA, see Edelgard Mahant, 'The Canada-United States Free Trade Agreement and the European Community: A Functionalist Comparison' (1990) 10:2 *Zeitschrift der Gesellschaft für Kanada-Studien* 113, 122–132.

making an assumption based on the existence of the Free Trade Area, the NAFTA was formed for the benefit of the Parties to the Agreement and only for the benefit of the Parties. This assumption based on the presumption that the Parties to the NAFTA are rational actors—they attempt to act efficiently and to maximize the benefits of their actions.[22] As rational actors, then, the Parties would not engage (and thereby invest resources) in negotiations with others unless they expected to achieve something in return and made commitments with this expectation.[23] Therefore, there is a certain amount of reciprocity built into every free trade agreement—reciprocity demanded by at least one of the Parties. It follows that the benefits from such an agreement must be intended to be limited to the Parties. In fact, one can assume that each substantive provision in a free trade agreement such as NAFTA exists because one or more of the Parties wanted to limit the pool of potential benefitors. This does not imply that non-Parties will necessarily be damaged by the Agreement, but in the words of one observer, '… although there are no indications that the NAFTA agreement will be used to raise protectionist walls against the rest of the world, care has been taken that the preferences derived from it are kept among the parties to the agreement and do not leak away to 'fourth' countries'.[24]

Based on this assumption, it comes as no surprise that the provisions contained in the NAFTA relating to the entrance, establishment, and operation of, banks are phrased so as to limit the benefits to NAFTA-Party financial institutions and NAFTA-Party financial service providers. Consequently, a distinction must be made between foreign banks (or bankers) operating in the territory of NAFTA Parties that are 'of a NAFTA-Party' and those that are not. This involves an investigation into the nationality rules[25] of the NAFTA Chapter Fourteen and is particularly important for banks new to the North American markets.[26]

---

[22] To use economic terms, they act in such a way as to maximize their utility and minimize their disutility in a manner so as to use a minimum of resources. See Nikolaj Petersen, 'National Strategies in the Integration Dilemma: An Adaptation Approach' (1998) 36:1 J Common Mkt Stud 33, 37 ('As rational actors, participants in regional integration must be presumed to want the benefits and avoid the drawbacks of integration'. See also Sanoussi Bilal, 'Political Economy Considerations on the Supply of Trade Protection in Regional Integration Agreements' (1998) 36:1 J Common Mkt Stud 1, explaining that the particular design of the free trade area influences the extent to which the area will be explicitly protectionist).

[23] Simply put, they could have unilaterally liberalized access to their markets had they not wanted something in return. However, instead of unilateral liberalizations, the NAFTA Parties negotiated a free trade agreement among themselves.

[24] Adriaan Ten Kate, 'Is Mexico a Back Door to the US Market or a Niche in the World's Largest Free Trade Area?', in Victor Bulmer-Thomas, Nikki Craske and Mónica Serrano (eds), *Mexico and the North American Free Trade Agreement: Who Will Benefit?* (St Martin's Press, New York, 1994), pp. 29–41, at 31. See also Petersen (note 22 *supra*), at 35, explaining that in market integration, 'the internal game dominates … completely the external game', making the process 'inward-looking'.

[25] The term 'nationality rules' is author's own. The idea corresponds to the 'rules of origin' used in the trade in goods, identifying for purposes of tariff/quota calculations the country in which the imported good is assumed to have been produced.

[26] Jun Yokoyama uses an alternative framework to analyze a similar problem. He looks at the European Community's program for liberalizing the internal insurance market in terms of

This chapter will approach the question of how Chapter Fourteen affects the legal rights of third country banks from a general level, focussing on the NAFTA's own provisions. The following chapter looks specifically at how the NAFTA provisions interact with the provisions of the World Trade Organization's rules on trade in financial services. The final chapter, reaches beyond the perspective of international trade law *per se*, and the analysis of the legal effects of Chapter Fourteen is completed with a cursory look at ramifications on the other aspects of a bank's international activities. These effects, identified as 'informal' to distinguish them from being either direct legal results of the Agreement or identifiable economic results, arise out of the process of negotiating NAFTA and from the fact of its existence.[27]

5.2   ANALYTICAL FRAMEWORK

The NAFTA provisions that determine the nationality of banks and banking service providers for purposes of the treaty are examined in the following pages. From this discussion, a third country bank will be able to determine if it is a 'NAFTA-Party bank' or a 'non-NAFTA Party bank'. The determination is of key importance, as it is only from the NAFTA itself that the benefits of Chapter Fourteen can be directly invoked.

For NAFTA-Party financial institutions and financial service providers, the effect of NAFTA will be as set out in Chapter 4 *supra*. The effect of NAFTA Chapter Fourteen for non-NAFTA Party financial institutions and service providers depends on whether the institution's (or provider's) nationality and any legal relationship that stems from such nationality. For an international trade law perspective such as that taken here, the critical line of division is based on the criterion of World Trade Organization membership. If the financial service institution or provider is a national of a non-WTO state, then the NAFTA does not affect its legal rights unless there are bilateral agreements between the state of nationality and one of the NAFTA Parties which are infringed. However, for financial service institutions and providers from states that are WTO Members, the Agreements under the WTO limit the extent to which NAFTA effects may alter the legal rights of such institutions and providers.[28]

(Contd.)

the effects this will have on Japan. To do so, Professor Yokoyama looks at the EC laws according to category—administrative law, private law, and international economic (GATS) law—and highlights the Japanese law's distinctions. Jun Yokoyama, 'The Creation of the European Insurance Market and Its Impact Upon Japan', Hitotsubashi J L & Pol 103 (Special Issue, June 1994). NAFTA's effects on China and Hong Kong are analyzed in yet another way: the terms-of-trade effects and the volume-of-trade effects. Xiaoning James Zhan, 'NAFTA's Likely Implications for China and Hong Kong' 23 *UNCTAD Bulletin* 6 (November–December 1993).

[27] See also Chapter 4, 4.4 *supra*, on how NAFTA is changing the financial services environment for NAFTA Party-banks.

[28] For readers unfamiliar with the WTO or the GATS, see Annex 2.

5.3 DETERMINING A BANK'S 'NATIONALITY': THE NAFTA RULES

The first step in determining how a bank from a third country will be affected by the NAFTA rules on trade in financial services is to establish that bank's 'nationality'. In the NAFTA context, the relevant question is whether or not the bank comes within the scope of the NAFTA definitions so as to be considered 'of' a Party to the Agreement.

Nationality rules in the NAFTA become comprehensible only by synthe-sizing the content of several Chapter Fourteen provisions. Article 1416 ('Definitions') clarifies the terms used in Chapter Fourteen as they are to be interpreted in this context: 'person of a Party'; 'financial service'; 'financial service provider of a Party'; 'financial institution'; 'financial institution of another Party'; 'investment'; 'investor of a Party'; and 'cross-border financial services provider of a Party'. As these terms are discussed in detail in Chapter 4 *infra*, the provisions only as they would affect third party banks are set out here.

To determine the nationality of a financial institution or financial service provider for purposes of NAFTA Chapter Fourteen, one must determine not only whether a particular entity is a 'financial institution' or a 'financial service provider', but also whether the institution is 'located in' a NAFTA Party territory and 'controlled' by NAFTA Party persons. Each of these will be addressed in turn.

5.3.1 Financial Institutions

The provisions of NAFTA Chapter Fourteen are intended to benefit financial institutions of another Party; investors of another Party and investments of such investors in financial institutions in the Party's terri-tory; and cross-border trade in financial services.[29] As explained earlier, 'financial institution' is defined to include '... any financial intermediary or other enterprise that is authorized to do business and regulated or super-vised as a financial institution under the law of the Party in whose territory it is located'.[30]

Under current laws of the NAFTA Parties, 'financial institution' includes 'commercial banks', 'banques', and 'instituciones de banca múltiple'.[31] To enjoy the benefits of Chapter Fourteen, a bank may operate as an in-corporated legal personality or as a partnership, a joint venture, a sole

---

[29] NAFTA Art. 1401:1.
[30] NAFTA Art. 1416 ('financial institution').
[31] NAFTA Annex VII (see various provisions). But note that national laws might put limitations on the legal form of a bank. See, e.g., Bank Act (Canada), S.C. 1991, c. 46 2 (Definition of 'foreign bank') (required that banks be incorporated entities).

proprietorship, or an 'other association', as allowed by the law of the Party under which it is licensed.[32]

Importantly, the *activities* of the bank are not limited by the NAFTA definition of 'financial institution'. Securities underwriting, insurance activities, and trusteeships are as valid as loaning funds and accepting deposits. While the national laws of each Party may prohibit banks from direct participation in certain areas of commercial activity, the NAFTA benefits themselves are not dependent on such limitations.

For third country banks, Chapter Fourteen's definition of financial institution means that if an institution qualifies as a 'bank' under a Party's national laws, the bank's investors, its investments in a NAFTA Party's territory, and its cross-border trade between Parties will be covered by Chapter Fourteen as long as the bank fulfills the other requirements set out by the Chapter.[33]

5.3.2 'Located In'

To qualify as a bank 'of another Party' under the NAFTA, the bank or a branch of the bank must be 'located in' the territory of a Party as well as be 'controlled by persons of another Party': 'financial institution of another Party means a financial institution, including a branch, located in the territory of a Party that is controlled by persons of another Party'.[34]

Using the principle of interpretation that attributes terms their ordinary usage, the phrase 'located in' found in the Article 1416 definition of 'financial institution of another party' could refer either to the physical presence of an enterprise in the NAFTA Party territory, to the legal existence of an entity in the territory, or to the activity level within the territory. The particular definition is left open to interpretation. Thus, this seemingly obvious limitation of the financial service benefits becomes one of the densest legal quagmires of Chapter Fourteen.

5.3.2.1 *Physical Presence*

A physical presence interpretation of 'located in' would focus on whether a bank has a tangible existence in one of the NAFTA Party's territories. The use of such an approach has the benefit of being clear and easy to apply in the majority of instances. Certainly a physical presence definition would encompass any bank with a building or office space used exclusively by it to conduct banking activities or by a branch it has established to conduct its commercial activities. Since the definition of 'financial institution' refers to 'any financial intermediary or other enterprise', the definition would most likely also include a bank or branch operating out of a shared space, as long as it is commercially active within the NAFTA Party territory.

---

[32] But see, GATS, United States Schedule of Specific Commitments, B. Preliminary notes to Financial Services Schedule ('… partnerships and sole proprietorships are generally not acceptable juridical forms for depository financial institutions in the United States').

[33] See discussion on 'control' and 'denial of benefits', 5.3.3 *infra*.

[34] NAFTA Art. 1416 ('financial institution of another Party').

The use of a physical presence analysis has great limitations in the modern world of financial service provisions, however. The number of banking services offered by banks that are less 'physical' than the traditional brick-and-mortar banking institution is increasing. The reliance on physical presence for a definition in the NAFTA is therefore less than satisfying for determining the location of a bank.[35]

5.3.2.2   Regulatory Existence

A further possible test for determining location could be based on a Party's regulation of a financial service institution. Regulatory existence is my term for an expanded view of legal existence. Thus, as with the criteria of legal existence, under a regulatory existence view, financial institutions can be considered 'located in' the territory in which they are incorporated or established as a partnership or a joint venture, to identify just a few possibilities. Regulatory existence would, however, go further. Even branches of a financial institution should fulfill the 'location in' qualifications of this rule by virtue of being registered with and supervised by national banking authorities.[36] The official acknowledgement of commercial viability under a strong regulatory system could be sufficient to show that the actual legal form of an entity is less important than the fact of doing business within a territory under a particular regulatory system.

One argument against the use of regulatory existence as a benchmark of 'location in' of a bank, is that the definition of 'financial institution' already requires that the financial intermediary be 'authorized to do business' and be 'regulated or supervised' as a financial institution in the Party in which it is located.[37] As this definition is incorporated into that for a 'financial institution of another Party', a regulatory existence in a Party territory is already required for an institution to benefit under Chapter Fourteen,[38] and a similar test for location in would be redundant.

5.3.2.3   Commercial Existence/Activity Level

Finally, a Party could look to a bank's activity level, or its 'commercial existence'. A commercial existence or activity level definition for 'located in' would look to the extent of a bank's financial transactions within a NAFTA Party territory. A Party could define a threshold value of transactions that must take place in its territory per unit of time, and any bank that achieved the level prescribed would be deemed 'located in' the Party.

---

[35] The problems of Automated Teller Machines and Internet banking sites are discussed at 5.3.2.4 *infra*.

[36] In the United States, foreign bank branches have been described as a 'hybrids'. Edward L. Symons Jr and James J. White, *Banking Law: Teaching Materials* (3rd edn, West Publishing, St Paul, MN, 1991), p. 781. Because the branches are owned by a foreign-licensed legal entity, but are simultaneously required to comply with reporting requirements and undergo individual examinations by US banking authorities, these branches could legitimately be classified as either independent or dependent.

[37] NAFTA Art. 1416 ('financial institution').

[38] NAFTA Article 1416 ('financial institution of another Party').

The use of activity level to determine a bank's 'location in' a Party's terri-tory has the advantage of avoiding problems encountered with new tech-nologies as well as complications posed by theoretical arguments over the importance of legal existence. While the use of activity level is complicated by the modern reality of internet banking, as such transactions are difficult to supervise, if it were in the bank's own interest to record electronic trans-actions, one could expect that the costs of recording the activity from a par-ticular geographic area would be borne by the institution itself.

Activity level is, moreover, already used by all three of the present NAFTA Parties in determining what is a foreign bank: representative offices of banks are not included in statistics on the number of 'foreign banks' in any of the NAFTA Parties mainly because these offices may not actively engage in banking.[39] If such offices were to satisfy the condition of 'location' for the Article 1416 definition, the interpretation of 'location' would have to be based on an out-dated, purely physical characteristic. At the same time, offshore branches of NAFTA Party banks would be granted the benefits of the treatment, at least to the extent of their activities with persons from the NAFTA Party territories.[40]

Activity level may also be a more politically appealing approach to deter-mining what banks should benefit from NAFTA liberalizations, as activities within a country tend to disproportionately benefit (or harm) that country. Similar to the reasoning used to justify claims of jurisdiction in the United States' legal systems,[41] activity level also has a firm basis for application in financial service regulation.

However, even activity level criteria are not perfect for deciding whether a bank is located in a NAFTA Party. One illustration of the problems related to activity levels in banking is trying to determine the result of a query into the location of a bank controlled by nationals of one NAFTA Party that does business from an office within that Party's territory, but whose activities are solely directed abroad: the 'Investment Edge Corporation' in the United States fits this hypothetical situation. Such a cor-poration is a bank holding company-type of entity established as a corpora-tion under federal banking law for the sole purpose of investing in equities and making loans to foreign companies. Although it is established in the United States, and is generally based within its parent bank's offices in the

---

[39] See, e.g., George Budzeika, 'Determinants of the Growth of Foreign Banking Assets in the United States', Federal Reserve Bank of New York Research Paper No. 9112 (May 1991), reviewing only foreign branches and agencies and subsidiaries of foreign banks; GAO, 'Foreign Banks: Assessing their Role in the US Banking System', GAO/GGD-96-26 (February 1996), pp. 23–38, discussing only foreign branches and agencies.

[40] The Federal Reserve Board published an article that in part describes the activities of US banks' offshore branch activities and foreign offshore banks' activities in the United States. Henry S. Terrell, 'US Branches and Agencies of Foreign Banks: A New Look', *Federal Reserve Bulletin* (October 1993), pp. 913–25. Mr Terrell explains, at 915, that offshore branches are often attractive for both the bank and the consumer (itself usually also a bank) because 'in some instances [the] deposits are not subject to reserve requirements and deposit insurance premia; avoidance of the costs of required reserves and deposit insur-ance allows the branches to offer higher interest rates on deposits'.

[41] See *infra*.

United States, an Investment Edge's business activities are not aimed at the United States. Should such an Investment Edge want to enter the Mexican or Canadian market, under a pure commercial presence test it could encounter arguments that it is not 'located in' a NAFTA Party, and is therefore ineligible for Chapter Fourteen benefits. If the intent to liberalize intra-NAFTA trade in financial services were followed, however, the Parties would not want to limit the benefits of the Agreement to this extent.

Another problem could arise from the timeframe within which a bank's activities are measured. An annual measure of commercial activity would introduce instability into the trade system by causing banks to be unsure of whether or not they will qualify for treatment as a Party bank in any given year. On the other hand, a one-time measurement could allow for the undesirable occurrence of falsely high activity for only so long as the bank was under supervision, and then a change in direction after receiving the recognition of Party-bank status. Though these disadvantages are perhaps only theoretical, they are brought up to show the problems that might be encountered by this test.

5.3.2.4   *Special Cases for 'Located In' Analyses*

A major difficulty with defining 'located in' for modern financial service providers (and one more likely to affect third country financial institutions than NAFTA Party banks) arises when the 'bank' is not represented by a tangible object in a territory. Nevertheless, as estimated by financial regulators in the United States, '(h)alf of all financial transactions are now handled outside of a bank',[42] making defining the limits of 'located in' increasingly important.

There are two developments in banking that make the determination of whether an entity is 'located in' a Party territory particularly difficult. These developments, however, are becoming so widespread that a developing a logical method for analyzing them is becoming unavoidable. The first development is that of the use of Automated Teller Machines for an increasing variety of transactions. The second is the offering of banking services over the Internet. Each of these will be examined in turn.

5.3.2.4.1   AUTOMATED TELLER MACHINES (ATMS)

Until now, the most obvious form of intangible banking has been the use of a bank's automated teller machine (ATM) within the territory of one Party.[43] ATMs began to be widely used in the United States in the 1980s. At

---

[42] Federal Reserve Bank of Atlanta, 'New Rules, Technical Tools Reshape Banking Industry' *Financial Update* (October–December 1995), p. 3

[43] The effect of ATM's on the way banking services are delivered is discussed in a paper prepared for the OECD Financial Experts' Meeting by an official of the Bank of Finland. See Jukka Vesala, 'Banking Industry Performance in Europe: Trends and Issues', in OECD, *The New Financial Landscape: Forces Shaping the Revolution in Banking, Risk Management and Capital Markets* (OECD, Paris, 1995), pp. 97–165, at 120–30, and Table 11 at 146. Vesala points out that the branch/ATM ratio throughout Europe suggests that there is a substitution effect encouraging the establishment of the cost-saving ATMs.

that time, banks assumed ATMs would be a substitute for branches, allowing the banks to save costs of physical infrastructure and personnel.
Although that has not been the case,[44] the use of ATMs by customers has
steadily increased, as has the number of machines in use.[45] More importantly, the ability of the machines themselves to perform banking transactions has grown tremendously. Already ATMs offer bank customers the
ability to withdraw cash, monitor accounts, cash checks, and even receive
loan papers.[46] In addition, customers often have the opportunity to purchase postage stamps, theater tickets, phone cards, and mass transit passes.
In the future, still more bank and non-bank products will be available
through ATMs.[47] This poses challenges for domestic regulators and the
international trade in financial services system as a whole.

From the perspective of international trade in financial services, the question of the relationship of an ATM to a bank is important. If ATMs are to be
viewed as branches, an ATM of a non-NAFTA Party bank could be considered physically present in a NAFTA Party (and thus 'located in' the territory of a Party under such a test) or it could be considered physically
present only where the parent bank is established (if a pure 'legal presence'
test were used).[48]

---

[44] Russell Redman, 'Sweetening the Appeal of ATMS', *Bank Systems + Technology* (November
1997) (text found on the internet at >www.financetech.com<). BankBoston executive vice
president explained the mistake bankers made when estimating the cost savings of ATMs:

> What consumers are saying is, 'This is great!' Instead of going to a branch four times
> a month, now they'll go to the branch twice but also go to the ATM six times, call the
> phone center twice and do PC banking maybe three nights a week … We thought it
> would be a one-for-one replacement [of branch visits], but in fact it isn't. It's a
> flat-out added cost.

[45] The main ATM networks in the United States expect huge increases in ATM activity.
'Cirrus ATMs are slated to process about 25 million transactions a month [in 1997], up from
20.5 million transactions in 1996; Plus ATMs are expected to process roughly 45 million
transactions, up from 17.5 million [in 1996]'. Redman, 'Sweetening the Appeal'. However,
one report notes a drop in transaction activity over ATM networks (as opposed to the use
of ATM machines in general) in the year 1997. David Balto, 'Regulatory, Competitive, and
Anittrust Challenges of ATM Surcharges' 70:2 BNA's Banking Rep 82 (13 July 1998).
Mr Balto attributes this drop in usage to the imposition of surcharges for ATM transactions
made over a machine not belonging to the customer's bank.

> To avoid surcharges, the vast majority [of customers] almost exclusively use their
> own bank's ATMs. Not suprisingly, the trend of ATM network growth has been
> reversed. Before surcharges were permitted those networks experienced consistent
> ATM transaction growth, typically at about 5 per cent a year. Surcharging reversed
> that trend. Last year ATM transactions decreased by about 10 per cent, and some
> networks experienced a much greater loss in transaction volume.

[46] Redman (note 44 *supra*).
[47] *Ibid.* citing a study of ATMs that Ernst & Young performed in 1997; the study reveals that
27 per cent of the banks plan to sell non-bank products from their ATMs in the near
future). Much of the impetus to cross-sell products comes from the need to cover the costs
of the computers themselves.
[48] The European Commission is also struggling with the question of whether an ATM is an
'establishment' of a bank. See Arthur Rogers, 'EU Parliamentarians Weigh Changes to
Allow Freer Cross-Border Banking Activity' 70:20 BNA's Banking Rep 826 (18 May 1998).

United States court rulings on whether ATMs should be considered 'branches' of banks for purposes of the interstate branching regulations have found that stations owned by single banks for the convenience of their customers are branches, but ATMs that are jointly used are not.[49] This jurisprudence could be appropriate in an institutional approach such as in the NAFTA Chapter Fourteen. Canadian financial officials do not consider branches and ATMs to be interchangeable, however.[50] There, the financial experts seem to look at the structural differences between the two different means of supplying a service to customers.

Whether an analysis can be drawn from these national approaches on establishing the location of an ATM to the location of a foreign bank by virtue of its ATM in the territory of a Party is not clear. However, it is unlikely that a free trade agreement would approve a claim of location merely through the customer's ability to access an account from a terminal: there are too many foreign banks that are part of the cash exchange networks to make such recognition of them reasonable from the perspective of limiting access to NAFTA benefits.

5.3.2.4.2   INTERNET BANKS

Even less 'physically present' is a bank whose services are accessible through a personal computer in a customer's home. Like the rapid growth of ATM banking in the 1980s, the 1990s have witnessed an explosive growth in the electronic supply of financial services by means of an electronic connection in the customer's home to the main banking corporation.[51] Having the advantage of offering 24-hour banking service, internet banking also equalizes to a certain extent the 'size' of banks. Thus, smaller banks profit from cyberspace presence just as the largest banks do.[52]

---

[49] See, e.g., *Independent Bankers Association of New York State v. Marine Midland Bank* 757 F.2d 453, finding that a jointly-used ATM is not a branch of a bank that does not own or rent it, because there is no 'establishment' for purposes of the McFadden Act § 36(c), (f). The McFadden Act, regulating the establishment of bank branches in the United States, has a wide definition of what is included as a 'branch' for purposes of that statute. Congressman McFadden himself explained his intended meaning in 1927 saying, 'Any place outside of or away from the main office where the bank carries on its business of receiving deposits, paying checks, lending money, or transacting any business carried on at the main office, is a branch'. Symons and White (note 36 *supra*), citing (1927) 68 *Congressional Record* 5816.

[50] See Finance Canada, 'Canadian Financial System', Chart 7 and accompanying text found on the Department's internet site at >www.fin.gc.ca<, showing the rise in the number of 'branches' and in the number of 'ATMs', and commenting that '... the number of bank branches has been flat for several years, while the level of Automated Banking Machines (ABMs) continued to grow rapidly'.

[51] Nearly every major bank in North America and Western Europe has some internet presence. Many banks offer a wide array of services. For a general introduction to the legal aspects of regulating the internet, see Mark D. Powell, 'Electronic Commerce: An Overview of the Legal and Regulatory Issues' (1997) 3:3 Int'l Trade L & Reg 85. Powell reports that one 1995 survey estimated commerce over the internet to have equalled $200 million, 'but it looks set to rise'; another study, by Forrester Research, estimates that the amount will have more than doubled by 1997 and that [b]y 2000 this will swell to $6.6 billion'.

[52] William Randle (see note 53 *infra*) remarks, 'When you're talking about competing in virtual space, as far as the customer is concerned, you're as close as any other bank—

Finally, the internet sites are even more likely than ATMs to become universal financial service providers in the future. A full range of banking services along with brokerage and insurance services are predicted to be offered through bank sites by the end of the twentieth century, if not sooner.[53]

As individual home computer-banking becomes more widespread the 'foreign' bank becomes more difficult to regulate even as the need for watchful regulatory attention grows.[54] With no permanent physical presence in a territory, no regulatory control by most of the supervisory agencies in the various territories in which a site can be accessed, and only a possibility of activity level being monitored if the banks themselves do so, internet banking does not fit well into any preexisting analytical framework for supervision. The increasing level of banking done through computer networks has made the definition of 'located in' as used in Article 1416 a much more important

---

(Contd.)

regardless of size—simply by picking up the telephone or going to the computer and hitting a keystroke …'. Bob Curley, 'Charting Virtual Territory', *Bank Systems + Technology* (November 1997) (text found on internet at >www.financetech.com<).

[53] As managing director of one bank's 'Direct Access Financial Services' division, William Randle proudly claimed in Fall 1997:

> We're going to add a lot of stuff to the Web bank over the next 12 months. The operation we've had out there since June of last year has been interesting. It's been transactional, it's been a real bank. But it's been very limited. We will add transfer capabilities within the next 30 days, and we'll add credit card, brokerage services, insurance—all of that will be coming next year. We intend to make it a full-service bank, and virtually anything we sell or deliver in a branch you'll be able to get over the Internet.

Curley (note 52 *supra*). The Bank of Montreal has been offering investment brokerage services over its internet site since March 1997. See John Shannon, 'Bank of Montreal Integrates Web Access into Remote Trading Service', *Bank Systems + Technology* (November 1997) (text found on internet at >www.financetech.com<).

[54] See 'Beware the Cyber-Regulator', *The Economist*, 23 August 1997, pp. 58–9; Finance Canada, *1997 Review of Financial Sector Legislation: Proposals for Changes* (June 1996), pp. 15–16, setting out proposals on increasing privacy protection regulations as a response to technological changes in banking. See also Powell (note 51 *supra*), at 85 ('The law is often accused of lagging behind changes inn [sic] society. [In electronic commerce], it seems it has been left standing').

[55] The Federal Reserve Bank of Atlanta foresees great technology-driven changes in banking by the next century:

> By the year 2000, more changes will occur. Direct payments as well as direct deposits may become routine … Banking from home will be possible through computers and telephones. And unsecured loans will be issued through ATM-like machines in a process that can take as little as 10 minutes. Carolina First already is operating such automated loan device in South Carolina.
> This is leading edge, but that's what we said about ATM's 25 years ago … .

Federal Reserve Bank of Atlanta, 'New Rules, Technical Tools Reshape Banking Industry' *Financial Update* (October–December 1995), p. 4, quoting Harold Brewer, chairman and chief executive officer of Brintech Inc. An executive vice president of Huntington National Bank (Columbus, OH), talked of the internet as a 'business region'. Curley (note 52 *supra*), (Interview of William M. Randle). In the United States, the ability to contact customers across the country from one physical location is particularly significant because of the legal restrictions on inter-State branching.

issue than it would be without electronic transfers of money and financial information,[55] yet the NAFTA Parties' banking authorities have not formally indicated how the 'location in' question will be answered.[56]

In the absence of direct answers, extrapolation from national law is once again a valuable exercise. There are, for example, a growing number of decisions by US courts addressing the question of personal jurisdiction in cases of internet activities which help in understanding the problems of applying traditional jurisprudence to legal contexts that could not have been imagined 30 years ago.[57] These courts faced the question of whether the 'minimal contacts' rule used in traditional situations would allow an out-of-State defendant to be sued in the plaintiff's State. The minimal contacts rule is one of the US standards used in determining the fairness of attaching personal jurisdiction to a non-resident civil defendant based on the defendant's commercial activities in State. Introduced in the landmark case of *International Shoe v. Washington*,[58] the principle of minimum contacts emphasizes the 'quality and nature of the activity in relation to the fair and orderly administration of the laws which it was the purpose of the due process clause to insure'.[59] Moreover, the reciprocity of rights from and obligations to the State of commercial presence must be taken into consideration:

> [the Due Process Clause of the 14th Amendment] does not contemplate that a state may make binding a judgment in personam against an individual or corporate defendant with which the state has no contacts, ties, or relations.

But to the extent that a corporation exercises the privilege of conducting activities within a state, it enjoys the benefits and protection of the laws of that state. The exercise of that privilege may give rise to obligations; and, so far as those obligations arise out of or are connected with the activities within the state, a procedure which requires the corporation to respond to a suit brought to enforce them can, in most instances, hardly be said to be undue.[60]

In the twentieth century, the personal jurisdiction issue continued to grow, particularly with the increasingly national and international economic expansion of trade. In *World-Wide Volkswagen Corp. v. Woodson*,[61] the majority of the US Supreme Court refined its 'minimal contacts' principle for application in federal courts. Addressing a case in which a family bought a car in

---

[56] The WTO has just started studying the problems posed by electronic trade mechanisms. While identifying the various aspects of the internet that might affect trade, the Secretariat's study does not comment on how to address the specifics of internet trade in banking services. WTO, *Electronic Commerce and the Role of the WTO* (WTO, Geneva, 1998).

[57] *Panavision International v. Toeppen* 141 F.3d 1316 (9th Cir. 1998); *Cybersell, Inc. v. Cybersell, Inc.* 130 F.3d 414 (9th Cir. 1997); *CompuServe v. Patterson* 89 F.3d 1257 (6th Cir. 1996); *Maritz, Inc. v. Cybergold* 947 F.Supp. 1328 (E.D. Mo. 1996); *Inset Systems v. Instruction Set* 937 F.Supp. 161 (D. Conn. 1996); *Bensusan Restaurant v. King* 937 F.Supp. 295 (S.D.N.Y. 1996). For an excellent introductory discussion of these cases see Corey B. Ackerman, 'Note: World-Wide Volkswagen, Meet the World Wide Web: An Examination of Personal Jurisdiction Applied to a New World' (1997) 71 St John's L Rev 403.

[58] 326 US 310 (1945).

[59] *Ibid.* at 319.

[60] *Ibid.*

[61] 444 US 286 (1980).

New York and, upon driving to their new home in Arizona, were injured in an auto accident in Oklahoma, Justice White wrote that the foreseeability that injury could be suffered in a particular location is not a sufficient criterion for suing a large corporation in a particular State:

> This is not to say, of course, that foreseeability is wholly irrelevant. But the foreseeability that is critical to due process analysis is not the mere likelihood that a product will find its way into the forum State. Rather, it is that the defendant's conduct and connection with the forum State are such that he should reasonably anticipate being haled into court there.[62]

Other Supreme Court opinions on this subject emphasize the ideas of 'purposeful availment' by the defendant of a State's legal system and 'reasonableness of jurisdiction' as elements on which to base jurisdiction:

> Jurisdiction ... may not be avoided merely because the defendant did not physically enter the forum state ... [I]t is an inescapable fact of modern commercial life that a substantial amount of business is transacted solely by mail and wire communications across state lines, thus obviating the need for physical presence within a State in which business is conducted. So long as a commercial actor's efforts are 'purposefully directed' toward residents of another State, we have consistently rejected the notion that an absence of physical contacts can defeat personal jurisdiction there.[63]

When the defendant is a foreign corporation, the US courts are more restrained in finding the legal linkages necessary for a plaintiff to bring the corporation into court.[64] The Supreme Court explained their restraint with the classic conception of the Court's unsuitability to make decisions that might affect international relations:

> The procedural and substantive interests of other nations in a state court's assertion of jurisdiction over an alien defendant will differ from case to case. In every case, however, those interests, as well as the Federal interest in its foreign relations policies, will be best served by a careful inquiry into the reasonableness of the assertion of jurisdiction in the particular case, and an unwillingness to find the serious burdens on an alien defendant outweighed by minimal interest on the part of the plaintiff or the forum State. 'Great care and reserve should be exercised when extending our notions of personal jurisdiction into the international field'.[65]

---

[62] *Ibid.* at 297.

[63] *Burger King v. Rudzewicz* 471 US 462, 476 (1985). See also *Hanson v. Denckla* 357 US 235, 253 (1958). See also *Kulko v. California Superior Court* 436 US 84, 96 (1978); *Keeton v. Hustler Magazine* 465 US 770, 780 ('Where, as in this case, respondent ... has continuously and deliberately exploited the New Hampshire market, it must reasonably anticipate being haled into court there ...').

[64] *Asahi Metal Industry v. Superior Court* 480 US 102 (1987). In this case, a Japanese motor cycle parts supplier shipped goods to a tire manufacturer in Taiwan. When a Californian motorcyclist sued for injuries suffered when his tire burst, the tire manufacturer cross-complained against Asahi in California court.

[65] *Ibid.* at 115, quoting Justice Harlan's dissent in *United States v. First National City Bank* 379 US 378, 404 (1965).

In deciding today's questions of internet commerce jurisdiction under the precedent of 'minimal contacts', the courts that have addressed this problem come to different conclusions, some finding that the establishment of a homepage should subject the business owner to liability throughout the United States, and another court hinting that, standing alone, the creation of an internet site 'is not an act purposefully directed toward the forum state'.[66] Each of these courts based its opinion on the personal jurisdiction jurisprudence developed through the years.[67]

In the context of NAFTA, one could ask whether the existence of a foreign bank's homepage on the World Wide Web be considered sufficient to establish a legal connection to the NAFTA territory based on the criteria of 'purposeful availment' by the bank of the NAFTA Parties' laws or by the bank's 'anticipation of being haled into court' there.

Alas, the use of the personal jurisdiction jurisprudence for a NAFTA Chapter Fourteen analysis is tempting (not in the least because it already exists) but inappropriate. The values that the personal jurisdiction jurisprudence prompts, 'notions of fair play and substantial justice', themselves are appropriate for any area of law. However, the purpose of the jurisdiction limits is to protect the defendant from being 'haled into court' in a foreign jurisdiction with which he or she had little connection. That is not the purpose of the Chapter Fourteen term 'located in'. Indeed, the purposes are opposites.

Under Chapter Fourteen, the 'located in' phrase is intended to limit the benefits of the treaty to insiders, not to protect unwilling outsiders from being 'caught' within its provisions. The foreign bank that has an internet site viewable by Canadian or Mexicans or persons in the United States would only claim to be located in those territories based on the Agreement in order to *profit* from the treaty's liberalizations among those countries. Thus, if the NAFTA Parties want to *limit* access to their markets, a minimum contacts rule is not the way to do so. The burden must instead be put on the foreign entity to show connections that make it reasonable to allow it to claim the benefits of the Agreement rather than the other way around.

Looking to the overall treaty goal of free cross border trade in financial services limited to NAFTA Parties and the two-part test for consideration as a NAFTA Party financial institution ('located in' and 'controlled by'), the most likely prognosis is that electronic 'presence' will not be sufficient to fulfill the definition of 'located in' under Chapter Fourteen.

---

[66] *Bensusan Restaurant v. King* 937 F.Supp. at 301 (in dicta; the holding of the case was that New York's long-arm statute did not provide for jurisdiction over this defendant). See also *Filetech, S.A. v. France Telecom* 157 F.3d 922, 932 (2d Cir. 1998), reversing the district court's finding that jurisdiction existed under the Sherman Act for a foreign telecommunications provider whose services were available to persons in the United States over its internet homepage.

[67] See *Panavision International v. Toeppen* 141 F.3d at 1319–1324, which is an excellent discussion of the law of both general and specific personal jurisdiction and how these relate to the use of the internet.

Even if future panels decide that physical presence is the relevant criteria for determining location, electronic presence would almost certainly not be an adequate basis for location. One indication that US authorities have considered such an argument can be found in a pre-NAFTA draft by the Office of the United States Trade Representative (USTR). In one USTR draft for the Uruguay Round negotiations, a proposed text for the agreement on trade in services contains a provision clarifying when a service would be eligible for national treatment, namely, 'whenever market access has been achieved'.[68] A subparagraph further defines the timing: '… a service provider of another Party shall be deemed to have achieved market access with respect to a Party whenever it has entered that Party's market, either through establishment, cross-border transactions, *or use of the service of the public telecommunications transport network*'.[69]

Evaluating this provision on face value, perhaps it would form a basis for electronic presence as a criterion. Yet, to do so would be to make a dangerous stretch of wording, because the internet was not developed in 1989. Cyberspace communications are causing troubles in many areas of the law precisely because, while similar to the older media of communication, it has specific technical qualities that make it unsuited to any controls yet developed. In financial services, the legal (as well as the technical) problems are just as difficult as they are in the area of freedom of expression.[70] Canadian regulators make an assumption that electronic banking transactions are cross-border provisions of services, and thus implicitly reject any consideration of 'establishment' by means of an internet presence.[71]

Under the regulatory existence criteria, the mere possibility that a customer could withdraw funds from her account by virtue of a private contractual arrangement between the bank and the ATM company would not automatically provide for a finding of the bank's being located where the ATM is placed. If there were no regulatory influence of the NAFTA Party on the bank itself, regulatory existence would be lacking. The internet bank licensed outside of the NAFTA territories and with no other presence of any sort there would suffer a similar fate. Without special arrangements, the supervisors of one country have no power to regulate the activities of

---

[68] Office of the US Trade Representative, United States Proposal for a General Agreement on Trade in Services, Art. 8.1 (opened to public on 24 October 1989).

[69] *Ibid*. Art. 8.1.2 (emphasis added).

[70] See 'Beware the Cyber-Regulator' (note 54 *supra*), at 58–9; 'The Internet's Most Wanted', *The Economist*, 23 August 1997, p. 59, stating that the Securities and Exchange Commission has formed a voluntary 'Cyberforce' to search for US securities laws violations on the internet and that the American Bankers Association also tries to control the bank-related web sites. In the area of free speech, the United States Supreme Court struck down a State law that would have prohibitted the transmission of pornographic materials over the Internet. *Reno v. ACLU* 521 US 844 (1997).

[71] Finance Canada, 'Foreign Bank Entry Policy—Consultation Paper 1' (text found on internet at >www.fin.gc.ca<) ('A related matter under consideration involves the rules for foreign banks that do not wish to establish a Canadian entity, but would like to provide services in Canada from *outside* the country. With the introduction of new delivery channels like the Internet, it is now feasible to serve customers worldwide … Such cross-border activities are of interest given their implications for Canadian consumers and financial institutions').

foreign financial institutions. The 'global' qualities of the medium of the internet have not changed this basic principle. Therefore, only the country in which it has a definite legal presence, regulates a foreign bank's home-page. A pure regulatory existence analysis would result in the clear exclusion of such banks from the provisions of NAFTA.

The commercial activities level analysis of 'located in' might lead to the NAFTA Parties' obligation to extend the benefits of NAFTA to a foreign bank. Depending on how many customers a certain internet bank had and what types of transactions could be made via electronic connection, the bank might meet the threshold that would give it 'presence' in a NAFTA Party territory.

The policy arguments for determining the status of internet banks under the NAFTA lead to a rejection of considering electronic presence as 'location in' a Party. The ease with which internet connections can be established and the lack of a Party's regulatory control of the bank make extension of the benefits of the Agreement irrational. While the international trade perspective of encouraging competition would be furthered by accepting the electronic presence as sufficient, the financial service law considerations of safety and systemic soundness would be jeopardized. Although the trade and financial service sectors must meld their interests, here, the interests of the financial service sector should carry more weight.

5.3.2.5   *Proposed Test for 'Located In'*

In any legal system, there must be a sufficient connection to the jurisdictional area before the rules of that area will apply to an actor there. In international trade law, regional agreements are designed so as to offer advantages to those belonging to the area while not extending those advantages to actors from outside the area. With these two considerations in mind, one can develop a guideline for determining how far NAFTA Chapter Fourteen should be made available to financial institutions that are not physically present and economically active in the territories of NAFTA Parties.

It could be argued that the test best suited to determining 'location in' is a combination of regulatory existence and activity level. The test would ask first, whether the financial service supplier or investor was subject to the supervisory authorities of one of the NAFTA Parties. Legal existence (by corporate charter or special license to do business) could lead to a presumption of regulatory existence, while submission to administrative supervision or payment of fees and taxes standing alone would have to be examined in detail to pass this test.

As a second prong of the test, the enterprise's commercial activity would be determinative. Even if there were regulatory presence in a NAFTA Party territory, the authorities could take into account the level of activity in the territory in the final decision on whether the firm were 'located in' that territory. If there were sufficient activity, such that significant benefits or harm arose from the single institution's (or investor's) actions, location would also be inferred. A *de minimus* standard agreed upon by the regulators of each Party would be a logical standard to develop for determining whether this level of activity has been reached.

Considering that most financial service providers will clearly be either 'located' or not 'located' in a NAFTA territory, such a two-prong test would allow the simple cases to be decided quickly and with a high degree of foreseeability while permitting difficult cases to be decided based on the needs of supervision and fairness. Moreover, the aims of liberalizing financial service activities would be promoted, as questionable cases would more likely be included than excluded from the benefits of Chapter Fourteen.

Finally, the 'location' of a bank may not be an effective criterion for determining the nationality of a bank at all (if indeed nationality is to be limited). Instead, regulators in the NAFTA Parties could more effectively use the issue of control over the bank (discussed below) as decisive. This test might then be subjected to a more rigorous examination to limit the extension of NAFTA benefits.

5.3.3   Control

The definition of financial institution of another Party has a second element. Not only is the institution to be 'located in' a Party's territory, but it must be 'controlled by Persons of another Party'.

5.3.3.1   *Controlling Entity: 'Person of a Party'*

The definition of a bank 'of another Party' further requires that a NAFTA Party legal entity has 'control' of the bank or branch: 'a financial institution of another Party means a financial institution, including a branch, located in the territory of a Party that is controlled by persons of another Party'.[72]

The applicability of NAFTA Chapter Fourteen provisions to a financial institution depends on the controlling person's being 'of another Party'. As a 'person of a Party', the controlling entity may be either a natural or a juridical person.[73] A branch of a third country's legal entity, on the other hand, is explicitly excluded from being a legitimate controller of a NAFTA bank.

Any bank or branch located in one Party that is incorporated or organized under the laws of another NAFTA Party and controlled by either a natural or legal, non-branch, person of another NAFTA Party is eligible for Chapter Fourteen benefits.[74] Canada has additional requirements for NAFTA treatment; the United States and Mexico do not.

---

[72] NAFTA Art. 1416 ('financial institution of another Party').

[73] NAFTA Art. 201 ('person of a Party'); NAFTA Art. 1416 ('person of a Party', referring to Chapter Two). In the text of the definition, the term 'persons of another Party' is used. Remarkably, there is no definition for this particular term. Rather, NAFTA Art. 1416 further defines 'person of a Party'. These terms being so similar, it is reasonable to view the difference as a result of sloppy drafting instead of an indication of meaningful distinction.

[74] See NAFTA Art. 1416 ('financial institution of a Party'; 'person of a Party'); NAFTA Art. 201 ('person of a Party').

The Canadian residency requirement is set out in Annex VII.[75] According to its Annex provisions, the Canadian government considers a natural person a 'resident of a Party' if he or she spends ('sojourns') at least 183 days per year in the territory of the Party.[76]

More significant is the definition of a legal person of a Party. For an entity, the Canadians require that the entity be not only formed under the laws of the Party, but also that it be controlled by natural person residents of the Party, as defined above, for Canadian recognition.[77]

5.3.3.2   *Level of Control*

One author discounts the role of the 'control' portion of the definition of 'financial institution of another Party' for banks wishing to establish in the United States and Mexico.[78] This author writes of two 'approaches' to the definition of 'person' in Chapter Fourteen. One (the approach taken by the Canadian government) focuses on the idea of 'control'. The other (used by the United States) focuses on the residency of the controlling institution itself. Thus, any bank incorporated in Canada or Mexico is eligible for the benefits of Chapter Fourteen in the United States, regardless of who ultimately controls it.[79]

Because Mexico presently requires foreign banks to establish as legal subsidiaries, there should be no problems under this rule for foreign banks located there to expand into the United States' territory on the beneficial terms of Chapter Fourteen.[80] On the other hand, there is no requirement of subsidiary-establishment to enter the United States market or (as of June 1999 the Canadian market). Because many foreign banks are present on the United States banking market in the form of branches, this definitional requirement will prevent a substantial number of these third country banks from entering Mexico directly as NAFTA Party financial institutions from the United States. Instead, United States-based branches will have to incorporate before entering the Mexican market under the NAFTA. However, with the change in Canada's foreign bank entry rules, the Canadian ultimate control considerations will not be applied to those foreign banks that take advantage of the opportunity to directly branch into that market,

---

[75] NAFTA Annex VII, Schedule of Canada, Section B, 2(f). See also description of Annex VII, in Chapter 3.

[76] NAFTA Annex VII, Schedule of Canada, Section B, 2(e).

[77] NAFTA Annex VII, Schedule of Canada, Section B, 2(f)(i).

[78] See Olin L. Wethington, *Financial Market Liberalization: The NAFTA Framework* (Shepard's/McGraw-Hill, New York, 1994), p. 70.

[79] *Ibid.* at 70 ('The residence rule ... is incorporated into the NAFTA through the definitive provisions, except where otherwise modified in the Agreement').

[80] This, of course, will change when the rules on legal form for market access change. When the Canadian regulations allowing for direct branching into their market come into effect, and the NAFTA rules are not otherwise amended, the result will be that this provision of NAFTA leads to more advantages by NAFTA Party banks relative to third banks than now exist. Still, only those branches from United States or Mexican banks would benefit from the NAFTA provisions. Third banks' branches in Canada would remain excluded from the ability to take advantage of the NAFTA.

because the United States and Mexico adhere only to the residency test for determining nationality.

5.3.3.3   Types of Control

Chapter Fourteen does not define what is meant by 'control' of a financial institution. In the context of investments within Chapter Eleven, control is referred to as including both direct and indirect control.[81] This approach of looking beyond purely legal control is consistent with Chapter Fourteen's general emphasis, and consequently can be extended to the definition of 'financial institution of another Party'. A person would thus control an institution either if the person owns a certain percentage of the corporation's securities (legal control) or if the person has the potential to influence the management of the corporation (control in fact).

The criterion of control is further defined by each Party for itself. For banks wishing to invoke NAFTA Chapter Fourteen in Canada, the elements for control are set out in Annex VII. For the other Parties, the requirements for control are not further defined in the text, leaving national law to determine the meaning of the term.

5.3.3.3.1   CANADIAN CONTROL TEST

Under Annex VII, the Canadians will recognize either control-in-fact or legal control by residents of NAFTA Parties as sufficient for attributing nationality to a financial institution under Chapter Fourteen. Under Canadian law, legal control is an ownership of 50 per cent of the voting stock, which enables the owner to elect a majority of the board of directors of a company.

Control-in-fact is based on 'beneficial ownership' of at least 50 per cent of the assets or stock, or on a person's (or group of affiliated persons') ability to 'direct the business and affairs' of the company.[82] Thus, nominal ownership of shares by a family member will be attributed to a person if that person actually determines how the shares are voted. Moreover, an individual (or enterprise) who does not hold any voting shares at all could still be in control of the corporation, if business decisions are made according to considerations that that individual (or enterprise) puts forward.

5.3.3.3.2   MEXICAN CONTROL TEST

In Mexico, the rules governing financial institutions assume a person or group of persons 'control' an institution when the individual's or group's

---

[81] See, e.g., NAFTA Art. 1139 ('investment of an investor of another Party') ('an investment owned or controlled directly or indirectly by an investor of such Party'). Although the text of the Agreement only refers to the presumption itself, under the same perspective of factual control, the presumption should be rebuttable.

[82] NAFTA Annex VII, Schedule of Canada, Section B, 2(b)–(c).

shareholdings are 30 per cent or more of the capital stock.[83] Alternatively, if a person or group of persons has 'control' over the assembly of shareholders, has the possibility of determining a majority of the members of the board of directors, or 'in any other way controls' the bank, control will be deemed to exist.[84]

5.3.3.3.3   UNITED STATES' CONTROL TEST[85]

In the United States, the law on control of a bank has been set out by the Board of Governors of the Federal Reserve in the Code of Federal Regulations (CFR). The CFR definitions are coherent with general corporate law principles as decided by the various State courts.[86] Generally, 'control' refers to the 'ability to exercise a restraining or directing influence over something'.[87]

Like its Canadian counterpart, US laws governing 'control' maintain a factual approach rather than a legal approach. Such an approach is consistent with US corporate law's overall pragmatism, and as such, does not generally give much weight to percentages of actual stock ownership. Because the block ownership of shares representing less than 50 per cent of outstanding shares can still give an individual control over a company, there is no absolute minimum level of stock ownership under which control could not be found.[88] On the other hand, beneficial ownership of over 25 per cent of the stock of a bank by a shareholder presents a court with a situation in which control will be presumed. Specifically, a relevant banking regulation states:

---

[83] Ley de Instituciones de Crédito, Title 2, Chapter I, Art. 17*bis*: '… se entenderá que un grupo de personas adquiere el control de una institución de banca múltiple cuando sea propietario de treinta por ciento o más de las acciones representativas del capital social de la propia institución …'.

[84] *Ibid.* continuing: '… un grupo de personas adquiere el control de una institución de banca múltiple cuando … tenga el control de la asamblea general de accionistas, esté en posibilidad de nombrar a la mayoría de los miembros del consejo de administración, o por cualquier otro medio controle a la institución de banca múltiple de que se trate'.

[85] With nothing in the text of the Agreement to support this supposed extinguishment of the requirement of control, it is questionable whether one could base a case on the claim that control of the controlling entity is superfluous for the United States. If the claim is accurate, however, there may never be a need to test the wording of the provision: any incorporated entity will be given NAFTA treatment in the United States. In the circumstance that the controlling entity must be a person of a Party, this following overview of the US law of control of a financial institution will be of assistance.

[86] The law of corporations is determined by each State rather than by the federal government in the United States. Although varying somewhat in the details, the body of corporate law has been largely harmonized, with a particularly strong emphasis coming from the courts of the State of Delaware.

[87] Henry Campbell Black, *Black's Law Dictionary* (6th edn, West Publishing, St, Paul, MN, 1990), p. 329 ('control').

[88] See 12 CFR § 225.124(e): '… A foreign bank holding company may … 'indirectly' control … voting shares if its noncontrolling interest in such company is accompanied by other arrangements that, in the Board's judgement, result in control of such shares by the bank holding company'. A recent case before New York's highest court involved a claim by the tax authorities that the brother of one of the owners of a closely held corporation had 'control' of the corporation despite his owning no shares at all. The Court of Appeals

Control of a bank or other company means ...:
(i) Ownership, control, or power to vote 25 percent or more of the outstanding shares of any class of voting securities of the bank or other company, directly or indirectly or acting through one or more other persons;
(ii) Control in any manner over the election of a majority of the directors, trustees, or general partners (or individuals exercising similar functions) of the bank or other company;
(iii) The power to exercise, directly or indirectly, a controlling influence over the management policies of the bank or other company, as determined by the Board after notice and hearing ...;
(iv) Conditioning in any manner the transfer of 25 percent or more of the outstanding shares of any class of voting securities of a bank or other company upon the transfer of 25 percent or more of the outstanding shares of any class of voting securities of another bank or other company.[89]

Even more restrictive are the rules for foreign bank holding companies. Such a company will be considered to indirectly own or control voting shares of a bank if that bank holding company acquires more than 5 per cent of any class of voting shares of another bank holding company.[90]

5.3.4   Financial Service Provider

Chapter Fourteen defines a financial service provider only as applies to a NAFTA-Party person: 'financial service provider of a Party means a person of a Party that is engaged in the business of providing a financial service within the territory of a Party'.[91]

Moreover, a financial service provider does not benefit from all of the Chapter Fourteen provisions. Thus, such a person benefits under Chapter Fourteen provisions for cross-border trade, national treatment, and

---

(Contd.)

found that the brother did dominate the corporation, finding that 'we should be concerned with "reality and not form ... with how the corporation operated and [the petitioner's] relationship to that operation"'. *Matter of Joseph Morris* 183 A.D.2d 5, 8; 588 N.Y.2d 927, 929 (1992), citing *Dewitt Truck Broker* 540 F.2d 681 (4th Cir. 1976). The highest Court refused to directly accept this finding, dismissing the case on other grounds. However, the Court did cite precedent that indicated that a non-shareholder could be found to be in control of a corporation. *In the Matter of Joseph Morris* 623 NE2d 1157 (N.Y. 1993), *citing Establissement Tomis v. Shearson Hayden Stone* 459 F.Supp. 1355, 1366, n.13 (S.D.N.Y. 1978).

[89] 12 CFR § 225.2(e)(1). See also 12 CFR § 1606.2 ('For purposes of [Title 12, § 16], an individual or entity shall be presumed to have control of a company or organization if the individual or entity directly or indirectly, or acting in concert with one or more subsidiaries, owns or controls 25 percent or more of its equity, or otherwise controls its management or policies'); 12 CFR § 583.7 (control of a savings association). The United States' law of securities regulation contains a reporting requirement for all acquisitions of 5 per cent of any one class of a business' stock. Although this 5 per cent does not necessarily indicate 'control', it does indicate the strict tests the US authorities are accustomed to using when checking who determines the activities of a corporation.

[90] 12 CFR § 225.124(e).

[91] NAFTA Art. 1416 ('financial service provider of a Party').

most-favored-nation treatment, but not under the right to establish a commercial presence in the territory of another Party.

The hallmark of this definition is that there is no prerequisite that a Party has recognized a financial service provider as such in its territory before the provider may claim rights accruing under NAFTA. Regulated financial service providers are only a subset of the possible 'financial service providers of a Party' for Chapter Fourteen. Unregulated persons can also receive the benefits aimed at such providers. Moreover, there is no requirement that a legal person be controlled by a person of a Party in order to fulfill the requirements of 'financial service providers'.

Nevertheless, the service provider is somewhat restricted by the Article 1416 definition. First, the 'person' providing the financial service, if a natural person, must be either a citizen or a permanent resident of a NAFTA Party in which the service is provided.[92] Thus, the presence requirement imposed by Canada's rule of a minimum of 183 days per year applies.[93]

Next, if the person is an enterprise, it may not be a branch of a foreign company.[94] Therefore, there must be incorporation or organization as a legal entity to be considered a 'financial service provider of a Party'. While this does not exclude a foreign person from controlling the service providing entity, other rules in the NAFTA would allow a Party to discriminate on the basis of foreign control.[95]

Finally, the financial service provider must be 'engaged in the business of providing a financial service'.[96] That is, it must be currently active in the financial sector of a Party. New entrants to a Party's market are thereby disqualified from claiming Chapter Fourteen benefits.

5.4   IF A THIRD PARTY BANK IS A 'FINANCIAL SERVICE INSTITUTION OF ANOTHER PARTY OR A 'FINANCIAL SERVICE PROVIDER OF A PARTY'

5.4.1   The Usual Effects of Being a 'NAFTA-Party Bank'

If the third party bank does fulfill the various tests set out by the Party in which it wants to provide a service, that Party must grant it the same status as all other 'financial institutions of another NAFTA Party' or 'financial service providers of a Party'. Thus, unless a specific limit is set out in the Annex VII reservations, each Party must allow this bank market access to establish in its territory, afford the bank treatment no less favorable than the Party does all other Party banks, and grant it conditions of competition no less favorable than its own domestic banks enjoy. The Party must also fulfill its own

---

[92] NAFTA Art. 1416 ('person of a Party').
[93] NAFTA Annex VII, Schedule of Canada, Section B, 2(e), (f).
[94] NAFTA Art. 1416 ('person of a Party').
[95] See 5.4.2 *infra*.
[96] NAFTA Art. 1415 ('financial service provider of a Party').

obligations of recognizing the new financial services the bank may introduce in local operations ensure its regulations' transparency (for example by providing the bank with information about the status of its application if asked), and offer the bank's investors access to investment dispute arbitration processes. Alternatively, the financial service provider must be afforded the opportunity to continue its cross-border trade in financial services, and the Party is to treat the provider in accordance with the principles of national treatment and most-favored-nation obligations.

Further, the third country NAFTA-Party bank has a right to bring complaints it has against the other Parties to the attention of the Party in which it is located in hopes that the Party will undertake measures to resolve the problems, whether through informal consultations or through the instigation of a formal dispute under NAFTA Chapter Twenty procedures. The controlling investor of the bank may alternatively call upon the investor-Party arbitration provisions to attempt to get relief directly.

Finally, every NAFTA-Party bank has the right to full and prompt compensation for another Party's expropriation of its property. The conditions under which the expropriation may be made and the procedures for compensation are also reviewable under the NAFTA framework.

In short, with the following notable exception, there is nothing in the NAFTA to suggest that non-Party controlled banks that are considered active NAFTA Party institutions or financial service providers would be subject to legal treatment any different than Party-controlled banks are. The effects set out above in Chapter 4 *supra* can be reasonably assumed to remain constant for all NAFTA Party institutions.[97]

5.4.2 Denial of Benefits on Diplomatic Grounds or for Shell Corporations

The incorporated Chapter Eleven provision on denial of benefits is the one limit on the application of the Chapter Fourteen advantages available to a third state bank. If a third state investor (or group of investors) owns or controls a bank and the NAFTA Party in which the bank is located either does not have diplomatic relations with that third party or has a regulation

---

[97] A question of practical importance is whether the recognition of a foreign bank as a NAFTA-Party bank by one NAFTA Party automatically makes the bank eligible to enter either of the other NAFTA Parties' banking market. Because NAFTA is a free trade area rather than a customs union, each NAFTA Party maintains exclusive control over its third-party foreign trade relations. Thus, eligibility of a foreign bank in one Party's territory is not an indication that the same foreign bank will be allowed in the other NAFTA Parties' banking markets. An example of this might be if Cuban-investors owned 51 per cent of the stock of a bank established in Canada and the bank applied for a license in both the United States and Mexico. Because the bank is controlled by non-Party investors, the denial of benefits provision is relevant. As the United States does not maintain diplomatic relations with Cuba, it could refuse to grant the bank market access, or any other benefit of the NAFTA Chapter Fourteen. Mexico, however, does have diplomatic relations with Cuba. Assuming there are no Mexican laws that would be circumvented by granting the bank's application and that the bank was already active in Canada, Mexico would be obliged to treat the bank as a NAFTA Party financial institution.

which would be circumvented by affording beneficial treatment under Chapter Fourteen to the bank, the Party may legitimately deny the bank NAFTA treatment. The third reason to deny benefits is if the bank is not commercially active in the Party's territory. In such a case the Party can deny the bank NAFTA treatment.[98] While the NAFTA's grounds for denial do not contradict the similar provisions of other international economic law instruments (such as the General Agreement on Trade in Services), the use of the activity level of an enterprise to deny benefits may disadvantage third party institutions.

This provision regulating 'shell corporations' permits a Party to deny Chapter Fourteen benefits to a bank if the 'enterprise has no substantial business activities' in another Party territory.[99] There is ambiguity as to whether the substantial business activities requirement means that a bank must be engaged in banking services in the other Party or whether it only refers to some type of commercial business. However, as the Chapter Fourteen definition of 'investor of another Party' is set out to mean one who is 'in the business of providing financial services',[100] a logical interpretation of the denial of benefits provision would require the bank's activities in the other Party's territory to be that of providing financial services. A requirement that banking services be provided would nullify the benefits of allowing entry of non-regulated financial service providers, as banks in all Parties must be regulated under national laws.

Significantly, the Chapter Eleven provisions require that two elements be present before benefits may be denied. Foreign ownership is the first, but not a sufficient criterion. Thus, a refusal to afford the NAFTA benefits to a bank solely based on the bank's foreign ownership is not valid. The necessary second finding is a finding that the bank is a 'shell' corporation—a bank established in one Party's territory solely in order to enter another Party's banking market via NAFTA, remaining inactive (or nearly so) in the territory where it originally established itself.

More precisely, a bank must have 'substantial' commercial activities in a NAFTA territory to be considered a NAFTA Party financial institution. The interpretation of 'substantial' business activity in this context introduces a potential for discriminatory effects. In so far as the definition of 'substantial' is to be made according to national law, non-NAFTA Party persons could have to be capable of proving a greater degree of activity than would someone from a financial service institution established and controlled by a NAFTA Party person to show 'location in' the Party.

If there is a shell corporation that tries to establish itself in a NAFTA Party on the grounds of the Agreement, a Party may refuse to issue it a license. Should a refusal be protested, the bank has only one choice: it may complain to its national government, which will in turn be able to initiate formal dispute settlement proceedings. Although the denial of benefits is an action taken under the authority of NAFTA Chapter Eleven, making the

---

[98] See discussion of NAFTA Art. 1113 (Denial of Benefits), *supra* (Part IV).
[99] NAFTA Art. 1113:2.
[100] NAFTA Art. 1416 ('investor of a Party').

investor-Party arbitration mechanism[101] available to the bank's investors as private parties in the normal case, here the investors are not 'persons of a Party', and thus do not come within the scope of the Chapter Eleven provisions.[102] The bank itself, as an investment, is barred from invoking the investor-Party mechanism from the beginning.[103]

5.5   IF A THIRD PARTY BANK IS NOT A 'FINANCIAL INSTITUTION OF ANOTHER PARTY' OR A 'FINANCIAL SERVICE PROVIDER OF A PARTY'

If a third party bank is controlled by non-residents of a NAFTA Party or by a branch of a non-Party business, the benefits of NAFTA do not need to be extended to the bank.[104] Thus, the bank has no rights under the NAFTA. Whether there are other legal effects from NAFTA on that bank thus depends on the external legal systems of which the bank, or as is more generally the case, the bank's state of nationality.

In international economic law, the law of the World Trade Organization (WTO) forms the most significant legal framework for global trade in financial services. The WTO regulates its Members' treatment of each other through several basic agreements, among them the General Agreement on Trade in Services (GATS), which includes rules on trade in financial services. As each of the present NAFTA Parties is a WTO Member, if a bank is a financial institution established in another country that is a Member of the WTO, the law of the WTO dictates that the obligations of that organization's provisions on trade in financial services must be complied with to the extent not excused by recognition as a free trade/economic integration area. Non-WTO Member banks, on the other hand, have rights only as afforded by bilateral or other multilateral financial service agreements, or by relevant customary international law.

Neither the NAFTA nor the WTO positively attempts to disadvantage non-Parties or non-Members, respectively, allowing the benefits of liberalized transactions to be globalized. Yet it is still important to uncover the issue of the effects of non-Membership in view of the positive and negative integration through the legal norms contained in the Agreement.

---

[101] See discussion of the investor-Party dispute settlement mechanism, see 3.15.6 *supra*.

[102] See NAFTA Arts 1116, 1117 (setting out that 'an investor of a Party' may use the investor-Party dispute settlement mechanism).

[103] NAFTA Art. 1117:4 ('An investment may not make a claim under this Section').

[104] If the NAFTA benefits are given non-Party institutions, however, Chapter Fourteens's most-favored-nation obligation requires that the treatment of the non-Party financial institution not be more advantageous than the treatment offered each of the other Parties' financial institutions 'in like circumstances'. See NAFTA Art. 1406:1 ('Each Party shall accord … treatment no less favorable than that it accords to … [financial institutions] of any other Party *or of a non-Party*, in like circumstances') (emphasis added).

5.5.1 Non-WTO Member Third Parties

As Members of the WTO, the NAFTA Parties must fulfill their obligations taken under the WTO Agreements only toward other WTO Members.[105] Non-WTO Members will receive treatment afforded directly through bilateral or multilateral agreements of which they and a NAFTA Party are signatories.

At present, the majority of the countries of the world are Members of the WTO.[106] However, certain important entities[107] are not.[108] As of April 1999, the non-Members of the WTO included Russia,[109] China,[110] and many of the Arab countries (significantly Saudi Arabia, Syria, Iran, and Iraq). The banks of any of these countries that are allowed access to the financial services markets of the NAFTA Parties as non-Party financial institutions will be affected by Chapter Fourteen only to the extent that commercial conditions change. Legally, these states have no basis outside bilateral treaty agreements to claim benefits from financial service liberalization nor are their rights violated in any way by the NAFTA preferences that the Parties extend only to one another's financial institutions and financial service providers.

5.5.2 WTO Member Third Parties

All three of the NAFTA countries were Contracting Parties to the General Agreement on Tariffs and Trade (GATT 1947) during the NAFTA negotiations, and are now original members of the GATT's legal successor, the World Trade Organization.[111] While Canada and the United States have long been active participants in the GATT 1947,[112] Mexico's accession is

---

[105] Marrakesh Agreement Establishing the World Trade Organization, Art. II:1 ('The WTO shall provide the common institutional framework for the conduct of trade relations among its Members in matters related to the agreements and associated legal instruments included in this Agreement').

[106] As of April 1999, there were 134 members of the WTO. There are, in addition, 29 on that date which had submitted applications to accede to the Organization. For the most recent membership list, see the official WTO internet site at >www.wto.org<.

[107] The WTO does not require formal statehood for membership. Rather, any 'State or separate customs territory' which possesses full control over its external trade policy is a potential Member of the WTO. Marrakesh Agreement, Art. XII.

[108] Several of these governments have applied for accession and are under consideration by the Ministerial Conference.

[109] Accession under consideration. WTO, *Annual Report 1997* (WTO: Geneva 1997), p. 95, listing the 29 governments for which Working Parties on Accession had been established as of July 1996; by October the number of applicants had increased to 31.

[110] *Ibid.*

[111] The WTO came into effect on 1 January 1995.

[112] Canada supported the multilateral trade system efforts from the beginning. See generally Frank Stone, *Canada, the GATT and the International Trade System* (Institute for Research on Public Policy, Montreal, 1984), pp. 22–3. When the 1947 Agreement was signed, Canadian Prime Minister King spoke on the radio of the importance of the GATT: 'I can think of no recent event more encouraging for the future than the successful conclusion of the General Agreement … The Agreement clearly charts our long-run course', in *ibid.* at 22, citing the

relatively recent, acceding in mid-1986.[113] The fact of the Parties' membership to both the GATT (at the time the NAFTA came into effect) and to the WTO (presently) is important in so far as they are bound by the trade rules of that organization to the same extent as they are bound to fulfill their obligations under the NAFTA.[114]

The principle of non-discrimination is essential to the existence of the World Trade Organization, and a key element of this principle is the rule that all Members grant each other Member treatment no less favorable than is granted any other trading partner. This 'most-favored-nation treatment' obligation is found in all three of the basic WTO Agreements, including in the agreement most relevant to financial services, the General Agreement on Trade in Services (GATS).[115] Article II of the GATS states unequivocally, 'With respect to any measure covered by this Agreement, each Member shall accord immediately and unconditionally to services and service suppliers of any other Member treatment no less favourable than that it accords to like services and service suppliers of any other country'.[116]

If the GATS were as unequivocal as this passage indicates, every NAFTA advantage to Party service suppliers would violate the international obligations of the Parties. This is not the case. The most-favored-nation treatment provision of the GATS allows for a major exception that is relevant to our analysis: the exception for preferential trade agreements in which the parties to the agreement may offer each other benefits only to each other. There are, however, limiting conditions imposed by the WTO on preferential agreements, and if the conditions are not fulfilled, the agreement will not be acknowledged as 'WTO-legal'. The determination of WTO-legality or -illegality, in turn, affects the rights of other WTO Members *vis-à-vis* the parties to the agreement.

To determine the effect of the NAFTA Chapter Fourteen provisions on non-NAFTA WTO Members, the basic question is therefore, *is the NAFTA a preferential trade agreement compatible with the overall WTO legal system?* Since the principle of most-favored-nation treatment that the WTO incorporates is clearly violated by a regional arrangement such as NAFTA, the NAFTA must form a legitimate exception to the rules of the WTO to be 'legal'. To

---

(Contd.)

radio address by Prime Minister King in London, 17 November 1947. The US Congress strongly indicated that it would reject the executive's attempts to enact the Havana Charter which would have established the International Trade Organization. Thus, the General Agreement on Tariffs and Trade came into effect through a 'Provisional Protocol of Application' instead. Nevertheless, the United States' participation in the GATT has been generally supportive since then.

[113] Accession of Mexico, Decision of 17 July 1986 (L/6024) BISD 33S/56 (1986). See also Report of the Working Party on the Accession of Mexico adopted on 15 July 1986 (L/6010) BIDS 33S/57 (1986).

[114] Those not familiar with the structure and legal principles of the GATT/WTO system, should refer initially to 1.2 *supra*.

[115] See General Agreement on Tariffs and Trade, Art. I; General Agreement on Trade in Services, Art. II; Agreement on Trade-Related Aspects of Intellectual Property Rights, Art. 4.

determine whether it is, an examination is made of the GATT and GATS provisions on regional trade arrangements and economic integration arrangements, respectively. The specific question of NAFTA's 'legality' under the WTO, is then addressed, and followed with general conclusions as to how WTO-Member non-Party banks' legal rights under the WTO framework are affected by NAFTA's Chapter Fourteen provisions.

5.5.2.1   WTO System Limits on Regional Trade Agreements

As in the NAFTA, the principles of non-discrimination (most-favored-nation and national treatment obligations) form the foundation for the multilateral trade rules in the WTO. Even these principles are not without exception. Perhaps the single most important exception to the entire WTO system is the allowance of preferential trade agreements between or among Members. Such arrangements enable the participants to apply discriminating measures to non-participating countries, even if those countries are Members of the WTO (and could thus contravene both the MFN and NTO obligations). Yet, the WTO, like the GATT before it, officially (though not very enthusiastically) supports the existence of such regional arrangements within its multilateral system.[117]

One reason for this apparently self-destructive exception is the WTO Members' (and their predecessors') acknowledgement of political reality. Before the GATT 1947 was put into effect, there was a plethora of regional preferential trade agreements in existence. Several customs unions between European nations had been established in the nineteenth century,[118] the Benelux customs union had been established in 1944,[119] and other existing preferential agreements were left over from the European powers' colonial relationships with African[120] and Asian[121] countries. The drafters of the Havana Charter for an International Trade Organization (Havana Charter), the forerunner of the General Agreement on Tariffs and Trade,[122] realized

---

[116] GATS Art. II:1.
[117] WTO, *Regionalism and the World Trading System* (WTO, Geneva, 1995), p. 55, commenting that the inclusion of a regional trade area exception to the principle of MFN in WTO Agreements 'reflects the belief that genuine customs unions and free trade areas are compatible with the principle of non-discrimination. The rationale for economic integration between several countries is analogous to the process of integration within a single sovereign state, which strongly suggests that genuine customs unions and free trade areas do not pose an *inherent* threat to efforts to promote continued integration in the world trading system'; 'Regional Integration and the WTO: Conflict or Compatibility?', address by Peter D. Sutherland, then-Director-General of the GATT to the Third Euro-Latin American Forum on 7 July 1994, São Paulo (text found in *GATT-WTO News*, GW/03, 7 July 1994, pp. 2–7, at 5), noting that the use of non-discrimination principles within regional trade areas 'is generally perceived to reinforce the GATT process … At the same time, regional integration initiatives are generally seen to be at their most effective when anchored to a GATT system that is strong and viable …'.
[118] WTO (note 117 *supra*), at 6.
[119] *Ibid.*
[120] French Union preferences.
[121] British Imperial preferences.
[122] The Havana Charter's technical development into the GATT 1947 was mainly due to the US Congress' refusal to accept membership in a supernational organization. The GATT

the difficulties they would encounter in establishing a new trade regime that required the dissolution of these existing preferential arrangements. Thus, they included an exception to the most-favored-nation principle for customs unions and free trade areas (and for members of interim agreements leading to the formation of either of these) in Article 44 of the Havana Charter.

It was not only for political reasons that the free trade area and customs union exception was included, however. The majority of the drafters were also convinced of the economic benefits of preferential trade areas. As one introduction to the Havana Charter explains:

> Article 44 [of the Charter] permits members to form customs unions or free-trade areas even though such action would be contrary to the strict terms of article 16 requiring nondiscriminatory treatment by each member of the trade of all other members. Customs unions have been almost universally regarded as legitimate exceptions to the principle of most-favored-nation treatment because of the economic benefits to the parties concerned and, indirectly, to the other countries of the world.[123]

While there was fierce debate among trade economists and certain academics as to the benefits or the harmfulness of such regional agreements on the multilateral trade system, the drafters' convictions of the overall compatibility of regional agreements in an international framework remained in the text as the Havana Charter gave way to Article XXIV of the General Agreement on Tariffs and Trade.[124] The exception for preferential agreements stuck, and within the first 15 years of the GATT the number of

---

(Contd.)

was one portion of the Charter, and this part was accepted provisionally by the President until the Uruguay Round established the WTO. For a more detailed account of the development of the Havana Charter to the GATT 1947, see John H. Jackson, 'The GATT-ITO Preparatory Work' in Jackson, *World Trade and the Law of GATT* (Bobbs-Merrill, Indianapolis, 1969), pp. 35–58, Ch. 2. The Charter's vision of an International Trade Organization was much broader than what finally became the effective GATT 1947. The present WTO is much more similar in scope to what the Havana Charter drafters envisioned.

[123] US Department of State, Havana Charter at 9.

[124] Professor Heinz Preusse encapsulates the basic arguments for and against regionalism in the international trade law circles:

> Those who argue in favour of regionalization interpret free trade areas and the like as building-blocks to multilateralism. They hold that free trade and integration areas will foster multilateral free trade globally. Their counterparts suspect that, with regional groupings gaining importance, multilateral free trade will collapse and economic and political stability will decline. According to this point of view, regionalization is bound to mutate to regionalism and will then become a stumbling-block to multilateralism.

> Heinz G. Preusse, 'Regional Integration in the Nineties: Stimulation or Threat to the Multilateral Trading System?' (1994) 28:4 J World Trade 147 (footnote omitted). See also *ibid.* at 149–53, setting out several of the empirical studies on the effects of regionalization of trade and regionalism.

preferential agreements between and among GATT Contracting Parties had multiplied. In 1962, 13 new regional agreements had been notified to the Secretariat and 12 more would be notified by 1970. At the end of 1993, as the GATT 1947 was about to be replaced by the World Trade Organization, 97 preferential trade agreements were either recognized or had applied for recognition under the GATT.[125]

Under the present package of treaties, Article XXIV of the GATT 1994 and the Understanding on the Interpretation of Article XXIV of the General Agreement on Tariffs and Trade 1994 govern the formation of preferential trade agreements in goods; Article V of the GATS governs preferential trade agreements in services.[126] There is also a special 'Decision' from 1979 allowing for preferential tariff arrangements among developing countries.[127] This so-called 'Enabling Clause' has been used widely by South American countries, among others, in order to gradually integrate their economies without being subjected to the rigorous requirements of the Article XXIV GATT and Article V GATS rules.[128]

As the main topic of this author's work is the on a preferential agreement that includes a developed country and affects trade in financial services, it is the GATS provision that is most relevant. Yet, as of the time of writing, Article XXIV GATT is the only one of these free trade area provisions that has been the subject of dispute before—and therefore interpreted by—the WTO/GATT legal bodies. Thus, the following will remain relevant to the later discussion of GATS Article V.[129]

5.5.2.1.1   CUSTOMS UNIONS AND FREE TRADE ZONES: GATT ARTICLE XXIV

While explicitly acknowledging 'the desirability of increasing freedom of trade by the development, through voluntary agreements, of closer integration between the economies of the countries parties to such agreements',[130] the GATT crafters also realized the danger of weakening the principle of MFN. The GATT rules were to ensure that regional arrangements remain

---

[125] See WTO, *Analytical Index: Guide to GATT Law and Practice* (WTO, Geneva, 1995), pp. 858–72, listing all regional agreements notified to the GATT Secretariat through 1994.

[126] For an overview of the provisions of GATT Art. XXIV and GATS Art. V and a discussion of how the Understanding changes the law of regional agreements, see Thomas Cottier, 'The Challenge of Regionalization and Preferential Relations in World Trade Law and Policy' (1996) 2 Europ Forg Aff L Rev 149, 157–163.

[127] Differential and More Favourable Treatment Reciprocity and Fuller Participation of Developing Countries (L/4903), 26S BISD 203 (1980), decision of 28 November 1979. See also GATT, Analytical Index, at 53–9.

[128] The Enabling Clause allows for preferential trade arrangements to be made among developing countries in an exception to the most-favored nation treatment obligation, but does not have the rigorous requirements that are found in Art. XXIV GATT (for instance that of liberalizing 'substantially all trade'). The review procedures for Enabling Clause trade preferences are traditionally very light, based on the assumption that developing country trade does not have a significant impact on world trade. Several of the South American regional trade arrangements were notified under this provision. See Chapter 8, 8.1 *infra*.

[129] See 5.5.2.1.2 *infra*.

[130] GATT Art. XXIV:4.

exceptions to the trade system. Thus, criteria are set out and must be complied with in order that GATT members who do so are officially recognized as parties to a preferential trade area. Addressing both customs unions and free trade areas, Article XXIV:8 of GATT begins:

> 8. For purposes of this Agreement:
> (a) A customs union shall be understood to mean the substitution of a single customs territory for two or more customs territories, so that
> (i) duties and other restrictive regulations of commerce (except, where necessary, those permitted under Articles XI, XII, XIII, XIV, XV and XX) are eliminated with respect to 'substantially all the trade' between the constituent territories of the union or at least with respect to substantially all the trade in products originating in such territories, and,
> (ii) subject to the provisions of paragraph 9, substantially the same duties and other regulations of commerce are applied by each of the members of the union to the trade of territories not included in the union;
> (b) A free-trade area shall be understood to mean a group of two or more customs territories in which the duties and other restrictive regulations of commerce (except, where necessary, those permitted under Articles XI, XII, XIII, XIV, XV and XX) are eliminated on substantially all the trade between the constituent territories in products originating in such territories.[131]

One notices first the limitations inherent in the definitions of such arrangements: tariffs 'and other restrictive regulations of commerce' must be 'eliminated on substantially all the trade between the constituent territories'.[132] On a facial reading, the preferential trade area is to be more than simply a duty-free zone. How much more is unclear.[133] It might seem that according to the terms of Article XXIV:8, even though the GATT itself would have allowed many non-tariff barriers, measures such as specifically designed technical standards, licensing requirements, and extended pre-importation inspections could not be used among preferential trade partners. However, such was not the result. Working party reports suggest that the limitations on preferential trade agreements cannot be stricter than is the overall GATT text.[134]

---

[131] GATT Art. XXIV:8.

[132] *Ibid.*

[133] The European Parliament's discussion of the NAFTA as a GATT-compatible free trade zone contains a concise assessment of the Art. XXIV text, 'These provisions are so vague as to be virtually irrelevant'. European Parliament, *Report of the Committee on External Economic Relations on the Free Trade Agreement between the United States of America, Canada and Mexico (NAFTA)*, A3-0378/92, DOC_EN/RR/217/217513 (18 November 1992), p. 14.

[134] See in particular EEC—Agreement of Association with Malta: Report of the Working Party, BISD 19S/90, 94–95 (adopted 29 May 1972), paras 14–16:

> A member of the Working Party, commenting on the importance to Malta of income originating from duties ... requested clarification of Maltese intentions with respect to differentiation between customs duties and taxes as referred to in the Declaration ... of the Agreement. The representative of Malta said that Malta had already taken the necessary steps ... to amend its customs duties ... However, Malta had no tariff bindings under the General Agreement and thus retained full freedom with regard to all its duties. The member who had raised this point expressed reservations as to the compatibility of such a change in the Maltese tariff

An additional criterion of Article XXIV:8 is that the trade barriers within a preferential trade area must be reduced on 'substantially all the trade' between members. Although its purpose is clearly to prevent governments from avoiding the requirements of MFN by simply forming regional trade areas for a particular product, this has become the single most controversial passage of GATT Article XXIV as regards free trade zones. In the past, the main arguments have been whether a quantitative[135] view or a qualitative[136] approach, or some combination of the two is the appropriate method for defining 'substantially all'. These debates center on free trade agreements

---

(Contd.)

with the intent of Article XXIV:8(a). If after entering a customs union Malta were to retain essentially the same level of charges on imports from all sources as presently existed in the Maltese tariff, but redefined as revenue duties, his delegation wondered how it could be said that trade was free of duties …

The parties denied the validity of this interpretation … in relation to the application of Article XXIV. There was nothing in the General Agreement to prohibit the levying of revenue duties … The freedom of action of any contracting party in the application of its fiscal policy was not limited by the General Agreement except where its direct or indirect protective effects might be detrimental to a concession. In the face of the provisions of Article XXIV, the existence of revenue duties, which by definition ruled out discriminatory application, could not be regarded as jeopardizing the establishment of free trade …

One member of the Working Party, agreeing in general with the views of the parties to the Agreement in this matter, stressed that there was no obligation to eliminate non-protective revenue duties on goods traded between members of a customs union ora free-trade area.

[135] The United Kingdom, for example, asserted:

[Article XXIV] had been drafted against the background of the possibility of a free trade area being established in Europe in which the United Kingdom, in particular, might wish to retain some barriers against certain imports from its partners mainly as a result of its preferential arrangements … It was important to note that the phrase used in Article XXIV was 'substantially all the trade' and not 'trade in substantially all products'. Some members might wish to avail themselves of this latitude in respect of different products.

BISD 9S/70, at 84, para. 51 (1960).
[136] The United States argued that 'substantially all' must contain a qualitative component if it is to have any meaning. Thus, they said, an entire sector of trade cannot legitimately be excluded from such a definition. A GATT Working Party formed to evaluate the compatibility of the European Free Trade Area (EFTA) with Art. XXIV faced both arguments.

It was … contended that the phrase 'substantially all the trade' has a qualitative as well as a quantitative aspect and that it should not be taken as following the exclusion of a major sector of economic activity. For this reason, the percentage of trade covered, even if it were established to be 90 per cent, was not considered to be the only factor to be taken into account. The Member States agreed that the quantitative aspect, in other words the percentage of trade freed, was not the only consideration to be taken into account.

European Free Trade Association: Examination of Stockholm Convention, L/1235, Report adopted 4 June 1960; found in BISD 9S/70, 83 (1961).

that exclude the entire agriculture sector of trade from liberalization.[137] The GATT Working Parties never conclusively accepted one perspective,[138] and the meaning of 'substantially all the trade' remains undefined in the World Trade Organization despite years of GATT disputes. However, in the interpretative Understanding contained in the WTO package, there is language to suggest that the qualitative arguments ought to win the sympathy of the reviewing committees in the future.[139] Whether the regional trade agreements committee will accept this suggestion remains to be seen.

GATT Article XXIV contains further controversial restrictions. One that is particularly important for the world trading system is the provision regulating the custom unions' external tariff. Article XXIV requires that the tariff not be 'on the whole ... higher or more restrictive than the general incidence of the duties and regulations' in the Member states prior to joining the customs union.[140] This protects the other WTO Members from economic damage due to the creation of a regional arrangement, and is thus one of the foundations upon which the theoretical economics of regional trade can find support in the multilateral system.

---

[137] The European Union's (EU) free trade association agreements with non-Union countries were the object of pointed criticism by the United States on the basis of these agreements' failure to provide for tariff-free trade in agricultural products among parner states. In the EEC Agreement with the Associated Overseas Territories, a typical example, the EEC argued that 'substantially all' should be interpreted quantitatively. Since the agreement would eliminate tariffs on 80 per cent of the total trade beteen the areas, the EEC argued, the fact that agricultural products were categorically excluded did not violate the requirements of Art. XXIV. Frank Schonenveld, 'The EEC and Free Trade Agreements: Stretching the Limits of GATT Exceptions to Non-Discriminatory Trade?' (1992) 26:5 J World Trade 59, 63–65, discussing the interpretation of 'substantially all' in the examination of several European Economic Community free trade agreements; see 'The European Economic Community' Reports adopted on 29 November 1957 (L/778), BISD 6S/70 (1958), at 98–101, setting out the various views on how 'substantially all' should be interpreted. See also 'Agreement Between the European Communities and Morocco' Report of the Working Party adopted on 11 November 1977 (L/4560), BISD 24S/88 (1978) ('new model' agreement between developed and developing country proposed; its exclusion of most agricultural products caused concern to some Working Party members); 'Agreement Between the European Communities and Tunisia' Report of the Working Party adopted on 11 November 1977 (L/4558), BISD 24S/97 (1978), pp. 102–103, para. 12. (Working Party member criticizes agreement's exclusion of most agricultural products, and notes that development objectives would be better pursued under the Generalized System of Preferences framework). Not only the European Community used quantitative arguments for excluding agriculture trade from regional agreements. See 'Agreement Between Finland and Hungary', Second Report of the Working Party adopted 23 May 1977 (L/4497), BISD 24S/107, 112, paras. 24–25 (1978), a critique of lack of coverage of agricultural products in agreement and reply that exports of such products were minimal percentage of total exports.

[138] The Working Party reviewing the European Free Trade Association's compatibility with the GATT left the interpretation of 'substantially all the trade' open. Examination of Stockholm Convention, BISD 9S/70, 86 para. 58 (adopted 4 June 1960).

[139] Understanding on the Interpretation of Art. XXIV of the General Agreement on Tariffs and Trade 1994, Preamble (*'Recognizing* also that such contribution is increased if the elimination between the constituent territories of duties and other restrictive regulations of commerce extends to all trade and diminished if any major sector of trade is excluded').

[140] GATT Art. XXIV:5(c).

In the case of a free trade zone (FTZ), such as the NAFTA is, the arguments differ only slightly from those encountered in customs union formation.[141] There is, for example, no discussion of how to determine whether a single external duty on third party goods is 'not on the whole higher or more restrictive than the general incidence' of the pre-agreement trade barriers maintained by each country because there is no single external barrier.[142] But there is an investigation into (and thus potential problem with) the corresponding passage for free trade areas. The GATT does not allow the addition to or erection of any new barriers by any of the Member counties against third parties.[143] This poses a particular difficulty for free trade areas, as rules of origin generally become more complex in order to prevent the benefits of the agreement from being readily available to third parties.[144] If this is the case, a third party could legitimately complain that the complexity of the rules of origin itself is a higher barrier to trade than existed before the FTZ. If this complaint were accepted, the members of the preferential agreement might have to adjust their plans to prevent such barriers from arising.

Procedural controversies remain as well. For instance, Members must maintain or lower their duties and regulations that will apply to fellow GATT Members outside of the preferential zone within a 'reasonable' length of time. Thus, the plan's time schedule for implementation comes under scrutiny, whether the plan is for a free trade area or a customs union. The issue of implementation time was one of the earliest dealt with by the Working Parties. While the Working Parties had voiced dissatisfaction with the long transitional periods planned for in some preferential trade agreements, until the Understanding on Article XXIV was written, there was no definitive number of years which was 'too long to be reasonable'. Now the Understanding on the Interpretation of Article XXIV states that preferential

---

[141] One author says there is only one difference between free trade zones and customs unions that is important for international trade law:

> ... the perspective of defining their treatment of traded goods. A free trade area removes tariffs and incidental barriers to traded goods between the member countries without the formation of a common outer tariff wall. A customs union both removes inter-member tariffs and establishes a common tariff wall. Despite frequent suggestions otherwise, from an international economic standpoint there is no other conceptual distinction between the two models ...

Frederick M. Abbott, 'The North American Free Trade Agreement and Its Implications for the European Union' (1994) 4:1 Transnat'l L & Contemp Probs 119, 121. For a discussion of the GATT tests for FTZs, see generally Kevin A. Wechter (note 3 *supra*), at 2611, 2612–2620.

[142] GATT Art. XXIV:5(a).

[143] GATT Art. XXIV:5(b).

[144] The possibility of entering an internally tariff-free market through the member with the lowest barrier has led to the implementation of 'rules of origin ... so complex and cumbersome as to be a barrier to trade in and of themselves ...': EEC-Agreement with Austria, BISD 20S/145, 149 para. 10 (1974) (doc. L/3900); see also Report of the Working Party on EEC—Agreement with Egypt (L/4054), BISD 21S/102, 106 para. 18 (1975) ('It was difficult to imagine why the parties would put themselves to so much trouble to draw up rules that hopefully would not represent increased barriers to third parties' trade').

[145] Understanding on the Interpretation of Art. XXIV of the General Agreement on Tariffs and Trade 1994, para. 3.

agreements ought to be formed within ten years.[145] If this would be unreasonable in a particular case, the involved parties are to notify the Council on Trade in Goods.[146]

Finally, the Members must vote their approval before the preferential trade area can become officially recognized by the WTO. Generally, decisions in the WTO are taken by consensus, and decisions under Article XXIV are not to form an exception to this practice. But failing a consensual acceptance of a free trade area or customs union, a vote of acceptance by a majority of the Members will be sufficient to make the decision valid.[147] Should the regional agreement not fulfill the Article XXIV requirements immediately, a two-thirds majority of the Members may approve the agreement on the condition that the area will become compatible with the Article in the future.[148]

Another possibility for the regional agreement to be recognized by the WTO system would be for the Parties to the Agreement to seek a waiver under GATT Article XXV. This waiver provision exempts the affected Members from certain obligations under the GATT, and thereby makes regional trade agreements possible even if they do not fulfill the qualifications set out in GATT Article XXIV. Like the Article XXIV:10 decision-making procedure, the acceptance of a waiver requires approval by a two-thirds majority of votes cast, but it additionally mandates that the votes cast represent at least half of the WTO Members. The United States has made use of the waiver provisions under the GATT system,[149] but for the broad scope of the NAFTA (covering, *inter alia*, services and intellectual property), such a waiver would not be sufficient to ensure the legality of all of its regional preferences.

Finally, regional agreements that are limited to developing countries may apply for WTO recognition under the 1979 Decision on Differential and More Favourable Treatment, Reciprocity and Fuller Participation of Developing Countries. Known as the Enabling Clause, this decision allows for regional tariff arrangements among developing countries under less stringent conditions than the GATT Article XXIV sets out. The limitation that only developing country-only arrangements can invoke this clause makes it irrelevant for a discussion of the NAFTA.

---

[146] *Ibid.*

[147] Marrakesh Agreement, Art. IX:1:

> The WTO shall continue the practice of decision-making by consensus followed under GATT 1947 ... Decisions of the Ministerial Conference and the General Council shall be taken by a majority of the votes cast, unless otherwise provided ...

[148] GATT Art. XXIV:10 ('The CONTRACTING PARTIES may by a two-thirds majority approve proposals which do not fully comply with the requirements of paragraphs 5 to 9 inclusive, provided that such proposals lead to the formation of a customs union or a free-trade area in the sense of this Article').

[149] The US-Canada Auto Pact, described at 1.3.1.2 *supra*, in Chapter 1, and the Caribbean Basin Economic Recovery Act of the United States were both established under GATT Art. XXV waiver procedures rather than as Art. XXIV regional agreements. Schoneveld (note 137 *supra*), at 66–7.

5.5.2.1.2   ECONOMIC INTEGRATION AREAS FOR SERVICES: GATS ARTICLE V

The rules governing preferential arrangements for trade in goods found in GATT Article XXIV have an equivalent provision in the area of services: GATS Article V. Article V of the services agreement, like its corollary in the area of trade in goods, provides for an exception to the rules of most-favored-nation obligation in the case of an acceptable arrangement between two or more Members of the WTO to liberalize internal trade. Article V, titled 'Economic Integration', provides:

> 1. This Agreement shall not prevent any of its Members from being a party to or entering into an agreement liberalizing trade in services between or among the parties to such an agreement, provided that such an agreement:
> (a) has substantial sectoral coverage, and
> (b) provides for the absence or elimination of substantially all discrimination, in the sense of Article XVII, between or among the parties, in the sectors covered under subparagraph (a), through:
> (i) elimination of existing discriminatory measures, and/or
> (ii) prohibition of new or more discriminatory measures,
> either at the entry into force of that agreement or on the basis of a reasonable time-frame, except for measures permitted under Articles XI, XII, XIV and XIV *bis*.[150]

Immediately noticeable is the parallel to GATT Article XXIV. The references to 'substantial sectoral coverage' and 'elimination of substantially all discrimination' are just two obvious similarities.[151] Article V also includes the 'reasonable time frame' requirement,[152] the prohibition on raising 'the overall level of barriers to trade in services ... compared to the level applicable prior to such an agreement',[153] and the notification requirement[154] that came originally from the GATT provisions.

5.5.2.1.3   DIFFERENCES BETWEEN GATT ARTICLE XXIV AND GATS ARTICLE V

There are slight differences between GATT Article XXIV and GATS Article V, however. Unlike the GATT negotiations, GATS was drafted with the benefit of experience—the negotiators were consequently able to preemptorily focus on at least some of the potential arguments.[155] Article V varies from its GATT twin in its self-contained clarifications. One of the most interesting aspects is the Article V footnote explanation attached to paragraph 1(a). The term 'substantial sectoral coverage', we are told, 'is understood in terms of

---

[150] GATS Art. V:1 (footnote omitted).

[151] GATS Art. V:1(a), (b). Compare with GATT Art. XXIV:8(a)(i), (b).

[152] GATS Art. V:1. Compare with GATT Art. XXIV:5(c).

[153] GATS Art. V:4. Compare with GATT Art. XXIV:5(a), (b).

[154] GATS Art. V:7(a). Compare with GATT Art. XXIV:7(a).

[155] Professor Abbott has little more faith in the usefulness of the GATS Art. V language as he does in the language of GATT Art. XXIV. Abbott (note 141 *supra*), at 127 ('The new GATS contains an exception provision permitting regional trading arrangements ... There is language intended to limit discriminatory abuses of this provision, but it is unlikely to be effective').

numbers of sectors, volume of trade affected and modes of supply. In order to meet this condition, agreements should not provide for *a priori* exclusion of any mode of supply'.[156] Notice that the substantial coverage explicitly disapproves of the complete exclusion of any 'mode of supply' but not of any single service sector. This is likely the outgrowth of the principle found under GATT Article XXIV of not requiring economic integration areas to liberalize internally more than the Members would be required to liberalize under the WTO Agreements in general.

Further, Article V prescribes that a services free trade agreement should not raise the 'overall level of barriers' to trade in the covered service sectors faced by other WTO Members[157] and should be 'designed to facilitate trade between the parties to the agreement',[158] Again a repetition of the rule for goods, GATS is here simply stating its overall goal that the preferential trade arrangement should be trade creating rather than trade diverting.[159] The WTO's official position of accepting that regional arrangements are not inherently incompatible with its multilateral structures is thus underlined.

Article V continues, addressing mixed membership of developed and developing countries in a regional preferential trade agreement. In such cases, paragraph 3 urges 'flexibility' in applying the conditions of 'substantial sectoral coverage' and 'elimination of substantially all discrimination' within the agreement (GATS Article V:3(a)). This, at least facially, opens a possibility of ignoring the footnote 1 prohibition on a priori mode of supply exclusions, even though the flexibility is to be used 'particularly with reference to subparagraph (b),' suggesting that all sectors should be included if possible, and that extended implementation of the liberalizations is the preferred method for taking into account the economic disadvantages faced by developing countries.

5.5.2.1.4 WTO PROCEDURE FOR REVIEW OF PREFERENTIAL AGREEMENTS

Since the coming into effect of the WTO, there are new procedures for examining preferential arrangements, involving a single committee reviewing all regional arrangements.[160] This committee examines the provisions of the arrangements, determines whether the provisions adhere to the WTO requirements, and estimates how the arrangement will affect other WTO

---

[156] GATS Art. V:1(a), n.1.
[157] GATS Art. V:4.
[158] *Ibid.*
[159] Arguably, such a provision should be much more prominent. Kenneth Dam's article 'Regional Arrangements and GATT', published in 1963, strongly argues for more attention to be paid to the overall world allocation effects of trade agreements. Dam's thesis is that trade law should encourage only those preferential trade agreements that will enhance world efficiency—i.e., trade creating agreements, and prohibit trade diverting agreements.
[160] Guidelines for the evaluation of Economic Integration Areas do exist for the Committee responsible. See e.g., WTO Committee on Regional Trade Agreements, 'Checklist of Systemic Issues Identified in the Context of the Examination of Regional Trade Agreements' WT/REG/W/12 (10 February 1997); WTO, 'Standard Format for Information on Economic Integration Agreements on Services', WT/REG/W/14 (6 May 1997); WTO, 'Annotated Checklist of Systemic Issues' WT/REG/W/16 (26 May 1997).

Members. The committee is then to issue a recommendation to the Members on whether the arrangement should be approved. A decision to adopt the report necessitates a two-thirds vote of approval by the Members.

Following the approval, the parties to the arrangement are to continue to report on the arrangement's operation and on '[a]ny significant changes and/or developments'.[161]

5.5.2.2   *The Effect of a Determination of 'WTO-Illegality'*

If a preferential agreement is positively determined to be 'WTO-illegal', the parties could first attempt to seek a waiver of their non-discrimination obligations under the Marrakesh Agreement Establishing the World Trade Organization, Article IX:3.[162] A waiver, however, is intended to be temporary and the basis for it reasserted in regular reviews, making it a poor alternative for GATT Article XXIV/GATS Article V.

Should the waiver not be granted or pursued, the parties to a WTO-illegal free trade agreement will be required to come into compliance with the most-favored-nation obligation of each WTO Agreement. Thus, the advantages to the parties must be eliminated, either by abandoning their regional agreement or by extending the preferences to all other WTO Members equally. If they refuse to do so, each party would be liable to the other WTO Members for violations of their obligations. Thus, the dispute settlement mechanism of the WTO could be invoked. This would most likely result in the issuing of a binding decision to remove the preferences. If the decision were ignored, then all non-party Members would be allowed to impose trade sanctions on the violating parties equal to the amount of damage the preferences cause.

Most of the banks of WTO Members, it must be noted, cannot initiate actions under the WTO Agreements directly (the WTO dispute settlement mechanism is only open to Member governments and banks' ability to invoke the WTO obligations in front of their own courts depends on the direct applicability of the WTO Agreements in national law). Instead, the banks must apply to their home government and attempt to motivate their government to pursue action in the WTO. Assuming that the government does so, the banks of non-party WTO Members will either gain the legal rights that the Party-banks enjoy under their (subsequently-multilateralized)

---

[161]   Understanding on the Interpretation of Art. XXIV of the General Agreement on Tariffs and Trade, 11.

[162]   Marakkesh Agreement, Art. IX:3 ('In exceptional circumstances, the Ministerial Conference may decide to waive an obligation imposed on a Member ... provided that:

   any such decision shall be taken by three-fourths [footnote 4] of the Members unless otherwise provided for in this paragraph'; footnote 4 reads: 'A decision to grant a waiver in respect of any obligation subject to a transition period or a period for staged implementation that the requesting Member has not performed by the end of the relevant period shall be taken only by consensus'). See also GATS Annex on Art. II Exceptions, 2 ('Any new exemptions applied for after the date of entry into force of the WTO Agreement shall be dealt with under paragraph 3 of Article IX of that Agreement').

preferential agreement, or will maintain their existing rights, but not be at a competitive disadvantage with any other banks.

5.5.2.3   The Effect of a Determination of WTO-Legality

If a preferential trade agreement were found to be WTO-legal, the effect on non-party WTO Member banks would be one of submitting to the loss of most-favored-nation treatment privileges. Thus, their governments would not be able to claim before a WTO dispute settlement panel that one of the Parties was in violation of its obligations by offering another Party's banks expedited application processes or by allowing persons of another Party to own a greater share of the country's banking assets.

However, non-Party Member banks do not face a complete loss of their WTO-based legal rights just because a preferential trade agreement is recognized as complying with the rules. The preferential trade area is only an exception to the rules on most-favored-nation treatment—it is not an exception to all WTO obligations. In a change from the GATT practice,[163] the WTO's dispute settlement mechanism can now be invoked on the basis of a claim of an Article XXIV violation even if the preferential arrangement has been reviewed and approved under WTO rules. The Understanding on the Interpretation of Article XXIV states:

> The provisions of Articles XXII and XXIII of GATT 1994, as elaborated and applied by the Settlement Understanding may be invoked with respect to any matter arising from the application of those provisions of Article XXIV relating to customs unions, free-trade areas or interim agreements leading to the formation of a customs union or free trade area.[164]

One author explains the significance of the newly established power of panels to examine preferential agreements' compliance with WTO obligations:

---

[163] See, e.g., EC—Tariff Treatment on Imports of Citrus Products from Certain Countries in the Mediterranean Region, L/5776, paras 4.15–4.16 (7 February 1985) (unadopted):

> ... In the opinion of the Panel, the examination—or re-examination—of Article XXIV agreements was the responsibility of the CONTRACTING PARTIES. In the absence of a decision by the CONTRACTING PARTIES and without prejudice to any decision CONTRACTING PARTIES might take in the future on such a matter, the Panel was of the view that it would not be appropriate to determine the conformity of an agreement with the requirements of Article XXIV on the basis of a complaint by a contracting party under Article XXIII:1(a) ... .
>
> The Panel considered that the practice, so far followed by the CONTRACTING PARTIES, never to use the procedures of Article XXIII:2 to make recommendations or rulings on the GATT-conformity of measures subject to special review procedures was sound. It felt that the purposes of these procedures served and the balance of interests underlying them would be lost if contracting parties could invoke the general procedures of Article XXIII:2 for the purpose of requesting decisions by the CONTRACTING PARTIES, on measures to be reviewed under special procedures.

[164] Understanding on the Interpretation of Art. XXIV, Art. 12.

The Understanding on the Interpretation of Article XXIV ... extends the jurisdiction of panels to include review of preferential trade agreements. [Text of
Article 12 of the Understanding omitted.] Similarly, the respective provisions of
the [GATS] can be invoked before a panel without any legal restriction ... The
examination is no longer limited to a review of *ex post* adoption general consistency [sic], but may now rely upon the facts of a particular regulatory problem.
This is a step of tremendous significance. For governments, this means that the
application of preferential trade rules may be subject to claims by third parties.
To companies, it means that reliance on privileges granted by such agreements
eventually found to be inconsistent with WTO law may not be stable and may
not offer lasting protection from third country competition.[165]

A panel finding of violation of a WTO provision by the preferential agreement would obligate the agreement's parties to either multilateralize that
particular preference or to eliminate it from their agreement. Additional compensation may or may not be necessary. If the party Members do not respond
to the panel's decision, non-party Members would have the opportunity to
retaliate with trade sanctions.[166] Thus, non-party Member banks would not
lose all of their legal rights under the WTO from a finding of 'WTO-legality'.

5.5.2.4   Is NAFTA 'Legal' Under WTO Rules?

The discussion about WTO-legality and illegality of regional arrangements
has been, and could well remain, theoretical. The reason is that until now
there have been no practical results of the GATT Working Party investigations in to preferential arrangements' consistency with the Article XXIV
requirements. While there are well over 100 preferential trade agreements
that have been notified to the WTO (and assumedly these are only a portion
of the preferential agreements actually in existence), only one—the
Customs Union Agreement between South Africa and Southern Rhodesia
from 1949—has ever been consensually approved by the GATT/WTO
Members.[167] The others simply exist and are thereby recognized *de facto*
when they are notified to the WTO, albeit with the frequent insertion of
'concerns' by the Working Party members about one or another portion of
the agreement. In the words of one author, the GATT's 'pragmatic ducking
if the issue' of European Community's compatibility with Article XXIV has
'established a precedent for Article XXIV analysis in future years' and
future arrangements.[168] Whether the effect of the provisions of the
Understanding on Article XXIV and/or the effect of GATS Article V
provisions are more apparent remains to be seen.

Despite their strengthening of the available procedures for testing preferential trade agreements' WTO-compatibility, it remains questionable how

---

[165] Cottier (note 126 *supra*), at 161.
[166] See generally the Understanding on the Rules and Procedures Governing the Settlement
of Disputes Arts 19, 21–3.
[167] Declaration of 18 May 1949, BISD II/29 (1949). See also Cottier (note 126 *supra*), at 149,
noting that 40 per cent of the 126 notified preferential agreements at that time had been
created since 1991.
[168] Kevin A. Wechter (note 3 *supra*), at 2611, 2615.

much these new procedures will be invoked. The actual decision-making process of the new committee is widely believed to be as heavily influenced by political considerations as the old methods of review were, and the dispute settlement process is itself still concerned with how its decisions will be received by the most powerful Members. Thus, there does not seem to be a significant likelihood that the new regional agreements will ever have a chance to be fully accepted or fully rejected. At the same time, should an approved-of regional agreement be complained of in formal dispute settlement proceedings, it is not at all clear that the potential political fallout from a finding of violation will be ignored by the panel or Appellate Body decision-makers. Facing the possibility that not only the immediate regional agreement's negotiated provisions might have to be abandoned, but with the possibility that all other preferential agreements' will be brought into question and also possibly disbanded—with the ensuing economic upset that could cause—panel members are likely to refrain from definitively suggesting that any agreement (or even a substantive provision of an agreement) is WTO-illegal.

Of course, the 'WTO legality' of the NAFTA as an agreement *could* be of critical importance to non-Party banks, as a finding of NAFTA's illegality would result in either the obligations of the NAFTA Parties being offered to all WTO Members under the principle of most-favored-nation treatment (and a consequent failure to achieve the goals of the NAFTA Parties),[169] or the abandonment of either the NAFTA or the WTO. The likelihood of the Parties' withdrawing from either the Agreement or the WTO is minimal, however, and there is no hypothesizing here on the potential ramifications of such events. The forced multilateralization of the NAFTA provisions would be the most likely result of a finding of illegality, and would have significant effects on international banking to the extent that NAFTA Chapter Fourteen rules are more liberal than the financial services framework of the GATS.

As of March 1998, the GATT Working Party on Regional Agreements and Arrangements investigating NAFTA had not come to a decision on the NAFTA's compatibility with GATT Article XXIV and GATS Article V.[170] With NAFTA's phasing in schedule of liberalizations extending in parts of the financial services sector for 15 years, the 'reasonable time' requirement poses particular difficulties. At the same time, it is an agreement between

---

[169] The goal of offering one another preferred access to, and greater freedom within, each other's markets.

[170] Indeed, though NAFTA's trade in goods provisions came into effect under the GATT 1947 regime and are thus clearly subject to GATT Art. XXIV limits, it is questionable whether NAFTA's services chapters must comply with GATS. The WTO including GATS came into effect on 1 January 1996—two years after the NAFTA. It was only in 1996 that global trade in services was subjected to the provisions of the WTO. As NAFTA's provisions were already in place and functioning, it is not so clear as to whether the service arrangements in NAFTA must fulfill the 'substantial sectoral coverage', 'reasonable time', and other requirements of GATS Art. V.

developed and a developing country. Thus, the 'flexibility' that stems from Mexico's membership in the NAFTA will lend a sound basis to the extended phase-in of the liberalizations.[171]

Among those familiar with the WTO regional integration rules there seems to be a widespread feeling that for NAFTA, perhaps more so than other regional preferential agreements, the status of being a unanimously-accepted WTO-compatible or a positively-declared WTO-incompatible agreement will never be achieved. One official commented that it is the case for NAFTA, because any such decision 'would have [both] precedential value and retroactive effects'.[172] Rather, the Agreement is likely to be generally approved with a critical commentary on certain aspects. In the end, non-Party banks are going to be left to work out for themselves how to overcome competitive hardships of not being a bank in a non-NAFTA-Party land.

---

[171] In an earlier discussion of the interpretation of 'reasonable length of time', Turkey defended the long phase in of its agreement with the EEC on the basis of its status as a developing economy. The Report of the Working Party records that the Turkish representative argued:

> Article XXIV of the General Agreement permitted the creation of a customs union between developed and developing countries. The modalities and time period for the formation of a customs union ... while remaining consistent with Article XXIV ..., must take into consideration the special conditions of the developing countries concerned, for their development and well-being were essential objectives of the same General Agreement ...

European Economic Community—Agreement of Association with Turkey: Report of the Working Party, 19S/102,103, para. 3 (adopted 25 October 1972). The Working Party made no conclusive decision on this argument, and while they 'expressed sympathy' for the need for development, still 'questioned whether the period for the formation of the customs union could be considered a 'reasonable length of time''. *Ibid.* at 108, paras. 13, 14. See also WTO (note 125 *supra*), *Analytical Index,* at 808–10, a discussion of 'within a reasonable length of time'. From a financial services policy perspective, the NAFTA's 15-year phase-in is reasonable, as it may prevent financial instability by allowing the markets to adapt to the changes gradually. In view of the importance that the financial service sector has on the rest of the economy, the security of gradual change is worth the time spent to bring it to completion. See Macario Schettino, *El TLC El Tratado de Libre Comerio: Qué Es y Cómo Nos Afecta* (Grupo Editorial Iberoamérica, Mexico City, 1994), p. 47 ('En el caso de servicios financieros, la lentitud y, finalmente, lo limitado de la apertura corresponde a la gran importancia de estos servicios sobre el resto de la economía').

[172] Government official responsible for NAFTA in the WTO; confidentiality protected. The same could be said for the European Union Agreements. On the European Agreements' compatibility with the WTO rules, see Nancy Scott, 'Compatibility of EU Regional Trade Agreements with WTO Rules in the Post-Uruguay Round' (1996) 2:6 Int'l Trade L & Reg 219.

6. Interaction of NAFTA Chapter Fourteen with the WTO Provisions on Trade in Financial Services

The following is a closer look at how the NAFTA provisions on financial services found in Chapter Fourteen of the Agreement interact with the World Trade Organization (WTO) provisions. Working under the assumption that the NAFTA will be accepted by the WTO as a legitimate preferential agreement (whether by a positive affirmation or by *de facto* approval through refraining from issuing a negative decision), the aim of this chapter is to determine the overall effects of the Chapter Fourteen on WTO Member banks based on the specific provisions of the two agreements.

This chapter begins with a discussion of how the NAFTA and the WTO General Agreement on Trade in Services (GATS) regulate trade in financial services. It starts with a comparison of the scope of the two treaties. This will assist in making a determination of to what extent the NAFTA Parties are obligated to both agreements for the same services. Then there is a short overview of the NAFTA Parties' specific commitments under the GATS to extend other WTO Members advantages in global trade in financial services. This is important, as within the WTO framework, the Members limit themselves to extending national treatment and market access advantages in financial services to only those areas they explicitly indicate, so non-NAFTA Member rights are limited. Finally, there is a schematic discussion of the two agreements from the point of view of the non-NAFTA WTO Member bank. Because any rights such a bank has *vis-à-vis* the NAFTA Parties comes from the WTO obligations of the Parties, it is necessary to find where the NAFTA might affect the legal rights of a non-Party under the WTO. Essentially, this is a determination of whether a non-Party bank could attempt to have its home government bring a dispute settlement proceeding against the NAFTA Parties in the WTO.

6.1   COMPARISON OF THE SUBSTANTIVE RULES ON TRADE IN FINANCIAL SERVICES UNDER NAFTA AND GATS

Assuming that the NAFTA is a WTO-legal free trade zone and economic integration area, the NAFTA forms a legitimate exception to the most-favored-nation (MFN) obligation of the WTO Agreements. Thus, the Parties to the NAFTA need not extend the benefits of Chapter Fourteen to third country banks. However, third countries do not lose all of their rights under the WTO Agreements. Rather, only their MFN-based rights are set aside by the NAFTA. In the specific area of financial services, the NAFTA Parties must continue to grant third country WTO Member banks the privileges offered them under the General Agreement on Trade in Services and its Annex on Financial Services, as well as the benefits affecting trade in financial services found in other areas of the WTO legal system.

To examine the effect Chapter Fourteen will have on third countries based on the WTO General Agreement on Trade in Services (GATS), the first step is to determine whether the treaties indeed cover the same activities. In the main they do, and it is interesting to proceed to consider not only the general principles of the World Trade Organization and the GATS itself, but also the specific rules governing trade in financial services and the NAFTA Parties' obligations under their GATS schedules of specific commitments. After examining these sources, the NAFTA provisions are categorized into three levels of GATS compatibility—complete compatibility, direct incompatibility, and potential incompatibility.

6.1.1   The General Agreement on Trade in Services: Framework Agreement

6.1.1.1   *Structure of the Agreement*

The Uruguay Round debates on the inclusion of a most-favored-nation treatment obligation, a national treatment obligation, and a market access obligation in the services sectors resulted in a GATS that has a quite different structure from that of the GATT. The General Agreement on Trade in Services is divided into five main parts: the scope and definitions; general obligations (including MFN and transparency); specific commitments (including NTO and market access); progressive liberalization commitments; and the structural provisions.[1] In addition, there are several sectoral annexes (including a one on financial services) which are integral to,[2] but not subject to all of the same obligations as, the

---

[1] See the outline of the GATS as set out in WTO, *The Results of the Uruguay Round of the Multilateral Trade Negotiations: The Legal Texts* (WTO, Geneva, 1995), pp. 325–6. There are numerous articles describing the GATS, some providing a general overview while others focus more particularly on problematic aspects of the Agreement. For a general overview see Drake, William J. and Kalypso Nicolaïdis, 'Ideas, interests, and institutionalization: 'trade in services' and the Uruguay Round' (1992) 46:1 Int'l Organization 37; Wendy Dobson and Pierre Jacquet, *Financial Services Liberalization in the WTO* (Institute for International Economics, Washington, DC, 1998), pp. 72–5.

[2] GATS Art. XXIX.

rest of the GATS.[3] Significantly, there are also 'schedules' for each Member listing that Member's reservations to the MFN commitment and the specific commitments on NTO and market access. These schedules are of tremendous importance, as they determine the legal obligations of each Member *vis-à-vis* the rest of the Members.[4] In a sense, these individually tailored lists create over 130 different GATS.

6.1.1.1.1 GATS' GENERAL OBLIGATIONS

The scope and definitions article[5] as well as the 'general' obligations are applicable to all Members. Thus, MFN,[6] Transparency,[7] Economic Integration Area rules,[8] Domestic Regulation,[9] and Recognition,[10] as well as provisions on Monopoly Suppliers,[11] Business Practices,[12] Payments and Transfers,[13] rules on use of Safeguards,[14] Subsidies,[15] and the General Exceptions[16] are all applicable to each Member. During the negotiations, it was also decided that if a country chooses not to afford full unconditional MFN to other Members, the exemptions must be listed in an Annex. A list attached to the Annex on Article II Exemptions therefore specifies the measures a particular Member retains the right to take. Any measures that discriminate among Members may otherwise be considered a violation of the Member's MFN obligation.[17] Such exemptions are to be limited to a

---

[3] The Annexes include the following:

   Annex on Article II Exemptions
   Annex on Movement of Natural Persons Supplying Services under the Agreement
   Annex on Air Transport Services
   Annex on Financial Services
   Annex on Negotiations on Maritime Transport Services
   Annex on Telecommunications
   Annex on Negotiations on Basic Telecommunications

   WTO (note 1 *supra*), at 326.
[4] The original Schedules for each Member can be found on the WTO CD-Rom. Modifications to the schedules resulted in a new set which can be found in WTO, Second Protocol. Plans for the WTO to put all the treaty materials on-line have not yet been realized.
[5] GATS Art. I.
[6] GATS Art. II.
[7] GATS Art. III.
[8] GATS Art. V.
[9] GATS Art. VI.
[10] GATS Art. VII.
[11] GATS Art. VIII.
[12] GATS Art. IX.
[13] GATS Art. XI.
[14] GATS Arts X, XII.
[15] GATS Art. XV.
[16] GATS Art. XIV.
[17] GATS, Art. II:2; GATS, Annex on Art. II Exemptions ('List of Article II Exemptions').

maximum of ten years,[18] with a review of the grounds for the exemption after five years.[19]

6.1.1.1.2   GATS' SPECIFIC COMMITMENTS

The portion of GATS devoted to specific commitments is mainly composed of the Market Access[20] and National Treatment Obligation[21] articles. Due to their intrusiveness in areas formerly thought of as purely 'national', they are treated differently than is the obligation of, for example, MFN. The specific commitments are only valid for a particular Member in so far as that Member has positively accepted the commitments.[22] There are lists, or 'schedules', attached to the GATS setting out each Member's commitments for National Treatment and for Market Access. Each of these, in turn, is further defined to specify the commitments as to the forms of supplying of the service: establishment, cross-border trade, presence of a natural person, or purchase in another Member territory.[23] Thus, it no longer makes sense to refer to the 'national treatment obligation for GATS Members in banking services'. Rather, there are 'Canadian national treatment obligations for banking services provided by a foreign firm by way of cross-border trade' and 'Indian market access obligations for the establishment of life insurance companies', to give just a couple of examples.

6.1.1.2   *Progressive Liberalization of Trade in Services*

The Articles relating to specific commitments are followed by an obligation to take part in further liberalization negotiations.[24] Provisions on the modification of specific commitment schedules are included as well. Modifications to Members' schedules may be made, but only after three years of having made the commitment and only at the cost of offering compensation on an MFN basis to any other Member that may be injured by the change.[25]

6.1.1.3   *GATS' Institutional Provisions*

Finally, there are the provisions on the implementation and administration of the Agreement.[26] These include the establishment of a Council to fulfill

---

[18] GATS, Annex on Art. II Exemptions 3, 4.
[19] GATS, Annex on Art. II Exemptions 6. If a Member decides after ten years that an exemption is to remain in force, that Member must apply to the WTO Ministerial Conference for a waiver. The waiver procedure, set out in the Marrakesh Agreement, would require a three-fourths majority vote to grant the waiver, and it would be reviewed annually. Marrakesh Agreement, Art. IX:3, 4.
[20] GATS Art. XVI.
[21] GATS Art. XVII.
[22] GATS Arts XVI:1, XVII:1.
[23] Further, these schedules may include the results of bilateral or plurilateral negotiations on 'qualifications, standards or licensing matters'. GATS Art. XVIII.
[24] GATS Art. XIX.
[25] GATS Art. XXI:1(a), (b).
[26] GATS Part V.

the administrative duties necessary for the functioning of the Agreement's implementation[27] and the dispute settlement provisions. GATS dispute settlement is unified with that of the entire WTO. It focuses on consultations[28] and, failing a successful settlement, gives Members a *de facto* right to approach the Dispute Settlement Body with allegations of violations of the Agreement[29] or with non-violation complaints of nullification and impairment.[30]

A denial of benefits provision limits the advantages of GATS Membership to the supply of services from WTO Members,[31] and a more complete listing of definitions is also included in the last part of GATS.[32]

6.1.1.4 Trade Elements of the GATS

The intrinsic trade law elements of the GATS are essentially the same as they are under GATT. That is, the principles of most-favored-nation treatment and the national treatment obligation can be found in both agreements. However, because GATS regulates trade in services and GATT regulates trade in goods, there are some differences worthy of notice.

6.1.1.4.1   OBJECT OF GATS PROTECTION: SERVICES AND SERVICE SUPPLIERS

First, the object of GATS protection is the 'services and service suppliers' of GATS Members.[33] The service sectors to which the GATS applies are, as emphasized above, determined by each Member's list, but the Agreement itself attempts to cover all services except those supplied by the government *qua* government,[34] those supplied under government procurement arrangements,[35] and air traffic rights.[36]

To determine whether a supplier or a service is eligible for the advantages of the Agreement, the service must be supplied or consumed by a natural person who is a citizen or permanent resident of a Member. Alternatively, the supplier or consumer may be a legal person owned by, controlled by, or affiliated with a person of a Member.[37]

---

[27] GATS Art. XXIV.
[28] GATS Art. XXII:1.
[29] GATS Art. XXIII:1.
[30] GATS Art. XXIII:3.
[31] GATS Art. XXVII.
[32] GATS Art. XXVIII.
[33] GATS Art. II:1.
[34] GATS Art. I:3(b), (c) (exempting 'services supplied in the exercise of governmental authority' from the definition of services).
[35] GATS Art. XIII:1 (exempting government procurement of services from MFN, NTO, and market access obligations).
[36] GATS Annex on Air Transport Services, para. 2; see also *ibid.* para. 6 (defining 'traffic rights').
[37] See GATS Art. XXVIII (m) (defining 'juridical person of another Member'); GATS Art. XXVIII (n) (defining 'owned', 'controlled', and 'affiliated').

6.1.1.4.2   IDEA OF 'LIKE'-NESS OF SERVICES AND SERVICE SUPPLIERS

Secondly, the most-favored-nation treatment and the national treatment obligation in GATS focus on 'like services and service suppliers' rather than, as in GATT, on 'like products'. Although impulsively satisfying, this criterion has a potential of being highly problematic in practice. A comparative element to relate the services/service suppliers is logical when requiring similar treatment, but the use of the adjective 'like' when describing an intangible service is difficult. Under the GATT panel decisions, the issue of 'like product' has been debated at length, and several approaches have been put forth as the most appropriate way to determine the likeness of a product. At present, the approach favored by the Appellate Body is that of comparing physical characteristics.[38] Without wanting to comment on the advisability of this approach in the goods context, it is clear that such an approach is completely unfit for the services context and would be ludicrous in the service supplier context. The drafters of the GATS appear to have adopted the GATT terminology without considering that the GATT analysis used to implement this terminology would be impossible to adopt.

6.1.1.4.3   IDEA OF MARKET ACCESS FOR SERVICES

Thirdly, GATS uses a concept termed 'market access' to refer to the overall idea of bringing a foreign service to customers in another Member state.[39] In the goods sectors, market access is limited by a combination of restrictions on the use of quantitative restrictions and regulations on the use of standards and other technical barriers to trade. In the services context, market access limitations are more subtle, due to the intangibility of the trade. National regulations, permit requirements, and conditions on investments are typical tools used to restrain service supplier entry into a market.

The WTO, as an organization for liberalizing trade, aims to encourage the market access of services in order to effectively liberate the flow of services. Under the GATS Article XVI, a Member obliges itself to grant other Members' service suppliers one or more form(s) of market access in those sectors for which there are specific commitments taken.[40]

6.1.1.4.4   REQUIREMENT OF 'TREATMENT NO LESS FAVORABLE'

The last element to mention is the level of treatment the MFN, NTO, and market access provisions require under GATS. These are the same as the MFN and NTO under GATT: treatment no less favorable than that afforded

---

[38] See 3.9.3 *supra*.

[39] See Joel P. Trachtman, 'Trade in Financial Services Under GATS, NAFTA and the EC: A Regulatory Jurisdictio Analysis' (1995) 34 Colum J Transnat'l L 37, 76 ('We may ... view 'market access' as a trade-oriented concept, which cares little abou regulatory values, focusing instead on the trade bottom line: is there access to the market?').

[40] GATS Art. XVI. The Understanding on Financial Services also has a market access provision, encouraging ('endeavour to') Members to offer market access for foreign financial service providers up to the point at which domestic providers would be disadvantaged. Trachtman (note 39 *supra*), at 79.

a Member's own services[41] or to any other services or service suppliers.[42] The GATS does go further than the GATT text, however, in defining more clearly that the meaning of 'no less favourable' refers to the 'conditions of competition'.[43]

6.1.1.5 Development of the GATS Regulation on Trade in Financial Services

The negotiations on financial services were among the most difficult of the Services discussions in the Uruguay Round. There are several factors accounting for the problems in coming to an agreed text to regulate the financial sector. First, more so than with the other service sectors, the developing countries opposed the inclusion of financial trade liberalization in the same institution that ruled trade in goods. The vulnerability of local banking and insurance institutions led to fears of a widespread collapse of national financial industries as the aggressive and efficient developed countries' institutions moved into their previously sheltered markets.

Moreover, banking, securities, and insurance activities have long been considered particularly sensitive to the national interest, which is why they are closely regulated and often protected from foreign competition in industrial and developing countries alike.[44] Arguments about security considerations as well as sovereignty concerns plagued those who attempted to foster an agreement on reducing trade barriers to financial services. Even the United States showed a surprising resistance to far-reaching liberalizations if such were to go beyond the granting of market access.[45]

Nevertheless, with the recognition that 'efficiency in trade in goods [was becoming] increasingly dependent on trade in services, such as in the area of information and financial services',[46] the negotiations began to proceed despite the complaints.

---

[41] GATS Art. XVII:1 ('each Member shall accord to services and service suppliers of any other Member, in respect of all measures affecting the supply of services, treatment no less favourable than that it accords to its own like services and service suppliers').

[42] GATS Art. II:1 ('each Member shall accord immediately and unconditionally to services and service suppliers of any other Member treatment no less favourable than that it accords to like services and services suppliers of any other country').

[43] GATS Art. XVII:3 ('Formally identical or formally different treatment shall be considered to be less favorable if it modifies the conditions of competition in favour of services or service suppliers of the Member compared to like services or service suppliers of any other Member').

[44] See Dobson and Jacquet (note 1 *supra*), at 8–12, summarizing objections to financial service liberalization attempts.

[45] Telephone conversation with Lukas Beglinger, Swiss government official and member of Switzerland's WTO delegation during the financial services negotiations (March 1998).

[46] Terence P. Stewart (ed.), *The GATT Uruguay Round*, Vol. 2, p. 2342.

By 1995, the United States had defined its opposition to an unconditional MFN obligation for their financial services liberalization. Instead, the United States was willing to offer conditional MFN, limiting their market openings to those WTO Members that reciprocated with open markets. Although the other WTO Members-to-be signed an alternative 'Understanding on Commitment in Financial Services', which in effect bound them to the principle of unconditional MFN and to a principle of improving the competitive position of foreign financial service providers in their territories, the hopes for world-wide participation in financial service liberalization were put on hold at the end of July 1995.[47]

At the First Ministerial Conference of the WTO in Singapore, a press brief on financial services lay out the ambitious objectives for the further development of the GATS Annex.[48] It states that beyond the technical work of defining more accurately the various types of financial services, '[the goals for] next year's talks are to make further progress, to bring the United States into the improved package, and for all countries to make their commitments non-discriminatory'.[49]

The statement does not elaborate on the method it would employ to achieve these goals, nor does it evaluate the possibility of non-achievement of them. The potential failure of the talks, however, remained a threat until the end.

The Members began meeting in early 1997 to prepare for the December session. One- or two-day bargaining rounds took place in April, August, and October 1997, allowing the Members to make non-binding offers and assess the climate of further liberalization. As November neared and several key states had not yet given an indication of what they were planning to offer in December, tension mounted.

The December negotiations began on the third of the month, amidst much uncertainty as to how the international financial markets would be shaped in the next nine days. By the beginning of the last week, most participants had circulated conditional revised offers, but the states considered critical to the process had not given any firm indication of their readiness to participate in further market openings. The United States refused to commit itself firmly until Brazil, India, Malaysia, and Japan had agreed to further liberalizations.

Finishing a few hours after midnight on the morning of 13 December 1997, the WTO Members were finally able to agree on a list of commitments. The results incorporated more liberalizations than had ever been achieved before on a multilateral level. With commitments from 102 Member states,

---

[47] See Roger Kampf, 'A Step in the Right Direction: The Interim Deal on Financial Services in the GATS' (1995) 1:5 Int'l Trade L & Reg 157, 163–5, summary of Member commitments from 28 July 1995 to November 1997.

[48] WTO, Press Brief: Financial Services (text found on internet at >www.wto.org<).

[49] *Ibid.*

including improved lists from 70 Members, the negotiations for the Fifth Protocol were declared a success.[50]

6.1.2 Note

The GATS is a relatively new agreement, and there is as yet only one dispute settlement decision interpreting this agreement[51] and none on the Financial Services Annex and accompanying texts. Therefore, the following predictions of how these agreements will be used are based mainly on past GATT practice.

6.1.3 Coverage of the Treaties

6.1.3.1 To Whom/To What the Treaties Apply

In determining the legal effects of NAFTA Chapter Fourteen on third parties, one first must ascertain that the two treaties apply to the same governmental and non-governmental bodies. Under both GATS and NAFTA, clearly the actions of the federal governments of Canada, Mexico, and the United States are regulated.[52] The measures by subnational governments are also included within the scope of both agreements.[53]

---

[50] WTO, Fifth Protocol (note 1 *supra*). WTO General Director Renato Ruggiero proclaimed the Fifth Protocol's completion 'a historic deal'. Esther Hauert (for the Swiss Federal Department of External Economic Relations), 'GATS—Committee on Trade in Financial Services CTFS: Abschluss der Verhandlungen über Finanzdienstleistungen' (19 December 1997) (on file with author). The United States praised the 'successful effort' behind the new 'dramatically improved' financial services agreement. The White House Office of the Press Secretary, 'Statement by Secretary Rubin and Ambassador Barshefsky Regarding the Successful Conclusion of WTO Financial Services Negotiations' 13 December 1997. Canada's reaction was similar, with Minister for International Trade Sergio Marchi proclaiming the result as 'a key step for the global trading system'(Canada Department of Foreign Affairs and International Trade, 'Canada Welcomes WTO Financial Services Agreement' (Press Release, 12 December 1997), as was Switzerland's: the conclusion of the negotiations was, 'in mehrer Hinsicht ein bedeutender Erfolg' announced the Federal Department of External Economic Relations' head of financial services negotiations P.L. Girard (BAWI, 'WTO/GATS: Abschluss der Verhandlungen über Finanzdienstleistungen', letter of 22 December 1997); see also European Union, 'Successful Conclusion of WTO Financial Services Negotiations' (text found on internet at >http://europa.eu.int<).

[51] European Communities—Regime for the Importation, Sale and Distribution of Bananas: Complaint by Ecuador, WT/DS27/R/ECU, 364–7, paras. 7.277–7.285 (22 May 1997). The case between Canada and the United States over Canada's advertising and postal rate regulations for split-run magazines did implicate GATS issues, but the Appellate Body upheld the panel's decision to solely analyze the dispute under GATS rules. Canada—Certain Measures Concerning Periodicals, WT/DS31/AB/R (30 June 1997), pp. 21–2.

[52] NAFTA Art. 105 ('The Parties shall ensure that all necessary measures are taken in order to give effect to the provisions of this Agreement …'); GATS Arts I:1, I:3(a)(i).

[53] NAFTA Article 105 ('The Parties shall ensure that all necessary measures are taken … including their observance, … by state and provincial governments'); GATS Art. I:3(a)(ii). With the subsequent exemption of State and Provincial measures from much of the scope of NAFTA (but not from the financial services provisions), the subnational reach of NAFTA has been extinguished to a large degree in practice.

Yet, the actions taken by non-governmental self-regulatory agencies or organizations are covered only in NAFTA[54] and the Understanding on Financial Services (the Understanding)—not in GATS. Moreover, the Understanding only extends the national treatment obligation of WTO Members to self-regulatory organizations in the financial services sectors.[55] By contrast, the NAFTA requires that any organization by which membership or participation is necessary for the supply of a service, abide by *all* the Chapter Fourteen principles.[56] This difference is important, as the NAFTA's broader scope here leaves non-NAFTA WTO Members with only a limited right to the advantages enjoyed by the NAFTA Parties. In light of the distinction between the obligations of market access and national treatment in the GATS Schedules, this is particularly problematic.

Consider, for example, the following. Assume that the US Securities and Exchange Commission (SEC) promulgated a rule requiring that to be listed on the New York Stock Exchange, all foreign banks must maintain a minimum reserve in the United States. This could be considered a market access issue rather than a national treatment problem, as the SEC has set out a prerequisite to forming the commercial relationship rather than a post-establishment operational requirement.[57] In this case, a Canadian or a Mexican bank (or any bank that fulfilled the requirements so as to be a 'financial institution of another Party') could bring this rule to the attention of its NAFTA Party government. Because the SEC is a self-regulatory body to which the NAFTA applies,[58] that government could then begin a NAFTA dispute settlement process. Consultations could lead to the formation of a panel under Article 1414 and Chapter Twenty, and ultimately to a panel decision ruling that the promulgated rule is incompatible with Chapter Fourteen. If necessary,

---

[54] NAFTA Art. 1402. Compare GATS Art. VIII (referring to 'monopoly and exclusive service suppliers') and the definition of 'monopoly supplier of a service' (GATS Art. XXVIII(h)) with NAFTA Art. 1416 definition of a 'self-regulatory organization'.

[55] Understanding on Financial Services, C.2:

> When membership or participation in, or access to, any self-regulatory body, securities or futures exchange or market, clearing agency, or any other organization or association, is required by a Member in order for financial service suppliers of any other Member to supply financial services on an equal basis with financial service suppliers of the Member, or when the Member provides directly or indirectly such entities, privileges or advantages in supplying financial services, the Member shall ensure that such entities accord national treatment to financial service suppliers of any other Member resident in the territory of the Member.

[56] NAFTA Art. 1402.

[57] See Aaditya Mattoo, 'National Treatment in the GATS: Corner-Stone or Pandora's Box?' (1997) 31:1 J World Trade 107, 113–19, discussion of the problematic distinction between market access and national treatment obligations in GATS.

[58] See 3.6.2.3 *supra* (explanation of scope of Chapter 14 application to self-regulatory bodies).

retaliation in the financial services sector may be used to enforce a decision of the dispute settlement panel.[59]

A similar bank of another nationality, suffering the same competitive disadvantage, may not be able to get such relief. Here, the operative agreements are the WTO Understanding on Commitments in Financial Services, the GATS, and the WTO dispute settlement procedures. A Thai bank, for example, falling under the Understanding on Commitments in Financial Services ('Understanding') rules, has the right to be granted treatment no less favorable than national banks by self regulatory organizations. But because the Understanding refers to the individual Members' lists of specific commitments, there may be only a national treatment commitment in the United States' schedule and no parallel market access commitment. Thus, it is conceivable that the Understanding provision would be interpreted so as to place no obligation on the self-regulatory body to offer equal market access opportunities to WTO Member banks as it does national banks. As the GATS itself does not cover self-regulatory bodies, a WTO Member bank could rely at most on the 'non-violation' clause of the GATS.[60] However, there is a higher burden of proof on the complainant in such cases. Thus, the seemingly minor difference in treaty scope may have potentially large commercial effects.

6.1.3.2   To What Types of Actions the Treaties Apply

The types of actions addressed by the treaties must be determined. Chapter Fourteen applies to Party measures 'relating to' financial service institutions, their investors and investments, and cross-border trade in financial services. The corresponding provision for the GATS is found in the Annex on Financial Services. There it sets out that the provisions apply to Member 'measures affecting the supply of financial services'.[61] The term

---

[59] NAFTA Art. 1415(a). In no case, however, may a Party retaliate for a violation of a Chapter Fourteen violation by affecting any sector other than financial services. Similarly, a non-financial services sector violation may not use measures affecting financial services as retaliation. NAFTA Art. 1415(c). This refusal to extend cross-border sanctions is different from the dispute settlement mechanism under the GATS. See 3.18 *supra*, discussing dispute settlement.

[60] The term 'non-violation' clause indicates that provision which forms a basis for a claim of GATS violation based on a disadvantage suffered by another Member's use of a measure that is not prohibited by the GATS text. The provision, found in GATS Art. XXIII:3 states:

> If any Member considers that any benefit it could reasonably have expected to accrue to it under a specific commitment of another Member under Part III of this Agreement is being nullified or impaired as a result of the application of any measure which does not conflict with the provisions of this Agreement, it may have recourse to the DSU.

See also GATT Art. XXIII:1(b) (non-violation provision for trade in goods).

[61] GATS Annex on Financial Services 1(a).

'measures' is broadly defined in both the NAFTA and WTO contexts to include not only laws and administrative rules, but also procedures and 'actions'.[62]

Another potential scope difference stems from the terms 'relating to', used in the NAFTA, and 'affecting' used in GATS.[63] Whereas NAFTA focuses on measures 'relating to' banks,[64] the GATS Annex looks at those 'affecting the supply of' banking services.[65] The general GATS' term 'affecting' has been interpreted widely.[66] Thus, certainly any measure that alters the relative conditions of competition faced by financial service providers is included. Conceivably, the 'relating to' language of the NAFTA is broader still. One must determine in any single case whether the measure in dispute is both 'affecting' the services and service suppliers and 'relating to' financial institutions or their investors. If the measure is 'related to', but not 'affecting', financial institutions, the non-NAFTA WTO Member has no right to demand relief under the GATS.[67] Such differences in scope are most likely to be felt when a bank is prevented from offering non-traditional services to its customers. If a NAFTA Party implemented legislation restricting a certain non-banking activity and if banks were commercially engaged in such activities as a separate area of profit-making, there could arise a constellation in which the legislation would be found not to 'affect the supply of financial services' but which would 'relate to financial institutions'. In this context, a NAFTA Party bank could have recourse to dispute settlement while a GATS Member bank could not.

---

[62] NAFTA defines 'measure' in Art. 201: 'measure includes any law, regulation, procedure, requirement or practice'. Chapter Fourteen contains no indication of varying the definition for financial services. The GATS definition of 'measure' is in Art. XXVIII(a): 'any measure by a Member, whether in the form of a law, regulation, rule, procedure, decision, administrative action, or any other form'. The term has the same definition for purposes of the Financial Services Annex. It is possible that the GATS language of 'any other form' extends farther than the NAFTA's 'practices' although it is not directly so stated. But given the intent of the GATS to liberalize trade in services, as well as the obvious intent to give the term a broad scope, any panel that interpreted 'measures' so narrowly as to exempt non-formal policies would be acting contrary to international law rules on interpretation of treaties.

[63] See also discussion of 'relating to', at 3.6.3 *supra*.

[64] NAFTA Art. 1401:1.

[65] GATS Annex on Financial Services 1(a).

[66] European Communities (note 51 *supra*). See particularly at 365–6, para. 7.281:

> In sum, we believe that, consistently with their general approach, the drafters consciously adopted the terms 'affecting' and 'supply of a service' to ensure that the disciplines of the GATS would cover any measure bearing upon conditions of competition in supply of a service, regardless of whether the measure directly governs or indirectly affects the supply of the service.

[67] Once again there is a possibility under GATS of bringing a non-violation complaint before the Dispute Settlement Body. GATS Art. XXIII:3. See also 3.18 *supra*.

6.1.3.3   Covered Activities: How the Approach to Liberalization of Trade in Financial Services Differs Between NAFTA and GATS

That the traditional banking activities of lending of funds and deposit-taking are covered by both the NAFTA and the GATS is clear. It is also clear that the NAFTA excludes financial government procurement while the Understanding includes government procurement of financial services in the GATS framework.[68] What is unclear is the extent to which the coverage of these treaties differs for the non-traditional activities of a bank. With the increasing expansion of banks' commercial activities, the protection of non-banking—or indeed non-financial—services offered by banks is potentially of great importance, and might result in a divergence in coverage of the two treaties. The following attempts to clarify the differing approaches to liberalization taken by the two treaties in hopes of more exactly understanding the boundaries of their scopes.

6.1.3.3.1   NAFTA AND GATS APPROACHES TO LIBERALIZATION

The NAFTA approach to protection is institutionally-based.[69] That is, Chapter Fourteen protects Party financial service providers and institutions (and the institutions' investors and the investors' investments in the institutions) themselves from Party measures that would discriminate based on nationality. Thus, the scope is determined in relation to the bank (or insurance company or security brokerage) rather than in relation to the service that is actually supplied.

The GATS framework, on the other hand, was written with an activity-based perspective: trade in financial services is protected, with 'insurance and insurance-related services' and 'banking and other financial services' defined by inclusive listings of activities.[70] Thus, the supplier of the financial service is protected by virtue of the fact that she supplies banking or insurance or securities services, not because she works for a financial service institution.

6.1.3.3.2   HOW THE NAFTA AND GATS APPROACHES AFFECT THE PROVISION OF NON-FINANCIAL SERVICES

The difference in approaches could lead to a difference in the NAFTA view of a non-financial service and the GATS view of the same service. Although a Canadian bank's securities and insurance affiliations would be covered by both the GATS' Financial Service Annex obligations and the NAFTA Chapter Fourteen provisions, the same bank's activities in a non-financial

---

[68] See NAFTA Art. 1401:3; WTO, Understanding on Commitments in Financial Services, para. 2.

[69] See Olin L. Wethington, *Financial Market Liberalization: The NAFTA Framework* (Shepard's/McGraw-Hill, New York, 1994), pp. 67–8.

[70] GATS Annex on Financial Services, para. 5(a) ('A financial service is any service of a financial nature offered by a financial service supplier of a Member. Financial services include all insurance and insurance-related services, and all banking and other financial services (excluding insurance)').

service sector would fall under the main GATS text provisions or under one of the specific annexes to the GATS that regulates a particular service sector. As an illustration, consider the following:

> Many banks have been taking over closed gasoline stations for the purpose of remodeling them into new branches. The stations offer ample parking space plus a high-traffic location picked by oil company experts. But generally the first things to go are the gas pumps.
>
> However, when Cass County Bank ... took over a gas station in 1975 ..., [its president] didn't take the general route. He decided that pumping gas could be an attractive plus.
>
> ...
>
> Most of the customers are Cass County Bank depositors who take advantage of a further discount: 4¢ per gallon is knocked off for people who have the bill debited from their checking account.[71]

If such a gas station business were allowed by the national banking authorities of a NAFTA Party, under the NAFTA Chapter Fourteen the gasoline sales by a NAFTA Party bank could be protected by the obligations of national treatment and most-favored-nation obligations. Under the GATS, because the activity is not a banking activity, the sales of gasoline would not come under the financial service provisions, rather, such sales would be most likely subject to the General Agreement on Tariffs and Trade, because gasoline is a good rather than a service. Thus, a non-Party bank would be at a disadvantage compared to a Party bank in the same situation, because it would have to familiarize itself with a wider range of legal provisions, and thus incur extra costs.

6.1.4   GATS Obligations of the NAFTA Parties

As set out earlier, the GATS obligations are of two types: general obligations, applying to all service sectors except those excluded in its Annex on Article II Exemptions; and specific commitments, applying only to the service sectors listed by the WTO Member in its Annex on Specific Commitments.[72] Determining the scope of GATS commitments in the financial services area for the NAFTA Parties depends first on whether any of the Parties has taken an Article II exemption for financial services or banking; and secondly on which financial service activities are contained on each Party's specific commitments schedule, and which modes of delivery of the services are subsumed under the market access and national treatment obligation lists.

In July 1995, seven months after the going into effect of the WTO Agreements for most of the original Members, the Financial Services

---

[71] 'Idea Exchange', *ABA Banking Journal* (December 1982), p. 22, found in Edward L. Symons Jr and James J. White, *Banking Law: Teaching Materials* (3rd edn, West Publishing, Minneapolis, 1991), p. 206.
[72] See 6.1.1.1.1, 6.1.1.1.2 *supra.*

negotiations were brought to a preliminary close.[73] However, due to the United States' dissatisfaction with the proposed commitments of other (mainly developing) countries in the area of market access for financial services, the commitments were to be reopened for revision starting 1 November 1997. From that point until 12 December 1997, Members were allowed to withdraw from prior commitments as well as to oblige themselves to make additional liberalizations in their financial service sectors.[74]

An account of the negotiations leading up to the December deadline is rife with dramatic tension.[75] Preliminary offers, political pressure, frustrating silences, and bargained concessions characterized the Members' search for a mutually agreeable commitment on liberalization. In the end, however, the efforts culminated in the Fifth Protocol—a document encompassing the most far-reaching financial liberalization yet achieved on among such a wide group of sovereign states. Among the most significant results of the negotiations for the revised commitments was the opening of some developing countries' markets, including several Latin American, south-east Asian, and African markets. It was this market access assurance that gave the United States the political opportunity to withdraw its

---

[73] See WTO, Second Decision on Commitments in Financial Services Adopted by the Council for Trade in Services on 21 July 1995, S/L/9 (24 July 1995) (dependent upon the acceptance of the Second Protocol to the GATS); WTO, Decision Adopting the Second Protocol to the General Agreement on Trade in Services Adopted by the Committee on Trade in Financial Services on 21 July 1995, S/L/13 (24 July 1995); WTO, Second Protocol to the General Agreement on Trade in Services, S/L/11 (24 July 1995).

[74] The Second Decision on Commitments in Financial Services states:

> *The Council for Trade in Services,*
>
> ...
>
> *Decides* as follows:
>
> 1. Notwithstanding Article XXI of the General Agreement on Trade in Services (GATS), a Member may during a period of sixty days beginning on 1 November 1997, modify or withdraw all or part of the Specific Commitments on Financial Services inscribed in its Schedule.
> 2. Notwithstanding Article II of the GATS and paragraphs 1 and 2 of the Annex on Article II Exemptions, a Member may, during the same period referred to in paragraph 1, list in that Annex measures relating to financial services which are inconsistent with paragraph 1 of Article II of the GATS.

A Trade in Services Council Decision taken at the end of May 1997 revised the ending date to December 12 rather than the orginally-planned end of December. WTO Council for Trade in Services, 'Decision on Financial Services Negotiations of May 29, 1997', S/L/39 (4 June 1997). The post-Uruguay Round negotiating process of the financial service commitments is explained by Roger Kampf of the European Commission in 'Liberalisation of Financial Services in the GATS and Domestic Regulation' (1997) 3:5 Int'l Trade L & Reg 155. See also WTO, 'Financial Service Talks Resume', 19 *WTO Focus* (May 1997), p. 1 ff; Dobson and Jacquet (note 1 *supra*), at 80–85.

[75] See Esther Hauert/Bundesamt für Aussenwirtschaft (Switzerland), 'GATS-Committee on Trade in Financial Services CTFS: Abschluss der Verhandlungen über Finanzdienstleistungen' (19 December 1997), pp. 2–5, description of the negotiating process in the weeks leading to 12 December 1997 by Swiss delegate).

standing MFN exception for new service providers.[76] In the following, the Specific Commitments of the NAFTA Parties will be set out as they appeared at the beginning of 1998, following the Fifth Protocol's completion. (The results of the Protocol did not take effect until 1 March 1999 and may be improved upon at any time, so the latest lists should be consulted before taking any decisions based on the following.) Upon their going into effect, the Fifth Protocol's commitments replace the earlier commitments.[77]

6.1.4.1 Canada's GATS Obligations

Canada's participation in the GATS negotiations was based on a view that a liberalization of its services market would be beneficial. Although its Provinces have strong regulatory powers in many of the important service sectors, leading to a significant MFN exception and a limited ability to offer foreign insurance and securities service providers national treatment and market access,[78] in banking Canada continues to bind itself multilaterally to opening its market to foreign service providers. Consequently, the Fifth Protocol of the GATS contains several significant liberalizations and improvements to the original Canadian schedule.

6.1.4.1.1 MFN EXEMPTIONS IN BANKING SERVICES

The Canadians will grant licenses to financial service suppliers 'on the basis of reciprocity'. In order to facilitate the Canadian banks' access to other markets, the Canadians here reserve the right to extend only conditional MFN treatment in licensing.[79] Thus, if a foreign government refuses to grant Canadian banks' applications for establishment, Canada can refuse to issue licenses to financial service providers from that country.

A further, perhaps minor, exception is the allowance that Québec may offer loan and investment companies from the United Kingdom and Ireland preferential treatment when giving licenses to carry on business. An historical preference, this exception is not likely to cause great distortions in world trade of financial services.[80]

---

[76] See WTO, 'Successful Conclusion of the WTO's Financial Services Negotiations' 15 December 1997 (text found on the internet at >www.wto.org<).

[77] WTO, Fifth Protocol (note 1 *supra*), para. 1. The issue of how the new commitments would stand in relation to the previous schedules was a concern discussed among the negotiators in anticipation of the December meeting. See WTO, 'Issues Concerning the Adoption of a Protocol to Conclude the Financial Services Negotiations', S/FIN/W/11 (1 May 1997), pp. 2–3, section setting forth possible methods of resolving the relationship between old and new commitments.

[78] See also 2.2 *supra*.

[79] The Fifth Protocol did not change Canada's earlier MFN exemptions. Those listed here are found in the schedule attached to the original Financial Service Annex.

[80] This exception is also a reservation in the NAFTA. See 3.9.4.1 *supra*.

6.1.4.1.2   SPECIFIC COMMITMENTS IN BANKING SERVICES

For the traditional banking activities of taking deposits, lending, leasing, making payments and transmissions, and providing guarantees and commitments, both market access and national treatment are fully granted to foreign banks located outside Canada that have Canadian customers either by virtue of cross-border supply or consumption abroad. For commercial presence within Canada, however, there are several limitations on these activities, enumerated in an exclusive list.

Limitations on market access   There are two major types of limitations on market access for foreign banks in Canada. The first is that of legal form and the second is that of ownership structure. In terms of legal form, until summer 1999 non-Canadian banks may only establish banking offices in Canada as a subsidiary.[81] Thus, the extra costs of establishing a separate juridical entity, as well as the lower capital asset level that comes from not being able to count the parent's capital in backup funds, are disadvantages that Canada may still impose on non-domestic banks. (This same restriction applies to NAFTA Parties' banks.) Under the new commitments in the Fifth Protocol, Canada will, however, allow direct branching for all foreign banks as according to the coming into effect of its new banking legislation for foreign banks. The Schedule of Specific Commitments foresees that Canada will be able to make a direct-branching commitment under GATS by 30 June 30 1999.[82]

The second main limitation on foreign banks wanting to enter the Canadian market is that of ownership structure. Applying to all federally regulated financial institutions—domestic or foreign-owned, Canada's widely-held rule requires that banks, trusts and loans, and insurance companies that have over C$750 million in capital 'have 35 per cent of their voting shares widely-held and listed and posted for trading on the Canadian stock exchange'.[83] Moreover, foreign-owned institutions are further limited in that the controlling shares of the subsidiary must be 'held directly by the foreign company incorporated in the jurisdiction where the foreign company, either directly or through a subsidiary, principally carries on business'.[84] Therefore, a Canadian subsidiary of a WTO Member bank must ensure that the parent bank controls the bank and that those shares are held in the country or national sub-unit of a country where the parent's main operations take place. Such a restriction ensures that a court will be able to reach the assets of the corporation should legal liabilities be incurred. The widely-held rule requires that the rest of the shares be distributed among various owners in order to prevent a further concentration of assets. Complete ownership of large banks is thus prohibited, albeit for Canadian as well as for foreign banks.

---

[81] Canada, Schedule of Specific Commitments—Revised Offer on Financial Services S/FIN/W/12/Add.7/Rev.2 at 11.

[82] See *ibid.* at 11.

[83] *Ibid.* at 3.

[84] *Ibid.*

The second ownership restriction is the '10 per cent rule' and applies specifically to banks. The relevant provision states, 'No one person (Canadian or foreign) may own more than 10 per cent of any class of shares of a Schedule I bank'.[85] This rule has been long-standing in Canadian banking law, and is aimed at preventing concentrations of power (both market power and political power).[86] Although this provision is facially non-discriminatory, it effectively limits the foreign-owned banks to operating as Schedule II institutions. As a Schedule II bank, however, the institution has the choice of either limiting itself to C$750 million in total equity or of ensuring that at least 35 per cent of its shares are widely held. The NAFTA does not alter this for Party banks.

For trust and loan companies and for credit unions and caisses populaires, Canada maintains limitations on market access for their laws that require incorporation for market access.[87] Beyond this, the various Provinces have limits on foreign control or acquisition of trust and loan companies within their authority.[88] Other types of non-insurance financial institutions have restrictions based on Provincial laws.[89]

For securities activities, the limitations on market access are more numerous. The Provincial governments regulate securities companies, and the list of limitations reflects this fact.[90] While all mutual funds that offer securities in Canada must have a resident custodian or sub-custodian, the other limits on cross border supply are specific to particular Provinces.[91] These include provisions requiring commercial presence for providing advisory and auxiliary financial services and for asset management. Quebec maintains a reservation for its public monopoly for managing the pension funds of public and para-public institutions.[92] Thus, in all of these areas, cross-border supply is essentially prohibited.

For the consumption abroad mode of service supply, there is a uniform requirement to 'register in order to trade through dealers and brokers that are neither resident nor registered in the province in which the trade is effected'.[93] This does not prohibit such trade, but does accord an advantage to those securities brokers that are located in Canada.

The limitations on market access by commercial presence are mainly restrictions on the legal form of the supplier. Securities dealers and brokers generally need to be incorporated under national or subnational laws.[94] In

---

[85] *Ibid.* at 11.
[86] See discussion of the 10 per cent rule 2.2.2.2 *supra*.
[87] Canada: Schedule ... Revised Offer (note 81 *supra*), at 11, 13 (for trust and loans, either federal or provincial incorporation may be required, except that this does not apply to British Columbia where ministerial approval is required for incorporation and for substantial changes in control; credit unions and caisses populaires 'and associations or groups thereof' must be incorporated 'in the jurisdiction in which they operate').
[88] See generally *ibid.* at 12.
[89] See generally *ibid.* at 13–16.
[90] *Ibid.* at 16–17.
[91] *Ibid.* at 15.
[92] *Ibid.*
[93] *Ibid.* at 16.
[94] *Ibid.*

several Provinces, the supplier may be 'formed ... under' such laws, but in order to be a member of the Montreal Exchange, a broker or dealer must be incorporated.[95] Finally, to provide advisory or auxiliary financial services in British Columbia, the service supplier must be incorporated under national or subnational laws.[96]

6.1.4.1.3   PRESENCE OF NATURAL PERSONS

The limitations on the presence of natural persons in traditional banking areas are no different than those set out for all other service sectors, except that members of the Montreal stock exchange must reside in Canada.[97]

6.1.4.1.4   LIMITATIONS ON NATIONAL TREATMENT

The limitations on Canada's offer of national treatment to foreign financial institutions (banking and non-insurance companies as well as insurance companies) include differences in categorizing transactions between related companies for value-added tax purposes and in the residency requirements for institutional managers.

For cross-border supply, consumption abroad, and commercial presence, companies' transactions with non-resident branches or other related companies may be considered transactions between unrelated companies for value-added tax assessment. Because the same type of transactions between similarly related firms that are both located in Canada would not be taxed, there is a discriminatory effect of such legislation.

Limitations on national treatment that are restricted to foreign banks arise only when a supplier of banking services has a commercial presence in Canada or to contexts where natural persons are present in the country. For banks, there are only two federal measures applying to commercial operations contained in the Fifth Protocol schedule: first, that at least one-half of the directors of a bank or trust and loan be either Canadian citizens or 'permanent residents ordinarily resident in Canada';[98] and second, that until 30 June 1999, foreign bank subsidiaries gain permission from the Minister of Finance to open more than one branch.[99] The rule on directors is not an unusual restriction on banks under general financial service regulations, as it aims to ensure that those making business decisions take into account the community's interest in which the bank is located. Such limitations also serve (more or less effectively) to maintain the Canadian 'character' of a bank. There are additional commitments for Provinces regarding the residency of trust and loan company and credit union directors.[100] Some Provinces have requirements that require a super-majority of the board of directors to live in Canada or in the Province.

---

[95] *Ibid.* at 16–17.
[96] *Ibid.* at 17.
[97] *Ibid.*
[98] *Ibid.* at 3.
[99] *Ibid.* at 11.
[100] *Ibid.* at 11–13.

The branching commitment is new and more significant from a trade perspective. Before the 1997 negotiations resulting in the Fifth Protocol, Canada maintained the right to require foreign bank subsidiaries to request permission from the Minister of Finance before opening more than one branch. As Canadian banks enjoy unlimited branching, this extra procedural step was a clear disadvantage to a foreign bank that wanted to expand operations, even if authorization was given. This restriction had been eliminated for NAFTA Party banks under Chapter Fourteen, but remained for WTO Members.[101] In the revised GATS schedule, Canada again inserts obligations based on its domestic legislation liberalizing the financial service sector to extend the benefits of such liberalization beyond Canadian institutions—and by doing so under the GATS, it does in a multilateral context what it was unwilling to do under pressure from the United States in a regional context.

In the final limitation on purely banking activities, certain provisions of the Income Tax Act of Canada have been specifically excluded from Canada's national treatment obligations. Investments in a venture capital corporation may be subject to less favorable tax treatment when the investor is non-Canadian than for Canadian investors.[102]

The presence of natural persons is generally unbound.[103] However, for business visitors, Canada does offer temporary entry rights for non-direct sales and commercial activities.[104]

Despite the several market access limitations, there are only two limitations on national treatment in the securities trading areas. For all Provinces except British Columbia, applicants for permission to trade in securities or futures or to advise or engage in auxiliary financial services must have been a resident of Canada for at least one year before the application and a resident of the Province in which operations are desired at the date of the application.[105] The second limitation is a residence requirement in the Province for representatives of dealers or advisers in Quebec.[106]

6.1.4.2   Mexico's GATS Obligations

Mexico's participation in the GATS negotiations, like in those of the NAFTA, was characterized by a basic willingness to liberalize its services market balanced by a fear of overwhelming competition from more highly developed service exporters. Under the Second Protocol, Mexico maintained a great deal of discretion to discriminate against foreign banks. The 1997 negotiations presented Mexico with the opportunity to further commit itself multilaterally to liberalization. However, by the end of the negotiations,

---

[101] See generally Canada: Schedule of Specific Commitments in: Second Protocol to the General Agreement on Trade in Services (Geneva, 6 October 1996).

[102] Canada: Schedule ... Revised Offer (note 81 *supra*), at 14.

[103] The term 'unbound' refers to the Member's unlimited ability to restrict this mode of supply.

[104] Canada: Schedule of Specific Commitments, Part I (Horizontal Commitments).

[105] Canada: Schedule ... Revised Offer (note 81 *supra*), at 17.

[106] *Ibid.* This is 'subject to certain exemptions'.

while Mexico did set forth some minor commitments by the close of the December meeting, its changes were modest.[107]

6.1.4.2.1   MFN EXEMPTIONS IN BANKING SERVICES

Mexico has taken no MFN exemptions for banking services.

6.1.4.2.2   SPECIFIC COMMITMENTS IN BANKING SERVICES

Mexico's specific commitments in the banking sector are characterized by a limited acceptance of positive duties. The headnote to the section on 'Banking and other financial services (excluding insurance)' set out the basic framework of foreign participation in the Mexican banking market. There is a list of permitted and non-permitted forms of banking institutions that may be set up by foreigners (including commercial banks, securities firms, limited purpose financial institutions, financial leasing companies, investment companies, and pension fund management companies, among others), and an assurance that representative offices of banks may establish in Mexico with prior permission from the national Ministry of Finance.[108] Representative offices, however, will not be allowed to engage in commercial financial activities other than placement.[109]

Limitations on market access   Mexico's scheduled entries for limitations on market access are littered with the phrase 'No consolidado', or 'unbound', for cross-border supply of services and for their consumption abroad, as well as for the presence of natural persons.[110] That means that for purposes of the WTO Members, Mexico reserves the right to limit these areas of trade in any manner it sees fit.

The commercial presence mode of supply, however, contains several important limitations that are explicitly listed. For the acceptance of deposits, the main limitation on market access is that only 'instituciones de banca múltiple', or commercial banks, may engage in deposit-taking from the public.[111] Representative offices of banks may not accept deposits.[112] A second restriction is Mexico's limit on the allowable total foreign

---

[107] The Swiss delegation was 'disappointed' in Mexico's refusal to more completely open its financial markets. Hauert (note 75 *supra*), at 5 ('Enttäuschend ist lediglich die Tatsache, dass sich gewisse Staaten (namentlich Korea, Mexiko, Philippinen) nicht vollumfänglich auf die im nationalen Gesetz vorgesehene oder in der Praxis durchgeführte Marktöffnung verpflichtet haben').

[108] Mexico—List of Specific Commitments—Offer on Financial Services, GATS/SC/56, B at 5 (April 1994).

[109] *Ibid.*

[110] The schedule of horizontal commitments submitted by Mexico also leaves the limitations on the presence of natural persons mainly unbound. The exception to this is the commitment that those directly responsible for the sale of a service and intra-company movement of officials are protected for visits of up to one year. See Canada (note 104 *supra*), Part I (Horizontal Commitments) at 1–4.

[111] Mexico—List of Specific Commitments—Offer on Financial Services, S/FIN/W/12/Add.39, at 6.

[112] *Ibid.*

ownership of deposit capital in Mexico. The original limit of 30 per cent of the aggregate capital ('capital social') was raised to 40 per cent of the common capital stock with voting rights in all Mexican deposit institutions under the Fifth Protocol.[113] Although foreign investors may own 100 per cent of the non-voting common stock capital, the less-than-majority-control limit casts a shadow on the improved commitment. Indeed, the schedule still states clearly, 'Se requiere que el control efectivo de la empresa lo mantengan los inversionistas mexicanos'—that is, effective control of investment must remain with Mexican investors.[114] In addition, no individual may hold more than 5 per cent of the capital stock of a commercial bank without special permission from the Secretary of Finance.[115] Even with such permission, a 20 per cent shareholding cannot be increased.[116]

For the loan activities of banks, the market access is the same as it is for deposit-taking, with the 40 per cent foreign ownership of voting capital stock and the 5 (up to a possible 20) per cent individual holding limits.[117] However, the terms are somewhat more liberal for non-bank institutions. Limited purpose financial institutions ('sociedades financieras de objeto limitado') may have up to 49 per cent foreign participation, although again effective Mexican control must be maintained.[118] Foreign government investment through legal persons is prohibited.[119]

Factoring by financial factoring companies ('empresas de factoraje financiero') is limited to institutions that have a 49 per cent limit on foreign investment in the voting paid-up capital and 30 per cent limit on non-voting paid-up capital.[120] Finally, no individual is allowed to hold more than 10 per cent of the paid-up capital of a lending institution.[121]

Financial leasing may be undertaken by either leasing companies or by commercial banks. Again, there is a possible limit of 49 per cent for foreign investor held voting paid-up capital for leasing companies ownership, and the 40 per cent of aggregate capital on foreign investments in commercial banks engaged in these activities.[122]

---

[113] Compare México—Lista de compromisos específicos, Suplemento 1: Revisión at 324 (Second Protocol commitments for deposit-acceptance, limiting foreign participation to 30 per cent of common stock in commercial banks involved in such activities) *with* Mexico—List of Specific Commitments—Offer on Financial Services, S/FIN/W/12/Add.39, at 6 (commitments for deposit-acceptance after the Fifth Protocol, limiting foreign participation to 40 per cent of common stock in commercial banks involved in such activities).

[114] Mexico (note 111 *supra*), at 6. One can reasonably ask whether this is an effective method of liberalizing investments particularly in financial services. There are few banks that are willing to invest as a minority shareholder in a foreign bank, particularly in an environment where both economic and political risks are high.

[115] *Ibid.* at 6.

[116] *Ibid.*

[117] *Ibid.* at 7.

[118] *Ibid.* at 8.

[119] *Ibid.*

[120] *Ibid.*

[121] *Ibid.*

[122] *Ibid.* at 9.

Securities activities are allowed to securities firms (*casas de bolsa*), securities specialists (*especialistas bursátiles*), commercial banks, and to foreign exchange firms (*casas de cambio*). While the particular activities allowed to each type of financial institution varies, the 40 per cent limit applies to all,[123] as does the 10 per cent limit on individual holdings (with a possible 20 per cent ownership upon permission from the Secretary of Finance).[124]

Investment companies are permitted to engage in asset management and portfolio, pension fund, and trust management services, as well as other activities. The foreign investor participation in these companies is subject to the 49 per cent limit on overhead capital ownership and the 10 per cent individual holding limit in paid-up capital. Moreover, indirect investment by foreign governments is not permitted and Mexican investors must have effective control of the company.[125]

There are various other subsectors and activities listed in Mexico's schedule, each falling under either the 40 per cent foreign investor ownership limitation combined with the 5 per cent individual holding limit or the 49 per cent foreign investor ownership limitation combined with the 10 per cent individual holding limit.[126] In each case, however, effective control by Mexican shareholders is required.[127]

Limitations on national treatment   Mexico's list of horizontal commitments includes a reference to the Mexican law prohibiting the ownership of coastal lands, and reserves the right to offer Mexican nationals research and development subsidies, as well as 'incentives' for small service businesses, and the right to limit subsidies offered natural persons based on citizenship.[128]

In the sector-specific commitments for financial services, the commitments in the cross-border, consumption abroad, and presence of natural persons modes remain unbound.[129] For commercial presence, however, there are no limitations on the national treatment for the listed commitments.[130]

---

[123] General securities trade including the trade in money market instruments and 'valores transferibles' is allowed to securities firms and securities specialists. Commercial banks and commercial exchange firms may engage in trade in 'Divisas'; commercial banks may also engage in trade of negotiable financial instruments.

[124] Mexico (note 111 *supra*), at 10, 14, 18.

[125] *Ibid.* at 16–17.

[126] Foreign exchange activities may be pursued by either commercial banks (with the 40 per cent limits, as for deposit-taking) or by foreign exchange firms. Such firms are subject to the 49 per cent ownership rules. *Ibid.* at 11. 'Other negotiable instruments and financial assets, including bullion' and money brokering activities are open to commercial banks (40 per cent rule). *Ibid.* at 13, 15. Foreign investors in holding companies come under the 40 per cent rule. *Ibid.* at 19. Guarantee institutions, re-guarantee institutions, and general deposit warehouses all are subject to the 49 per cent limitation on foreign investment. *Ibid.* at 20–21.

[127] Mexico (note 108 *supra*), at 11, 13, 15, 19–21.

[128] *Ibid.*, Part I, at 1 (April 1994).

[129] Mexico (note 111 *supra*) at 5–21.

[130] *Ibid.*

6.1.4.3   United States' GATS Obligations

The United States entered the GATS financial services negotiations as one of the most open markets in the world and as a highly competitive exporter of financial services. So not surprisingly, its main objective was to gain a commitment from the governments of several potentially lucrative financial service markets to grants of market access to US service providers. Throughout the extended negotiations, the United States attempted to pressure other Members into taking further commitments to liberalize. With the end of the first set of negotiations drawing near, the pressure was intensified as a reaction to what the United States considered insufficient commitments by several developing countries in the areas of market access to and national treatment in the financial services markets.[131] When the other Members did not respond favorably, the the United States adopted an attitude in support of conditional MFN: instead of agreeing to immediately and unilaterally extend every WTO Member the same treatment as it every other Member, the United States reserved the right to treat Member financial institutions based on a principle of reciprocity in market access and national treatment advantages. This caused great concern among the other WTO trading partners, who saw the United States' actions as blows to the principle of unconditional MFN in general, and worried that this particular exception would cripple the Financial Services Agreements.[132] Nevertheless, at the end of the June 1995 meeting, the United States remained opposed to extending unconditional MFN treatment to other Members. Although voicing its continued commitment to the cause of multilateral financial liberalization,

---

[131] See US Department of Treasury, National Treatment Study (1994), pp. 7–11, highlighting 'Continuing Problem Areas' in US efforts to open foreign financial markets as of 1994, and setting out the future goals for liberalization. The 1997 renegotiations of the WTO Members' financial services obligations was a continuation of the United States' emphasis on the developing countries' agreement to further market openings. In July 1997, Deputy US Trade Representative Jeffrey Lang answered a reporter's question about the 'particular obstacles' to the negotiations by stating:

> ... We have always used the term 'critical mass' precisely to avoid answering those kind of questions, and to be able to mix and match offers so that if countries cannot move on one part of the negotiation but can move a little further than expected on another part, we can take account of that, ... but I would say that the major emerging markets in Asia and Latin America are absolutely critical. We are simply unable to make ambitious MFN-based commitments ... without substantial commitments from the major emerging markets in Latin America and Asia and a few other parts of the world, including I might say in the countries of Central Europe.

USIA, 'Transcript: Lang on Financial Services Negotiations' (14 July 1997) (text found on internet at >www.usia.go...n<).

[132] Although it was the US' refusal to agree to unconditional MFN principles demonstrated a further weakening of the country's traditional multilateralism, the practical effects of the exception itself were not felt by the main actors in the international banking field. At the time the exception was taken, the United States gave an assurance to the European Union, Japan, and Switzerland that the banks of these countries would continue to receive national treatment.

the United States did not sign either the Understanding or the Second Protocol. It also maintained an MFN exception for their treatment of new financial services.

In April 1997, as the WTO Members began preparing for renewed talks on financial services, the United States indicated its continued demand for reciprocal concessions.[133] At the December 1997 meetings, the United States was vindicated: the Fifth Protocol to the GATS, which went into effect on 1 March 1999, includes 56 new or improved commitments for financial ervices by the developing countries as well as the industrialized Members, and the United States is among them.[134]

The major change in the United States' GATS commitments stemming from the Fifth Protocol came in its acceptance of unconditional MFN in the offering of new financial services by foreign banks. The rescission of this exemption came as a great relief to the other WTO Members, as it was interpreted as a resumption of the traditional belief in an unrestricted MFN ideology. Yet in reality, the Fifth Protocol only relieved the symptoms of the principle of the United States' new preference for conditional MFN—there was a revocation of their exception, but only after other countries made additional market access commitments.

6.1.4.3.1   MFN EXEMPTIONS IN BANKING SERVICES

The United States government has few MFN exemptions affecting the banking services sector trade directly. One is the exemption allowing US registered broker-dealers with Canada as the principle place of business to keep its required reserves in Canada and be supervised by Canadian authorities.[135] The requirement of State permission to establish State-licensed branches and agencies and to pursue other discriminatory State practices forms a second group of exceptions.[136] The last two exceptions require reciprocity to receive authority to 'act as a sole trustee of an indenture for a bond offering in the United States' and to be designated a primary dealer in federal debt securities.[137]

---

[133] See *WTO Focus* (note 74 *supra*), at 1ff, 8 ('The United States, which did not sign on to the 1995 financial services agreement, said it was hoping to table an m.f.n. based offer, with full market access and national treatment provisions, at the earliest possible date. It said that new and significant market access opportunities must be reflected in the offers of other countries, even though it recognized that some governments may need transition periods …').

[134] Although prior to the December 1997 meetings, the United States was generally seen as one of the most open banking markets of the world, research done by two economists before the results of the negotiations were known find the overall openness of the US financial service (i.e., including insurance and securities markets as well as banking) only moderate, surpassed by the EU, Switzerland, Canada, and Australia. Eva Carceles Poveda and Susanne Droege, 'International Trade in Financial Services: An Assessment of the GATS' (1997) 52:4 *Aussenwirtschaft* 603, 619–25.

[135] United States of America—List of Article II (MFN) Exemptions, S/FIN/W/12/Add.5/Rev.2, at 32.

[136] *Ibid.* at 33.

[137] *Ibid.* at 33–4.

6.1.4.3.2   SPECIFIC COMMITMENTS IN BANKING SERVICES

In the preliminary comments to the revised schedule of specific commitments in banking services, the United States sets forth the following noteworthy sentence: 'Commitments in this subsector are undertaken in accordance with the Understanding on Commitments in Financial Services (the 'Understanding'), subject to the limitations and conditions set forth in these headnotes and the schedule below'.[138]

The Understanding's provisions oblige Members to not only apply all commitments according to MFN basis, but to also agree to treat government procurement of financial services according to MFN principles, to allow new financial services to be supplied by Member institutions, and to refrain from introducing new legislation that places limitations on financial institutions, even if such measures would be permissible under the Member's schedule.

Limitations on market access   For cross-border supply, the United States' commitments only guarantee foreign suppliers the right to transfer financial information, provide data processing, and to supply advisory and non-intermediation 'auxiliary' banking services from outside US territory.[139] The consumption abroad mode of supply is also protected for persons seeking most banking services outside the United States, but does not include the right for non-US institutions that have no presence in the United States to solicit customers in US territory.[140]

In its market access schedule lists, the presence of natural persons mode of supply is unbound except for the commitments applying to all service sectors. Instead, the United States focused its exemptions on the commercial presence mode of supply and on the States' restrictions on foreign branches' activities and powers. One of the most important restrictions is the limitation on retail banking (and, in turn, its grandfathering exception). Only foreign bank subsidiaries may engage in such activities:

> In order to accept or maintain domestic retail deposits of less than $100,000, a foreign bank must establish an insured bank subsidiary. This requirement does not apply to a foreign bank branch that was engaged in insured deposit-taking activities on December 19, 1991.[141]

Another significant limitation on market access is the US right to require that national banks that are affiliates and subsidiaries of foreign banks have

---

[138] United States of America—Schedule of Specific Commitments—Revised Conditional Offer, S/FIN/W/12/Add.5/Rev.2, (12 December 1997), p. 2.

[139] See *ibid.* B.2 at 17; Understanding on Commitments in Financial Services B.3(c) (referring to GATS, Annex on Financial Services 5(a)).

[140] United States of America (note 138 *supra*), B.2 at 17; Understanding (note 139 *supra*), B.4(c), referring to GATS, Annex on Financial Services 5(a)(v)–5(a)(xvi).

[141] United States of America (note 138 *supra*), at 18.

US citizens for more than 50 per cent of the members of the board of directors.[142] In addition, foreign banks and their subsidiaries are the sole foreign owners of Edge corporations.[143]

Because the State governments in the United States are responsible for allowing banks to branch into their jurisdiction, the United States government left unbound the issue of establishment of branches and acquisitions of banks by banks located in another State.[144] However, in the attached 'Additional Commitments Paper II', the US government reaffirmed its support for domestic financial service reform among the States in order to allow for unlimited branching.[145]

The most detailed set of restrictions on commercial presence are those explaining State measures that diverge from the market access provision of GATS. Establishment of foreign banks is not permitted in all States, and where it is allowed, may be permitted under conditions less favorable than those governing the establishment of a domestic bank. Expansion of banks, the particular activities allowed, and the residency or nationality of the boards of directors of banks are other areas that the United States left unbound for certain States.[146]

The remaining limitations on market access concern security activities. Trade in onion futures may not be entered into by foreign financial institutions.[147] Requirements for acting as a 'sole trustee for a bond offering in the United States' and measures affecting 'the use of simplified registration and periodic reporting forms for securities issued by small business corporations' are left unbound.[148]

Limitations on national treatment   Like the limitations on market access, the United States limited its variance with national treatment to the commercial presence form of service supply and remained largely unbound in the area of presence of natural persons. The major condition on the United States' commitments to afford national treatment stems from the dual system of banking that characterizes the US market. The preliminary comments to the banking sector commitments provides that for purposes of the following commitments, 'national' treatment is to be based on treatment by the 'home

---

[142] *Ibid.*

[143] *Ibid.*

[144] *Ibid.* at 19.

[145] *Ibid.,* 'Attachment to the United States Schedule: Additional Commitments Paper II', at 31, para. 2:

> (2) The Administration noting that even before the adoption of the Riegle-Neal banking legislation, many states had taken action to liberalize interstate acquisitions of banks on a basis that provided national treatment to foreign banks, welcomes further initiatives by states to provide additional access on a non-discriminatory basis.

[146] See generally United States of America (note 138 *supra*), at 19-26.

[147] *Ibid.* at 27.

[148] *Ibid.* at 27.

State' of the foreign bank located in the United States.[149] Treatment may, therefore, vary among foreign banks based on the 'nationality' (that is residency) of the bank's main office, as interpreted under the US domestic banking regulations.

Within the subsector specific commitments, there are only two non-State-specific limitations set out on the NTO. The first is that only foreign banks need to register to provide customers with securities advice and investment management.[150] Because of this requirement, the foreign banks will have to bear extra costs that similarly active domestic banks do not have to pay. The next limitation is based on the new Federal Reserve System rules: foreign banks are no longer allowed to be members of the Federal Reserve System, and therefore cannot vote for directors of the Foreign Reserve Bank.[151] The Fifth Protocol negotiations succeeded to remove the prior limitation excepting the law that foreign banks are required to pay for the costs of the mandatory Federal Reserve examinations from NTO.

The United States limited its NTO obligations for a variety of State measures that treat foreign banks less favorably than domestic banks. Such limitations include registration requirements for certain activities and restrictions on commodity transactions.[152] Despite the differential treatment, these measures generally apply only to foreign bank branches and agencies—not to subsidiaries of foreign banks—suggesting that their basis lies in prudential concerns more than in purely non-competitive intent.

6.2   INDIVIDUAL NAFTA FINANCIAL SERVICES PROVISIONS FROM THE WTO PERSPECTIVE

The great majority of the NAFTA Chapter Fourteen obligations are completely compatible with the Parties' obligations as GATS signatories. This should not be surprising, as the goal of each of the agreements was to provide for freer trade in financial services. Moreover, the NAFTA was written simultaneously with the GATS, and many of the drafters were the same individuals.

Still, some NAFTA provisions have a different emphasis or are more extensive than the similar terms of the GATS and other leave room for potential conflicts in the way they are applied. The latter group of provisions'

---

[149]   *Ibid.* B.3 at 17:

> 3. National treatment commitments in these subsectors are subject to the following limitation: National treatment will be provided based upon the foreign bank's 'home state' in the United States, as that term is defined under the International Banking Act, where that Act is applicable. A domestic bank subsidiary of a foreign firm will have its own 'home state' and national treatment will be provided based upon the subsidiary's home state, as determined under applicable law.

[150]   United States of America (note 138 *supra*), at 18.
[151]   *Ibid.*
[152]   See generally *ibid.* at 22–3, 25.

compatibility with the rules of the WTO will be left to the interpreters of Chapter Fourteen—the dispute settlement panels, the Financial Services Committee, and those individual banking entities within the Parties that take an interest in influencing the development of North American financial services law.

The following discusses the provisions of the GATS (including that agreement's Annex on Financial Services) and their NAFTA counterparts. These provisions will be examined from the perspective of whether the NAFTA causes its Parties to violate their obligations as WTO Members, in order to determine Chapter Fourteen's legal effects on non-Party WTO Member banks. In general, one can assume that where the NAFTA provisions are more liberal than the corresponding WTO or GATS provisions, the effects on non-Party banks will be a disadvantageous lowering of their relative competitive position *vis-à-vis* Party banks, but that these effects will not violate the banks' protectable legal rights under the WTO. On the other hand, where the NAFTA provisions correspond to the GATS provisions, there may be legal rights under the WTO that can be protected from infringement by the NAFTA through WTO dispute settlement procedures.

6.2.1 Complete Incompatibility Between NAFTA and GATS: Where Non-NAFTA WTO Member Banks' Rights Under WTO Law Are Clearly Violated

There is only one provision of the GATS that is directly contravened by the WTO Members' formation of the NAFTA: the most-favored-nation obligation of GATS Article II. Although this obligation is one of the basic obligations on which the entire WTO system is dependent, even this provision is subject to a legitimizing exception for economic integration areas.[153]

6.2.1.1 *Most-Favored-Nation Obligation and Economic Integration Areas (GATS Articles II–III)*

In the GATS general obligations, the Most-Favored-Nation Treatment Obligation of Article II is qualified by the Article V allowance for regional integration agreements in which the members of the agreement may legitimately offer each other more favorable treatment than that they each offer other WTO Members as long as the requisite degree of market integration is foreseen.[154]

If NAFTA is recognized as fulfilling the GATS Article V requirements, a non-Party WTO Member will not be permitted to object to the NAFTA Parties' preferential treatment offered one another's banks not being offered to its banks. For MFN purposes, within the WTO the North American Free

---

[153] See under 5.5.2 *supra* for a further discussion of the WTO rules on free trade areas and economic integration agreements.
[154] There must be an elimination of 'substantially all' trade barriers within a 'reasonable' time. See 5.5.2 *supra*.

Trade Agreement Parties are to be treated as a single unit, within which services may move more freely than they could if the service were from outside the unit, the external trade of which is controlled by each Party for itself. Thus, the main questions posed in an international trade analysis of NAFTA Chapter Fourteen commitments are: to what extent does recognition under GATS Article V (as a legitimate regional integration agreement for services) relieve the NAFTA Parties from their GATS obligations toward non-Party WTO Members, and does Chapter Fourteen allow the NAFTA Parties to fulfill their remaining GATS requirements?

6.2.1.2   Extent To Which GATS Article V Relieves the NAFTA Parties From Their Obligations Toward Non-Party WTO Members

In general terms, recognition by the WTO as a legitimate GATS Article V regional integration area should have no effect on the regional agreement's parties' external MFN obligations, on their non-MFN-related obligations in the GATS itself, or on their outstanding commitments in the Marrakesh Agreement. All Members must continue to act in accordance with their other duties to the international trade community.[155]

---

[155] There is still some question to the exact extent of the Art. XXIV excusal of GATT obligations. See, e.g., the GATT Working Party report on 'The European Economic Community' (1958) BISD 6S/70, 77–8 (L/778, adopted 29 November 1957):

> 3. The [EEC Members] considered that the opening phrase of paragraph 5 of Article XXIV provided a general exception under which they were entitled to deviate from the other provisions of the General Agreement, including Articles XI to XIV, in so far as the application of these provisions would constitute obstacles to the formation of the customs union and to the achievement of its objectives ... .
> 4. Most members of the Sub-Group had a different interpretation of Article XXIV. In their view countries entering a customs union would continue to be governed by the provisions of Article XI ... as well as by the other provisions of the Agreement which provided certain exceptions permitting the use of quantitative restrictions where necessary to deal with balance-of-payments difficulties.

For a concise and helpful explanation see Frederick M. Abbott, 'GATT and the European Community: A Formula for Peaceful Coexistence' (1990) 12 Mich J Int'l L 1, 14–15. Professor Abbott writes:

> Article XXIV does not expressly address deviations from the National Treatment principle and there is no good reason to conclude that the drafters of the General Agreement intended that [regional trade areas] be permitted to grant internal preferences to locally produced goods. However, on a purely semantic level, a case for an interpretation of article XXIV which permits derogation from the National Treatment principle can be made, though such interpretation is by no means widely accepted. This is not to say that there is absolutely no scholarly support for the proposition that article XXIV permits derogations from provisions of the GATT other than the MFN principle as it applies to tariffs and related charges and regulations ... .

Ibid. (footnotes omitted). Professor Abbott, however, admits to only having discovered one author who even indirectly supports the view that Art. XXIV would exempt members of a regional agreement from any GATT provisions other than the MFN obligation. *Ibid.* at 15, n.37.

Help in determining to what extent GATS Article V relieves the NAFTA Parties from their MFN obligations can be found in part from the text of Article V itself. Paragraph 4 of this Article protects non-party WTO Members from protectionism-based trade blocs. It does so by limiting the validity of GATS Article V arrangements to those arrangements that do not negatively affect the position of a third party service or service provider. The level of treatment is set out to be that existing prior to the coming into effect of the trade agreement. The relevant parts of the sentence read, 'Any agreement [liberalizing trade in services] ... shall not in respect of Members outside the agreement raise the overall level of barriers to trade in services within the respective sectors or subsectors compared to the level applicable prior to such an agreement'.[156]

Thus, if 'barriers to trade' is broadly defined (as the overall purpose of the treaty would indicate it should be), the GATS Article V exception to the most-favored-nation treatment obligation must be strictly limited so as to prevent a trade area from violating the other general GATS principles. Examples of such remaining obligations include not only the general obligation of national treatment, but also the fostering of transparency[157] and neutrality[158] in domestic regulation and the non-discriminatory use of safeguard measures against imports.[159] That also would keep special commitments in force.

In the case of NAFTA Chapter Fourteen, trade in banking services between the Parties was liberalized with very little concern for how the liberalization would affect non-Parties, but with clear agreement among the negotiators that the multilateral trade principles should be followed.[160] In this context, the result is positive for non-Party banks. Formerly nearly

---

[156] As applied specifically to the NAFTA Chapter Fourteen, this sentence leaves a great deal of ambiguity. Because NAFTA is a free trade zone and not a customs union, each NAFTA Party has control over its own non-NAFTA commercial relations. Thus, to investigate the *overall* level of barriers to trade in services' seems to require the balancing of the United States', Canada's, and Mexico's level of barriers to trade in banking services from before the NAFTA and after the NAFTA implementation. GATS V(3) (emphasis supplied); Bernard Hoekman, 'The General Agreement on Trade in Services' reproduced in John H. Jackson, William Davey and Alan Sykes (eds), *International Economic Law: Cases and Materials* (3rd edn, West Publishing, St Paul, 1995), pp. 921–30, at 928, calling attention to the difference between the GATS' non-recognition of the difference between free trade zones and customs unions, and the resulting difference in interpretation of 'overall level of barriers'. Because Mexico's banking sector was completely closed to active foreign commercial presence, it would be unreasonable to attribute an overall raising of barriers regardless of any realistic assessments of potential raising of barriers in Canada and the United States. However, even in the making of a comparison of trade barriers in banking services before and after NAFTA, one is immediately confronted with the problem that is explicit in the second half of GATS Article V(3), namely, that the barriers to trade in banking services prior to the NAFTA agreement were not subject to any WTO regulations at all.
[157] GATS Art. III.
[158] GATS Art. VI.
[159] GATS Art. X.
[160] Telephone conversation with Keith Palzer, legal adviser for US NAFTA financial services negotiating team.

excluded from Mexico and severely handicapped in Canada, foreign banks in those two countries have long been disadvantaged even without NAFTA. At the same time, the NAFTA did nothing to close the United States' open market structure for foreign banks. Thus, there is virtually nothing in the NAFTA that would *additionally* hinder a non-NAFTA bank from entering any of the Parties' banking markets from a purely legal point of view.

Incorporating the language of the GATS Article XVII national treatment obligation, the relevant question becomes whether there has been a change in the 'conditions of competition' to the advantage of the NAFTA-Party banks.[161] This would have to be viewed in the context of a particular bank, and would necessarily involve economic analysis and a critical evaluation of the business climate.

6.2.2 Complete Compatibility Between NAFTA and GATS: Where NAFTA Does Not Affect the Legal Rights of Non-NAFTA Member Banks Under WTO Law

The following is an overview of those provisions of GATS and NAFTA that are completely compatible with one another. Non-Party Members of the WTO therefore would have no cause of action against the NAFTA Parties based on one of these articles.

6.2.2.1 *Cross-Border Trade (GATS Article I and NAFTA Article 1404)*

Cross border trade is one of the modes of service supply that the GATS aims to liberalize. However, as a mode of supply, Members must explicitly indicate the types of services that they intend to commit themselves to permit to enter their markets through this form. The NAFTA coverage of cross-border trade, while only obligating the Parties to not worsen their present practices, is an unconditional requirement for the Parties.

In their GATS Schedules of Specific Commitments, Canada and the United States broadly bound themselves to ensuring that WTO Member financial service suppliers be permitted to deliver their services by means of cross-border supply methods. Thus, their NAFTA obligations do not interfere with their WTO obligations.

---

[161] GATS Art. XVII:3. An approach to interpretation that emphasizes consistency in meaning for the same words throughout the Agreement has gained ground in the GATS, and is a trend those making NAFTA interpretations should follow. See European Communities (note 51 *supra*), at 373, para. 7.304 ('Therefore, we find that the obligation contained in Art. II:1 of GATS to extend "treatment no less favorable" should be interpreted *in casu* to require providing no less favourable conditions of competition'). This panel decision is important as it is the only report that interprets the GATS terms, and it clears up a problematic term usage. Under GATT law, numerous panel reports pointed out the potential for different interpretations of the same term used in different GATT provisions. By stating that in the GATS the term 'no less favorable' is to be interpreted the same whether referring to MFN or NTO, the *Bananas* panel made a great achievement in assisting the coherence of the treaty.

Mexico left its GATS commitments for cross-border supply modes unbound for banking service delivery. Thus, Mexico may restrict other WTO Member's banks from engaging in cross border trade to the extent it sees fit. Under the NAFTA, however, Mexico is required to continue to offer Party-banks access to its market through cross-border supply. For non-Party Member banks, this constellation of obligations could result in disadvantages. Yet, because Mexico's refusal to include cross-border supply within the scope of its GATS commitments is legitimate, there is no actual violation of a non-Party's WTO rights caused by this potential competitive inequality.

6.2.2.2   *Progressive Liberalization (GATS Articles XIX–XXI and NAFTA Annex 1404.4)*

The GATS that came into effect in 1995 was a 'framework agreement'. Even with the additional commitments that have since come into effect, the GATS is not an instrument that completely covers the international service trade. Knowing that it was only a good first step, the GATS was agreed to and signed by the Members on the condition that further liberalizations were to be negotiated in the future. Together Articles XIX through XXI of the GATS are a clear symbol of this open-endedness.[162] Composing Part IV (Progressive Liberalization) of the GATS, these provisions set out the framework requirements of future negotiating rounds in the service sectors. Starting no later than in the year 2000, and 'periodically thereafter', the Members 'shall enter into successive rounds of negotiations, ... with a view to achieving a progressively higher level of liberalization'.[163] The schedules of specific commitments completed by each Member at the end of the Uruguay Round, the Second Protocol, and/or the Fifth Protocol are the basis from which further developments in financial services are to proceed. While the existing commitments may be withdrawn or modified,[164] any

---

[162] See Kampf (note 74 *supra*), at 158:

> ... it becomes clear from the Preamble and Article XIX [GATS] that there is no obligation to liberalise trade in services immediately, but that liberalisation should be achieved progressively in successive rounds of negotiations. The liberalisation process has to take account of national policy objectives and in particular each member's level of development. In addition, special concessions are made to developing country members ... The adherence to the principle of progressive liberalisation of trade in services was clearly reaffirmed by all WTO members at the Singapore Ministerial Conference in December 1996 [footnote omitted]. Full liberalisation of trade in financial services was therefore certainly not the aim of Uruguay Round negotiations and should not realistically be expected to be achieved by December 12, 1997 ... Each round of negotiations is, however, due to achieve some important improvements so as to increase the general level of commitments without reducing the liberalisation already reached today.

[163] GATS Art. XIX:1.
[164] GATS Art. XXI:1(a).

Member who by doing so lessens the benefits other Members would have enjoyed in the absence of the withdrawal or modification must compensate those injured on an MFN basis.[165]

The December 1997 completion of the third broad attempt at liberalization of financial services in the WTO framework was a success for the Organization and for GATS' commitment to further liberalizations. Yet, the closing of those negotiations was just the finishing of one step in a continuing program. Even now, with expanded coverage under the GATS, work will continue in hopes of ever-freer trade in financial services throughout the trading world.

Chapter Fourteen of NAFTA is more complete than was the GATS Annex on Financial Services. Yet even Chapter Fourteen did not accomplish all that the negotiators had hoped it would. Consequently, the NAFTA Parties also provided for further attempts to liberalize their financial service markets in two of Chapter Fourteen's Annex provisions. In Annex 1404.4 there is an obligation to 'consult on further liberalization of cross-border trade in financial services'. Annex 1413.6 also requires consultations on certain provisions of Mexico's commitments. Neither of these NAFTA provisions would have an adverse affect on a non-Party, WTO Member.

6.2.2.3   *Transparency (GATS Article III and NAFTA Article 1411)*

Drafted with the conviction that visibility reduces protectionism, the GATS Article III provision on transparency has the goal that each World Trade Organization Member's laws and regulations affecting trade in services are made public and available to interested persons. Specifically, the Article states that Members 'shall publish promptly and, ... at the latest by the time of their entry into force, all relevant measures of general application which pertain to ... the operation of this Agreement'.[166]

Allowing for deviations from this strict rule in cases of emergency or impracticability,[167] the obligation to foster transparency of rules is one of the bases of the GATS and is a particularly important principle for trade in services (where discrimination is even more likely to take place within a country's domestic legal system than is the case with trade in physical goods).

In addition to publishing their measures, Members of the WTO 'shall promptly and at least annually inform the Council for Trade in Services of the introduction of any new, or any changes to existing, laws, regulations or administrative guidelines which specifically affect trade in services covered by its specific commitments'.[168]

---

[165]   GATS Art. XXI:2. Nullification of benefits will only have to be compensated if the injured Party requests negotiations on compensation. The aim of these negotiations is to reach agreement on maintaining 'a general level of mutually advantageous commitments not less favourable to trade than that provided for in Schedules of specific commitments prior to such negotiations'. GATS Art. XXI:2(a).

[166]   GATS Art. III:1.

[167]   GATS Art. III:1.

[168]   GATS Art. III:3.

In addition, each Member is to set up an information center responsible for 'promptly' giving specific information to the other WTO Members on the reported changes.[169]

A comparison of the requirements of GATS Article III with the parallel provision in NAFTA Chapter Fourteen reveals no exclusivity in fulfilling the obligations of each treaty. The requirements of publication of new measures and the establishment of information centers to distribute detailed information are also present in the NAFTA.[170] However, NAFTA Article 1411 is not only more detailed than the GATS Article III, it is also targeted at involving *all* interested persons in the rule-making processes of the NAFTA Parties—not just persons of NAFTA Parties. The GATS obligation is phrased in terms of government-to-government (that is, Member-to-Member) notification. Thus, assuming that private persons will maintain vigilant watch over the implementation of the treaty requirements, the NAFTA has a higher potential for achieving non-discrimination in domestic measures.

Article 1411 begins, for instance, by requiring that notice of proposed measures of 'general application' be published 'in order to allow an opportunity for such persons to comment on the measure'. This idea of allowing for comments on proposals before a rule is made suggests (without an explicit requirement) that the rule makers of the Party take the comments into consideration before deciding whether to enact the proposed rule.[171]

Furthermore, the Chapter Fourteen Transparency provision is oriented toward informing interested persons of the regulations as much as it is a notification obligation. The second paragraph specifies that the relevant authorities 'shall' assist interested persons in applying for permission to establish a financial institution by making the application requirements 'available to interested persons'.[172] The following paragraphs continue in this strain, providing individual financial service providers with a right of access to non-confidential information regarding the application process.[173]

The NAFTA's inclusion of a right to a certain degree of due process within Chapter Fourteen is of great importance to all financial institutions. Aimed also at preventing willful delays on the part of

---

[169] GATS Art. III:4.
[170] NAFTA Arts 1411:1, 1411:6.
[171] This pro-active characteristic of comment periods is also found in the domestic administrative law of the United States. See Administrative Procedure Act of 1941, 5 U.S.C. § 553(c) ('After notice required [in § 553(b)], the agency shall give interested persons an opportunity to participate in the rule making through submission of written data, views, or arguments with or without opportunity for oral presentation …').
See also Bernard Schwartz, *Administrative Law* (3rd edn, Little, Brown & Co, Boston, 1991), pp. 189–207.
[172] NAFTA Art. 1411:2.
[173] The status of an application must be told the affected applicant upon request. NAFTA Art. 1411:3.

grudging authorities, the transparency provision imposes time limits on the application examination and affirmative duties of the licensing authorities. First, the authority must make its decision within 120 days of receiving the completed application, unless this time limit is 'not practicable'.[174] In that case, the authority is to notify the applicant and 'endeavor to make the decision within a reasonable time thereafter'.[175] By requiring more transparency than does the GATS, and by not limiting the rights of access to information to NAFTA Party persons, NAFTA surpasses the standard set by GATS, and thereby does not contravene the GATS transparency obligation in any way.

6.2.2.4   *Protection of Privacy (GATS Annex on Financial Services 2(b) and NAFTA Article 1411:5)*

Neither NAFTA nor GATS obligations extend so far as to require a Party to violate an individual's privacy. The GATS Annex on Financial Services ensures a protection of an individual's privacy as well as of commercially valuable information.[176] The text of the Annex's provision is nearly identical to that of the corresponding NAFTA clause:

> Nothing in the Agreement shall be construed to require a Member to disclose information relating to the affairs and accounts of individual customers or any confidential or proprietary information in the possession of public entities.[177]

The NAFTA Chapter Fourteen rule, set out in Article 1411:5, allows both private and public entities to refuse a request for information if the information relates to a person's financial affairs or personal accounts.[178] Additionally, officials may refuse to give information to other Parties if the release of such information would endanger the success of law enforcement efforts, other public interests, or would injure a commercial entity's lawful activities.[179]

For both the GATS and NAFTA, the same circumstances allow refusals from giving information on request, and the same interests are protected. Thus, in the area of privacy protection, there is no danger of non-Parties being disadvantaged by the NAFTA.

---

[174] NAFTA Art. 1411:4.
[175] *Ibid.*
[176] GATS Annex on Financial Services 2(b).
[177] *Ibid.*
[178] NAFTA Art. 1411:5(a)
[179] NAFTA Art. 1411:5(b).

6.2.2.5   *Competition Rules (GATS Articles VIII and IX and NAFTA Chapter Fifteen)*

The WTO does not yet include obligations based on competition rules.[180] While GATS does prohibit violations of MFN and a Member's Specific Commitments by monopolies (and dictates that Members 'shall' participate in further negotiations on competition policy), the provisions on limiting other restrictive business practices are hortatory. 'Members recognize that certain business practices ... may restrain competition and thereby restrict trade in services',[181] and are thus to 'enter into consultations with a view to eliminating [such restrictive] practices'.[182] The Understanding treats monopoly rights of national financial service providers similarly.[183] The lack of consensus on incorporating antitrust and other competition rules in the WTO prevented stronger obligations under that framework.

The NAFTA obligations extend farther than the GATS competition provisions, with a Chapter of the Agreement devoted to competition issues.[184] Chapter Fifteen requires each Party to 'adopt or maintain measures to proscribe anti-competitive business conduct and take appropriate action with respect thereto'.[185] While monopoly suppliers may be allowed, NAFTA is similar to GATS in stating that such a monopoly is not to endanger the Party's fulfillment of its other obligations under the Agreement. However, the enforceability of the Chapter Fifteen obligations is weak: a violation of the suggestion to adhere to fair competition practices may not be a basis for dispute settlement proceedings.[186]

6.2.2.6   *Movement of Natural Persons (GATS Annex on Movement on Natural Persons and NAFTA Chapter Sixteen)*

The GATS does not prevent Members from regulating the control of natural persons into or within their territories. Despite the indivisibility of providing

---

[180] There is a great deal of literature on the various aspects of competition law (and the lack thereof) on trade. For more on the WTO Membership's activities regarding competition rules, see WTO, 'Trade and Competition Policy', in *Annual Report 1997* (WTO: Geneva 1997), pp. 29–91; Aaditya Mattoo and Arvind Subramanian, 'Multilateral Rules on Competition Policy: A Possible Way Forward' (1997) 31:5 J World Trade 95; Bernard M. Hoekman and Petros C. Mavroidis, 'Antitrust-Based Remedies and Dumping in International Trade', Policy Research Working Paper 1347 (The World Bank, 1994); *ibid.*, 'Policy Externalities and High-Tech Rivalry: Competition and Multilateral Cooperation Beyond the WTO' (1996) 9 Leiden J Int'l L 273; Michael J. Trebilcock, 'Competition Policy and Trade Policy: Mediating the Interface' (1996) 30:4 J World Trade 71. For a general overview of the problems of antitrust law, see Barry E. Hawk (ed.), *International Antitrust Law & Policy* (Juris Publishing/Sweet & Maxwell, New York/London, 1996).

[181] GATS Art. XI:1.
[182] GATS Art. XI:2.
[183] Understanding on Commitments in Financial Services, B.1 ('Each Member shall list in its schedule ... existing monopoly rights and shall endeavour to eliminate them or reduce their scope').
[184] See NAFTA Chapter Fifteen ('Competition Policy, Monopolies and State Enterprises').
[185] NAFTA Art. 1501:1.
[186] NAFTA Art. 1501:3.

some services and the temporary presence of natural persons supplying the services, the GATS Members were not willing to open their borders to unlimited temporary (let alone permanent) workers. Instead, the Annex on Movement of Natural Persons Supplying Services Under the Agreement sets out that the Members are to negotiate for concessions on movement and list their commitments on the Schedule of Specific Commitments.[187]

The Understanding on Financial Services extends the general GATS principles to the banking sector (and other financial services).[188] There, the 'Temporary Entry of Personnel'[189] is protected for selected senior managers[190] and specialists[191] of financial service suppliers that have a commercial presence in the territory of a Member.[192] In addition, such persons are to be allowed entry in order to assist in the establishment of the supplier in the territory.[193]

The NAFTA is also reserved about allowing movements of labor between Parties' territories.[194] Chapter Sixteen (Temporary Entry for Business Persons) states, '... this Chapter reflects the preferential trading relationship between the Parties, the desirability of facilitating temporary entry on a reciprocal basis and of establishing transparent criteria and procedures for temporary entry ...'.[195]

Yet, it goes on to emphasize, '... the need to ensure border security and to protect the domestic labor force and permanent employment in their respective territories'.[196]

The NAFTA framework for movement of natural persons is based on a general obligation to grant temporary entry to businesspersons, including financial service personnel.[197] Subject to standard national interest exceptions

---

[187] Annex on Movement of Natural Persons Supplying Services Under the Agreement 3.
[188] Understanding on Commitments in Financial Services.
[189] Understanding on Commitments in Financial Services 9.
[190] The relevant provision permits the temporary entry of personnel of established financial service providers of another Member for: 'senior managerial personnel possessing proprietary information essential to the establishment, control and operation of the services of the financial service supplier'. Understanding on Commitments in Financial Services B.9(a)(i).
[191] The specialists allowed temporary entry under the Understanding are those '... in the operation of the financial service supplier' (Understanding B.9(a)(ii)) and, 'subject to the availability of qualified personnel in its territory: (i) specialists in computer services, telecommunication services and accounts of the financial service supplier; and (ii) actuarial and legal specialists'. Understanding B.9(b).
[192] Understanding on Commitments in Financial Services B.9(a).
[193] *Ibid.* Also note that the Third Protocol contains additional specific obligations effective 31 January 1996 for those GATS Members who had accepted it by then. 'Third Protocol to the General Agreement on Trade in Services' S/L/12, para. 3 (24 July 1995). Of the NAFTA Parties, only Canada is a member of this protocol.
[194] This is mainly due to US and Canadian fears of immigration from Mexico.
[195] NAFTA Art. 1601.
[196] *Ibid.*
[197] NAFTA Appendix 1603.A.1 ('Business Visitors') (declaring the validity of the Chapter for 'financial services personnel' (insurers, bankers or investment brokers) engaging in commercial transactions for an enterprise located in the territory of another Party).

(public health, public safety, national security),[198] Parties are to provide persons of the other Parties with documents to allow employment in the territory, and give other Parties information on the national immigration regulations, both in legal and explanatory formats.[199]

Even within these relatively narrow parameters of liberal movement, the NAFTA Parties' obligations for movement of natural persons under the GATS are minimal and will prove difficult to enforce. Significantly, dispute settlement proceedings may not be brought for individual cases of refused entry under NAFTA.[200] There must be a charge of 'pattern of practice' as well as an exhaustion of administrative remedies before a NAFTA panel will be established.[201] Certainly intended as a protection from administratively overwhelming numbers of complaints, this limitation sets a very high burden on future efforts to enforce the entry of persons obligations. Although GATS disputes over the movements of natural persons could be brought, there is no specific conflict with the NAFTA's refusal to allow similar disputes under its framework.

6.2.2.7 Movement of Capital (GATS Articles XI and XII and NAFTA Article 1109)

As a compromise between the interests of facilitating the free flow of services and the protection of Members' right to control their macroeconomies, the GATS provides for a principle of liberal capital movements, underlain with a flexible protection for balance of payments levels. Under the GATS Articles XI and XII, Members are only to restrict the movement of capital for payments and international transfers as according to their Schedules of Specific Commitments[202] or in the case of 'serious balance-of-payments and external financial difficulties or threat thereof'.[203] Also, if a Member requires the assistance of the International Monetary Fund (IMF), the IMF may request that the Member be allowed to impose exchange action measures counter to its specific commitments.[204]

The use of emergency measures to protect financial reserves is allowed under strict rules of non-discrimination and the principle of least violation necessary. The latter includes requirements that the measures be temporary, that the measures be used so as to avoid unnecessary damage to other Members' interests, and that the measures be narrowly tailored to the circumstances demanding relief.[205]

---

[198] NAFTA Art. 1603:1.
[199] NAFTA Art. 1604:1.
[200] NAFTA Art. 1606:1.
[201] NAFTA Art. 1606:1(a).
[202] GATS Art. XI:1.
[203] GATS Art. XII:1.
[204] GATS Art. XI:2.
[205] GATS Art. XII:2:

> The restrictions referred to in paragraph 1:
> (a) shall not discriminate among Members;

The NAFTA provides for liberalized movement of capital by the incorporation of MFN, market access, and national treatment obligations for financial services institutions. Additionally, it has a specific article to ensure the unencumbered flow of 'all transfers relating to an investment of an investor of another Party'.[206] NAFTA Article 1109 describes more specifically the types of transfers to be allowed 'freely and without delay',[207] and lists exceptions for transfers that would violate national laws.[208]

As the GATS provisions are more general than those of the NAFTA, there should be no conflict of regulations governing the free flow of capital.

6.2.2.8   General Exceptions (GATS Articles XIV and XIVbis and NAFTA Chapter Twenty-One and Article 1114:2)

The GATS obligations are subject to a list of exceptions, allowing Member governments to implement or to continue using public policy measures that would otherwise violate the GATS. GATS Article XIV (General Exceptions) contains a list of five grounds for ignoring GATS obligations. These exceptions are similar to the GATT Article XX exceptions, allowing for narrowly-tailored measures[209] to protect 'public morals or to maintain public order',[210] life forms,[211] and 'to secure compliance with laws or regulations which are not inconsistent with the provisions of this Agreement'.[212]

Article XIVbis (Security Exception) adds three further possible reasons to act not in accordance to the GATS. The national security interest and the interest in world peace are included in this provision.[213]

The exceptions generally applicable to NAFTA financial services obligations stem from Chapter Twenty-One and Chapter Fourteen.[214] Like the GATS General Exceptions, Chapter Twenty-One of NAFTA provides that Parties may avoid their NAFTA obligations under certain conditions. None of the conditions would contradict the WTO obligations of the Parties if invoked.

(Contd.)

> (b) shall be consistent with the Articles of Agreement of the International Monetary Fund;
> (c) shall avoid unnecessary damage to the commercial, economic and financial interests of any other Member;
> (d) shall not exceed those necessary to deal with the circumstances described in paragraph 1;
> (e) shall be temporary and be phased out progressively as the situation specified in paragraph 1 improves.

[206] NAFTA Art. 1109.
[207] NAFTA Art. 1109:1.
[208] NAFTA Art. 1109:4–6.
[209] Three of the exceptions are allowances for measures 'necessary to' achieving an aim, and the other two are limited to taxation questions. See GATS Art. XIV(a)–(e).
[210] GATS Art. XIV(a).
[211] GATS Art. XIV(b) ('protect human, animal or plant life or health').
[212] GATS Art. XIV(c).
[213] GATS Art. XIVbis:1(a)–(c).
[214] See 3.17 *supra* (general exceptions).

On the contrary, the GATT general exceptions provision (Article XX GATT) is directly integrated for purposes of NAFTA trade in goods and technical barriers to trade.[215] The trade in services and telecommunications provisions of NAFTA are covered by exceptions for 'health and safety and consumer protection'.[216] These are reasons found in GATT Article XX as well.[217]

Because NAFTA's financial services trade is organized in a separate chapter from trade in other services, Chapter Twenty-One limits the exceptions applying to it.[218] The exceptions applicable to the financial service provisions found in the general exceptions of Chapter Twenty-One include exclusions for balance of payment difficulties,[219] for contravening obligations under tax conventions,[220] and for threats to national security.[221]

The environmental and life-form protections of the GATS agreement are included indirectly as exceptions from Chapter Fourteen through this Chapter's incorporation of the Chapter Eleven (Investment) provisions prohibiting the encouragement of investment by relaxation of 'domestic health, safety or environmental measures'.[222] Thus, there are no general exceptions under either agreement that are peculiar.

6.2.2.9   *Prudential Exceptions (GATS Annex on Financial Services 2a and NAFTA Article 1410)*

In financial service law, the term 'prudential' refers to the protection of the economic safety and security of an institution or system. The GATS Annex on Financial Services contains a 'prudential exception' that limits the use of measures to protect depositors and the stability of the system only in so far as the measures are used 'as a means of avoiding the Member's commitments or obligations under the Agreement'.[223] Although the text seems self-contradictory[224] (if a measure does not conform to the obligations, the Member

---

[215] NAFTA Art. 2101:1.
[216] NAFTA Art. 2101:2.
[217] GATT Art. XX(b).
[218] See, e.g., NAFTA Art. 2101:2(c) (exceptions applying only to the Cross-Border Trade in Services Chapter of NAFTA). Compare NAFTA Art. 2104:5 ('Restrictions on Transfers Other than Cross-Border Trade in Financial Services') with NAFTA Art. 2104:6-7 ('Restrictions on Cross-Border Trade in Financial Services').
[219] NAFTA Art. 2104:6–7.
[220] NAFTA Art. 2103.
[221] NAFTA Art. 2102.
[222] NAFTA Art. 1114:2 (incorporated by Art. 1401:2).
[223] GATS, Annex on Financial Services 2(a). The full provision reads:

> Notwithstanding any other provisions of the Agreement, a Member shall not be prevented from taking measures for prudential reasons, including for the protection of investors, depositors, policy holders or persons to whom a fiduciary duty is owed by a financial system supplier, or to ensure the integrity and stability of the financial system. Where such measures do not conform with the provisions of the Agreement, they shall not be used as a means of avoiding the Member's commitments or obligations under the Agreement.

[224] One commentator also notes that the prudential exception in GATS is 'not well defined'. Kampf (note 74 *supra*), at 158.

may use it only so as not to avoid its commitments), the intent is straightforward. Each Member retains the right to use otherwise GATS-violative measures to protect the safety and soundness of its financial system.[225]

Chapter Fourteen of the NAFTA also provides for exceptions to the Parties' obligations if there are prudential reasons for not abiding by the agreement. Article 1410 is specifically focussed on protecting investors and depositors and the national financial systems as a whole.[226] This is accomplished through language that reflects the strong financial service law influence on the provision. As such, the NAFTA does not conflict with the GATS Annex in providing a prudential exception.

6.2.2.10   *Expropriation Rules (No GATS Provisions, NAFTA Article 1110)*

The GATS rules on treatment of financial services do not mention expropriation at all. Indeed, the entire WTO framework avoids the topic of nationalizations and expropriations and treats investments only in so far as trade-related investments in goods are contained by the provisions of the Agreement on such measures.[227] As the WTO obligations of the Parties do not include limits on the use of expropriation, the NAFTA provisions cannot conflict with any specific WTO duties. It could even be debated whether the general GATS principles of MFN and Transparency are required for expropriations: although customary international law would suggest that expropriations must be made non-discriminatorily, this is not set forth as a consideration in the trade context.

For third country banks in the NAFTA territory, then, the lack of explicit protection from non-compensated (if not discriminatory) expropriations is a disadvantage that the NAFTA Party banks do not face. Mexico's historic use of the Calvo Clause doctrine, set aside in the NAFTA for the investors of NAFTA Parties, turns this disadvantage into a potentially great barrier to operations on equal terms for all in that country. As a result of the NAFTA, NAFTA Party banks have a more certain investment environment, which in turn allows for a greater competitiveness. Such an enhanced competitiveness is not, however, incompatible with the GATS.

6.2.3   Potential Incompatibility of NAFTA and GATS: Where Non-NAFTA WTO Member Banks' Rights Under WTO Might Be Violated

Despite the overriding compatibility of the NAFTA with the WTO obligations of the Member Parties, there are several provisions in the two

---

[225] See Kampf (note 47 *supra*), at 157, 163, '… the so-called prudential carve-out in paragraph 2 of the Annex is of particular importance: it permits supervisory authorities of any WTO member to apply prudential measures to protect investors or to ensure the integrity and stability of the financial system'.

[226] See discussion of Art. 1410, at 3.17 *supra*.

[227] See the Agreement on Trade-Related Investment Measures, found in: WTO (note 1 *supra*), at 163–7.

agreements that could come into conflict. The following discrepancies are not unavoidable, but are set out in order to draw attention to sensitive areas of the agreements that are perhaps not as visible as the conflicts with MFN.

6.2.3.1   *Grandfather Rights in Regional Integration Areas (GATS Article V:6)*

The rules regarding GATS-compatible regional integration arrangements include one provision that poses a problem to NAFTA. Article V:6 states:

> A service supplier of any other Member that is a juridical person constituted under the laws of a party to an agreement referred to in paragraph 1 shall be entitled to treatment granted under such agreement, provided that it engages in substantive business operations in the territory of the parties to such agreement.[228]

This provision is a so-called 'grandfathering' (or standstill) clause for all non-party WTO Member service providers established as a legal entity within the regional integration area. Although offering grandfather rights to established businesses is not unusual in the WTO context,[229] it presents a potential—albeit unlikely—conflict with NAFTA Chapter Fourteen's incorporation of the Chapter Eleven Denial of Benefits provision.

Under NAFTA, a Party may deny a non-Party controlled financial institution the benefits of NAFTA if one of three findings is made: if the enterprise is owned or controlled by a non-Party and the two states do not have diplomatic relations; if the Party has regulations that would be nullified if the Chapter Fourteen benefits were extended to such an enterprise; and if the enterprise has no 'substantial business activities' in the territory of the Party in which it is established.[230] Because of the careful wording of this Denial of Benefits provision in NAFTA, unless a Party neglected to maintain a WTO waiver against a state with whom it did not have diplomatic relations, the provision will not conflict with GATS Article V:6.

However, consider the following: an Indian bank (non-NAFTA Party, WTO Member investor) owns a subsidiary bank in Canada. The bank in Canada is actively conducting financial transactions on a large scale (thus, is engaging in substantial banking activity by any definition of the term), including lending to high-technology firms in India. Drawn by the profit potential of the United States banking market, the bank applies to the Department of the Treasury for a national banking license on grounds of the NAFTA. Calling on NAFTA Article 1113:1(b), the banking authorities deny the license due to the potential that the businesses in India receiving

---

[228]   GATS Art. V:6.

[229]   Indeed, 64 of the 70 participants in the negotiations on the Fifth Protocol to the GATS now have standstill, or grandfathering, commitments. See USTR, 'World Trade Organization (WTO) Financial Services Negotiations: Banking /Securities Commitments' Press Release (December 1997) (list of countries 'Grandfathering acquired rights of foreign banks').

[230]   NAFTA Art. 1113.

loans from the bank in the United States would violate United States patents while developing their products. The United States might argue, for instance, that its efforts to force India into implementing its intellectual property protection obligations would be circumvented if it allowed this bank to establish itself in the United States.

Under the GATS Article V:6, the bank is entitled to 'treatment granted under' the free trade area (NAFTA). One could argue this mandates extending all benefits of the treaty.

However, one can also plausibly ARGUE that the NAFTA is not denying that the bank is a NAFTA Party institution, and is therefore not denying 'treatment'. Rather, it is denying the bank the *benefits* of the NAFTA as allowed by incorporation of Article 1113 into Chapter Fourteen ('A Party may deny the benefits of this Chapter to an investor of another Party ...'). Taking the view that 'treatment' includes the benefits of the treaty as well as the limitations under the treaty, the NAFTA provision does not conflict with GATS Article V:6.

6.2.3.2   Obligations on Domestic Regulations (GATS Article VI and NAFTA Chapter Eighteen and Article 1411)

Article VI of the GATS governs domestic regulatory administration for WTO Members. Intended to prevent internal regulatory processes from becoming trade barriers, Article VI imposes a duty of impartiality and reasonability on the administration of laws and rules. Application for licenses or permission to provide services, technical standards to be complied with, and judicial review procedures within a Member's service sector are to be non-discriminatory in law and fact.

In aiming to prevent invisible hurdles to foreign service supplies, the GATS does not conflict directly with the related rules found under NAFTA. Chapter Eighteen of the NAFTA contains the general guidelines for the administrating of measures 'of general application respecting any matter covered by this Agreement'.[231] That Chapter sets out the due process elements of giving notice of measures to interested persons, 'consistent, impartial and reasonable' administration of NAFTA provisions, opportunity for being present at legal proceedings and presenting evidence according to normal domestic procedural rules, and the right of a person to have access to judicial review of decisions that are contrary to his or her interest.

Chapter Fourteen itself contains similar provisions. Because NAFTA's financial service regulations are generally applicable, however, the national treatment obligation and establishment provisions reinforce the neutrality in the administration of NAFTA more than could the GATS' parallel provisions. The Parties' non-conforming measures are specifically set out in the Annex on financial services.

The one area where problems could arise between the GATS and NAFTA would be in the processing of applications for financial service provision

---

[231] NAFTA Art. 1802:1.

licenses. Under GATS VI:3, the applicant for a license to provide a service must be informed of the status of the application 'within a reasonable period of time'. The corresponding obligation in the NAFTA, found in Article 1411 ('Transparency'), sets out a maximum time limit for notification of 120 days from the day the application is complete.[232] If there were two banks applying for a license to establish in a NAFTA Party territory, and one of the banks was a NAFTA Party financial institution and the other was not, these time limits could conflict. Because administrative resources are scarce, it is possible that the licensing authority would not be able to complete the processing of two simultaneously-submitted applications within four months. If this were the case, the licensing authority might choose to complete the processing of the NAFTA Party financial institution before it began on the non-NAFTA Party institution's request. Regardless of the definition given 'reasonable time' by future GATS panels, the conditions of competition are skewed by such timing differences. Although it is probable that the NAFTA Parties could claim these preferences as allowed under the GATS Article V exception to the MFN obligation, the vagueness of exactly what type of variations are allowed under Article V makes the situation a potential problem.

6.2.3.3   Recognition (GATS Article VII and NAFTA Article 1406:2–3)

The GATS, similar to NAFTA, encourages the liberalization of trade in financial services by supporting a Member's acceptance of another Member's 'standards or criteria for the authorization, licensing or certification of services suppliers'.[233] As recognition of such factors would seriously intrude on a Member's ability to control the quality of services offered within its territory, the recognition is not obligatory to the extent transparency is. Moreover, the recognition provision is not subject to an unconditional MFN requirement. Rather, a Member may selectively recognize one Member's qualification standards without being further obliged to recognize all Members' standards.

Still, other WTO Members are not left to a system of purely bilateral standards. Under the principle of conditional MFN, the other Members have a right to present their standards to the recognizing Member and to prove that these standards are equally effective as the recognized Member's standards in achieving the qualitative goals set out.[234] The recognizing Member must give all Members such an opportunity, and is obliged to negotiate toward a separate recognition agreement with each other interested Member.[235]

In addition to the general GATS provision on recognition, the principle of allowing for unequal recognition is included in the specific Annex on Financial Services. There, the prudential measures applied to financial

---

[232] NAFTA Art. 1411:4.
[233] GATS Art. VII:1; NAFTA Art. 1406.
[234] GATS Art. VII:2.
[235] *Ibid.*

services by one Member may be recognized as fulfilling another Member's prudential requirements.[236] Again, this recognition may be granted unilaterally, subject only to the conditional MFN element of a right to negotiate a comparable agreement.[237]

A similar requirement exists in Chapter Fourteen of the NAFTA for the conditional MFN recognition of prudential measures.[238] The Article 1406 provisions on MFN treatment contain three paragraphs setting out the requirements for recognition. Significantly, it acknowledges that NAFTA Parties 'may recognize prudential measures ... unilaterally'.[239] Such recognition is also contingent upon other Parties' rights to demonstrate their own standards' effectiveness and to negotiate a compatible arrangement of recognition.[240]

Based on a textual comparison, these provisions do not conflict. Yet if the NAFTA Parties were to develop an expedited application review process for NAFTA Party banks, or if they exclusively recognize the standards set by NAFTA Party banking authorities without any sign of a thorough investigation into the ramifications of such recognition, there could be a conflict with the other GATS-Members' right to negotiate for the same recognition.[241]

6.2.3.4   Dispute Settlement (WTO Understanding on the Settlement of Disputes and NAFTA Chapter Twenty)

The dispute settlement provisions of NAFTA raised concern among some GATT Parties when the structure became known.[242] Most of the contention centered on the allowance of complaining NAFTA Parties to choose either the WTO dispute settlement procedures or the NAFTA dispute settlement procedures to decide disagreements that affect both Agreements.[243] However, NAFTA dispute settlement processes are mandatory for Parties if

---

[236] GATS, Annex on Financial Services 3(a).
[237] GATS, Annex on Financial Services 3(b).
[238] NAFTA Art. 1406:2-4.
[239] NAFTA Art. 1406:2(a). Recognition may also arise from harmonization of laws or based on a bilateral agreement. NAFTA Art. 1406:2(b), (c).
[240] NAFTA Art. 1406:3.
[241] However, according to an authority in the US Office of the Comptroller of the Currency, neither Mexican nor Canadian banking regulations are yet recognized as fulfilling the United States' banking authorities' prudential regulations, and are thus not offered any special treatment during the application process to establish a bank or branch in the United States. Interview with author (January 1997).
[242] See European Parliament, 'Report of the Committee on External Economic Relations on the Free Trade Agreement between the United States of America, Canada and Mexico (NAFTA)' DOC_EN/RR/217/217513 (18 November 1992) (A3-0378/92), p. 4, beginning with a Motion for Resolution that contained the 'concern' that 'NAFTA's rules on dispute settlement could undermine the effectiveness of the GATT dispute settlement mechanism'. The statement by a former member of the Office of the United States Trade Representative gives these fears at least some credibility. See Sanford E. Gaines, 'Comments on Dispute Settlement Issues under NAFTA' (1993) 1:1 US-Mex LJ 35 ('The clear intention of the parties is that the NAFTA obligations prevail among the three parties as to matters explicitly covered in NAFTA, to the extent that there may be some inconsistency between the NAFTA obligations and GATT obligations').
[243] See European Parliament (note 242 *supra*), at 4.

the defendant Party chooses to form its defense by invoking an environ-mental exception,[244] a defense based on certain NAFTA provisions on sanitary and phytosanitary measures,[245] or on certain NAFTA standards-related measures chapter provisions.[246] Moreover, NAFTA Article 2005:6 excludes simultaneous legal actions on the same set of facts.[247]

The compatibility of such a NAFTA provision with the WTO Dispute Settlement procedures is questionable because under the WTO Agreements each Member has a right to enter consultations within the WTO Framework if it feels the benefits under one of the WTO Agreements have been 'nullified or impaired'.[248] This nullification and impairment extends beyond the bilateral relations and the specific Members' commit-ments to each other during negotiations. In the WTO Understanding on Rules and Procedures Governing the Settlement of Disputes (DSU), the interests of third WTO Members are to be protected during the formal panel process between two WTO disputants.[249] Article 10 of the DSU provides for the possibility that a WTO Member bring its own case to a dispute settlement panel on the same basis as an on-going bilateral dispute settlement.[250] In addition, the Article states that a Member may also make written and oral submissions to the established panel during a dispute[251] and receive the original disputants' submissions.[252] Such 'rights to be heard' protect the atmosphere of voluntary compliance without subjecting a Member to overwhelming compensatory burdens.

---

[244] NAFTA Art. 2005:3.

[245] NAFTA Art. 2005:4 (if the dispute concerns 'a measure adopted or maintained by a Party to protect its human, animal or plant life or health, or to protect its environment, and (b) that raises factual issues concerning the environment, health, safety or conservation, including directly related scientific matters').

[246] *Ibid.*

[247] The restriction on simultaneous dispute settlement processes is not effective if the complainant has taken the case to the GATT dispute settlement forum and the respondant claims that the complaint is one that should be governed by NAFTA Art. 104 (Relation to Environmental and Conservation Agreements), by NAFTA Chapter 7, Section B (Sanitary and Phytosanitary Measures), or by NAFTA Chapter 9 (Standards-Related Measures). See NAFTA Art. 2005:6, referring to NAFTA Art. 2005:3–4.

[248] See generally, Understanding on the Rules and Procedures Governing the Settlement of Disputes (DSU), Art. 4:2 (providing that all Members agree to 'accord sympathetic consideration to and afford adequate opportunity for consultation regarding any representations made by another Member concerning measures affecting the operation of any covered agreement taken within the territory of the former').

[249] DSU Art. 10:4. See also Chi Carmody, 'Of Substantial Interest: Third Parties Under GATT' (1997) 18:4 Mich J Int'l L 615, describing historical and present third party participation in GATT/WTO dispute settlement and encouraging such intervention when there is a 'substantial interest' for the third party in doing so.

[250] DSU Art. 10:4:

> If a third party considers that a measure already the subject of a panel proceeding nullifies or impairs benefits accruing to it under any covered agreement, that Member may have recourse to normal dispute settlement procedures under this Understanding. Such a dispute shall be referred to the original panel wherever possible.

[251] DSU Art. 10:2.

[252] DSU Art. 10:3.

These third Member rights could be impaired by the NAFTA's separate dispute settlement mechanism, as the NAFTA has no explicit mechanism to allow non-NAFTA persons access to its panel processes. If a NAFTA dispute settlement panel were selected as the forum for voicing a complaint falling under both treaties, a non-NAFTA WTO Member would be excluded from voicing a claim in the same action. A separate claim would have to be brought, with the accompanying risk of having less support for the claim than if more than one Member had voiced complaints to the WTO panel. Moreover, once the NAFTA becomes the forum for dispute settlement, the NAFTA Parties themselves are bound to continue the dispute within this framework to the exclusion of beginning a process under GATS rules.[253]

Even with this potential impairment of rights, when viewed in comparison to the European Union's formal dispute settlement institution (the European Court of Justice) and its procedures, the NAFTA dispute settlement structure appears preferable. The European Union (EU) Member States are not permitted to bring complaints against either the European Community (EC) or other Member States to the WTO Dispute Settlement Body in most, if not in all, types of trade.[254] This is true

---

[253] NAFTA Art. 2005:6 provides that '[o]nce dispute settlement procedures have been initiated under Article 2007 or dispute settlement proceedings have been initiated under the GATT, the forum selected shall be used to the exclusion of the other ...'.

[254] Arts 9, 12, and 30 of the Treaty of Rome establish the fundamental rules on the liberalization of inter-EC trade in goods. Art. 170 of the same treaty gives the European Court of Justice the competence to decide disputes arising between Member States over alleged violations of the Treaty. As the EC rules are supreme in the area of trade in goods, it has been determined necessary that Member State complaints be taken to the European Court of Justice rather than to the WTO. See Case 21-24/72, *International Fruit Company NV v. Produktschap voor goenten en fruit* (1972) ECR I-1219 (12 December 1972); C-Case 70/87, *Vereinigung der Oelmühlenindustrie der EWG (Fediol) v. Commission*, p. 1781 (22 June 1989) (para. 21: 'Der Umstand schliesslich, dass das GATT in Artikel XXIII ein besonderes Verfahren für die Beteiligung von Streitigkeiten zwischen Vertragsparteien vorsieht, ist nicht geeignet, die Auslegungsbefugnis des Gerichtshofs auszuschliessen ...'); Case C-280/93, *Germany v. Council* (1994) ECR I-4973 (refusing to overturn an EC Regulation on the basis of its alleged violation of GATT because the GATT provisions were not sufficiently precise); Opinion 1/94, WTO/GATT/GATS/ TRIPs, (1994) ECR I-5267. But see also Bundesfinanzhof Order of 9 January 1996, in which Germany's Federal Court for Financial Law rejected the EC Regulation as a violation of Germany's international law obligations under GATT. Whether a Member State could bring a complaint in an area of trade, such as intellectual property, in which there are 'mixed competences' of the EC and the Member States is unclear. In the absence of any Community rule directing an outcome, it is possible that a Member State could bring a case to the WTO on its own. However, in the proposals coming out of the Summer 1997 conference in Amsterdam, the European Council indicates a tendency to bring the areas of 'mixed competences' under the same rubric as that which determines the treatment of goods. See Treaty of Amsterdam Amending the Treaty on European Union, the Treaties Establishing the European Communities and Certain Related Acts, TA/en 57, at 63, para. 20, proposing an amendment to Art. 113:

    20. In Article 113, the following paragraph shall be added:
      '5. The Council, acting unanimously on a proposal from the Commission and after consulting the European Parliament, may extend the application of paragraphs 1 to 4 to international negotiations and agreements on services and intellectual property insofar as they are not covered by these paragraphs.'

despite the fact that each Member State as well as the EC itself is a Member of the WTO.[255] NAFTA Parties may, but simply do not have to. The choice facing the NAFTA Parties will be made based on tactics. The choice facing the EU Member States is whether to renew their attempts at bringing the direct effect of the WTO Agreements into Community law.

A second area of conflict that NAFTA dispute settlement could pose to the WTO is that of differing interpretations of similar treaty obligations. It is conceivable that a NAFTA dispute settlement will address a complaint in a manner that is different from that of a WTO panel, and the potential difference in result does give cause for thought. First, as the European Parliament claims, the WTO dispute settlement mechanism might lose authority, 'if only because within NAFTA, the United States can wield considerably more influence than is possible in GATT'.[256] This danger, however, is less problematic for the individual financial service entity than is that of legal uncertainty. If the NAFTA panel were to interpret and apply WTO rules as well as NAFTA rules, a degree of dichotomy may be introduced in the 'WTO-lex'.[257] Thus, enterprises that trade with NAFTA Parties and non-NAFTA Parties could encounter conflicting norms governing their transactions.

---

[255] Marrakesh Agreement Establishing the World Trade Organization, Art. XI:1 (European Community is an original member of the WTO as are all former Contracting Parties to the GATT 1947).

[256] European Parliament stated: 'If the NAFTA countries were to develop a different "jurisprudence" from that of the GATT, the authority of the GATT would be undermined'. Report of the Committee on Exteral Economic Relations at 14.

[257] Countries that allow direct effect of WTO rules are also potential misconstruers of these rules. Indeed, a recent Swiss Supreme Court's interpretation of the compatibility of Switzerland's tariff quotas with GATT's principle of tariffication arguably was not consistent with how the WTO itself would read the provision. Bundesgerichtsentscheid 2A.496/1996 (14 July 1997) (unpublished opinion). See also Mitsuo Matsushita, 'State Trading in Japan', in Thomas Cottier and Petros Mavroidis (eds), *State Trading in the 21st Century* 258-265 (University of Michigan Press, Ann Arbor MI, 1998), pp. 258–65, discussing the Kyoto District Court's distortion of GATT law in the *Kyoto Necktie Case*, 31 *Shomu Geppo* 207, judgement of 29 June 1984. Thus, NAFTA panels are not the only threat to a tightly-controlled application of WTO provisions. Piet Eeckhout brings up the problem of differing opinions on treaty provisions in his discussion of the issue of direct effect of the WTO Agreements by the European Union:

> [T]he complex character of the GATT's rules and mechanisms ... is, if anything, increased by the WTO Agreement ... It is therefore questionable whether domestic courts, ... should become day-to-day operators and interpreters of the WTO Agreement ... The result could be that the Community's courts become the courts of the WTO, and that is probably undesirable.

'The Domestic Legal Status of the WTO Agreement: Interconnecting Legal Systems' (1997) 34 Common Mkt. L. Rev. 11, 50 (footnotes omitted).

Differences of law always cause such conflicts, but are particularly troublesome when the texts themselves are the same or use similar terms. Commercial actors from outside the NAFTA Parties are likely to be put at a greater disadvantage in such a situation, as there will be no formal mechanism to inform them of NAFTA legal interpretations. Moreover, they will remain outside of the system, unable to add their views to the development of the interpretation. This point is reverted to in the Conclusion.[258]

---

[258] See Chapter 9 *infra*.

7. Indirect Effects of Chapter Fourteen on Third Country Banks

One can well imagine that the obligations of ensuring non-discriminatory market access and an equality of conditions of competition, while perhaps offering economic equality, will not result in a completely integrated market place for banking services within the NAFTA Parties' territories. Moreover, the lack of unified monetary policy will prevent the formation of a single North American market for financial services.[1] However, Chapter Fourteen does offer several intangible opportunities for its Parties' banks that third banks are not in a position to exploit.

Knowledge of the other market's legal system, familiarity with the business and financial environments, and cultural awareness are all important factors in successful long-term financial activity.[2] Entry into retail markets requires an even deeper knowledge of a country and its people.[3] Seen in this broader business context, one important consequence

---

[1] See Jeffrey A. Hart and Aseem Prakash, 'Globalisation and Regionalisation: Conceptual Issues and Reflections' (1996) 6 Int'l Trade L & Reg 205, 211, criticizing the NAFTA's lack of 'institutionalised behaviour regarding the monetary policy' as a barrier to unimpeded trade flows, particularly for financial services.

[2] See Elizabeth Laderman and Ramon Moreno, 'NAFTA and U.S. Banking', Fed. Res. Bank of San Francisco Weekly Letter 92-40 (13 November 1992), pp. 1–3, at 2:

> Traditional commercial banking requires the development of long-term relationships between bankers and their corporate clients. Such relationships give bankers information on borrowers and the deep knowledge of credit markets that is required to make sound and profitable credit decisions. In the absence of such close relationships with clients in Mexico, US banks initially may be reluctant to incur the costs of setting up subsidiaries in Mexico, even if NAFTA allows them to do so.

[3] The argument that 'there might exist strong incumbency advantages to domestic firms deriving from long familiarity with local culture, customs, tastes, language and legal systems' is particularly true for the retail banking market, but even foreign banks who have been present on a market for a certain time will be able to enjoy such advantages over new foreign entrants. Edward M. Graham and Robert Z. Lawrence, 'Measuring the International Contestability of Markets: A Conceptual Approach' (1996) 30:5 J World Trade 5, 6.

of the NAFTA negotiations on third states' banks arises out of the negotiation process itself.[4]

Although NAFTA was primarily aimed at economic, rather than political and social, integration, the process of negotiating and agreeing on sectoral liberalization inherently leads to a certain degree of harmonization among the participants' views. During the early negotiation preparation phase, the government negotiating teams and interested public in each Party had to find out about the corresponding groups from the other Parties. Information collected and ideas developed during this time then was deepened or altered through personal contacts during the formal negotiations. This simple awareness-building and 'getting-to-know-one-another' experience forms a foundation for understanding and future working together. Even where the participants did not accurately interpret the ideas conveyed by the others about the different domestic environments, all gained a greater possibility of empathizing with the others.

The governmental and public debate on the NAFTA (as a whole and on Chapter Fourteen on its own) spurred dialogues among private firms and individuals of each country. This occurred to a greater or lesser extent, depending on the particular sector and geographic area, but again, understanding among the Parties and their publics was the result. Neither required by nor dependent on the Agreement as such, this dialogue may well lead to benefits which, while unquantifiable, do give the Parties an advantage of a common understanding that non-Party persons do not enjoy. At the same time, such understanding may make commercial partnerships more likely and, when they occur, more successful.

The opportunity to have alliances in the other Parties' financial services markets could be competitively very important, particularly for banks that have internationally active customers but that do not want to invest heavily in an unfamiliar environment, or that are individually too small to afford the necessary financial outlay to establish a foreign operation.[5] At the same time, the harmonization of liberal regulatory norms could remove the advantages enjoyed by foreign banks operating in already liberal markets due to a phenomenon of 'distorted comparative advantage': in a harmonized

---

[4] See Nikolaj Petersen, 'National Strategies in the Integration Dilemma: An Adaptation Approach' (1998) 36:1 J. Common Mkt. Stud. 33, 35 ('the integration process is progressive by having a developmental aspect to it').

[5] Writing in the context of European integration, one author explains the particular benefits of business partnerships between foreign banks in a regional trade area:

> … strategic partnerships will play a more important role in the financial sector than in manufacturing industry, where a merger will still be a way of achieving a better position in the market. Partnerships will be formed for the purpose of offering a full range of products and eliminating the disadvantages of being small. Transnational partnerships and partnerships between local specialists in various segments will be created. This means that the financial service sector in the future will be a market not only for big operators but also for small innovative operators.

> Thomas Hagdahl, 'Doing Business in a Wider Europe', in Mary Robinson and Jantien Findlater (eds), *Creating a European Economic Space: Legal Aspects of EC-EFTA Relations* (1990), pp. 229–37, at 236.

regulatory world, trade in financial services actually decreases due to the lack of incentives to take advantage of regulatory differentials.[6]

Following the NAFTA's coming into effect, the Parties were required to establish formal inquiry points for businesses interested in taking advantage of the market entry liberalizations contained in the Agreement. The required transparency set out by Chapter Fourteen provisions, however, is not the only government-sponsored trade facilitation. There has been an increase in government activity (particularly at the sub-national level) in collecting and making available economic data and information on the commercial environment in the partner countries and partner sub-national units.[7] There have even been financial assistance programs started to give money both to entrepreneurs entering the other Parties' markets and to researchers studying the Agreement's effects and the opportunities it holds.

Efforts are also underway to remedy the holes left in the Agreement by bringing together business leaders, lawyers, academics, and sub-national politicians from all Parties to work out voluntary guidelines on how to conduct everyday business.[8] Those interested in Chapter Fourteen are among those actively trying to improve on the Agreement privately,

---

[6] Thomas Helbling, 'Explaining the Presence of Foreign Financial Intermediaries in Switzerland', in Niklaus Blattner, Hans Genberg, and Alexander K. Swoboda (eds), *Banking in Switzerland* (Physica-Verlag, Heidelberg, 1993), pp. 145–96, at 166, n.21, citing Arndt (1988) and Ryan (1990).

[7] See Bruce Waddell, 'NAFTA Problems and Solutions for US Business', the text of which is on the internet at >www.flash.net<, setting out the steps a small or medium-sized US business needs to take in order to start commercial activities in Mexico, and listing the various government offices that are equipped to give information and assistance to interested persons.

[8] In the financial services context, the NAFTA makes only a minimal effort to harmonize banking practices among the Parties. Yet, during consultations with bankers in North America, researchers find that it is often the differing levels of technology and individual ways of completing routine transactions that hinder trade. Public international trade law, protecting banks against state-led discrimination, it would seem, is limited in its usefulness to the ordinary bank's everyday operations. To be sure, without the trade law principles of establishment and national treatment, foreign banks would certainly face high—in many cases prohibitive—barriers to doing business. Yet, with technology making electronic trans-actions ever more prevalent and banking ever more global, there is a certain realistic damper thrown on the financial service liberalization achievements without strong support from and involvement of the private sector itself. For an analysis of why an international regulatory system that is led by the banks themselves may be preferable to one dictated by governments or international organizations, see Raj Bhala, 'Equilibrium Theory, the FICAS Model, and International Banking Law' (1997) 38:1 Harv Int'l LJ 1, arguing that a self-regulatory system optimizes the chances of achieving a stable dynamic equilibrium of a regulatory structure).

[9] One example of such a conference was that organized by the National Law Center for Inter-American Free Trade in Arizona. There, representatives of the United States Council on International Banking, the Canadian Bankers Association, and the Mexican Bankers Association met to discuss methods of harmonizing check-clearing and -return practices among the NAFTA participants. Guidelines were drafted amidst an open question-and-answer exchange among the participants. See 'Transcript of the First Meeting', in Mordy Karsch and Boris Kozolchyk (transcript eds), *Toward Seamless Borders*, Vol. 1 (1993), p. 352 (Appendix A). There are also many regional or sectoral initiatives to

whether in conferences,[9] by exchange visits, or via internet discussion groups and websites.

These institutional structures and political relations formed within the NAFTA governments may result in a comfort level for NAFTA Party banks that non-Party banks will not enjoy. Individuals from the private and regulatory banking communities in Canada, the United States, and Mexico have the opportunity to establish contacts, if not friendships, making future co-operation less burdensome.

Similarly, informal discussion groups, led as often by efficiency-seeking practitioners as by academic interests, could form the more promising basis for greater legal harmonization among the three Parties than the efforts of official government negotiating teams ever could.[10] The involvement in such trilateral networking will give an additional advantage to those banks that become familiar with the trading environment among NAFTA parties. These banks will find that the opportunities to profit from increased levels of trade have grown already and are likely to continue to grow, not because of nationality, but because of informal structures.

Before NAFTA came into effect, one Canadian researcher noted the lack of trade between the western Canadian Provinces and Mexico with concern. It is not only that trade increases the amount of money, he noted, but also just as important, trade builds relationships that are self-regenerating.

> The dearth of trade between ... two regions means that Mexican business people have virtually no significant interface with the business sector of Western Canada when compared to their relationships with American and some European business partners. If there is truth in the adage that 'people do business with people they know', and if knowing is the prelude

---

(Contd.)

discover the profitable business opportunities in continental trade that have opened due to NAFTA or that are only now being noticed. See Ted Chambers, 'Western Canada—Mexico Trade: Realizing Strategic Opportunities', the text of which is on the Internet at >www.freenet.calgary.ab.ca<. At a meeting in April 1997 of 'mayors, economic development officials and business leaders who want to foster trade opportunities' a plan was developed for a North American 'trade corridor' aimed at increasing freight traffic from Winnipeg, Canada to Guadalajara, Mexico by developing highway and railway lines. An 'intermodal transportation' facility will be co-ordinated by the officials of the more than 100 municipalities along the corridor. See 'KC Delegation Pushes Trade Among Mexico, US, Canada', *Kansas City Business Journal* (14 April 1997), the text of which is on the Internet at >www.amcity.com<.

[10] For an insight into the areas of banking law in which such harmonizing efforts might make a difference to the daily business of competitive banking, see Jacqueline S. Akins, 'Selected Statutes and Regulations Affecting Day-to-Day Bank Operations' (1994) 48 Cons Fin LQ Rep. 368, discussing, *inter alia*, laws regulating a bank's advertising, advice-giving, disclosures, backroom operations, and banking secrecy.

to trust which is a big part of Latin culture where sustained and consistent personal contact means so much, then there is a great deal of work to be done.[11]

The same reasoning leads to the idea that those outside a free trade area are disadvantaged in practice by a lack of closer personal ties to the relevant business community within the area.

On a theoretical level, four processes have been noticed as characteristic of economically-defined regions: innovation; clustering; institutional learning; and economies of association.[12] These processes may also be descriptive of has started to occur in services, including financial services, in North America. Examining the aspects of innovation and institutional learning, for example, highlights the importance of the increased contacts among and between producer, supplier, and consumers of banking services that will arise from the NAFTA as an integration process. These contacts will themselves help the NAFTA's banking system become not only more developed and increasingly flexible, but also more interlinked as a distinctive system.[13] Moreover:

> ... economic, technical, institutional and social spheres of a society or a system, by continuously interacting and reciprocal conditioning, tend to evolve jointly. Such a process will shape solid traditions and habits, which in turn

---

[11] Chambers (note 9 *supra*).

[12] Philip Cooke, 'Regions in a Global Market: the Experiences of Wales and Baden-Württemberg' 4:2 Rev. Int'l Pol Econ 349, 357, referring to works by Ohmae, de Vet, Rhodes, Archibugi and Michie, Lundvall, and Krugman. Cooke describes the earlier works for the reader in the context of automobile manufacturing regions:

> ... it is increasingly suggested that regions ... have a new role as economic locomotives in the increasingly 'borderless worlds' of the European and North American trade blocs (Ohmae 1990, 1995). To repeat, the argument goes like this, following Ohmae, de Vet (1993) and Rhodes (1995). As national state economies, typical of the first half of the present century, lose their ability to protect their industry with tariff barriers and subsidies within trade blocs, so weak industries decline and economies become more *specialized*. The latter point is commented upon by numerous economists who note what they call the 'stickiness' of regional economic structures and, as de Vet (1993) notes, the tendency for them to become even more 'sticky' or sectorally distinctive as time goes by.
>
> What is being said here is, clearly, that spatial distinctiveness of economic activity will become the norm. We may disagree about the detail ... of the likely future centres of key economic activity. Key here is the absence of a notion of polycentricity associated with specialization by different regions or cities in similar industries, but with the *processes* ... it is difficult to disagree.

[13] *Ibid.* at 358–9, 360–4. See particularly at 362:

> ... it is essential to link the phenomenon of innovation to the cluster structure of the industry and to the regional innovation *system*. The focus is thus on the relationships and flows between the various actors and parts of the innovation system: firms, institutions for research and higher education, private R&D laboratories, technology transfer agencies, chambers of commerce and so on. In other words, it is crucial to examine the 'systemness' of the regional innovation system.

influence industrial structure and performance, characteristics of institutions and technological trajectories.[14]

Finally, the NAFTA Party banks that have used the new informal networks have an advantage of time. Although not necessarily a critical factor, being the first (or among the first) of a group of firms to enter a market is almost always advantageous in many respects. The so-called 'incumbency advantages' include the ability to possess, even if for a short time, monopoly or oligopoly profits.[15] More importantly, within this period, the incumbent bank has an opportunity to learn about the commercial environment and thereby attract customers who will then develop a loyalty to the institution. The first bank will also be able to establish distribution systems and partner businesses that will already be in place when future competition starts to enter the market.[16] Once established in a market, the bank will then attract complementary firms and a suitable labor pool, both of which create external scale economies. This might lead to a banking 'cluster' that includes competitors as well as complementary businesses, but the first to arrive will have a definite potential advantage. One economist who studies the phenomenon of geographic clustering of foreign direct investment writes:

> Incumbency advantages created by external scale economies are reinforced by the fact that a cluster not only supplies goods and services but also demands them ... The combined effect of 'supply side' incumbency advantages (borne basically of economies of scale) and 'demand side' ones (borne basically of logistical advantages) are such that, in formal models of clusters, these clusters become stable equilibria in the spatial coordinates of a suitable cartesian space.[17]

---

[14] *Ibid.* at 362.

[15] See Edward M. Graham, 'The (Not Wholly Satisfactory) State of the Theory of Foreign Direct Investment and the Multinational Enterprise', in Jerome L. Stein (ed.), *The Globalization of Markets: Capital Flows, Exchange Rates and Trade Regimes* (Physica-Verlag, Heidelberg, 1997), pp. 99–122, at 108, explaining that this assumes the possibility of extracting monopoly or oligopoly rents). The financial services market of any country would allow for such a possibility as the entrance costs—gaining permission from the governmental authorities to begin banking operations as well as the time and effort required to investigate the regional market and the infrastructure's capital costs—are substantial in any highly regulated service industry. Moreover, there is often no suitable substitute for banking products, allowing for considerable market power by a bank over a potential customer.

[16] Chambers (note 9 *supra*); Edward M. Graham and Robert Z. Lawrence, 'Measuring the International Contestability of Markets: A Conceptual Approach' (1996) 30:5 J World Trade 5, 6, explaining that contestability of markets is inherently constrained by incumbency advantages that include 'economies of scale (fixed costs), advantages due to superior knowledge of incumbents (e.g. learning by doing) and advantages due to market niches with particular consumer loyalty'.

[17] Graham (note 15 *supra*), at 115.

Within this equilibrium (by virtue of being a stable system), the incumbent bank will maintain its predominant position.[18] Thus, in the case of NAFTA, if non-Party banks wait to take advantage of the general liberalizations, they will be at an additional competitive disadvantage due to the indirect effects of the Chapter Fourteen regime.

---

[18] See also *ibid.* at 102–6 (Graham's discussion of the 'OLI', or 'eclectic' paradigm); see particularly his explanation of 'ownership advantages', where he sets out what elements constitute 'ownership advantages' for firms engaged in foreign direct investment:

> [Besides economies of scale and marketing skills,] [m]ost authors would now include as ownership advantages other intangible assets such as proprietary product and process technologies, ability to create new technologies, organizational and managerial skills beyond those associated with marketing, and intellectual property not technical in nature, e.g., well recognized brand names. Dunning includes also what he terms 'advantages of common governance', including advantages that established enterprises might have over new entrants (accumulated learning effects, economies of scope, ability to obtain inputs on favorable terms, etc.) ... .

Ibid. at 103, referring to J.H. Dunning, *American Investment in British Industry* (Unwin, London, 1958).

Part IV
The Effects of NAFTA Expansion and
Concluding Remarks

8. Possible Effects of a NAFTA Expansion on Banks

The converging of interests that led Canada, Mexico, and the United States to negotiate the North American Free Trade Agreement was perhaps unique in its details, but the interests it embodies (industrialized countries' prospective alliance building with emerging economies; securing attempts at domestic liberalization through external obligations; promoting 'deeper' integration through regional agreements with fewer original members) are widely shared at a general level. Further, the NAFTA Parties themselves have expressed interest from the beginning in the idea of broadening the membership of the Agreement. As South American economies grow and begin to be recognized as future centers of economic growth (especially as the newly developing South Asian economies reveal signs of weakness), North American (as well as European) attention is being turned upon Chile, Argentina, and Brazil as desirable trading partners.[1] Although the North American interest has waned since the leaders of the American nations announced their optimistic plans for a Free Trade Area that would stretch from Anchorage to Tierra del Fuego, there continues to be official statements of the expansion of NAFTA to more than its three original Parties.[2] The following introduces the current status of plans to expand the North

---

[1] As a manager of the New York investment firm of at Brown Brothers Harriman & Co remarked, 'Europe is overbanked, Asians are repatriating their money, and Middle Eastern oil prices are not what people in that region would like. But in Latin America we are seeing a lot of new wealth being created'. Quoted by Aline Sullivan, 'In Latin America, New Wealth Shakes Out Old Family Habits' International Herald Tribune, 12 May 1998, p. 20, reporting on the new and growing interest in Latin American markets among private bankers due to the increases in wealth of many individuals in the region as well as a new trend to invest in high-yield portfolios. The commercial interest in Latin America, with the exception of Brazil, has not seemed to be significantly affected by the negative economic developments of 1998s Asian Crisis. While new loans to the region 'ground to a halt' in the second quarter of 1998, 'there was no large-scale capital flight during the first half of the year' from Argentinian and Mexican banks. Daniel Pruzin, 'BIS Report Cites Retreat in Bank Funds from Asia, Slowdown in Latin America' (1998) 71:21 BNA's Banking Rep 883.

[2] See 8.3, 8.4 *infra*.

American Free Trade Agreement to Central and South America and then presents a glimpse into how changes in the composition of NAFTA may effect non-Parties' banks.[3]

8.1   THE GROWTH OF NAFTA

8.1.1   Latin American Integration Efforts

As a regional integration agreement, the NAFTA is not alone in the Western Hemisphere. There are numerous free trade area agreements comprised by the countries of Latin America.[4] Among the more than 30 bilateral and regional trade agreements[5] are: the Latin American Integration Association (LAIA), which itself contains the sub-groupings of the Common Market of the Southern Cone (Mercosur)[6] and the Andean Group,[7] along with the members of each and Mexico; the Central American Common Market (CACM);[8] the Caribbean Community and Common Market (CARICOM)[9] and its sub-group the Organization of Eastern Caribbean States (OECS-CARICOM);[10] and the

---

[3] The problem of how a single state's membership in multiple regional free trade areas could effect the WTO/GATT system is not discussed here. It is, however, an interesting is not discussed here concept and is worthy of further study. The present author has only seen one article addressing this issue: Waldemar Hummer and Dietmar Prager, 'Zur GATT-Kompatibilität von Mehrfachmitgliedschaft in regionalen Präferenzzonen–dargestellt am Beispiel Mexikos in der NAFTA/ALADI und Lichtensteins im EWR/Zollanschlussvertrag Schweiz' (1997) 35:4 *Archiv des Völkerrechts* 367.

[4] See Hummer and Prager (note 3 *supra*), at 377, stating that there are 26 different free trade areas in Latin America and the Caribbean. See also *ibid.* at 377–85, explaining the special forms of the overlapping regional trade agreements in Latin America. Another author emphasizes the rapidity at which the South American integration is proceeding, and even talks of 'blitz' tactics by Mercosur. Pascual Covarrubias Meyer, 'Whether for Chilean NAFTA or NAFTA 'Light' Accession: The Necessity of Fast Track Authority' (1998) 4:1 NAFTA: L & Bus Rev Am 137. In the same vein, a Senator from Chile begins an article with the observation, 'Trade negotiations seem to be on the rise in the Americas. Hardly a month goes by without a trade pact being signed or a new initiative announced. Existing integration schemes are revised and new groupings are formed'. Miguel Otero-Lathrop, 'MERCOSUR and NAFTA: the Need for Convergence' (1998) 4:3 NAFTA: L & Bus Rev Am 116.

[5] Meyer (note 4 *supra*), at 142.

[6] Members are Argentina, Brazil, Paraguay, and Uruguay. See also Gustavo A. Bizai, 'Mercosur: Towards the Common Market—Developments in 1995' (1996) 1 Int'l Trade L Rev 13, setting out in a short summary the main provisions of the Treaty of Asunción forming Mercosur and those of the amendments to the treaty, particularly the Protocol of Ouro Preto, which established the institutional structure of the customs union. For a more trade-oriented discussion of Mercosur, see Sam Laird, 'MERCOSUR: Objectives and Achievements', WTO Staff Working Paper TPRD9702.WPF (23 May 1997) (WTO Working Papers may be downloaded from the WTO internet site at >www.wto.org<).

[7] Members are Bolivia, Colombia, Ecuador, Peru, and Venezuela.

[8] Members are Costa Rica, El Salvador, Guatemala, Honduras, and Nicaragua.

[9] Members are Bahamas, Barbados, Belize, Guyana, Jamaica, Surinam, and Trinidad and Tobago.

[10] Members are Antigua and Barbuda, Dominica, Grenada, Montserrat, St Kitts and Nevis, St Lucia, and St Vincent and Grenadines.

Group of Three (G3).[11] Although in the history of Latin American attempts at integration have not shown much success in integrating the economies,[12] recent efforts to revise the agreements take a different, perhaps more effective approach to integration.[13] Most significantly, there is a new emphasis on improving the competitiveness of the Latin American economies rather then on encapsulating them behind a wall of trade barriers to the outside: today's Latin American regional integration is combining reforms in external trade methods with market liberalizations in the domestic economies[14]

---

[11] Members are Mexico, Colombia, and Venezuela.

[12] The Jamaican Ambassador to the United States, who was simultaneously Permanent Representative of the Organization of American States and the Chairman of the Organization's Working Group on the Enterprise for the Americas Intiative, sets out a short history of the many attempts at integration undertaken by the states of the Americas:

> Regional integration in Latin America was conceived of in the late 1930s, gathered momentum in the 1940s and 1950s, and witnessed its first tangible manifestation in the early 1960s … Not long after the countries of Latin America won their independence from the industrialized colonial powers, they began to examine various strategies of economic cooperation and integration. In 1939, Argentina and Brazil negotiated a treaty of "industrial complementation and free commerce". In early 1941, representatives of Argentina, Bolivia, Brazil, Paraguay and Uruguay attended a Regional Conference at which a number of economic agreements were signed in an effort to harmonize economic relations among the countries. In particular, Argentina proposed the creation of a "customs union" which would encompass the La Plata countries and bordering nations. These efforts toward Latin American integration repeatedly ended in failure.

Richard Bernal, 'Regional Trade Arrangements in the Western Hemisphere' (1993) 8:4 Am Univ J Int'l L & Pol'y 683, 684—685 (footnotes omitted).

[13] See generally, Sam Laird, 'Latin American Trade Liberalization' (1995) 4:2 Minn J Global Trade 195, discussing trade liberalization in the context of the American regional agreements from an international trade perspective; Eduardo Gitli and Gunilla Ryd, 'Latin American Integration and the Enterprise for the Americas Initiative' (1992) 26:4 J World Trade 25; Bernal (note 12 *supra*); Mario A. Gutiérrez, 'Is Small 'Beautiful' for Economic Integration? The Americas' (1996) 30:4 J World Trade 173, setting out an economic perspective on the integration of 'small economies' and how such integration affects trade; including many statistical charts comparing the economic indicators of the Central and South American countries as well as the major trade arrangements). See also Frank J. Garcia, 'Decisionmaking and Dispute Resolution in the Free Trade Area of the Americas: An Essay in Trade Governance' (1997) 18:2 Mich J Int'l L 357.

[14] Gitli and Ryd (note 13 *supra*), at 33; Bernal (note 12 *supra*), at 689. During the 1980s, inter-regional trade actually declined for some of the Latin American trade areas. Gitli and Ryd (note 13 *supra*), at 28 reporting that LAIA's inter-regional trade went from 14 per cent in 1980 to 10 per cent in 1989 and CACM's internal trade declined from 25 to 15 per cent in the same time frame. The 1990s, by contrast, were seen as times of tremendous trade growth. A report leaked from within the World Bank recorded its author's belief in the fortification of the Mercosur bloc, based on an analysis of that agreement's effects on trade. Alexander Yeats, 'Does Mercosur's Trade Performance Justify Concerns About the Effects of Regional Trade Arrangements? YES!'. However, the study was widely condemned (as well as held to be its author's personal opinion by the World Bank itself) as an inaccurate assessment of the liberalizations taking place in South America. The critics emphasize that Latin American trade has grown significantly both within the regional arrangements with third countries. See Miguel Rodriguez Mendoza, 'Which Mercosur

and is being pursued parallel to, rather than instead of, multilateral trade liberalization.[15]

8.2   THE ENTERPRISE OF THE AMERICAS INITIATIVE

8.2.1   The Miami Summit

The NAFTA was introduced to the other states of the Western Hemisphere as the first stage in an effort at hemispheric economic integration known as the Enterprise for the Americas Initiative (EAI). During the First Summit of the Americas in mid-December 1994, the leaders of 34 American countries proclaimed they would support the formation of a Free Trade Area of the Americas (FTAA) as a part of the EAI's program.[16] The First Summit (known as the Miami Summit) lay out the conceptual framework of the FTAA and established an organization within which the negotiations were to be prepared. Twelve working groups were to investigate the status of various sectors of American commercial activity, under the oversight of the Vice Ministers of Trade, who would in turn report to the Trade Ministers. The guiding principles for the organization are contained in the Miami Summit's Declaration of Principles and the accompanying 'Plan of Action'.[17] These Principles capture the essence of the American (broadly defined) view of how 'modern' trade should be:

> Our continued economic progress depends on sound economic policies, sustainable development, and dynamic private sectors. A key to prosperity is

---

(Contd.)

Anyway?' and Robert Devlin, 'In Defense of Mercosur' (Mr Rodriguez is the Chief Trade Adviser to the Organization of American States and Mr Devlin is the Chief of Integration, Trade and Hemispheric Issues Division at the Inter-American Development Bank) (both texts found on the internet at >www.aduaneiras.com.br<).

[15] Otero-Lathrop (note 4 *supra*), at 116 ('... even if substantial regionalization is taking place, this regionalization does not necessarily reverse the trend towards globalization and multilateralization in the region'). The efforts to further liberalize regional trade cannot be attributed to the requirements of the WTO rules on regional integration arrangements as most of the Latin American arrangements, including Mercosur, were notified under the provisions of the November 1979 Decision known as the 'Enabling Clause' rather than under the Article XXIV GATT and/or Art. V GATS provisions. The notification of MERCOSUR under this provision therefore caused the United States to demand that the WTO use Art. XXIV review procedures rather than the lesser Enabling Clause when reviewing that custom union's compatibility with the WTO rules. Telephone conversation with WTO representative of Trade and Development Division, 9 March 1999. But see also Laird (note 13 *supra*), at 4 attributing the Article XXIV GATT review procedures to the tardiness of the enabling clause review committee within the Trade and Development Division.

[16] See 'Summit of the Americas: Declaration of Principles and Plan of Action' found in (1995) 34:3 ILM 808. See also the official internet site for the FTAA at >www.alca-ftaa.org<. The First Summit of the Americas took place in Miami, Florida.

[17] Both of these documents can be downloaded from the FTAA internet site given at note 16 *supra*.

trade without barriers, without subsidies, without unfair practices, and with an increasing stream of productive investments Eliminating impediments to market access for goods and services among our countries will foster our economic growth. A growing world economy will also enhance our domestic prosperity. Free trade and increased economic integration are key factors for raising standards of living, improving working conditions of people in the Americas and better protecting the environment.[18]

Significant in the Declaration is the comprehensive approach to the integration: not only is movement in goods, services, capital, and persons to be facilitated, but the societies of the American states are to be made more democratic,[19] the peoples healthier and better educated,[20] the environment more protected,[21] and governments more responsive to civil society.[22] Compared to this, even NAFTA's ambitious goals seem moderate.

8.2.2 Trade Ministerials

Following the Miami Summit, the trade ministers began meeting at so-called 'Trade Ministerials'. These Ministerials produced Joint Declarations in which the progress reports and action plans for the working groups were announced.

---

[18] Summit of the Americas: Declaration of Principles (passage from section titled 'To Promote Prosperity Through Economic Integration and Free Trade').

[19] The Declaration, for example, opens with a firm statement on the states' commitment to democracy:

> The elected Heads of State and Government of the Americas are committed to advance the prosperity, democratic values and institutions, and security of our Hemisphere ... Although faced with differing development challenges, the Americas are united in pursuing prosperity through open markets, hemispheric integration, and sustainable development.
>
> We reiterate our firm adherence to the principles of international lawand the purposes and principles enshrined in the United Nations Charter ... including the principles of sovereign equality of states, non-intervention, self-determination, and peaceful resolution of disputes.

[20] See, e.g., *ibid*. at section titled 'To Eradicate Poverty and Discrimination in Our Hemisphere' ('With an aim of attaining greater social justice for all our people, we pledge to work individually and collectively to improve access to quality education and primary health care and to eradicate extreme poverty and illiteracy').

[21] See, e.g., *ibid*. at section titled 'To Guarantee Sustainable Development and Conserve Our Natural Environment for Future Generations' ('... we will create cooperative partnerships to strengthen our capacity to prevent and control pollution, to protect ecosystems and use our biological resource on a sustainable basis, and to encourage clean, efficient and sustainable energy production and use').

[22] See concluding paragraphs of Declaration ('... we invite the cooperation and participation of the private sector, labor, political parties, academic institutions and other non-governmental actors and organizations ..., thus strengthening the partnership between governments and society').

8.2.2.1   Denver Ministerial

The first of these Ministerials took place in Denver, Colorado, six months after the First Summit. It was there that the Trade Ministers officially agreed to a work program for pursing the FTAA.[23]

8.2.2.2   Cartegena Ministerial

The Ministers met the following year in Cartegena, Columbia. The Cartegena Ministerial focused mainly on the various approaches to forming a regional integration area within the framework of the World Trade Organization.[24] In addition, however, the Ministers specifically emphasized the need to further involve the 'smaller economies' in trade relations, and called on the Working Groups to pursue the possibilities for doing so.

8.2.2.3   Belo Horizonte Ministerial

The third meeting of the Trade Ministers occurred in Brazil, in the city of Belo Horizonte. By that time, the Second Summit of the Americas was already beginning to be organized, and the Ministerial Declaration is pointed to concretizing plans for that Summit.[25] Among other decisions taken in Belo Horizonte was that to make the Santiago Summit the official beginning of the formal FTAA negotiating process.[26] For that purpose, a Preparatory Committee was established, with each country represented through its Vice Minister of Trade.[27]

8.2.2.4   San Jose Ministerial

The fourth Trade Ministerial took place in San Jose, Costa Rica. Just one month before the Second Summit of the Americas, this Trade Ministerial was significant in its recommendations on how to structure the upcoming negotiations.[28] As a first step, the Trade Ministers established a Trade Negotiations Committee, composed of the Vice Trade Ministers.[29] In addition, the 12 working groups of the past four years were transformed

---

[23] See The Denver Ministerial Declaration, Joint Declaration issued at the Summit of the Americas Trade Ministerial, Denver, Colorado, Unites States of America (30 June 1995). Text of this Declaration can be found on the FTAA internet site (note 16 *supra*).

[24] See The Cartegena Ministerial Declaration, Joint Declaration issued at the Summit of the Americas Second Ministerial Trade Meeting, Cartegena, Columbia (26 March 1996). Text of this Declaration can be found on the FTAA internet site (note 16 *supra*).

[25] See The Belo Horizonte Ministerial Declaration, issued at the Summit of the Americas Third Trade Ministerial Meeting, Belo Horizonte, Brazil (16 May 1997). Text of this Declaration can be found on the FTAA internet site (note 16 *supra*).

[26] *Ibid.* at para. 4.

[27] *Ibid.* at para. 6.

[28] See The San Jose Ministerial Declaration, Joint Declaration issued at the Summit of the Americas Fourth Trade Ministerial, San Jose, Costa Rica (19 March 1998). Text of this Declaration can be found on the FTAA internet site (note 16 *supra*).

[29] *Ibid.* at para. 10.

into nine 'negotiating groups', each with a Chairman and Vice-Chairman chosen with the aim to ensure 'geographic balance'.[30] Annexed to the Joint Declaration of San Jose is a list of 'General Principles and Objectives'.[31] In the 'General Principles' list, the Ministers agreed to apply consensus decision-making rules to the negotiations, to maintain transparency in the negotiations, and to aim at WTO-compatibility for the results of the negotiations. Moreover, the Trade Ministers made two statements on the relationship between the future FTAA and other regional agreements (necessarily including NAFTA):

f. The FTAA can co-exist with bilateral and sub-regional agreements, to the extent that the rights and obligations under these agreements are not covered by or go beyond the rights and obligations of the FTAA.
g. Countries may negotiate and accept the obligations of the FTAA individually or as members of a sub-regional integration groups negotiating as a unit.[32]

8.2.3   Second Summit of the Americas

The Second Summit of the Americas took place in April 1998 in Santiago, Chile. It was with the Santiago Declaration made on the 19th of that month that the American heads of state officially began negotiations on the Free Trade Area of the Americas:

Today, we direct our Ministers Responsible for Trade to begin negotiations for the FTAA, in accordance with the March 1998 Ministerial Declaration of San José. We reaffirm our determination to conclude the negotiation of the FTAA no later than 2005, and to make concrete progress by the end of the century. The FTAA agreement will be balanced, comprehensive, WTO-consistent and constitute a single undertaking.[33]

8.3   THE FTAA AND THE EXPANSION OF NAFTA

Despite the heralded beginnings and continued annual ministerial meetings, between 1994 and 1999 little tangible progress has been made on realizing the EAI's goal of establishing a FTAA. The same is true of the plans to extend NAFTA membership to other American states. Five years into the effective life of the Initiative, the number of NAFTA Parties remains as it was originally, and indeed looks less likely to increase than it did at the beginning of 1994. The lack of progress with the NAFTA and that of the FTAA, while not to be seen as identical, are related to each other.

---

[30] *Ibid.* at para. 11.
[31] See *ibid.* Appendix.
[32] *Ibid.* under 'General Principles'.
[33] Santiago Declaration, issued at the Second Summit of the Americas, Santiago, Chile (19 April 1998).

One problem lies in the United States' refusal to take more than a first-step in seriously considering Chile as a NAFTA Partner. Having indicated to Chile that it would be the first nation to be offered an invitation to accede to the NAFTA, the United States reversed its policy and has refused to act, to the frustration of Canada and Mexico. By 1997, the then-Chairman of Canada's House of Commons Standing Committee on Foreign Affairs made the comment, 'I think the chance of seeing any agreement with Chile or with NAFTA is extremely remote'.[34]

At the same time, Chile's present attitude toward NAFTA accession is also tepid, at best, but this appears to be strongly related to its problems with the United States.[35]

---

[34] William C. Graham, 'NAFTA Vis à Vis the EU—Similarities and Differences and Their Effects on Member Countries' (1997) 23 Can-US LJ 123, 131. See also Richard O. Cunningham, 'NAFTA In the Global Context' (1997) 23 Can-US LJ 379, 392 ('... NAFTA is momentarily stalled. Even when (and if) passage of Fast Track gets NAFTA moving again, progress is likely to be slow until well into the first decade of the next century').

[35] In part, Chile's unwillingness to join NAFTA is due to Chile's traditionally strong economic ties to Europe and the Asian-Pacific countries. In part it must be seen as an outgrowth of Chile's reluctance to submit itself to US demands for liberalizations in certain economic sectors. And, in part Chile's attitude of indifference is based on a desire to pursue 'open regionalism' in its foreign policy in order to maximize its trade benefits. See Otero-Lathrop (note 4 *supra*), at 121–2. particularly at 121 ('NAFTA is undoubtedly an important element in the internationalization of the Chilean economy because NAFTA ensures Chile a part in the 'global economy powerful triad,' but by no means is NAFTA the only instrument that can facilitate Chile's economic relationship with the global economy ... [U]nlike the Mexican case, accession to NAFTA is not a life or death matter in Chile'). There have also been NGO-led efforts to protest Chile's possible accession to the NAFTA. Some argue that the NAFTA is harmful to the cultural identity of the indigenous peoples of the Parties while other groups complain that Chile's government is undemocratic. See 'Aukin Wallmapu Ngulam-Consejo de Todos las Tierras, 'Mapuche Declaration on NAFTA in Chile' (text found on the internet at >www.xs4all.nl<):

> Considering that the free trade agreement is essentially economicist [sic], serving to accumulate wealth for a small minority and to create poverty and exclusion for the great majority of Indigenous and non-Indigenous people, Being a new form of expansion of colonialism and neocolonialism expressed in the economic sphere,
> ...
> We do not accept the entry of Chile into the free trade agreement, because its principle purpose is the exploitation of the territories in which we Indigenous people live; as well as the extraction of natural resources ...
> We do not agree with Chile's entry into the free trade agreement because our knowledge, the intellectual property of the Indigenous peoples will continue to be usurped with greater efficiency, in view of the fact that biotechnology has become the mechanism and tool of usurpation and extraction of our knowledge at the service of the northern country's [sic] nationals.
> ...
> We oppose the free trade agreement because the economy and development which have occurred under its framework has not respected nor taken into account our own development and economy which is grounded in our culture and specific identity.

(2 December 1994, Temuco, Chile): 'Citizen Groups Oppose NAFTA Extensions' (1995) 4:10A *Trade News* (8 July) (text found on internet at >www.envirolink.org<) 'On July 5, nearly 350 citizen groups from Chile, the United States, Canada and Mexico sent messages to their

The reluctance of the US cannot be attributed to only one cause, particularly as the recent political history in the United States has been dominated by domestic politics (as demonstrated by Congress' refusal to grant the President so-called 'Fast-Track' negotiating authority).[36] Yet, as regards NAFTA expansion, certainly one strong influence on the US refusal to accept proposals is the realization that the United States would likely encounter procedural disadvantages from any broadening of membership. The voting process, for instance, would have to be reworked so as to accommodate extra NAFTA Parties. Retaining the present one-country-one-vote decision making structure would put the United States at a disadvantage due to the potentially large majority of southern developing economies with interests that are at odds with those of the United States (and perhaps Canada). Bluntly stated, the United States could no longer use its size to dominate the decisions taken in the NAFTA.

In view of the accession of multiple South American states, a related question is whether the accession would be of Mercosur as a unit or of the countries of Mercosur individually, and further whether the votes would be individual or conglomerated. One lawyer familiar with US trade policy has indicated that the United States is likely to be very dissatisfied with an arrangement of more Parties with equal votes, as it would dramatically decrease the US's own authority within the NAFTA:

> The US has a nearly paranoid fear ... of being ganged up on. So you could not have a situation in NAFTA, for example, of a panel of seven, where everyone gets two members, and you flip for the chairman. The US fantasy is that even if the US chooses the chairman, we would always be ganged up on, four to three.
>
> The reverse selection ... is done not for its elegance and as a neat solution ..., but rather because it means that for the US to lose a Chapter 20 decision in NAFTA, it has to lose either on the basis of votes by US citizens the other country chooses, or votes by other countries' citizens the US chose ...
>
> It is a beautiful solution, until NAFTA gets beyond three or four countries. Indeed if there is an extension of NAFTA, you start talking about weighted voting, at which point Mexico and Canada weigh in and say they get the right in any such extension to the same number of votes as the US has, because they had it in the beginning.
>
> ...

(Contd.)

respective heads of state opposing plans to extend the ... [NAFTA]. ... Signatories included human rights organizations, labor unions, consumer groups, churches and other religious groups, academics and indigenous American organizations ...'; 'NAFTA Opponents Continue to Organize' (1995) 4:10b *Trade News* (27 July) (text found on internet at >www.envirolink.org<). '... in the United States, the Citizens Trade Campaign ... is lobbying against Chile's admission to NAFTA ... Opposition to Chilean entry has also focused on the threat to democracy possibly posed by the Chilean military ...'). It is, however, unlikely that these complaints have prevented the NAFTA expansion.

[36] For a good overview of the problems posed to further American trade integration by the Fast-Track debate, see Meyer (note 4 *supra*), at 138–42.

Now obviously, ... we cannot keep agreeing to one-country, one-vote. If you get into a western hemisphere free trade area, we are one country out of, depending on how you count them, 30 or more countries. So it is called the OAS and it is not traditionally the favorite model of the United States.[37]

A further problem arises from the dispute settlement procedures, which the United States strongly desires to keep within its power.[38] Because NAFTA's rules on accession require that all Parties agree on the new Party,[39] Chile's accession will not be able to proceed without US approval. However, US President Bill Clinton's loss of fast-track negotiating authority in late 1997,[40] combined with a general dissatisfaction with the NAFTA in the US Congress, are additional factors that will hinder progress on the development of an FTAA in the near future.[41]

As a result of United States foot-dragging within the NAFTA, Canada and Mexico have completed bilateral free trade agreements with Chile. These agreements incorporate goods and services sectors, and are likely to enhance trade between the countries, but cannot be equated with

---

[37] Gary Horlick, 'Sovereignty and International Trade Regulation' (1994) 20 Can-US LJ 57, 59–61.

[38] *Ibid*. Another expert feels that potential changes to the dispute settlement processes of NAFTA Chapter Nineteen would have to be changed to accommodate more Parties:

> ... [O]ne of the more interesting questions is whether the binational panel system can or should be extended as more countries accede to NAFTA. US industries interested in invoking antidumping and countervailing duty laws oppose its extension. It is likely that most new NAFTA members will want the system to be continued, since they view it, as Canada did, as offering some protection against inappropriate application of US trade remedy laws ... The author's experience on the first binational panel reviewing a Canadian agency's decision suggests that it requires some effort to understand how a foreign legal system works ...
> Nonetheless, that experience also suggests that there is no inherent 'cultural' barrier to the extension of the binational panel system to additional countries.

> William Davey, *Pine & Swine: Canada-United States Trade Dispute Settlement: The FTA Experience and NAFTA Prospects* (Centre for Trade Policy and Law, Ottawa, 1996), p. 288.

[39] NAFTA also allows any Party to opt out of extending the benefits of the Agreement to the newcomer upon the accession of the new Party. NAFTA Art. 2204:2.

[40] President Clinton decided in November 1997 to withdraw a bill requesting Congress to extend his fast-track negotiating authority that year. Seen as 'the President's biggest reversal since the health-care proposal failed in 1994', Clinton's failure to secure enough votes from his own political party for trade negotiating authority lessened the chances of any major trade packages being formed with foreign economic partners. The failure of the bill was due to many factors besides trade, however. See ''Fast Track' is Derailed', *New York Times*, 1 November 1997 (editorial) (text found on the internet at >www.sice.oas.org<). See also Meyer (note 4 *supra*), at 142–6, explaining how the loss of fast track approval may effect regional integration in the Americas. For a look at how fast track authority affected the NAFTA negotiations, see Robert J. Kirchhoff, 'The Fast Trade Adoption of the NAFTA: Special and National Interests', in Bernard D. Reams Jr and Jon S. Schultz (eds), *The North American Free Trade Agreement (NAFTA): Documents and Materials Including a Legislative History of the North American Free Trade Agreement Implementation Act: Public Law* (W. S. Hin, Buffalo, 1994), pp. 103–82, at 113–65.

[41] See also 'Throwing Sand in the Gears', *The Economist*, 30 January 1999, p. 65, describing the swell of protectionist sentiment in the United States and stating that a grant of fast track authority is now highly improbable to occur before 2001.

plurilateral free trade agreements in their potential for generating large positive trade effects. Neither have the bilateral agreements had a significant impact in motivating the United States to act. The expansion of NAFTA to even four Parties by the turn of the century (much less the complete incorporation of all Latin American states into an American Free Trade Agreement, or 'AFTA', by 2005) seems less and less likely.

Nevertheless, there still remains a potential that the NAFTA (or a successor FTAA or an AFTA) will someday include more (if not all) members of the Western Hemisphere. For that reason, the possible effects of an expansion of the North American Free Trade Agreement to other Latin American countries are cursorily addressed here.

8.3.1   Possible FTAA Structure

The exuberant proclamations made by North American leaders in the early years of the NAFTA negotiating process indicated their support for the initial expansion of NAFTA by accession. Nevertheless, the guidelines proposed for the FTAA negotiations at the March 1998 FTAA Ministerial Meeting in San José leave the ultimate design open. Existing regional agreements, it proclaims, may 'coexist' with the larger integration area[42] and parties to the different regional agreements may negotiate either independently or as a bloc.[43]

The choice to leave undecided the question of how NAFTA, Mercosur, and the Andean Pact will be treated in the scheme of hemispheric integration is politically expedient but ultimately untenable due to the structural differences in the various scenarios. The 'convergence question' may prove the most difficult one of the integration process, and deserves close observation by third parties as well as by the Americans. A Chilean author discusses the problem:

> It is tempting to assume that the various agreements and groupings that are beginning to crystallize in Latin America form building blocks for regional integration and for the emergence of a hemispheric free-trade area. However, this would present a rather idealized image of a very complex reality. Subregions are advancing at very different paces. Memberships and commitments to specific groupings are ambiguous or contradictory ..., and tend to overlap. Problems of compatibility may emerge from simultaneous participation in NAFTA and subregional schemes in Latin America.
>
> The alternatives ... involve difficult dilemmas and problematic trade-offs for the Latin American countries. Successive bilateral negotiations could lead to friction and practical problems. Overlapping arrangements can cause mismatches in the phasing of tariff reductions, inconsistencies between different dispute settlement mechanisms, and difficulties in the implementation of disparate rules of origin. The likelihood of jurisdictional disputes seems high, especially concerning the application of most favored nation status.[44]

---

[42] San José Ministerial Declaration at para. 8 and in Annex I, 'General Principles' f.
[43] *Ibid.* in Annex I, 'General Principles' g.
[44] Otero-Lathrop (note 4 *supra*), at 119.

There are conceptually two possibilities for expanding NAFTA: a country-by-country accession to the Agreement as foreseen in Article 2204 of NAFTA (or a variation on this possibility that would allow the other American regional trade areas to join the NAFTA as a single Party); or a subsumation of NAFTA into a larger free trade area composed of the several American regional trade areas.

The effects of NAFTA on any bank is determined by the bank's own profit structure and business interests. If the NAFTA is expanded, this remains true, but changes the analysis to the extent that there would be more competition among the NAFTA banks in any NAFTA Party market. The result is a polarization of the possible effects of the present NAFTA on banks. The extent of such polarization depends on the specific conditions under which new NAFTA Parties accede. If, on the other hand, the NAFTA formation turns out to be just one step toward what will be a hemispheric-wide free trade area, the effects of such an area on third country banks could be more dramatic. This in turn depends on the way any hemispheric agreement would be structured.

According to one of the United States' negotiators, the drafters of Chapter Fourteen did not consciously consider the expansion of NAFTA in developing rules for the financial services system.[45] This is despite the official proclamation of the Parties' leaders that NAFTA was to have an open-door policy toward willing accessors. Nevertheless, the negotiators did try to word the provisions to allow for expansion, even if not directly pointed in that direction.[46] Their attempts were substantially realized: if NAFTA does expand, the financial service practices of the Parties would not be much affected. The Parties would simply have to extend their obligations under the Agreement to the newcomers or reserve the right (at the time of the accession) to refuse to extend such treatment to the new Party.

There is discussed in the following the potential effects of a NAFTA expansion in two separate constellations: first, in a NAFTA of many members, each joining through the accession provisions of the Agreement; and secondly, in a Free Trade Area of the Americas with NAFTA as a member of a larger agreement. The distinction is made in order to reflect the significance of governance structures in preferential trade agreements for the agreements' effects on non-parties.[47]

---

[45] Robert Herzstein, legal adviser to Mexico during the NAFTA negotiations (January 1997).

[46] *Ibid.*

[47] See Sanoussi Bilal, 'Political Economy Considerations on the Supply of Trade Protection in Regional Integration Agreements' (1998) 36:1 J Common Mkt Stud 1, studying the way integration areas' institutional governance structures can further or hinder protectionist impulses. One commentator asserts that in her opinion, FTAA negotiations will take place neither as a state-by-state accession to the NAFTA nor as a bloc-to-bloc negotiation, but rather as a new negotiation process among separate states, albeit with 'a huge amount of coordination and cooperation and solidarity among the NAFTA countries'. M. Jean Anderson, 'Implications of NAFTA's Extension to Chile and Other Countries—A US View' (1997) 23 Can-US LJ 227, 234 (speech given at the Proceedings of the Canada-United States Law Institute Conference, NAFTA Revisited). But see Graham (note 34 *supra*), at 123, 132 ('How can you talk about a free trade arrangement ... if the United States is going about it independently[,] Canada is going about it independently, and Mexico is going about it independently when, meanwhile, we have our NAFTA').

8.4 THE EFFECT OF NAFTA ACCESSIONS

8.4.1 Effect of NAFTA Expansion on Parties' Banks

One of the main effects of such an accessionary-led extension of the NAFTA would be that the most favored nation (MFN) and national treatment obligation (NTO) principles would be applicable to a larger group of banks. For the current Party banks, such an expansion would not change the legal environment significantly. The United States already offers most Latin American countries non-discriminatory treatment, at least to the extent granted to NAFTA Parties under Chapter Fourteen. The exception is in the underwriting of government bonds, and this would then have to be either extended or placed in the Annex VII reservations. Canada and Mexico's markets are also in part opened to the South American countries through bilateral trade agreements that exist parallel to the NAFTA. Canada and Mexico both, for instance, have free trade agreements with Chile, and Mexico also has bilateral agreements with almost all Latin American countries that are significant trading nations.

The expansion of NAFTA could bring about much more substantial changes for the accessor Parties, however. This is particularly so for those that presently have closed markets. These new Parties would have to alter their banking systems to the benefit of the other NAFTA Parties, if the systems are less liberal than Chapter Fourteen requires. The Chapter Fourteen transparency requirement and the possibility that investors of another Party could bring a NAFTA challenge directly against a government for certain violations could be a significant factor in attracting Party banks to those markets, as would the codified protection against non-compensated expropriations.

Most South American banking systems have already started to follow a liberal policy of market access by foreign banks. The expansion of NAFTA to include these territories will therefore not have many legal ramifications for Party banks, even if the actual competitive environment for the banks already present in these markets becomes much more severe. The United States Department of Treasury's study of the banking policies of foreign authorities reveals a substantially open and nondiscriminatory attitude to foreign financial service providers in Chile, Columbia, and Venezuela.[48] While Brazil's banking market forms an exception to this generalization, with its absolute stop on new foreign bank entries in effect since 1988 and with discriminatory treatment in existing regulations,[49] the Brazilian government's commitments under the GATS Fifth Protocol

---

[48] See US Treasury Department, *'South America' National Treatment Study 1994* (GPO, Washington, DC, 1994), pp. 107–9 (Synopsis of the detailed review of Argentina, Brazil, Columbia, Chile, and Venezuela).

[49] *National Treatment Study* (note 48 *supra*), at 169–70. Nevertheless, there is a substantial foreign bank presence in Brazil. The United States alone is represented by six banks with more than 100 branches, as of 30 December 1993. *Ibid* at 169.

schedule relaxed the restrictions on new establishments as of the going into effect of the Protocol in February 1999.[50]

8.5   EFFECTS OF NAFTA EXPANSION ON NON-PARTY BANKS

From the perspective of a non-Party banking entity (as opposed to that of the Party government), the effects of NAFTA expansion are qualitatively similar to the overall effects of Chapter Fourteen itself. Primarily, then, the impact will depend largely on whether the bank is considered a 'NAFTA Party bank' or not. If it is, an expanded NAFTA will provide quantitatively greater rights of entry, establishment, and cross-border activity by virtue of having more borders opened. Similarly, the banks will have the right to 'treatment no less favorable' than that received by domestic banks or by other Party banks in more markets, and there will be legal protection for access to the procedural rules and agency processes in more countries.

If, on the other hand, a bank is not a 'NAFTA Party bank', the disadvantages of the NAFTA become greater with the addition of countries under its rules. If, for instance, any of the other South American markets is substantially opened to the NAFTA Party banks through the expansion, while keeping restrictions applicable to other states, there could be significant competitive disadvantages to those banks not considered 'NAFTA Party banks'.

From the political economy perspective, the growth of NAFTA into a larger free trade area would worsen the problem of convincing it to remain a liberal trading partner. The 'size effect' of regional integration arrangements has been determined to increase the relative strength of an area, affording it the opportunity to protect its markets at the cost of non-parties.[51] At the same time, by virtue of remaining a free trade zone, the outside bank must attempt to lobby the various party governments to minimize protectionist tendencies. This is logistically a difficult task, and becomes both more difficult and more expensive to undertake, while at the same time becoming less likely to succeed, with each additional party to the agreement. Although the recent history of American economic

---

[50] According to the proposed commitments, Brazil has agreed to allow for new establishments in the banking sector through either branches or subsidiaries subject to Presidential approval. The Fifth Protocol to the GATS went into effect on 1 March 1999. See 'The WTO's Financial Services Commitments Will Enter Into Force as Scheduled', WTO Press Release, PRESS/120 (15 February 1999).

[51] See generally Bilal (note 47 *supra*), at 3 ('the purpose of this article is to discuss the role of the institutional setting in determining the external trade policy stance endogenously adopted by a trade bloc. Contrary to much prevailing wisdom [citations omitted], this article argues that institutional designs in an RIA can lead to an increase in the responsiveness of trade authorities to protectionist demands').

integration has not proven to be bloc-like, the potential of a size-effect cannot be completely ignored as a threat.

Perhaps even more importantly, NAFTA would have effects on the international regulation of trade in financial services. As the most significant example, one can look at dispute settlement. Through the expansion of countries that applied the NAFTA rules, the NAFTA dispute settlement system would gain in prominence as a forum for resolving international banking disputes. Instead of applying to only three countries, the dispute settlement panels of an expanded NAFTA would be interpreting the terms of, and making decisions about, financial services trade throughout two continents. This in itself may have a noticeable effect on non-Party banks that are not a part of the system.

Finally, no matter what the accessors' legal obligations, the non-legal considerations such as discussion groups and privately-organized cross-border business associations might exclude such banks from their dialogues. On this level, third country banks would not necessarily face disadvantages due to the structures of a regional agreement. Rather, they would be competitively disadvantaged simply by not being involved in the development of a new, pan-American banking law culture.[52]

8.6   POTENTIAL EFFECTS OF A FREE TRADE AREA OF THE AMERICAS

Assume for the sake of argument, that the statements made at the Second Summit of the Americas on negotiating a FTAA are to be realized. If the Free Trade Area of the Americas succeeds in taking on a shape that is legally distinct from the NAFTA, the effects on third country banks could be somewhat different than if the NAFTA merely expanded through accessions. The effects will first depend on the particular content of the agreement's financial services trade provisions. Mercosur, for instance, does not include free trade in banking among its framework provisions.[53] Yet the agreement is gaining in importance in South American trade relations[54] and must be recognized as a potentially strong force in determining the direction of further integration efforts. If the FTAA was formed through the agglomeration of various free trade areas (for example Mecosur, NAFTA, and the Andean Pact as three equal members), it would be likely that a 'lowest common denominator' approach to the integration would determine the sectoral coverage. Thus, the banking sector would not be covered and banks, regardless of nationality, would be left unaffected.

---

[52] See the Chapter 9 *infra* for further development of this idea.

[53] Meyer (note 4 *supra*), at 162.

[54] See Anderson (note 47 *supra*), at 232–3 ('A few years ago I used to hear people say MERCOSUR was not real. MERCOSUR was one of those fuzzy agreements … That, I believe, is a big mistake … In my experience talking to businesses in North America, they are organizing their activities with MERCOSUR very much in mind').

(The question of whether such a result is politically realistic in view of the United States' desire to ensure financial services market access is a separate matter.)[55]

In addition to the specific areas of trade covered, the way an FTAA would affect banks will also depend on the its overall approach to integration: the role of governance institutions; the effect of dispute settlement mechanisms; the method of decision-making; and the basic relations of the FTAA to third countries.[56] If an FTAA agreement were designed to protect American businesses against European or Asian competition, non-member

---

[55] See *ibid.* at 234 ('There is real aversion ... to the idea that what comes out in a Free Trade Agreement for the Americas might be a compromise between NAFTA and MERCOSUR ... NAFTA, to the United States, is going to be the standard than an agreement ought to meet in terms of legal commitments and obligations, and enforceability of those commitments and obligations').

[56] For an insight on the potential 'shape' of a FTAA, see Garcia (note 13 *supra*). Mr Garcia uses the regime theory developed by Kenneth Abbott and Duncan Snidal that looks at 'mesoinstitutions' to propose the governance structure of a future Free Trade Area of the Americas agreement. All of these authors categorize international institutions according to their function in relation to the members of the treaty under which the institution is created. There are 'facilitative organizations', or those that 'reduce the transaction costs of concluding mutually beneficial agreements, primarily through improving information and communication, and facilitate the self-enforcement of these agreements in view of changing circumstances'; and there are 'productive organizations', which 'carry out substantive activities themselves, thus "producing" work of importance to the regime: rules, technical assistance, information, resolutions to disputes, legitimacy, and financial support in addition to performing facilitative duties'. *Ibid.* at 364, 365.

Basing his opinions on the 'Declaration of Principles and Plan of Action' issued by the participating governments at the Miami Summit of the Americas, Garcia predicts that a FTAA governance body would be primarily facilitative, and that the Parties would not give up a significant amount of sovereignty to the institution. *Ibid.* at 385–7. He also predicts that decision-making will be based on consensus (at least in the short-term), given that the United States is unlikely to allow itself to be bound to decisions made against its will. *Ibid.* at 392. Moreover, dispute settlement will probably be based on a NAFTA-type mechanism in which the Parties retain ultimate control over the outcome in a formal arbitration setting:

> While NAFTA and CARICOM are the only hemispheric [regional trading agreements] in which the decisions of the arbitral panel are not themselves binding on the parties, the NAFTA approach in particular is bound to be disproportionately influential due to NAFTA's market power.

Ibid. at 394, citing Charles M. Gastle, 'Policy Alternatives for Reform of the Free Trade Agreement of the Americas: Dispute Settlement Mechanisms' (1995) 26 L & Pol'y Int'l Bus 735, 821 ('NAFTA DSM 'clearly will become the basis' of the FTAA DSM'); Sergio López-Ayllón, 'Comments', in Paul Demaret, Jean-François Bellis and Gonzalo García Jiménez (eds), *Regionalism and Multilateralism after the Uruguay Round: Convergence, Divergence and Interaction* (Institut d'études Juridiques Européennes, University of Liège, Liège, 1997), pp. 251–264, at 261 (the NAFTA model will be 'an inevitable point of reference' for further regional integration efforts in the Americas). But see Donald R. Mackay, 'The North American Free Trade Agreement: Its Possible Extension to South American Countries', in Demaret *et al.* (*supra*), pp. 235–49, at 236 ('trade and economic integration in the Americas cannot be built around the NAFTA as the core'); Meyer (note 4 *supra*), at 146–51, predicting that a future FTAA would be more similar to Mercosur than to the NAFTA because of the low priority the United States has given to the negotiations.

banks would be in danger of encountering a new set of barriers and member banks would profit accordingly.[57] If, alternatively, an agreement were formed mainly to lower barriers to trade internally (as NAFTA is), the impact of such an agreement on non-member banks would be absolutely positive to the extent that the newly-fostered trade created more economic activity, and relatively negative to the extent that these banks would not enjoy the preferences that the American competitors did.

However, there is also a chance that non-member banks would be harmed absolutely by an Americas-wide free trade agreement just as they would be from an expansion of NAFTA. Again, this would arise from the formal and informal co-perative efforts that harmonize previously separated markets. As under the NAFTA, the process of forming a Free Trade Area of the Americas would bring the political and industrial leaders of the party-states into contact with each other. These relations would form the basis for further interactions that would assist individuals and businesses to take advantage of treaty benefits.[58] Similarly, academic, regional, and special interest groups would form to informally expand the agreement's importance. While this would enable member banks to create a system-specific dialogue, again adding to the advantages that the formal agreement text provides, third country entities would be less likely to participate in such developments. Their non-participation in such dialogues could cause subtle disadvantages in the competitive field.

---

[57] One South American author, while emphasizing the global openness of American trade integration, also recalls that it 'seems to coincide with increasing polarization of the global economy around the 'triad' of the European Union (EU), the North American Free Trade Agreement (NAFTA), and Japan and its Asian partners'. Otero-Lathrop (note 4 *supra*), at 116.

[58] See, e.g., 'Chile, Fed, OCC Enter Into Cooperation Statement', 70:16 BNA's Banking Rep 646 (20 April 1998), reporting a jointly released statement by the banking regulators of the United States and Chile setting out a program of supervisory co-operation of each country's banks involved in cross-border financial service supply.

9. Conclusion

9.1 SUMMARY OF RESULTS

The North American Free Trade Agreement is the first plurilateral trade agreement to regulate the trade in financial services without simultaneous political unification. Looking back on the first half of the 1990s, one sees that it was the context of the overall NAFTA negotiations that allowed such a leap forward in the financial services trade liberalization process. The advantages to be secured in the goods area made Mexican accession to Chapter Fourteen economically and politically viable.[1] It was Mexico's acceptance of financial service liberalization, in turn, that promoted the United States' and Canadian interests in dealing with Mexico. This allowed for a broadening of the strong economic ties between Canada and the United States to include the Mexican nation despite its economic instability. Other nations, watching the NAFTA process, themselves became more interested in Mexico as an emerging nation, and began to consider it a potential trading partner.

Politically, NAFTA also changed the attitudes of the Parties to the extent that financial service trade liberalizations have continued well beyond the Chapter Fourteen boundaries. While Canadian willingness to liberalize its financial industry markets had been signaled by the late 1980s, the United States' disillusionment with the multilateral trade negotiations led to a real threat of a US refusal to participate in further global liberalization efforts. Had the NAFTA not been approved, it is quite likely that the Uruguay Rounds would not have been approved either. Although the United States did not commit fully to the GATS Annex on Financial Services until the

---

[1] One commentator writes of the possibilities that regional trade liberalization create:

> ... [L]eaders have used political support for regional solidarity to achieve liberalization that would be politically impossible if pursued unilaterally. De Melo, Panagariya, and Rodrik (1993, section 3) model the process whereby governments can adopt rules or institutions in a regional context to insulate themselves from pressure by private-sector lobbies for intervention on their behalf.

Jeffrey A. Frankel, *Regional Trading Blocs in the World Economic System* (Institute for International Economics, Washington, DC, 1997), p. 217. Frankel refers to Jaime de Melo, Arvind Panagariya, and Dani Rodrik, 'New Regionalism: A Country Perspective', in Jaime de Melo and Arvind Panagariya (eds), *New Dimensions in Regional Integration* (CUP, New York, 1993).

December 1997 'Fifth Protocol' negotiations were completed, the eventual retraction of the US reciprocity-exemption to the most-favored-nation obligation under the new results may be seen as a success for supporters of global banking liberalization.

The Mexico's subsequent financial liberalizations bilaterally and in the multilateral GATS framework were also fostered by the successful completion of the NAFTA and Chapter Fourteen. Able to expose its financial service industries to the potential competition of United States and Canadian providers within the bounds of the NAFTA and its reciprocal advantages to Mexicans, even the impressive authority of the Mexican government would have had difficulties in ignoring the strong internal resistance to a full-scale, non-reciprocal opening of their markets on a global scale. Politically, NAFTA paved the way for these future openings.

Perhaps more importantly from a global trade perspective, the NAFTA also remains the only agreement in which Mexico has retreated from the Calvo Doctrine.[2] While it may be hoped that this remains of symbolic importance, Mexico's commitment to abide by international law in the area of expropriations could prove a crucial safeguard against future regress from economic openness in that country. Regulatory takings and state-required conditioning of a bank's active operations might be considered violations of NAFTA (and would therefore be compensable) even though the WTO contains no provisions against them. Depending on the degree to which these restrictions affected a financial service provider, NAFTA Party banks could be greatly advantaged by the existence of these Chapter Fourteen rights.

Moreover, NAFTA increased the contestability of the North American banking markets. Consequently, Chapter Fourteen heightens the potential for new entrants to any of the three markets. In turn, the consumer welfare benefits are increased even in the absence of many actual entries of foreign banks.[3] This 'invisible presence of competition'[4] was made possible in Mexico by the NAFTA's establishment and cross-border trade provisions, and is furthered by the obligations of Canada and the United States in their markets. The mere possibility of competition, economists remind us, forces existing firms to behave competitively, because any extraordinary profits will attract competition.[5]

---

[2] Michael Gestrin and Alan M. Rugman, 'The North American Free Trade Agreement and Foreign Direct Investment' (1994) 3:1 Transnat'l Corp 77, 79 ('... the expropriation and compensation provisions (article 1110) ... seek to establish a minimum North American standard. The acceptance of these articles by Mexico is historically significant in so far as these represent a weakening of the Calvo doctrine').

[3] Edward M. Graham and Robert Z. Lawrence, 'Measuring the International Contestability of Markets: A Conceptual Approach' (1996) 30:5 J World Trade 5, 7.

[4] This term is used at *ibid*.

[5] *Ibid.* at 8:

> The central idea of contestability rests on the assumption that although, in fact, the actual number of sellers in any given market may be limited (and thus, by any standard measure of industry structure such as the Herfindahl Index, the market may be 'concentrated'), if the market is contestable, there are virtually unlimited numbers of potential sellers into the market ...

Thus goes the reasoning, if a market is contestable, the market clearing price and quantity will be as though perfect competition prevailed.

The consequences of NAFTA Chapter Fourteen on the global financial services system, and particularly on third country banks, could easily be overlooked because of the more recent and much more publicized negotiations leading to the Financial Services Agreement under the WTO. Still, the effects of the NAFTA are significant and worthy of attention. First, while the North American Free Trade Agreement establishes commitments to liberalize within the region, the advantages offered to Party banks are, with few exceptions, open to all banks. The nationality of the holder of ultimate control is to a large degree immaterial. Thus, the positive obligations in furtherance of liberalized trade in financial service found in NAFTA assists third country banks nearly as much as they do the NAFTA banks themselves (and of the few provisions that would limit benefits to NAFTA Party institutions, some have subsequently been neutralized by the progress made on the multinational level in the WTO negotiations on financial services). In addition, domestic reforms of the financial systems—to a large extent made in reaction to Chapter Fourteen—have eliminated many of the internal barriers to trade in financial services that had been preserved within the NAFTA Parties' territories. Again, third country banks will benefit from such liberalizations.

There are other important results of NAFTA on non-Party banks, too. These are the results of NAFTA from the world trade system perspective. On its own, NAFTA Chapter Fourteen dramatically changed the global legal framework of the banking, insurance, and securities industries. Suddenly, there was an extensive set of legal rules and procedures binding major international trading nations in an area previously regarded as one of the most sensitive (and perhaps, last) precincts of sovereignty. Equally important, a developing country had agreed to be bound to obligations to liberalize its financial services industry. In doing so, it also became the first of the Calvo Clause adherents to agree to abandon its previous right to nationalize foreign property without facing international scrutiny of its actions.

Finally, the NAFTA Chapter Fourteen provisions set in motion a myriad of regional efforts to further trade in banking services. Thus, Chapter Fourteen (and the NAFTA as a whole) is more than a list of commitments. It is itself a dynamic system-building process. Evolutionary process developments for the North American region are furthered by the effects NAFTA's completion is having on the informal communities of scholars and practitioners within the NAFTA territory.[6] It is not yet clear what the ultimate impact of these discussion groups, conferences, and academic studies will be—in which direction the financial service system of North America is being pointed—but the fact that they are occurring is a symbol

---

[6] Philip Cooke describes the process of regional development as 'evolutionary'. Philip Cooke, 'Regions in a Global Market: the Experiences of Baden-Württemberg' (1997) 4:2 Rev Int'l Pol Econ 349. The three 'dimensions of culture' that underlie the process of 'collaborative manufacturing' are also important to the evolution of a collaborative production of banking services. These three dimensions are trust on the individual person level, a willingness to co-operate within the enterprise, and a recognition of network relationships among firms (as opposed to a heirarchical corporate organization). *Ibid.* at 359.

that the banking environment of the Parties is evolving within the NAFTA dynamic.

The consequences of NAFTA Chapter Fourteen for non-Party banks, then, could be more significant than the ownership preferences and the formal procedural protections. Non-Party banks may not be able to determine the further development of the North American financial services system, and thus are threatened with being left to follow the market rather than to lead it.

9.2   REFLECTION

There are many more issues that could be analyzed in the context of NAFTA and its effects on banks. One of the most fundamental issues to be examined is the relationship of financial services to trade and trade principles. Now that the NAFTA is firmly established and the WTO is well on its way to regulating banking services, it might seem that questioning the premises is moot. Nevertheless, it is important to re-examine the financial service liberalization methods in light of the concrete results they have had.

While there is no doubt that regulations on financial service suppliers affect trade in goods and trade in other services, there may be doubts as to whether the 'liberalization' of financial service provision ought to be accomplished through a trade agreement.[7] At the risk of regressing into an overly formal distinction of subject matter, it could be proposed that financial service law and trade law are two related but distinct subject matters. Their basic organizing principles differ and their goals differ. Their shared effect on trade, standing alone, does not seem to be reason enough to subsume the banking, insurance and securities law disciplines into the law of international trade.

In conversations with government officials and persons in the private sector, it is not uncommon for the banking experts to refer to 'the trade people'. It is less common for these 'trade people' to refer to their counterparts as 'the financial service people'. What does that indicate? Without wanting to delve into a linguistic investigation, and not wanting to read too much into more or less casual conversation styles, it is nevertheless striking that at least those most familiar with the laws regulating the financial service markets think of themselves and their area of expertise as something separate from trade while the trade lawyers (perhaps overly-exuberant with the expanse of legal area now covered by their WTO) happily absorb any legal subject matter into their liberalization framework. Financial services are global—indeed perhaps the most global—of commodities. Yet, they are not so much 'traded' as 'produced', 'distributed', and 'consumed'. More importantly, the services are 'regulated' at least as

---

[7]   See, e.g., Joel P. Trachtman, 'Trade in Financial Services under GATS, NAFTA and the EC: A Regulatory Jurisdiction Analysis' (1995) 34 Colum J Transnat'l L 37; Joel P. Trachman. 'Recent Initiatives in International Financial Regulation and Goals of Competitiveness, Effectiveness, Consistency and Cooperation' (1991) 12 NW J Int'l L & Bus 241.

much as, and probably much more than, they are 'protected'. Thus, disconcertingly, the use of trade principles seems simultaneously too narrow and too broad—and the trade law system has not seemed to notice.

Trade principles are too narrow because with the pace of technological development, governments (and therefore necessarily trade negotiators and trade agreements) cannot hope to keep up. The regulations that would prohibit trade can often be easily circumvented with untraceable electronic commerce. While perhaps not the most efficient way of achieving a global market, to some extent, technology has superseded legal texts liberalizing international financial service supply.[8]

Trade principles are too broad because the regulation of financial services by governments in a growing number of nations is based mainly on the protection of the stability of the financial system and the security of the accounts. It is not solely or even mainly about protecting the system from foreigners. Certainly there is also a barrier to foreign banks involved. A preference for national banks to survive while less efficient than a foreign bank, however, must be seen in a more neutral light than the ugly glare cast by the word 'protectionism' coming from the mouths of trade people.[9]

---

[8] Richard J. Herring and Robert E. Litan, *Financial Regulation in the Global Economy* 46 (Brookings Institution, Washington, DC, 1995), p. 46, thoroughly analyze the context in which modern financial regulators find themselves in their excellent work, Financial Regulation in the Global Economy. The authors stress the importance of technological change as a factor shaping the way financial institutions work, and therefore the way regulators must regulate:

> … the costs of withdrawing from an integrated world financial market are rising. Technological advances have limited the scope for autonomous regulatory action that raises the cost of financial services. The introduction of personal computers, modems, and international direct-dial telephone systems has sharply limited a government's options for insulating its financial sector from the integrated international financial system. Unless a government chooses to impose draconian controls on cross-border flows of information and people, sophisticated transactors can readily shift from costly domestic financial services to cheaper foreign substitutes.

[9] The debates within the United States over the advantages and disadvantages of the Glass-Steagall Act are telling in this respect. Having little, if anything, to do with protectionism, the exchanges among banking professionals and banking regulators show a clear discrepancy between those arguing for a 'free market' approach and those wanting to maintain tighter controls on bank activities. The two positions are polarized because the different interests (commercial competitiveness and safety of the banking system) have been assumed to be mutually exclusive. This assumption stems from the clash of an economic idea with a socio-political idea—neither of which necessarily has to do with the rubric of liberalization. One official from a financial institution argues that the banks have seized upon a single issue, Glass-Steagall repeal, to represent liberalization, when a more effective step toward liberalization would focus on issues such as interstate branching. In addition, the regulatory concerns surrounding these other issues are more easily assuaged.

> Many of the country's largest banks … argue that they are unfairly confined to traditional banking activities—activities that are no longer profitable …
> Their complaint has some superficial appeal. Only one US bank is numbered among the world's largest 30, suggesting that US banks have become globally uncompetitive. It is rarely mentioned, however, that Japan, the country with the most banks in the top 10, has its own version of Glass-Steagall …

A banking system, by virtue of its inseparable role in the monetary system is much more so than any goods-producing industry, the hallmark of a state and a government's ultimate ability to control the economic and social conditions in a country.[10] It is, to borrow a term from Hugh Collins, part of a state's 'cultural identity'.[11] The term 'cultural identity', although distinctly anti-liberal, 'provides in a compendious term the source of values and politics'.[12] It *is* and needs to *be*, whether the market wants it to exist or not. And, just as the individual person cannot exist without the socially-determined meaning given to her identity, neither can a state. Consequently, if a government must allow for all or even most of the banks of its nationality to face more efficient competition—and thereby face the possibility of bankruptcy—the government risks losing not only its ability to govern, but also its reason for governing.

(Contd.)

> Despite all arguments for expanded powers, ... no one has yet demonstrated a compelling need to let federally insured banks move ... into other businesses ... That some banks have been so incompetent in handling their core business certainly does not recommend that we encourage them to expand into other enterprises.
>
> Nor would entrance into the securities business be the panacea than many bankers seem to think it would be ...
>
> ...
>
> There are legitimate reasons to push for banking reform, but reform must satisfy the twin goals of improving efficiency and liquidity while also protecting depositors, taxpayers, and borrowers.
>
> The change that would best satisfy these goals would be a repeal of the current prohibition against interstate braching. ... (This) would stimulate consolidations and offer efficiencies of scale that could significantly improve operating margins without increasing risks.
>
> ...
>
> Another reform that merits serious consideration would be loosening the constraints that currently prohibit industrial companies from controlling or owning major interests in commercial bank ...

Philip A. Lacovara, 'Modernizing Banking ... But With Care' (1992) 15 GAO J 15, 18–20. But see Geza Feketekuty, *International Trade in Services: An Overview and Blueprint for Negotiations* (Ballinger, Cambridge, MA, 1988), p. 32, who writes, 'To a significant degree, control over the movement of services and maintenance of democratic freedoms are incompatible'.

[10] See *Osborn v. Bank of the United States* 22 U.S. 738, 9 Wheat. 738, (1824):

> The bank is not considered as a private corporation, whose principle object is individual trade and individual profit; but as a public corporation, created for public and national purposes. That the mere business of banking is, in its own nature, a private business, and may be carried on by individuals or companies having no political connection with the government, is admitted; but the bank is not such an individual or company. It was not created for its own sake, or for private purposes ... It is an instrument which is 'necessary and proper' for carrying on the fiscal operations of government.

9 Wheat. at 860–861, cited in *First Nat'l Bank in St. Louis v. Missouri* 263 U.S. 640, 663 (1924) (Justice Vandevanter in dissent).

[11] Hugh Collins, 'European Private Law and the Cultural Identity of States' (1995) 3 Europ Rev Priv L 353.

[12] *Ibid.* at 357.

Of course there are safeguards built into trade agreements to prevent a complete collapse of a state's national banking system. However, the fundamental problem remains: the trade people—many of whose experience in financial service law is as limited as their banking counterparts' familiarity with trade law—seem to see banking services as just another good or just another service. Therefore, they apply trade rules and assume, by virtue of their Ricardian values, that more 'trade' in such services is *per se* 'better' for the whole world. The present author does not mean to denigrate the trade community (considering herself a 'trade person'). The author only wishes to emphasize that it is imperative that trade people consider more carefully the implications of their actions. Not every area of law was meant to be subject to the liberalizing effects of MFN, market access, and cross-border trade. The recognition of the necessary existence of cultural identity has the result that the goal of a rational market must be tempered by the realization that there is another legitimate goal: that of allowing for difference—in the case of banking, the allowance of limits on financial freedom.

Many are critical of mixing the disciplines of financial services and trade. Joel Trachtman has written of this, defining it as a difference between areas of 'regulation'. Professor Trachtman's introduction to his carefully written article addressing the liberalization of trade in financial services from a regulatory perspective explains:

> Trade discourse does not concern itself with the flow of money *per se*, but with the flow of goods or services, or other factors. We often consider commercial banking or investment banking as services that involve the flow of money. Services in general, and heavily regulated services in particular, are not completely amenable to some of the traditional trade disciplines ... such as reduction of tariffs, prohibition of quantitative restrictions, most-favored-nation treatment, and national treatment. Although regulatory barriers may be analogized to quantitative restrictions—or absolute prohibitions—they cannot be simply eliminated.
>
> Thus, coexisting and competing with this trade perspective on international movement of services, at least in the area of financial services, is a regulatory perspective. The regulatory perspective is concerned about the possibility for regulatory arbitrage, or simply for regulatory failure, due to the limitations of national regulation based on national jurisdiction. BCCI has come to symbolize this type of failure. The regulatory perspective is concerned more with the goals of regulation than with the goals of free trade and competition in financial services, although free trade and competition may have important positive or negative effects on the ability to achieve regulatory goals.[13]

The problem with addressing the regulation of financial services in a plurilateral or multilateral forum of traders is that the particular interests inherent in the regulation of, for instance, banking may not be recognized. In an increasingly globalized financial services market, the particular needs of various regulators—each intrinsically linked to a particular level of development, a particular legal background, a particular role in the particular

---

[13] Joel P. Trachtman (note 7 *supra*), at 41–2.

social context—and the particular interests of these regulators become more and more difficult to identify. The search for the legitimacy of those interests from a regulatory standpoint becomes even more obscure. In short, a trade panel trying to determine whether a particular rule or action by national banking supervisors is a legitimate barrier to trade faces an almost impossible task.

This is not an argument against liberalizing the banking industry, but rather an argument against putting such a liberalization in the same framework as the liberalization of the trade in auto parts or the trade in construction services. The trade principles of market access and most-favored-nation treatment are simply not as useful for liberalizing a banking market as they are for liberalizing other economic sectors. The criteria for applying these principles were developed in a different context that offered suitable reference points. Moreover, the aims of these principles are different.

What the NAFTA Chapter Fourteen negotiations represent is the colliding of two separate systems of law: the trade system and the financial services system. Chapter Fourteen as the product of the negotiations, is the result of the collision. It now forms an area of commonality between these otherwise independent systems. And this for better or for worse. Chapter Fourteen does not extinguish the differences between the systems (i.e., NAFTA was not a fusion of systems), but rather now forms a third system—a 'trade in financial services' subsystem for each of the two main systems. It is within this new system area that an interactive process of defining system-specific terms into a new 'language' will begin.

The significance of this system's defining process from the vantage point of the remaining trade law system and financial service law system is that the new language will necessarily be the product of imprecise translations of the original two languages.[14] The trade law principles will not—indeed cannot and should not—have exactly the same meaning for trade in financial services as they do for trade in goods. Trade lawyers can only *apply* their language to the financial system. They cannot understand the financial service system. Thus, the financial service principles will be somewhat distorted.

At the same time, the financial system lawyers will be attempting to apply their language to trade rules. Understanding the terms of these rules only as they are able to as financial service lawyers, the trade rules will become distorted.

---

[14] Professor Guenther Teubner has eloquently and forcefully argued that a 'productive misunderstanding' occurs when different language games interact. Guenther Teubner, 'Breaking Frames: The Global Interplay of Legal and Social Systems' (1997) 45 Am J Comp L 149, 161, citing Teubner, 'Autopoiesis and Steering: How Politics Profits From the Normative Surplus of Capital', in R. Veld *et al.* (eds), *Autopoiesis and Configuration: New Approaches to Societal Steering* (Kluwer, Dordrecht, 1991), pp. 127–41.

The result is a new language based on 'productive misunderstanding'.[15] It is not a 'bad' language or a 'wrong' language. Neither is it a 'good' language. It is simply a 'new' language. And, it is the language in which the terms of Chapter Fourteen must necessarily be interpreted.[16] Terms from one system may not retain their original meanings in the new system, as the old meanings become distorted in the new broader context.

A telling example of how terminologies can be wrongly mixed is the principle of national treatment as applying to trade in banking services under the NAFTA. The idea of national treatment is perhaps the most important principle in trade law, and indeed has corresponding principles in other areas of law. In a trade context, the principle can be summarized as the requirement that national authorities treat foreign banks such that the foreign banks enjoy no less advantageous conditions of competition than do domestic banks. The national treatment obligation, as found in the NAFTA, forbids regulatory authorities from discriminating against foreign banks 'in like circumstances'. This makes sense from the trade point of view. If two banks are to compete in a market, they should both be subject to the same competitive conditions, including the same regulatory costs.

However, there are at least two problems with using a pure trade-orientation to determine how to apply the national treatment principle in the NAFTA in the context of banking services. One is that (at least for financial services) the technical wording of the NTO provision is uninformative. The

---

[15] The term 'productive misunderstanding' was developed by Professor Teubner to explain the process by which the terms of one system are misunderstood by those persons from another system in such a way that the terms take on a new, slightly different meaning. 'The "mis" describe [*sic*] the innovation, while the "understanding" tells us that it builds on another meaning and not into the blue air'. Teubner (note 14 *supra*), at 161. The member of the other system does, however, gain a better understanding of the foreign system—thus a productive misunderstanding.

[16] Writing about the intervention of law in global economic transactions, Teubner (note 14 *supra*), warns of a danger of two 'languages' trying to interact on a single relation.

> The structures of global economic transactions are essentially non-legal: they build on factual chances of action and create new chances of action or of trust in future changes of chances. In ongoing business relations it is wise to keep the lawyers out. They will distort business realities. [citation omitted] Why? Not only do they replace the search for profit by the *quaestio juris*. Not only do they replace the cost-benefit calculus by the maxim of treating like cases alike. Worse, they misread factual chances of action as legal 'property,' and they misunderstand mutual trust in future behaviour as contractually binding 'obligations,' as 'rights' and 'duties.' And if their rigid and formalist claims and counter-claims are re-read in the ongoing transaction relation they will destroy precarious trust relations. The difference between economic chances of action and legal property and between trust and obligations is due to their different grammar. The lawyers observe economic action under the code legal/illegal and misread economic processes and structures as sources of law. Vice versa, clever economic actors misread legal norms under the economic code as bargaining chips, as new opportunities for profit making. We observe not exchange that leads to the mutual containment of law and the economy but a mutual distortion of law and economy. Their elements link up to each other, but nevertheless legal acts remain identifiable as against economic acts and legal norms against economic expectations.

more intractable problem is that the NTO principle itself cannot be applied without tremendous reliance on the allowable exceptions to it. It is only by *not* applying it that the principle is viable.

It is with these distortions of old meanings in the new context that the difficulties arise for those outside the NAFTA Chapter Fourteen system. As non-members of the process of creating the new language, non-Party banks will not be able to influence the development of the language. Their understanding of the system, and thus their ability to operate in the system, will thus be limited to an observation of and a translation of the Chapter Fourteen language into their own languages.

The informal exchanges among members of the financial services law system are thus just one part of the development of NAFTA-specific law. The other part is the exchange between the trade lawyers and the financial services lawyers. The two sets of dialogues certainly influence one another, however, and those not participating in either group are doubly disadvantaged.

Recognizing that the phenomenon of system interaction is an important step to minimizing the distortions that must occur in translating the terms of the NAFTA system. Attempts to understand the Chapter Fourteen provisions as a new language, rather than as a trade language with some importation of financial terms or as a financial language in a trade framework, is the creative challenge that those both within and outside of the NAFTA have to face.

Part V
Appendix

Appendix

CHAPTER FOURTEEN FINANCIAL SERVICES

Article 1401: Scope and Coverage

1. This Chapter applies to measures adopted or maintained by a Party relating to:
   (a) financial institutions of another Party;
   (b) investors of another Party, and investments of such investors, in financial institutions in the Party's territory; and
   (c) cross-border trade in financial services.
2. Articles 1109 through 1111, 1113, 1114 and 1211 are hereby incorporated into and made a part of this Chapter. Articles 1115 through 1138 are hereby incorporated into and made a part of this Chapter solely for breaches by a Party of Articles 1109 through 1111, 1113 and 1114, as incorporated into this Chapter.
3. Nothing in this Chapter shall be construed to prevent a Party, including its public entities, from exclusively conducting or providing in its territory:
   (a) activities or services forming part of a public retirement plan or statutory system of social security; or
   (b) activities or services for the account or with the guarantee or using the financial resources of the Party, including its public entities.
4. Annex 1401.4 applies to the Parties specified in that Annex.

Article 1402: Self-Regulatory Organizations

Where a Party requires a financial institution or a cross-border financial service provider of another Party to be a member of, participate in, or have access to, a self-regulatory organization to provide a financial service in or into the territory of that Party, the Party shall ensure observance of the obligations of this Chapter by such self-regulatory organization.

Article 1403: Establishment of Financial Institutions

1. The Parties recognize the principle that an investor of another Party should be permitted to establish a financial institution in the territory of a Party in the juridical form chosen by such investor.
2. The Parties also recognize the principle that an investor of another Party should be permitted to participate widely in a Party's market through the ability of such investor to:
   (a) provide in that Party's territory a range of financial services through separate financial institutions as may be required by that Party;

(b)   expand geographically in that Party's territory; and

(c)   own financial institutions in that Party's territory without being subject toownership requirements specific to foreign financial institutions.

3. Subject to Annex 1403.3, at such time as the United States permits commercial banks of another Party located in its territory to expand through subsidiaries or direct branches into substantially all of the United States market, the Parties shall review and assess market access provided by each Party in relation to the principles in paragraphs 1 and 2 with a view to adopting arrangements permitting investors of another Party to choose the juridical form of establishment of commercial banks.

4. Each Party shall permit an investor of another Party that does not own or control a financial institution in the Party's territory to establish a financial institution in that territory. A Party may:

(a)   require an investor of another Party to incorporate under the Party's law any financial institution it establishes in the Party's territory; or

(b)   impose terms and conditions on establishment that are consistent with Article 1405.

5. For purposes of this Article, 'investor of another Party' means an investor of another Party engaged in the business of providing financial services in the territory of that Party.

Article 1404: Cross-Border Trade

1. No Party may adopt any measure restricting any type of cross-border trade in financial services by cross-border financial service providers of another Party that the Party permits on the date of entry into force of this Agreement, except to the extent set out in Section B of the Party's Schedule to Annex VII.

2. Each Party shall permit persons located in its territory, and its nationals wherever located, to purchase financial services from cross-border financial service providers of another Party located in the territory of that other Party or of another Party. This obligation does not require a Party to permit such providers to do business or solicit in its territory. Subject to paragraph 1, each Party may define 'doing business' and 'solicitation' for purposes of this obligation.

3. Without prejudice to other means of prudential regulation of cross-border trade in financial services, a Party may require the registration of cross-border financial service providers of another Party and of financial instruments.

4. The Parties shall consult on future liberalization of cross-border trade in financial services as set out in Annex 1404.4.

Article 1405: National Treatment

1. Each Party shall accord to investors of another Party treatment no less favorable than that it accords to its own investors, in like circumstances, with respect to the establishment, acquisition, expansion, management, conduct, operation, and sale or other disposition of financial institutions and investments in financial institutions in its territory.

2. Each Party shall accord to financial institutions of another Party and to investments of investors of another Party in financial institutions treatment no less favorable than that it accords to its own financial institutions and to investments of its own investors in financial institutions, in like circumstances, with respect to the establishment, acquisition, expansion, management, conduct, operation, and sale or other disposition of financial institutions and investments.

3. Subject to Article 1404, where a Party permits the cross-border provision of a financial service it shall accord to the cross-border financial service providers of another Party treatment no less favorable than that it accords to its own financial service providers, in like circumstances, with respect to the provision of such service.

4. The treatment that a Party is required to accord under paragraphs 1, 2, and 3 means, with respect to a measure of any state or province:

    (a) in the case of an investor of another Party with an investment in a financial institution, an investment of such investor in a financial institution, or a financial institution of such investor, located in a state or province, treatment no less favorable than the treatment accorded to an investor of the Party in a financial institution, an investment of such investor in a financial institution, or a financial institution of such investor, located in that state or province, in like circumstances; and

    (b) in any other case, treatment no less favorable than the most favorable treatment accorded to an investor of the Party in a financial institution, its financial institution or its investment in a financial institution, in like circumstances.

          For greater certainty, in the case of an investor of another Party with investments in financial institutions or financial institutions of such investor, located in more than one state or province, the treatment required under sub-paragraph (a) means:

    (c) treatment of the investor that is no less favorable than the most favorable treatment accorded to an investor of the Party with an investment located in such states or provinces, in like circumstances; and

    (d) with respect to an investment of the investor in a financial institution or a financial institution of such investor, located in a state or province, treatment no less favorable than that accorded to an investment of an investor of the Party, or a financial institution of such investor, located in that state or province, in like circumstances.

5. A Party's treatment of financial institutions and cross-border financial service providers of another Party, whether different or identical to that accorded to its own institutions or providers in like circumstances, is consistent with paragraphs 1 through 3 if the treatment affords equal competitive opportunities.

6. A Party's treatment affords equal competitive opportunities if it does not disadvantage financial institutions and cross-border financial services providers of another Party in their ability to provide financial services as compared with the ability of the Party's own financial institutions and financial services providers to provide such services, in like circumstances.

7. Differences in market share, profitability or size do not in themselves establish a denial of equal competitive opportunities, but such differences may be used as evidence regarding whether a Party's treatment affords equal competitive opportunities.

Article 1406: Most-Favored-Nation treatment

1. Each Party shall accord to investors of another Party, financial institutions of another Party, investments of investors in financial institutions and cross-border financial services providers of another Party treatment no less favorable than that it accords to the investors, financial institutions, investments of investors in financial institutions and cross-border financial service providers of any other Party or of a non-Party, in like circumstances.

2. A Party may recognize prudential measures of another Party or of a non-Party in the application of measures covered by this Chapter. Such recognition may be:
  (a) accorded unilaterally;
  (b) achieved through harmonization or other means; or
  (c) based upon an agreement or arrangement with the other Party or non-Party.
3. A Party according recognition of prudential measures under paragraph 2 shall provide adequate opportunity to another Party to demonstrate that circumstances exist in which there are or would be equivalent regulation, oversight, implementation of regulation, and if appropriate, procedures concerning the sharing of information between the Parties.
4. Where a Party accords recognition of prudential measures under paragraph 2(c) and the circumstances set out in paragraph 3 exist, the Party shall provide adequate opportunity to another Party to negotiate accession to the agreement or arrangement, or to negotiate a comparable agreement or arrangement.

Article 1407: New Financial Services and Data Processing

1. Each Party shall permit a financial institution of another Party to provide any new financial service of a type similar to those services that the Party permits in its own financial institutions, in like circumstances, to provide under its domestic law. A Party may determine the institutional and juridical form through which the service may be provided and may require authorization for the provision of the service. Where such authorization is required, a decision shall be made within a reasonable time and the authorization may only be refused for prudential reasons.
2. Each Party shall permit a financial institution of another Party to transfer information in electronic or other form, into and out of the Party's territory, for data processing where such processing is required in the ordinary course of business of such institution.

Article 1408: Senior Management and Boards of Directors

1. No Party may require financial institutions of another Party to engage individuals of any particular nationality as senior managerial or other essential personnel.
2. No Party may require that more than a simple majority of the board of directors of a financial institution of another Party be composed of nationals of the Party, persons residing in the territory of the Party, or a combination thereof.

Article 1409: Reservations and Specific Commitments

1. Articles 1403 through 1408 do not apply to:
  (a) any existing or non-conforming measure that is maintained by
      (i)   a Party at the federal level, as set out in Section A of its Schedule to Annex VII.
      (ii)   a state or province, for the period ending on the date specified in Annex 1409.1 for that state or province, and thereafter as described by the Party in Section A of its Schedule to Annex VII in accordance with Annex 1409.1, or
      (iii) a local government;
  (b) the continuation or prompt renewal of any non-conforming measure referred to in subparagraph (a); or
  (c) an amendment to any non-conforming measure referred to in subparagraph (a) to the extent that the amendment does not decrease the conformity of the measure, as it existed immediately before the amendment, with Articles 1403 through 1408.

2. Articles 1403 through 1408 do not apply to any non-conforming measure that a Party adopts or maintains in accordance with Section B of its Schedule to Annex VII.

3. Section C of each Party's Schedule to Annex VII sets out certain specific commitments by that Party.

4. Where a Party has set out a reservation to Article 1102, 1103, 1202 or 1203 in its Schedule to Annex I, II, III or IV, the reservation shall be deemed to constitute a reservation to Article 1405 or 1406, as the case may be, to the extent that the measure, sector, subsector or activity set out in the reservation is covered by this Chapter.

Article 1410: Exceptions

1. Nothing in this Part shall be construed to prevent a Party from adopting or maintaining reasonable measures for prudential reasons, such as:
   (a) the protection of investors, depositors, financial market participants, policyholders, policy-claimants, or persons to whom a fiduciary duty is owed by a financial institution or cross-border financial service provider;
   (b) the maintenance of the safety, soundness, integrity or financial responsibility of financial institutions or cross-border financial service providers; and
   (c) ensuring the integrity and stability of a Party's financial system.

2. Nothing in this part applies to non-discriminatory measures of general application taken by any public entity in pursuit of monetary and related credit policies or exchange rate policies. This paragraph shall not affect a Party's obligations under Article 1106 (Performance Requirements) with respect to measures covered by Chapter Eleven (Investment) or Article 1109 (Transfers).

3. Article 1405 shall not apply to the granting by a Party to a financial institution of an exclusive right to provide a financial service referred to in Article 1401(3)(a).

4. Notwithstanding Article 1109(1), (2) and (3), as incorporated into this Chapter, and without limiting the applicability of Article 1109(4), as incorporated into this Chapter, a Party may prevent or limit transfers by a financial institution or cross-border financial services provider to, or for the benefit of, an affiliate of or person related to such institution or provider, through the equitable, non-discriminatory and good faith application of measures relating to maintenance of the safety, soundness, integrity or financial responsibility of financial institutions or cross-border financial service providers. This paragraph does not prejudice any other provision of this Agreement that permits a Party to restrict transfers.

Article 1411: Transparency

1. In lieu of Article 1802(2)(Publication), each Party shall, to the extent practicable, provide in advance to all interested persons any measure of general application that the Party proposes to adopt in order to allow an opportunity for such persons to comment on the measure. Such measure shall be provided:
   (a) by means of official publication;
   (b) in other written form; or
   (c) in such other form as permits an interested person to make informed comments on the proposed measure.

2. Each Party's regulatory authorities shall make available to interested persons their requirements for completing applications relating to the provision of financial services.

3. On the request of an applicant, the regulatory authority shall inform the applicant of the status of its application. If such authority requires additional information from the applicant, it shall notify the applicant without undue delay.

4. A regulatory authority shall make an administrative decision on a completed application of an investor in a financial institution, a financial institution or a cross-border financial service provider of another Party relating to the provision of a financial service within 120 days, and shall promptly notify the applicant of the decision. An application shall not be considered complete until all relevant hearings are held and all necessary information is received. Where it is not practicable for a decision to be made within 120 days, the regulatory authority shall notify the applicant without undue delay and shall endeavor to make the decision within a reasonable time thereafter.

5. Nothing in this Chapter requires a Party to furnish or allow access to:

(a) information related to the financial affairs and accounts of individual customers of financial institutions or cross-border financial service providers; or

(b) any confidential information, the disclosure of which would impede law enforcement or otherwise be contrary to the public interest or prejudice legitimate commercial interests of particular enterprises.

6. Each Party shall maintain or establish one or more inquiry points no later than 180 days after the date of entry into force of this Agreement, to respond in writing as soon as practicable, to all reasonable inquiries from interested persons regarding measures of general application covered by this Chapter.

Article 1412: Financial Services Committee

1. The Parties hereby establish the Financial Services Committee. The principal representative of each Party shall be an official of the Party's authority responsible for financial services set out in Annex 1412.1.

2. Subject to Article 2001(2)(d)(Free Trade Commission), the Committee shall:

   (a) supervise the implementation of this Chapter and its further elaboration;
   (b) consider issues regarding financial services that are referred to it by a Party; and
   (c) participate in the dispute settlement procedures in accordance with Article 1415.

3. The Committee shall meet annually to assess the functioning of this Agreement as it applies to financial services. The Committee shall inform the Commission of the results of each annual meeting.

Article 1413: Consultations

1. A Party may request consultations with another Party regarding any matter arising under this Agreement that affects financial services. The other Party shall give sympathetic consideration to the request. The consulting Parties shall report the results of their consultations to the Committee at its annual meeting.

2. Consultations under this Article shall include officials of the authorities specified in Annex 1412.1.

3. A Party may request that regulatory authorities of another Party participate in consultations under this Article regarding that other Party's measures of general application which may affect the operations of financial institutions or cross-border financial service providers in the requesting Party's territory.

4. Nothing in this Article shall be construed to require regulatory authorities participating in consultations under paragraph 3 to disclose information or to take any

action that would interfere with individual regulatory, supervisory, administrative or enforcement matters.

5. Where a Party requires information for supervisory purposes concerning a financial institution in another Party's territory or a cross-border financial service provider in another Party's territory, the party may approach the competent regulatory authority in the other Party's territory to seek the information.

6. Annex 1413.6 shall apply to further consultations and arrangements.

Article 1414: Dispute Settlement

1. Section B of Chapter Twenty (Institutional Arrangements and Dispute Settlement Procedures) applies as modified by this Article to the settlement of disputes arising under this Chapter.

2. The Parties shall establish by January 1, 1994 and maintain a roster of up to 15 individuals who are willing and able to serve as financial services panelists. Financial services roster members shall be appointed by consensus for terms of three years, and may be reappointed.

3. Financial services roster members shall:
   (a) have expertise or experience in financial services law or practice, which may include the regulation of financial institutions;
   (b) be chosen strictly on the basis of objectivity, reliability and sound judgment; and
   (c) meet the qualifications set out in Article 2009(2)(b) and (c) (Roster).

4. Where a Party claims that a dispute arises under this Chapter, Article 2011 (Panel Selection) shall apply, except that:
   (a) where the disputing Parties so agree, the panel shall be composed entirely of panelists meeting the qualifications in paragraph 3; and
   (b) in any other case,
       (i) each disputing Party may select panelists meeting the qualifications set out in paragraph 3 or in Article 2010(1) (Qualifications of Panelists), and
       (ii) if the Party complained against invokes Article 1410, the chair of the panel shall meet the qualifications set out in paragraph 3.

5. In any dispute where a panel finds a measure to be inconsistent with the obligations of this Agreement and the measure affects:
   (a) only the financial services sector, the complaining Party may suspend benefits only in the financial services sector;
   (b) the financial services sector and any other sector, the complaining Party may suspend benefits in the financial services sector that have an effect equivalent to the effect of the measure in the Party's financial services sector; or
   (c) only a sector other than the financial services sector, the complaining Party may not suspend benefits in the financial services sector.

Article 1415: Investment Disputes in Financial Services

1. Where an investor of another Party submits a claim under Article 1116 or 1117 to arbitration under Section B of Chapter Eleven (Investment—Settlement of Disputes between a Party and an Investor of Another Party) against a Party and the disputing Party invokes Article 1410, on request of the disputing Party, the Tribunal shall refer the matter in writing to the Committee for a decision. The Tribunal may not proceed pending receipt of a decision or report under this Article.

2. In a referral pursuant to paragraph 1, the Committee shall decide the issue of whether and to what extent Article 1410 is a valid defense to the claim of the investor. The Committee shall transmit a copy of its decision to the Tribunal and to the Commission. The decision shall be binding on the Tribunal.

3. Where the Committee has not decided the issue within 60 days of the receipt of the referral under paragraph 1, the disputing Party or the Party of the disputing investor may request the establishment of an arbitral panel under Article 2008 (Request for an Arbitral Panel). The panel shall be constituted in accordance with Article 1414. Further to Article 2017 (Final Report), the panel shall transmit its final report to the Committee and to the Tribunal. The report shall be binding on the Tribunal.

4. Where no request for the establishment of a panel pursuant to paragraph 3 has been made within 10 days of the expiration of the 60–day period referred to in paragraph 3, the Tribunal may proceed to decide the matter.

Article 1416: Definitions

For purposes of this Chapter:

cross-border financial service provider of a Party means a person of a Party that is engaged in the business of providing a financial service within the territory of the Party and that seeks to provide or provides financial services through the cross-border provision of such services;

cross-border provision of a financial service or **cross-border trade in financial services** means the provision of a financial services:

    (a)   from the territory of a Party into the territory of another Party,

    (b)   in the territory of a Party by a person of that Party to a person of another Party, or

    (c)   by a national of a Party in the territory of another Party,

but does not include the provision of a service in the territory of a Party by an investment in that territory;

financial institution means any financial intermediary or other enterprise that is authorized to do business and regulated or supervised as a financial institution under the law of the Party in whose territory it is located;

financial institution of another Party means a financial institution, including a branch, located in the territory of a Party that is controlled by persons of another Party;

financial service means a service of a financial nature, including insurance, and a service incidental or auxiliary to a service of a financial nature;

financial service provider of a Party means a person of a Party that is engaged in the business of providing a financial service within the territory of that Party;

investment means 'investment' as defined by Article 1139 (Investment—Definitions), except that, with respect to 'loans' and 'debt securities' referred to in that Article:

    (a)   a loan to or debt security issued by a financial institution is an investment only where it is treated as regulatory capital by the Party in whose territory the financial institution is located; and

    (b)   a loan granted by or debt security owned by a financial institution, other than a loan to or debt security of a financial institution referred to in subparagraph (a), is not an investment;

       for greater certainty:

    (c)   a loan to, or debt security issued by, a Party or a state enterprise thereof is not an investment; and

    (d)   a loan granted by or debt security owned by a cross-border financial service provider, other than a loan to or debt security issued by a financial institution, is an investment if such loan or debt security meets the criteria for investments set out in Article 1139;

investor of a Party means a Party or state enterprise thereof, or a person of that Party, that seeks to make, makes, or has made an investment;

new financial service means a financial service not provided in the Party's territory that is provided within the territory of another Party, and includes any new form of delivery of a financial service or the sale of a financial product that is not sold in the Party's territory;

person of a Party means 'person of a Party' as defined in Chapter Two (General Definitions) and, for greater certainty, does not include a branch of an enterprise of a non-Party;

public entity means a central bank or monetary authority of a Party, or any financial institution owned or controlled by a Party; and

self-regulatory organization means any non-governmental body, including any securities or futures exchange or market, clearing agency, or other organization or association, that exercises its own or delegated regulatory or supervisory authority over financial service providers or financial institutions.

Annex 1401.4

Country-Specific Commitments

For Canada and the United States, Article 1702(1) and (2) of the *Canada—United States Free Trade Agreement* is hereby incorporated into and made a part of this Agreement.

Annex 1403.3

Review of Market Access

The review of market access referred to in Article 1403(3) shall not include the market access limitations specified in Section B of the Schedule of Mexico to Annex VII.

Annex 1404.4

Consultations on Liberalization of Cross-Border Trade

No later than January 1, 2000, the Parties shall consult on further liberalization of cross-border trade in financial services. In such consultations the Parties shall, with respect to insurance:

(a) consider the possibility of allowing a wider range of insurance services to be provided on a cross-border basis in or into their respective territories; and

(b) determine whether the limitations on cross-border insurance services specified in Section A of the Schedule of Mexico to Annex VII shall be maintained, modified or eliminated.

Annex 1409.1

Provincial and State Reservations

1. Canada may set out in Section A of its Schedule to Annex VII by the date of entry into force of this Agreement any existing non-conforming measure maintained at the provincial level.

2. The United States may set out in Schedule A of its Schedule to Annex VII by the date of entry into force of this Agreement any existing non-conforming measures

maintained by California, Florida, Illinois, New York, Ohio and Texas. Existing non-conforming state measures of all other states may be set out by January 1, 1995.

Annex 1412.1

Authorities Responsible for Financial Services

The authority of each Party responsible for financial services shall be:
  (a)   for Canada, the Department of Finance of Canada;
  (b)   for Mexico, the Secretaria de Hacienda y Credito Publico; and
  (c)   for the United States, the Department of the Treasury for banking and other financial services and the Department of Commerce for insurance services.

Annex 1413.6

Further Consultations and Arrangements

SECTION A—LIMITED SCOPE FINANCIAL INSTITUTIONS

Three years after the date of entry into force of this Agreement, the Parties shall consult on the aggregate limit on limited scope financial institutions described in paragraph 8 of Section B of the Schedule of Mexico to Annex VII.

SECTION B—PAYMENTS SYSTEM PROTECTION

1. If the sum of the authorized capital of foreign commercial bank affiliates (as such term is defined in the Schedule of Mexico to Annex VII), measured as a percentage of the aggregate capital of all commercial banks in Mexico, reaches 25 percent, Mexico may request consultations with the other Parties on the potential adverse effects arising from the presence of commercial banks of the other Parties in the Mexican market and the possible need for remedial action, including further temporary limitations on market participation. The consultations shall be completed expeditiously.

2. In considering the potential adverse effects, the Parties shall take into account:
  (a)   the threat that the Mexican payments system may be controlled by non-Mexican persons;
  (b)   the effects foreign commercial banks established in Mexico may have on Mexico's ability to conduct monetary and exchange-rate policy effectively; and
  (c)   the adequacy of this Chapter in protecting the Mexican payments system.

3. If no consensus is reached on the matters referred to in paragraph 1, any Party may request the establishment of an arbitral panel under Article 1414 or Article 2008 (Request for an Arbitral Panel). The panel proceedings shall be conducted in accordance with the Model Rules of Procedure established under Article 2012 (Rules of Procedure). The Panel shall present its determination within 60 days after the last panelist is selected or such other period as the Parties to the proceeding may agree. Article 2018 (Implementation of Final Report) and 2019 (Non-Implementation—Suspension of Benefits) shall not apply in such proceedings.

Selected Bibliography

TREATY SOURCES

Carter, Barry E. and Phillip R. Trimble, *International Law: Selected Documents* (Little, Brown & Co, Boston, 1991)

Holbein, James R. and Donald J. Musch (eds), *NAFTA: Final Text, Summary, Legislative History and Implementation Directory* (Oceana Publications, New York, 1994).

World Trade Organization, *The Results of the Uruguay Round of Multilateral Trade Negotiations: The Legal Texts* (WTO, Geneva, 1995).

BOOKS

Abbott, Frederick M., *Law and Policy of Regional Integration: The NAFTA and Western Hemispheric Integration in the World Trade Organization System* (Kluwer Law and Taxation Publishers, Cambridge, MA, 1995).

Anderson, Kym, and Richard Blackhurst, (eds), *Regional Integration and the Global Trading System* (Harvester Wheatsheaf, New York, 1993).

Baxter, Ian F.G., *Law of Banking* (4th edn, Thomson Canada/Carswell, Toronto, 1992).

Bello, Judith H., Alan F. Holmer and Joseph J. Norton (eds), *The North American Free Trade Agreement: A New Frontier in International Trade and Investment in the Americas* (American Bar Association, 1994).

Bhagwati, Jagdish, and Robert E. Hudec (eds), *Fair Trade and Harmoniztion: Prerequisites for Free Trade?*, Vol. 2 (MIT Press, Cambridge, MA, 1996).

Bhagwati, Jagdish, and Anne O. Krueger, *The Dangerous Drift to Preferential Trade Agreements* (American Enterprise Institute for Public Policy Research, Washington, DC, 1995).

Blattner, Niklaus Hans Genberg, and Alexander K. Swoboda (eds), *Banking in Switzerland* (Physica-Verlag, Heidelberg, 1993).

Bothwell, Robert, *Canada and the United States: The Politics of Partnership* (University of Toronto Press, Toronto, 1992).

Bulmer-Thomas, Victor, Nikki Craske and Mónica Serrano (eds), *Mexico and the North American Free Trade Agreement: Who Will Benefit?* (St Martin's Press, New York, 1994).

Cicurel, Ronald, (ed.), *1991 Die Schweizerischen Wirtschaft: Geschichte in Drei Akten* (SQP Publications, St Sulpice, 1991).

415

Davey, William J., *Pine & Swine Canada—United States Trade Dispute Settlement: The FTA Experience and NAFTA Prospects* (Centre for Trade Policy and Law, Ottawa, 1996).

Demaret, Paul, Jean-François Bellis and Gonzalo García Jiménez (eds), *Regionalism and Multilateralism after the Uruguay Round: Convergence, Divergence and Interaction* (Institut d'études Juridiques Européennes, University of Liège, Liège, 1997).

Dowd, K., (ed.), *The Experience of Free Banking* (Routledge, London, 1992).

Ebke, Werner F., and Joseph J. Norton (eds), *Festschrift in Honor of Sir Joseph Gold* (Verlag Recht und Wirtschaft, Heidelberg, 1990).

England, Catherine, (ed.), *Governing Banking's Future: Markets vs. Regulation* (Kluwer Academic Publishers, Deventer, 1991).

Fernández Jilberto, Alex E., and André Mommen (eds), *Liberalization in the Developing World: Institutional and Economic Changes in Latin America, Africa and Asia* (Routledge, London, 1996).

Fry, Earl H., *The Expanding Role of State and Local Governments in US Foreign Affairs* (Council on Foreign Relations, New York, 1998).

Fundación Konrad Adenauer, *Competencia Economica y Tratado de Libre Comercio* (Konrad Adenauer Stiftung, Mexico City, 1994).

Gall, Gerald L., *The Canadian Legal System* (4th edn, Carswell, Toronto, 1995).

Gelfand, Brian F., *Regulation of Financial Institutions* (Carswell, Toronto, 1996).

Glick, Leslie Alan, *Understanding the North American Free Trade Agreement* (Kluwer, Boston, 1993).

Guggisberg, Brigitte, *Das Protektionspotential der EG und die Effekte auf Drittstaaten* (Verlag Rüegger, Zurich, 1997).

Herring, Richard J., and Robert E. Litan, *Financial Regulation in the Global Economy* (Brookings Institution, Washington, DC, 1995).

Hilf, Meinhard, and Ernst-Ulrich Petersmann (eds), *National Constitutions and International Economic Law* (Kluwer Law and Taxation Publishers, Deventer, 1993).

Hufbauer, Gary Clyde, and Jeffrey Schott, 'The Mexican Financial System', in *North American Free Trade: Issues and Recommendations* (Institute for International Economics, Washington, DC, 1992).

Jackson, John H., William J. Davey and Alan O. Sykes Jr, *Legal Problems of International Economic Relations: Cases, Materials and Text* (3rd edn, West Publishing, St Paul, MN, 1995).

Jackson, John H., and Alan Sykes (eds), *Implementing the Uruguay Round* (Clarendon Press, Oxford, 1997).

Kapteyn, P.J.G., and P. VerLoren van Themaat, *Introduction to the Law of the European Communities* (3rd edn, Kluwer Law International, London, 1998).

Kilgus, Ernst, *Die Grossbanken: Eine Analyse under den Aspekten von Macht und Recht* (Verlag Paul Haupt, Bern, 1979).

Krueger, Anne O., *American Trade Policy: A Tragedy in the Making* (AEI Press, Washington, DC, 1995).

Lüderitz, Alexander, and Jochen Schröder (eds), *Internationales Privatrecht und Rechtsvergleichung im Ausgang des 20. Jahrhunderts: Bewahrung oder Wende?* (Alfred Metzner Verlag, Frankfurt, aM, 1977).

Lustig, Nora, Barry P. Bosworth and Robert Z. Lawrence (eds), *Assessing the Impact: North American Free Trade* (Brookings Institution, Washington, DC, 1992).

Mason, T. David, and Abdul M. Turay (eds), *Japan, NAFTA and Europe: Trilateral Cooperation or Confrontation?* (St Martin's Press, New York, 1994).

Matscher, Franz, and Ignaz Seidl-Hohenveldern (eds), *Europa im Aufbruch: Festschrift Fritz Schwind zum 80. Geburtstag* (Manzsche Verlags- und Universitäts-buchhandlung, Vienna, 1993).

Mishkin, F.S., *The Economics of Money, Banking, and Financial Markets* (4th edn, Harper Collins, New York, 1995).

Moncarz, Raul, (ed.), *International Trade and the New Economic Order* (Pergamon, New York, 1995).

Mottet, Louis H., (ed.), *Geschichte der Schweizer Banken: Bankier-Persönlichkeiten aus fünf Jahrhunderten* (Verlag Neue Zürcher Zeitung, Zurich, 1987).

NAFTA: Issues, Industry, Sector Profiles and Bibliography (Nova Science Publishers, 1994).

Norton, J.J., *et al* (eds), *NAFTA and Beyond. A New Framework for Doing Business in the Americas* (Maritinus Nijhoff, Dordrecht, 1995).

OECD, *Banks Under Stress* (OECD, Paris, 1992).

OECD, *The New Financial Landscape: Forces Shaping the Revolution in Banking, Risk Managementand Capital Markets* (OECD, Paris, 1995) (OECD Documents).

OECD, *Regulatory Reform and Interational Market Openness* (OECD, Paris, 1996) (OECD Proceedings).

Petersmann, Ernst-Ulrich, (ed.), *International Trade Law and the GATT/ WTO Dispute Settlement System* (Kluwer Law International, London, 1997).

Ratner, David L., and Thomas Lee Hazan, *Securities Regulation: Cases and Materials* (5th edn, West Publishing, St Paul, MN, 1996).

Schwartz, Jürgen, (ed.), *The External Relations of the European Community, In Particular EC-US Relations* (Nomos Verlaggesellschaft, Baden-Baden, 1989).

Senti, Richard, *NAFTA: Die Nordamerikanische Freihandelszone* (Schulthess Polygraphischer, Zurich, 1996).

Smith, Roy C., and Ingo Walter, *Global Banking* (OUP, New York, 1997).

Stadler, Christoph, *Die Liberalisierung des Dienstleistungshandels am Beispiel der Versicherungen: Kernelemente bilateraler und multilateraler Ordnungsrahmen einschliesslich des GATS* (Duncker & Humblot, Berlin, 1992).

Stein, Jerome L., *The Globalization of Markets: Capital Flows, Exchange Rates and Trade Regimes* (Physica Verlag, Heidelberg, 1997).

Stone, Frank, *Canada, the GATT and the International Trade System* (Institute for Research on Public Policy, Montreal, 1984).

Symons, Edward L. Jr, and James J. White, *Banking Law: Teaching Materials* (3rd edn, West Publishing, St Paul, MN, 1991).

Thürer, Daniel, and Stephan Kux, *GATT 94 und die Welthandelsorganisation: Herausforderung für die Schweiz und Europa* (Schulthess Polygraphischer Verlag, Zurich, 1996).

von Bertrab, Hermann, *Negotiating NAFTA: A Mexican Envoy's Account* (Praeger, Westport, CT, 1997).

Weintraub, Sidney, Chandler Stolp and Leigh Boske, *US-Mexican Free Trade: the Effect on Textiles and Apparel, Petrochemicals, and Banking in Texas* (Policy Report No. 5) (US-Mexican Policy Studies Program, Austin, TX, 1993).

Wethington, Olin L., *Financial Market Liberalization* (Shepard's/McGraw-Hill, New York, 1994).

Witker, Jorge, (ed.), *Legal Aspects of the Trilateral Free Trade Agreement* (Universidad Nacional Autónoma de México, Mexico City, 1992).

Wyatt, Derrick, and Alan Dashwood, *European Community Law* (3rd edn, Sweet & Maxwell, London, 1993).

COLLECTED INFORMATION

Committee on Banking and Financial Services of the House of Representatives (United States), *Compilation of Basic Banking Laws* (Revised to 1 May 1995) (US Government Printing Office, Washington, DC, 1995).

Department of the Treasury (United States), *National Treatment Study* (1994).
Holbein, James R., and Donald J. Musch (eds), *North American Free Trade Agreements: Dispute Settlment* (Oceana Publications, Dobbs Ferry, NY) (looseleaf).
Reams, Bernard D. Jr, and Jon S. Schultz (eds), *The North American Free Trade Agreement (NAFTA): Documents and Materials Including a Legislative History of the North American Free Trade Agreement Implementation Act: Public Law*, Vols. 1–28 (1994).
WTO, *GATT Analytical Index* (6th edn, WTO, Geneva, 1994).

ARTICLES (LISTED BY SUBJECT)

International Trade in Services

USTR, WTO Implementation Report: Services (Internet)
BAWI, 'WTO: GATS-Nachverhandlungen über Finanzdienstleistungen und über natürliche Personen als Dienstleistungserbringer Schlussbericht' (Geneva, 28 July 1995).
Ascher, Bernard, 'Multilateral Negotiations on Trade in Services: Concepts, Goals, Issues' (1989) 19:2 Ga J Int'l & Comp L 392.
Auerback, Raymond M., 'Governing Law Issues in International Financial Transactions' (1993) 27:2 Int'l Lawyer 303.
Bachman, Kenneth L., Scott N. Benedict and Ricardo A. Anzaldúa, 'Financial Services under the North American Free Trade Agreement: An Overview' (1994) 28:2 Int'l Lawyer 291.
Broadman, Harry G., 'International Trade and Investment in Services: A Comparative Analysis of the NAFTA' (1993) 27:3 Int'l Lawyer 623.
Carceles Poveda, Eva, and Susanne Droege, 'International Trade in Financial Services: An Assessment of the GATS' (1997) 52:4 *Aussenwirtschaft* 603.
Drake, William J., and Kalypso Nicolaïdis, 'Ideas, interests, and institutionalization: 'trade in services' and the Uruguay Round' (1992) 46:1 Int'l Organization 37.
Footer, Mary E., 'GATT and the Multilateral Regulation of Banking Services' (1993) 27:2 Int'l Lawyer 343.
Feketekuty, Geza, 'Does the Theory of Comparative Advantage Apply to Trade in Services?', in International Trade in Services: An Overview and Blueprint for Negotiations, Ch. 6 'Does International Trade Theory Apply to Services?' (Ballinger, Cambridge, MA, 1988), pp. 100–27.
Forschungsinstitut für Wirtschaftsverfassung und Wettbewerb, e.V., (ed.), *Die Bedeutung der WTO für die europaische Wirtschaft* (Carl Heymanns Verlag, Cologne, 1997).
Gibbs, Murray, and Mina Mashayekhi, 'Elements of a Multilateral Framework of Principles and Rules for Trade in Services', in *United Nations, Uruguay Round: Papers on Selected Issues* (UNCTAD, Geneva, 1989), pp. 81–127.
Graham, Edward M., 'The (Not Wholly Satisfactory) State of the Theory of Foreign Direct Investment and the Multinational Enterprise', in Jerome L. Stein (ed.), *The Globalization of Markets: Capital Flows, Exchange Flows and Trade Regimes* (Physica Verlag, Heidelberg, 1997), pp. 99–122.
Grey, Richard de C., '"1992", Service Sectors and the Uruguay Round', in *UN, Trade in Services: Sectoral Issues* (UNCTAD/ITP/26, UNCTAD 1989), pp. 407–30.
Heather, Thomas, 'Comments on Financial Services, Other Services, and Temporary Entry Rules' (1993) 1:1 US-Mex LJ 73 (Symposium: The Problems and Prospects of a North American Free Trade Agreement).

Hirsch, Seev, 'Services and Service Intensity in International Trade' (1989) 125 *Weltwirtschaftliches Archiv* 45.

Hoekman, 'Conceptual and Political Economy Issues in Liberalizing International Transactions in Services' (1993) 48:2 *Aussenwirtschaft* 203.

Jackson, John H., 'Introduction and Basic Policy Goals' and 'Statement', in *International Competition in Services: A Constitutional Framework* (American Enterprise Institute for Public Policy Research, Washington, DC, 1988), pp. 3–19, 43–7.

Kampf, Roger, 'Liberalisation of Financial Services in the GATS and Domestic Regulation' (1997) 3:5 Int'l Tr L & Reg 155.

Kennett, Wendy, 'The European Community and the General Agreement on Trade in Services', in Nicholas Emiliou and David O'Keeffe, *The European Union and World Trade Law: After the GATT Uruguay Round* (John Wiley & Sons, Chichester/New York/Toronto, 1996), pp. 136–48.

MacNeil, Iain, 'The Legal Framework in the United Kingdom for Insurance Policies Sold by EC Insurers Under Freedom of Services' (1995) 44:1 Int'l & Comp LQ 19.

Mattoo, Aaditya, 'National Treatment in the GATS: Corner-Stone or Pandora's Box?' (1997) 30:1 J World Trade 107.

Meron, Theodor, 'The World Bank and Insurance' (1977) XLVII The British YB Nt'l L 301.

Moncarz, Raul, (ed.), *International Trade and the New Economic Order* (Pergamon, New York, 1995), which includes: Mancarz, 'An Introduction'; Abdel Agami, 'Accounting Issues in Free Trade Agreements'; Sovathana Sokhom, 'The Trade War of the Twenty-First Century'; Sayeeda Bano & Peter Lane, 'The Significance and Determinants of Trade in Services: Canada and the World Economy'; Carl L. Dyer, Kathleen Rees, & Jan Hathcote, 'US Trade Policy in Retrospect: A Synopsis from the Continental Congress to Current Costs'.

Mukherjee, Neela, 'Exporting Labour Services and Market Access Commitments under GATS in the World Trade Organization: An Analysis from the Perspective of Developing Countries' (1996) 30:5 J World Trade 21.

Nicolaides, Phedon, 'The Problem of Regulation in Traded Services: The Implications for Reciprocal Liberalization' (1989) 44:1 *Aussenwirtschaft* 29.

Nicolaides, Phedon, 'The Emerging International Regime For Services' (1990) 46:1 *The World Today*.

O'Connor, Walter F., 'The International Tax Implications of Transborder Data Flow' (1989) 15:1 Int'l Tax J 73.

Powell, Jane Louise, '1992: Single European Market Implications for the Insurance Sector' (1990) 13:2 Boston College Int'l & Comparative L Rev 371.

Reidenberg, Joel R., 'The Privacy Obstacle Course: Hurdling Barriers to Transnational Financial Services' (1992) 60:6 Fordham L Rev S137.

Rolfe, Robert J., and W. Chase Idol III, 'The Taxation of Offshore Captive Insurance Companies' (1990) 16:2 Int'l Tax J 113.

Sapir, André, 'The General Agreement on Trade in Services: from 1994 to the Year 2000' (1999) 33:1 J World Trade 51.

Sauvé, Pierre, 'A First Look at Investment in the Final Act of the Uruguay Round' (1994) 28:5 J World Trade 4.

Sauvé, Pierre, 'Qs and As on Trade, Investment and the WTO' (1997) 31:4 J World Trade 55.

Schlegelmilch, Rupert, 'International Rules on Foreign Direct Investment: A New Challenge for the World Trade Organization' (1996) 6 Int'l Trade L & Reg 212.

Schott, Jeffrey J., and Murray G. Smith (eds), *The Canada-United States Free Trade Agreement: The Global Impact*, Ch. 6 'Services and Investment' (Institution for International Economics, Washington, DC, 1988), pp. 137–55.

Schwietert, Aloys, 'Financial Services Ergebnisse aus der Sicht der Banken', in Daniel Thürer and Stephan Kux (eds), *GATT 94 und die Welthandelsorganisation: Herausforderung für die Schweiz und Europa* (Schulthess Polygraphischer: Zurich/Nomos Verlags, Baden-Baden, 1996), pp. 189–92.

Senti, Richard, 'Das Allgemeine Dienstleitungsabkommen', in Forschungsinstitut für Wirtschaftsverfassung und Wettbewerb, e.V. (ed.), *Die Bedeutung der WTO für die europaische Wirtschaft* (Carl Heymanns Verlag, Cologne, 1997), pp. 67–92.

Stalson, Helena, '1 Introduction and Summary'/'2 US Services in International Trade', in H. Stalson, *US Service Exports and Foreign Barriers: An Agenda for Negotiations* (National Planning Association, 1985), pp. 1–5, 6–15.

Votre, Kenneth A., 'Trade in Services: Proposals for the Liberalization of International Trade in Insurance' (1993) 13:3 Bridgeport L Rev 537.

Wegen, Gerhard, 'Transnational Financial Services—Current Challenges for an Integrated Europe' (1992) 60:6 Fordham L Rev S91.

Werner, Welf, 'Liberalisierung von Finanzdienstleitsungen: Atlantische Positionen und Konzepte auf dem Weg zur Interimslösung im multilateralen Dienstleistungsabkommen (GATS)' (1996) 51:3 *Aussenwirtschaft* 327.

Wood, Philip R., 'Comparative Financial Law: A Classification of the World's Jurisdictions' (manuscript completed 1996, for publication in *Festschrift*).

Yokoyama, Jun, 'The Creation of the European Insurance Market and its Impact upon Japan' (1994) Hitotsubashi J of L and Politics, Special Issue 103.

Regional Integration

Abbott, Frederick M., 'Integration Without Institutions: The NAFTA Mutation of the EC Model and the Future of the GATT Regime' (1992) 40:4 Am J Comparative L 917.

Abbott, Frederick M., 'Regional Integration Mechanisms in the Law of the United States: Starting Over' (1993) 1 Global Legal Studies J 155.

Abbott, Frederick M., 'The NAFTA Environmental Dispute Settlement System as Prototype for Regional Integration Arrangements' (manuscript on file with author).

Abbott, Frederick M., 'The North American Free Trade Agreement and Its Implications for the European Union' (1994) 4:1 Transnat'l L & Contemp Prob 119.

Abbott, Frederick M., 'GATT and the European Community: A Formula for Peaceful Coexistence' (1990) 12:1 Mich J Int'l L 1.

American Society of International Law, 'Multilateral and Regional Efforts to Integrate Markets: The Uruguay Round, NAFTA, Asia Pacific Economic Cooperation Initiatives and the European Communities', in Proceedings of the 87th Annual Meeting (1993) (Mark David Davis, Reporter), pp. 340–56.

Bello, Judith H., and Alan F. Holmer, 'The NAFTA: Its Overarching Implications' (1993) 27:3 Int'l Lawyer 589 (Annual Symposium: The North American Free Trade Agreement (NAFTA)).

Bernal, Richard, 'Regional Trade Arrangements in the Western Hemisphere' (1993) 8:4 Am Univ J Int'l L & Policy 683.

Bhagwati, Jagdish, 'Is Free Trade Passé After All?' (1989) 125 *Weltwirtschaftliches Archiv* 17.

Bilal, Sanoussi, 'Political Economy Considerations on the Supply of Trade Protection in Regional Integration Agreements' (1998) 36:1 J Common Market Stud 1.

Bizai, Gustavo A., 'Mercosur: Towards the Common Market—Developments in 1995' (1996) 1 Int'l Trade L Rev 13.

Chichilnisky, Graciela, 'Trade Regimes and GATT: Resource Intensive vs. Knowledge Intensive Growth', in Jerome L. Stein (ed.), *The Globalization of*

Markets: Capital Flows, Exchange Flows and Trade Regimes (Physica Verlag, Heidelberg, 1997), pp. 63–97.

Cooke, Philip, 'Regions in a Global Market: the Experiences of Wales and Baden-Württemburg' (1997) 4:2 Rev Int'l Pol Econ 349.

Cottier, Thomas, 'The Challenge of Regionalization and Preferential Relations in World Trade Law and Policy' (1996) 2 Europ Foreign Aff Rev 149.

Dam, Kenneth W., 'Regional Economic Arrangements and the GATT: the Legacy of a Misconception' (1963) 30:4 Univ of Chicago L Rev 615.

Friedman, Sheldon, 'The EC vs. NAFTA: Levelling Up vs. Social Dumping' (1993) 68:3 Chic-Kent L Rev 1421.

Garten, Jeffrey E., 'Is America Abandoning Multilateral Trade?' 74:6 *Foreign Affairs* 50 (Nov.–Dec. 1995) pp. 789–872.

GATT, 'Article XXIV', in *Analytical Index: Guide to GATT Law and Practice* (6th edn, GATT, Geneva, 1994) pp. 789–872.

Gitli, Eduardo, and Gunilla Ryd, 'Latin American Integration and the Enterprise for the Americas Initiative' (1992) 26:4 J World Trade 25.

Gutiérrez, Mario A., 'Is Small "Beautiful" for Economic Integration? The Americas' (1996) 30:4 J World Trade 173.

Hart, Jeffrey A., and Aseem Prakash, 'Globalisation and Regionalisation: Conceptual Issues and Reflections' (1996) 6 Int Trade L & Reg 205.

Helbing, Thomas, 'Explaining the Presence of Foreign Financial Intermediaries in Switzerland', in Niklaus Blattner, Hans Genberg and Alexander Swoboda (eds), *Banking in Switzerland* (Physica Verlag, Heidelberg, 1993), pp. 145–201.

Hoekman, Bernard M., and Michael P. Leidy, 'Holes and Loopholes in Regional Trading Arrangements and the Multilateral Trading System' (1992) 47:3 *Aussenwirtschaft* 325.

Hummer, Waldemar and Dietmar Prager, 'Zur GATT-Kompatibilität von Mehrfachmitgliedshaften in regionalen Präferenzzonen—dargestellt am Beispiel Mexikos in der NAFTA/ALADI und Lichtensteins im EWR/Zollanschlussvertrag Schweiz' (1997) 35:4 *Archiv des Völkerrechts* 367.

Johnson, Chris Alan, 'Protectionism Toward Transplants and Obligations Under GATT, FCN Treaty and OECD Instruments: Trojan Horse or Engine for Growth?' (1994) 4.1 Transnat'l L & Contemp Problems 279 (Symposium: Regional Economic Integration in the Global Marketplace).

Krause, Lawrence, 'Trade Policy in the 1990s: Good-bye Bipolarity, Hello Regions' 46:5 *The World Today* 83 (May 1990).

Krueger, Anne O., '5 The North American Free Trade Agreement, the Western Hemisphere Free Trade Agreement, and the Multilateral Trading System', in A. O. Krueger, *American Trade Policy: A Tragedy in the Making* (AEI Press, Washington, DC, 1995), pp. 84–101.

Laird, Sam, 'Latin American Trade Liberalization' (1995) 4:2 Minn J Global Trade 195.

de León, Ignacio, and Marianella Morales, 'From Aid to Trade: A New Appraisal of the Economic Relations Between the European Union and Latin America' (1997) 2 Euro For Aff Rev 63.

Matsui, Robert, 'Introduction' (1994) 27:4 UC Davis L Rev 791 (address by trade representative).

McCarthy, Colin L., 'Regional Integration of Developing Countries at Different Levels of Economic Development—Problems and Prospects' (1994) 4:1 Transnat'l L & Contemp Problems 1 (Symposium: Regional Economic Integration in the Global Marketplace).

Nicolaides, Phedon, 'Trade Policy in the 1990s II: Avoiding the Trap of Regionalism' 46:5 *The World Today* 85 (May 1990).

Nunnenkamp, Peter, 'The World Trading System at the Crossroads: Multilateral Trade Negotiations in the Era of Regionalism' (1993) 48:2 *Aussenwirtschaft* 177.

OECD, 'Policy Dialogue with the Dynamic Non-Member Economies' (Report on the Workshop on 'Regional Integration and its Place in the Multilateral Trading System', Paris, 10–11 July 1995) (from internet >http://www. oecd.org<).

Palmeter, David, 'Rules of Origin in Customs Unions and Free Trade Areas', in Kym Anderson and Richard Blackhurst (eds), *Regional Integration and the Global Trading System* (Harvester/Wheatsheaf, New York, London, 1993), pp. 326 *et seq.*

Petersen, Nikolaj, 'National Strategies in the Integration Dilemma: An Adaptation Approach' (1998) 36:1 J Common Market Stud 33.

Preusse, Heinz G., 'Regional Integration in the Nineties: Stimulation or Threat to the Multilateral Trading System?' (1994) 28:4 J World Trade 147.

Purnell, David R., '1993 International Trade Update: The GATT and NAFTA' (1994) 73:1 Nebr L Rev 211.

Roessler, Frieder, 'Diverging Domestic Policies and Multilateral Trade Integration', in Jagdish Bhagwati and Robert E. Hudec (eds), *Fair Trade and Harmonization: Prerequisites for Free Trade?* (MIT Press, Cambridge, MA, 1996), pp. 21–56.

Sagasser, Bernd, 'Das Nordamerikanische Freihandelsabkommen NAFTA' 39:7 Recht der int'l Wirtschaft 573 (1993).

Salvatore, Dominick, 'NAFTA and the EC: Similarities and Differences', in Khosrow Fatemi and Dominick Salvatore (eds), *The North American Free Trade Agreement* (Elsevier Science, Oxford, 1994).

Samuels, Michael A., 'The Decline of Multilateralism—Can We Prevent It?' 46:1 *The World Today* 6 (January 1990).

Schoneveld, Frank, 'The EEC and Free Trade Agreements: Stretching the Limits of GATT Exceptions to Non-Discriminatory Trade?' (1992) 26:5 J World Trade 59.

Schreuer, Christopher, 'Regionalism v. Universalism' (1995) 6:3 Eur J Int'l L 477.

Senti, Richard, 'Im Widerstreit zwischen GATT und Integration: Art. XXIV des GATT und die Entwicklung der wirtschaftlichen Integrationsräume' (ETH Zurich, Feb. 1993).

Senti, Richard, 'Die Integration als Gefahr für das GATT' (1994) 49:1 *Aussenwirtschaft* 131.

Snyder, Edward C., 'The Menem Revolution in Argentina: Progress Toward a Hemispheric Free Trade Area' (1994) 29:1 Texas Int'l LJ 95.

Steinberg, Richard H., 'Antidotes to Regionalism: Responses to Trade Diversion Effects of the North American Free Trade Agreement' (1993) 29:2 Stanford J Int'l L 315.

Supper, Erich, 'Regionalismus und die WTO' in: Forschungsinstitut für Wirtschaftsverfassung und Wettbewerb, e.V. (ed.), *Die Bedeutung der WTO für die europäische Wirtschaft* (Carl Heymanns Verlag, Cologne, 1997), pp. 93–105.

Thakur, Ramesh, 'The North American Free Trade Agreement' (1993) 47:1 Austrl J Int'l Aff 77.

Trachtman, Joel P., 'Unilateralism, Bilateralism, Regionalism, Multilateralism, and Functionalism: A Comparison with Reference to Securities Regulation' (1994) 4:1 Transnat'l L & Contemp Problems 69 (Symposium: Regional Economic Integration in the Global Marketplace).

Wechter, Kevin A., 'NAFTA: A Complement to GATT or a Setback to Global Free Trade?' (1993) 66:6 So Ca L Rev 2611.

WTO, 'No evidence of polarization of world trade among three 'blocs' and no clash between world and regional trade systems—says new WTO report', *WTO Focus*, No. 3 (May–June 1995).

Yarbrough, Beth V., and Robert M. Yarbrough, 'Regionalism and Layered Governance: The Choice of Trade Institutions' (1994) 48:1 J Int'l Affairs 95.

Zhan, Xiaoning James, 'NAFTA's Likely Implications for China and Hong Kong' 23 *UNCTAD Bulletin* 6 (Nov.–Dec. 1993).

Mexico/Mexican Banking System

Altschuler, Irwin P. and Claudia G. Pasche, 'The North American Free Trade Agreement: the Ongoing Liberalization of Trade with Mexico' (1993) 28:1 Wake Forest L Rev 7 .

Banco de México, *The Mexican Economy 1996* (1996), pp. 220–25.

Bankverein, 'Mexikanischer Peso: Spiegelbild Wechselhafter Stimmungen' (1996) 3 *Der Monat* 30.

Banowsky, David W., and Carlos A. Gabuardi, 'Secured Credit Transactions in Mexico' (1994) 28:2 Int'l Lawyer 263.

Bartlett, David, and Wendy Hunter, 'Market Structures, Political Institutions, and Democratization: The Latin American and East European Experiences' (1997) 4:1 Rev Int'l Pol Econ 87.

Basáñez, Miguel, and Roderic A. Camp, 'La Nacionalización de la Banca y la Opinión Pública en México' (1984) 25:2 *Foro Internacional* 202.

Bilateral Commission on the Future of United States—Mexican Relations (Report of), Ch. 1: 'The Nature of the Relationship', in *The Challenge of Independence: Mexico and the United States* (University Press of America 1989), pp. 9–33.

Castañeda, Jorge G., 'Mexico's Circle of Misery' 75 *Foreign Affairs* 93 (July–Aug. 1996).

Cecena, Montserrat Romero, 'El Efecto Tequila en Algunos Mercados Emergentes de America Latina: Un Analisis de Cointergracion', Ejecutivos de Finanzas, 1 May 1997 (Instituto Mexicana de Ejecutivos de Finanzas, 1997).

Clayton, Tomás Anthony, José Humberto Días-Guerrero and José Trinidad Garci-Cervantes, 'Foreign Investment in Mexico: Mexico Welcomes Foreign Investors' (1992) 12:1 Chicano-Latino L Rev 13.

Committee on Banking, Finance and Urban Affairs House of Representatives (Hearing Before the), 'Abuses Within the Mexican Political Regulatory and Judicial Systems and Implications for the North American Free Trade Agreement (NAFTA)', Serial No. 103-93 (US Government Printing Office, Washington, DC, 1994) (List of Participants, including industry members, of the NAFTA Financial Services negotiations) (filed under Correspondences).

Dakolias, Maria, 'A Strategy for Judicial Reform: The Experience in Latin America' (1995) 36 Va J Int'l L 167.

Davis, Bronwen, 'Mexico's Commercial Banking Industry: Can Mexico's Recently Privatized Banks Compete with the United States Banking Industry After the Enactment of the North American Free Trade Agreement?' (1993) 10:1 Ariz J Int'l & Comp L 77.

Faesler, Julio, 'Mexico's Trade with the European Economic Community Countries' (1968) 101:2 Weltwirtsch Archiv 124.

Fernández Jilberto, Alex E., and Barbara Hogenboom, 'Mexico's Integration in NAFTA: Neoliberal Restructuring and Changing Political Alliances', in Alex E. Fernández Jilberto and André Mommen (eds), *Liberalization in the Developing World: Institutional and Economic Changes in Latin America, Africa and Asia* (Routledge, London/New York, 1996), pp. 138–60.

Goddard, Jorge Adame, 'Relaciones Entre el Tratado de Libre Comercio y la Legislación Mexicana' (1992) 16 *Revista de Investigaciones Jurídicas* 9.

Greenwold, Stephen, 'The Government Procurement Chapter of the North American Free Trade Agreement' (1994) 1994:4 Public Proc L Rev 129.

Heredia, Carlos A., 'NAFTA and Democratization in Mexico' (1994) 48:1 J Int'l Affairs 13.

Hufbauer, Gary Clyde, and Jeffrey Schott, 'The Mexican Financial System', in *North American Free Trade: Issues and Recommendations* (Institute for International Economics, Washington, DC, 1992).

Kate, Adriaan Ten, 'Is Mexico a Back Door to the US Market or a Niche in the World's Largest Free Trade Area?', in Victor Bulmer-Thomas, Nikki Craske and Mónica Serrano (eds), *Mexico and the North American Free Trade Agreement: Who Will Benefit?* (St Martin's Press, New York, 1994), Ch. 3, pp. 29–41.

'Liberalismo Contra Democracia: Recent Judicial Reform in Mexico' (1995) 108 Harv L Rev 1919 (note).

Mandig, D. Michael, 'The Judicial Cooperation Project Between Arizona and Sonora' (1995) 3 US-Mex LJ 83.

McGee, Henry W. Jr, 'Mexican Perspectives on Economic, Political and Cultural Implications of Free Trade' (1992) 12:1 Chicano-Latino L Rev 1.

Molina Pasquel, Roberto, 'The Mexican Banking System' (1956–57) 11 Miami LQ 470.

Moody-O'Grady, Kristin, 'Dispute Settlement Provisions in the NAFTA and the CAFTA: Progress or Protectionism?' (1994) 18:1 *Fletcher Forum of World Affairs* 121.

Philip, George, 'Mexican Politics and the North American Free Trade Agreement' (1995) 47:12 *The World Today* 204.

Reig, María Sol Martín, 'The Mexican Presidential Elections of the 21st of August 1994' (1994) 25:3 *Revue Générale de Droit* 605.

Ritch, James E., Jr, 'Legal Aspects of Lending to Mexican Borrowers' (1981) 7:3 No Carol J Int'l L & Commercial Reg 315.

Rodríguez, Carlos del Río, 'Judicial Review Seen From a Mexican Perspective' (1989–90) 20 Cal Western Int'l LJ 7.

Rogers, John E., 'The Prospects for Modernization of Financing of Mexican Business' (1994) 2 US-Mex LJ 139.

Rojas, Miguel Jauregui, 'A New Era: The Regulation of Investment in Mexico' (1993) 1:1 US-Mex LJ 41 (Symposium: The Problems and Prospects of a North American Free Trade Agreement).

Sachs, Jeffrey, Aaron Tornell and Andrés Velasco, 'The Collapse of the Mexican Peso: What Have We Learned?' 22 *Economic Policy* 15 (April 1996).

Silva, Ricardo Méndez, 'México ante el Mercado Común de América del Norte' (1980) VII *Anuario Jurídico* 145.

Skiles, Marilyn E., 'Stabilization and Financial Sector Reform in Mexico', Federal Reserve Bank of New York, Research Paper No. 9125 (August 1991).

Smith, James F., 'Confronting Differences in the United States and Mexican Legal Systems in the Era of NAFTA' (1993) 1:1 United States-Mexico L.J. 85 (Symposium: The Problems and Prospects of a North American Free Trade Agreement).

Smith, Robert Freeman, 'The American Revolution and Latin America: An Essay in Imagery, Perceptions, and Ideological Influence' (1978) 20:4 J Interamerican Studies and World Affairs 42.

Solís Soberon, Fernando, and Ignacio Trigueros, 'Bancos', in UN, *Mexico: Una Economía de Servicios* (UNCTAD/ITP/58, UN, 1991), pp. 93–113.

Stephenson, John M. (moderator), 'Corporate and Securities Laws in Mexico and the United States. Panel Discussion: Securities Law Questions and Comments on the Comparison of Corporate and Securities Laws in Mexico and the United States' (1995) 3 US-Mex LJ 30.

Tobler, Hans Werner, 'Das Verhältnis Mexiko—USA: Zwischen Konflikt und Kooperation', in Kurt R. Spillmann (ed.), *Zeitgeschichtliche Hintergründe Aktueller*

Konflikte V—Vorlesung für Hörer aller Abteilungen—Sommersemester 1995 (Zürcher Beiträge zur Sicherheitspolitik und Konfliktforschung, No. 37, Zurich, 1995).

Treviño, Julio C., 'The New Mexican Legislation on Commercial Arbitration' (1994) 11:4 J Int'l Arb 5.

Treviño, Julio C., 'Mexico: The Present Status of Legislation and Governmental Policies on Direct Foreign Investment' (1984) 18:2 Int'l Lawyer 297.

Trigueros, Ignacio, 'The Mexican Financial System and NAFTA', in Victor Bulmer-Thomas, Nikki Craske and Mónica Serrano (eds), *Mexico and the North American Free Trade Agreement: Who Will Benefit?* (St Martin's Press, New York, 1994), Ch. 4, pp. 43–57.

Trigueros, Ignacio, 'El Sistema Financiero Mexicano y el TLC', in Victor Bulmer-Thomas, Nikke Craske and Mònica Serrano (eds), *México Frente al TLC: Costos y Beneficios* (El Colegio de México, Mexico, 1994).

Vargas, Jorge A., 'NAFTA, the Chiapas Rebellion, and the Emergence of Mexican Ethnic Law' (1994–95) 25:1 Calif West Int'l LJ 1.

Warman, Fanny, and A.P. Thirlwall, 'Interest Rates, Saving, Investment and Growth in Mexico 1960–1990: Test of the Financial Liberalisation Hypothesis' (1994) 30:3 J Developmental Stud 629.

White, William R., 'The Implications of the FTA and NAFTA for Canada and Mexico', Technical Report No. 70 (Bank of Canada, undated).

Witker, Jorge, and Rich Robins, 'A Critical Analysis of the Post-1994 Elections: Mexican Foreign Investment Regulatory Scheme', in Seymour J. Rubin and Dean Alexander (eds), *NAFTA and Investment* (Kluwer Law, Boston 1995), pp. 111–145.

Canada/Canadian Banking System

Anwar, Syed Tariq, 'The Impact of NAFTA on Canada's Automobile Industry: Issues and Analysis' (1996) 19:3 *World Competition* 115.

Bothwell, Robert, 'Free Trade and Its Discontents', in *Canada and the United States: The Politics of Partnership* (University of Toronto Press, Toronto, 1992), pp. 139–56.

Canada, Department of Finance, *1997 Review of Financial Sector Legislation: Proposals for Changes* (June 1996).

Cross, John T., 'The Constitutional Federal Question in the Lower Federal Courts of the United States and Canada' (1993) 17 Hastings Int'l & Comp L Rev 143.

Dymond, William, 'The Canada-US Free Trade Agreement: Implications for the Global Trading Regime', in T. David Mason and Abdul M. Turay (eds), *Japan, NAFTA and Europe: Trilateral Cooperation or Confrontation?* (St Martin's Press, New York, 1994), pp. 38–57.

Finance Canada, *The Canadian Financial System (1995)* (>http://www.fin.gc.ca/toce/1995/fctshtsum95%2De.html<).

Finance Canada, Foreign Bank Entry Policy—Consultation Papers 1 and 2 (1997) (>http://www.fin.gc.ca/foreign/foreign1%2De.html<).

Financial Service Task Force, 'Discussion Paper' (1997) (>http://finservtask-force.fin.gc.ca/disce/exesum_e.htm< or >...disce/sect2_e.htm<).

Fry, Earl H., 'The Impact of Federalism on the Development of International Economic Relations: Lessons from the United States and Canada' (1989) 43:1 Australian Outlook/Austrl J Int'l Aff 17.

Groven, Robert C., 'Setting Our Sites: The United States and Canadian Investor Visa Programs' (1995) 4:2 Minn J of Global Trade 271.

Howse, Robert, 'State Trading in Canada', in Thomas Cottier and Petros C. Mavroidis (eds), *Trade Liberalization and Property Ownership: State-Trading in the 21st Century* (University of Michigan Press, Ann Arbor, 1988), pp. 181–209).

Mahant, Edelgard, 'The Canada-United States Free Trade Agreement and the European Community: a Functionalist Comparison' (1990) 10:2 *Zeitschrift der Gesellschaft für Kanada-Studien* 113.

McCormack, James, 'Financial Market Integration: The Effects on Trade and the Response of Trade Policy' Policy Staff Paper 94/01 (Department of Foreign Affairs and International Trade, Canada, February 1994) (found at >http://www.dfait-maeci.gc.ca/english/foreignp/dfait/policy'1/94_01_e/<).

Merkin, William S., Ann H. Hughes, Ralph R. Johnson and Julius Katz, 'US-Canada Free Trade Agreement 1986–1987' (1996) 1 Int'l Negotiation 257.

Ogilvie, M.H., 'Financial Institutions Reform in Canada' (1992) J of Business L 615.

Redish, Angela, 'The Government's Role in Payment Systems: Lessons from the Canadian Experience', in Catherine England (ed.), *Governing Banking's Future: Markets vs. Regulation* (Kluwer Academic Publishers, Deventer, 1991).

Thomas, Hugh, 'Banks and Other Deposit-Taking Institutions', in Hugh Thomas, *Financial* Institutions Management (draft, May 1996, Ch. 1) (>http://www.business.mcmaster.ca/finance/thomas/fim-1.html<).

Thomas, Kenneth P., 'Capital Mobility and Trade Policy: the Case of the Canada-US Auto Pact' (1997) 4:1 Rev Int'l Pol Econ 127.

Smith, Murray G., 'Trade Policies in Canada', in Jorge Witker (ed.), *Legal Aspects of the Trilateral Free Trade Agreement* (Universidad Nacional Autónoma de México, Mexico, 1992), pp. 11–41.

Stone, Frank, '2 The Pre-War Background'/'3 The Post-War Multilateral Trade System: Origins and Main Elements'/'8 The Organization for Economic Co-operation and Development'/'11 The Generalized System of Preferences (GSP)', in Frank Stone, *Canada, the GATT and the International Trade System* 5-17, 18-23+, 84-97, 132-137+ (Montreal: The Institute for Research on Public Policy 1984), pp. 5–17, 18–23 *et seq*, 84–97, 132–7 *et seq*.

Ursel, Dale, 'Bank Confidentiality in Canada' (1992) 14 Comp L YB of Int'l Business 239.

White, William R., 'The Implications of the FTA and NAFTA for Canada and Mexico' Technical Report No. 70 (Bank of Canada, undated).

Winham, Gilbert R., 'NAFTA and the Trade Policy Revolution of the 1980s: a Canadian Perspective' (1994) XLIX:3 Int'l J 472 (Canadian Institute of International Affairs).

Wonnacott, Ronald J., 'Canada's Role in NAFTA: To What Degree has it been Defensive?', in Victor Bulmer-Thomas, Nikki Craske and Mónica Serrano (eds), *Mexico and the North American Free Trade Agreement: Who Will Benefit?* (St Martin's Press, New York, 1994), Ch. 11, pp. 163–75.

United States Banking System

ACIR (Advisory Commission on Intergovernmental Relations), State Regulation of Banks in an Era of Deregulation (A-110; September 1988).

Ackerman, Corey B., 'Note: World-Wide Volkswagen, Meet the World Wide Web: An Examination of Personal Jurisdiction Applied to a New World' (1997) 71 St John's L Rev 403.

Akins, Jacqueline S., 'Selected Statutes and Regulations Affecting Day-to-Day Bank Operations' (1994) 48 Cons Fin L 368.

Baxter, Lawrence G., 'The Rule of Too Much Law? The New Safety/Soundness Rulemaking Responsibilities of the Federal Banking Agencies' (1993) 47 Consumer Finance Law QR 210.

Bierman, Leonard, and Donald R. Fraser, 'The Canada-United States Free Trade Agreement and US Banking: Implications for Policy Reform' (1988) 29 Va J Int'l Law 1.

Brill, Robert M., and James J. Bjorkman, 'Federal Court Jurisdiction over International Banking Transactions' (1993) 110 Banking LJ 118.

Burand, Deborah, 'Regulation of Foreign Banks' Entry into the United States Under the FBSEA: Implementation and Implications' (1993) 24:4 L & Policy in Int'l Business 1089.

Caskey, John P., 'Explaining the Boom in Check-Cashing Outlets and Pawnshops' (1995) 49 Consumer Finance L QR 4.

Corrigan, E. Gerald, 'Commercial Banking in the United States: A Look Back and a Look Ahead: After a Turbulent Decade, Baking Faces a Long and Difficult Road to Renewal' (1992) 15 *GAO Journal* 10.

Curley, Bob, 'Charting Virtual Territory', *Banking Systems + Technology* (Nov. 1997) (downloaded from >http://www.financetech.com/db/_area/archives2/bst/1997/9711/22.htm<).

Dunne, Gerald T., 'The Glass-Steagall Wall: Subtle Hazards Revisited' (1994) 111 Banking LJ 115.

Dunne, Gerald T., 'Toward a Truly National System' (1993) 110 Banking LJ 3 (headnote).

Ferraté, Alejandro, 'Foreign Direct Investment in Costa Rica After the "Death" of CBI' (1996) 2:2 J Int'l Leg Stud 119.

Franzen, Corrine A., 'Increasing the Competitiveness of US Corporations: Is Bank Monitoring the Answer?' (1993) 2:2 Minn J of Global Trade 271.

Garwood, Griffith L., and Dolores S. Smith, 'The Community Reinvestment Act: Evolution and Current Issues' *Federal Reserve Bulletin* 251 (April 1993).

Haubrich, Joseph G., 'Bank Diversification: Laws and Fallacies of Large Numbers', Federal Reserve Bank of Cleveland Working Paper 9417 (December 1994).

Indick, Murray A., and Satish M. Kini, 'The Interstate Banking and Branching Efficiency Act: New Options, New Problems' (1995) 112 Banking LJ 100.

Kelley, Edward W. Jr, 'The Future of Electronic Payments' (BOG of Federal Reserve, New York, 31 October 1996).

Kies, W.J., 'Bank Expansion Through Foreign Branches under the Federal Reserve Act' (an Address Before the Association of the Reserve City Bankers' Fourth Annual Convention, Detroit, MI, 12 May 1916).

Lacovara, Philip A., 'Modernize Banking … But With Care: A Historical Reminder that Expanded Powers Could Lead to Expanded Problems' (1992) 15 *GAO Journal* 15.

Lance, Donna L., 'Can the Glass-Steagall Act be Justified Under the Global Free Market Policies of the NAFTA?' (1995) 34:2 Washburn LJ 297.

Lea, Haynes Pell, 'The Ramifications of the International Banking Act of 1978 on North Carolina: The Need to Adopt Legislation Enabling Foreign Banks to Establish Federal Agencies and Limited Branches' (1981) 7:1 No Carol J Int'l L & Comm Reg. 67.

Lichtenstein, Cynthia C., 'US Restructuring Legislation: Revising the International Banking Act of 1978, For the Worse?' (1992) 60 Fordham L Rev S37.

Loss, Louis, and Joel Seligman, 'Securities Regulation', in David L. Ratner and Thomas Lee Hazan, *Securities Regulation: Cases and Materials* (5th edn, West Publishing, St Paul, MN, 1996), pp. 76–81

Lynyak, Joseph T. III, 'Foreign Bank Supervision: The Regulation K Amendments' (1994) 111 Banking LJ 464.

Moudi, Henri, 'The State of US Banking in the Global Arena' (1992) 10:2 Boston Univ Int'l LJ 255.

Note, 'The New American Universal Bank' (1997) 110:6 Harv L Rev 1310.

Nunes, M.A., 'Foreign Banks Come Sailing In As United States Banks Tack Slowly Upwind' (1990) 13:1 Houston J Int'l L 39.

O'Connor, Walter F., 'Tax on Foreign Banks: How Times Have Changed' (1989) 15 Int'l Tax J 323.

Phillips, Susan M., 'Supervisory and Regulatory Responses to Financial Innovation and Industry Dynamics' (BOG of Federal Reserve, 25 November 1996).

Price, William, 'A Nonbanker's Perspective on Banking Reform' (1992) 15 *GAO Journal* 29.

Redman, Russell, 'Sweetening the Appeal of ATMs', *Bank Systems + Technology* (November 1997), downloaded from >http://www.financetech.com/db/_area/archives2/bst/1997/9711/08.htm<.

Roderer, David W., and William B.F. Steinman, 'The Authority for Banks to Sell Annuities and Insurance Related Products' (1994) 48 Consumer Finance L QR 395.

Simmons, Craig A., and Stephen C. Swain, 'Girding for Competition' (1992) 15 *GAO Journal* 3.

Symons, Edward L. Jr, 'The United States Banking System' (1993) 19:1 Brooklyn J Int'l L 1.

Sullivan, Edward D., 'Glass-Steagall Update: Proposals to Modernize the Structure of the Financial Services Industry' (1995) 112 Banking LJ 977.

Wagman, Sarah A., 'Laws Separating Commercial Banking and Securities Activities as an Impediment to Free Trade in Financial Services: A Comparative Study of Competitiveness in the International Market for Financial Services' (1994) Mich J Int'l L 999.

European Union/EU Banking System (including EG Banking)

Abbott, Frederick M., 'The North American Free Trade Agreement and Its Implications for the European Union' (1994) 4:1 Tranat'l L & Comp Problems 119 (Symposium: Regional Economic Integration in the Global Marketplace).

Bellamy, Christopher, 'Free Movement of Capital in the Community: An Outline of the Implications for EFTA', in Mary Robinson and Jantien Findlater (eds), *Creating a European Economic Space: Legal Aspects of EC-EFTA Relations* (Irish Center for European Law, Trinity College, Dublin, 1990), pp. 239–60.

Carter, Barry, 'A Code of Conduct for EC-US Relations', in Jürgen Schwartz (ed.), *The External Relations of the European Community, In Particular EC-US Relations* (Nomos Verlags, Baden-Baden, 1989), pp. 131–9.

Commission of the European Communities, 'Green Paper: Financial Services: Meeting Consumers' Expectations' (COM(96) 209 final; Brussels, 22.05.1996).

Eizenstat, Stuart E., 'US Relations with the European Union and the Changing Europe' (1995) 9:1 Emory Int'l L Rev 1.

European Parliament, 'Report of the Committee on External Economic Relations on the Free Trade Agreement between the United States of America, Canada and Mexico (NAFTA)' DOC_EN/RR/217/217513, (18 November 1992)(A3-0378/92).

Fischer, Peter, 'Die Ordnungsprinzipien des nordamerikanischen und europäischen Wirtschaftsraumes in rechtsvergleichender Sicht', in Franz Matscher and Ignaz Seidl-Hohenveldern (eds), *Europa im Aufbruch: Festschrift Fritz Schwind zum 80. Geburtstag* (Manzsche Verlags- und Universitätsbuchhandlung, Vienna, 1993), pp. 251–68.

García Jiménez, Gonzalo, 'The New Commercial Strategy of the European Union towards Latin America: In Search of Market Access through a Regional and Specific Approach', in Paul Demaret, Jean-François Bellis and Gonzalo García Jiménez (eds), *Regionalism and Multilateralism after the Uruguay Round:*

Convergence, Divergence and Interaction (Institut d'études Juridiques Européennes, University of Liège, Liège, 1997), pp. 265–94.

Grenon, Jean-Yves, 'L'Accord de Libre-échange Nord-Américain: Comparé à la communauté économique européenne' (1993) 367 *Revue du Marché Commun et de l'Union Européen* 306.

Hagdahl, Thomas, 'Doing Business in a Wider Europe', in Mary Robinson and Jantien Findlater, *Creating a European Economic Space: Legal Aspects of EC-EFTA Relations* (1990), pp. 229–37.

Hammen, Horst, 'Beschränkung von Beteiligungen der Kreditinstitute an Nichtbankunternehmen' (1996) 160 *Zeitschrift für Handelsrecht* (ZHR) 133.

Holland, Kenneth M., '1 NAFTA and the Single European Act', in T. David Mason and Abdul M. Turay (eds), *Japan, NAFTA and Europe: Trilateral Cooperation or Confrontation?* (St Martin's Press, New York, 1994), pp. 1–37.

James, A., 'Exporting Insider Trading Laws: The Enforcement of US Insider Trading Laws Internationally' (1995) 9:1 Emory Int'l L Rev 345.

Kampf, Roger, 'Ein beachtlicher (Teil-)Erfolg: Finanzdienstleistungen als integraler Bestandteil des GATS', in Daniel Thürer and Stephan Kux, *GATT 94 und die Welthandelsorganisation: Herausforderung für die Schweiz und Europa* (Schulthess Polygraphischer Verlag, Zurich, 1996), pp. 167–87.

Kuijper, Pieter, 'The Conclusion and Implementation of the Uruguay Round Results by the European Community' (1995) 6:2 Eur L Int'l L 222.

Malet, Jaime, 'Movement Towards Financial Integration and Monetary Union in the European Communities' (1990) 13:1 Houston J Int'l L 79.

Matthews, Barbara C., 'The Second Banking Directive: Conflicts, Choices, and Long-Term Goals' (1992) 2:1 Duke J Comp & Int'l L 89.

Mayer, Pierre, 'The Private International Law Aspects of European Integration' (June 1994) Hitotsubashi J of Law and Politics 93.

Napier, Brian, (ed.), 'A European Passport for Investment Services' (March 1994) J of Business L 195.

Newman, Karl, (ed.), 'Current Developments/European Community Law: Company Law and Trade in Securities' (1995) 44 Int'l & Comp LQ 214.

Powell, Jane Louise, '1992: Single European Market Implications for the Insurance Sector' (1990) 13:2 Boston Coll Int'l & Comp L Rev 371.

Rossini, Christine, 'Cross-Border Banking in the EC: Host Country Powers Under the Second Banking Directive' (1995) 4 European Rev of Private L 571.

Scheer, Craig M., 'The Second Banking Directive and Deposit Insurance in the European Union: Implications for US Banks' (1994) 28:1 Geo Wash J Int'l L & Economics 171 (note).

Schwok, René, and Christophe Bonte, 'European Economic Area and Switzerland-European Union Bilateral Agreements in Comparative Perspective: What Lessons?', in Paul Demaret, Jean-François Bellis and Gonzalo García Jiménez (eds), *Regionalism and Multilateralism after the Uruguay Round: Convergence, Divergence and Interaction* (Institut d'études Juridiques Européennes, University of Liège, Liège, 1997), pp. 27–58, followed by Comment by Jonas W. Myhre.

Siegel, Shari, 'Slouching Toward Integration: International Banking Before and After 1992' (1989) 11:1 Cardozo L Rev 147.

Strange, Susan, 'The Persistence of the Problems in EC-US Relations: Conflicts of Perception?', in Jürgen Schwartz (ed.), *The External Relations of the European Community, In Particular EC-US Relations* (Nomos Verlags, Baden-Baden, 1989), pp. 109–18.

Wegen, Gerhard, 'Transnational Financial Services—Current Challenges for an Integrated Europe' (1992) 60:6 Fordham L Rev S91.

Woods, Therese M., 'The EEC-Mexican Agreement: Time for Reevaluation?' (1989) 12:3 Fordham Int'l LJ 541.

International Banking System

Alford, Duncan E., 'Basle Committee Minimum Standards: International Regulatory Response to the Failure of BCCI' (1992) 26:2 Geo Wash J Int'l L & Economics 241.

Aubert, Maurice, and Donald Cronson, 'Bank Secrecy and Supervision of Swiss Foreign Bank Affliates' (1992) 14 Comp L YB of Int'l Business 205.

Bhala, Raj, 'Equilibrium Theory, the FICAS Model, and International Banking Law' (1997) 38:1 Harv Int'l LJ 1.

Blair, William, 'Extraterritorial Orders Affecting Banks: The English Experience', 1991–92) Banking & Finance L Rev 429.

Blattner, Niklaus, 'Banking', in Peter Zweifel (ed.), *Services in Switzerland: Structure, Performance, and Implications of European Economic Integration* (Springer-Verlag, Berlin/Heidelberg, 1993), pp. 163–82.

Byron, H. Thomas III, 'A Conflict of Laws Model for Foreign Branch Deposit Cases' (1991) 58:2 Univ Chic L Rev 671.

Camil, Jorge, 'The Nationalized Banking System and Foreign Debt' (1984) 18:2 Int'l Lawyer 323.

City of Bits, '4.9 Banking Chambers' >http://www-mitpress.mit.edu/ City_of_Bi..._Architecture/BankingChambersATMs.html<.

Cornford, Andrew J., 'Banking Under a Regime for World Trade in Services' 18 *UNCTAD Bulletin* 1 (Jan.–Feb. 1993).

Durić, Hans-Peter, *Die Freihandelsabkommen EG-Schweiz: Die rechtliche Problematik* (undated), pp. 104–5.

EDA, *Die Schweiz in Europa: Gestern Heute Morgen* (EDA, Bern, 1992).

EDA/EVD, *EWR Botschaft: Kurzfassung* (EDA, Bern, undated).

Epstein, Gerald, and Herbert Gintis, 'International Capital Markets and National Economic Policy' (1995) 2:4 Rev Int'l Pol Econ 693.

Faber, Mike, 'Guidelines on the Treatment of Foreign Direct Investment', in UNCTAD, *International Monetary and Financial Issues for the 1990s*, Vol. 3 (UNCTAD, 1993), pp. 85–100.

Garten, Helen A., 'Universal Banking and Financial Stability' (1993) 19:1 Brooklyn J Int'l L 159.

Gibson, L. Todd, 'The Foreign Bank Supervision Enhancement Act of 1991: Short Run Consequences En Route to the Long Term Goal' (1995) 27:1 Case West Res J Int'l L 119.

Greenspan, Alan, 'Banking in the Global Marketplace' (speech by Chairman, BOG in Tokyo, 18 November 1996).

Harris, Stephen L., and Charles A. Pigott, 'A Changed Landscape for Financial Services' 206 *OECD Observer* 28 (June–July 1997).

Hawley, F. William, 'Perspective of the Private Sector—Banking' (1989) 19:2 Ga J Int'l & Comp L 404.

Helbling, Thomas, 'Explaining the Presence of Foreign Financial Intermediaries in Switzerland', in Niklaus Blattner, Hans Genberg and Alexander K. Swoboda (eds), *Banking in Switzerland* (Physica Verlag, Heidelberg, 1993), pp. 145–97.

Helleiner, Eric, 'Explaining the Globalization of Financial Markets: Bringing the States Back In' (1995) 2:2 Rev Int'l Pol Econ 315.

Hultman, Charles W., 'Regulation of International Banking: A Review of the Issues' (1992) 26:5 J World Trade 79.

Issing, Otmar, 'Geldpolitik in einer Welt globalisierter Finanzmärkte' (1996) 51:3 *Aussenwirtschaft* 295.

Kurosawa, Yoshitaka, 'Institutional Investors: Global Scale Securities Markets and Insurance, Trust, and Annuity Groups' (1993) 16 Hastings Int'l & Comp L Rev 231.

Licht, Georg, and Dietmar Moch, 'Innovation and Information Technology in Services', Discussion Paper No. 97-20 (Zentrum für Europäische Wirtschaftsforschung GmbH (ZEW), Mannheim, 1997).

Marcuss, Stanley J., 'Jurisdiction with Respect to Foreign Branches and Subsidiaries: Judicial Power in the Foreign Affairs Context Under Section 414 of the Foreign Relations Restatement' (1992) 26:1 Int'l Lawyer 1.

Mottet, Louis H., 'Die Schweiz und Ihre Banken', in Louis H. Mottet (ed.), *Geschichte der Schweizer Banken: Bankier-Persönlichkeiten aus fünf Jahrhunderten* (Verlag Neue Zürcher Zeitung, Zurich, 1987), pp. 9–38.

Norton, Joseph Jude, 'The Multidimensions of the Convergence Processes Regarding the Prudential Supervision of International Banking Activities—The Impact of the Basle Supervisors Committee's Efforts Upon, Within and Without the European Union' in Werner F. Ebke & Joseph J. Norton (eds), *Festschrift in Honor of Sir Joseph Gold* (Verlag Recht und Wirtschaft, Heidelberg, 1990), pp. 249–307.

OECD, *The New Financial Landscape: Forces Shaping the Revolution in Banking, Risk Management and Capital Markets* (OECD, Paris, 1995).

Peters, Rebecca G., 'Money Laundering and Its Current Status in Switzerland: New Disincentives for Financial Tourism' (1990) 11:1 NW J Int'l L & Business 104.

Semkow, Brian W., 'Syndicating and Rescheduling International Financial Transactions: A Survey of the Legal Issues Encountered by Commercial Banks' (1984) 18:4 Int'l Lawyer 869.

Senti, Richard, 'Multilaterale Wirtschaftsdiplomatie der Schweiz Seit 1945', in Ronald Cicurel (ed.), *1291 1991 Die Schweizerischen Wirtschaft: Geschichte in Drei Akten* (SQP Publications, St Sulpice, 1991), pp. 172–5.

Seymann, Marilyn R., 'Banking's Role in Emerging Secondary Markets' (1993) 47 Consumer Finance L QR 253.

Sheldon, George, and Urs Haegler, 'Economies of Scale and Scope and Inefficiencies in Swiss Banking', in Niklaus Blattner, Hans Genberg and Alexander Swoboda (eds), *Banking in Switzerland* (Physica Verlag, Heidelberg, 1993) pp. 103–129.

Silard, Stephan A., 'International Law and the Conditions for Order in International Finance: Lessons for the Debt Crisis', in Werner F. Ebke and Joseph J. Norton (eds), *Festschrift in Honor of Sir Joseph Gold* (Verlag Recht und Wirtschaft, Heidelberg, 1990), pp. 387–402.

Swiss Quality Banking: Guide to the Swiss Economy and Business Opportunities, 6th issue, Sept. 1994 (various articles).

Tanner, Jakob, 'Banken und Franken: Zur Geschichte des Schweizerischen Finanzplatzes im 19. und 20. Jahrhundert', in Ronald Cicurel (ed.), *1291 1991 Die Schweizerischen Wirtschaft: Geschichte in Drei Akten* (SQP Publications, St Sulpice, 1991), pp. 168–71.

Trachtman, Joel P., 'Recent Initiatives in International Financial Regulation and Goals of Competitiveness, Effectiveness, Consistency and Cooperation' (1991) 12 NW J Int'l L & Bus 241.

Weber, Ernst-Juerg, 'Schweizerische Finanz- und Währungsgeschichte: Vorlesungsunterlagen' (University of Zurich, Zurich, 1996), pp. 1–29 (mimeo).

Weber, Ernst-Juerg, 'Free Banking in Switzerland After the Liberal Revolutions in the Nineteenth Century', in K. Dowd (ed.), *The Experience of Free Banking* (Routledge, London, 1992), pp. 188–205.

NAFTA and the Banking System

Appleton, Barry, 'Investment', in *Navigating NAFTA: A Concise User's Guide to the North American Free Trade Agreement* (Carswell, Toronto, undated), pp. 79–89.

Bachman, Kenneth L., Scott N. Benedict, Ricardo A. Anzaldua, 'Financial Services Under the North American Free Trade Agreement: An Overview', in Judith H. Bello, Alan F. Holmer and Joseph J. Norton (eds), *The North American Free Trade Agreement: A New Frontier in International Trade and Investment in the Americas* (American Bar Association, Washington, DC, 1994), pp. 209–31.

Bachman, Kenneth L., Scott N. Benedict and Ricardo A. Anzaldúa, 'Financial Services under the North American Free Trade Agreement: An Overview' (1994) 28:2 Int'l Lawyer 291.

Broadman, Harry G., 'International Trade and Investment in Services: A Comparative Analysis of the NAFTA' (1993) 27:3 Int'l Lawyer 623.

Busse, Matthias, 'NAFTA's Impact on the European Union' (1996) 51:3 *Aussenwirtschaft* 363.

Eklund, Cheri D., 'A Primer on the Arbitration of NAFTA Chapter Eleven Investor-State Disputes' (1994) 11:4 J Int'l Arb 135.

Fasken Martineau Barristers and Solicitors, 'Financial Services', in *The North American Free Trade Agreement: A Guide for Business: What It Says and How It Will Work* (Fasken Martineau, 1993), pp. 19–23.

Gestrin, Michael, and Alan M. Rugman, 'The North American Free Trade Agreement and Foreign Direct Investment' (1994) 3:1 Transnat'l Corporations 77.

Glick, Leslie Alan, 'F. Financial Services', in L A Glick, *Understanding the North American Free Trade Agreement* (Kluwer, Boston, 1993), pp. 28–32.

Glick, Leslie Alan, 'Recent Legislative Developments Affecting US-Mexico Trade and Investment' (1995) 3 US-Mex LJ 37.

Kennish, Tim, 'NAFTA and Investment—A Canadian Perspective', in Seymour J. Rubin and Dean Alexander (eds), *NAFTA and Investment* (Kluwer, Boston, 1995), pp. 1–35.

Kozolchyk, Boris, 'Introduction to the Guidelines for the Clearing of Checks Between Canada, the United States, and Mexico' (1993) 1 *Banking and Commercial Credit* 340.

Laderman, Elizabeth, and Ramon Moreno, 'NAFTA and US Banking', *FRBSF Weekly Letter*, 13 November 1992, pp. 92–40 (Federal Reserve Board of San Francisco).

Levin, Richard C., and Susan Erickson Marin, 'NAFTA Chapter 11: Investment and Investment Disputes' (Summer 1996) NAFTA L & Bus Rev of the Americas 82.

MacAllister, Karen, 'NAFTA: How the Banks in the United States and Mexico Will Respond' (1994) 17 Hous J Int'l L 273.

Massee, Michael, 'Foreign Bank Supervision Enhancement Act of 1991 and NAFTA: Will an Expanded Federal Role in the Supervision of Foreign Banks and a Continental Market Combine to Spur Reform of the Domestic Banking Industry?' (1993) 1 *Toward Seamless Borders* 245.

McNevin, Valerie J., 'Policy Implications of the NAFTA for the Financial Services Industry' (1994) 5 Colo J Int'l Env'l L & Pol 369.

Miller, Steven, 'Citibank has jump on competition', *NAFTA Watch* (download).

Nadal Egea, Alejandro, 'Balance-of-Payments Provisions in the GATT and NAFTA' (1996) 30:4 J World Trade 4.

Napier, Brian, (ed.), 'NAFTA: A New Framework for Regulation and Supervision of Financial Services in the Americas' (1994) J of Business L 394.

Nederkoorn, Heinz, 'Die Finanzdienstleistungen im Nordamerikanischen Freihandelsabkommen (NAFTA)' (1993) 48:3 *Aussenwirtschaft* 337.

Nelson, Todd, 'Secured Financing Project' (internet at >http://www.natlaw.com/pubs/sfproj.htm<).

Powers, Linda, 'NAFTA and the Regulation of Financial and Other Services' (1993) 1:1 US-Mex LJ 65.

Simser, Jeffrey, 'Financial Services Under NAFTA: A Starting Point' (1994–95) 10 Banking & Finance L Rev 185.

Trachtman, Joel P., 'Trade in Financial Services under GATS, NAFTA and the EC: A Regulatory Jurisdictional Analysis' (1995) 34 Columbia J Transnt'l L 39.

Weintraub, Sidney, Chandler Stolp and Leigh Boske, 'Banking', in *US-Mexican Free Trade: the Effect on Textiles and Apparel, Petrochemicals, and Banking in Texas* (US-Mexican Policy Studies Program, Policy Report No. 5, Austin, TX, 1993), pp. 81–111.

Zamora, Stephen T., 'Comments on the Regulation of Financial and Legal Services in Mexico under NAFTA' (1993) 1:1 US-Mex LJ 77 (Symposium: The Problems and Prospects of a North American Free Trade Agreement).

Zangari, B.J., (ed.), 'Financial Service Provisions', in *NAFTA: Issues, Industry, Sector Profiles and Bibliography* (Nova Science Publishers, 1994), pp. 31–41.

Other NAFTA

Abbott, Frederick M., 'NAFTA and the Future of United States—European Community Trade Relations: The Consequences of Asymmetry in an Emerging Era of Regionalism' (1993) 16 Hastings Int'l & Comp L Rev 489.

Abbott, Frederick M., 'The NAFTA as Architecture for Political Decision' (Draft, 21 May 1997: Project on Domestic Politics and International Law; St. Helena, CA (forthcoming)).

Ackerman, Bruce, and David Golove, 'Is NAFTA Constitutional?' (1995) 108:4 Harv L Rev 799.

Alexander, Dean, 'The Likely Impact of NAFTA on Investment in Selected Goods and Services Sectors in Mexico, Canada, and the US', in Seymour J. Rubin and Dean Alexander (eds), *NAFTA and Investment* (Kluwer, Boston, 1995), pp. 147–60.

Alexander, Dean, 'Selected United States-Mexico-Canada Cross-Border Investment and Trade Deals: 1994', in Seymour J. Rubin and Dean Alexander (eds), *NAFTA and Investment* (Kluwer, Boston, 1995), pp. 207–17.

Amsterdam, Robert R., and Peter W. Klestadt, 'NAFTA: A Symbol of Change', *Global Focus* (Winter 1994) (>http://www.amperlaw.com/1-2aa.html<).

Azulaye, Carole A., 'Mexico Modifies its Labeling Requirements Pursuant to NAFTA', NAFTA: L & Bus Rev Ams 83 (Spring 1995).

Baker, Steven W., 'Wearing Apparel Under NAFTA: Determining Origin for Preference Purposes' (1998) 4:1 NAFTA: L & Bus Rev Ams 105.

Barber, Michael, 'NAFTA Disute Resolution Provisions: Leaving Room for Abusive Tactics By Airlines Looking Southward' (1996) 61 J Air L & Commerce 991.

Bello, Judith H., 'The Current Status of the North American Free Trade Agreement' (1994) 2 US-Mex LJ 6.

Brown, Preston, and Carolyn Karr, 'The Transformation of the Maquiladora Under the North American Free Trade Agreement', in Seymour J. Rubin and Dean Alexander (eds), *NAFTA and Investment* 37-63 (Kluwer, Boston, 1995), pp. 37–63.

Buchanan, Ruth, 'Border Crossings: NAFTA, Regulatory Restructuring, and the Politics of Place' (1997) 11:2 Global Leg Stud J 371 (>http://www.law.ind…/no2/buchanan.html<).

Compa, Lance, 'International Labor Rights and the Sovereignty Question: NAFTA and Guatemala, Two Case Studies' (1993) 9 Am U J Int'l L & Pol'y 117.

Covarrubias Meyer, Pascual, 'Whether for Chilean NAFTA (or NAFTA "Light") Accession: The Necessity of Fast Track Authority' (1998) 4:1 NAFTA: L & Bus Rev Ams 137.

Cross, Michael S., 'Towards a Definition of North American Culture', in Stephen J. Randall, Herman Konrad and Sheldon Silverman (eds), *North America Without Borders?* (University of Calgary Press, Calgary, 1992), pp. 303–12.

Diaz, Luis Miguel, 'Private Rights Under the Environment and Labor Agreements' (1994) 2 US-Mex LJ 11.

Endsley, Harry B., 'Dispute Settlement Under the CFTA and NAFTA: From Eleventh Hour Innovation to Accepted Institution' (1995) 18 Hastings Int'l & Comp L Rev 659.

Esty, Daniel C., 'Making Trade and Environmental Policies Work Together: Lessons from NAFTA' (1994) 49:1 *Aussenwirtschaft* 59.

Fierro, Héctor Fix, and Sergio López Ayllón, 'El Tratado de Libre Comercio de América del Norte y la Globalizaciòn del Derecho', in Jorge Witker (ed.), *El Tratado de Libre Comercio de America del Norte: Análisis, Diagnóstico y Propuestas Jurídicos*, Vol. 1 (Instituto de Investigaciones Jurídicas, Mexico, 1993).

Foster, Kent S., and Dean Alexander, 'Selected United States-Mexico-Canada Cross-Border Investment and Trade Deals: 1992–1993', in Seymour J. Rubin and Dean Alexander (eds), *NAFTA and Investment* (Kluwer, Boston, 1995), pp. 185–205.

Garcia, Frank J., 'Decisionmaking and Dispute Resolution in the Free Trade Area of the Americas: An Essay in Trade Governance' (1997) 18:2 Mich J Int'l L 357.

García Moreno, Víctor Carlos and César Emiliano Hernández Ochoa, 'Towards a Free Trade Agreement Between Mexico and the United States: Legal Implications, in Jorge Witker (ed.), *Legal Aspects of the Trilateral Free Trade Agreement* (Universidad Nacional Autónoma de México, Mexico City, 1992), pp. 45–75.

Glover, Stephen I., and JoEllen Lotvedt, 'The Mexican Telecommunications Market: The Interplay of Internal Reform and NAFTA' (1997) 3:1 NAFTA: L & Bus Rev Ams 23.

Göll, Edgar, 'NAFTA als neues Instrument regionaler Wirtschaftskooperation' (1994) 49:2 *Europa Archiv* 43.

Gordon, Michael W., 'Some Comments and Comparisons: GATT and NAFTA' (1993) 1 US-Mex LJ 25.

Herzstein, Robert E., 'The Labor Cooperation Agreement Among Mexico, Canada and the United States: Its Negotiation and Prospects' (1995) 3 US-Mex LJ 121.

Hagen, Katherine A., 'Fundamentals of Labor Issues and NAFTA' (1994) 27 UC Davis L Rev 917.

Hufbauer, Gary Clyde, and Jeffrey Schott, 'Implications for Nonmember Countries', in *North American Free Trade: Issues and Recommendations* (Institute for International Economics, Washington, DC, 1992), pp. 111–29.

Inman, Harry A., 'US-Mexican Trade: New Initiatives Are Needed Now' (1981) 7:3 No Carol J Int'l & Comp Reg 355.

Kozolchyk, Boris, 'Introduction to the Guidelines for the Clearing of Checks between Canada, the United States, and Mexico' (1993) 1 *Toward Seamless Borders* 340–351.

Lustig, Nora Claudia, 'NAFTA: Setting the Record Straight', Brookings Policy Brief No. 20 (1997) (internet download at >http://www.brook.e...olicy/Polbrf20.htm<).

Lutz, Robert E., 'Current Developments in the North American Free Trade Agreement: A Guide for Future Economic Integration Efforts' (1997) 18 Whittier L Rev 313 (13th Annual International Law Symposium: Negotiating the Free Trade Labyrinth: Your Map to the 21st Century).

Mackay, Donald R., 'The North American Free Trade Agreement: Its Possible Extension to South American Countries', in Paul Demaret, Jean-François Bellis and Gonzalo García Jiménez (eds), *Regionalism and Multilateralism after the Uruguay Round: Convergence, Divergence and Interaction* (Institut d'études Juridiques Européennes, University of Liège, Liège, 1997), pp. 235–49, followed by Comment by Sergio López-Ayllón.

Méndez, Manuel O., and John H. Knox, 'NAFTA's Effect on State Agencies and Administrative Law', 7th Annual Advanced Administrative Law Course; State Bar of Texas, Austin September 1995) (found on internet 9 September 1997).

NAFTA: Law and Business Review of the Americas, 'Summit of the Americas' 88 (Spring 1995).

NAFTA: Law and Business Review of the Americas, 'Member States Developments: Canada' 114 (Spring 1995).

NAFTA: Law and Business Review of the Americas, 'Implementation: Mexico' 139 (Winter 1995).

The North American Institute (NAMI), NAMI Reports, revised 7 November 1996 by Kevin Drennan; including:

Austin, Jack (Senator), 'Canadian Federalism Revisited'

Barragá, Esteban Moctezuma, 'The New Federalism in Mexico'

'Discussion: A New Model for Sub-National Regions in North America'

'Discussion: Evolving Federalism: The Role of the State in North America'

'Discussion: Managing the Nation-State: Subsidiarity and Fiscal Federalism'

'Discussion: NAFTA After Two Years: How Fare the New Institutions'

'Discussion: The State of the North American Community'

Finbow, Robert, 'The Labor Side Agreement'

Harcourt, Michael (The Hon.), 'Introduction'

Inkeles, Alex, 'Opening Comments'

Lutz, Robert E., 'Resolving Trade Disputes'

McKinnon, Ronald, 'Capital Markets and Fiscal Federalism in Canada and the United States'

Mendelson, Michael, 'The Erosion of National Social Capital in Canada'

Pachter, Marc, 'The Unsuitable North Americans'

Phillips, Alfredo, 'Keynote Speech: The Role of NADBank as a New Institution'

Rom, Mark Carl, 'Welfare Programs: Sinking Swiftly and Silently'

Rosaldo, Renato, 'The Requisites of Community'

SuáDá, Francisco (Dip.), 'Funding Infrastructure Needs and Fiscal Federalism in Mexico'

'Summary of Recommendations'

Swinton, Katherine, 'Federalism and Regionalism in Canada: Rebalancing or Offloading?'

Vargas, Luz Lajous (Senator), 'Reshaping Mexican Politics and Institutions'

Weingast, Barry, 'Market-Preserving Federalism'

Wirth, John D., 'Environmental Cooperation'

Osmond, Carol S., and Claire Wright, 'The NAFTA Marking Rules of Origin' (1996) 1 Int'l Trade Law & Reg 9.

Pethke, Ralph, 'Die präferentiellen Ursprungsregeln in der Nordamerikanischen Freihandelszone (NAFTA)' (1998) 44:2 *Recht der Internationalen Wirtschaft* 128.

Public Citizen, 'NAFTA's Broken Promises: The Border Betrayed—Recommendations' (internet print-out).

Quinter, Peter, 'NAFTA: A Practical Appraisal' Export Observer (1996) (>http://www.unzexport.com/observer/nov96/practical.html<).

Radio Free America, '(Transcript) Tom Valentine with Glen Kealey and Shelley Ann Clarke' 23 March 1994, broadcast over WWCR, Nashville, TN, Band 49 at 5810 (>http://www.turnercom.com/jdk/cana14.html<).

Sheenen, James M., 'How's NAFTA Now?' (Competitive Enterprise Institute), internet printout.

Simpson, John P., 'North American Free Trade Agreement—Rules of Origin' (1994) 28:1 J World Trade 33.

Smith, James F., 'NAFTA and Human Rights: A Necessary Linkage' (1994) 27 UC Davis L Rev 793.

Stankovsky, Jan, 'NAFTA a její v'yznam pro Evropu' (1995) 2 *Mezinàrodnì vztahy* 66.

Stevens, Geneva E., 'Telecommunications Under the NAFTA and Its Effect on Canada's Telecommunications Industry' (1997) 3:1 NAFTA: L & Bus Rev Ams 93.

Van Pelt, Laura J., 'Countervailing Environmental Subsidies: A Solution to the Environmental Inequities of the North American Free Trade Agreement' (1994) 29:1 Texas Int'l LJ 123.

Vogel, Sarah M., 'The Effects of NAFTA Upon North Dakota State Law' (1994) 70:3 No Dakota L Rev 485.

Waddell, Bruce, 'NAFTA Problems and Solutions for US Business' >http://www.flash.net/~mexis/experts/nafta_waddell_01.html<.

Whalley, John, and Colleen Hamilton, 'The Intellectual Underpinnings of North American Economic Integration' (1995) 4:1 Minn J Global Trade 43.

Witker, Jorge, and Rich Robins, 'A Critical Analysis of the Post-1994 Elections: Mexican Foreign Investment Regulatory Scheme', in Seymour J. Rubin and Dean Alexander (eds), *NAFTA and Investment* (Kluwer, Boston, 1995), pp. 111–45.

Witker, Jorge, (ed.), 'Introducción', in Jorge Witker, *El Tratado de Libre Comercio de América del Norte: Análisis, diagnóstico y propuestas jurídicos*, Vol. 1 (Universidad Nacional Autònoma de México, Mexico, 1993).

Dispute Settlement (WTO/NAFTA/theory)

Applegate, J. Todd, 'Chapter 19 of the NAFTA: Are Binational Panels Constitutional?' (1997) 3:3 NAFTA: L & Bus Rev Ams 129.

Carmody, Chi, 'Of Substantial Interest: Third Parties under GATT' (1997) 18:4 Mich J Int'l L 615.

Deyling, Robert P., 'Free Trade Agreements and the Federal Courts: Emerging Issues' (1996) 27 St Mary's LJ 353.

Hauser, Heinz and Andrea Martel, 'Das WTO-Streitschlichtungsverfahren: Eine ver-handlungsorientierte Perspektive' (1997) 52:4 *Aussenwirtschaft* 525.

Juenger, Friedrich K., 'Governmental Interests—Real and Spurious—in Multistate Disputes' (1988) 21:3 UC Davis L Rev 515.

Moody-O'Grady, Kristin, 'Dispute Settlement Provisions in the NAFTA and the CAFTA: Progress or Protectionism?' (1994) 18:1 *Fletcher Forum of World Affairs* 121.

Parra, Carlos Angulo, 'Comments on the Potential Influence of NAFTA on Procedures for the Settlement of Disputes' (1993) 1 US-Mex LJ 29, followed by Michael Gordon, 'Some Comments'.

Pescatore, Pierre, 'The New WTO Dispute Settlement Mechanism', in Paul Demaret, Jean-François Bellis and Gonzalo García Jiménez (eds), *Regionalism and Multilateralism after the Uruguay Round: Convergence, Divergence and Interaction* (Institut d'études Juridiques Européennes, University of Liège, Liège, 1997), pp. 661–86.

Petersmann, Ernst-Ulrich, 'The Dispute Settlement System of the World Trade Organization and the Evolution of the GATT Dispute Settlement System Since 1948' (1994) 31 Common Market L Rev 1157.

Reisman, W. Michael, 'Control Mechanisms in International Dispute Resolution' (1995) 3 US-Mex LJ 130.

Reisman, Michael, and Mark Wiedman, 'Contextual Imperatives of Dispute Resolution Mechanisms: Some Hypotheses and their Applications in the Uruguay Round and NAFTA' (1995) 29:3 J World Trade 5.

Rojas, Hector, 'The Dispute Resolution Process Under NAFTA' (1993) 1:1 US-Mex LJ 19 (Symposium: The Problems and Prospects of a North American Free Trade Agreement).

Schaefer, Matt, 'Are Private Remedies in Domestic Courts Essential for International Trade Agreements to Perform Constitutional Functions with Respect to Sub-Federal Governments?' (1996–97) 17:2/3 NW J Int'l L & Bus 609.

Thompson, William R., 'The Evolution of Political-Economic Challenges in the Active Zone' (1997) 4:2 Rev Int'l Pol Econ 286.

Wellens, Karel, 'Chapter 1: Fundamental Elements of the Court's Function', in Karel Wellens, *Economic Conflicts and Disputes Before the World Court (1922–1995): A Functional Analysis* 15-26 (Kluwer Law International, The Hague, 1996), pp. 15–21.

Wellens, Karel, 'Conclusion', in Karel Wellens, *Economic Conflicts and Disputes Before the World Court (1922–1995): A Functional Analysis* (Kluwer Law International, The Hague, 1996), pp. 251–95.

International Law (General)

Buxbaum, Richard M., 'The Reciprocal Influences of Facts and Norms', in Joseph Jude Norton (ed.), *Public International Law and the Future World Order: Liber Amicorum in honor of A.J. Thomas, Jr* (Rothman & Co, Littleton, CT, 1987), pp. 16-3-16-27.

Cutler, A. Claire, 'Artifice, Ideology and Paradox: the Public/Private Distinction in International Law' (1997) 4:2 Rev Int'l Pol Econ 261.

Koch, Harald, 'Private International Law: A 'Soft' Alternative to the Harmonization of Privte Law?' (1995) 3:2 Europ Rev Priv L 329.

Lim, Chin, and Olufemi Elias, 'The Role of Treaties in the Contemporary International Legal Order' (1997) 66:1 Nordic J Int'l L 1.

Plofchan, Thomas K., Jr, 'A Concept of International Law: Protecting Systemic Values' (1992) 33:1 Va J Int'l L 197.

Slaughter, Anne-Marie, 'International Law in a World of Liberal States' (1995) 6 Europ J Int'l L 503.

Wolf, James C., 'The Jurisprudence of Treaty Interpretation' (1988) 21:3 UC Davis L Rev 1023.

Wunschik, Johann, *Die Wirkung der völkerrechtlichen Verträge für dritte Staaten* (Emil Horat, Bern, 1930) (dissertation, University of Bern).

International Economic Law (General)

Ambrosius, Gerold, 'Internationale Wirtschaftsbeziehungen', in Gerold Ambrosius, Dietmar Petzina and Werner Plumpe (eds), *Moderne Wirtschaftsgeschichte: Eine Einführung für Historiker und Ökonomen* (Oldenburg, Munich, 1996), pp. 305–36.

Bellmann, Christophe, and Richard Gerster, 'Accountability in the World Trade Organization' (1996) 30: 6 J World Trade 31.

Carlisle, Charles R., 'Is the World Ready for Free Trade?' 75:6 *Foreign Affairs* 113 (Nov.–Dec. 1996).

Charnovitz, Steve, 'The World Trade Organization and Social Issues' (1994) 28:5 J World Trade 17.

Cooke, Philip, 'Regions in a Global Market: the Experiences of Wales and Baden-Württemberg' (1997) 4:2 Rev Int'l Pol Econ 349.

Croome, John, *Reshaping the World Trading System: A history of the Uruguay Round* (World Trade Organization, Geneva, 1995).

van Dijk, P., 'Nature and Function of Equity in International Economic Law' (1986) 7 *Grotiana* 4.

Fried, Jonathon T., 'Two Paradigms for the Role of International Trade Law' (1994) 20 Canada-US LJ 39.

Graham, Edward M., and Robert Z. Lawrence, 'Measuring the International Contestability of Markets: A Conceptual Approach' (1996) 30:5 J World Trade 5.

Gupta, Kanhaya L., and Robert Lensink, 'Introduction' and 'Banking Efficiency and Private Investment', in Kanhaya L. Gupta and Robert Lensink, *Financial Liberalization and Investment* (Routledge, London, 1996), pp. 1–9, 86–95.

Hart, Michael, 'Coercion or Cooperation: Social Policy and Future Trade Negotiations' (1994) 20 Canada-US LJ 351.

Hart, Michael, 'The WTO and the Political Economy of Globalization' (1997) 31:5 J World Trade 75.

Immenga, Ulrich, 'Entwicklung einer internationalen Wettbewerbsordnung— ein Instrument der Handelspolitik?', in Forschungsinstitut für Wirtschafts- verfassung und Wettbewerb, e.V. (ed.), *Die Bedeutung der WTO für die europäische Wirtschaft* (Carl Heymanns Verlag:, Cologne, 1997), pp. 107–20.

Investment Policy Advisory Committee (INPAC), 'The Uruguay Round of Multilateral Trade Negotiations', in Bernard D. Reams Jr and Jon S. Schultz (eds), *The North American Free Trade Agreement (NAFTA): Documents and Materials Including a Legislative History of the North American Free Trade Agreement Implementation Act: Public Law*, Vol. 27, Doc. 44 (1994), pp. 103–82.

Jackson, John H., 'Helms-Burton, the US, and the WTO', *ASIL Insight* (>http://www.asil.org/insight7.htm<).

Jackson, John H., 'US Constitutional Law Principles and Foreign Trade Law and Policy', in Meinhard Hilf and Ernst-Ulrich Petersmann (eds), *National Constitutions and International Economic Law* (Kluwer Law and Taxation Publishers, Deventer, 1993), pp. 65–89.

Kim, Yong K., 'The Beginnings of the Rule of Law in the International Trade System Despite US Constitutional Constraints' (1996) 17:4 Mich J Int'l L 967.

Kitson, Michael and Jonathon Michie, 'Conflict, Cooperation and Change: the Political Economy of Trade and Trade Policy' (1995) 2:4 Rev Int'l Pol Econ 632.

Leebron, David W., 'Implementation of the Uruguay Round Results in the United States', in John H. Jackson and Alan Sykes (eds), *Implementing the Uruguay Round* (Clarendon Press, Oxford, 1997), pp. 175–242.

Mattoo, Aaditya, and Arvind Subramanian, 'Multilateral Rules on Competition Policy: A Possible Way Forward' (1997) 31:5 J World Trade 95.

Merryman, John Henry, 'The Retention of Cultural Property' (1988) 21:3 UC Davis L Rev 477.

Mestmäcker, Ernst-Joachim, 'Rechtsfragen einer Ordnung der Weltwirtschaft', in Bodo Börner, Hermann Jahrreiss and Klaus Stern (eds), *Einigkeit und Recht und Freiheit: Festschrift für Karl Carstens*, Vol. 1 (Carl Heymanns Verlag, Cologne, 1984), pp. 417–27.

Morrison, Fred L., and Rüdiger Wolfrum, 'The Impact of Federalism on the Implementation of International Trade Obligations', in Meinhard Hilf and Ernst-Ulrich Petersmann (eds), *National Constitutions and International Economic Law* (Kluwer Law and Taxation Publishers, Deventer, 1993), pp. 519–35.

Oppermann, Thomas, '"Neue Weltwirtschaftsordnung" und Internationales Wirtschaftsrecht', in Bodo Börner, Hermann Jahrreiss and Klaus Stern (eds), *Einigkeit und Recht und Freiheit: Festschrift für Karl Carstens*, Vol. 1 (Carl Heymanns Verlag, Cologne, 1984), pp. 449–64.

Petersmann, Ernst-Ulrich, 'Why Do Governments Need the Uruguay Round Agreements, NAFTA and the EEA?' (1994) 49:1 *Aussenwirtschaft* 31.

Rikhze, Indar Jit, 'American Postures in Multilateral Negotiations' (1996) 1 Int'l Negotiation 295.

Roessler, Frieder, 'Diverging Domestic Policies and Multilateral Trade Integration', in Jagdish Bhagwati and Robert E. Hudec (eds), *Fair Trade and Harmonization: Prerequisites for Free Trade? Legal Analysis*, Vol. 2 (1996), pp. 21–56.

Rupert, Mark E., '(Re)Politicizing the Global Economy: Liberal Common Sense and Ideological Struggle in the US NAFTA Debate' (1995) 2:4 Rev Int'l Pol Econ 658.

Sassen, Saskia, 'Toward a Feminist Analytics of the Global Economy' (1996) 14:1 Global Leg Stud J 7 (from internet at >http://www.law.ind...14/ no1/ saspgp.html<).

Schaefer, Matt, and Thomas Singer, 'Multilateral Trade Agreements and US States: An Analysis of Potential GATT Uruguay Round Agreements' (1992) 26:5 J World Trade 45.

Seidl-Hohenveldern, Ignaz, 'Internationales Enteignungsrecht', in Alexander Lüderitz and Jochen Schröder (eds), *Internationales Privatrecht und Rechtsvergleichung im Ausgang des 20. Jahrhunderts: Bewahrung oder Wende?* (Alfred Metzner Verlag, Frankfurt aM, 1977), pp. 265–84.

Siebert, Horst, '9. Zölle, Handelshemmnisse und Welthandelsordnung', in Horst Sibert, *Aussenwirtschaft* (6th edn, Gustav Fischer, Jena, 1994), pp. 168–88.

Steger, Debra, 'Canadian Implementation of the Agreement Establishing the World Trade Organization', in John H. Jackson and Alan Sykes (eds), *Implementing the Uruguay Round* (Clarendon Press Oxford, 1997), pp. 243–83.

Stoll, Peter-Tobias, 'Freihandel und Verfassung. Einzelstaatliche Gewährleistung und die konstitutionelle Funktion der Welthandelsordung (GATT/WTO)' (1997) Zeitschrift f ausländisches und öffentliches R & VR 33.

Miscellaneous

Carothers, Thomas, 'Democracy Without Illusions' 76:1 *Foreign Affairs* 85 (Jan.–Feb. 1997).

Christensen, Benedicte Vibe, 'Development as an International Financial Center', in *Switzerland's Role as an International Financial Center* (IMF Occasional Paper No. 45, July 1986).

Collins, Hugh, 'European Private Law and the Cultural Identity of States' (1995) 3 Europ Private L Rev 353.

Compa, Lance A., 'The First Labor Cases: A New International Labor Rights Regime Takes Shape' (1995) 3 US-Mex LJ 159.

De George, Richard T., 'The Many Faces of Sovereignty' (1997) 17 *Rechtstheorie* 93.

Domínguez, Jorge I., 'Latin America's Crisis of Representation' 76:1 *Foreign Affairs* 100 (Jan.–Feb. 1997).

Dunning, John H., 'Governments and the Macro-Organization of Economic Activity: An Historical and Spatial Perspective' (1997) 4:1 Rev Int'l Pol Econ 42.

Falk, Richard A., 'Designing a New World Order', in *A Study of Future Worlds* (1975), pp. 150–223.

Fernández Jilberto, Alex E., and André Mommen, 'Setting the Neoliberal Development Agenda: Structural Adjustment and Export-Led Industrialization', in Alex E. Fernández Jilberto and André Mommen (eds), *Liberalization in the Developing World: Institutional and Economic Changes in Latin America, Africa and Asia* (London, Routledge, 1996), pp. 1–27.

Fry, Earl H., 'State and Local Governments in the International Arena', in John Kincaid (ed.), *The Annals of the American Academy of Political and Social Science*, No. 509 (May 1990), pp. 118–27.

Garten, Jeffrey E., 'Business and Foreign Policy' 76:3 *Foreign Affairs* 67 (May–June 1997).

Höffe, Otfried, 'Zwei Gesellschaftsverträge für Europa: Elf Thesen', Kolloquium: Geneva, 10 March 1995 (1. Fassung, manuscript).

Humphrey, James D. II, 'Student Note: Foreign Affairs Powers and "The First Crisis of the 21st Century": Congressional vs. Executive Authority and the Stabilization Plan for Mexico' (1995) 17 Mich J Int'l L 181.

Hirsch, Joachim, 'Nation-state, International Regulation and the Question of Democracy' (1995) 2:2 Rev Int'l Pol Econ 267.

Krädtke, Michael, 'Globalisierung und Standortkonkurrenz' (1997) 2 *Leviathan* 202.

Krugman, Paul, 'Dutch Tulips and Emerging Markets' (1995) 74:4 *Foreign Affairs* 28.

Luke, Timothy W., and Gearóid Ó. Tuathail, 'On Videocameralistics: the Geopolitics of Failed States, the CNN International and (UN)governmentality' (1997) 4:4 Rev Int'l Pol Econ 709.

MacCormick, Neil, 'Sovereignty, Democracy, Subsidiarity' (1994) 25 *Rechtstheorie* 281.

Mathews, Jessica T., 'Power Shift' 76:1 *Foreign Affairs* 50 (Jan.–Feb. 1997).

Naím, Moisés, 'Latin America the Morning After' (1995) 74:4 *Foreign Affairs* 45.

Norton, Patrick M., 'A Law of the Future or a Law of the Past? Modern Tribunals and the International Law of Expropriation' (1991) 85 Am J Int'l L 474.

OECD, Regulatory Reform and International Market Openness (OECD, Paris, 1996).

OECD, 'The OECD Report on Regulatory Reform: Summary' (May 1997) (>http://www.oecd.org<).

Otani, Yoshio, 'State Sovereignty and Common Interests in the International Community' (1994) Hitotsubashi J L & Politics 19 (Special Issue).

Peters, Christopher J., 'Foolish Consistency: On Equality, Integrity and Justice in Stare Decisis' (1996) 105 Yale LJ 2031.

Powell, Mark D., 'Electronic Commerce: An Overview of the Legal and Regulatory Issues' (1997) 3:3 Int'l Trade L & Reg 85.

Samuels, Barbara C. II, 'Emerging Markets Are Here to Stay' 74:6 *Foreign Affairs* 143 (Nov.–Dec. 1995).

Selgin, George A. and Lawrence H. White, 'How Would the Invisible Hand Handle Money?' (1994) 32 J Econ Lit 1718.

Sono, Kazuaki, 'Sovereignty, This Strange Thing: Its Impact on Global Economic Order' (1979) 9:3 Geo J Int'l & Comp L 549.

Sunstein, Cass R., 'Incompletely Theorized Arguments' (1995) 108 Harv L Rev 1733.

Sunstein, Cass R., 'Forward: Leaving Things Undecided' (1996) 110:1 Harv L Rev 4.

Vagts, Detlev F., 'Switzerland, International Law and World War II' (1997) 91:3 Am J Int'l L 466.

Walser, Rudolf, 'Die Schweiz vor der Herausforderung einer erweiterten Europäischen Union: Einige Gedankensplitter' (1994) 49:4 *Aussenwirtschaft* 461.

Zobl, Dieter, 'Zusammenfassung der Rechtsprechung: Das schweizerische Bankprivatrecht 1994-1996' (1997) 69:4 Schw Zeitschrift f Wirtschaftsrecht 148.

Index

International Banking, Finance and Economic Law

1. J.J. Norton, Chia-Jui Cheng and I. Fletcher (eds): *International Banking Regulation and Supervision: Change and Transformation in the 1990s*. 1994
   ISBN 1-85333-998-9

2. J.J. Norton, Chia-Jui Cheng and I. Fletcher (eds): *International Banking Operations and Practices: Current Developments*. 1994
   ISBN 1-85333-997-0

3. J.J. Norton: *Devising International Bank Supervisory Standards*. 1995
   ISBN 1-85966-1858

4. Sir Joseph Gold: *Interpretation: The IMF and International Law*. 1996
   ISBN 90-411-0887-4

5. R. Smits: *The European Central Bank: Institutional Aspects*. 1997
   ISBN 90-411-0686-3

6. M. Andenas, L. Gormley, C. Hadjiemmanuil and I. Harden (eds): *European Economic and Monetary Union: The Institutional Framework*. 1997
   ISBN 90-411-0687-1

7. T. Wan: *Development of Banking Law in the Greater China Area: PRC and Taiwan*. 1999
   ISBN 90-411-0948-X

8. R.P. Buckley: *Emerging Markets Debt: An Analysis of the Secondary Market*. 1999
   ISBN 90-411-9716-8

9. P. Cartwright (ed.): *Consumer Protection in Financial Services*. 1999
   ISBN 90-411-9717-6

10. T. Traisorat: *Thailand: Financial Sector Reform and the East Asian Crises*. 1999
    ISBN 90-411-9734-6

KLUWER LAW INTERNATIONAL – THE HAGUE, LONDON, BOSTON

11. M.I. Steinberg: *International Securities Law: A Contemporary Analysis.*
    1999   ISBN 90-411-9738-9

12. M. Giovanoli and G. Heinrich (eds.): *International Bank Insolvencies: A
    Central Bank Perspective.* 1999   ISBN 90-411-9728-1